AFRICA 68-69

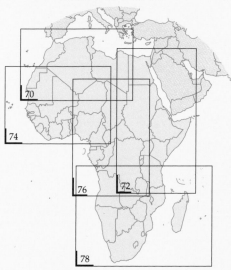

EUROPE 80-81

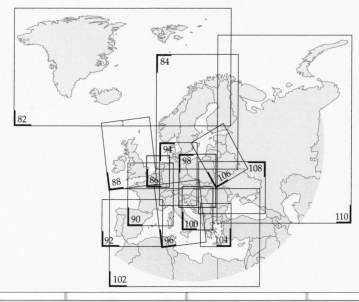

ESSENTIAL
WORLD
ATLAS

Christmas 200?

To Uncle John —
Merry Christmas!
I hope you have many
more exciting explorations.

Love,
Margaret

LONDON, NEW YORK, MUNICH,
MELBOURNE, DELHI

A DORLING KINDERSLEY PUBLISHING BOOK
www.dk.com

FOR THE SECOND EDITION

EDITOR-IN-CHIEF Andrew Heritage
SENIOR MANAGING ART EDITOR Philip Lord
SENIOR CARTOGRAPHIC MANAGER David Roberts
SENIOR CARTOGRAPHIC EDITOR Simon Mumford
PROJECT CARTOGRAPHERS James Anderson
SYSTEMS COORDINATOR Philip Rowles
PRODUCTION Joanna Bull

DORLING KINDERSLEY CARTOGRAPHY

PROJECT CARTOGRAPHY AND DESIGN
Julia Lunn, Julie Turner

CARTOGRAPHERS
James Anderson, Roger Bullen, Martin Darlison,
Simon Mumford, John Plumer, Peter Winfield

DESIGN
Katy Wall

INDEX-GAZETTEER
Natalie Clarkson, Ruth Duxbury, Margaret Hynes, Margaret Stevenson

PRODUCTION
Hilary Stephens, David Proffit

EDITORIAL DIRECTION
Andrew Heritage

ART DIRECTION
Chez Picthall

First American edition 1997. Reprinted with revisions 1998. Second Edition 2001.
Reprinted with revisions 2003.
Previously published as the Concise World Atlas

Published in the United States by Dorling Kindersley Publishing, Inc., 375 Hudson Street,
New York, New York 10014
Copyright © 1997, 1998, 2001, 2003 Dorling Kindersley Limited

A Penguin Company

A CIP catalog record for this book is available from the Library of Congress

ISBN 0-7894-9358-6

Reproduced by GRB, Italy
Printed and bound in Slovakia by TBB s.r.o.

For the very latest information, visit:
www.dk.com and click on the Maps & Atlases icon

KEY TO MAP SYMBOLS

PHYSICAL FEATURES

Elevation

	4,000m/13,124ft
	2,000m/6,562ft
	1,000m/3,281ft
	500m/1,640ft
	250m/820ft
	100m/328ft
	0
	Below sea level

△ Mountain

▽ Depression

△ Volcano

)(Pass/tunnel

▨ Sandy desert

DRAINAGE FEATURES

——— Major perennial river

——— Minor perennial river

- - - Seasonal river

——— Canal

| Waterfall

⬭ Perennial lake

⬭ Seasonal lake

▨ Wetland

ICE FEATURES

▢ Permanent ice cap/ice shelf

▢ Winter limit of pack ice

▢ Summer limit of pack ice

BORDERS

▬▬▬ Full international border

▬ ▬ ▬ Disputed *de facto* border

• • • • Territorial claim border

✕▬✕▬✕ Cease-fire line

▬ ▬ ▬ Undefined boundary

——— Internal administrative boundary

COMMUNICATIONS

——— Major road

——— Minor road

——— Rail

✈ International airport

SETTLEMENTS

▣ Over 500,000

◉ 100,000 - 500,000

○ 50,000 - 100,000

○ Less than 50,000

● National capital

◉ Internal administrative capital

MISCELLANEOUS FEATURES

+ Site of interest

⌐⌐⌐ Ancient wall

GRATICULE FEATURES

——— Line of latitude/longitude/Equator

– – – Tropic/Polar circle

25° Degrees of latitude/longitude

NAMES

Physical features

Andes

Sahara   Landscape features

Ardennes

Land's End   Headland

Mont Blanc
4,807m   Elevation/volcano/pass

Blue Nile   River/canal/waterfall

Ross Ice Shelf   Ice feature

PACIFIC
OCEAN

Sulu Sea   Sea features

Palk Strait

Chile Rise   Undersea feature

Regions

FRANCE   Country

JERSEY   Dependent territory
(to UK)

KANSAS   Administrative region

Dordogne   Cultural region

Settlements

PARIS   Capital city

SAN JUAN   Dependent territory capital city

Chicago

Kettering   Other settlements

Burke

INSET MAP SYMBOLS

▢	Urban area
⬭	City
▢	Park
▪	Place of interest
▫	Suburb/district

Contents

The
World Today

Flags of the World 6-7
The Political World 8-9
The Physical World 10-11
Time Zones 12-13
Geology & Structure 14-15
World Climate 16-17
Ocean Currents 18-19
Life Zones 20-21
Population 22-23
Languages 24-25
Religion 26-27
The Global Economy 28-29
Global Conflict 30-31

The World's
Regions

North &
Central America

North & Central America 34-35
Western Canada & Alaska 36-37
Eastern Canada 38-39
USA: The Northeast 40-41
USA: The Southeast 42-43
 Bermuda
USA: Central States 44-45
USA: The West 46-47
 Los Angeles & Hawaii

USA: The Southwest 48-49
Mexico 50-51
Central America 52-53
The Caribbean 54-55
 Jamaica, St. Lucia, & Barbados

South America

South America 56-57
Northern South America 58-59
Western South America 60-61
 Galapagos Islands
Brazil 62-63
Southern South America 64-65
The Atlantic Ocean 66-67

Africa

Africa .68-69
Northwest Africa 70-71
Northeast Africa 72-73
West Africa 74-75
Central Africa 76-77
 Sao Tome & Principe
Southern Africa 78-79

Europe

Europe .80-81
The North Atlantic 82-83
Scandinavia & Finland 84-85
The Low Countries 86-87
The British Isles 88-89
 London

continued...

EUROPE *continued*

France, Andorra, & Monaco 90-91
  Paris, Andorra, & Monaco
Spain & Portugal 92-93
  Azores & Gibraltar
Germany & the Alpine States . . .94-95
  Liechtenstein
Italy 96-97
  San Marino & Vatican City
Central Europe 98-99
Southeast Europe 100-101
  Bosnia & Herzegovina
The Mediterranean 102-103
  Malta & Cyprus
Bulgaria & Greece 104-105
The Baltic States & Belarus 106-107
Ukraine, Moldova,
  & Romania 108-109
European Russia 110-111

NORTH & WEST ASIA

North & West Asia 112-113
Russia & Kazakhstan 114-115
Turkey & the Caucasus 116-117
The Near East 118-119
  West Bank
The Middle East 120-121
Central Asia 122-123

SOUTH & EAST ASIA

South & East Asia 124-125
Western China & Mongolia . . .126-127

Eastern China & Korea 128-129
  Hong Kong (Xianggang)
Japan .130-131
  Tōkyō & Nansei-Shotō
South India & Sri Lanka 132-133
North India, Pakistan,
  & Bangladesh 134-135
Mainland Southeast Asia 136-137
Maritime Southeast Asia 138-139
  Singapore
The Indian Ocean 140-141

AUSTRALASIA & OCEANIA

Australasia & Oceania 142-143
The Southwest Pacific 144-145
Western Australia 146-147
Eastern Australia 148-149
  Sydney
New Zealand 150-151
The Pacific Ocean 152-153
Antarctica 154
The Arctic Ocean 155

INDEX – GAZETTEER

Overseas Territories
  & Dependencies 156-159
Glossary of Geographical
  Terms 160-161
Continental Factfiles 162-163
Geographical Comparisons . . .164-166
Index-Gazetteer of Places
  & Countries 167-256

FLAGS OF THE WORLD

NORTH & CENTRAL AMERICA

 ANTIGUA & BARBUDA PAGES 54-55

 BAHAMAS PAGES 54-55

 BARBADOS PAGES 54-55

 BELIZE PAGES 52-53

 CANADA PAGES 36-39

 COSTA RICA PAGES 52-53

 CUBA PAGES 54-55

 DOMINICA PAGES 54-55

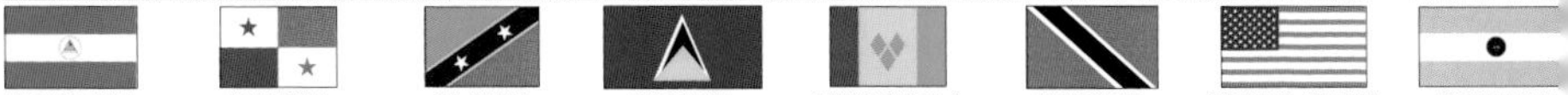

SOUTH AM

 NICARAGUA PAGES 52-53

 PANAMA PAGES 52-53

 ST. KITTS & NEVIS PAGES 54-55

 ST. LUCIA PAGES 54-55

 ST.VINCENT & THE GRENADINES PAGES 54-55

 TRINIDAD & TOBAGO PAGES 54-55

 UNITED STATES OF AMERICA PAGES 40-49

 ARGENTINA PAGES 64-65

AFRICA

 SURINAME PAGES 58-59

 URUGUAY PAGES 64-65

 VENEZUELA PAGES 58-59

 ALGERIA PAGES 70-71

 ANGOLA PAGES 78-79

 BENIN PAGES 74-75

 BOTSWANA PAGES 78-79

 BURKINA FASO PAGES 74-75

 DEM. REP. CONGO PAGES 76-77

 DJIBOUTI PAGES 72-73

 EGYPT PAGES 72-73

 EQUATORIAL GUINEA PAGES 76-77

 ERITREA PAGES 72-73

 ETHIOPIA PAGES 72-73

 GABON PAGES 76-77

 GAMBIA PAGES 74-75

 MALAWI PAGES 78-79

 MALI PAGES 74-75

 MAURITANIA PAGES 74-75

 MAURITIUS PAGES 78-79

 MOROCCO PAGES 70-71

 MOZAMBIQUE PAGES 78-79

 NAMIBIA PAGES 78-79

 NIGER PAGES 74-75

 SUDAN PAGES 72-73

 SWAZILAND PAGES 78-79

 TANZANIA PAGES 72-73

 TOGO PAGES 74-75

 TUNISIA PAGES 70-71

 UGANDA PAGES 72-73

 ZAMBIA PAGES 78-79

 ZIMBABWE PAGES 78-79

 CYPRUS PAGES 102-103

 CZECH REPUBLIC PAGES 98-99

 DENMARK PAGES 84-85

 ESTONIA PAGES 106-107

 FINLAND PAGES 84-85

 FRANCE PAGES 90-91

 GERMANY PAGES 94-95

 GREECE PAGES 104-105

 MALTA PAGES 96-97

 MOLDOVA PAGES 108-109

 MONACO PAGES 90-91

 NETHERLANDS PAGES 86-87

 NORWAY PAGES 84-85

 POLAND PAGES 98-99

 PORTUGAL PAGES 92-93

 REPUBLIC OF IRELAND PAGES 88-89

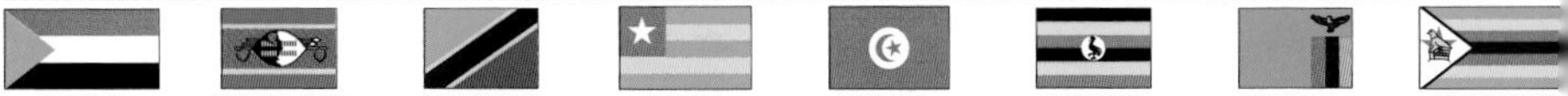

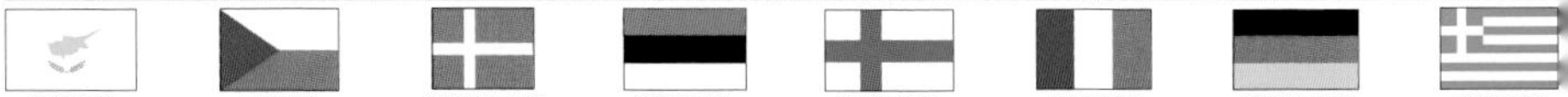

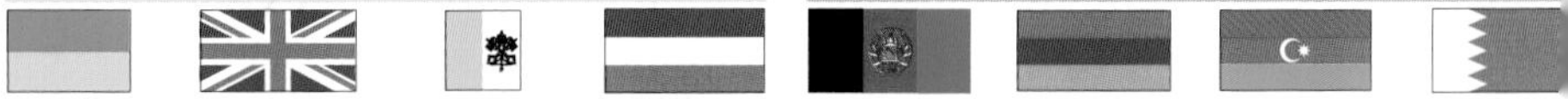

ASIA

 UKRAINE PAGES 108-109

 UNITED KINGDOM PAGES 88-89

 VATICAN CITY PAGES 96-97

 SERBIA & MONTENEGRO (YUGOSLAVIA) PAGES 100-101

 AFGHANISTAN PAGES 122-123

 ARMENIA PAGES 116-117

 AZERBAIJAN PAGES 116-117

 BAHRAIN PAGES 120-121

 INDONESIA PAGES 138-139

 IRAN PAGES 120-121

 IRAQ PAGES 120-121

 ISRAEL PAGES 118-119

 JAPAN PAGES 130-131

 JORDAN PAGES 118-119

 KAZAKHSTAN PAGES 114-115

 KUWAIT PAGES 120-121

 OMAN PAGES 120-121

 PAKISTAN PAGES 134-135

 PHILIPPINES PAGES 138-139

 QATAR PAGES 120-121

 SAUDI ARABIA PAGES 120-121

 SINGAPORE PAGES 138-139

 SOUTH KOREA PAGES 128-129

 SRI LANKA PAGES 132-133

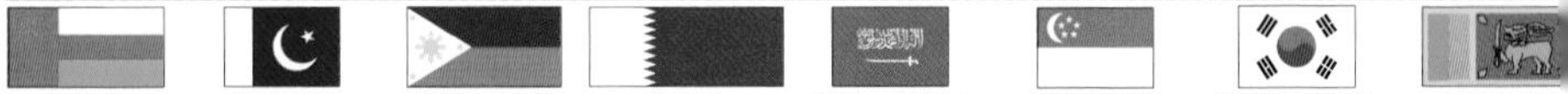

AUSTRALIA & OCEANIA

 VIETNAM PAGES 136-137

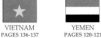 YEMEN PAGES 120-121

 AUSTRALIA PAGES 146-149

 FIJI PAGES 144-145

 KIRIBATI PAGES 144-145

 MARSHALL ISLANDS PAGES 144-145

 MICRONESIA PAGES 144-145

 NAURU PAGES 144-145

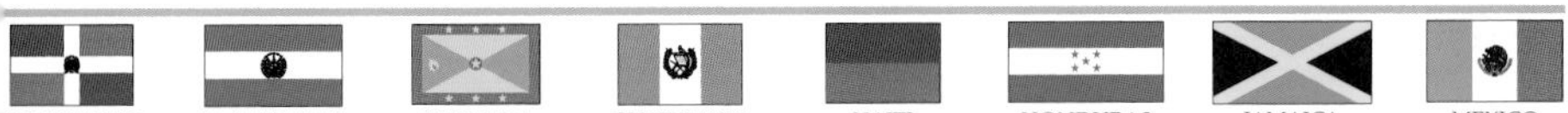

DOMINICAN REPUBLIC PAGES 54-55
EL SALVADOR PAGES 52-53
GRENADA PAGES 54-55
GUATEMALA PAGES 52-53
HAITI PAGES 54-55
HONDURAS PAGES 52-53
JAMAICA PAGES 54-55
MEXICO PAGES 50-51

BOLIVIA PAGES 60-61
BRAZIL PAGES 62-63
CHILE PAGES 64-65
COLOMBIA PAGES 58-59
ECUADOR PAGES 60-61
GUYANA PAGES 58-59
PARAGUAY PAGES 64-65
PERU PAGES 60-61

BURUNDI PAGES 72-73
CAMEROON PAGES 76-77
CAPE VERDE PAGES 74-75
CENTRAL AFRICAN REPUBLIC PAGES 76-77
CHAD PAGES 76-77
COMOROS PAGES 78-79
CONGO PAGES 76-77
CÔTE D'IVOIRE PAGES 74-75

GHANA PAGES 74-75
GUINEA PAGES 74-75
GUINEA-BISSAU PAGES 74-75
KENYA PAGES 72-73
LESOTHO PAGES 78-79
LIBERIA PAGES 74-75
LIBYA PAGES 70-71
MADAGASCAR PAGES 78-79

NIGERIA PAGES 74-75
RWANDA PAGES 72-73
SAO TOME & PRINCIPE PAGES 76-77
SENEGAL PAGES 74-75
SEYCHELLES PAGES 78-79
SIERRA LEONE PAGES 74-75
SOMALIA PAGES 72-73
SOUTH AFRICA PAGES 78-79

EUROPE

ALBANIA PAGES 100-101
ANDORRA PAGES 90-91
AUSTRIA PAGES 94-95
BELARUS PAGES 106-107
BELGIUM PAGES 86-87
BOSNIA & HERZEGOVINA PAGES 100-101
BULGARIA PAGES 104-105
CROATIA PAGES 100-101

HUNGARY PAGES 98-99
ICELAND PAGES 82-83
ITALY PAGES 96-97
LATVIA PAGES 106-107
LIECHTENSTEIN PAGES 94-95
LITHUANIA PAGES 106-107
LUXEMBOURG PAGES 86-87
MACEDONIA PAGES 100-101

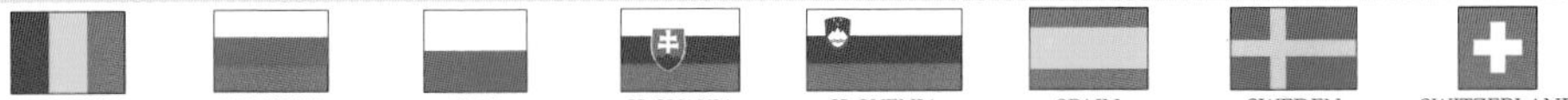

ROMANIA PAGES 108-109
RUSSIAN FEDERATION PAGES 110-111
SAN MARINO PAGES 96-97
SLOVAKIA PAGES 94-95
SLOVENIA PAGES 94-95
SPAIN PAGES 92-93
SWEDEN PAGES 84-85
SWITZERLAND PAGES 94-95

ANGLADESH PAGES 134-135
BHUTAN PAGES 134-135
BRUNEI PAGES 138-139
CAMBODIA PAGES 136-137
CHINA PAGES 126-129
EAST TIMOR PAGES 138-139
GEORGIA PAGES 116-117
INDIA PAGES 132-135

RGYZSTAN AGES 122-123
LAOS PAGES 136-137
LEBANON PAGES 118-119
MALAYSIA PAGES 138-139
MALDIVES PAGES 132-133
MONGOLIA PAGES 126-127
MYANMAR (BURMA) PAGES 136-137
NEPAL PAGES 134-135
NORTH KOREA PAGES 128-129

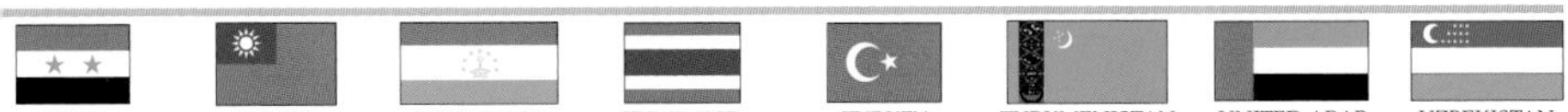

SYRIA PAGES 118-119
TAIWAN PAGES 128-129
TAJIKISTAN PAGES 122-123
THAILAND PAGES 136-137
TURKEY PAGES 116-117
TURKMENISTAN PAGES 122-123
UNITED ARAB EMIRATES PAGES 120-121
UZBEKISTAN PAGES 122-123

NEW ZEALAND PAGES 150-151
PALAU PAGES 144-145
PAPUA NEW GUINEA PAGES 144-145
SAMOA PAGES 144-145
SOLOMON ISLANDS PAGES 144-145
TONGA PAGES 144-145
TUVALU PAGES 144-145
VANUATU PAGES 144-145

THE POLITICAL WORLD

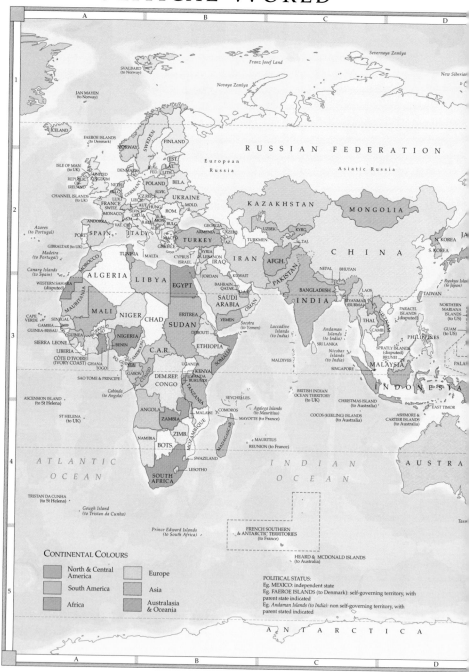

CONTINENTAL COLOURS

- North & Central America
- South America
- Africa
- Europe
- Asia
- Australasia & Oceania

POLITICAL STATUS:
Eg. MEXICO: independent state
Eg. FAEROE ISLANDS (to Denmark): self-governing territory, with parent state indicated
Eg. Andaman Islands (to India): non self-governing territory, with parent stated indicated

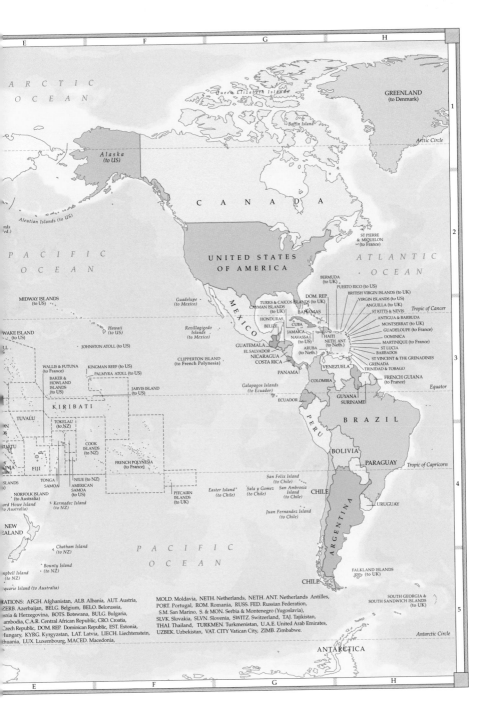

ARCTIC
OCEAN

Queen Elizabeth Islands

GREENLAND
(to Denmark)

Baffin Island

Arctic Circle

Alaska
(to US)

Aleutian Islands (to US)

C A N A D A

ST PIERRE
& MIQUELON
– (to France)

PACIFIC
OCEAN

UNITED STATES
OF AMERICA

ATLANTIC
OCEAN

MIDWAY ISLANDS
(to US)

Guadelupe
(to Mexico)

BERMUDA
(to UK)

PUERTO RICO (to US)

BRITISH VIRGIN ISLANDS (to UK)

VIRGIN ISLANDS (to US)

ANGUILLA (to UK)

Tropic of Cancer

WAKE ISLAND
(to US)

Hawaii
(to US)

Revillagigedo
Islands
(to Mexico)

MEXICO

TURKS & CAICOS ISLANDS (to UK)

CAYMAN ISLANDS
(to UK)

BAHAMAS

HONDURAS

CUBA

BELIZE

JAMAICA

NAVASSA I.
(to US)

HAITI

DOM. REP.

ST KITTS & NEVIS

ANTIGUA & BARBUDA

MONTSERRAT (to UK)

GUADELOUPE (to France)

DOMINICA

MARTINIQUE (to France)

ST LUCIA

BARBADOS

JOHNSTON ATOLL (to US)

GUATEMALA

EL SALVADOR

NICARAGUA

COSTA RICA

NETH. ANT.
(to Neth.)

ARUBA
(to Neth.)

ST VINCENT & THE GRENADINES

GRENADA

TRINIDAD & TOBAGO

CLIPPERTON ISLAND
(to French Polynesia)

WALLIS & FUTUNA
(to France)

KINGMAN REEF (to US)

PALMYRA ATOLL (to US)

BAKER &
HOWLAND
ISLANDS
(to US)

JARVIS ISLAND
(to US)

PANAMA

VENEZUELA

COLOMBIA

Galapagos Islands
(to Ecuador)

FRENCH GUIANA
(to France)

Equator

KIRIBATI

TUVALU

TOKELAU
(to NZ)

COOK
ISLANDS
(to NZ)

ECUADOR

GUYANA

SURINAME

PERU

BRAZIL

FIJI

FRENCH POLYNESIA
(to France)

BOLIVIA

PARAGUAY

Tropic of Capricorn

TONGA

SAMOA

NIUE (to NZ)

AMERICAN
SAMOA
(to US)

San Felix Island
(to Chile)

Sala y Gomez
Island
(to Chile)

San Ambrosia
Island
(to Chile)

NORFOLK ISLAND
(to Australia)

Kermadec Island
(to NZ)

PITCAIRN
ISLANDS
(to UK)

Easter Island
(to Chile)

CHILE

URUGUAY

NEW
ZEALAND

Juan Fernandez Island
(to Chile)

Chatham Island
(to NZ)

ARGENTINA

Bounty Island
(to NZ)

PACIFIC
OCEAN

mpbell Island
(to NZ)

quarie Island (to Australia)

CHILE

FALKLAND ISLANDS
(to UK)

SOUTH GEORGIA &
SOUTH SANDWICH ISLANDS
(to UK)

NATIONS: AFGH. Afghanistan, ALB. Albania, AUT. Austria,
ZERB. Azerbaijan, BELG. Belgium, BELO. Belorussia,
snia & Herzegovina, BOTS. Botswana, BULG. Bulgaria,
ambodia, C.A.R. Central African Republic, CRO. Croatia,
Czech Republic, DOM. REP. Dominican Republic, EST. Estonia,
Hungary, KYRG. Kyrgyzstan, LAT. Latvia, LIECH. Liechtenstein,
thuania, LUX. Luxembourg, MACED. Macedonia,

MOLD. Moldavia, NETH. Netherlands, NETH. ANT. Netherlands Antilles,
PORT. Portugal, ROM. Romania, RUSS. FED. Russian Federation,
S.M. San Marino, S. & MON. Serbia & Montenegro (Yugoslavia),
SLVK. Slovakia, SLVN. Slovenia, SWITZ. Switzerland, TAJ. Tajikistan,
THAI. Thailand, TURKMEN. Turkmenistan, U.A.E. United Arab Emirates,
UZBEK. Uzbekistan, VAT. CITY Vatican City, ZIMB. Zimbabwe.

Antarctic Circle

ANTARCTICA

THE PHYSICAL WORLD

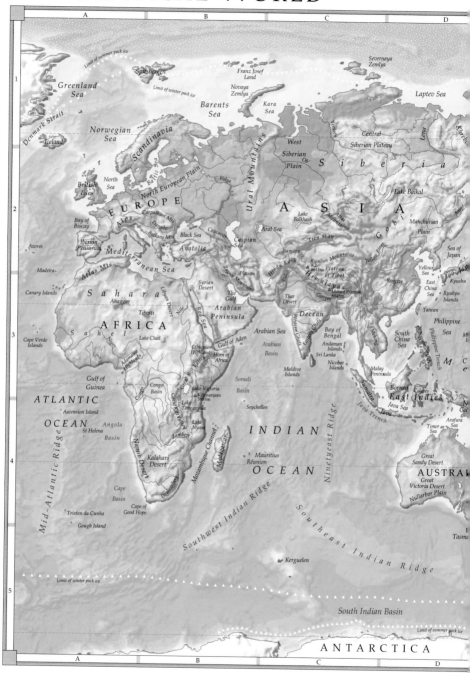

Limit of summer pack ice
Spitsbergen
Franz Josef Land
Severnaya Zemlya
Laptev Sea
Greenland Sea
Limit of winter pack ice
Novaya Zemlya
Barents Sea
Kara Sea
Denmark Strait
Iceland
Norwegian Sea
Scandinavia
West Siberian Plain
Ob
Central Siberian Plateau
Yenisey
Lena
Khatanga
Siberia
British Isles
North Sea
Baltic Sea
North European Plain
Ural Mountains
Volga
Lake Baikal
Amur
EUROPE
Alps
Carpathian Mts
Danube
Balkans Mts
Black Sea
Caucasus
Caspian Sea
Aral Sea
Lake Balkhash
Altai Mountains
Tien Shan
Gobi
ASIA
Manchurian Plain
Bay of Biscay
Iberian Peninsula
Anatolia
Pamirs
Hindu Kush
Kunlun Mountains
Yellow River
Sea of Japan
Azores
Mediterranean Sea
Iranian Plateau
Zagros Mountains
8611m K2
Plateau of Tibet
Yellow Sea
Yangtze
East China Sea
Kyushu
Madeira
Atlas Mts
Syrian Desert
Himalayas
Mount Everest 8848m
Ryukyu Islands
Canary Islands
Sahara
Ahaggar
Libyan Desert
Nile
The Gulf
Arabian Peninsula
Thar Desert
Ganges
Deccean
Taiwan
Tibesti
Red Sea
Western Ghats
Eastern Ghats
Philippine Sea
AFRICA
Sahel
Niger
Lake Chad
Ethiopian Highlands
Gulf of Aden
Arabian Sea
Bay of Bengal
Andaman Islands
Sri Lanka
South China Sea
Philippine Trench
M
Cape Verde Islands
Mahanadi
Horn of Africa
Arabian Basin
Nicobar Islands
Malay Peninsula
Gulf of Guinea
Congo Basin
Congo
Great Rift Valley
Lake Victoria
Kilimanjaro 5895m
Somali Basin
Maldive Islands
Sumatra
Borneo
East Indies
Celebes
Gu
ATLANTIC
Ascension Island
Seychelles
Java Trench
Arafura Sea
OCEAN
St Helena
Angola Basin
Lake Tanganyika
INDIAN
Timor Sea
Mid-Atlantic Ridge
Namib Desert
Lake Nyasa
Zambezi
Madagascar
Mozambique Channel
Mauritius
Réunion
Ninetyeast Ridge
Great Sandy Desert
AUSTRAL
Kalahari Desert
OCEAN
Great Victoria Desert
Nullarbor Plain
Cape Basin
Drakensberg
Tristan da Cunha
Cape of Good Hope
Southwest Indian Ridge
Southeast Indian Ridge
F
Tasm
Gough Island
Kerguelen
Limit of winter pack ice
South Indian Basin
Limit of summer pack ice
ANTARCTICA

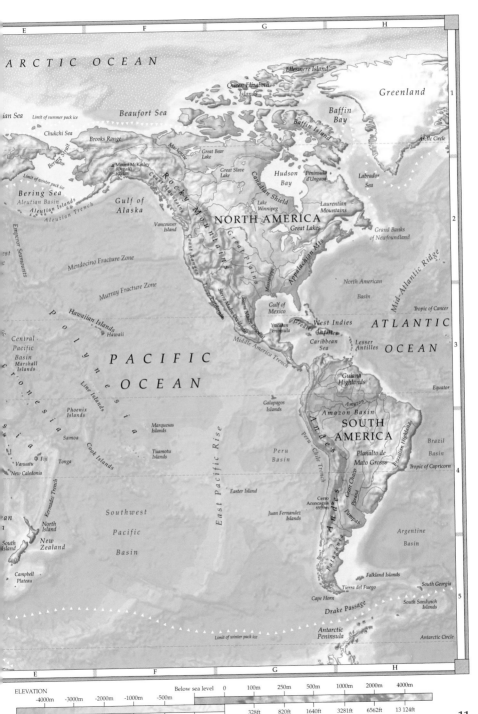

ELEVATION

| Below sea level | 0 | 100m | 250m | 500m | 1000m | 2000m | 4000m |

-4000m -3000m -2000m -1000m -500m

-13 124ft -9843ft -6562ft -3281ft -1640ft -820ft/-250m 0 328ft 820ft 1640ft 3281ft 6562ft 13 124ft

TIME ZONES

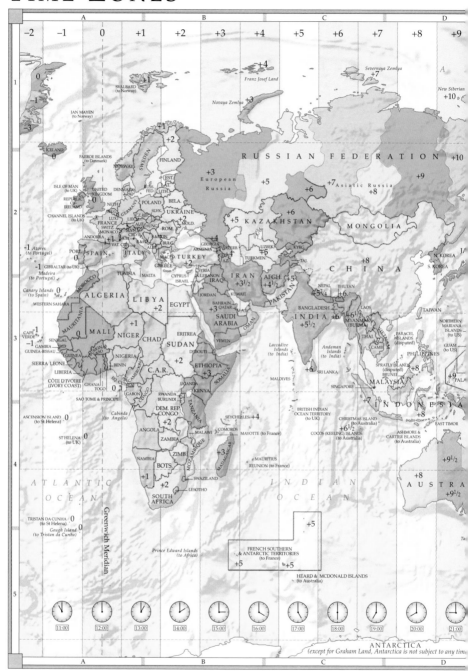

The numbers represented thus: +2/-2, indicate the number of hours each time zone is ahead or behind GMT (Greenwich Mean Time)

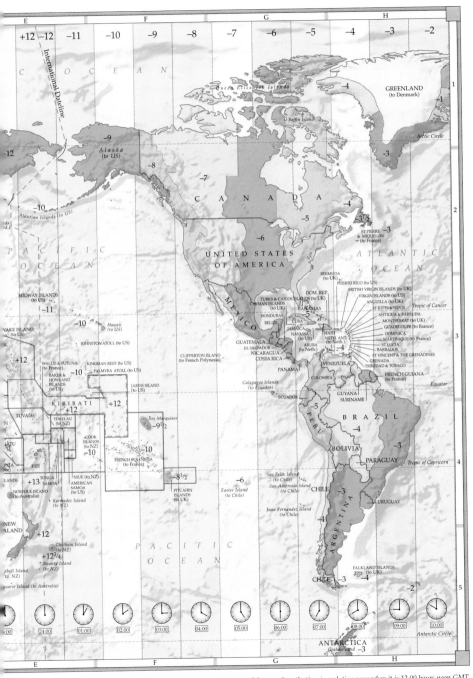

The clocks and 24-hour times given at the bottom of the map show the time in each time zone when it is 12.00 hours noon GMT

GEOLOGY & STRUCTURE

EURASIAN PLATE

Ural Mountains

Alps

ANATOLIAN PLATE

IRANIAN PLATE

Himalayas

ARABIAN PLATE

PHILIPP PLATE

AFRICAN PLATE

INDO-AUSTRALIAN PLATE

ANTARCTIC PLATE

GEOLOGICAL REGIONS   Continental shield   Igneous rock types   MOUNTAIN RANGES   Hercynian (290 to 362 Ma)   Ma= milli
                      Sedimentary rocks   Coral formation   Alpine (5 to 23 Ma)   Caledonian (386 to 439 Ma)   year

| E | F | G | H |

NORTH AMERICAN PLATE

JUAN DE FUCA PLATE

Rocky Mountains

Arctic Circle

Tropic of Cancer

CARIBBEAN PLATE

COCOS PLATE

LINE

ARCK

LOMON ATE

FIJI PLATE

PACIFIC PLATE

NAZCA PLATE

Andes

SOUTH AMERICAN PLATE

Equator

Tropic of Capricorn

ANTARCTIC PLATE

SCOTIA PLATE

Antarctic Circle

● Earthquake zone	▲ Volcanic zone	PLATE BOUNDARIES	—— Sliding plates	▲▲▲ Colliding plates
● Hot spot	▲▲▲ Rift valley		—— Spreading plates	– – – Uncertain plate boundary

15

WORLD CLIMATE

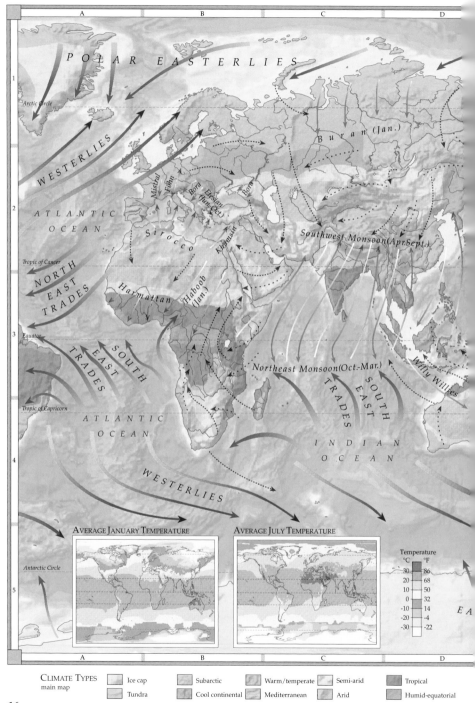

POLAR EASTERLIES

Arctic Circle

WESTERLIES

ATLANTIC
OCEAN

Buran (Jan.)

Mistral
Föhn
Bora
Etesian
(Jun.-Oct.)
Bora

Tropic of Cancer

Sirocco

Khamsin

Southwest Monsoon (Apr.-Sept.)

NORTH
EAST
TRADES

Harmattan

Haboob
(Jan.)

Equator

SOUTH
EAST
TRADES

Northeast Monsoon (Oct.-Mar.)

Willy Willies

Tropic of Capricorn

ATLANTIC
OCEAN

SOUTH
EAST
TRADES

INDIAN
OCEAN

WESTERLIES

AVERAGE JANUARY TEMPERATURE

AVERAGE JULY TEMPERATURE

Antarctic Circle

Temperature
°C	°F
30	86
20	68
10	50
0	32
-10	14
-20	-4
-30	-22

E A

CLIMATE TYPES
main map

Ice cap

Tundra

Subarctic

Cool continental

Warm/temperate

Mediterranean

Semi-arid

Arid

Tropical

Humid-equatorial

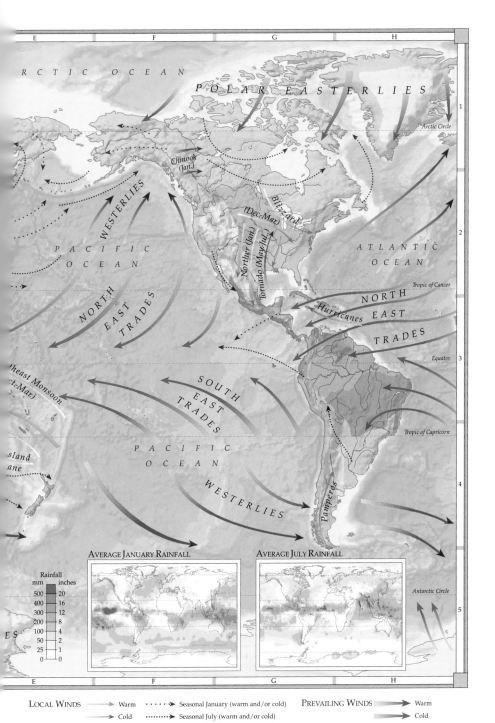

E   F   G   H

ARCTIC OCEAN

POLAR EASTERLIES

Arctic Circle

1

Chinook
(Jan.)

WESTERLIES

Blizzard
(Dec-Mar.)

Norther (Jan.)

Tornado (May-Jul.)

PACIFIC
OCEAN

ATLANTIC
OCEAN

2

NORTH

EAST

TRADES

Tropic of Cancer

Hurricanes

NORTH

EAST

TRADES

theast Monsoon
ct-Mar.)

SOUTH
EAST
TRADES

Equator

3

island
ane

PACIFIC
OCEAN

Tropic of Capricorn

4

WESTERLIES

Pampero

AVERAGE JANUARY RAINFALL

AVERAGE JULY RAINFALL

Rainfall	
mm	inches
500	20
400	16
300	12
200	8
100	4
50	2
25	1
0	0

Antarctic Circle

5

E S

E   F   G   H

LOCAL WINDS   → Warm   ·····➤ Seasonal January (warm and/or cold)   PREVAILING WINDS   ➤ Warm

                 → Cold   ·········➤ Seasonal July (warm and/or cold)   ➤ Cold

OCEAN CURRENTS

Greenland Sea

Summer limit of pack ice

Winter limit of pack ice

Laptev Sea

Denmark Strait

North Atlantic Drift

Barents Sea

Kara Sea

North Sea

Baltic Sea

EUROPE

ASIA

Black Sea

Canary Current

Mediterranean Sea

Sea of Japan

Yellow Sea

East China Sea

Kuro Siwo

AFRICA

Red Sea

The Gulf

Gulf of Aden

Arabian Sea

Bay of Bengal

South China Sea

Philippine Sea

Equatorial Counter-current

Doldrums

Gulf of Guinea

Celebes Sea

South Equatorial Current

Doldrums

Java Sea

Banda Sea

Benguela Current

Mozambique Channel

South Equatorial Current

Timor Sea

Arafura Sea

ATLANTIC OCEAN

INDIAN OCEAN

AUSTRA

West Australian Current

ANNUAL MEAN OCEAN TEMPERATURE

20 to 30°C/68° to 86°F	Annual mean extent of sea ice (below -2°C/28°F)
10 to 20°C/50° to 68°F	Permanent ice shelf
0 to 10°C/32° to 50°F	Prevailing warm ocean current
-2° to 0°C/28° to 32°F	Prevailing cold ocean current

Winter limit of pack ice

Summer limit of pack ice

ANTARCTICA

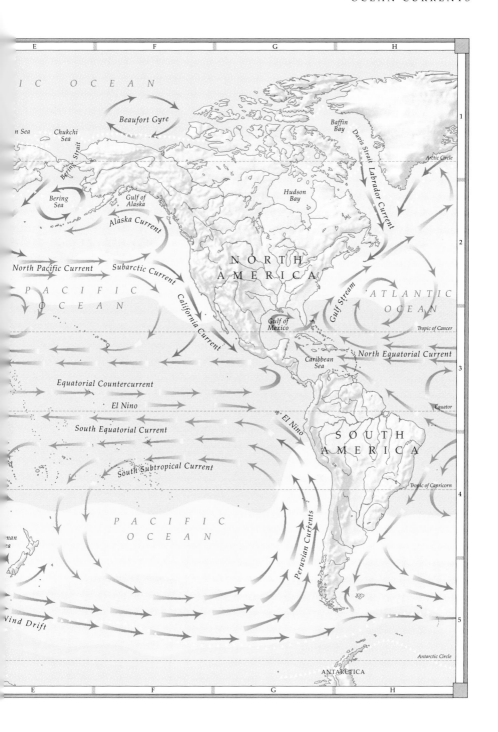

LIFE ZONES

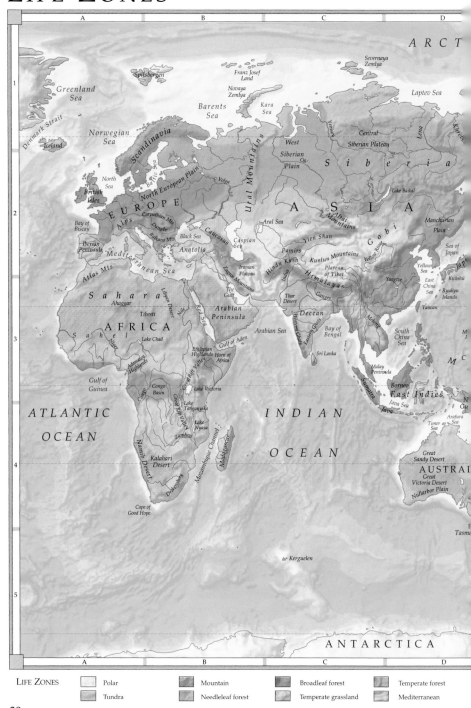

A R C T

Severnaya
Zemlya

1
Greenland
Sea

Spitsbergen

Franz Josef
Land

Novaya
Zemlya

Barents
Sea

Kara
Sea

Laptev Sea

Denmark Strait

Norwegian
Sea

Iceland

Scandinavia

Baltic Sea

West
Siberian
Plain

Central
Siberian Plateau

Yenisey

Lena

Khatila

North
Sea

North European Plain

Volga

S i b e r i a

British
Isles

Ural Mountains

Ob

Lake Baikal

2
E U R O P E

Bay of
Biscay

Alps

Carpathian Mts

Danube

Balkans Mts

Black Sea

Caucasus

A   S   I   A

Aral Sea

*Altai
Mountains*

Manchurian
Plain

Iberian
Peninsula

Mediterranean Sea

Anatolia

Caspian
Sea

Tien Shan

Pamirs

Gobi

Yellow River

Sea of
Japan

Japan

Atlas Mts

Iranian
Plateau

Hindu Kush

Kunlun Mountains

Plateau
of Tibet

Yellow
Sea

Yangtze

East
China
Sea

Kyūshū

Ryukyu
Islands

Zagros Mountains

Indus

Himalayas

S a h a r a

Ahaggar

Libyan Desert

Nile

Red Sea

Tric
Gulf

Ganges

Thar
Desert

Taiwan

Tibesti

Arabian
Peninsula

Deccan

Mekong

3
A F R I C A

S   a   h   e   l

Niger

Lake Chad

Ethiopian
Highlands

Gulf of Aden

Horn of
Africa

Arabian Sea

Western Ghats

Eastern Ghats

Bay of
Bengal

South
China
Sea

M

Sri Lanka

M   C

Adamawa
Highlands

Great Rift Valley

Malay
Peninsula

Gulf of
Guinea

Congo
Basin

Congo

Lake Victoria

Lake
Tanganyika

Lake
Nyasa

Borneo

Sumatra

East Indies

N

Gu

ATLANTIC

Great Ruaha Valley

I N D I A N

Java Sea

Java

Timor
Sea

Arafura
Sea

OCEAN

Zambezi

Mozambique Channel

Madagascar

O C E A N

Great
Sandy Desert

4
Kalahari
Desert

Namib Desert

AUSTRAL

Great
Victoria Desert

Drakensberg

Nullarbor Plain

Cape of
Good Hope

I

Tasm

Kerguelen

5

A N T A R C T I C A

LIFE ZONES

Polar
Tundra

Mountain
Needleleaf forest

Broadleaf forest
Temperate grassland

Temperate forest
Mediterranean

20

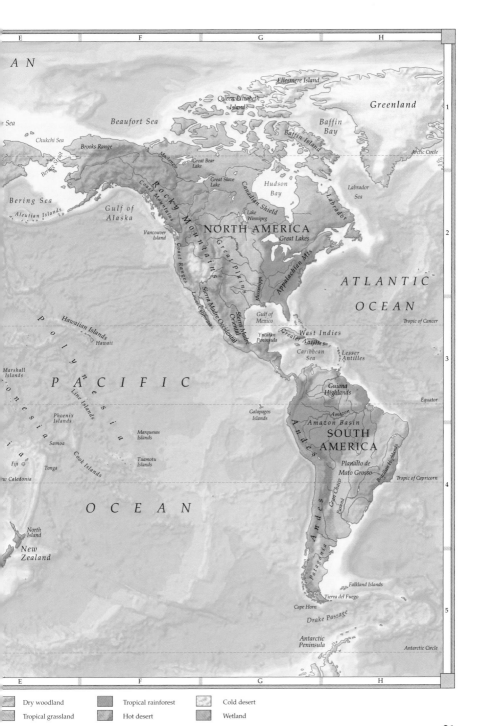

Dry woodland	Cold desert
Tropical grassland	Tropical rainforest	Wetland
	Hot desert	

POPULATION

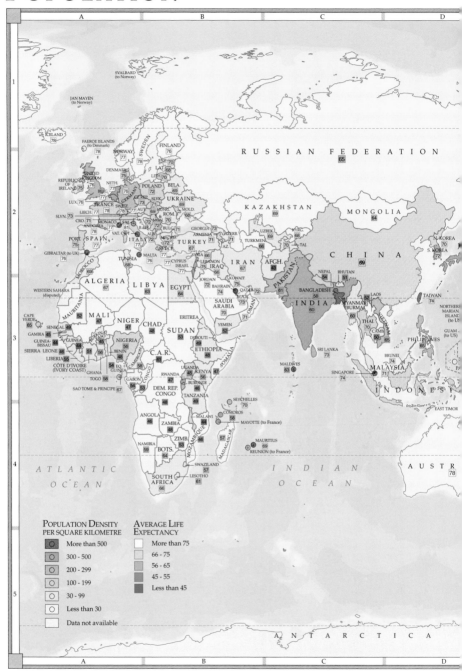

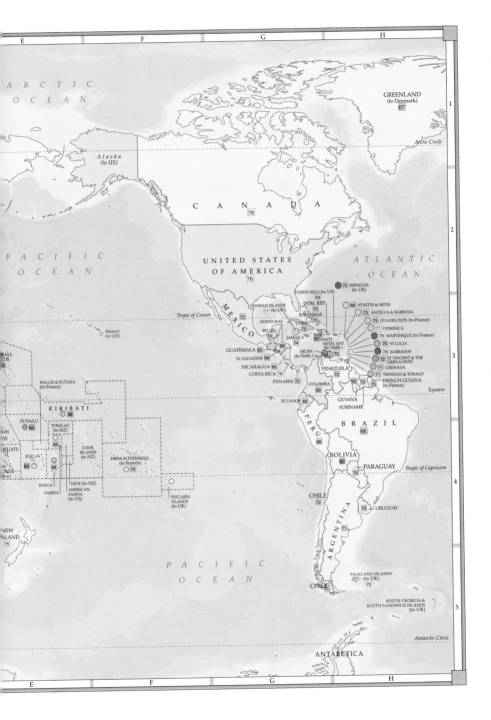

E F G H

ARCTIC
OCEAN

GREENLAND
(to Denmark)
67

Arctic Circle

Alaska
(to US)

1

CANADA
78

PACIFIC
OCEAN

UNITED STATES
OF AMERICA
76

ATLANTIC
OCEAN

2

PUERTO RICO (to US)
74

BERMUDA
(to UK)
75

CAYMAN ISLANDS
(to UK)
77

DOM. REP.
70

ST KITTS & NEVIS
66

Tropic of Cancer

MEXICO
72

BAHAMAS
73

ANTIGUA & BARBUDA
73

Hawaii
(to US)

HONDURAS
70

CUBA
75

GUADELOUPE (to France)
75

BELIZE
74

DOMINICA
77

ALL
DS.
3.

JAMAICA
74

HAITI
(to Neth.)
57

NETH. ANT.
(to Neth.)

MARTINIQUE (to France)
76

WALLIS & FUTUNA
(to France)

GUATEMALA
65

ARUBA
(to Neth.)
76

73

ST LUCIA
70

EL SALVADOR
68

BARBADOS
76

KIRIBATI
68

NICARAGUA
65

VENEZUELA
72

ST VINCENT & THE
GRENADINES
72

TUVALU
63

COSTA RICA
76

GRENADA
71

ON
DS.

TOKELAU
(to NZ)
68

PANAMA
72

COLOMBIA
69

65

TRINIDAD & TOBAGO
71

FRENCH GUIANA
(to France)
75

NUATU

COOK
ISLANDS
(to NZ)

ECUADOR
69

GUYANA

Equator

NIA
nce)

63

FIJI
68

FRENCH POLYNESIA
(to France)
70

SURINAME

PERU
66

BRAZIL
66

TONGA

SAMOA

NIUE (to NZ)
AMERICAN
SAMOA
(to US)

PITCAIRN
ISLANDS
(to UK)

BOLIVIA
60

PARAGUAY
70

Tropic of Capricorn

NEW
ALAND
76

CHILE
72

ARGENTINA

URUGUAY
73

PACIFIC
OCEAN

71

CHILE

FALKLAND ISLANDS
(to UK)
76

SOUTH GEORGIA &
SOUTH SANDWICH ISLANDS
(to UK)

5

Antarctic Circle

ANTARCTICA

E F G H

23

LANGUAGES

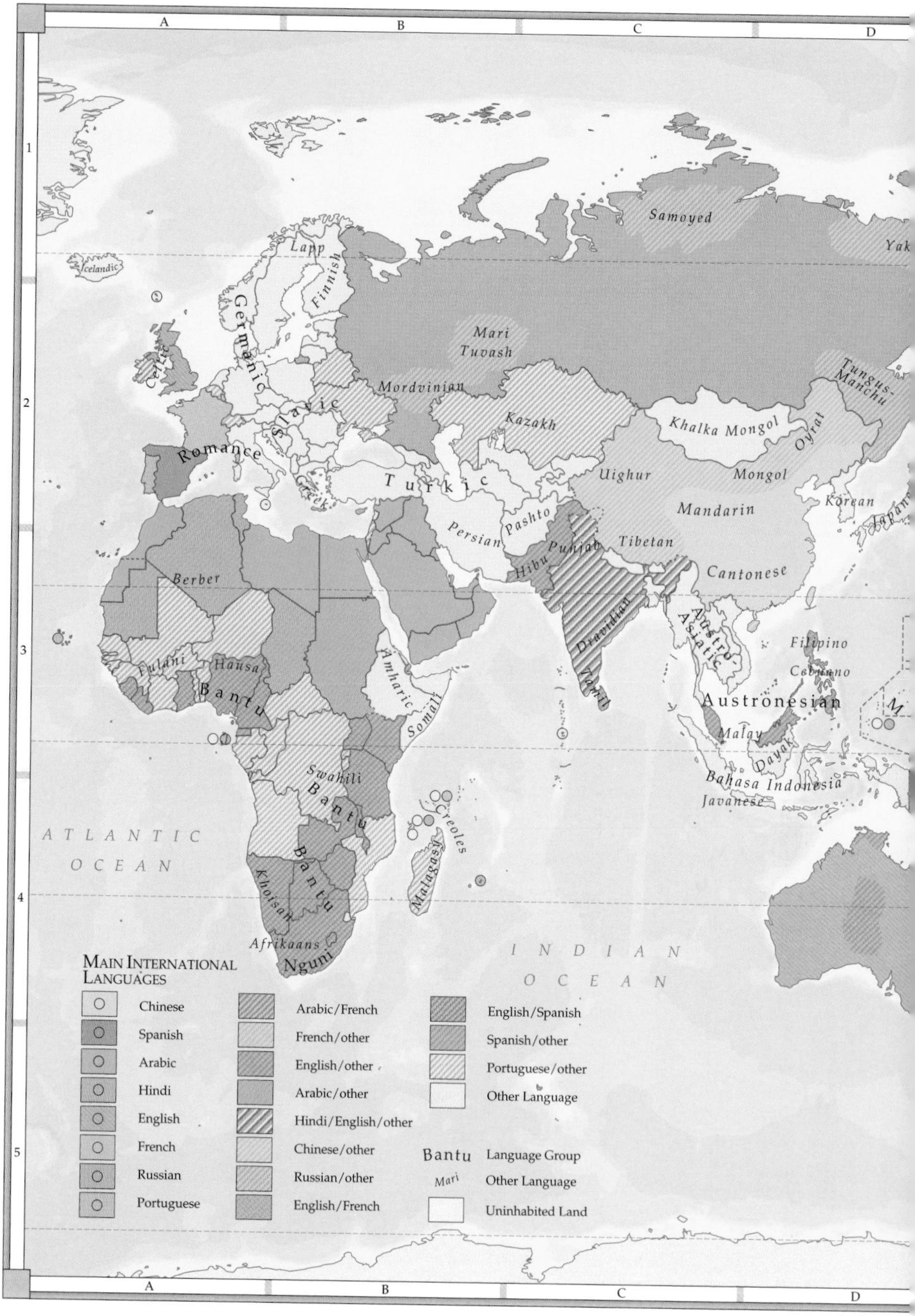
A
B
C
D
1
2
3
4
5
Icelandic
Lapp
Finnish
Germanic
Celtic
Slavic
Romance
Greek
Turkic
Mari
Tuvash
Mordvinian
Samoyed
Kazakh
Khalka Mongol
Oyrat
Tungus-Manchu
Uighur
Mongol
Mandarin
Korean
Persian
Pashto
Punjab
Tibetan
Cantonese
Dravidian
Tamil
Austro-Asiatic
Filipino
Cebuano
Austronesian
Malay
Dayak
Bahasa Indonesia
Javanese
Berber
Fulani
Hausa
Bantu
Amharic
Somali
Swahili
Bantu
Creoles
Malagasy
Bantu
Khoisan
Afrikaans
Nguni
ATLANTIC OCEAN
INDIAN OCEAN
MAIN INTERNATIONAL LANGUAGES
Chinese
Spanish
Arabic
Hindi
English
French
Russian
Portuguese
Arabic/French
French/other
English/other
Arabic/other
Hindi/English/other
Chinese/other
Russian/other
English/French
English/Spanish
Spanish/other
Portuguese/other
Other Language
Bantu Language Group
Mari Other Language
Uninhabited Land

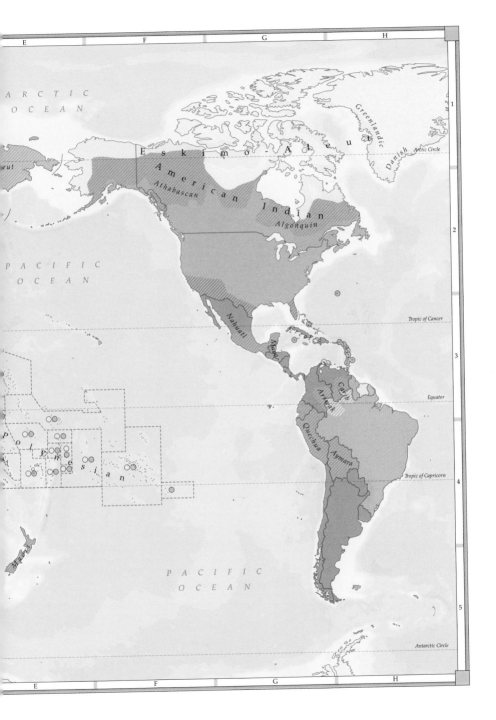

MAJORITY RELIGIONS

- ◯ Marxism / Maoism
- ◯ Protestant Christianity
- ◯ Catholic Christianity
- ◯ Orthodox Christianity
- ◯ Shi'a Islam
- ◯ Sunni Islam
- ◯ Hinduism
- ◯ Judaism
- ◯ Theravada Buddhism
- ◯ Mahayana Buddhism
- ◯ Tibetan Buddhism
- ◯ Other

STATE POLICY

- ▲ Secular ideologies governing
- ● Communist states during 20th century
- ■ Non-pluralist states

THE GLOBAL ECONOMY

ECONOMIC PERFORMANCE

GNP per capita, 1995 ($US)

- more than 20 000
- 10 000 to 20 000
- 5000 to 10 000
- 1000 to 5000
- 500 to 1000
- 250 to 500
- less than 250
- data not available

Human Development Index (HDI)

- high human development
- poor human development

HDI is one of the best indicators of economic development. The single index is reached by measuring life expectancy at birth, per capita purchasing power, literacy rates and years of schooling

E   F   G   H

EAN

GREENLAND
(to Denmark)

Arctic Circle

Alaska
(to US)

C A N A D A

PACIFIC
OCEAN

UNITED STATES
OF AMERICA

ATLANTIC
OCEAN

Hawaii
(to US)

M
E
X
I
C
O

BERMUDA
(to UK)

TURKS & CAICOS ISLANDS (to UK)
CAYMAN ISLANDS
(to UK)
HONDURAS
BELIZE
GUATEMALA
EL SALVADOR
NICARAGUA
COSTA RICA
PANAMA

DOM. REP.
BAHAMAS
CUBA
JAMAICA
HAITI

PUERTO RICO
(to US)

ST KITTS & NEVIS
ANTIGUA & BARBUDA
GUADELOUPE (to France)
DOMINICA
MARTINIQUE (to France)
ST LUCIA
BARBADOS
ST VINCENT &
THE GRENADINES
GRENADA
TRINIDAD & TOBAGO

Tropic of Cancer

ARUBA
(to Neth.)

NETH. ANT.
(to Neth.)

VENEZUELA

FRENCH GUIANA
(to France)

Equator

HALL
NDS

NAURU

KIRIBATI

TUVALU

TOKELAU
(to NZ)

SAMOA

UATU

TONGA

NIA
nce)

FIJI

FRENCH POLYNESIA
(to France)

PITCAIRN
ISLANDS
(to UK)

COLOMBIA

ECUADOR

P
E
R
U

GUYANA
SURINAME

B R A Z I L

BOLIVIA

PARAGUAY

CHILE

A
R
G
E
N
T
I
N
A

URUGUAY

Tropic of Capricorn

NEW
EALAND

PACIFIC
OCEAN

FALKLAND ISLANDS
(to UK)

CHILE

Antarctic Circle

ANTARCTICA

E   F   G   H

GLOBAL CONFLICT

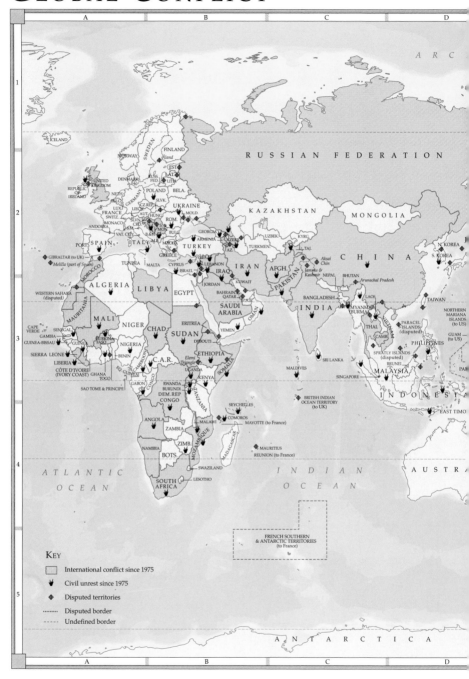

KEY

International conflict since 1975

Civil unrest since 1975

Disputed territories

.... Disputed border

----- Undefined border

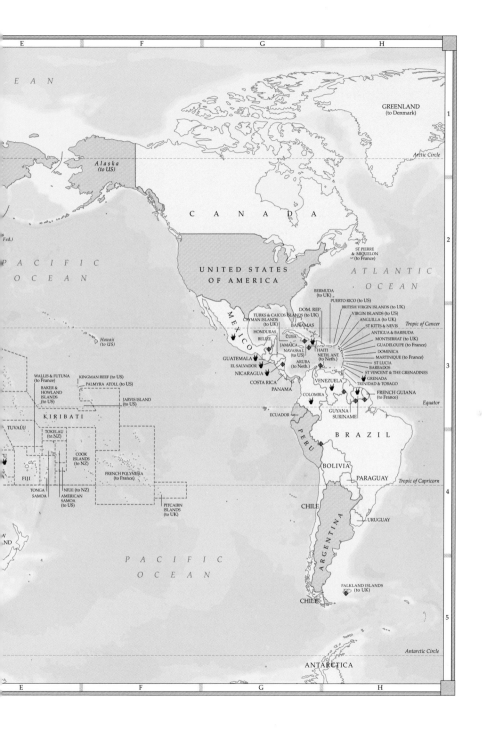

GREENLAND
(to Denmark)

Arctic Circle

Alaska
(to US)

C A N A D A

Fed.)

P A C I F I C

O C E A N

ATLANTIC

UNITED STATES
OF AMERICA

OCEAN

ST PIERRE
& MIQUELON
~ (to France)

BERMUDA
(to UK)

PUERTO RICO (to US)

BRITISH VIRGIN ISLANDS (to UK)

VIRGIN ISLANDS (to US)

ANGUILLA (to UK)

ST KITTS & NEVIS

Tropic of Cancer

Hawaii
(to US)

MEXICO

TURKS & CAICOS ISLANDS
(to UK)

CAYMAN ISLANDS
(to UK)

HONDURAS
BELIZE

CUBA

BAHAMAS

DOM. REP.

HAITI

JAMAICA

NAVASSAL
(to US)

NETH. ANT.
(to Neth.)

ANTIGUA & BARBUDA

MONTSERRAT (to UK)

GUADELOUPE (to France)

DOMINICA

MARTINIQUE (to France)

ST LUCIA

BARBADOS

ST VINCENT & THE GRENADINES

GRENADA

TRINIDAD & TOBAGO

GUATEMALA

EL SALVADOR

ARUBA
(to Neth.)

NICARAGUA

COSTA RICA

VENEZUELA

PANAMA

COLOMBIA

FRENCH GUIANA
(to France)

Equator

WALLIS & FUTUNA
(to France)

KINGMAN REEF (to US)

PALMYRA ATOLL (to US)

BAKER &
HOWLAND
ISLANDS
(to US)

JARVIS ISLAND
(to US)

ECUADOR

GUYANA
SURINAME

K I R I B A T I

TUVALU

B R A Z I L

PERU

TOKELAU
(to NZ)

COOK
ISLANDS
(to NZ)

BOLIVIA

FIJI

FRENCH POLYNESIA
(to France)

PARAGUAY

Tropic of Capricorn

TONGA
SAMOA

NIUE (to NZ)

AMERICAN
SAMOA
(to US)

PITCAIRN
ISLANDS
(to UK)

CHILE

URUGUAY

W
ND

P A C I F I C

O C E A N

ARGENTINA

FALKLAND ISLANDS
(to UK)

CHILE

Antarctic Circle

ANTARCTICA

THE WORLD'S REGIONS

NORTH & CENTRAL AMERICA

EUROPE

Barents Sea

Mohns Ridge

SVALBARD (to Norway)

JAN MAYEN (to Norway)

Iceland

Denmark Strait

Greenland Sea

Reykjanes Basin

North Atlantic Mid-Ocean Canyon

Kong Christian IX Land

Kong Frederik VI Kyst

Kong Christian X Land

NUUK

Kong Frederik VIII Land

GREENLAND (to Denmark)

Davis Strait

Labrador Sea

Labrador Basin

Labrador

Smallwood Reservoir

Labrador Mountains

Nansen Basin

Nansen Cordillera

North Pole

Makarov Basin

Lomonosov Ridge

Alpha Cordillera

Kap Morris Jesup

Lincoln Sea

Wandel Sea

Ellesmere Island

Queen Elizabeth Islands

Baffin Bay

Baffin Island

Lancaster Sound

Gulf of Boothia

Foxe Basin

Southampton Island

Hudson Bay

Belcher Islands

James Bay

ARCTIC OCEAN

Laptev Sea

East Siberian Sea

Merdeleyev Ridge

Chukchi Plateau

Chukchi Sea

Canada Basin

Beaufort Sea

Banks Island

Victoria Island

Prince of Wales Island

Great Bear Lake

Great Slave Lake

Lake Athabasca

Reindeer Lake

Lake Winnipeg

Peninsula of Ungava

Wrangel Island

Limit of summer pack ice

Arctic Circle

Mackenzie

Mackenzie Mountains

Athabasca

CANADA

Saskatoon

Regina

Calgary

Edmonton

ASIA

Bering Sea

Bering Strait

Saint Lawrence Island

Nunivak Island

Norton Sound

Yukon

Brooks Range

Mount McKinley ▲6194m

Alaska (to US)

Alaska Range

Anchorage

Rocky Mountains

Mount Logan ▲5959m

Juneau

Coast Mountains

Vancouver

Vancouver Island

Victoria

Seattle

Mount Rainier ▲4392m

Cascadia

Eugene

Nurist

Bristol Bay

Nunivak Island

Kodiak Island

Gulf of Alaska

Alaska Trench

Alexander Archipelago

Queen Charlotte Islands

Aleutian Basin

Aleutian Islands

Aleutian Trench

PACIFIC OCEAN

0 km   1000
0 miles   1000

POPULATION   ● National capital

○ Less than 50,000   ○ 50,000 -100,000   ◉ 100,000 - 500,000   ■ Over 500,000

ATLANTIC

OCEAN

Bermuda Rise

Sargasso Sea

Nares Plain

BERMUDA (to UK)

Hatteras Plain

Blake Plateau

BAHAMAS
NASSAU

TURKS & CAICOS ISLANDS (to UK)

Greater Antilles

VIRGIN ISLANDS (to US)
BRITISH VIRGIN ISLANDS (to UK)
PUERTO RICO (to US)
ANGUILLA (to UK)
ANTIGUA & BARBUDA
GUADELOUPE (to France)
DOMINICA

DOMINICAN REPUBLIC
SANTO DOMINGO

ST KITTS & NEVIS
MONTSERRAT (to UK)
MARTINIQUE (to France)
ST LUCIA
ST VINCENT & THE GRENADINES
GRENADA

Lesser Antilles

BARBADOS

TRINIDAD & TOBAGO

PORT-OF-SPAIN

HAITI
PORT-AU-PRINCE

CUBA

HAVANA

Straits of Florida

Miami

Tampa

Jacksonville

Columbia

Raleigh

Richmond
WASHINGTON DC
Baltimore
Philadelphia
New York
Boston
Albany

Cape Cod

Niagara Falls
Lake Erie

Atlanta

Columbus
Cleveland

Detroit
Lansing

Milwaukee
Madison
Chicago

Des Moines
Lincoln
Topeka

Denver

El Paso

Phoenix
Grand Canyon

Los Angeles
San Diego

Nashville

Memphis

Jackson

Baton Rouge
New Orleans

Little Rock

Oklahoma City

Austin

San Antonio

Dallas

Houston

Corpus Christi

Monterrey

Rio Grande

Red River

Arkansas

Missouri

Mississippi

Mississippi Delta

Gulf of Mexico

Yucatan Peninsula

JAMAICA
KINGSTON

CAYMAN ISLANDS (to UK)

ARUBA (to Neth.)
NETHERLANDS ANTILLES (to Neth.)

Caribbean Sea

Colombian Basin

SOUTH
AMERICA

Andes

BELIZE
BELMOPAN

GUATEMALA
GUATEMALA CITY

HONDURAS
TEGUCIGALPA

EL SALVADOR
SAN SALVADOR

NICARAGUA
MANAGUA

Lake Nicaragua

COSTA RICA
SAN JOSE

PANAMA
PANAMA CITY

Cocos Ridge

Panama Basin

Guatemala Basin

Colón Ridge

Galapagos Islands (to Ecuador)

MEXICO

Sierra Madre Oriental

Sierra Madre Occidental

MEXICO CITY
Volcán Pico de Orizaba 5700m

Guadalajara

Acapulco

Middle America Trench

Lower California

Gulf of California

Revillagigedo Islands (to Mexico)

CLIPPERTON ISLAND (to French Polynesia)

Clarion Fracture Zone

East Pacific Rise

PACIFIC

OCEAN

Gallego Rise

N

Tropic of Cancer

Equator

UNITED STATES
OF AMERICA

Mount Whitney 4418m

Rocky Mountains

Great Plains

Colorado

30°

20°

10°

10°

120°

110°

100°

90°

80°

70°

66

56

153

153

35

WESTERN CANADA & ALASKA

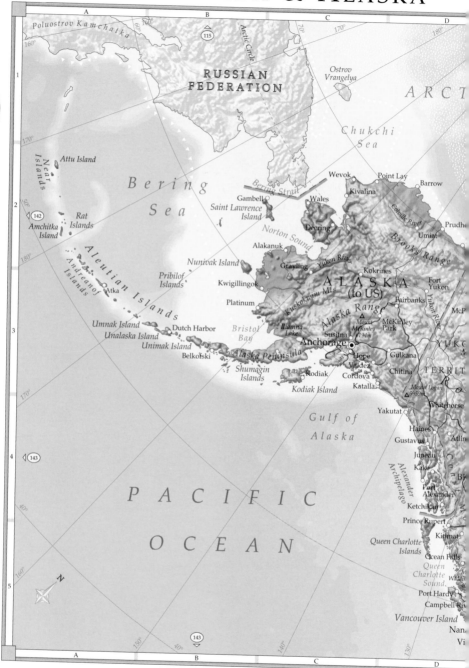

NORTH & CENTRAL AMERICA

RUSSIAN
FEDERATION

Poluostrov Kamchatka

Arctic Circle

Ostrov
Vrangelya

ARCT

*Chukchi
Sea*

Wevok
Point Lay
Barrow

Kivalina

Wales

Gambell

Deering

Umiat
Prudh

*Near
Islands*

Attu Island

*Bering
Sea*

Saint Lawrence
Island

Norton Sound

Alakanuk

Brooks Range

Cobulk River

Amchitka
Island

*Rat
Islands*

Nunivak Island

Grayling

Yukon River

Kokrines

Fort
Yukon

ALASKA
(to US)

Fairbanks

McP

Aleutian Islands

*Andreanof
Islands*

Atka

Pribilof
Islands

Kwigillingok

Platinum

Kuskokwim Mts

Yukon River

YUKC

Umnak Island

Dutch Harbor

*Bristol
Bay*

Iliamna
Lake

Alaska Range

Mount
McKinley
6194m

McKinley
Park

TERRIT

Unalaska Island
Unimak Island

Belkofski

Susitna

Anchorage

Hope
Valdez
Cordova
Katalla

Gulkana

Chitina

Mount Logan
5959m

Whitehorse

Alaska Peninsula

*Shumagin
Islands*

Rodiak

Kodiak Island

Yakutat

Haines

Atlin

*Gulf of
Alaska*

Gustavus

Juneau
Kake

*Alexander
Archipelago*

Bl

P A C I F I C

Port
Alexander

Ketchikan

Prince Rupert

Kitimat

Queen Charlotte
Islands

Ocean Falls

*Queen
Charlotte
Sound*

Port Hardy

Campbell Ri

Vancouver Island

Nan.
Vi

O C E A N

N

0 km   400
0 miles   400

POPULATION

○ Less than 50,000   ○ 50,000 –100,000   ● 100,000 – 500,000   ■ Over 500,000

● Internal administrative capital

Alert

155

GREENLAND
(to Denmark)

Knud Rasmussen Land

Ellesmere Island

Axel Heiberg
Island

Ellef Ringnes
Island
Isachsen

Amund
Ringnes
Island

Baffin

Bay

Prince Patrick
Island

Mould Bay

Queen Elizabeth Islands

Bathurst
Island Cornwallis
Island

Devon Island

82

Melville
Island

Resolute

Lancaster Sound

Davis Strait

Arctic Circle

Banks
Island

*Viscount Melville
Sound*

Somerset
Island

*Prince of
Wales Island*

*Bothia
Peninsula*

Baffin Island

Cumberland Sound

Holman

*Victoria
Island*

Amundsen
Gulf

McClintock Channel

Gulf of Boothia

Igloolik

Nettilling
Lake

Iqaluit

Pelly Bay

King William
Island

Boothia
Peninsula

*Melville
Peninsula*

Amadjuak
Lake

Cambridge Bay

Kugluktuk

Gjoa Haven

Repulse Bay

*Foxe
Basin*

Hope

Great
Bear
Lake Echo Bay

NUNAVUT

Garry Lake

Baker Lake

Back

*Southampton
Island*

Coral
Harbour

Hudson Strait

**NORTHWEST
TERRITORIES**

Edzo Yellowknife Reliance

Mansel
Island

Coats
Island

*Péninsule
d'Ungava*

Fort Simpson

Great Slave
Lake

Lutselk'e

Rankin Inlet

Whale Cove

QUEBEC

Providence

rt Liard

Hay River Fort Smith

Arviat

Hudson

Churchill

Bay

rt Nelson

Lake Athabasca

Fort St. John

Fort Vermilion

A

Wollaston Lake

Reindeer Lake

Belcher
Islands

38

** B I A**

L B E R T A

N

Fort
McMurray

Fox Mine

*Southern
(Indian Lake)*

*James
Bay*

Grande Prairie

Buffalo
Narrows

SASKATCHEWAN

Thompson

A

George

Athabasca

North Saskatchewan

Flin Flon

*Lake
Winnipeg*

Athaba sca

MANITOBA

The Pas

ONTARIO

Edmonton

Mount Robson
3954m

Ledic

Saskatchewan

D

Red Deer

Prince Albert

Kamloops

Calgary

Kindersley

Saskatoon

Yorkton

Lake
Manitoba

Kelowna

Regina

Qu'Appelle

Winnipeg

er

Cranbrook

Medicine Hat

Brandon
Weyburn

Lake Superior

Lethbridge

Melita

Lake Michigan

Milk River

Estevan

U N I T E D   S T A T E S   O F

45

A M E R I C A

Lake Huron

E   F   G   H

ELEVATION

				Below sea level	0	100m	250m	500m	1000m	2000m	4000m

-4000m -3000m -2000m -1000m -500m

328ft 820ft 1640ft 3281ft 6562ft 13 124ft

-13 124ft -9843ft -6562ft -3281ft -1640ft -820ft/-250m 0

EASTERN CANADA

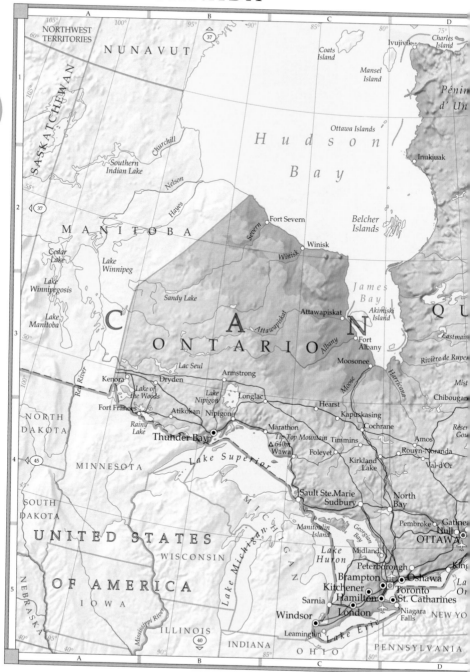

NORTHWEST
TERRITORIES

NUNAVUT

SASKATCHEWAN

Coats
Island

Ivujivik

Charles
Island

Pénin
d' Un

Mansel
Island

Inukjuak

H u d s o n

B a y

Southern
Indian Lake

Churchill

Nelson

Ottawa Islands

Hayes

Fort Severn

Belcher
Islands

MANITOBA

Winisk

Winisk

James
Bay

Cedar
Lake

Lake
Winnipeg

Lake
Winnipegosis

Sandy Lake

Attawapiskat

Akimiski
Island

QU

C   A   N

Lake
Manitoba

O N T A R I O

Attawapiskat

Albany

Fort
Albany

Eastmain

Rivière de Ruper

Lac Seul

Moosonee

Mist

Kenora

Dryden

Armstrong

Moose

Harricana

Chibougan

Lake of
the Woods

Lake
Nipigon

Longlac

Hearst

Kapuskasing

Réser
Gou

NORTH
DAKOTA

Fort Frances

Rainy
Lake

Atikokan

Nipigon

Marathon

Tip Top Mountain
△ 640m

Timmins

Cochrane

Amos

Rouyn-Noranda

Thunder Bay

Lake Superior

Wawa

Foleyet

Kirkland
Lake

Val-d'Or

MINNESOTA

SOUTH
DAKOTA

Sault Ste.Marie

Sudbury

North
Bay

Pembroke

Gatine

Hull

OTTAWA

UNITED STATES

WISCONSIN

Manitoulin
Island

Georgian
Bay

Lake
Huron

Midland

Peterborough

King

NEBRASKA

OF AMERICA

IOWA

Lake Michigan

Brampton

Kitchener

Sarnia

Hamilton

Oshawa

Toronto

St. Catharines

La
Or

Windsor

London

Niagara
Falls

NEW YO

Mississippi River

ILLINOIS

Leamington

Lake Erie

INDIANA

OHIO

PENNSYLVANIA

0 km   400
0 miles   400

POPULATION   ● National capital   ◉ Internal administrative capital

○ Less than 50,000   ○ 50,000 -100,000   ◉ 100,000 - 500,000   ■ Over 500,000

E 65° 60° F 55° 60° 50° G 45° H

82

Resolution
Island

Button Islands

Akpatok
Island

L a b r a d o r   S e a

55°

66

Rivière à la Baleine

Nain

Hopedale
Makkovik Cape Harrison

Cartwright

Scheffervile

N E W F O U N D L A N D

Smallwood
Reservoir Lake Melville

Churchill

St.Anthony

& L A B R A D O R

C   D   A

50°

3

66

r e n t i a n   M o u n t a i n s

Havre-St-Pierre

Sept-Îles

Île d'Anticosti

Corner Brook

Gander

Grand Falls St.John's

Newfoundland

Cape Race

45°

Gaspé

Baie-Comeau

St Lawrence

Matane

*Péninsule de
Gaspé*

Chicoutimi

Rimouski

Rivière-du-Loup

Edmundston

*Gulf of
St. Lawrence*

*Îles de la
Madeleine*

Bathurst

Channel-Port
aux Basques

Cabot Strait

ST PIERRE
& MIQUELON
(to France)

50°

Charlesbourg

Québec

St-Georges

Fredericton

NEW
BRUNSWICK

Moncton

Oromocto

Amherst

PRINCE
EDWARD
ISLAND

Charlottetown

New Glasgow

Glace Bay

Sydney

*Cape Breton
Island*

66

4

Sherbrooke

MAINE

Saint John

Bay of Fundy

Truro

NOVA SCOTIA

Dartmouth
Halifax

Sable Island

40°

NEW
HAMPSHIRE

Yarmouth

Liverpool

A T L A N T I C

5

CHUSETTS

Cape Cod

O C E A N

55°

RHODE ISLAND
70°

65° 40° 60°

66

N

E   F   G   H

ELEVATION
-4000m   -3000m   -2000m   -1000m   -500m   Below sea level   0   100m   250m   500m   1000m   2000m   4000m

328ft   820ft   1640ft   3281ft   6562ft   13 124ft

-13 124ft   -9843ft   -6562ft   -3281ft   -1640ft   -820ft/-250m   0

39

USA: THE NORTHEAST

0 km	200	
0 miles		200

POPULATION   ● National capital   ◎ Internal administrative capital

○ Less than 50,000   ○ 50,000 -100,000   ◉ 100,000 - 500,000   ◼ Over 500,000

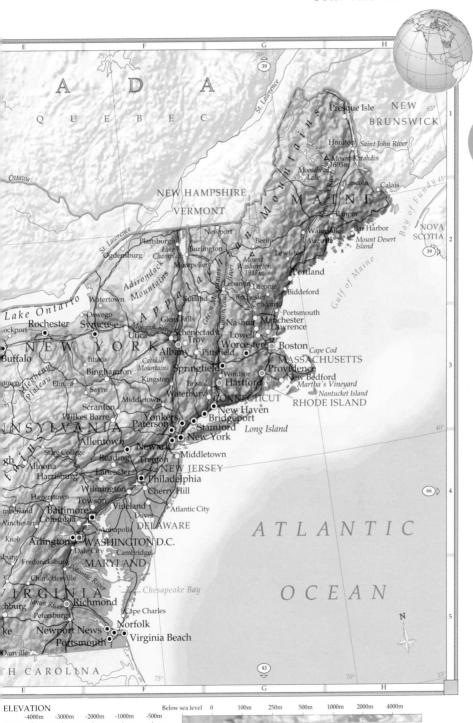

A   D   A

QUEBEC

St. Lawrence

Presque Isle   NEW
BRUNSWICK

Ottawa

Houlton   *Saint John River*

△ Mount Katahdin
1605m
Moosehead
Lake   Lincoln   Calais

NEW HAMPSHIRE
VERMONT   MAINE

Newport   Berlin   Bangor   *Bay of Fundy*
Plattsburgh   Bar Harbor   NOVA
Ogdensburg   Lake   Burlington   Waterville   Mount Desert   SCOTIA
Champlain   Montpelier   Augusta   Island
St. Lawrence   △ Mount   Lewiston   *Gulf of Maine*
Adirondack   Washington   Portland
Watertown   Mountains   1917m
Oswego   Rutland   Lebanon   Laconia   Biddeford
Lake Ontario   Rochester   Rochester   Portsmouth
Lockport   Syracuse   Glens Falls   Concord
ckport   Utica   Schenectady   Nashua   Manchester
Buffalo   NEW YORK   *Mohawk River*   Troy   Lowell   Lawrence
Ithaca   Albany   Pittsfield   Worcester   Boston
Binghamton   Caatskill   Springfield   MASSACHUSETTS   Cape Cod
town   Allegheny   Mountains   Windsor   Providence
Plateau   Elmira   Kingston   Bristol   Hartford   New Bedford
en   Sayre   Middletown   Waterbury   *Martha's Vineyard*
Scranton   CONNECTICUT   Nantucket Island
Wilkes Barre   New Haven   RHODE ISLAND
NSYLVANIA   Yonkers   Bridgeport
Paterson   Stamford   *Long Island*
gh   Allentown   Newark   New York
State College   Reading   Trenton   Middletown
Altoona   Lancaster   NEW JERSEY
Harrisburg   Philadelphia
Hagerstown   Wilmington   Cherry Hill
mberland   Towson   Vineland   Atlantic City
Winchester   Baltimore   Dover
Columbia   DELAWARE   ATLANTIC
Knob   Annapolis
Arlington   WASHINGTON D.C.
burg   Fredericksburg   Dale City   Cambridge
MARYLAND   OCEAN
Charlottesville   *Potomac River*
Chesapeake Bay
IRGINIA   *James River*   Richmond
hburg   Petersburg   Cape Charles
ke   Newport News   Norfolk   N
Danville   Portsmouth   Virginia Beach

TH CAROLINA

ELEVATION
-4000m   -3000m   -2000m   -1000m   -500m   Below sea level   0   100m   250m   500m   1000m   2000m   4000m

-13 124ft   -9843ft   -6562ft   -3281ft   -1640ft   -820ft/-250m   0   328ft   820ft   1640ft   3281ft   6562ft   13 124ft

USA: THE SOUTHEAST

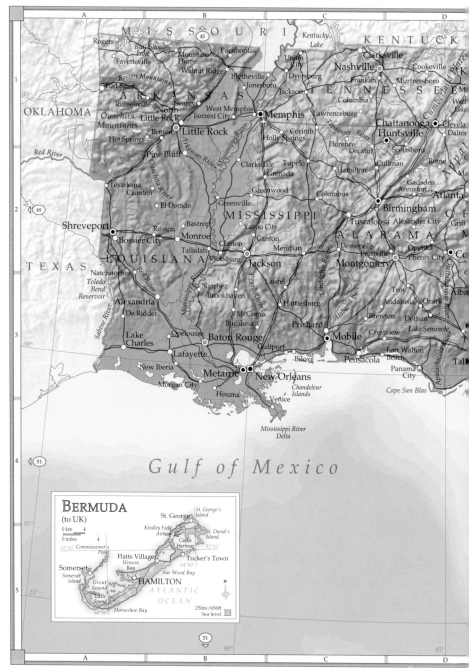

Gulf of Mexico

BERMUDA
(to UK)

0 km 4
0 miles 4

Commissioner's Point

St. George's Island
St. George
Kindley Field Airbase
St. David's Island
Castle Harbour
Flatts Village
Tucker's Town
Hinson Bay
Sue Wood Bay
Somerset
Somerset Island
Great Sound
Little Sound
HAMILTON
Horseshoe Bay

ATLANTIC OCEAN

250m/656ft
Sea level

0 km 200
0 miles 200

POPULATION

○ Less than 50,000   ○ 50,000 -100,000   ◉ 100,000 - 500,000   ◼ Over 500,000

◉ Internal administrative capital

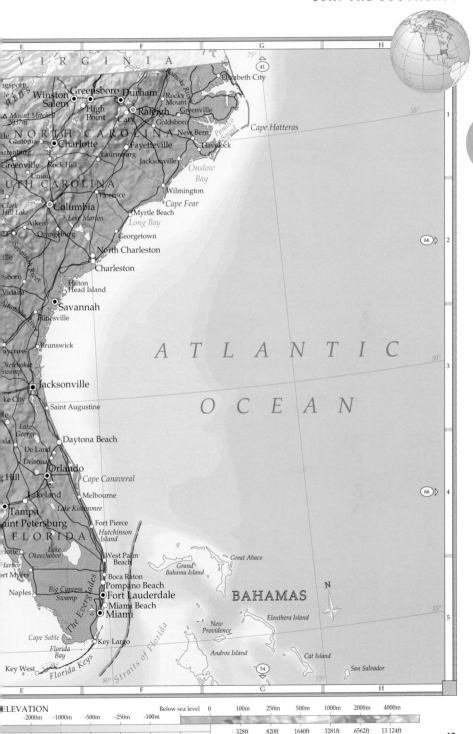

ELEVATION

					Below sea level	0	100m	250m	500m	1000m	2000m	4000m
-2000m	-1000m	-500m	-250m	-100m								
-6562ft	-3281ft	-1640ft	-820ft	-328ft	-164ft/-50m	0		328ft	820ft	1640ft	3281ft	6562ft	13 124ft

USA: Central States

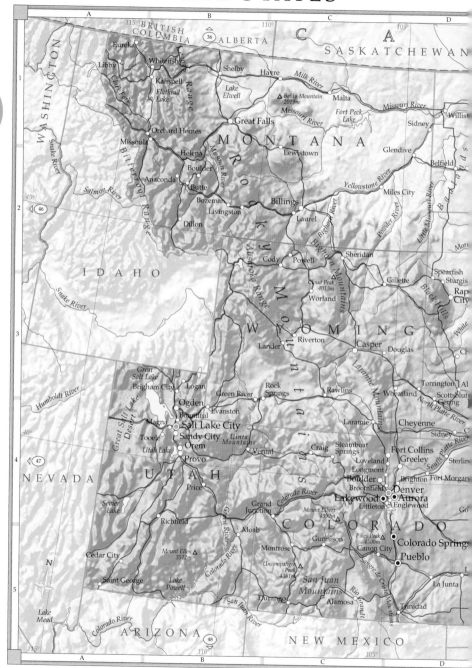

Map labels include:

BRITISH COLUMBIA · ALBERTA · SASKATCHEWAN · CANADA

Eureka · Libby · Whitefish · Kalispell · Flathead Lake · Shelby · Havre · Milk River · Lake Elwell · Baldy Mountain 2019m · Malta · Fort Peck Lake · Missouri River · Sidney · Willis

Great Falls · Missouri River · Orchard Homes · Missoula · Helena · Boulder · Lewistown · Glendive · Belfield

MONTANA

Anaconda · Butte · Bozeman · Livingston · Billings · Laurel · Yellowstone River · Miles City · More

Dillon · Cody · Powell · Sheridan · Spearfish · Sturgis

IDAHO · Snake River · Worland · Cloud Peak 4013m · Bighorn Mountains · Gillette · Rap City · Black Hills

Lander · Riverton · Casper · Douglas

WYOMING

Rock Springs · Green River · Rawlins · Wheatland · Torrington · Scottsbluff · Gering

Great Salt Lake · Brigham City · Logan · Laramie · Cheyenne

Ogden · Evanston · North Platte River · Sidney

Magna · Bountiful · Salt Lake City · Uinta Mountains · Craig · Steamboat Springs · Fort Collins · Greeley · Sterlin

Tooele · Sandy City · Orem · Vernal · Loveland · Longmont

Utah Lake · Provo · Boulder · Brighton · Fort Morgan

NEVADA · UTAH · Price · Broomfield · Denver · Aurora · Lakewood · Littleton · Englewood · Go

Sevier Lake · Richfield · Grand Junction · Colorado River · Mount Elbert 4399m · Pikes Peak 4300m · Colorado Springs

COLORADO

Moab · Gunnison · Canon City · Pueblo

Cedar City · Mount Ellen 3512m · Montrose · Uncompahgre Peak 4361m

Saint George · Lake Powell · Durango · San Juan Mountains · Alamosa · Trinidad · La Junta

Lake Mead · Colorado River · San Juan River · Rio Grande

ARIZONA · NEW MEXICO

POPULATION

0 km — 200
0 miles — 200

○ Less than 50,000 · ○ 50,000 – 100,000 · ◉ 100,000 – 500,000 · ■ Over 500,000

⊚ Internal administrative capital

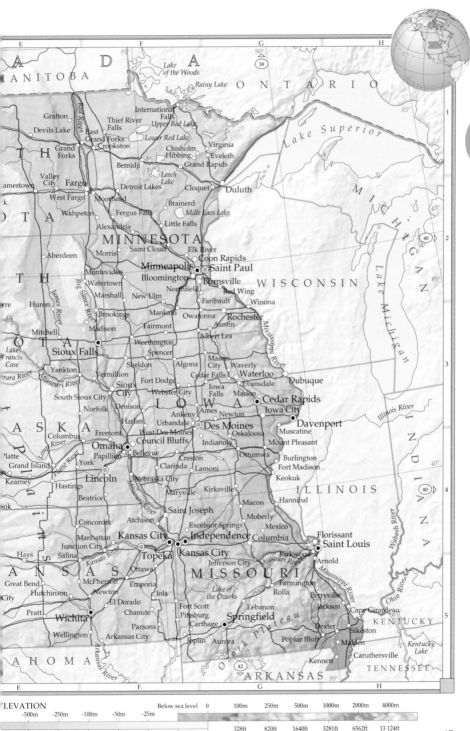

ELEVATION

-500m	-250m	-100m	-50m	-25m	Below sea level	0	100m	250m	500m	1000m	2000m	4000m
-1640ft	-820ft	-328ft	-164ft	-82ft	33ft/-10m	0	328ft	820ft	1640ft	3281ft	6562ft	13 124ft

USA: THE WEST

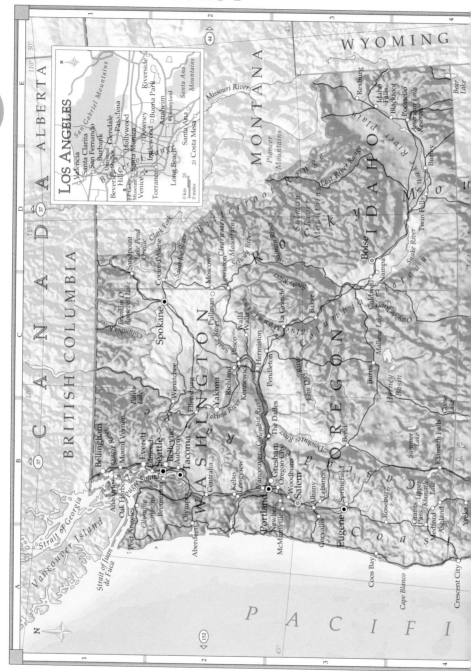

WYOMING

MONTANA

IDAHO

OREGON

WASHINGTON

CANADA

ALBERTA

BRITISH COLUMBIA

Missouri River

Rexburg
Idaho Falls
Blackfoot
Pocatello
American Falls Reservoir
Bear Lake
Burley
Twin Falls
Snake River
Boise
Nampa
Caldwell
Owyhee River
Malheur Lake
Burns
Harney Basin
Goose Lake
Klamath Falls
Summer Lake
Upper Klamath Lake
Bend
Roseburg
Grants Pass
Medford
Ashland
Yreka
Crescent City
Cape Blanco
Coos Bay

Pioneer Mountains
Salmon River Mountains
Lost River Range
Sawtooth Range
Snake River Plateau
Blue Mountains
La Grande
Baker
Pendleton
John Day River
Deschutes River
The Dalles
Columbia River
Gresham
Portland
Vancouver
Oregon City
Woodburn
Salem
Newberg
McMinnville
Albany
Lebanon
Springfield
Eugene
Corvallis

Bitterroot Range
Clearwater Mountains
Selway River
Salmon River
Clearwater River
Lewiston
Moscow
Pullman
Walla Walla
Pasco
Hermiston
Kennewick
Richland
Yakima River
Yakima
Ellensburg
Wenatchee
Spokane
Coeur d'Alene
Sandpoint
Lake Pend Oreille
Clark Fork
Saint Joe River
Columbia River
Franklin D. Roosevelt Lake
Banks Lake

Seattle
Bellevue
Tacoma
Everett
Edmonds
Auburn
Mount Vernon
Bellingham
Anacortes
Oak Harbor
Port Angeles
Olympic Mountains
Bremerton
Olympia
Centralia
Kelso
Longview
Aberdeen
Puget Sound
Skagit River

Vancouver Island
Strait of Georgia
Strait of Juan de Fuca

PACIFI

C

0 km   200
0 miles   200

POPULATION

○ Less than 50,000
○ 50,000 -100,000
◉ 100,000 - 500,000
■ Over 500,000

● Internal administrative capital

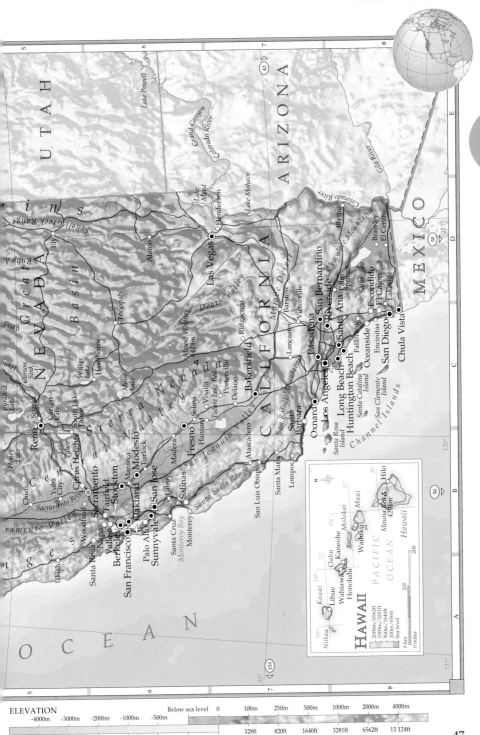

USA: The Southwest

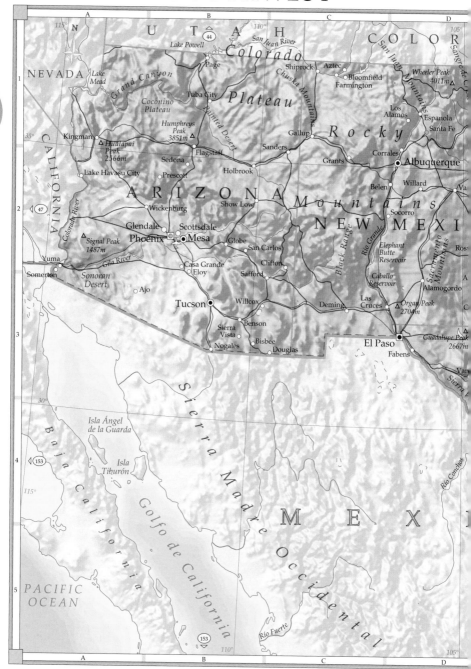

POPULATION

○ Less than 50,000   ○ 50,000 -100,000   ◉ 100,000 - 500,000   ■ Over 500,000

◉ Internal administrative capital

ELEVATION

				Below sea level	0	100m	250m	500m	1000m	2000m	4000m
-2000m	-1000m	-500m	-250m	-100m							

						328ft	820ft	1640ft	3281ft	6562ft	13 124ft
-6562ft	-3281ft	-1640ft	-820ft	-328ft	-164ft/-50m	0					

MEXICO

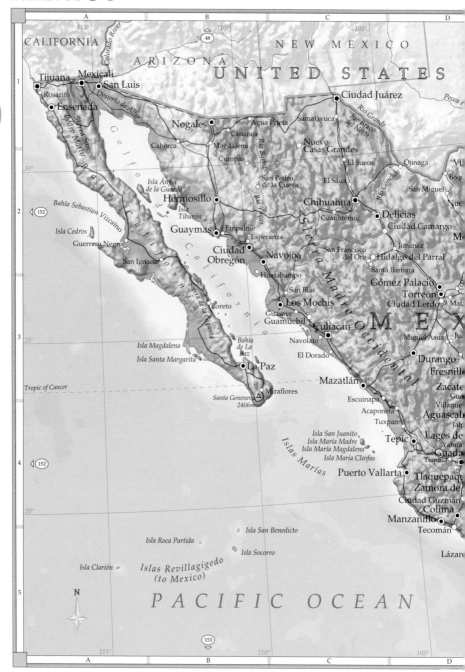

CALIFORNIA

ARIZONA

NEW MEXICO

UNITED STATES

Tijuana
Rosarito
Ensenada
Mexicali
San Luis
Nogales
Caborca
Cananea
Magdalena
Cumpas
Agua Prieta
Samalayuca
Ciudad Juárez
Pecos r
Río Grande del Norte
Nuevo Casas Grandes
El Sueco
Ojinaga
San Miguel
Vi
Boqu
Nue

Desierto de Altar

Colorado River

Sierra San Pedro Mártir

Bahía Sebastián Vizcaíno

Isla Cedros

Guerrero Negro

San Ignacio

Golfo de California

Isla Ángel de la Guarda

Isla Tiburón

Hermosillo

Río Yaqui

Río Bavispe

San Pedro de la Cueva

El Sáuz

Chihuahua

Cuauhtémoc

Delicias

Ciudad Camargo

M

Río Conchos

Guaymas
Empalme
Esperanza

Ciudad Obregón
Navojoa

Huatabampo

San Francisco del Oro

Jiménez

Hidalgo del Parral

Santa Bárbara

Sierra Madre

Gómez Palacio

Torreón

Ciudad Lerdo

Mat

San Blas

Los Mochis

Guasave

Guamúchil

Culiacán

M E

X

Navolato

Miguel Asua

Jua

Loreto

Isla Magdalena

Isla Santa Margarita

Bahía de La Paz

La Paz

El Dorado

Durango

Fresnill

occidental

Tropic of Cancer

Santa Genoveva
2406m

Miraflores

Mazatlán

Escuinapa

Acaponeta

Tuxpan

Zacate

Gua

Villanue

Aguascal

Jal

Islas Marías

Isla San Juanito
Isla María Madre
Isla María Magdalena
Isla María Cleofas

Tepic

Yahua

Tequila

Guada

Lagos de

Puerto Vallarta

Tlaquepaq

Zamora de

Ciudad Guzmán

Colima

Manzanillo

Tecomán

Lázar

Isla Roca Partida

Isla San Benedicto

Isla Socorro

Isla Clarión

Islas Revillagigedo
(to Mexico)

N

PACIFIC OCEAN

0 km   300

0 miles   300

POPULATION   ● National capital

○ Less than 50,000   ○ 50,000 -100,000   ◉ 100,000 - 500,000   ◻ Over 500,00

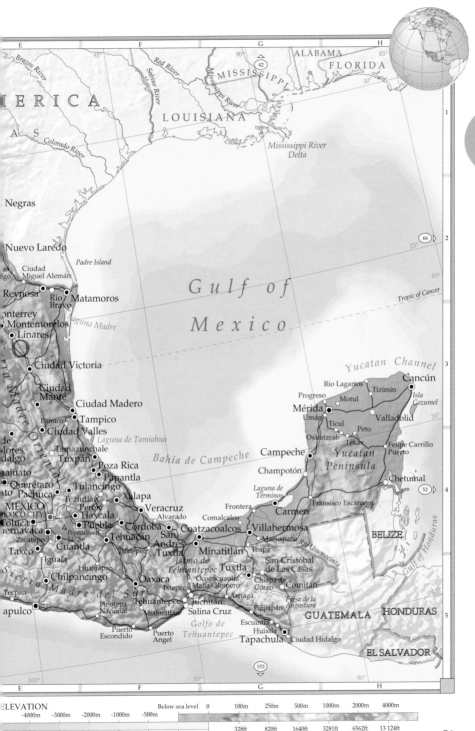

ALABAMA

FLORIDA

Brazos River

Sabine River

Red River

MISSISSIPPI

LOUISIANA

IERICA

AS

Colorado River

Mississippi River

Mississippi River
Delta

Negras

Nuevo Laredo

Padre Island

25°   66   2

as
go   Ciudad
Miguel Alemán

85°

Reynosa   Río
Bravo   Matamoros

Gulf of

Tropic of Cancer

onterrey

Montemorelos

Linares

Laguna Madre

Mexico

Ciudad Victoria

3

Yucatan Channel

Ciudad
Mante

Río Lagartos   Cancún

Tizimín   Isla
Cozumel

Ciudad Madero   Progreso   Motul

Pánuco   Tampico   Mérida   Valladolid   20°

Ciudad Valles   Umán

lores   Laguna de Tamiahua   Ticul   Peto

dalgo   Tamazunchale   Oxkutzcab   Tekax

aajuato   Tuxpán   Papantla   Bahía de Campeche   Campeche   Felipe Carrillo
Puerto

Querétaro   Poza Rica   Champotón   Yucatan
Peninsula   Chetumal

to   Pachuca   Tulancingo   Champotón   Peninsula

Teziutlán   Xalapa   Laguna de
Términos   52   4

MÉXICO   Perote   Veracruz   Fransisco Escárcega

XICO CITY   Tlaxcala   Alvarado   Frontera

Toluca   Puebla   Córdoba   Comalcalco   Carmen

iernavaca   Popocatépetl   Coatzacoalcos   Villahermosa   BELIZE

Zacatepec   5452m   Tehuacán   San   Macuspana

Taxco   Cuautla   Andrés   Minatitlán   Teapa   San Cristóbal
de Las Casas

Iguala   Tuxtepec   Tuxtla   Istmo de   Tuxtla   Chiapa de
Corzo   Comitán

Chilpancingo   Huajuapan   Tehuantepec   Ixtepec   Ocozocuautla   15°

Sierra   Oaxaca   Matías Romero   Presa de la
Angostura   5

apulco   Tehuantepec   Juchitán   Arriaga   GUATEMALA   HONDURAS

Pinotepa
Nacional   Miahuatlán   Salina Cruz   Pijijiapán

Puerto
Escondido   Puerto
Angel   Golfo de
Tehuantepec   Escuintla
Huixtla   EL SALVADOR

Tapachula   Ciudad Hidalgo

100°   95°   153   90°   51
E   F   G   H

CENTRAL AMERICA

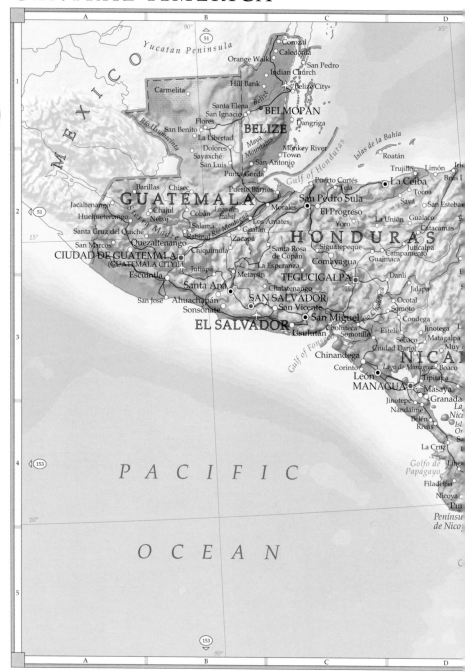

M E X I C O

Yucatan Peninsula

Corozal
Caledonia
Orange Walk
San Pedro
Indian Church
Hill Bank
Belize City
Carmelita
Santa Elena
San Ignacio
BELMOPAN
Flores
Dangriga
San Benito
BELIZE
La Libertad
Maya
Dolores
Monkey River
Sayaxché
Town
San Luis
San Antonio
Mountains
Punta Gorda
Gulf of Honduras
Islas de la Bahía
Barillas   Chisec
Puerto Barrios
Roatán
Trujillo   Limón   Iric
Puerto Cortés
GUATEMALA
Lago de
Morales
San Pedro Sula
Tela
La Ceiba
Brus I
Jacaltenango
Chajul
Zabal
Tocoa
Coban
El Progreso
Savá   San Esteba
Huehuetenango
Nebaj
Salamá
Los Amates
Yoro
La Unión   Gualaco
Santa Cruz del Quiche
Rabinal
Gualán
Catacamas
San Marcos
Chiquimula
Zacapa
HONDURAS
Quezaltenango
Santa Rosa
Siguatepeque
Juticalpa
CIUDAD DE GUATEMALA
de Copán
Campamento
(GUATEMALA CITY)
Comayagua
Guaimaca
Escuintla
Jutiapa
Metapán
La Esperanza
Danlí
San José
Santa Ana
Chalatenango
TEGUCIGALPA
Jalapa
Ahuachapán
San Salvador
Ocotal
Sonsonate
San Vicente
Somoto   Condega
EL SALVADOR
San Miguel   Choluteca
Estelí   Jinotega
Usulután   Somotillo
Sébaco   Matagalpa
Gulf of Fonseca
Chinandega   Ciudad Darío
Muy
Corinto
Lago de Managua   Boaco
NICA
León   Tipitapa
MANAGUA   Masaya
Jinotepe   Granada   *La*
Nandaime   *Nica*
Belén   *Isl*
Rivas   *Or*
Sa
La Cruz
Golfo de   Libe
Papagayo
Filadelfia
Nicoya   *Pu*
Penínsu
de Nico

P A C I F I C

O C E A N

| 0 km | 200 |
| 0 miles | 200 |

POPULATION   ● National capital

○ Less than 50,000   ○ 50,000 -100,000   ◉ 100,000 - 500,000   ◼ Over 500,000

52

E F G H

54

N

80°

Bajo Nuevo
(to Colombia)

Cayo de Serranilla
(to Colombia)

15°

Caratasca

o Lempira

Cayo de Serrana
(to Colombia)

55

75°

C a r i b b e a n

Cayos Miskitos

Tuapi

Puerto Cabezas

Isla de Providencia
(to Colombia)

S e a

Prinzapolka

Barra de Río Grande

Isla de San Andrés
(to Colombia)

Laguna de Perlas

Islas del Maíz

Bluefields

Punta Gorda

San Juan del Norte

Gulf of

Darien

COSTA RICA

Siquirres

Istmo de Panamá

El Porvenir

58

SAN JOSÉ Limón

Cartago

Portobelo

Colón

Ailigandí

Guabito

Cristóbal

Cordillera de San Blas

10°

Chirripó
Grande
3819m

Cordillera de
Talamanca

Almirante

Laguna
de Chiriquí

Panama Canal

Lago Gatún

Lago Bayano

Puerto Obaldía

Cortés

Golfo de los
Mosquitos

Balboa

San Miguelito

Serranía del Darién

Buenos Aires

Volcán Barú 3475m

Capira

PANAMÁ
(PANAMA CITY)

Chimán

palma
nado

Boquete

Cordillera Central

Penonomé

Archipiélago
de las Perlas

La Palma

Isla
del Rey

Yaviza

C O L O M B I A

Almar Sur

La Concepción

P A N A M Á

Aguadulce

El Real

la de Osa

David

Santiago

Garachiné

Golfo Dulce

Golfo
de Chiriquí

Guarumal

Ocú

Chitré

Las Tablas

Golfo

de Panamá

Jaqué

Isla de Coiba

Isla
Cébaco

Península de
Azuero

58

80°

E F G H

ELEVATION

					Below sea level	0	100m	250m	500m	1000m	2000m	4000m
-4000m	-3000m	-2000m	-1000m	-500m								
							328ft	820ft	1640ft	3281ft	6562ft	13 124ft
-13 124ft	-9843ft	-6562ft	-3281ft	-1640ft	-820ft/-250m	0						

THE CARIBBEAN

N

United States of America

The Everglades

Gulf of Mexico

Grand Bahama Island
Freeport
Marsh Harbour
Great Abaco

Bimini Islands
Berry Islands
Northeast Providence Channel

Nicholls Town
NASSAU
Eleuthera Island

New Providence
Rock Sound

Andros Town

Exuma Sound
Cat Island

Tropic of Cancer

Andros Island

BAHAMAS
San Salvador

Florida Keys
Cay Sal
Straits of Florida

Anguilla Cays
George Town
Rum Cay

LA HABANA (HAVANA)
Guanabacoa
Cárdenas

Great Exuma Island
Long Island

Artemisa
Matanzas
Sagua la Grande

Clarence Town
Crooked Island

Pinar del Río
Consolación del Sur
La Fé

Cienfuegos
Santa Clara
Nacetas

Archipiélago de Camagüey
Crooked Island Passage

Acklins Island

Crooked Island

Mayaguana Passage

Caico

Nueva Gerona
Isla de la Juventud
Archipiélago de los Canarreos

Cayo Largo
Bahía de Cochinos

Sancti Spíritus
Morón
Ciego de Ávila

C U B A

Ragged Island Range

Little Inagua

Camagüey
Nuevitas

Lake Rosa
Matthew Town

Archipiélago de los Jardines de la Reina

Las Tunas
Holguín

Manzanillo
Bayamo

Cayman Brac

Palma Soriano

Guantánamo

G r e a t

Santiago de Cuba

Guantánamo Bay (to US)

Windward Passage

Gona

Little Cayman
GEORGE TOWN
Grand Cayman

NAVASSA ISLAND (to US)

Île de la Gonâve
Jérémie
PORT PRIN

CAYMAN ISLANDS (to UK)

Montego Bay

Cayes

Spanish Town
Portmore
KINGSTON

JAMAICA

Jamaica Channel

Pedro Cays

C a r i b b e a n

HONDURAS

NICARAGUA

JAMAICA

Montego Bay
Lucea
Falmouth
Runaway Bay
St Ann's Bay

Caribbean Sea

Cambridge
The Cockpit Country
Christiana
Ewarton
Ocho Rios
Annotto Bay
Buff Bay

Savanna-La-Mar
Mandeville
Spanish Town
Port Antonio
Blue Mountain Peak 2256m

Black River
May Pen
Old Harbour
KINGSTON
Portmore
Morant Bay

Portland Bight

Caribbean Sea

0 km   20
0 miles   20

2000m/6562ft
1000m/3281ft
500m/1640ft
200m/656ft
Sea level

COSTA RICA

COLOM

0 km   200
0 miles   200

POPULATION   ● National capital

○ Less than 50,000   ○ 50,000 -100,000   ◉ 100,000 - 500,000   ■ Over 500,00

54

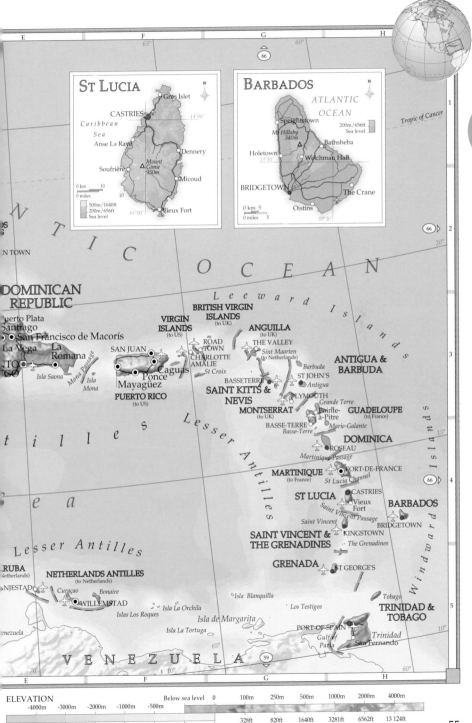

ST LUCIA

- Gros Islet
- CASTRIES
- 14°00'
- *Caribbean Sea*
- Anse La Raye
- Dennery
- Soufrière
- △ Mount Gimie 950m
- Micoud
- 0 km 10
- 0 miles 10
- 500m/1640ft
- 200m/656ft
- Sea level
- Vieux Fort
- 61°00'

BARBADOS

- *ATLANTIC OCEAN*
- Speightstown
- Mt Hillaby 340m △
- Bathsheba
- Holetown
- 13°10'
- Welchman Hall
- 200m/656ft Sea level
- BRIDGETOWN
- The Crane
- Oistins
- 0 km 5
- 0 miles 5
- 59°30'

Tropic of Cancer

ATLANTIC OCEAN

N TOWN

DOMINICAN REPUBLIC
Puerto Plata
Santiago
San Francisco de Macorís
La Vega
La Romana
Isla Saona
Mona Passage
Isla Mona

Leeward Islands

BRITISH VIRGIN ISLANDS (to UK)
VIRGIN ISLANDS (to US)
ROAD TOWN
CHARLOTTE AMALIE
St Croix
ANGUILLA
THE VALLEY
Sint Maarten (to Netherlands)

SAN JUAN
Caguas
Ponce
Mayagüez
PUERTO RICO (to US)

BASSETERRE
SAINT KITTS & NEVIS
MONTSERRAT (to UK)
PLYMOUTH
BASSE-TERRE
Basse-Terre

Barbuda
ST JOHN'S
Antigua
ANTIGUA & BARBUDA
Grande Terre
Pointe-à-Pitre
Marie-Galante
GUADELOUPE (to France)

Antilles

Lesser Antilles

DOMINICA
ROSEAU
Martinique Passage

MARTINIQUE (to France)
St Lucia Channel
FORT-DE-FRANCE

ST LUCIA
CASTRIES
Vieux Fort
Saint Vincent Passage

Saint Vincent
SAINT VINCENT & THE GRENADINES
KINGSTOWN
The Grenadines

BARBADOS
BRIDGETOWN

Windward Islands

Sea

Lesser Antilles

ARUBA (Netherlands)
ANJESTAD
NETHERLANDS ANTILLES (to Netherlands)
Curaçao
Bonaire
WILLEMSTAD
Islas Los Roques
Isla La Orchila
Isla Blanquilla
Los Testigos

GRENADA
ST GEORGE'S

Tobago
TRINIDAD & TOBAGO

Isla de Margarita
Isla La Tortuga
PORT-OF-SPAIN
Gulf of Paria
Trinidad
San Fernando

VENEZUELA
Venezuela

ELEVATION
-4000m -3000m -2000m -1000m -500m Below sea level 0 100m 250m 500m 1000m 2000m 4000m
328ft 820ft 1640ft 3281ft 6562ft 13 124ft
-13 124ft -9843ft -6562ft -3281ft -1640ft -820ft/-250m 0

55

SOUTH AMERICA

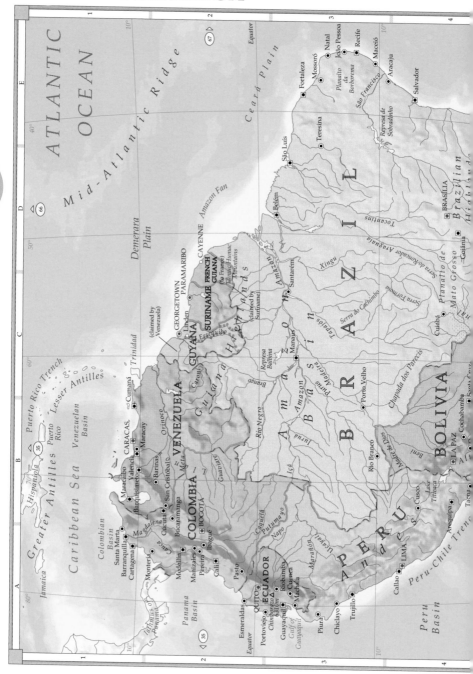

0 km 500

0 miles 500

POPULATION   ● National capital

○ Less than 50,000   ○ 50,000 -100,000   ◉ 100,000 - 500,000   ◼ Over 500,000

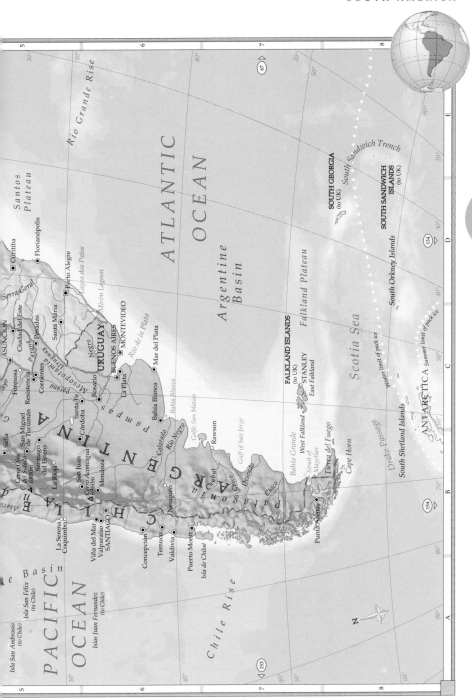

ATLANTIC OCEAN

PACIFIC OCEAN

Rio Grande Rise

Santos Plateau

Argentine Basin

Falkland Plateau

Scotia Sea

SOUTH GEORGIA
(to UK)

South Sandwich Trench

SOUTH SANDWICH
ISLANDS
(to UK)

South Orkney Islands

Winter limit of pack ice

ANTARCTICA Summer limit of pack ice

FALKLAND ISLANDS
(to UK)
STANLEY
East Falkland
West Falkland

South Shetland Islands

Drake Passage

Cape Horn

Tierra del Fuego

Strait of Magellan

Bahía Grande

Punta Arenas

Chile Rise

Curitiba
Florianópolis
Porto Alegre
Lagoa dos Patos
Serra Geral
Santa Maria
Ciudad del Este
ASUNCIÓN
Formosa
Resistencia
Posadas
Corrientes
Paraná
Mesopotamia
Santa Fe
Rosario
Córdoba
La Plata
URUGUAY
BUENOS AIRES
MONTEVIDEO
Río de la Plata
Mar del Plata
Bahía Blanca
Bahía Blanca
Negro
Mirim Lagoon

Salta
San Miguel
de Tucumán
Santiago
del Estero
Cerro Ojos
del Salado
6880m
La Rioja
San Juan
Cerro Aconcagua
6960m
Mendoza
San Luis
A R G E N T I N A
Pampas
Colorado
Río Negro
Neuquén
Chubut
Río Chico
Río Chico
Deseado
Golfo San Jorge
Golfo San Matías
Rawson
Patagonia

La Serena
Coquimbo
Viña del Mar
Valparaíso
SANTIAGO
Concepción
Temuco
Valdivia
Puerto Montt
Isla de Chiloé
C H I L E
Andes

Isla San Ambrosio
(to Chile)
Isla San Félix
(to Chile)
Islas Juan Fernández
(to Chile)

N

67
154
154
153

57

NORTHERN SOUTH AMERICA

A · B · C · D

80°
75°
70°

Caribbean Sea

Lesser A

ARUBA
(to Netherlands)

NETHERLANDS
ANTILLES
(to Netherlands)

Península de la Guajira

Puerto López
Curaçao
Bonaire

Islas
Los Roques

Ríohacha
Santa Marta
Maicao
Golfo de
Venezuela
Coro
Punto Fijo
Puerto
Cumarebo

Barranquilla
Ciénaga
Dabajuro
Sabaneta

Soledad
Pico Cristóbal Colón
5775m
La Concepción
Maracaibo
Puerto
Cabello
CA

Cartagena
Sabanalarga
Cabimas
San Felipe
Mara

Valledupar
Ciudad
Ojeda
Carora
Barquisimeto
Valencia
San

El Carmen
de Bolívar
Machiques
Lago de
Maracaibo
Valera
Acarigua

Sincelejo
Magangué
San Carlos
del Zulia
Mérida
Guanare
Calabozo
V
la

Monteria
Cereté
El Vigía
Pico Bolívar
5007m
Barinas
Río Guanare

Planeta Rica
Aguachica
Ocaña
San Cristóbal
Río Apure
San

Caucasia
Cúcuta
Río Arauca
V E

53
Golfo de
Panamá
Pamplona

PANAMA
Dabeiba
Yarumal
Bucaramanga
Arauca
Río Meta
Puerto

Panama
Canal
Bello
Barrancabermeja
Río Orinoco
Puerto

Medellín
Puerto Berrío
Sogamoso

Nuquí
Itagüí
Tunja
Yopal

PACIFIC
Quibdó
Manizales
Zipaquirá

OCEAN
Pereira
Armenia
BOGOTÁ
Río Meta
Puerto

Buenaventura
Tuluá
Ibagué
Girardot
Villavicencio
Río Guaviare
Puerto Inír

Buga
Espinal
C O L O M B I A

Palmira
Cali
Neiva
San José del Guaviare

Popayán
Garzón

Tumaco
Pitalito

Nevada de Cumbal
4764m
Pasto
Mocoa
Florencia
Río Vaupés
Mitú

60
Ipiales
Orito
Río Apaporis

Equator

Río Putumayo
Río Caquetá
Río Japurá

E C U A D O R
Río Napo

Río Icá

P E R U
Amazon

80°
75°
70°

0 km   200
0 miles   200

POPULATION   ● National capital

○ Less than 50,000   ○ 50,000 -100,000   ◉ 100,000 - 500,000   ◼ Over 500,000

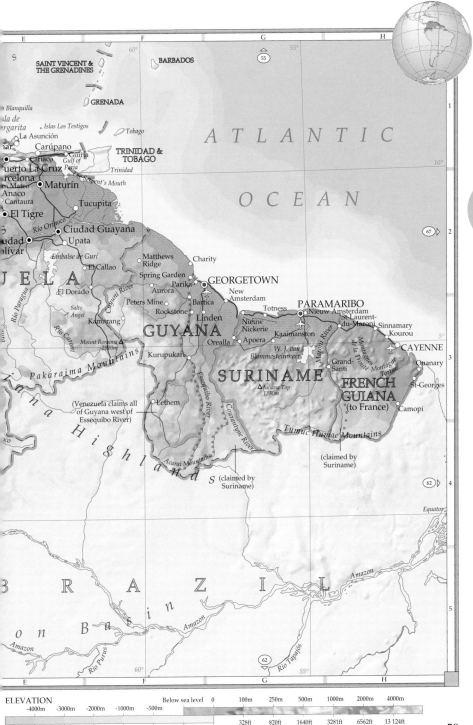

SAINT VINCENT &
THE GRENADINES

BARBADOS

GRENADA

Blanquilla
sla de
rgarita La Asunción
Islas Los Testigos
ar *Tobago*
Carúpano
Cariaco Güiria
Gulf of
Paria
TRINIDAD &
TOBAGO
uerto La Cruz
rcelona
Trinidad
Serpent's Mouth
Mateo
Maturín
Anaco
Cantaura
Tucupita
El Tigre

Río Orinoco
Ciudad Guayana
udad
Upata
olívar

Embalse de Guri
Matthews
Ridge
Charity

UELA
El Callao
Spring Garden
Aurora
Parika
GEORGETOWN

El Dorado
Peters Mine
New
Amsterdam

Salto
Angel
Rockstone
Bartica

Kamarang
Linden
Totness
PARAMARIBO

GUYANA
Nieuw Amsterdam
St-Laurent-
du-Maroni
Sinnamary

Mount Roraima △
2810m
Nieuw
Nickerie
Kaaimanston
Kourou

Pakaraima Mountains
Orealla
Apoera
W. J. van
Blommesteinmeer
CAYENNE

Kurupukari
SURINAME
Grand-
Santi
St-Georges

(Venezuela claims all
of Guyana west of
Essequibo River)
Lethem
△Juliana Top
1230m
FRENCH
GUIANA
(to France)
Camopi

Highlands
Tumuc Humac Mountains

Acarai Mountains
(claimed by
Suriname)

(claimed by
Suriname)

B R A Z I L

Amazon

Amazon

o
B
a
s
i
n
Amazon

Amazon
Río Purús
Río Tapajós

ATLANTIC

OCEAN

ELEVATION
-4000m   -3000m   -2000m   -1000m   -500m   Below sea level   0   100m   250m   500m   1000m   2000m   4000m

-13 124ft   -9843ft   -6562ft   -3281ft   -1640ft   -820ft/-250m   0   328ft   820ft   1640ft   3281ft   6562ft   13 124ft

WESTERN SOUTH AMERICA

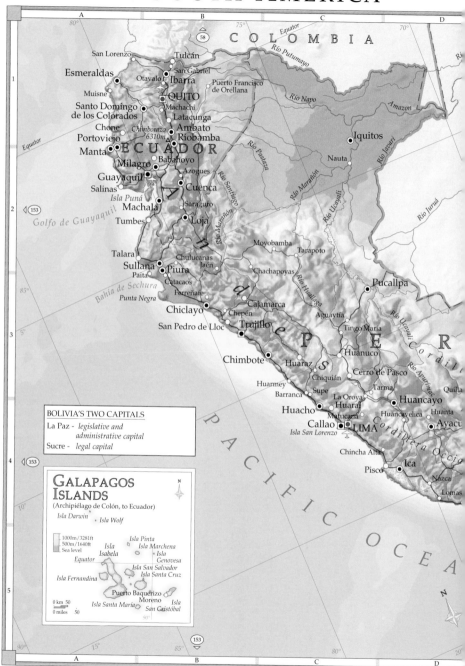

BOLIVIA'S TWO CAPITALS

La Paz - *legislative and administrative capital*
Sucre - *legal capital*

GALAPAGOS ISLANDS
(Archipiélago de Colón, to Ecuador)

Isla Darwin • *Isla Wolf*

| 1000m/3281ft |
| 500m/1640ft |
| Sea level |

Isla Pinta
Isla Marchena
Isla Isabela
Isla Genovesa
Equator
Isla San Salvador
Isla Santa Cruz
Isla Fernandina
Puerto Baquerizo Moreno
Isla Santa María
Isla San Cristóbal

0 km 50
0 miles 50

POPULATION   ● National capital
○ Less than 50,000   ○ 50,000 -100,000   ◉ 100,000 - 500,000   ◼ Over 500,000

0 km 400
0 miles 400

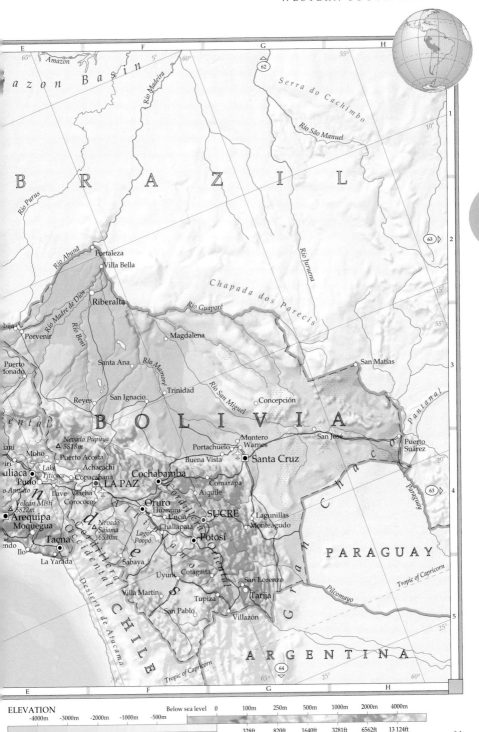

65°
E
Amazon
5°
F
60°
G
55°
H
10°
1

Serra do Cachimbo

a z o n   B a s i n

Rio Madeira

Rio São Manuel

B   R   A   Z   I   L

Rio Purus

63
2
10°

Rio Abuñá

Fortaleza
Villa Bella

Chapada dos Parecis

Rio Madre de Dios

Riberalta

Rio Guaporé

15°
55°

bija

Porvenir

Rio Beni

Magdalena

Puerto
Ionado

Santa Ana

Rio Mamoré

San Ignacio

Trinidad

Rio San Miguel

Concepción

San Matías
3

Reyes

ental

B   O   L   I   V   I   A

San José

Pantanal

Nevado Pupuya
△ 5818m

Montero
Warnes

Puerto
Suárez

Moho

Puerto Acosta

Achacachi

Portachuelo

Buena Vista

Santa Cruz

Gran   Chaco

20°

iri
iliaca
uliaca

*Lake
Titicaca*

Copacabana

Cochabamba

Comarapa

Paraguay

63

Ilave
Viacha

LA PAZ

Aiquile

o Apurío
Volcán Misti
△ 5822m

Corocoro

Oruro

Huanuni

Cordillera

Arequipa
Moquegua

Nevado
Sajama
△ 6520m

Uncia

SUCRE

Lagunillas

Central

Challapata

Monteagudo

Tacna

*Lago
Poopó*

Potosí

Oriental

Ilo

La Yarada

Sabaya

PARAGUAY

C   H   I   L   E

Uyuni

Cotagaita

San Lorenzo

Tropic of Capricorn

endo

Desierto de Atacama

Villa Martín

Tupiza

Tarija

Pilcomayo

25°

San Pablo

Villazón

A   R   G   E   N   T   I   N   A

Tropic of Capricorn

64

70°

65°

60°

E
F
G
H

ELEVATION

| -4000m | -3000m | -2000m | -1000m | -500m | Below sea level | 0 | 100m | 250m | 500m | 1000m | 2000m | 4000m |

| | | | | | | | 328ft | 820ft | 1640ft | 3281ft | 6562ft | 13 124ft |

-13 124ft   -9843ft   -6562ft   -3281ft   -1640ft   -820ft/-250m   0

BRAZIL

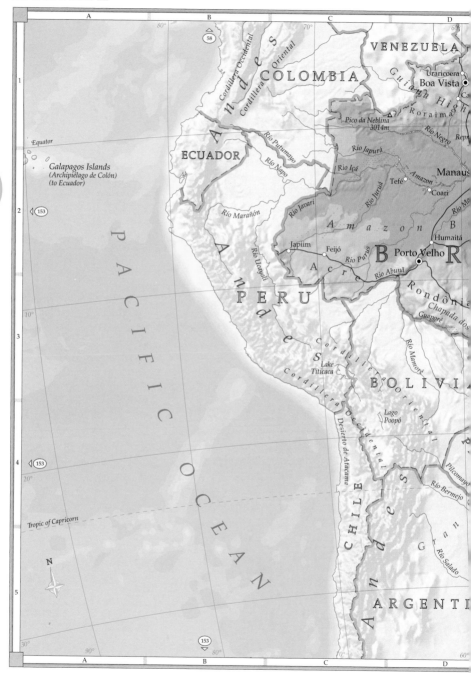

A

B

C

D

58

80°

70°

60°

VENEZUELA

Cordillera Occidental

Cordillera Oriental

COLOMBIA

Uraricoera

Boa Vista

Ca

Guiana High

Roraima

Pico da Neblina
3014m

Rio Negro

Rep

1

ECUADOR

Rio Putumayo

Rio Japurá

Rio Napo

Rio Içá

Manaus

Equator

Rio Juruá

Tefé

Amazon

Coari

Galapagos Islands
(Archipiélago de Colón)
(to Ecuador)

Rio Marañón

Rio Javari

A m a z o n

Rio Ma

2

153

Rio Ucayali

Japiim

Feijó

Rio Purús

Humaitá

B

A c r e S

B

Porto Velho

R

P A C I F I C

P E R U

Rio Abunã

Rondônia

Chapada dos

Guaporé

3

Cordillera

Rio Mamoré

Lake
Titicaca

Cordillera

B O L I V I A

Desierto de Atacama

Lago
Poopó

Cordillera Oriental

O C E A N

4

153

20°

C H I L E

Pilcomayo

Rio Bermejo

Tropic of Capricorn

A n d e s

G

Rio Salado

N

5

153

30°

90°

80°

70°

60°

ARGENTI

A

B

C

D

0 km   600

0 miles   600

POPULATION   ● National capital

○ Less than 50,000   ○ 50,000 -100,000   ◉ 100,000 - 500,000   ■ Over 500,000

ELEVATION

					Below sea level	0	100m	250m	500m	1000m	2000m	4000m
-4000m	-3000m	-2000m	-1000m	-500m								
-13 124ft	-9843ft	-6562ft	-3281ft	-1640ft	-820ft/-250m	0	328ft	820ft	1640ft	3281ft	6562ft	13 124ft

SOUTHERN SOUTH AMERICA

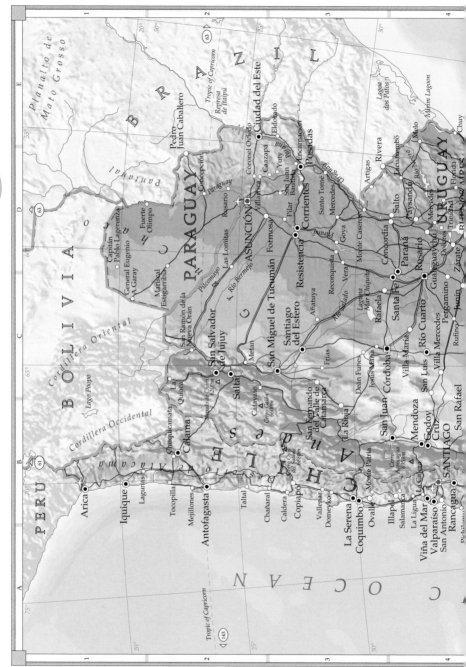

POPULATION ● National capital

○ Less than 50,000   ○ 50,000 -100,000   ◉ 100,000 - 500,000   ◼ Over 500,000

0 km   200

0 miles   200

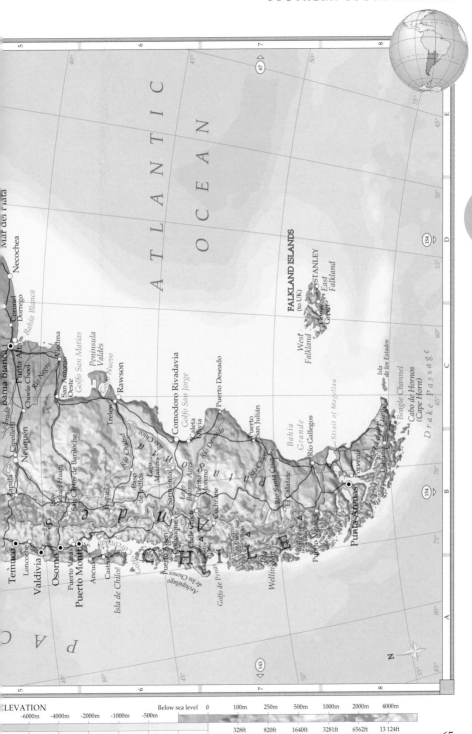

5   6   7   8

40°

45°   67

50°

E

45°

50°

Mar del Plata

Necochea

A T L A N T I C

O C E A N

45°

Coronel
Dorrego

D

154

55°

FALKLAND ISLANDS
(to UK)

STANLEY

Bahía Blanca

Punta Alta

Bahía Blanca

West
Falkland

Choele Choel

Río Negro

San Antonio
Oeste

Golfo San Matías

Península
Valdés

Golfo Nuevo

Rawson

East
Falkland

Goose
Green

C

60°

Cipolletti

Viedma

Neuquén

Zapata

Trelew

Comodoro Rivadavia

Golfo San Jorge

Puerto Deseado

Isla
de los Estados

Río Chubut

Caleta
Olivia

Strait of Magellan

D r a k e   P a s s a g e

San Carlos de Bariloche

Río Chico

Sarmiento

Puerto
San Julián

Bahía
Grande

Beagle Channel

Cabo de Hornos
(Cape Horn)

65°

Ushuaia

Esquel

Paso
de Indios

Lago
Musters

Río Deseado

Río Gallegos

Tierra del Fuego

70°

El Bolsón

Lago
Buenos Aires

Perito
Moreno

Río Chico

Porvenir

Temuco

Loncoche

Ideal
Miñel Huapi

Cochrane

Río Santa Cruz

El Calafate

Punta Arenas

154

75°

Valdivia

Osorno

Puerto Varas

Puerto Montt

Ancud

Castro

Coyhaique

Puerto Aisén

Chile Chico

Monte
Sur

Puerto Natales

B

C H I L E

Corcovado

Archipiélago
de los Chonos

Golfo de Penas

Wellington

N

Isla de Chiloé

P A C

P

80°

85°

50°

55°

A

143

N

5   6   7   8

ELEVATION

| -6000m | -4000m | -2000m | -1000m | -500m | Below sea level | 0 | 100m | 250m | 500m | 1000m | 2000m | 4000m |

| -19 686ft | -13 124ft | -6562ft | -3281ft | -1640ft | -820ft/-250m | 0 | 328ft | 820ft | 1640ft | 3281ft | 6562ft | 13 124ft |

THE ATLANTIC OCEAN

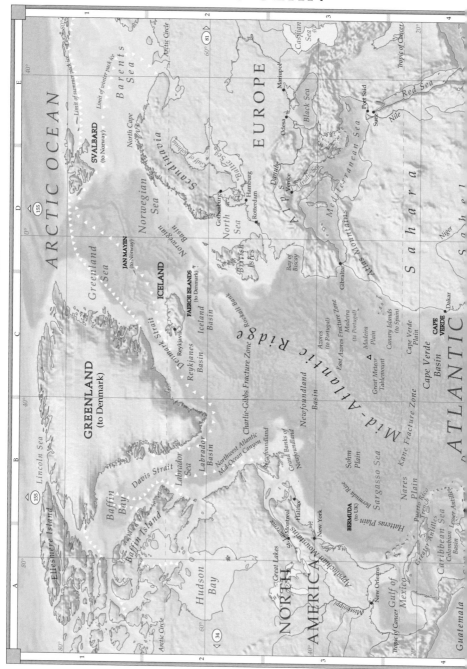

ARCTIC OCEAN

EUROPE

Barents Sea

Caspian Sea

Black Sea

Mediterranean Sea

Red Sea

Nile

Suez

Port Saïd

Mariupol'

Odesa

Danube

Venice

Adriatic Sea

Gibraltar

Atlas Mountains

Sahara

Sahel

Niger

Dakar

CAPE VERDE

Svalbard (to Norway)

Scandinavia

Gulf of Bothnia

North Cape

Norwegian Sea

Gulf of Finland

Baltic Sea

North Sea

Hamburg

Gothenburg

Rotterdam

Göteborg

British Is.

Bay of Biscay

Azores (to Portugal)

East Azores Fracture Zone

Madeira (to Portugal)

Canary Islands (to Spain)

Great Meteor Tablemount

Cape Verde Plain

Cape Verde Basin

ATLANTIC

Kane Fracture Zone

JAN MAYEN (to Norway)

Greenland Sea

ICELAND

FAEROE ISLANDS (to Denmark)

Iceland Basin

Reykjavik

Reykjanes Basin

Denmark Strait

Charlie-Gibbs Fracture Zone

Rockall Bank

Rockall Trough

Mid-Atlantic Ridge

Newfoundland Basin

GREENLAND (to Denmark)

Labrador Sea

Labrador Basin

Northwest Atlantic Mid-Ocean Canyon

Davis Strait

Baffin Bay

Baffin Island

Lincoln Sea

Ellesmere Island

Hudson Bay

Newfoundland

Grand Banks of Newfoundland

Sohm Plain

Sargasso Sea

Nares Plain

Bermuda Rise

BERMUDA (to UK)

Hatteras Plain

Puerto Rico Trench

Nares Plain

Appalachian Mountains

Great Lakes

Montreal

Halifax

New York

New Orleans

Mississippi

Gulf of Mexico

NORTH AMERICA

Tropic of Cancer

Arctic Circle

Caribbean Sea

Greater Antilles

Lesser Antilles

Colombian Basin

Guatemala

Limit of summer pack-ice

Limit of winter pack-ice

Arctic Circle

Tropic of Cancer

• Major port

0 km ————— 1000

0 miles ————— 1000

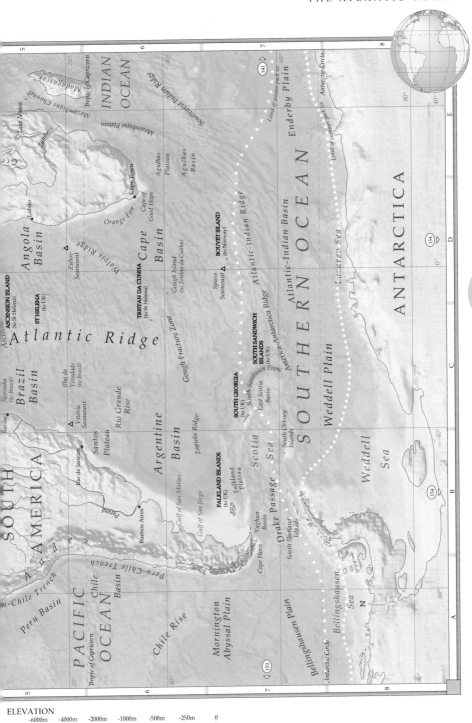

INDIAN OCEAN

Lake Nyasa

Madagascar

Mozambique Channel

Zambezi

Mozambique Plateau

Tropic of Capricorn

Southwest Indian Ridge

Limit of winter pack ice

Antarctic Circle

ENDERBY Plain

Limit of summer pack ice

Lobito

Cape Town

Orange Fan

Cape of Good Hope

Agulhas Plateau

Agulhas Basin

Angola Basin

Zubov Seamount

Walvis Ridge

BOUVET ISLAND (to Norway)

Atlantic-Indian Ridge

Atlantic-Indian Basin

Lazarev Sea

ANTARCTICA

Ascension

ASCENSION ISLAND (to St Helena)

ST HELENA (to UK)

TRISTAN DA CUNHA (to St Helena)

Cape Basin

Gough Island (to Tristan da Cunha)

Spiess Seamount

SOUTHERN OCEAN

Atlantic Ridge

Atlantic Ridge

Brazil Basin

Noronha (to Brazil)

Recife

Ilha da Trindade (to Brazil)

Vitória Seamount

Rio Grande Rise

Santos Plateau

Gough Fracture Zone

Zapiola Ridge

Argentine Basin

SOUTH GEORGIA (to UK)

South Sandwich Trench

East Scotia Basin

America-Antarctica Ridge

SOUTH SANDWICH ISLANDS (to UK)

Weddell Plain

Weddell Sea

SOUTH AMERICA

Rio de Janeiro

Paraná

Buenos Aires

Gulf of San Matías

Gulf of San Jorge

FALKLAND ISLANDS (to UK)

Falkland Plateau

Scotia Sea

South Orkney Islands

Andes

Drake Passage

Yaghan Basin

Cape Horn

South Shetland Islands

Bellingshausen Plain

Bellingshausen Sea

PACIFIC OCEAN

Peru-Chile Trench

Chile Trench

Chile Basin

Tropic of Capricorn

Peru Basin

Chile Rise

Mornington Abyssal Plain

Antarctic Circle

ELEVATION

-6000m	-4000m	-2000m	-1000m	-500m	-250m	0
-19 686ft	-13 124ft	-6562ft	-3281ft	-1640ft	-820ft	0

67

AFRICA

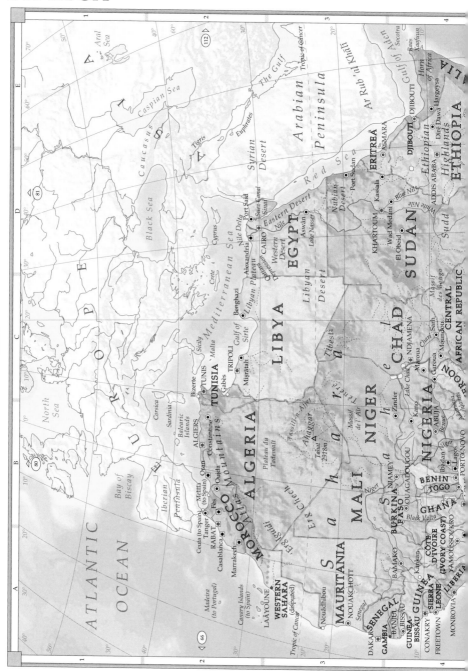

POPULATION ● National capital

○ Less than 50,000   ○ 50,000 -100,000   ◉ 100,000 - 500,000   ▣ Over 500,000

68

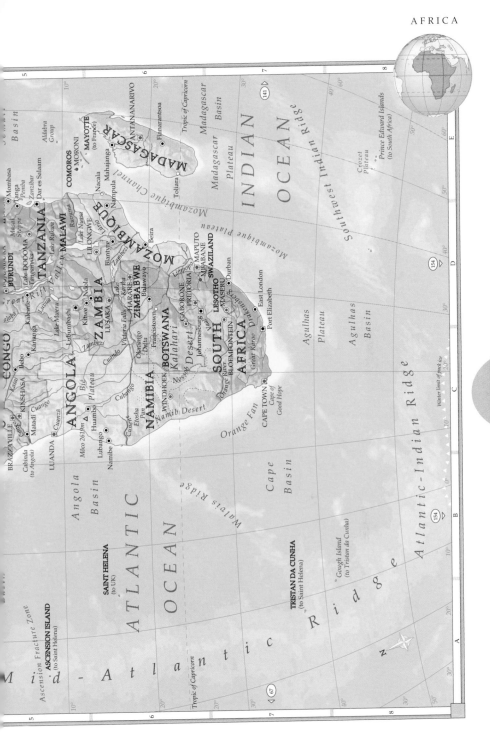

ATLANTIC OCEAN

INDIAN OCEAN

MADAGASCAR

MOZAMBIQUE

TANZANIA

ZAMBIA

ANGOLA

NAMIBIA

BOTSWANA

ZIMBABWE

SOUTH AFRICA

MALAWI

BURUNDI

CONGO

LESOTHO

SWAZILAND

COMOROS

MAYOTTE
(to France)

Mid-Atlantic Ridge

Atlantic-Indian Ridge

Southwest Indian Ridge

Walvis Ridge

Kalahari Desert

Namib Desert

Madagascar Basin

Madagascar Plateau

Mozambique Channel

Mozambique Plateau

Agulhas Plateau

Agulhas Basin

Cape Basin

Angola Basin

Orange Fan

Great Rift Valley

Crozet Plateau

Prince Edward Islands
(to South Africa)

Winter limit of pack ice

ASCENSION ISLAND
(to Saint Helena)

SAINT HELENA
(to UK)

TRISTAN DA CUNHA
(to Tristan da Cunha)

Gough Island
(to Tristan da Cunha)

BRAZZAVILLE

KINSHASA

LUANDA

DODOMA

LILONGWE

LUSAKA

HARARE

GABORONE

PRETORIA

MBABANE

MASERU

BLOEMFONTEIN

WINDHOEK

MAPUTO

MORONI

ANTANANARIVO

Mombasa

Tanga

Pemba

Zanzibar

Dar es Salaam

Mahajanga

Toliara

Fianarantsoa

Nacala

Nampula

Beira

Blantyre

Lake Nyasa

Lake Rukwa

Lake Tanganyika

Masai Steppe

Ruvuma

Ndola

Kitwe

Lubumbashi

Kananga

Kalemie

Lake Mweru

Iebo

Kasai

Matadi

Cabinda
(to Angola)

Cuanza

Mico 2619m

Huambo

Bié Plateau

Lubango

Namibe

Cunene

Cubango

Etosha Pan

Nossob

Okavango Delta

Cuando

Zambezi

Victoria Falls

Lake Kariba

Bulawayo

Francistown

Johannesburg

Vaal

Orange River

Great Karoo

Cape of Good Hope

CAPE TOWN

Port Elizabeth

East London

Durban

Limpopo

Save

Kariba

Luangwa

Congo

Cango

Cuango

Alabra Group

Tropic of Capricorn

Tropic of Capricorn

141

154

154

67

69

NORTHWEST AFRICA

ATLANTIC

OCEAN

PORTUGAL

SPAIN

Tagus

40°

20°

15°

10°

35°

Strait of Gibraltar

GIBRALTAR
(to UK)

Tanger   Ceuta (to Spain)

Ksar-el-Kebir   Tetouan

Melilla
(to Spain)

Oran   Chlef

Mostaga

Madeira
(to Portugal)

Madeira   Porto Santo

Funchal   *Ilhas*
Desertas

Chefchaouen

Salé   Kenitra   Fès   Oujda

Sidi Bel

Tlemcen

RABAT

Casablanca

Jerada

Chott

El-Jadida   Mohammedia

Khouribga

Moyen Atlas

Hauts Plateaux

Safi   Beni   Mellal

Atlas   *Mountains*

Atlas Sahar

Essaouira   Marrakech

Haut

El-Rachidia

Tigni

30°

Islas Canarias
(Canary Islands)
(to Spain)

Béchar

MOROCCO

Ouarzazate

Agadir

Grand Erg Occ

El

La Palma

Santa Cruz de
Tenerife   Lanzarote

Tiznit

Gomera   *Fuerteventura*

Hierro   *Tenerife*

Las Palmas
de Gran Canaria

Gran
Canaria

Tan-Tan

Hamada du Dra

A L G E

LAÂYOUNE

El Mahbas   Tindouf

Pl
du T

Boujdour

Smara

Adrar

I-n-Sa

Bou Craa

'Erg Iguîdi

Reggane

WESTERN
SAHARA
(disputed territory
under Moroccan occupation)

Galtat-Zemmour

Erg Chech

Tanezrouft

Tropic of Cancer

Ad Dakhla

25°

66

20°

Lagouira

Ouarâne

S

a

MAURITANIA

Azaouâd

MALI

15°

Senegal

15°

SENEGAL

Niger

10°

5°

0°

A   B   C   D

0 km   400

0 miles   400

POPULATION   ● National capital

○ Less than 50,000   ○ 50,000 -100,000   ◉ 100,000 - 500,000   ◼ Over 500,000

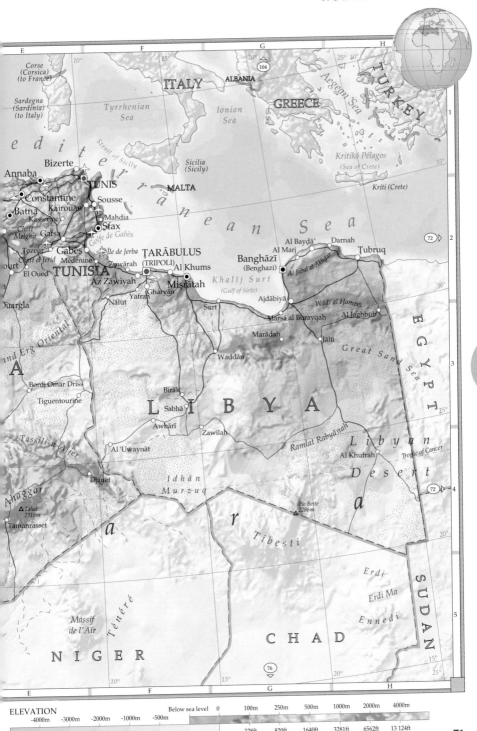

ELEVATION

Below sea level						100m	250m	500m	1000m	2000m	4000m
-4000m	-3000m	-2000m	-1000m	-500m	0						
-13 124ft	-9843ft	-6562ft	-3281ft	-1640ft	-820ft/-250m	0	328ft	820ft	1640ft	3281ft	6562ft	13 124ft

NORTHEAST AFRICA

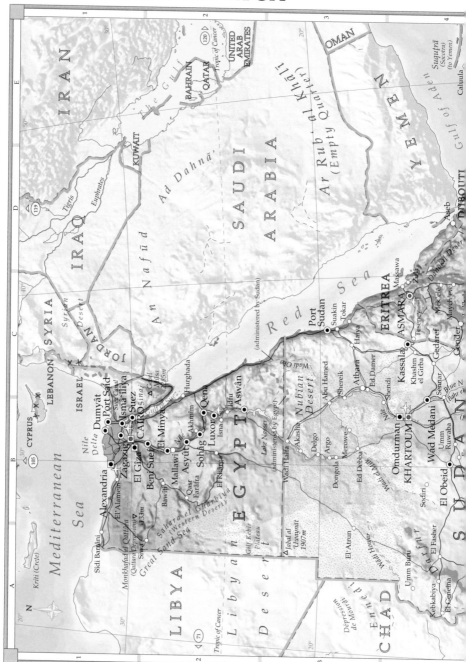

IRAN

IRAQ

SYRIA

LEBANON

ISRAEL

JORDAN

CYPRUS

Kríti (Crete)

Mediterranean Sea

KUWAIT

BAHRAIN

QATAR

UNITED ARAB EMIRATES

OMAN

Suqutrā (Socotra) (to Yemen)

The Gulf

An Nafūd

Ad Dahnā'

SAUDI ARABIA

Ar Rub' al Khālī (Empty Quarter)

YEMEN

Gulf of Aden

Caluula

DJIBOUTI

Aseb

Red Sea

ERITREA

ASMARA

Massawa

Zula

Dahlak Desert

Mayd'ew

Mek'elē

Keren

Tesseney

Tigris

Euphrates

Syrian Desert

Tropic of Cancer

(administered by Sudan)

Port Sudan

Suakin

Tokar

Hafya

Kassala

Gedaref

Gonder

Wadi Oko

Nubian Desert

Hurghada

Jabal Mūsa 2285m

Port Said

Dumyât

Ismâ'îlîya

Suez

Sinai

Nile Delta

Alexandria

El Alamein

Sîdi Barâni

CAIRO

El Gîza

Zagazig

Benha

El Minya

Mallawi

Asyûṭ

Sohâg

Akhmîm

Qena

Luxor

Isna

Idfu

Aswân

Lake Nasser

(administered by Egypt)

Wadi Halfa

Akasha

Delgo

Argo

Dongola

Ed Debba

Merowe

Abu Hamed

Shereik

Atbara

Ed Damer

Shendi

Khashm el Girba

Sennar

Wad Medani

Omdurman

KHARTOUM

Umm Ruwaba

El Obeid

Sodiri

Umm Badr

Kebkabiya

El Geneina

El Fasher

Blue Nile (Bahr el A...)

SUDAN

DARFUR

CHAD

ENNEDI

Dépression de Mourdi

Wadi Howar

El'Atrun

LIBYA

Libyan Desert

Western Desert

Great Sand Sea

Sahara el Gharbîya

Siwa

Bawîti

Qasr Farâfra

El Nasya

Gilf Kebir Plateau

△ *Jabal al Uwaynāt 1907m*

Monkhafad el Qattâra (Qattara Depression) ▽ 133m

Tropic of Cancer

N

△ 71

119

105

120

Blue Nile

0 km   400

0 miles   400

POPULATION

 ● National capital

○ Less than 50,000   ○ 50,000 -100,000   ◉ 100,000 - 500,000   ◼ Over 500,000

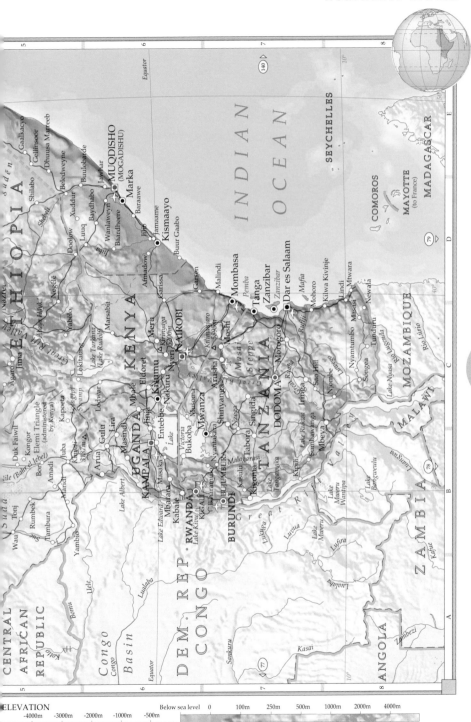

CENTRAL AFRICAN REPUBLIC

ETHIOPIA

SUDAN

KENYA

UGANDA

RWANDA

BURUNDI

DEM. REP. CONGO

TANZANIA

ZAMBIA

ANGOLA

MALAWI

MOZAMBIQUE

MADAGASCAR

SEYCHELLES

COMOROS

MAYOTTE (to France)

INDIAN OCEAN

MUQDISHO (MOGADISHU)

NAIROBI

KAMPALA

DODOMA

BUJUMBURA

KIGALI

Mombasa

Dar es Salaam

Zanzibar

Tanga

Pemba

Mafia

Equator

Gaalkacyo
Gellinsoor
Dhuusa Mareeb
Shilabo
Beledweyne
Buulobarde
Marka
Baraawe
Xuddur
Baydhabo
Kismaayo
Jamaame
Buur Gaabo
Afmadow
Garissa
Garsen
Malindi
Lamu
Kilwa Kivinje
Lindi
Mtwara
Newala
Nyamtumbo
Tunduru
Songea
Mbeya
Iringa
Morogoro
Sao Hill
Njombe
Masasi
Mpanda
Tabora
Kigoma
Singida
Shinyanga
Mwanza
Musoma
Arusha
Moshi
Meru
Nyeri
Nakuru
Kisumu
Eldoret
Mbale
Gulu
Lira
Masindi
Arua
Kabale
Entebbe
Bukoba
Nansio
Kilimanjaro 5895m
Marsabit
Negēlē
Ägaro
Jīma
Negēlē
Kabelo

ELEVATION

73

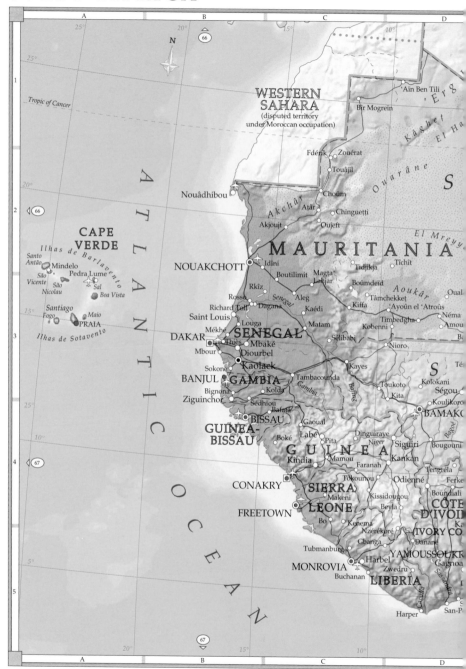

N

66

25°   20°   15°   10°

Tropic of Cancer

**WESTERN
SAHARA**
(disputed territory
under Moroccan occupation)

Aïn Ben Tili

Bîr Mogreïn

'Erg Î

Kâghet

El Ha

Fdérik   Zouérat

Touâjîl

Ouarâne

S

20°

66

Nouâdhibou

Choûm

Akchâr   Atâr   Chinguetti

Akjoujt   Oujeft

El Mreyy

**CAPE
VERDE**

Ilhas de Barlavento

Santo
Antão   Mindelo
Pedra Lume
São   Sal
Vicente   São   Boa Vista
Nicolau

Santiago
Fogo   Maio
PRAIA

Ilhas de Sotavento

M A U R I T A N I A

NOUAKCHOTT   Idîni

Boutilimit   Magta
Lahjar   Tidjikja   Tîchît   Aoukâr

Rkîz   Boûmdeïd   Tâmchekket   Oual
Rosso   Senegal   Aleg   Kiffa   Ayoûn el 'Atroûs   Néma
Richard Toll   Dagana   Kaédi   Timbedgha   Amou
Saint Louis   Kobenni   Nioro   Ba
Louga   Matam   Sélibabi

DAKAR   Mékhé   SENEGAL   Kayes   S   Té
Thiès   Mbaké   Toukoto   Kolokani
Mbour   Diourbel   Tambacounda   Kita   Ségou
Sokone   Kaolack   Gambia   Kouloro
BANJUL   GAMBIA   Kolda   BAMAKO
Bignona   Sédhiou   Bafata
Ziguinchor   Gambia   Bagoé

BISSAU   Gaoual   Labé   Dinguiraye   Niger   Siguiri   Bougouni
**GUINEA-
BISSAU**   Boké   Pita   Mamou   Kankan
Kindia   Faranah   Tengréla
Tokoumou   Odienné   Ferke
CONAKRY   Mamou   Kissidougou   Boundiali
SIERRA   Makeni   Beyla   CÔTE
FREETOWN   LEONE   D'IVOI
Bo   Kenema   IVORY CO
Nzérékoré   Ka
Gbanga   Danané
Tubmanburg   YAMOUSSOUKR
MONROVIA   Harbel   Zwedru   Gagnoa
Buchanan   LIBERIA
Harper   San-P

A T L A N T I C   O C E A N

0 km   400

0 miles   400

POPULATION   ● National capital

○ Less than 50,000   ○ 50,000 -100,000   ● 100,000 - 500,000   ■ Over 500,000

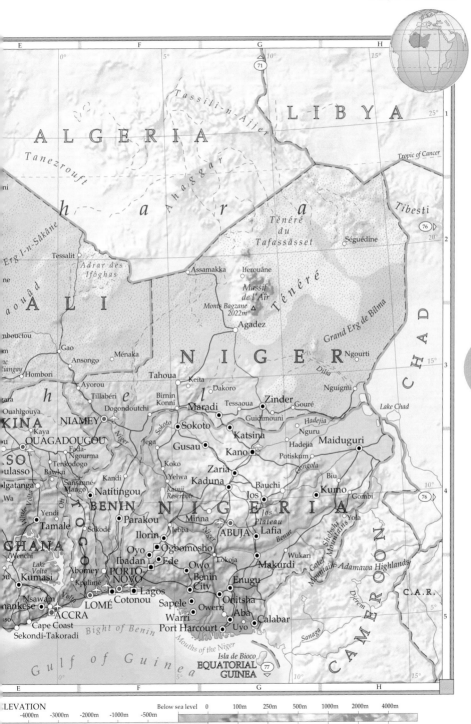

CENTRAL AFRICA

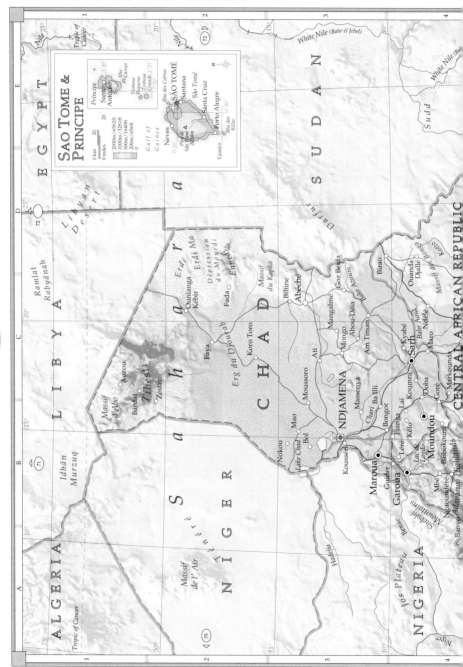

POPULATION   ● National capital

○ Less than 50,000   ○ 50,000 -100,000   ◉ 100,000 - 500,000   ◼ Over 500,000

0 km   400
0 miles   400

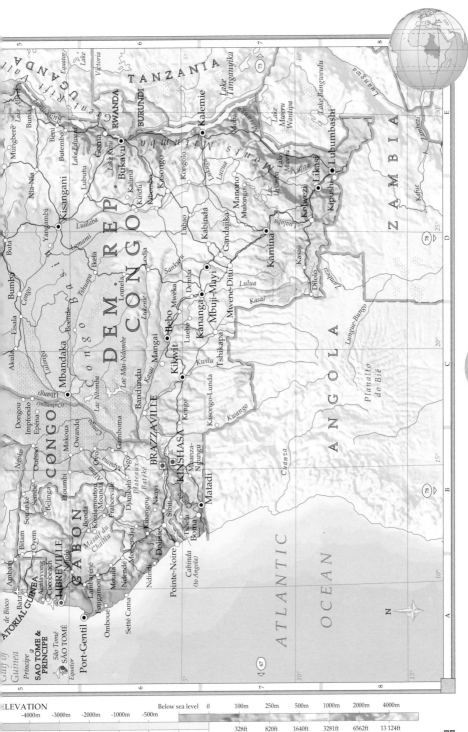

SOUTHERN AFRICA

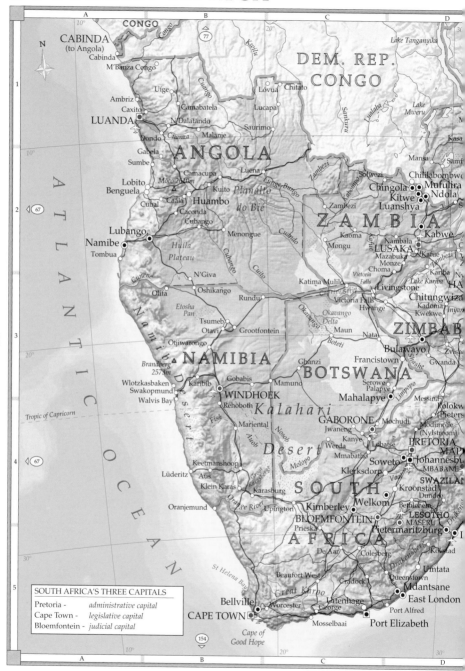

CONGO

CABINDA
(to Angola)
Cabinda

M'Banza Congo

Ambriz
Caxito
Uíge
Camabatela
Lóvua
Chitato

DEM. REP.
CONGO

Lake Tanganyika

LUANDA
N'Dalatando
Lucapa
Saurimo

Dondo
Cuanza
Malanje

Gabela
Sumbe
Camacupa
Luena
ANGOLA

Mansa
Samf

Lobito
Benguela
Moço 2620m
Kuito
Planalto
do Bié

Lake
Mweru

Kasa

Cubal
Caála
Huambo
Caconda

Zambezi
Lunga-Bungo

Solwezi
Chililabombwe
Chingola
Mufulira
Kitwe
Ndola
Luanshya

Cubango
Zambezi

ZAMBIA

Lubango

Namibe
Tombua

Huíla
Plateau

Menongue

Cubango

Cuito

Kaoma
Mongu

Kabwe

Nambala
LUSAKA
Mazabuka
Monze
Choma

Kafue

N'Giva
Oshikango

Cunene

Olifa

Rundu

Katima Mulilo

Victoria
Falls

Livingstone

Lake Kariba
Kariba

Katima

Ha

Etosha
Pan

Tsumeb
Otavi
Grootfontein

Okavango
Delta

Maun

Victoria Falls
Hwange

Chitungwiza
Kadoma
Kwekwe

Inyi

Otjiwarongo

Boteti

Nata

ZIMBAB

Brandberg
2573m

NAMIBIA

Ghanzi

Francistown

Bulawayo

Zvisha
Gwanda

Wlotzkasbaken
Swakopmund
Walvis Bay

Karibib
Gobabis
Mamuno

BOTSWANA

Serowe
Palapye
Mahalapye

Messina

Kolokw
Pieters

Tropic of Capricorn

WINDHOEK
Rehoboth

Kalahari

Limpopo

Fish

Mariental

GABORONE
Jwaneng
Mochudi
Kanye
Lobatse

Modimolle
(Nylstroom)

PRETORIA
MAP

Auob

Nosob

Desert

Werda
Mmabatho

Soweto

MBABANE

Johannesb

Keetmanshoop

Molopo

Klerksdorp

SWAZILAN

Lüderitz
Aus
Klein Karas

Karasburg

SOUTH

Kroonstad
Dundee

Oranjemund

Orange River
Upington

Kimberley

Welkom

Bethlehem

LESOTHO

MASERU

BLOEMFONTEIN
Prieska

Pietermaritzburg

AFRICA

De Aar
Colesberg

Drakensberg

Kokstad

I

Beaufort West

Cradock

Umtata

Queenstown

Mdantsane

St Helena Bay

Great Karoo

Worcester
George

Uitenhage

East London

Bellville

CAPE TOWN
Mosselbaai

Port Alfred

Port Elizabeth

Cape of
Good Hope

SOUTH AFRICA'S THREE CAPITALS

Pretoria - *administrative capital*
Cape Town - *legislative capital*
Bloemfontein - *judicial capital*

0 km   400

0 miles   400

POPULATION   ● National capital

○ Less than 50,000   ◉ 50,000 -100,000   ◉ 100,000 - 500,000   ▣ Over 500,000

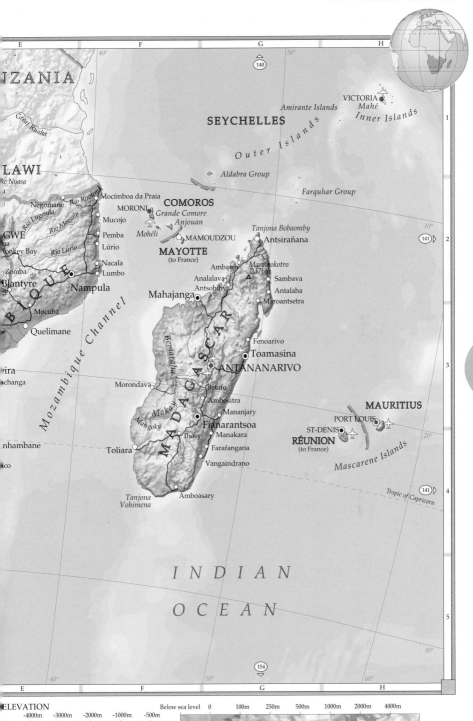

ZANIA

Great Ruaha

LAWI

ke Nyasa

GWE
na
onkey Bay
Zomba
Blantyre

BIQUE

Mocuba

Quelimane

eira

achanga

nhambane

ico

Negomane
Rio Rovuma
Rio Lugenda
Rio Messalo
Rio Lúrio

Mocímboa da Praia
Mucojo
Pemba
Lúrio
Nacala
Lumbo
Nampula

SEYCHELLES

Amirante Islands

VICTORIA
Mahé
Inner Islands

Outer Islands

Aldabra Group

Farquhar Group

COMOROS
MORONI
Grande Comore
Anjouan
Mohéli
MAMOUDZOU
MAYOTTE
(to France)

Tanjona Bobaomby
Antsirañana

Ambanja
Analalava
Antsohihy
Mahajanga

Maromokotro
2376m
Sambava
Antalaha
Maroantsetra

Fenoarivo
Toamasina

Bemaraha

ANTANANARIVO

Morondava
Betafo
Ambositra
Mananjary
Fianarantsoa
Ihosy
Manakara
Toliara
Farafangana
Vangaindrano

Makay

Mangoky

Tanjona
Vohimena
Amboasary

Mozambique Channel

MADAGASCAR

MAURITIUS
PORT LOUIS
ST-DENIS
RÉUNION
(to France)

Mascarene Islands

Tropic of Capricorn

INDIAN

OCEAN

40°
50°
10°
20°
30°

140
141
141
154

E   F   G   H

EUROPE

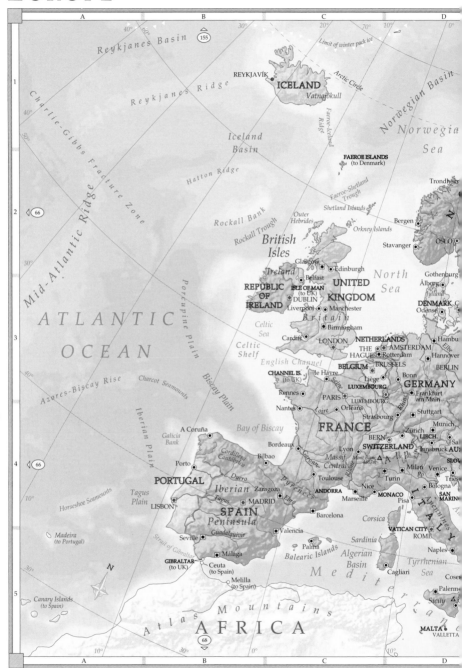

Reykjanes Basin

155

Reykjanes Ridge

REYKJAVÍK

Limit of winter pack ice

Arctic Circle

ICELAND
Vatnajökull

Iceland
Basin

Norwegian Basin

66

Faeroe-Iceland Ridge

FAEROE ISLANDS
(to Denmark)

Norwegian
Sea

Hatton Ridge

Trondheim

Faeroe-Shetland Trough

Shetland Islands

Bergen

Rockall Bank

Outer
Hebrides

Orkney Islands

Stavanger

OSLO

Rockall Trough

British
Isles

North
Sea

Gothenburg

Mid-Atlantic Ridge

Porcupine Plain

Glasgow
Edinburgh

Ireland
Belfast

UNITED
KINGDOM

Ålborg
Jylland

DENMARK

ATLANTIC

REPUBLIC
OF
IRELAND

ISLE OF MAN
(to UK)
DUBLIN

Liverpool
Manchester

Britain

Odense

OCEAN

Celtic
Sea

Cardiff

Birmingham

LONDON

NETHERLANDS

Hambu

Elbe

Celtic
Shelf

THE
HAGUE

AMSTERDAM
Rotterdam

Hannover

BERLIN

English Channel

BELGIUM

BRUSSELS

Azores-Biscay Rise

Charcot Seamounts

Biscay Plain

CHANNEL IS.
(to UK)

le Havre

Liège

Bonn

GERMANY

Rennes

Seine

LUXEMBOURG
LUXEMBOURG

Frankfurt
am Main

Iberian Plain

Nantes

PARIS

Orléans

Rhine

Stuttgart

Loire

Strasbourg

A Coruña

Galicia
Bank

Bay of Biscay

FRANCE

Munich

Zürich

LIECH.

Bordeaux

BERN

SWITZERLAND

Innsbruck

AU:

66

Porto

Cordillera
Cantábrica

Bilbao

Garonne

Lyon

Massif
Central

Mont Blanc
4807m

Alps

Milan

Turin

Po

SLOV

Venice

Trie

Bologna

PORTUGAL

Duero

Pyrenees

Toulouse

Rhône

Nice

Horseshoe Seamounts

Tagus
Plain

Iberian

Zaragoza

Ebro

ANDORRA

Marseille

MONACO

Pisa

SAN
MARIN

LISBON

Tagus

MADRID

SPAIN

Barcelona

Corsica

VATICAN CITY
ROME

Madeira
(to Portugal)

Peninsula

Guadalquivir

Valencia

Naples

Seville

Sardinia

Algerian
Basin

Tyrrhenian
Sea

Málaga

Palma

Balearic Islands

GIBRALTAR
(to UK)

Strait of Gibraltar

Ceuta
(to Spain)

Cagliari

Cose

Canary Islands
(to Spain)

Melilla
(to Spain)

Mediterranean

Palerm

Sicily

N

Atlas Mountains

AFRICA

68

MALTA
VALLETTA

0 km   500

0 miles   500

POPULATION ● National capital

○ Less than 50,000   ○ 50,000 -100,000   ◉ 100,000 - 500,000   ◼ Over 500,00

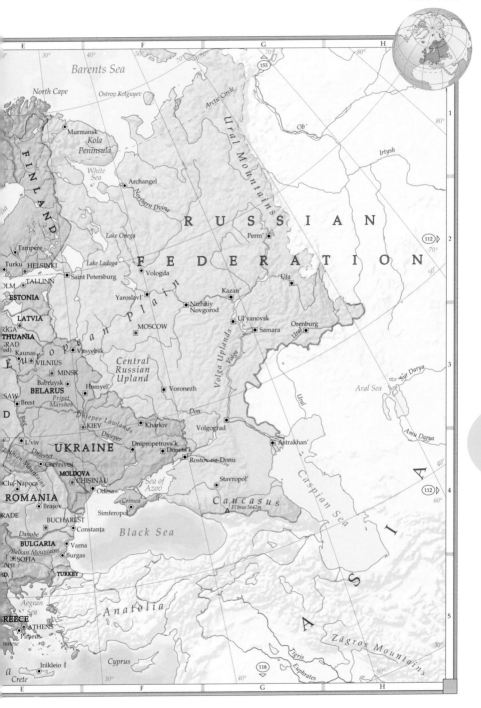

Barents Sea

North Cape

Ostrov Kolguyev

Arctic Circle

155

Ob'

80°

FINLAND

Murmansk

Kola
Peninsula

Irtysh

White
Sea

Archangel

Northern Dvina

Ural Mountains

R U S S I A N

Perm'

112

70°

Tampere

Lake Onega

Lake Ladoga

Vologda

F E D E R A T I O N

Ufa

50°

Turku HELSINKI

Saint Petersburg

Kazan'

OLM TALLINN

Yaroslavl'

Nizhniy
Novgorod

Orenburg

ESTONIA

MOSCOW

Ul'yanovsk

Ural

LATVIA

Samara

RIGA

Volga Uplands

Aral Sea

THUANIA

Vitsyebsk

Central
Russian
Upland

Syr Darya

RAD
ed).

Kaunas

VILNIUS

MINSK

Amu Darya

SAW

Babruysk

Homyel'

Voronezh

Don

Ural

40°

Brest

BELARUS

Pripet
Marshes

Dnieper Lowlands

Kharkiv

Volgograd

Astrakhan'

KIEV

Dnieper

L'viv

Dniester

UKRAINE

Dnipropetrovs'k

Donets'k

60°

Chernivtsi

Rostov-na-Donu

Caspian Sea

Cluj-Napoca

MOLDOVA

CHIŞINĂU

Stavropol'

112

ROMANIA

Odesa

Sea of
Azov

60°

RADE

Braşov

Crimea

Caucasus

Simferopol

El'brus 5642m

BUCHAREST

Constanţa

Black Sea

30°

Danube

BULGARIA

Varna

Balkan Mountains

OPIE SOFIA

Burgas

D.

TURKEY

Aegean
Sea

Anatolia

Zägros Mountains

REECE ATHENS

Piraeus

30°

Irákleio

Cyprus

118

Tigris

50°

Crete

Euphrates

a

E   F   G   H

81

THE NORTH ATLANTIC

Hudson
Bay

Southampton
Island

Foxe
Basin

N U N A V U T

Gulf of Boothia

Devon
Island

Ellesmere Isl

Nares Strait

Qaanaaq

Knud Rasmu

Innaanganeq

Savissivik

C A N A D A

Qimusseriarsuaq

Baffin
Bay

Kullorsuaq

Upernavik

Péninsule
d'Ungava

QUEBEC

Hudson Strait

Frobisher Bay

Cumberland Sound

Baffin Island

Limit of summer pack ice

Davis Strait

Uummannaq
Qeqertarsuaq
Qeqertarsuaq
Qeqertarsuup Tunua
Qasigiannguit

Arnaud

Ungava
Bay

George

Sisimiut

Kong Frederik IX
Land

G R E E N L A N

(to Denmark)

Maniitsoq

NUUK

Kong Christian IX Land
Gunn

Mont Forel
3360m

Paamiut

Ivittuut

Ammassalik

Kong Frederik VI Kyst

Den

Labrador
Sea

Qaqortoq
Nanortalik

Nunap Isua
(Kap Farvel)

Limit of winter pack ice

Reykjanes Basin

NEWFOUNDLAND & LABRADOR

A T L A N T I

O C E A N

0 km   400

0 miles   400

POPULATION   ● National capital

○ Less than 50,000   ○ 50,000 -100,000   ◉ 100,000 - 500,000   ◼ Over 500,000

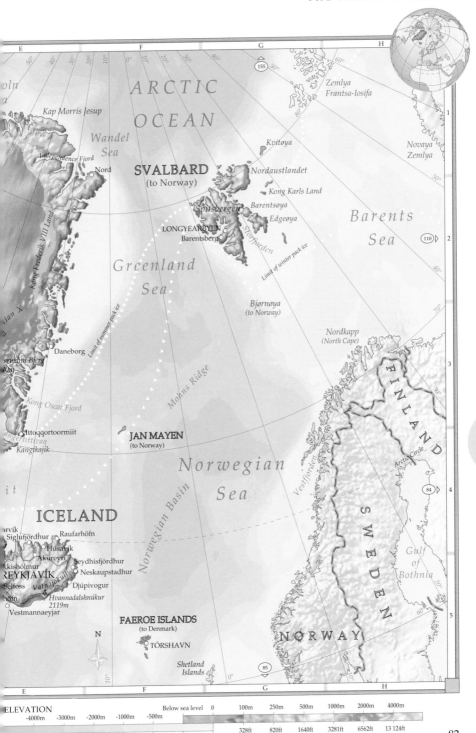

ARCTIC OCEAN

Kap Morris Jesup

Wandel Sea

Independence Fjord

Nord

SVALBARD
(to Norway)

Kvitøya

Nordaustlandet

Kong Karls Land

Zemlya
Frantsa-Iosifa

Novaya
Zemlya

Kong Frederik VIII Land

Spitsbergen

Barentsøya

Edgeøya

Barents
Sea

LONGYEARBYEN
Barentsberg

Storfjorden

Limit of winter pack ice

Greenland
Sea

Kaiser Wilhelm II Land

Daneborg

Limit of summer pack ice

Bjørnøya
(to Norway)

Nordkapp
(North Cape)

Germania Bjerg
10m

Kong Oscar Fjord

Mohns Ridge

FINLAND

Ittoqqortoormiit

Kangikajik

JAN MAYEN
(to Norway)

Norwegian
Sea

Vestfjorden

Arctic Circle

ICELAND

Siglufjördhur

Raufarhöfn

Húsavík

Akureyri

Seydhisfjördhur

Neskaupstadhur

Djúpivogur

Norwegian Basin

S W E D E N

Gulf
of
Bothnia

REYKJAVÍK

Selfoss

Vatnajökull

Höfn

Hvannadalshnúkur
2119m

Vestmannaeyjar

N

FAEROE ISLANDS
(to Denmark)

TÓRSHAVN

NORWAY

Shetland
Islands

ELEVATION

| | | | | | | Below sea level | 0 | 100m | 250m | 500m | 1000m | 2000m | 4000m |
| -4000m | -3000m | -2000m | -1000m | -500m | | | | | | | | | |

328ft   820ft   1640ft   3281ft   6562ft   13 124ft

-13 124ft   -9843ft   -6562ft   -3281ft   -1640ft   -820ft/-250m   0

83

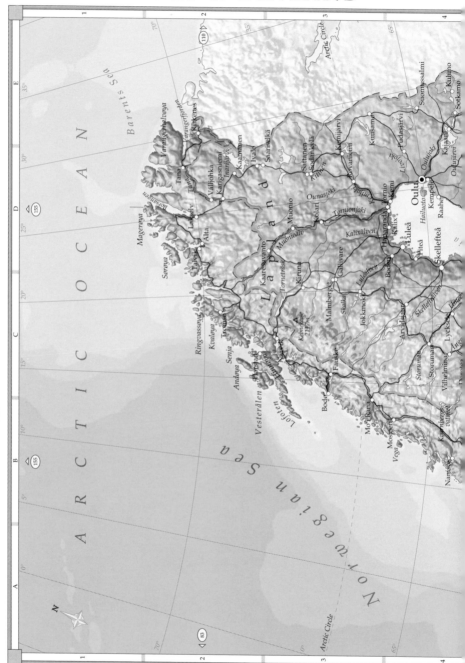

0 km		200	
0 miles			200

POPULATION ● National capital

○ Less than 50,000   ○ 50,000 -100,000   ◉ 100,000 - 500,000   ◼ Over 500,000

RUSS. FED.

BELARUS

Ladozhskoye
Ozero

Saimaa

Joutseno
Imatra

Kouvola

Poŕvoo Kotka

HELSINKI

Jyväskylä

Tampere
Lappeenranta

Pieksämäki

Nokia
Lahti

Hämeenlinna

Hyvinkää
Vantaa
ESPOO

Pori
Kankaanpää
Salo

Rauma
Turku
(Åbo)

Hanko
(Hangö)

Åland
Ålands hav

Norrtälje

Hiiumaa

Saaremaa

Gulf of Finland

ESTONIA

Lake Peipus

Gulf of Riga

LATVIA

Western Dvina

LITHUANIA

Neman

Courland Lagoon

Gulf of Danzig

KALININGRAD
(to Russian
Federation)

Wisła

POLAND

GERMANY

Oder

Elbe

Weser

Ems

Härnösand
Sundsvall

Hudiksvall

Söderhamn

Gävle

Uppsala
STOCKHOLM

Norrtälje

Gotland

Visby

Baltic Sea

Bornholm
Rønne

Borgholm

Öland

Kalmar

Karlskrona

Handöbukten

Ronneby

Ange
Sveg
Idre

Ljusdal

Mora

Bollnäs
Rättvik
Leksand

Falun
Borlänge
Ludvika

Sala
Avesta

Sandviken
Tierp

Södertälje

Nyköping

Norrköping

Linköping

Jönköping

Växjö

Kristianstad

Lund
Helsingborg
Malmö

Härjedalen

Sveg

Klarälven

Filipstad

Örebro

Karlstad

Kristinehamn

Motala

Mariestad

Vättern

Askersund

Vänern
Mellerud

Amål
Säffle
Grums

Lidköping

Skövde
Falköping

Trollhättan
Uddevalla

Borås

Mölndal
Kungsbacka

Varberg

Halmstad
Laholm

Ljungby

Vänersborg

Göteborg
(Gothenburg)

Ölme

KØBENHAVN
(Copenhagen)

DENMARK

Sjælland

Møn

Falster
Nykøbing

Lolland

Storebælt

Slagelse

Odense

Fyn

Kolding

Vejle
Horsens

Århus

Randers

Viborg

Herning

Holstebro

Ringkøbing Fjord

Varde

Esbjerg

Ribe

Jylland

Ålborg

Hjørring

Frederikshavn

Læsø

Kattegat

Skagerrak

North
Sea

NORWAY

Bergen

Stavanger

Sandnes

Moi
Egersund

Kristiansand

Lillesand

Setesdal

Arendal

Porsgrunn

Skien

Drammen
Sandvika
OSLO

Ski
Moss

Halden

Strömstad

Fredrikstad

Lillestrøm

Hamar

Ringsaker

Gjøvik

Gol

Fagernes

Lillehammer

Dombås

Trondheim

Otta

Kongsberg

Notodden

Hønefoss

Horten

Larvik

Kongsvinger

Eidsvoll

Elverum

Haugesund

Odda

Voss

Hardangerfjorden

Sognefjorden

Flåm

Leirvik

Bokṇafjorden

Jotunheimen

Glittertind
▲ 2465m

Galdhøpiggen
2469m ▲

Glåma

Folldal

Röros

ELEVATION

| | | | | | Below sea level | 0 | 100m | 250m | 500m | 1000m | 2000m | 4000m |

-2000m -1000m -500m -250m -100m

328ft 820ft 1640ft 3281ft 6562ft 13 124ft

-6562ft -3281ft -1640ft -820ft -328ft -164ft/-50m 0

The Low Countries

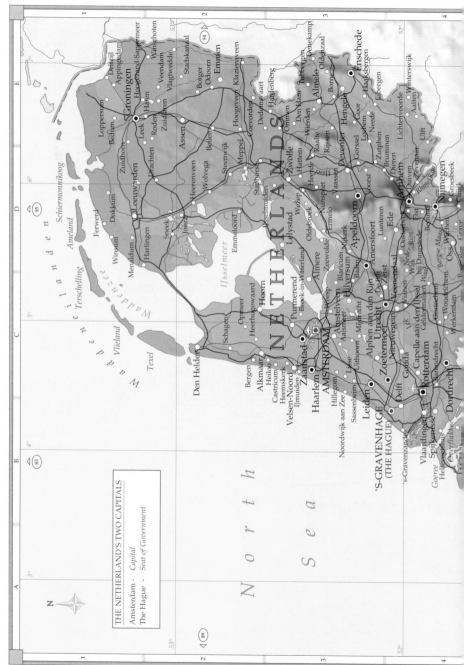

THE NETHERLAND'S TWO CAPITALS

Amsterdam - *Capital*
The Hague - *Seat of Government*

North Sea

0 km   50
0 miles   50

POPULATION   ● National capital

○ Less than 50,000   ○ 50,000 -100,000   ◉ 100,000 - 500,000   ◼ Over 500,000

ELEVATION

| Below sea level | 0 | 100m | 250m | 500m | 1000m | 2000m | 4000m |

-500m -250m -100m -50m -25m

328ft 820ft 1640ft 3281ft 6562ft 13 124ft

-1640ft -820ft -328ft -164ft -82ft 33ft/-10m 0

THE BRITISH ISLES

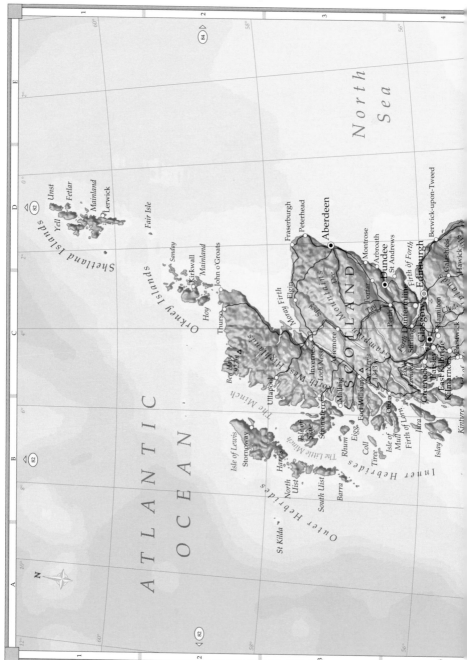

North Sea

Atlantic Ocean

Shetland Islands
Unst
Yell
Fetlar
Mainland
Lerwick
Fair Isle

Orkney Islands
Sanday
Kirkwall
Mainland
Hoy
John o'Groats

Thurso
Ullapool
Moray Firth
Elgin
Fraserburgh
Peterhead
Aberdeen
Montrose
Arbroath
Forfar
Dundee
St Andrews
Firth of Tay
Perth
Dunfermline
Firth of Forth
Edinburgh
Berwick-upon-Tweed
Galashiels
Hawick
Tweed

SCOTLAND
Grampian Mountains
Dee
Spey
Tay

Inverness
Aviemore
Loch Ness
Ben Nevis
1343m
Mallaig
Fort William
Oban
Stirling
Glasgow
Hamilton
Clyde
Greenock
Paisley
East Kilbride
Kilmarnock
Cheswick

North West Highlands
The Minch
The Little Minch
Isle of Lewis
Stornoway
Harris
Ben Hope
927m

Skye
Stromeferry
Isle of
Raasay
Eigg
Rhum
Coll
Tiree
Isle of
Mull
Firth of Lorn
Jura
Islay
Kintyre

Inner Hebrides
Outer Hebrides
North Uist
South Uist
Barra
St Kilda

N

0 km   100
0 miles   100

POPULATION   ● National capital   ○ Internal administrative capital
○ Less than 50,000   ○ 50,000 -100,000   ◉ 100,000 - 500,000   ▣ Over 500,000

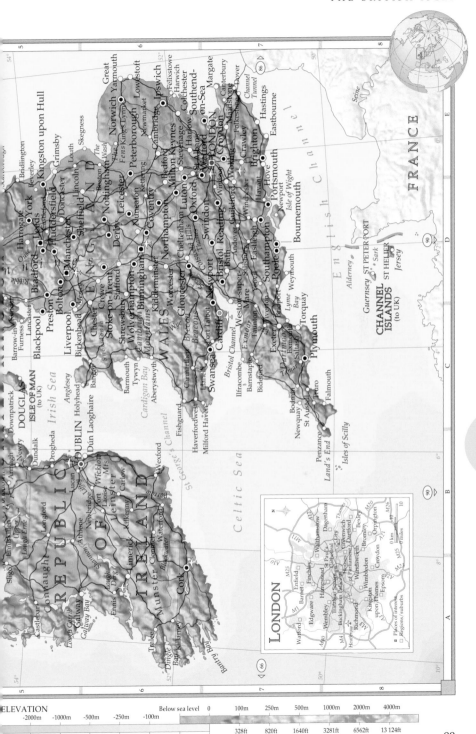

ELEVATION

					Below sea level	0	100m	250m	500m	1000m	2000m	4000m
-2000m	-1000m	-500m	-250m	-100m								
							328ft	820ft	1640ft	3281ft	6562ft	13 124ft
-6562ft	-3281ft	-1640ft	-820ft	-328ft	-164ft/-50m	0						

FRANCE, ANDORRA & MONACO

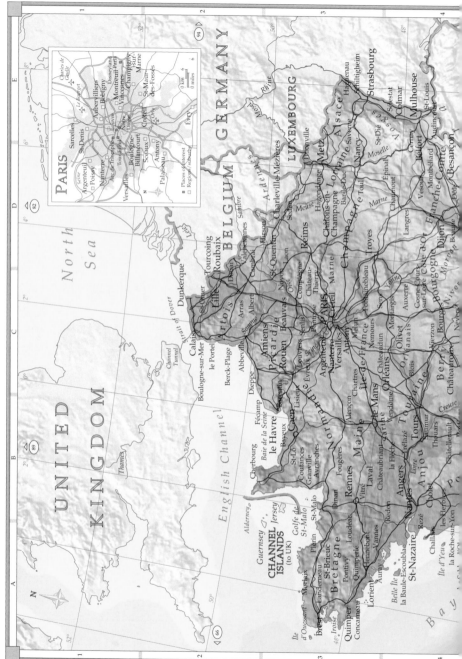

POPULATION
● National capital

○ Less than 50,000   ○ 50,000 -100,000   ◉ 100,000 - 500,000   ▣ Over 500,000

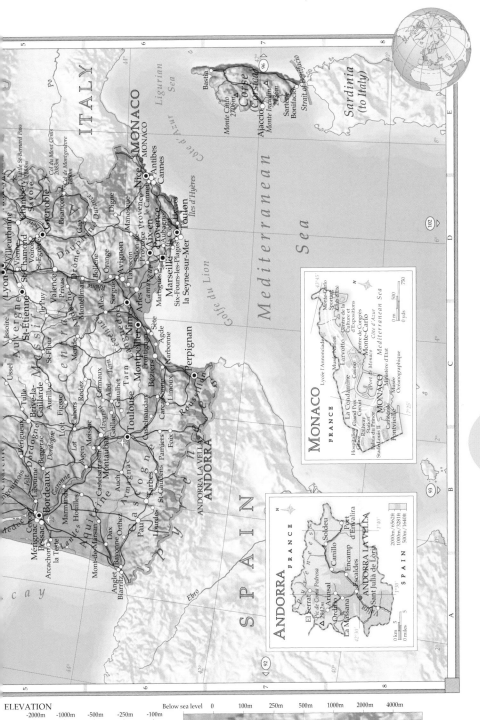

ELEVATION

					Below sea level	0	100m	250m	500m	1000m	2000m	4000m
-2000m	-1000m	-500m	-250m	-100m								
								328ft	820ft	1640ft	3281ft	6562ft	13 124ft
-6562ft	-3281ft	-1640ft	-820ft	-328ft	-164ft/-50m	0						

SPAIN & PORTUGAL

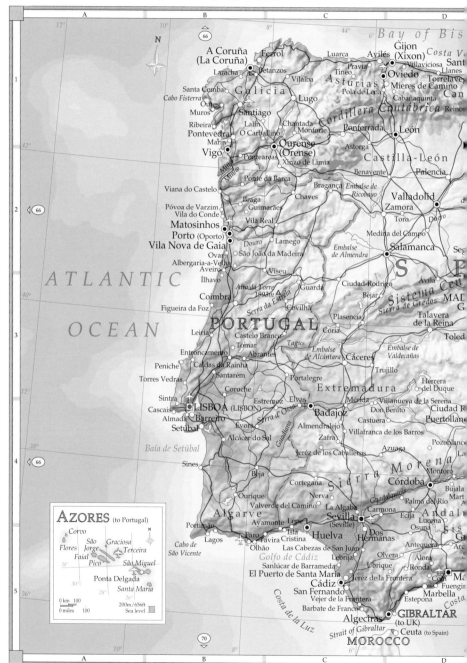

A Coruña
(La Coruña)
Ferrol
Betanzos
Laracha
Vilalba
Luarca
Tineo
Pravia
Gijon
(Xixon)
Villaviciosa
Costa V.
Sant
Llanes
Santa Comba
Cabo Fisterra
Oules
Muros
Santiago
Lalín
O Carballiño
Ribeira
Pontevedra
Marín
Vigo
Ponteareas
Chantada
Monforte
Lugo
Pola de Lena
Mieres de Camino
Oviedo
Torrelave
Can
Cordillera Cantábrica
Reinos
Ponferrada
León
Astorga
Castilla-León
Benavente
Palencia

Galicia

Miño
Minho
Xinzo de Limia
Ourense
(Orense)
Ponte da Barca
Braganza
Embalse de
Ricobayo
Valladolid
Zamora
Toro
Duero
Viana do Castelo
Chaves
Braga
Guimarães
Vila Real
Medina del Campo
Salamanca
Seg
Póvoa de Varzim
Vila do Conde
Matosinhos
Porto (Oporto)
Vila Nova de Gaia
Ovar
São João da Madeira
Albergaria-a-Velha
Aveiro
Ílhavo
Douro
Lamego
Viseu
Embalse
de Almendra
S
E
P

ATLANTIC
Coimbra
Figueira da Foz
Alto da Torre
1993m
Serra da Estrela
Guarda
Béjar
Ciudad-Rodrigo
Ávila
Sistema Cen
Sierra de Gredos
MAI
G

OCEAN
Leiria
Castelo Branco
Covilhã
Coria
Plasencia
Talavera
de la Reina
Toled

PORTUGAL
Tomar
Entroncamento
Abrantes
Tagus
Embalse
de Alcántara
Cáceres
Embalse de
Valdecañas
Peniche
Caldas da Rainha
Torres Vedras
Santarém
Portalegre
Trujillo
Herrera
del Duque
Coruche
Extremadura
Sintra
LISBOA (LISBON)
Cascais
Almada
Barreiro
Setúbal
Estremoz
Serra d'Ossa
Elvas
Évora
Mérida
Villanueva de la Serena
Badajoz
Don Benito
Castuera
Ciudad R
Puertollan
Alcácer do Sal
Almendralejo
Zafra
Villafranca de los Barros
Pozoblanco
Guadiana

Baía de Setúbal
Jeréz de los Caballeros
Azuaga
Morena
Montoro
Sines
Beja
Cortegana
Sierra
Córdoba
Bujala
Mart
Ourique
Nerva
Guadalquivir
Palma del Río
Andal
Valverde del Camino
La Algaba
Carmona
Ecija
Lucena
Gi
Algarve
Ayamonte
Lepe
Sevilla
(Seville)
Dos
Hermanas
Osuna
Antequera
Arc
Portimão
Lagos
Faro
Isla
Cristina
Tavira
Huelva
Las Cabezas de San Juan
Olvera
Álora
Ronda
Cabo de
São Vicente
Olhão
Golfo de Cádiz
Lebrija
Ubrique
Sanlúcar de Barrameda
El Puerto de Santa María
Cádiz
San Fernando
Vejer de la Frontera
Jeréz de la Frontera
Com
Ma
Fuengir
Marbella
Estepona
Costa
Barbate de France
Algeciras
Strait of Gibraltar
GIBRALTAR
(to UK)
Ceuta (to Spain)
Costa de la Luz
MOROCCO

AZORES (to Portugal)
Corvo
São
Flores
Jorge
Graciosa
Faial
Pico
Terceira
São Miguel
Ponta Delgada
Santa Maria
30°
28°
26°
0 km 100
0 miles 100
200m/656ft
Sea level

POPULATION   ● National capital

○ Less than 50,000   ○ 50,000 -100,000   ◉ 100,000 - 500,000   ■ Over 500,000

0 km 100
0 miles 100

ELEVATION

-4000m	-3000m	-2000m	-1000m	-500m	Below sea level	0	100m	250m	500m	1000m	2000m	4000m

| | | | | | | | 328ft | 820ft | 1640ft | 3281ft | 6562ft | 13 124ft |

| -13 124ft | -9843ft | -6562ft | -3281ft | -1640ft | -820ft/-250m | 0 |

GERMANY & THE ALPINE STATES

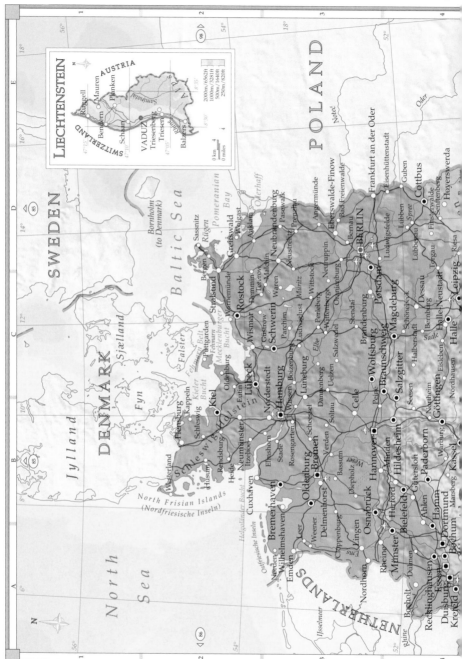

LIECHTENSTEIN

AUSTRIA

SWITZERLAND

Ruggell
Mauren
Planken
Bendern
Schaan
VADUZ
Triesenberg
Triesen
Balzers
Saminatal

2000m/6562ft
1000m/3281ft
500m/1640ft
250m/820ft

0 km   4
0 miles   4

POLAND

SWEDEN

DENMARK

Jylland

Sjælland

Fyn

Falster

Bornholm
(to Denmark)

Baltic Sea

North
Sea

NETHERLANDS

Frankfurt an der Oder
Eisenhüttenstadt
Cottbus
Finsterwalde
Senftenberg
Hoyerswerda
Guben
Lübben
Lübbenau
Forst
Riesa
Eberswalde-Finow
Bad Freienwalde
Angermünde
Prenzlau
Pasewalk
BERLIN
Bernau
Ludwigsfelde
Potsdam
Leipzig
Halle
Halle-Neustadt
Eisleben
Dessau
Bernburg
Schönebeck
Magdeburg
Halberstadt
Wernigerode
Nordhausen
Göttingen
Northeim
Neuruppin
Wittstock
Stendal
Brandenburg
Wolfsburg
Braunschweig
Salzgitter
Seesen
Osterburg
Neubrandenburg
Waren
Müritz
Perleberg
Wittenberge
Salzwedel
Uelzen
Celle
Hannover
Hildesheim
Minden
Herford
Bielefeld
Gütersloh
Paderborn
Warburg
Kassel
Marsberg
Greifswald
Wolgast
Usedom
Anklam
Demmin
Rostock
Warnemünde
Stralsund
Sassnitz
Rügen
Bergen
Ribnitz
Güstrow
Parchim
Ludwigslust
Schwerin
Wismar
Grevesmühlen
Boizenburg
Dannenberg
Soltau
Verden
Rosengarten
Scheessel
Hamburg
Lüneburg
Neumünster
Lübeck
Neustadt
Eutin
Oldenburg
Fehmarn
Kiel
Kieler
Bucht
Mecklenburger
Bucht
Fehmarn
Belt
Langeland
Kappeln
Flensburg
Schleswig
Rendsburg
Husum
Heide
Itzehoe
Elmshorn
Stade
Cuxhaven
Bremerhaven
Wilhelmshaven
Emden
Leer
Aurich
Norden
Papenburg
Meppen
Lingen
Nordhorn
Rheine
Osnabrück
Münster
Ahlen
Hamm
Dortmund
Bochum
Essen
Duisburg
Krefeld
Recklinghausen
Dülmen
Bocholt
Delmenhorst
Bremen
Oldenburg
Bassum
Diepholz
Wilhelmshaven
Wesermünde
Weener
Wasserland
Sylt
North Frisian Islands
(Nordfriesische Inseln)
Helgoländer Bucht
Ostfriesische Inseln
Ijsselmeer
Oderhaff
Pomeranian
Bay
Elbe
Weser
Ems
Rhine
Spree
Saale
Oder
Noteć
Müggelspree

0 km   100
0 miles   100

POPULATION   ● National capital

○ Less than 50,000   ○ 50,000 -100,000   ◉ 100,000 - 500,000   ■ Over 500,000

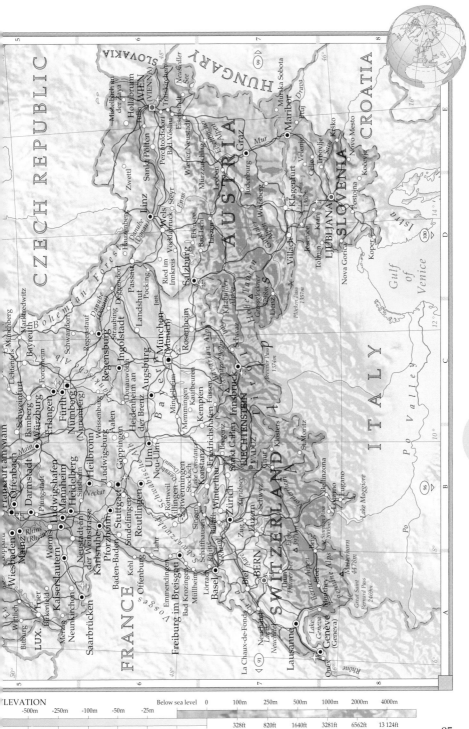

ELEVATION

| -500m | -250m | -100m | -50m | -25m | Below sea level | 0 | 100m | 250m | 500m | 1000m | 2000m | 4000m |

| -1640ft | -820ft | -328ft | -164ft | -82ft | 33ft/-10m | 0 | 328ft | 820ft | 1640ft | 3281ft | 6562ft | 13 124ft |

ITALY

SLOVAKIA
HUNGARY
GERMANY
AUSTRIA
SWITZERLAND
LIECHTENSTEIN
FRANCE
SLOVENIA
CROATIA
BOSNIA & HERZEGOVINA

SAN MARINO

Dogana
Serravalle
Fiorina
Falciano
Monte Titano
739m
Murata
Montegiardino
ITALY
Gualdicciolo
Borgo Maggiore
SAN MARINO
ITALY
Chiesanuova
500m/1640ft
200m/656ft
100m/325ft
0 km 2
0 miles 2

Trieste
Istra
Montfalcone
Portogruaro
Tarvisio
Cortina d'Ampezzo
Gemona del Friuli
Udine
Venezia (Venice)
Gulf of Venice
Chioggia
Foci del Po
Ravenna
Comacchio
Rimini
SAN MARINO
Forlì
Cesena
Fano
Pesaro
Falconara Marittima
Ancona
Civitanova Marche
Fermo
Ascoli Piceno
Giulianova
Teramo
Pescara
Chieti
L'Aquila
Terni
Foligno
Todi
Perugia
Viterbo
Civitavecchia
Grosseto
Orbetello
Portoferraio
Isola d'Elba
Piombino
Cecina
Livorno
Pisa
Viareggio
Massa
Carrara
La Spezia
Lago Trasimeno
Arezzo
Sansepolcro
Firenze (Florence)
Prato
Pistoia
Lucca
Siena
Chianti
Toscana
Grosseto
Archipelago Toscano
Corse (Corsica) (to France)
Ligurian Sea
MONACO
San Remo
Ventimiglia
Imperia
Finale Ligure
Savona
Golfo di Genova
Genova (Genoa)
Appennino Ligure
Mondovì
Cuneo
Savigliano
Moncalieri
Susa
Rivoli
Torino (Turin)
Gran Paradiso 4061m
Aosta
Mont Blanc 4807m
Little St-Bernard Pass 2188m
Grand Saint Bernard Pass
Asti
Alessandria
Casteggio
Pavia
Vercelli
Novara
Monza
Milano (Milan)
Varese
Lago Maggiore
Lago di Como
Lombardia
Bergamo
Sesto San Giovanni
Brescia
Lago di Garda
Verona
Cremona
Mantova
Piacenza
Parma
Reggio nell'Emilia
Modena
Bologna
Carpi
Ferrara
Imola
Faenza
Rovigo
Padova
Vicenza
Monselice
Mestre
Treviso
Pordenone
Adige
Bassano del Grappa
Trento
Bolzano
Merano
Edolo
Arco
Dolomitiche
Alpi
Bressanone
Brenner Pass 1374m
Inn
Lake Constance
Rhine
Rhône
Lake Geneva
Emilia
Po
Piemonte
Appennino

POPULATION

● National capital
○ Less than 50,000
○ 50,000 -100,000
◉ 100,000 - 500,000
■ Over 500,000

0 km 100
0 miles 100

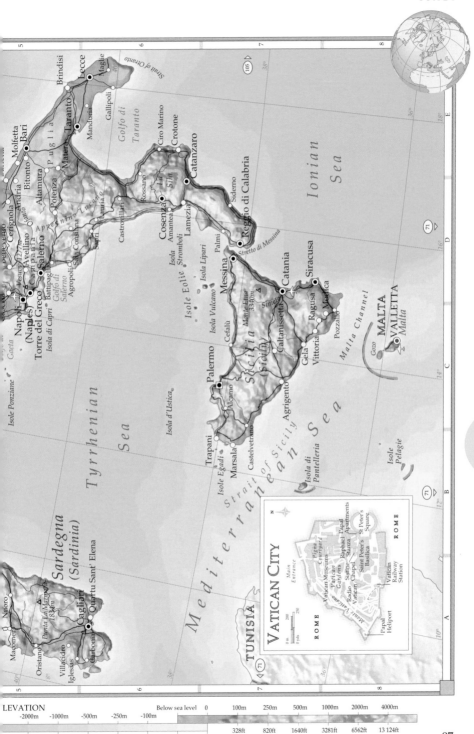

Strait of Otranto

Brindisi
Lecce
Maglie
Gallipoli
Mandúria
Taranto
Matera
Molfetta
Bari
Bitonto
Andria
Altamura
Cerignola
Avellino
Potenza
Melfi
P u g l i a
Golfo di Taranto
Ciro Marino
Crotone
Catanzaro
Rossano
La Sila
Siderno
Reggio di Calabria
Castrovillari
Cosenza
Amantea
Lamezia
Palmi
Appennino Lucano
Campania
Salerno
Vésuvio 1277m
Napoli (Naples)
Torre del Greco
Battipaglia
Golfo di Salerno
Agrópoli
Sapri
Castellabate
Gaeta
Isole Ponziane
Isola di Capri
Isola d'Ustica
Stretto di Messina
Messina
Isole Eolie
Isola Stromboli
Isola Lipari
Isola Vulcano
Monte Etna 3340m
Catania
Siracusa
Modica
Pozzallo
Simeto
Cefalù
Palermo
Álcamo
Caltanissetta
Gela
Vittória
Ragusa
Agrigento
Castelvetrano
Marsala
Isole Egadi
Trápani
S i c i l i a (Sicily)
Strait of Sicily
Isola di Pantelleria
Isole Pelagie

Ionian Sea

Tyrrhenian Sea

Mediterranean Sea

Malta Channel
MALTA
VALLETTA
Malta
Gozo

TUNISIA

Sardegna (Sardinia)
Núoro
Macomer
Oristano
Villacidro
Iglésias
Gúspini
Punta La Marmora 1834m
Cágliari
Quartu Sant'Elena

71

71

71

VATICAN CITY
ROME

Main Entrance
Piano Courtyard
Vatican Museums
Vatican Gardens
Radio Vatican
Sistine Chapel
Raphael Stanza
Papal Apartments
Saint Peter's Basilica
St Peter's Square
Vatican Railway Station
Papal Heliport

0m   200
0 yds   250

ROME

ELEVATION

					Below sea level	0	100m	250m	500m	1000m	2000m	4000m
-2000m	-1000m	-500m	-250m	-100m								
-6562ft	-3281ft	-1640ft	-820ft	-328ft	-164ft/-50m	0		328ft	820ft	1640ft	3281ft	6562ft	13 124ft

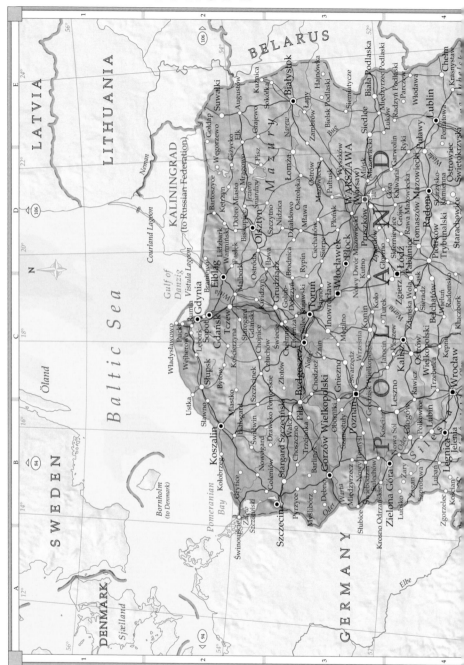

POPULATION   ● National capital

○ Less than 50,000   ◎ 50,000 -100,000   ◉ 100,000 - 500,000   ◼ Over 500,000

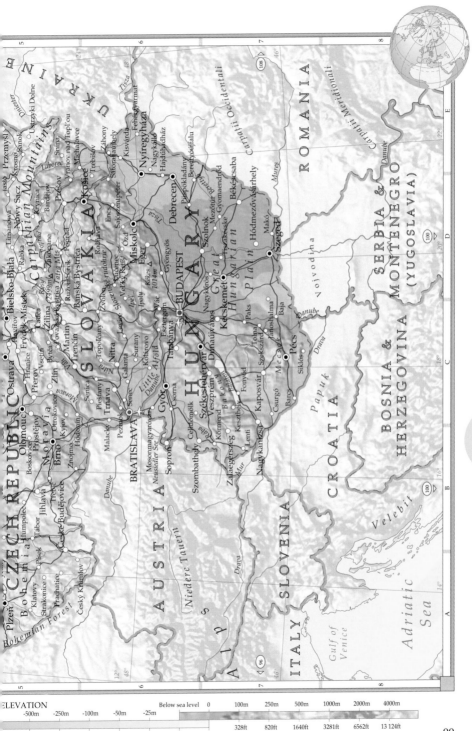

ELEVATION

-500m	-250m	-100m	-50m	-25m	Below sea level	0	100m	250m	500m	1000m	2000m	4000m
-1640ft	-820ft	-328ft	-164ft	-82ft	33ft/-10m	0	328ft	820ft	1640ft	3281ft	6562ft	13 124ft

SOUTHEAST EUROPE

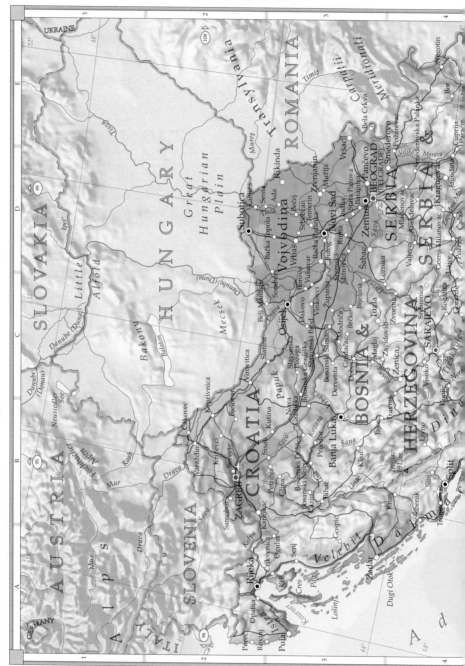

UKRAINE

SLOVAKIA

AUSTRIA

GERMANY

ITALY

SLOVENIA

HUNGARY

Great Hungarian Plain

Little Alföld

Bakony

Mecsek

Transylvania

ROMANIA

Carpații Meridionali

Subotica

Vojvodina

Novi Sad

BEOGRAD (BELGRADE)

SERBIA

SERBIA

Zemun

Pančevo

Smederevo

CROATIA

ZAGREB

Osijek

Banja Luka

BOSNIA & HERZEGOVINA

SARAJEVO

Tuzla

Zenica

Dinara

Split

Zadar

Rijeka

Velebit

Dalma

Dugi Otok

Lošinj

Cres

Adri

POPULATION ● National capital

○ Less than 50,000 ○ 50,000 -100,000 ◉ 100,000 - 500,000 ■ Over 500,000

0 km 100

0 miles 100

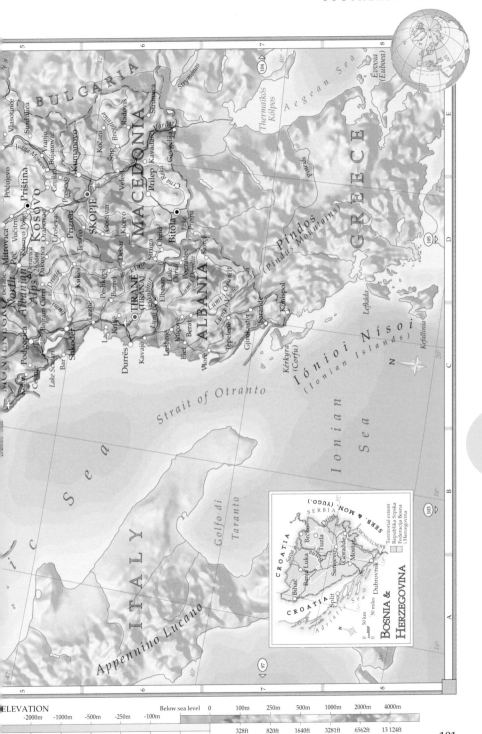

BULGARIA

Vlasotince
Surdulica
Podujevo
Priština
Kosovo
Peć
Dečane
Mitrovica
Vučitrn
Gnjilane
Preševo
Bujanovac
Vranje
Južna Morava
Kumanovo
Kočani
Brég
Radoviš
Strumica
Strymónas
Štip
Kriva
Vardar
Kavadarci
Gevgelija
Veles
Prilep
MACEDONIA
SKOPJE
Gostivar
Kičevo
Tetovo
Prizren
Orahovac
Uroševac
Kačanik
Ohrid
Lake Ohrid
Bitola
Lake Prespa
Struga
Black Drin
Crna Reka

North Albanian Alps
Bajram Curri
Prokletije
2556m
Drini
Tropojë
Kukës
Peshkopi
Burrel
Debar
Lumi Drinit
Lake Ohrid
Lini
Pogradec
Ohri
Përrenjas
Librazhd

MONTENEGRO
Podgorica
Cetinje
Bar
Shkodër
Lake Scutari
Lezhë
Lac
Krujë
Burrel
TIRANE
(TIRANA)
Elbasan
Shkumbini
Lumi Devollit
Berat
Lumi Osumit
Korçë

Durrës
Kavajë
Lushnjë
Fier
Vlorë
ALBANIA
Tepelenë
Gjirokastër
Lumi Vjosës

Sarandë
Konispol
Lefkáda

Pindos
(Pindus Mountains)
GREECE
Piniós

Thermaïkós
Kólpos
Aegean Sea
Évvoia
(Euboea)

Kérkyra
(Corfu)
Iónioi Nísoi
(Ionian Islands)
Kefallinía

Strait of Otranto
Golfo di Taranto
ITALY
Appennino Lucano

Ionian Sea

Adriatic Sea

N

BOSNIA & HERZEGOVINA

Territorial extent
Republika Srpska
Federacija Bosna
i Hercegovina

CROATIA
SERBIA & MON. (YUGO.)
MONTENEGRO
Bihać
Banja Luka
Brčko
Tuzla
Bijeljina
Sava
Drina
Sarajevo
Goražde
Mostar
Split
Dubrovnik
Adriatic Sea
CROATIA

0   50 km
0   50 miles

N

ELEVATION

					Below sea level	0	100m	250m	500m	1000m	2000m	4000m
-2000m	-1000m	-500m	-250m	-100m								
-6562ft	-3281ft	-1640ft	-820ft	-328ft	-164ft/-50m	0		328ft	820ft	1640ft	3281ft	6562ft	13 124ft

THE MEDITERRANEAN

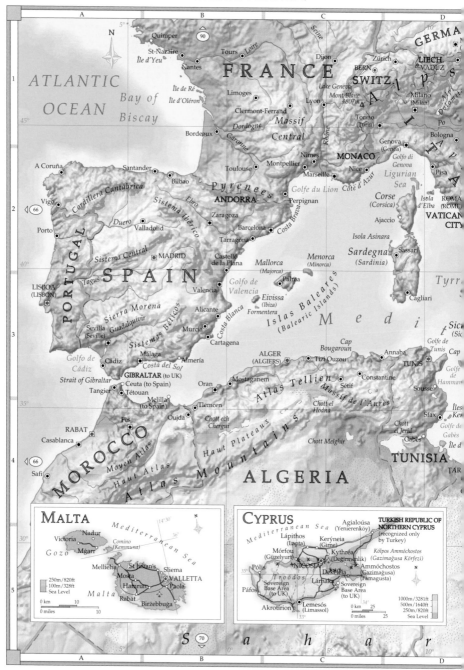

ATLANTIC OCEAN

FRANCE

Quimper
St-Nazaire
Île d'Yeu
Nantes
Tours
Loire
Dijon
Zürich
BERN
SWITZ.
LIECH.
VADUZ
GERMA

ATLANTIC
OCEAN

Bay of Biscay

Île de Ré
Île d'Oléron
Limoges
Lake Geneva
Lyon
Mont Blanc
4807m
Milano
(Milan)
Torino
(Turin)

A Coruña
Bordeaux
Dordogne
Garonne
Massif
Central
Rhône
Nîmes
MONACO
Genova
(Genea)
Golfo di
Genova
Po
Bologna

Santander
Bilbao
Toulouse
Montpellier
Marseille
Nice
Côte d'Azur
Ligurian
Sea
Pisa

Vigo
Cordillera Cantábrica
Pyrenees
ANDORRA
Perpignan
Golfe du Lion
Corse
(Corsica)
Isola
d'Elba
ROMA
(ROME)

Porto
Duero
Valladolid
Sistema Ibérico
Ebro
Zaragoza
Barcelona
Costa Brava
Ajaccio
Isola Asinara
VATICAN
CITY

Tagus
Sistema Central
MADRID
Castelló
de la Plana
Mallorca
(Majorca)
Menorca
(Minorca)
Sardegna
(Sardinia)
Sassari
Tyrr

LISBOA
(LISBON)
SPAIN
Valencia
Golfo de
Valencia
Palma
Cagliari

Sierra Morena
Sevilla
(Seville)
Guadalquivir
Sistemas Béticos
Alicante
Costa Blanca
Eivissa
(Ibiza)
Formentera
Islas Baleares
(Balearic Islands)
M e d i
Sic
(Sic

Golfo de
Cádiz
Cádiz
Málaga
Costa del Sol
Almería
Murcia
Cartagena
Cap
Bougaroun
Golfe de
Tunis
Cap

GIBRALTAR (to UK)
Ceuta (to Spain)
ALGER
(ALGIERS)
Tizi Ouzou
Annaba
TUNIS
Golfe de
Hamman

Strait of Gibraltar
Tangier
Tétouan
Oran
Mostaganem
Sétif
Constantine
Sousse

Melilla
(to Spain)
Tlemcen
Atlas Tellien
Massif de l'Aurès
Îles
Sfax
Ke

RABAT
Fès
Oujda
Chott ech
Chergui
Chott el
Hodna
Chott
el Jerid
Golfe de
Gabès

Casablanca
MOROCCO
Haut Plateaux
Chott Melghir
TUNISIA
Gabès
Île d

Safi
Moyen Atlas
Haut Atlas
Atlas Mountains
ALGERIA
TAR

MALTA

Mediterranean Sea

Victoria
Nadur
Gozo
Mgarr
Comino
(Kemmuna)

Mellieħa
St Julian's
Sliema
Mosta
VALLETTA
Ħamrun
Paola
Rabat
Malta
Birżebbuġa

250m/820ft
100m/328ft
Sea Level

0 km   10
0 miles   10

CYPRUS

Mediterranean Sea

Agialoúsa
(Yenierenköy)

TURKISH REPUBLIC OF
NORTHERN CYPRUS
(recognized only
by Turkey)

Lápithos
(Lapta)
Kerýneia
(Girne)
Mórfou
(Güzelyurt)
Kythréa
(Degirmenlik)
Kólpos Ammóchostos
(Gazimağusa Körfezi)

Pólis
NICOSIA
Ammóchostos
(Gazimağusa)
(Famagusta)
Dekéleia
Sovereign
Base Area
(to UK)
Lárnaka

Tróodos
Páfos
Lemesós
(Limassol)
Sovereign
Base Area
(to UK)
Akrotírion

1000m/3281ft
500m/1640ft
250m/820ft
Sea Level

0 km   25
0 miles   25

S a h a r a

0 km   400
0 miles   400

POPULATION   ● National capital

o Less than 50,000   o 50,000 -100,000   ● 100,000 - 500,000   ■ Over 500,000

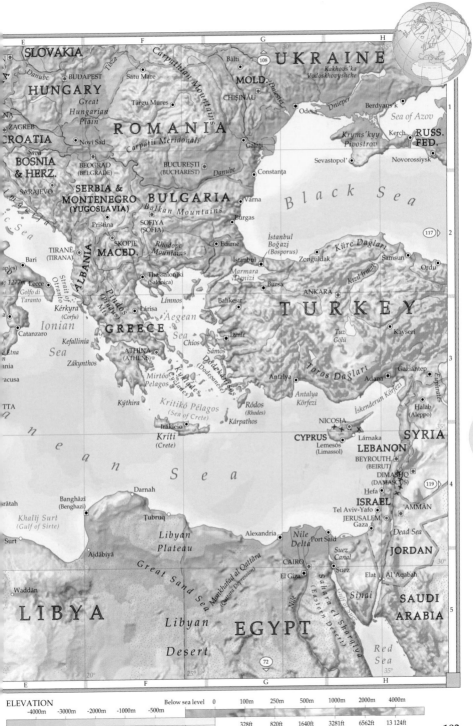

ELEVATION

					Below sea level	0	100m	250m	500m	1000m	2000m	4000m
-4000m	-3000m	-2000m	-1000m	-500m								
							328ft	820ft	1640ft	3281ft	6562ft	13 124ft
-13 124ft	-9843ft	-6562ft	-3281ft	-1640ft	-820ft/-250m	0						

BULGARIA & GREECE

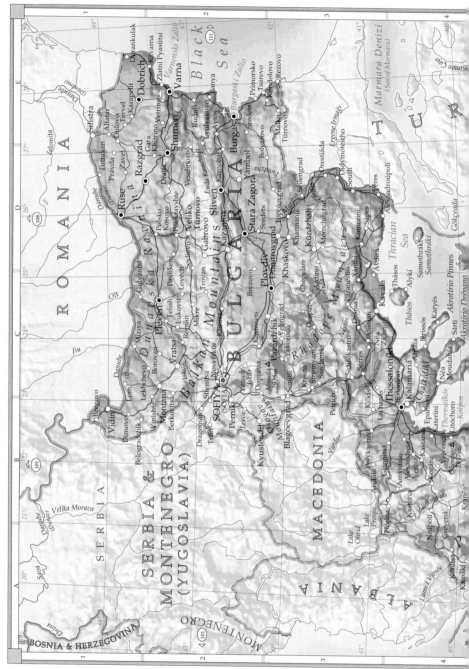

0 km 100

0 miles 100

POPULATION ● National capital

○ Less than 50,000　○ 50,000 -100,000　◉ 100,000 - 500,000　◼ Over 500,000

Ródos (Rhodes)
Lindos
116
Kattavía
Kárpathos
Kárpathos
Chalki
Ródos (Rhodes)
Kos
Nísyros
Tílos
Stária
Kásos
Agía Marína
Léros
Arkoí
Lípsoi
Agathonísi
Thérma
Kálimnos
Dodekánisos (Dodecanese)
Pátmos
Astypálaia
Sými
Anáfi
Akna Floúda
Amorgós
Amorgós
Naxós
Íos
Thíra
Thíra
Thíra

Plomári
Sámos Sámos
Ikaría
Chíos
Psará
Antípsara
Chíos

Kritikó Pélagos
(Sea of Crete)

Neápoli
Sitía
Ágios Nikólaos
Ierápetra
Mýrtos
Díkti
Kríti (Crete)
Iráklio
Iráklio
Zarós
Tympáki
Váronmos
Gávdos
Sfak.
Lefk. Orí
Chaniá
Kastélli
Kántanos
Stákia

Mirtóo Pélagos
Andros
Andros
Tínos
Tínos
Mýkonos
Ermoúpoli
Sýros
Kéa
Kéa
Kýthnos
Kýklades (Cyclades)
Páros
Páros
Náxos
Kastro
Sérifos
Sífnos
Sfnos
Mílos
Mílos
Folégandros
Kýthnos

Vóre Sporádes
Skýros
Skýros
Kými
Évvoia (Euboea)
Istiaía
Chalkída
Alíveri
Mýkonos
Marathónas
Keratéa
Lávrio
Lávrio
ATHINA (ATHENS)
Peiraías
(Piraeus)
Paianía
Aígina
Aígina
Epídavros
Póros
Ýdra
Ermióni
Dalmoniá
Kýthira
Kýthira
Neápoli
Karavás
Leonídi
Potamós
Antikýthira

GREECE
Lamía
Agrínio
Amfíssa
Thérmo
Métora
Malesína
Vília
Megalópoli
Megára
Sálona
Korónthos
Korinth
Pátra
Káto Achaía
Aígio
Xylókastro
Lechaína
Gastoúni
Pýrgos
Pelopónnisos
Trípoli
Neméa
Árgos
Náfplio
Lerna
Spárti
Gýtheio
Gerolimenas
Areópoli
Lampeía
Kalámata
Messíni
Koróni
Pýlos
Kyparissía
Zacháro
Olympía
Kalo

Lefkáda
Kefallinía
Argostóli
Vasilikí
Lixoúri
Pátra
Néos Chorió
Póros
Kerí
Zákynthos
Iónioi Nísoi (Ionian Islands)

Ionian Sea

Mediterranean Sea

N

ELEVATION

| | | | | Below sea level | 0 | 100m | 250m | 500m | 1000m | 2000m | 4000m |

-2000m -1000m -500m -250m -100m

-6562ft -3281ft -1640ft -820ft -328ft -164ft/-50m 0 328ft 820ft 1640ft 3281ft 6562ft 13 124ft

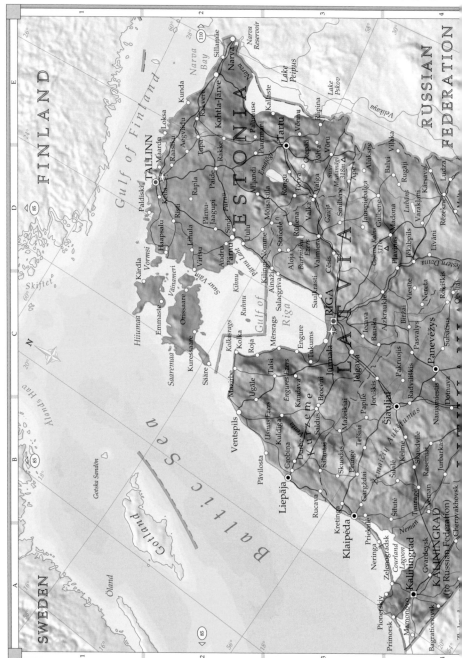

POPULATION
● National capital

○ Less than 50,000　　○ 50,000 -100,000　　◉ 100,000 - 500,000　　◼ Over 500,000

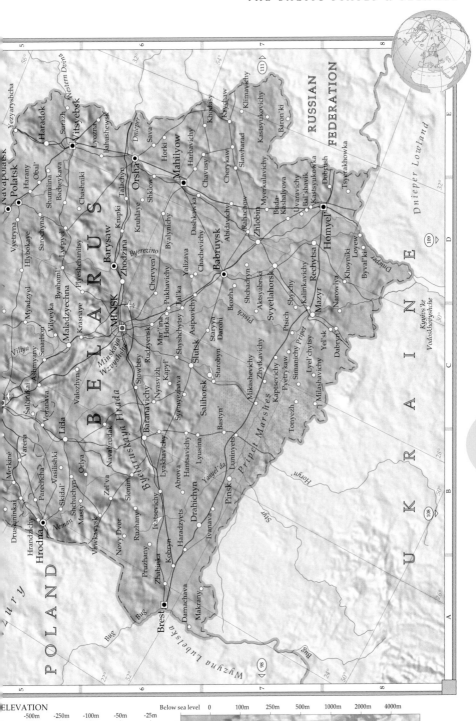

ELEVATION

					Below sea level	0	100m	250m	500m	1000m	2000m	4000m
-500m	-250m	-100m	-50m	-25m								
-1640ft	-820ft	-328ft	-164ft	-82ft	33ft/-10m	0	328ft	820ft	1640ft	3281ft	6562ft	13 124ft

UKRAINE, MOLDOVA & ROMANIA

18° · 20° · 106 · 52° · 24° · 26° · 28°

BELARUS

Pripet

Pripet Marshes

POLAND

Małopolska

Wyżyna Lubelska

Kovel' · Sarny · Olevs'k

1

50°

Wisła · *Bug* · *Stýr* · *Słuch*

Volodymyr-Volyns'kyy · Volyns'kyy · Kivertsi · Korosten

Novovolyns'k · **Luts'k** · **Rivne**

Sokal' · Dubno · Novohrad-Volyns'kyy

Zhovkva · Chervonohrad · Slavuta · Shepetivka · Rad

Yavoriv · **L'viv** · Kremenets' · Izyaslav · Polonne · Zhy

Horodok · Zolochiv · Zbarazh · Starokostyantyniv · B

Sambir · Khodoriv · Berezhany · **Ternopil'** · **Khmel'nyts'kyy**

Drohobych · Zhydachiv · **U** · **K** · **Vinnytsya**

Boryslav · Stryy · Kalush · Chortkiv · R

2

SLOVAKIA

Tatra Mountains

Slovenské Rudohorie

98

Dolyna · **Ivano-Frankivs'k**

Uzhhorod · Nadvirna · Kam''yanets'-Podil's'kyy · Zhmerynka

Mukacheve · Kolomyya · *Podil's'ka Vysoci*

Berehove · Khust · **Chernivtsi** · Mohyliv-Podil's'kyy · *Dniester*

Vynohradiv · Negresti-Oaş · Hora Hoverla 2061m · Darabani · Soroca

3

HUNGARY

Great Hungarian Plain

Satu Mare · Rădăuţi · Dorohoi · **Botoşani** · **Bălţi** · Ribniţa

Carei · **Baia Mare** · Solca · Suceava · **MOLDOVA**

Marghita · Baia Sprie · Borşa · Năsăud · Fălticeni

Şimleu Silvaniei · Zalău · **Bistriţa** · Târgu-Neamţ · Paşcani · **Iaşi** · Ungheni · Stras

Oradea · Dej · Reghin · Topliţa · Bicaz · **Roman** · Hînceşti

Aleşd · Beiuş · **Cluj-Napoca** · Gheorgheni · **Piatra-Neamţ** · **CHIŞINĂU**

Salonta · Turda · Ludus · **Târgu Mureş** · **Bacău** · (KISHINEV) · Tigh

Curtici · Ineu · *Munţii* · Abrud · Aiud · Cristuru · Miercurea-Ciuc · Vaslui

4

Sânnicolau Mare · **Arad** · *Apuseni* · Alba Iulia · Mediaş · Secuiesc · Târgu Ocna · **Bârlad** · Comrat

Lipova · Deva · **R** · **O** · **M** · **A** · **N** · **I** · **A** · Rupea · Adjud

Jimbolia · Lugoj · Hunedoara · **Sibiu** · Făgăraş · Târgu Secuiesc · Cahul · Ciad

100 · **Timişoara** · Oţelu Roşu · Haţeg · Vârful · Codlea · Sfântu Gheorghe · Taraclia

Bocşa · Cisnădie · Moldoveanu 2544m · **Braşov** · Focşani · Tecuci · **Galaţi** · Reni · **Brăila**

Orăştie · Reşiţa · Petroşani · Câmpulung · Râşnov · Râmnicu Sărat · Izma

Anina · Târgu Jiu · Călimăneşti · Sinaia · Câmpina · **Buzău** · Măcin · Isaccea · Tulce

Orşova · Moldova Nouă · Curtea · de Argeş · Mizil · **Ploieşti** · Babadag

Drobeta-Turnu Severin · **Râmnicu Vâlcea** · **Piteşti** · Moreni · Urziceni · Ţăndărei · Hârşova

Carpaţii · Motru · Strehaia · **Târgovişte** · Titu · *Ialomiţa* · Slobozia · Feteşti · **Consta**

5

SERBIA & MONTENEGRO (YUGOSLAVIA) · Filiaşi · Drăgăşani · *Meridionali* · Buftea · **BUCUREŞTI** · **Călăraşi** · Medgidia

Craiova · Slatina · (BUCHAREST) · Olteniţa · Eforie Sud

Balş · Caracal · Roşiori de Vede · Alexandria · Techirghiol · Mangalia

Băileşti · Corabia · Turnu · Măgurele · Giurgiu · *Dunavska Ravnina*

Calafat · *Danube (Dunărea)* · Zimnicea · **BULGARIA**

0 km · 100 · 0 miles · 100

POPULATION ● National capital

○ Less than 50,000 · ○ 50,000 -100,000 · ◉ 100,000 - 500,000 · ■ Over 500,000

Dnieper

Horodnya
Shchors
Shostka
Hlukhiv
Chernihiv
Krolevets'
Konotop
Nizhyn
Bakhmach
chu
Desna
Nosivka
Romny
Sumy
Brovary
Pryluky
Yahotyn
Pyryatyn
Okhtyrka
Zolochiv
Derhachi
Kautos'ke
khovyshche
Hrebinka
Lubny
Myrhorod
Lyubotyn
Kharkiv
Kup"yans'k
serkva
Kaniv
lav
Zolotonosha
Merefa
I   N   E
dyshche
Cherkasy
Hlobyne
Poltava
Donets
Izyum
Kreminna
Starobil's'k
rodka
Smila
Chyhyryn
Kremenchuts'ke
Vodoskhovyshche
Rubizhne
Syeverodonets'k
al'ne
Shpola
Svitlovods'k
Slov"yans'k
Kramators'k
Lysychans'k
Luhans'k
Oleksandrivka
Oleksandriya
Dniprodzerzhyns'ke
Vodoskhovyshche
Zolote
lala Vyska
Znam"yanka
Novomoskovs'k
Kostyantynivka
anivs'k
Kirovohrad
Dniprodzerzhyns'k
Pavlohrad
Horlivka
Stakhanov
Zhovti Vody
Dnipropetrovs'k
Yenakiyeve
Krasnodon
Vil'shanka
Dolyns'ka
P"yatykhatky
Synel'nykove
Makiyivka
Krasnyy Luch
zeto
Pervomays'k
Bobrynets'
Kryvyy Rih
Pokrovs'ke
Donets'k
Torez
Arbyzynka
Inhulets'
Amvrosiyivka
Novyy Buh
Ordzhonikidze
Nikopol
Zaporizhzhya
Orikhiv
Volnovakha
Dokuchayevs'k
Voznesens'k
Marhanets'
Polohy
Don
Kam"yanka-Dniprovs'ka
Dniprorudne
Tokmak
Novoazovs'k
Kakhovs'ka
Vodoskhovyshche
Molochans'k
Mariupol'
Mykolayiv
Kakhovka
Melitopol'
Gulf of Taganrog
Yeya
Zhovtneve
Dnieper
(Dnipro)
Akinovka
Prymors'k
Berdyans'k
Ochakiv
Kherson
Tsyurupyns'k
desa
Hola Prystan'
Chaplynka
Novotroyits'ke
nivs'k
Kalanchak
Heniches'k
Sea of Azov
Armyans'k

RUSSIAN
FEDERATION

Srednerusskaya
Vozvyshennost'

Don

RUSSIAN
FEDERATION

Karkinits'ka Zatoka
Rozdol'ne
Krasnoperekops'k
Dzhankoy
Zatoka
Syvash
Kerch
Kerch Strait
Chornomors'ke
Krasnohvardiys'ke
Nyzhn'ohirs'kyy
Kuban'
Yevpatoriya
Kryms'kyy
Pivostriv
Lenine
Saky
Feodosiya
Simferopol'
Bakhchysaray
Krymski Hory
Sevastopol'
Alushta
Yalta
Alupka

B l a c k   S e a

ELEVATION

-2000m	-1000m	-500m	-250m	-100m	Below sea level 0	100m	250m	500m	1000m	2000m	4000m
-6562ft	-3281ft	-1640ft	-820ft	-328ft	-164ft/-50m 0	328ft	820ft	1640ft	3281ft	6562ft	13 124ft

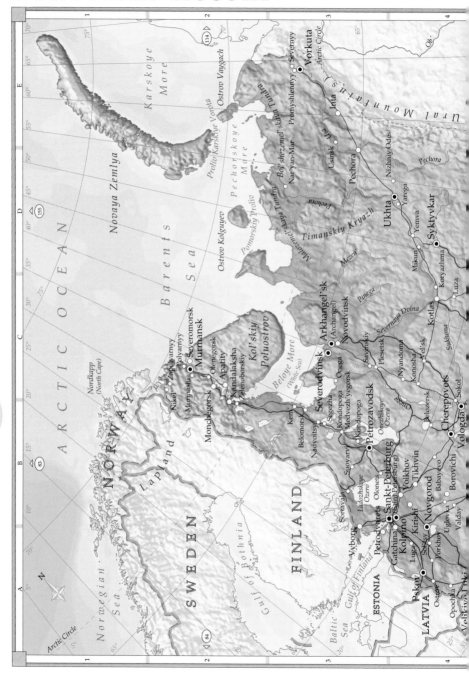

ARCTIC OCEAN

Karskoye More

Nordkapp (North Cape)

Novaya Zemlya

Ostrov Vaygach

Proliv Karskiye Vorota

Pechorskoye More

Pechorskiy Proliv

Pomorskiy Proliv

Ostrov Kolguyev

B a r e n t s   S e a

Severnyy

Vorkuta

Arctic Circle

Promyshlennyy

Inta

Usinsk

Nar'yan-Mar

Nizhniy Odes

Pechora

Pechora

Bol'shezemel'skaya Tundra

Mal'zemel'skaya Tundra

Ural Mountains

Ukhta

Yarega

Syktyvkar

Timanskiy Kryazh

Mezen'

Mikun'

Yemva

Koryazhma

Luza

Luza

Kol'skiy Poluostrov

Beloye More (White Sea)

Pinega

Arkhangel'sk (Archangel)

Novodvinsk

Severnaya Dvina

Kotlas

Sukhona

Sol'vychegodsk

NORWAY

SWEDEN

Lapland

Nikel

Zapolyarnyy

Polyarnyy

Severomorsk

Murmansk

Murmashi

Olenegorsk

Apatity

Monchegorsk

Kandalaksha

Zelenoborskiy

Kem'

Belomorsk

Nadvoitsy

Segezha

Medvezh'yegorsk

Kondopoga

Kondopoga

Onega

Savinskiy

Plesetsk

Nyandoma

Konosha

Vel'sk

Severodvinsk

Petrozavodsk

Onezhskoye Ozero

Vytegra

Belozersk

Cherepovets

Vologda

Sokol

Sovayarv

Olonets

Lodeyskoye Ozero

Syamozero

Suoyarvi

FINLAND

Gulf of Bothnia

Vyborg

Petrodvorets

Gatchina

Sankt-Peterburg (Saint Petersburg)

Kolpino

Luga

Sol'tsy

Kirishi

Volkhov

Tikhvin

Babayevo

Borovichi

Uglovka

Valday

Novgorod

Pskov

Ostrov

Opochka

Velikiye Luki

ESTONIA

LATVIA

Baltic Sea

Gulf of Finland

Torkhov

Porkhov

Lovat'

N

0 km   400

0 miles   400

POPULATION   ● National capital

○ Less than 50,000   ○ 50,000 -100,000   ◉ 100,000 - 500,000   ◼ Over 500,000

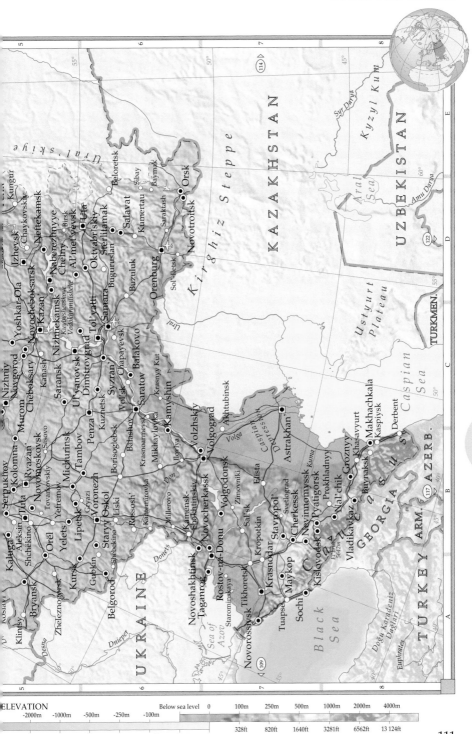

ELEVATION

					Below sea level	0	100m	250m	500m	1000m	2000m	4000m
-2000m	-1000m	-500m	-250m	-100m								
							328ft	820ft	1640ft	3281ft	6562ft	13 124ft
-6562ft	-3281ft	-1640ft	-820ft	-328ft	-164ft/-50m	0						

NORTH & WEST ASIA

ARCTI
Franz Josef Land
155
Severna
Ostrov Komsomolets
Ostrov Oktyabr'skoy Revolyutsii
Ostrov Bol'shevi
Poluostrov T
North Si

Summer limit of pack ice

Winter limit of pack ice

Norwegian
Sea   North Cape
Murmansk
Kola
Peninsula
White Sea

Barents
Sea

Ostrov
Kolguyev
Poluostrov
Yamal
Novaya Zemlya
East Nopaya Zemlya Trench
Kara Sea
Noril'sk
Kureyka
Cent
Sibe
Plat

Arctic Circle
81

Archangel
Northern
Dvina

RUSSIAN
F
S
i

West Siberian
Plain
Ob'
Lower Tunguska
Stony Tunguska
Angara
Chulym
Yenisey

Lake
Onega
Lake Ladoga
Vologda
Saint Petersburg
Yaroslavl
Nizhniy
Novgorod
Perm'
Yekaterinburg
Irtysh
Tomsk
Krasnoyar
Kaliningrad
MOSCOW
Central
Russian
Upland
Kazan'
Ufa
Chelyabinsk
Omsk
Novosibirsk
Novokuznetsk
KALININGRAD
(to Russ. Fed.)
Ul'yanovsk
Samara
Ishim
Irtysh
Baltic Sea
Voronezh
Saratov
Orenburg
Ural'sk
ASTANA
Sayanskiy Khrebet
A
EUROPE
Volgograd
Ural
Kirghiz
Steppe
Karaganda
Semipalatinsk
Altai Mountains
Rostov-na-Donu
Don
Astrakhan'
Volga
Kazakh Uplands
Ozero
Zaysan
S
Danube
Stavropol'
Caspian Sea
Aral'sk
Aral
Sea
KAZAKHSTAN
Lake
Balkhash
Black Sea
El'brus
5642m
Caucasus
GEORGIA
Ustyurt
Plateau
Syr Darya
Kyzylorda
Taraz
Almaty
Il
Istanbul
Küre Dağları
ANKARA
ARMENIA
TBILISI
AZERB.
BAKU
Dashkhovuz
Amu Darya
UZBEKISTAN
Kyzyl
Kum
BISHKEK
Tien Shan
KYRGYZSTAN
YEREVAN
TASHKENT
TURKMENISTAN
Kara Kum
Anatolia
TURKEY
Lake
Van
Tabriz
ASHGABAT
DUSHANBE
TAJIKISTAN
Adana
Gaziantep
Mosul
TEHRAN
Qom
Kunlun Mountains
CYPRUS
Aleppo
SYRIA
IRAQ
Isfahan
KABUL
Hindu Kush
Jalalabad
Khyber Pass
BEIRUT
LEBANON
DAMASCUS
BAGHDAD
Syrian Desert
Tigris
Euphrates
IRAN
Iranian
Plateau
Herat
AFGHANISTAN
Thar Desert
Himalayas
ISRAEL
AMMAN
JERUSALEM
JORDAN
Basra
Zagros Mountains
Shiraz
Zahedan
Ganges
An Nafud
KUWAIT
KUWAIT
Bandar-e 'Abbas
Indus Fan
Ganges Fan
Tropic of Cancer
MANAMA
BAHRAIN
RIYADH
QATAR
DOHA
Gulf
Dubai
U.A.E.
ABU
DHABI
MUSCAT
Sur
Murray Ridge
SAUDI ARABIA
Arabian
Peninsula
At Ta'if
Ar Rub' al Khali
OMAN
Arabian
Sea
Bay of
Bengal
AFRICA
Nile
Red Sea
SANA
Ta'izz
Aden
YEMEN
Gulf of Aden
Socotra
(to Yemen)
69

0 km   800
0 miles   800

POPULATION   ● National capital

○ Less than 50,000   ○ 50,000 -100,000   ◉ 100,000 - 500,000   ▣ Over 500,000

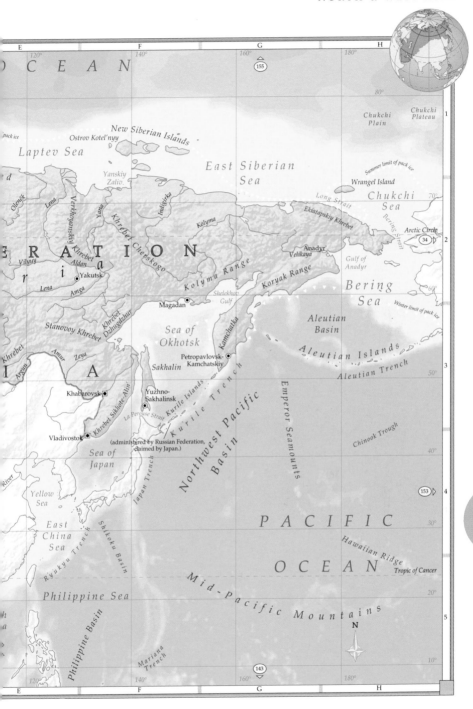

RUSSIA & KAZAKHSTAN

NETH.

NORWAY

DENMARK

SWEDEN

GERMANY

Baltic Sea

Gulf of Bothnia

FINLAND

SVALBARD
(to Norway)

Winter limit of pack ice

Summer limit of pack ice

Zemly

A R C

Nordkapp
(North Cape)

Barents
Sea

Murmansk

KALININGRAD
(to Russ. Fed.)

Kaliningrad

POLAND

Kandalaksha

Kol'skiy Poluostrov

Novaya Zemlya

Karskoye More

Ostrov

LITH. LAT. EST.

Sankt-Peterburg

Ladozhskoye Ozero

Severodvinsk

Ostrov Kolguyev

Poluostrov Yamal

BELARUS

Pskov

Novgorod

Petrozavodsk

Onezhskoye Ozero

Arkhangel'sk

Nar'yan-Mar

MOLDOVA

Smolensk

Cherepovets

Vel'sk

Severnaya Dvina

Beloye More

Pechora

UKRAINE

MOSKVA
(MOSCOW)

Tver

Vologda

Ukhta

Vorkuta

Ural'skiye Gory

Salekhard

Obskaya Guba

Bryansk

Tula

Yaroslavl'

Kineshma

Kotlas

Syktyvkar

Belgorod

Ryazan'

Vladimir

Nizhniy Novgorod

Kirov

Nadym

Nyagan'

Zapadno-

Voronezh

Tambov

Glazov

Solikamsk

Sibirskaya

Sea of Azov

Penza

Kazan'

Izhevsk

Perm'

Serov

Khanty-Mansiysk

Ravnina

Mikhaylovka

Ul'yanovsk

Tol'yatti

Rostov-na-Donu

Saratov

Balakovo

Naberezhnyye Chelny

Yekaterinburg

Surgut

Nizhnevarto

RUSSI

Krasnodar

Volgograd

Samara

Ufa

Tyumen'

Tobol'sk

Ob'

Chul

Sochi

Stavropol'

Ural'sk

Sterlitamak

Chelyabinsk

Caucasus 5642m

Orenburg

Magnitogorsk

Ishim

Petropavlovsk

Omsk

Tomsk

Nal'chik

Astrakhan

Aktobe

Orsk

Novosibirsk

Kra

GEORGIA

Vladikavkaz

Groznyy

Atyrau

Alga

Rudnyy

Kostanay

Ken

ARM.

Makhachkala

Emba

Kokshetau

AZERBAIJAN

Fort-Shevchenko

Chelkar

Atbasar

Shchuchinsk

Novosibirsk

Aktau

Zhanaozen

KAZAKHSTAN

ASTANA

Pavlodar

Barnaul

Novokuznetsk

Ustyurt Plateau

Aral Sea

Aral'sk

Ayteke Bi

Temirtau

Semipalatinsk

Leninogorsk

Caspian Sea

Syr Darya

Zhezkazgan

Kazakhskiy

Saran'

Karaganda

Shar

Zyryanovs

IRAN

TURKMENISTAN

Amu Darya

UZBEKISTAN

Dzhusaly

Kyzylorda

Melkosopochnik

Ust'-Kamenogorsk

Gora 4506m

Altai Mou

Kyzyl Kum

Balkhash

Ayaguz

Ozero Zaysan

Turkistan

Kentau

Ozero Balkhash

Taldykorgan

Karatau

Tekeli

Arys

Shu

Shymkent

Taraz

Almaty
(Alma-Ata)

CHINA

TAJIKISTAN

Kirghiz Range

Tien Shan

AFGHANISTAN

KYRGYZSTAN

| 0 km | 800 |
| 0 miles | 800 |

POPULATION   ● National capital

○ Less than 50,000   ○ 50,000 -100,000   ◉ 100,000 - 500,000   ◼ Over 500,00

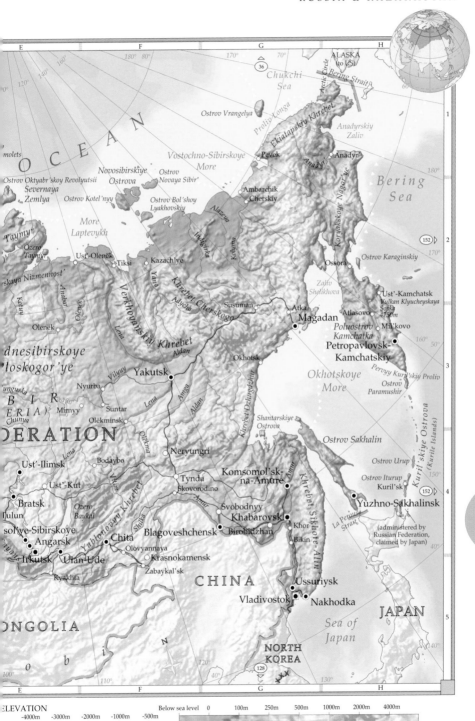

ELEVATION

				Below sea level	0	100m	250m	500m	1000m	2000m	4000m
-4000m	-3000m	-2000m	-1000m	-500m							
-13 124ft	-9843ft	-6562ft	-3281ft	-1640ft	-820ft/-250m	0	328ft	820ft	1640ft	3281ft	6562ft	13 124ft

TURKEY & THE CAUCASUS

ROMANIA

UKRAINE
Kryms'kyy
Pivostriv

Pacul Razim
Pacul Sinoie

N

Danube

BULGARIA

B l a c k   S e a

Varnenski
Zaliv

Burgaski
Zaliv

Maritsa

Kırklareli
Edirne

Çorlu
Ergene Nehri
Tekirdağ

İstanbul Boğazı
(Bosporus)

Cide
İnebolu

Bartın

Sinop
Gerze

Küre Dağları

Zonguldak

Bafra

Sams

Karabük
Kastamonu

Devrek
Çankırı
Kargı

İstanbul

İzmit   Adapazarı
Çerkeş

Çanık Dağ

Marmara Denizi
(Sea of Marmara)
Bandırma   Yalova

Bolu   Gerede
Merzifon

Çanakkale

İznik Gölü

Bursa
Bilecik

Çankırı

Kızıl Irmak

Çorum

Çanakkale
Boğazı
(Dardanelles)

Balıkesir

Bozüyük   Eskişehir
ANKARA

Kalecik
Alaca

Tok
Yıld

Edremit
Ayvalık

Kütahya

Kırıkkale

Sorgun

Lésvos

Simav
Gediz

T

U

R

Şarkışla
Boğazlıyan

Menemen
Akhisar
Manisa

Uşak
Afyon

Polatlı

Hirfanlı
Barajı

İncesu
Bünyan

Chíos
İzmir

Kulu

Tuz Gölü

Nevşehir
Kayseri

Gü

Sámos

Alaşehir
Nazilli

Cihanbeyli
Akşehir
Aksaray

Ödemiş
Aydın

Dinar

Beyşehir
Gölü

Göksun
G

Söke
Büyükmenderes Nehri

Denizli
Burdur

Isparta

Konya

Niğde

Kahram

Milás
Tavas
Burdur
Gölü

A

Suğla Gölü

Ereğli

Bodrum
Muğla

n

Karaman

Ceyhan

Tarsus
Osma

Marmaris

Dalaman
Antalya
a

t

o

l

Toros

Mut
Mersin
Adana
Ki

Dodekánisos
(Dodecánese)

Fethiye
Kaş

Manavgat

Dağları

İskenderun

Finike
Antalya
Körfezi

Alanya

Silifke

Antakya
Kırık

Ródos
(Rhodes)

Anamur

Kárpathos

CYPRUS

TURKISH REPUBLIC OF
NORTHERN CYPRUS
(recognised only by Turkey)

Oran

M e d i t e r r a n e a n
S e a

LEBANON

0 km   200

0 miles   200

POPULATION   ● National capital

○ Less than 50,000   ○ 50,000 -100,000   ◉ 100,000 - 500,000   ◼ Over 500,000

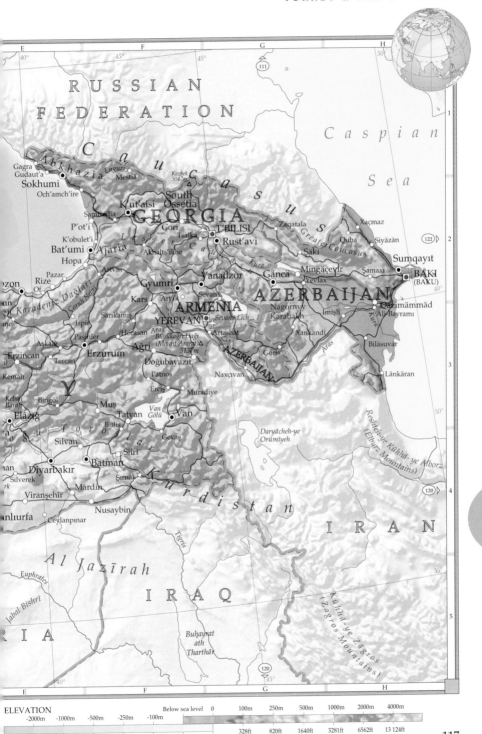

RUSSIAN

FEDERATION

Caucasus

Caspian

Sea

Gagra
Gudaut'a
Sokhumi
Och'amch'ire

Abkhazia

Enguri
Mestia

Kazbek
5047m △

K'ut'aisi

South
Ossetia

GEORGIA

Samtredia

P'ot'i

K'obulet'i

Bat'umi · Ajaria

Hopa

Gori

Tsalka

T'BILISI

Rust'avi

Zaqatala

Xaçmaz

Lesser

Quba

Siyäzän

Akhalts'ikhe

Säki

Greater Caucasus

Sumqayıt

Pazar

Rize

Of

ozon

un

ane

Karadeniz Dağları

Çoruh Nehri

Artvin

Gyumri

Vanadzor

Gäncä

Mingäçevir

Yevlax

Şamaxı

BAKI
(BAKU)

Ca

ucasus

Kura

Kars

Aralık

Sevan

ARMENIA

Nagornyy
Karabakh

İmişli

Qazimämmäd
Äli-Bayramı

Sarıkamış

YEREVAN

Sevana Lich

Xankändi

Biläsuvar

İspir

Aşkale

Paşınler

Horasan

Aras

Büyükağrı Dağı
(Mount Ararat) △
5137m

Artashat

Goris

Aras

AZERBAIJAN

Erzincan

Tercan

Erzurum

Ağrı

Doğubayazıt

Naxçıvan

Länkäran

Kemah

Patnos

Ercis

Muradiye

*Reshteh-ye Kühhä-ye Alborz
(Elburz Mountains)*

Keban
Barajı

Bingöl

Muş

Tatvan

Van
Gölü

Van

*Daryácheh-ye
Orúmíyeh*

Eläzığ

Bitlis

Gevaş

Silvan

Siirt

Diyarbakır · Batman

Silverek

Şırnak

Mardin

IRAN

Viranşehir

Nusaybin

Kurdistan

nlıurfa

Ceylanpınar

Tigris

Al Jazīrah

Euphrates

Jabal Bishrī

IRAQ

RIA

*Buhayrat
ath
Tharthār*

*Kühhä-ye Zagros
(Zagros Mountains)*

ELEVATION

| -2000m | -1000m | -500m | -250m | -100m | Below sea level | 0 | 100m | 250m | 500m | 1000m | 2000m | 4000m |

| -6562ft | -3281ft | -1640ft | -820ft | -328ft | -164ft/-50m | 0 | 328ft | 820ft | 1640ft | 3281ft | 6562ft | 13 124ft |

THE NEAR EAST

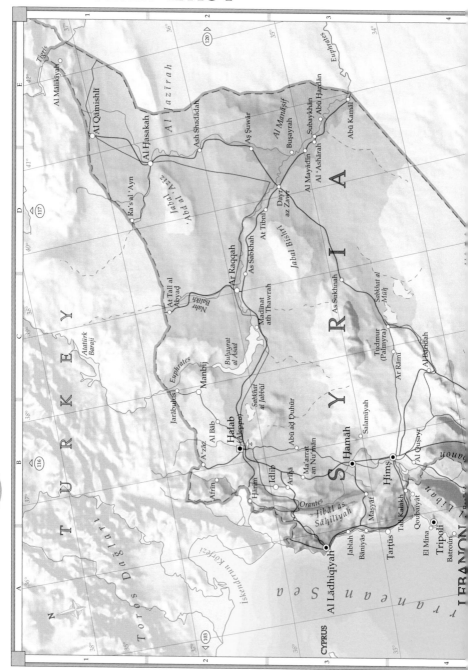

0 km 100
0 miles 100

POPULATION ● National capital

○ Less than 50,000 ○ 50,000 -100,000 ◉ 100,000 - 500,000 ◼ Over 500,000

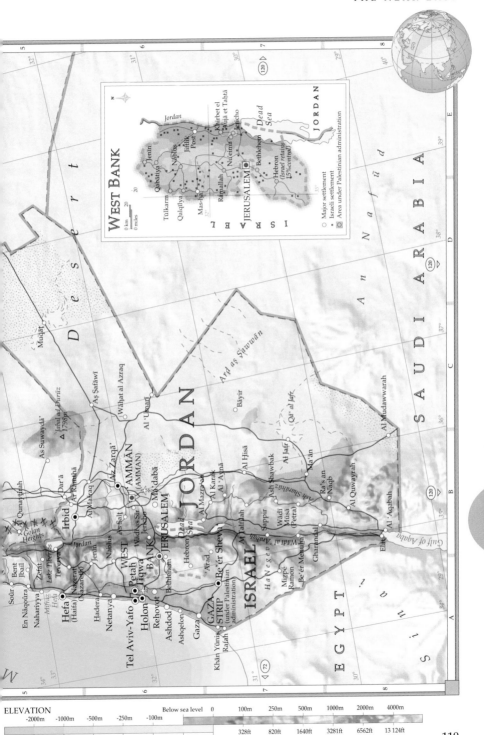

WEST BANK

0 km   20
0 miles   20

○ Major settlement
▪ Israeli settlement
◉ Area under Palestinian administration

ELEVATION

						Below sea level	0	100m	250m	500m	1000m	2000m	4000m
-2000m	-1000m	-500m	-250m	-100m									
-6562ft	-3281ft	-1640ft	-820ft	-328ft	-164ft/-50m	0		328ft	820ft	1640ft	3281ft	6562ft	13 124ft

119

THE MIDDLE EAST

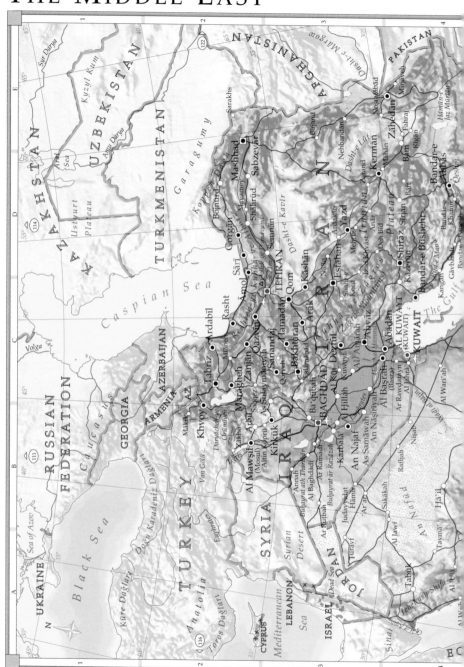

POPULATION • National capital

○ Less than 50,000 ◉ 50,000 -100,000 ◉ 100,000 - 500,000 ◼ Over 500,000

0 km   400

0 miles   400

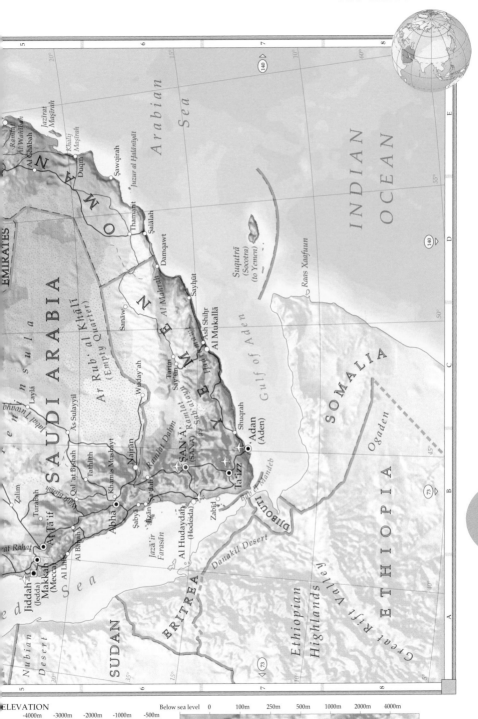

Arabian Sea

INDIAN OCEAN

EMIRATES

SAUDI ARABIA

Peninsula

Ar Rub' al Khālī
(Empty Quarter)

OMAN

YEMEN

Raṃlat
Al Wahībah

Jazīrat Maṣīrah

Khalīj Maṣīrah

Al Ghābah

Duqm

Sawqirah

Juzur al Ḥalāniyāt

Thamarīt

Ṣalālah

Damqawt

Al Mahrah

Sayḥūt

Sanāw

Al Ghaydah

Wadī Ḥaḍramawt

Saywūn

Tarīm

Ash Shiḥr

Al Mukallā

Suquṭrā
(Socotra)
(to Yemen)

Raas Xaafuun

Gulf of Aden

SOMALIA

Ogaden

Wuday'ah

Layla

Zālim

Turabah

Al Ḥillah

Layla

As Sulayyil

Qal'at Bīshah

Taṭhlīth

Najrān

Khamis Mushayṭ

Abhā

Shabwah

Ramlat as Sab'atayn

SANʻĀʼ
(SANA)

Ta'izz

Shuqrah

Adan
(Aden)

Bāb el Mandeb

DJIBOUTI

ERITREA

ETHIOPIA

Ethiopian Highlands

Great Rift Valley

Danakil Desert

Zabid

Jazā'ir Farasān

Al Hudaydah
(Hodeida)

Al Birkah

Jāzān

Ṣabyā

Jiddah
(Jedda)

Makkah
(Mecca)

Al Līth

Raḥaṭ

Nubian Desert

SUDAN

Sea

ELEVATION

					Below sea level	0	100m	250m	500m	1000m	2000m	4000m
-4000m	-3000m	-2000m	-1000m	-500m								
-13 124ft	-9843ft	-6562ft	-3281ft	-1640ft	-820ft/-250m	0	328ft	820ft	1640ft	3281ft	6562ft	13 124ft

121

CENTRAL ASIA

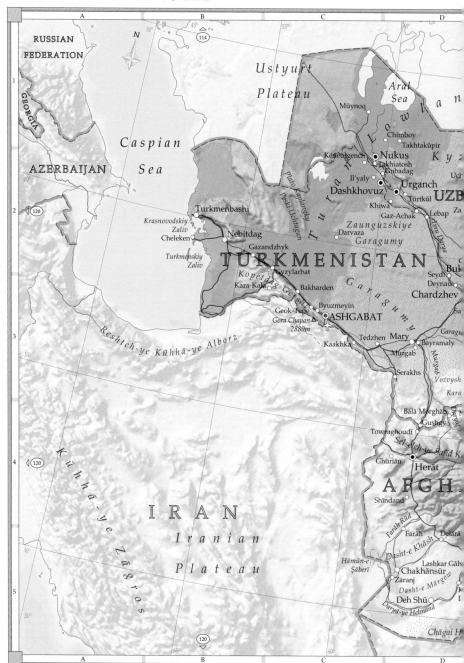

RUSSIAN
FEDERATION

GEORGIA

Ustyurt

Plateau

Aral
Sea

Müynoq

Chimboy

Takhtaküpir

Caspian

Kerieugench

Sea

Takhiatosh

Nukus

Gubadag

AZERBAIJAN

Il'yaly

Urganch

Dashkhovuz

UZB

Khiwa

Türtkül

Turkmenbashi

Gaz-Achak

Lebap

Za

*Krasnovodskiy
Zaliv*

Cheleken

Nebitdag

Darvaza

Zaunguzskiye

Garagumy

Gazandzhyk

*Turkmenskiy
Zaliv*

TURKMENISTAN

Buk

Gyzylarbat

Seydi

Kara-Kala

Kopet dag Gerisi

Bakharden

Garagum

Deynau

Chardzhev

Geok-Tepe

Byuzmeyin

Sa

Gora Chapan
2889m

ASHGABAT

Reshteh-ye Kŭhhā-ye Alborz

Kaakhka

Tedzhen

Mary

Garagu

Bayramaly

Mürgab

Vozvysh

Serakhs

Murgab

Kara

Bālā Morghāb

Gushgy

Towraghoudī

Selseleh-ye Safīd K

Ghūriān

Herāt

Kŭhhā-ye Zāgros

IRAN

Iranian

Shindand

AFGH.

Plateau

Fariāb Rūd

Farāh

Delārā

Dasht-e Khāsh

Hāmūn-e
Şāberī

Lashkar Gāh

Chakhānsūr

Zaranj

Dasht-e Mārgow

Deh Shū

Daryā-ye Helmand

Chāgai H

0 km 200

0 miles 200

POPULATION   ● National capital

○ Less than 50,000   ○ 50,000 -100,000   ◉ 100,000 - 500,000   ◼ Over 500,000

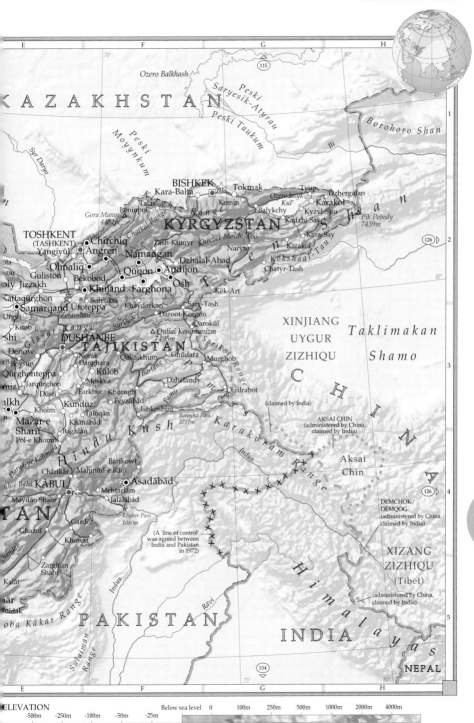

KAZAKHSTAN

Ozero Balkhash
Peski Saryesik-Atyrau
Peski Taukum
Peski Moyynkum
Ili
Borohoro Shan

Syr Darya

BISHKEK
Kara-Balta · Tokmak
Talas · Leninpol · Kemin
Gora Manas · Kadzhi-Say
4482m · Balykchy
Tyup
Dzhergalan
Ozero Issyk-Kul'
Karakol
TOSHKENT
(TASHKENT)
Yangiyŭl · Chirchiq
Angren
Olmaliq
Bekobod · Quqon · Andijon
Guliston
Jizzakh
Khŭjand · Farghona
KYRGYZSTAN
Tash-Kumyr
Khrebet Moldo-Too
Dzhalal-Abad
Naryn
Osh
Kadzhi-Say
Kyzyl-Suu
Kara-Say
Pik Pobedy
7439m
Karakol
Kokshaal-Tau
Chatyr-Tash
Kattaqŭrghon
Samarqand · Uroteppa
Zeravshan
Kitob
Urgut
Gissar Range
shi
Denow
Boysun
Qŭrghonteppa
miz
Jarqŭrghon
alkh
Kholm
Mazār-e
Sharīf
Pol-e Khomri

Sulyukta
Khaydarkan
Daroot-Korgon
Qullai Kommunizm
7495m
DUSHANBE
TAJIKISTAN
Norak
Danghara
Kŭlob
Moskva
Farkhor · Khorugh
Feyzābād
Kunduz
Khānābād
Baghlān
Bārīkowt
Chārīkār · Mahmūd-e Rāqī
Qarokŭl
Sary-Tash
Kēk-Art
XINJIANG
UYGUR
ZIZHIQU
Taklimakan
Shamo
CHINA
Qal'aikhum · Ghŭdara
Murghob
Dzhelandy
Qizilrabot
Ishkoshim
Baroghil Pass
3777m
Karakoram Range
(claimed by India)
AKSAI CHIN
(administered by China,
claimed by India)
Aksai
Chin
DEMCHOK/
DÊMQOG
(administered by China,
claimed by India)

KĀBUL
Maydān Shahr
Ghaznī
Gardēz
Khowst
Zarghūn
Shahr
Kalat
dldak
oba Kākar Range
Asadābād
Mehtarlām
Jalālābād
Khyber Pass
1080m
(A 'line of control'
was agreed between
India and Pakistan
in 1972)
Indus
Ravi
Sulaiman
Range
PAKISTAN
Himalayas
XIZANG
ZIZHIQU
(Tibet)
(administered by China,
claimed by India)
INDIA
NEPAL

ELEVATION

				Below sea level	0	100m	250m	500m	1000m	2000m	4000m
-500m	-250m	-100m	-50m	-25m							
-1640ft	-820ft	-328ft	-164ft	-82ft	33ft/-10m	0	328ft	820ft	1640ft	3281ft	6562ft	13 124ft

SOUTH & EAST ASIA

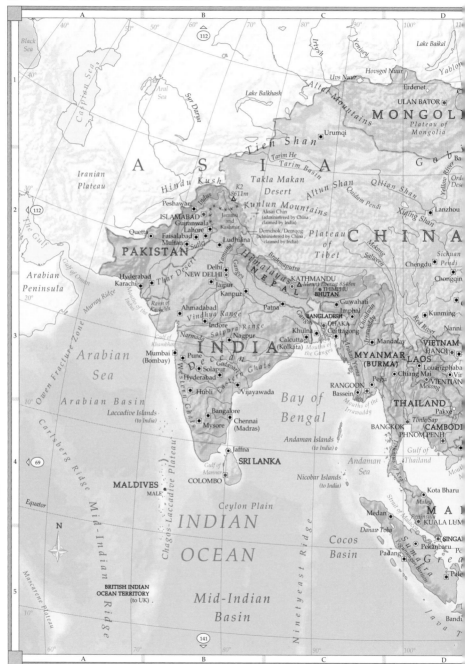

0 km   1000

0 miles   1000

POPULATION   • National capital

○ Less than 50,000   ○ 50,000 -100,000   ◉ 100,000 - 500,000   ◼ Over 500,000

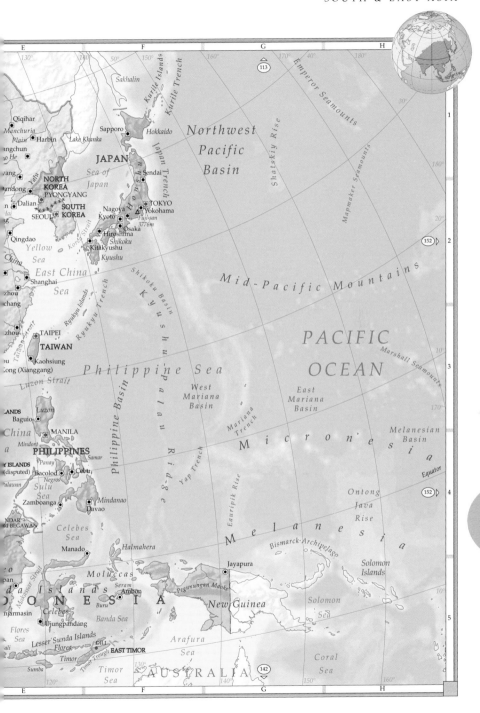

E   F   G   H

130°   140°   50°   150°   160°   170°   40°   180°

Sakhalin

Kurile Islands

Kurile Trench

113

Emperor Seamounts

1

Qiqihar

Manchuria
Plain   Harbin   Lake Khanka

angchun

lo He

Sapporo   Hokkaido

*Northwest
Pacific
Basin*

Shatskiy Rise

30°

Mapmaker Seamounts

yang

JAPAN   *Sea of
Japan*

Sendai

Japan Trench

NORTH
KOREA

PYONGYANG

andong   Yalu

Dalian

SOUTH
KOREA

SEOUL

Honshu

TOKYO
Yokohama

Nagoya
Kyoto   Osaka

*Fuji-san
3776m*

180°

20°

152

2

Qingdao

Hiroshima
Kitakyushu

Shikoku

Kyushu

*Yellow
Sea*

Korea Strait

East China

Shanghai

Sea

Ryukyu Islands

Shikoku Basin

Mid-Pacific Mountains

zhou

chang

zhou

TAIPEI

TAIWAN

Taiwan Strait

Ryukyu Trench

Kyushu

Philippine Sea

*West
Mariana
Basin*

*East
Mariana
Basin*

PACIFIC

OCEAN

Marshall Seamounts

10°

3

Kaohsiung

ong (Xianggang)

Luzon Strait

LANDS

Baguio

Luzon

China

a

Mindoro

MANILA

PHILIPPINES

Samar

Philippine Basin

Palau Ridge

*M i c r o n e s
i
a*

170°

Y ISLANDS
(disputed)   Bacolod

Panay   Cebu

Mariana Trench

Yap Trench

Eauripik Rise

*Melanesian
Basin*

Equator

152

4

alawan

*Sulu
Sea*

Zamboanga

Negros

Mindanao

Davao

*Ontong
Java
Rise*

NDAR
RI BEGAWAN

*Celebes
Sea*

Manado

Halmahera

*M e l a n e s
i
a*

Bismarck Archipelago

*Solomon
Islands*

o

pan

Moluccas

Seram
Ambon

Pegunungan Maoke

Jayapura

*Solomon
Sea*

10°

jarmasin   Manakasar Strait

Buru

New Guinea

DONESIA

Celebes

Ujungpandang

Banda Sea

5

*Flores
Sea*

Lesser Sunda Islands

Flores

Timor

DILI

EAST TIMOR

*Arafura
Sea*

*Coral
Sea*

Sumba

Timor
Trough

*Timor
Sea*

AUSTRALIA

142

120°   130°   140°   150°   160°

E   F   G   H

WESTERN CHINA & MONGOLIA

POPULATION   ● National capital   ○ Internal administrative capital

0 km   400

0 miles   400

○ Less than 50,000   ○ 50,000 -100,000   ◉ 100,000 - 500,000   ◼ Over 500,000

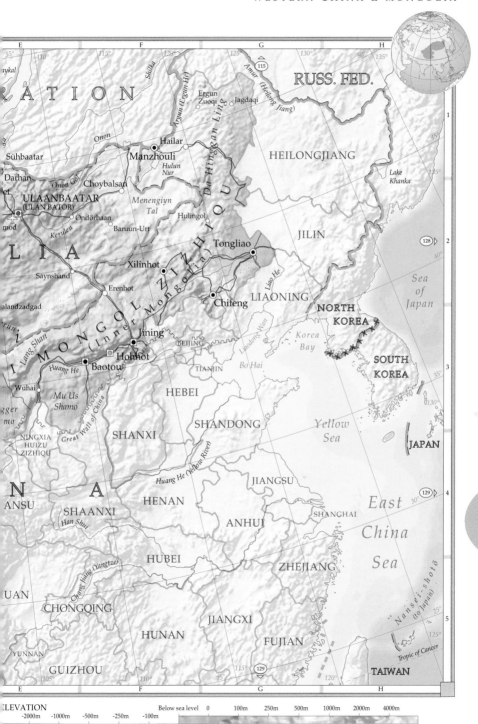

RUSS. FED.

ERATION

Baykal

Sühbaatar

Darhan

ULAANBAATAR
(ULAN BATOR)

mod

Öndörhaan

Baruun-Urt

Saynshand

alandzadgad

Wuhai

NINGXIA
HUIZU
ZIZHIQU

Onon

Onon Gol

Hailar

Manzhouli

Hulun
Nur

Choybalsan

Menengiyn
Tal

Kerülen

Erenhot

Jining

Hohhot

Baotou

Huang He

Mu Us
Shamo

Great Wall of China

SHANXI

Ergun
Zuoqi

Jagdaqi

HEILONGJIANG

Hulingol

Tongliao

Xilinhot

Chifeng

LIAONING

BEIJING

TIANJIN

HEBEI

SHANDONG

Huang He (Yellow River)

Lake
Khanka

JILIN

Liao He

NORTH
KOREA

Korea
Bay

Bo Hai

Sea
of
Japan

SOUTH
KOREA

JAPAN

Yellow
Sea

JIANGSU

East
China
Sea

ANSU

A

SHAANXI

Han Shui

HENAN

ANHUI

SHANGHAI

UAN

CHONGQING

HUBEI

Chang Jiang (Yangtze)

JIANGXI

ZHEJIANG

YUNNAN

GUIZHOU

HUNAN

FUJIAN

Nansei-shotō
(to Japan)

Tropic of Cancer

TAIWAN

LIA

I MONGOL ZIZHIQU (Inner Mongolia)

Da Hinggan Ling

Liang Shan

i

Amur (Heilong Jiang)

Shilka

Argun (Ergun He)

Liaodong Wan

Liaodong Bandao

ELEVATION

| -2000m | -1000m | -500m | -250m | -100m | Below sea level | 0 | 100m | 250m | 500m | 1000m | 2000m | 4000m |

| -6562ft | -3281ft | -1640ft | -820ft | -328ft | -164ft/-50m | 0 | 328ft | 820ft | 1640ft | 3281ft | 6562ft | 13 124ft |

127

EASTERN CHINA & KOREA

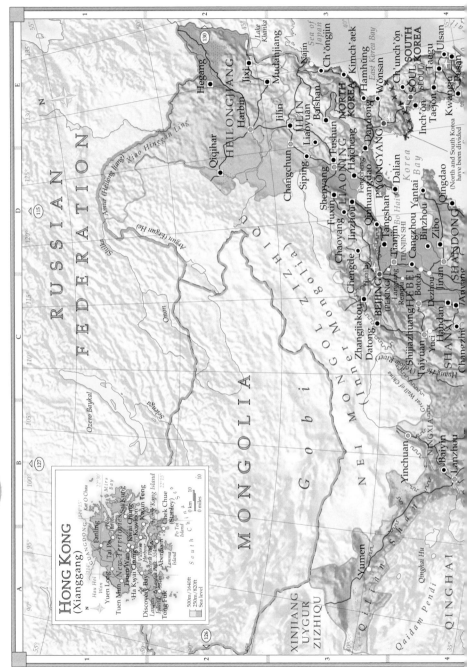

HONG KONG
(Xianggang)

POPULATION ● National capital ◎ Internal administrative capital

○ Less than 50,000 ◯ 50,000 -100,000 ● 100,000 - 500,000 ■ Over 500,000

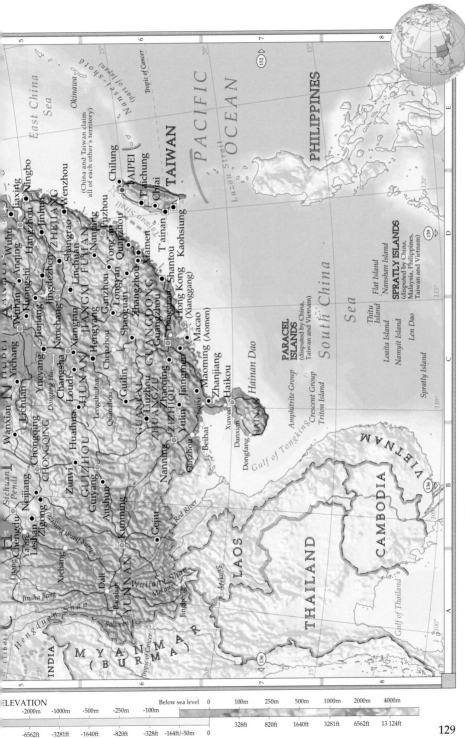

East China
Sea

Okinawa (to Japan)

Nansei-shoto *(Ryukyu Islands)*

Tropic of Cancer

PACIFIC

OCEAN

152

PHILIPPINES

TAIWAN

Chilung
TAICHUNG
TAIPEI
Chiai

Kaohsiung

T'ainan

(China and Taiwan claim
all of each other's territory)

Luzon Strait

139

SPRATLY ISLANDS
(disputed by China,
Malaysia, Philippines,
Taiwan and Vietnam)

Nanshan Island
Flat Island

Thitu
Island

South China

Loaita Island
Len Dao
Namyit Island

Sea

Spratly Island

PARACEL
ISLANDS
(disputed by China,
Taiwan and Vietnam)

Amphitrite Group
Crescent Group
Triton Island

Ningbo
Jiaxing
Hangzhou
Wuhu
Anqing
Wuhan
Wanxian
Yichang
HUBEI
ANHUI
Wenzhou
Jinhua
Shangrao
ZHEJIANG
Nanchang
Jingdezhen
Huangshi
Jiujiang
JIANGXI
FUJIAN
Fuzhou
Xiangtan
Linchuan
Nanping
Changsha
Loudi
Yong'an
Quanzhou
Ganzhou
Shaoguan
HUNAN
Longyan
Xiamen
Yichun
Hengyang
Chenzhou
Zhangzhou
Shantou
Lengshuitan
GUANGDONG
Shaoyang
Hong Kong
(Xianggang)
Guilin
Liuzhou
Guangzhou
Dongguan
GUANGXI
Zhaoqing
Macao (Aomen)
ZHUANG ZU
Yulin
Jiangmen
Huaihua
Zunyi
GUIZHOU
Nanning
Maoming
Zhanjiang
Zhaotong
Guiyang
Qinzhou
Haikou
Beihai
Anshun
HAINAN Hainan Dao
Xuwen
Danxian
Dongfang
Gulf of Tongking

Chongqing
CHONGQING
Neijiang

Gejiu

Red River

Kunming

YUNNAN

VIETNAM

CAMBODIA

LAOS

THAILAND

136

Wuliang Shan

Mekong

Gulf of Thailand

MYANMAR
(BURMA)

136

INDIA

Hengduan Shan

Salween

Baoshan

Dali

Xichang

Jinsha Jiang

Leshan
Zigong
Yibin
Chengdu
Sichuan
Pendi
SICHUAN
Liang

Tropic of Cancer

JAPAN

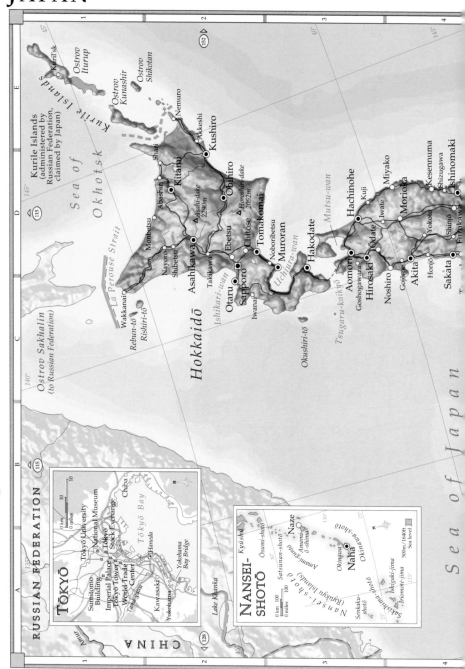

Sea of Okhotsk

Kuril'sk
Ostrov Iturup
Ostrov Shikotan
Ostrov Kunashir
Kurile Islands

Kurile Islands (administered by Russian Federation, claimed by Japan)

Nemuro
Akkeshi
Kushiro
Shari
Kitami
Abashiri
Mombetsu
Asahi-dake 2290m
Hokoshiri-dake 2052m
Obihiro
Nayoro
Shibetsu
Asahikawa
Takikawa
Ebetsu
Chitose
Tomakomai
Noboribetsu
Muroran
Uchiura-wan
Hakodate
Otaru
Sapporo
Iwanai
Wakkanai
Rebun-tō
Rishiri-tō
Okushiri-tō
Ishikari-wan
La Perouse Strait

Hokkaidō

Ostrov Sakhalin (to Russian Federation)

Mutsu-wan
Tsugaru-kaikyō
Hachinohe
Miyako
Kesennuma
Shizugawa
Ishinomaki
Morioka
Iwate
Kuji
Yokote
Shinjō
Furukawa
Aomori
Odate
Goshogawara
Hirosaki
Noshiro
Gojōme
Akita
Honjō
Sakata

Sea of Japan

RUSSIAN FEDERATION

Amur

CHINA

Lake Khanka

TŌKYŌ

Chiba
Tōkyō University
National Museum
Tōkyō Stock Exchange
Sumitomo Building
Tōkyō Tower
Imperial Palace
World Trade Center
Tōkyō
Hameda
Yokohama Bay Bridge
Kawasaki
Yokohama
Yokosuka
Tōkyō Bay

0 km 10
0 miles 10

NANSEI-SHOTŌ

Kyūshū
Ōsumi-shotō
Satsunan-shotō
Naze
Amami
Ō-shima
Amami-guntō
Tokara-shotō
Okinawa
Naha
Okinawa-shotō
Miyako-shotō
Ishigaki-jima
Iriomote-jima
Yonaguni-jima
Senkaku-shotō
Sakishima-shotō

Nansei-shotō (Ryūkyū Islands)

500m/1640ft
Sea level

0 km 100
0 miles 100

0 km 200
0 miles 200

POPULATION

● National capital

○ Less than 50,000   ○ 50,000 -100,000   ◉ 100,000 - 500,000   ◼ Over 500,000

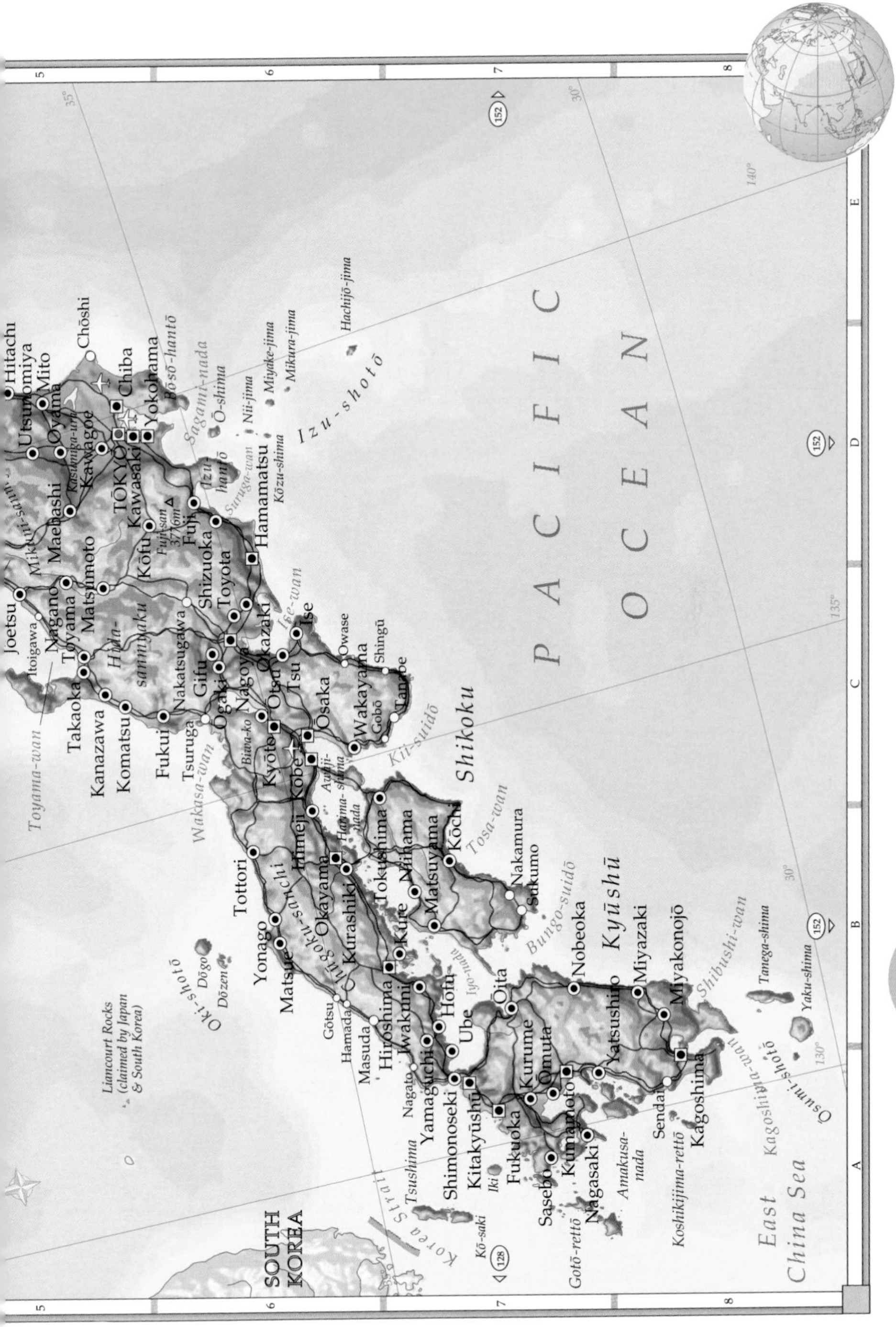

PACIFIC

OCEAN

SOUTH
KOREA

Shikoku

Kyūshū

East
China Sea

Hitachi
Utsunomiya
Oyama
Mito
Choshi
Kawagoe
Bōsō-hantō
TOKYO
Kawasaki
Yokohama
Koshigaya-uri
Mikuni-sanm
Maebashi
Nagano
Toyama
Matsumoto
Kōfu
Fuji
Izu
hantō
Suruga-wan
Izu-shotō
Hachijō-jima
Mikura-jima
Miyake-jima
Nii-jima
Ō-shima
Kōzu-shima
Sagami-nada
Fujisan △ 3,776m
Joetsu
Itoigawa
Hida-
sanmyaku
Shizuoka
Toyota
Okazaki
Hamamatsu
Takaoka
Kanazawa
Komatsu
Fukui
Tsuruga
Gifu
Nakatsugawa
Ogaki
Nagoya
Ōtsu
Okayama
Ise
Owase
Shingū
Tanabe
Gobō
Wakayama
Osaka
Tsu
Ise-wan
Kōbe
Akashi
Wakasa-wan
Kyōto
Himeji
Harima-
nada
Biwa-ko
Awaji-
shima
Tosa-wan
Kii-suidō
Nakamura
Sukumo
Kōchi
Miyama
Matsuyama
Tokushima
Toyama-wan
Tottori
Yonago
Matsue
Chūgoku-sanchi
Okayama
Kurashiki
Kōbe
Hiroshima
Iwakuni
Kure
Oki-shotō
Dōgo
Dōzen
Liancourt Rocks
(claimed by Japan
& South Korea)
Hōfu
Ube
Ōita
Nobeoka
Miyazaki
Shibushi-wan
Tanega-shima
Yaku-shima
Gōtsu
Masuda
Hamada
Nagato
Yamaguchi
Shimonoseki
Kitakyūshū
Ōmuta
Kurume
Natsushiro
Miyakonojō
Sendai
Kagoshima
Ōsumi-shotō
Ōsumi-kaikyō
Kagoshima-wan
Iki
Fukuoka
Saga
Kumamoto
Amakusa-
nada
Koshikijima-rettō
Gotō-rettō
Nagasaki
Sasebo
Tsushima
Kō-saki
Korea Strait
Iyo-nada
Suō-nada
Bungo-suidō

ELEVATION

-4000m	-3000m	-2000m	-1000m	-500m		Below sea level	0	100m	250m	500m	1000m	2000m	4000m
-13 124ft	-9843ft	-6562ft	-3281ft	-1640ft	-820ft/-250m	0		328ft	820ft	1640ft	3281ft	6562ft	13 124ft

131

SOUTHERN INDIA & SRI LANKA

Kalyān
Mumbai (Bombay)
Pune
Ahmadnagar
Bārāmati
Nizāmābād
Nānded
Karīmnagar
Jago
Andhra Pradesh
Vizianagar
INDIA
Solāpur
Secunderābād
Visākh
Sāngli
Gulbarga
Hyderābād
Rājah
Kolhāpur
Deccan
Rāichūr
Krishna
Vijayawad
Karnātaka
Kurnool
Machilīp
Belgaum
Gadag
Pānji
Chīrāla
Hubli
Nandyal
Ongole
Tungabhadra
Reservoir
Tādpatri
Kāvali
Dāvangere
Anantapur
Nellore
Shimoga
Cuddapah
Udupi
Bhadrāvati
Tumkūr
Chennai (Madras)
Mangalore
Bangalore
Vellore
Kānchīpuram
Kāsargod
Mandya
Krishnagiri
Tiruppattūr
Cannanore
Mysore
Pondicherry
Calicut
Erode
Salem
Neyveli
Coimbatore
Tamil Nādu
Trichūr
Tiruchchirāppalli
Ernākulam
Dindigul
Madurai
Jaffna
Cochin
Pālk Strait
SRI LA
Alleppey
Rājapālaiyam
Mannar
Vavuniya
Quilon
Trincomale
Trivandrum
Tuticorin
Anurādhapura
Nāgercoil
Gulf of Mannar
Batti
Puttalam
Matale
Negombo
Kandy
COLOMBO
Sri Jayawardan
Kalutara
Ratnapura
Galle
Matara

Arabian
Sea

Western
Ghats

Malabar Coast

Eastern Ghats

Coromandel Coast

Godāvari

Amīndīvi
Islands
Lakshadweep
(Laccadive Islands)
(to India)
Kavaratti
Island
Kalpeni
Island
Nine Degree Channel
Minicoy Island
Eight Degree Channel

Ihavandippolhu
Atoll

MALDIVES

Faadhippolhu
Atoll
Horsburgh
Atoll
Ari Atoll
Male' Atoll
MALE'
Felidhu Atoll
Mulaku Atoll
Kolhumadulu
Atoll
Hadhdhunmathi Atoll

INDIA

North Huvadhu Atoll
South Huvadhu
Atoll
Gan
Addu Atoll

Equator

0 km   300
0 miles   300

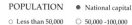

POPULATION   ● National capital

○ Less than 50,000   ○ 50,000 -100,000   ◉ 100,000 - 500,000   ■ Over 500,000

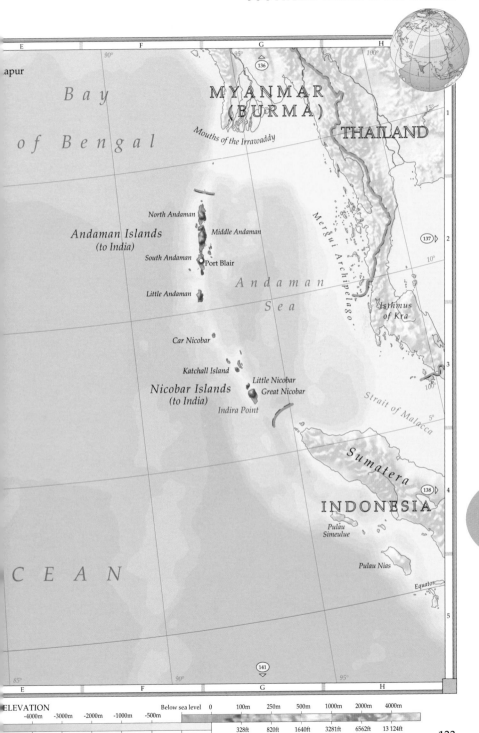

ELEVATION

					Below sea level	0	100m	250m	500m	1000m	2000m	4000m
-4000m	-3000m	-2000m	-1000m	-500m								
-13 124ft	-9843ft	-6562ft	-3281ft	-1640ft	-820ft/-250m	0	328ft	820ft	1640ft	3281ft	6562ft	13 124ft

NORTHERN INDIA, PAKISTAN & BANGLADE:

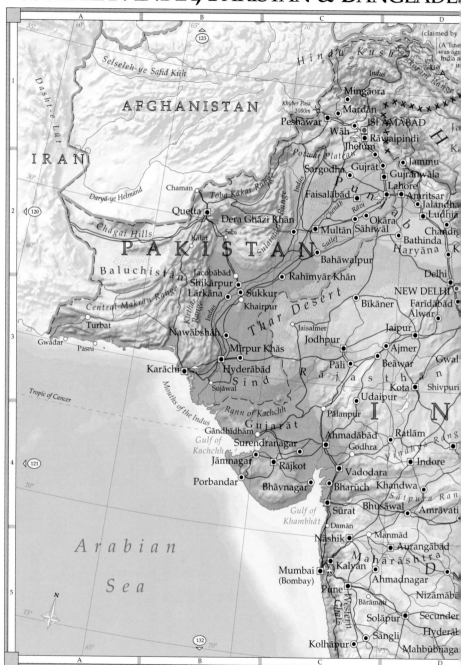

(claimed by

(A "line
was ag:
India a

35°

A 60° B 65° C 70° D 75°

123

Selseleh-ye Safid Kūh

1

Dasht-i Lūt

AFGHANISTAN

Hindu Kush

Indus

Mingāora

Mardan

Khyber Pass
1080m

Peshāwar

Wāh

ISLAMABAD

Rāwalpindi

Jhelum

Jammu

IRAN

30°

Chaman

Toba Kākar Range

Quetta

Dera Ghāzi Khān

Sargodha

Gujrāt

Gujrānwāla

Lahore

Amritsar

Jalandha

Ludhiā

Potwar Plateau

Indus

Faisalābād

Chenāb

Rāvi

Okāra

Sāhīwāl

Chandī

Daryā-ye Helmand

60°

2

120

Chāgai Hills

PAKISTAN

Kālat

Sibi

Multān

Sutlej

Bathinda

Haryāna

K

Baluchistan

Jacobābād

Shikārpur

Lārkāna

Sukkur

Khairpur

Bahāwalpur

Rahīmyār Khān

Bīkāner

Delhi

NEW DELHI

Farīdābād
Alwar

Central Makrān Range

Kirthar Range

Indus

Turbat

Nawābshāh

Thar Desert

Jaisalmer

Jodhpur

Jaipur

25°

Gwādar

Pasni

3

Mīrpur Khās

R

Pāli

Ajmer

Beāwar

Gwal

Karāchi

Hyderābād

Sind

a

j

a

s

t

h

ā

n

Kota

Shivpuri

Sujāwal

Mouths of the Indus

Rann of Kachchh

Udaipur

I

N

Tropic of Cancer

Pālanpur

20°

4

121

Gāndhīdhām

*Gulf of
Kachchh*

Surendranagar

Gujarāt

Ahmadābād

Godhra

Ratlām

Aravalli Range

Indore

Jāmnagar

Rājkot

Vadodara

Khandwa

Sātpura Ran

Porbandar

Bhāvnagar

Bharūch

Bhusāwal

Amrāvati

*Gulf of
Khambhāt*

Sūrat

Damān

Nāshik

Manmād

Aurangābād

A r a b i a n

Maharashtra

D

Mumbai
(Bombay)

Kalyān

Ahmadnagar

Nizāmābā

5

S e a

N

15°

Pune

Bārāmati

Solāpur

Secunder

Hyderāb

65°

132

70°

Kolhāpur

Sāngli

Mahbūbnaga

A B C D

0 km   300

0 miles   300

POPULATION   ● National capital

○ Less than 50,000   ◉ 50,000 -100,000   ◉ 100,000 - 500,000   ■ Over 500,000

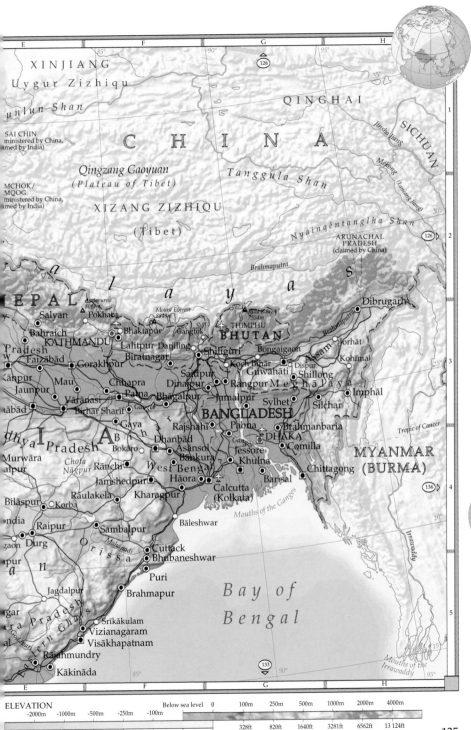

XINJIANG
Uygur Zizhiqu

QINGHAI

unlun Shan

SAI CHIN
ministered by China,
aimed by India)

C H I N A

SICHUAN

Jinsha Jiang

Qingzang Gaoyuan
(Plateau of Tibet)

Tanggula Shan

Mekong (Lancang Jiang)

MCHOK/
MQOG
ministered by China,
aimed by India)

XIZANG ZIZHIQU
(Tibet)

Nyainqêntanglha Shan

126

ARUNACHAL
PRADESH
(claimed by China)

Brahmaputra

a l a y a s

Dibrugarh

EPAL
Salyan
Pokhara

Mount Everest
8848m

Assam

Brahmaputra

Jorhāt

Bahraich

KATHMANDU
Bhaktapur
Gangtok

THIMPHU

BHUTAN

Bongaigaon

Pradesh
Faizābād
Gorakhpur
Lalitpur
Biratnagar
Darjiling
Shiliguri
Koch Bihar
Dispur

Assam
Kohima

Jaunpur
Mau
Chhapra
Saidpur
Dinajpur
Rangpur
Guwāhāti
Shillong
M e g h ā l a y a

Imphāl

Kānpur
Vārānasi
Patna
Bhāgalpur
Jamalpur
Sylhet
Silchar

ābād
Birhar Sharif
Ganges

BANGLADESH

Tropic of Cancer

dhya Pradesh
Gaya
Rajshahi
Pabna
Brahmanbaria

Murwāra
Bokaro
Dhanbad
Asansol
DHAKA
Comilla

MYANMAR
(BURMA)

alpur
Chota
Nagpur
Rānchi
Bankura
Jessore
Khulna

Bilāspur
Jamshedpur
West Bengal
Hāora
Barisal
Chittagong

Raūlakela
Kharagpur
Calcutta
(Kolkata)

India
Korba

Bāleshwar

Mouths of the Ganges

Raipur
Sambalpur

Durg
Mahānadi

Orissa
Cuttack
Bhubaneshwar

Irrawaddy

Jagdalpur
Puri

Brahmapur

B a y o f
B e n g a l

Srīkākulam
Vizianagaram
Visākhapatnam

Rājahmundry

Kākināda

Mouths of the
Irrawaddy

ELEVATION

| | | | | | | Below sea level | 0 | 100m | 250m | 500m | 1000m | 2000m | 4000m |

-2000m -1000m -500m -250m -100m

328ft 820ft 1640ft 3281ft 6562ft 13 124ft

-6562ft -3281ft -1640ft -820ft -328ft -164ft/-50m 0

MAINLAND SOUTHEAST ASIA

POPULATION   ● National capital

○ Less than 50,000   ○ 50,000 -100,000   ◉ 100,000 - 500,000   ◼ Over 500,000

0 km   200
0 miles   200

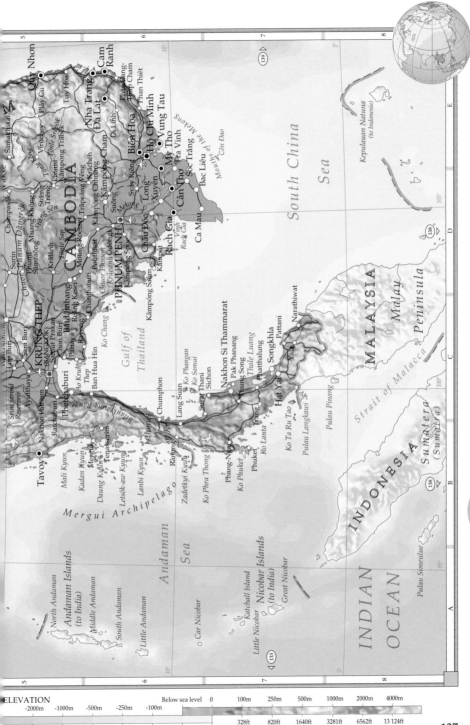

Qui Nhơn
Cam Ranh
Plây Cu
Tuy Hòa
Nha Trang
Đà Lạt
Phan Rang-Tháp Chàm
Bi'n Hòa
Phan Thiết
Di Linh
Hồ Chí Minh
Vũng Tàu
Mỹ Tho
Biên Hòa
Sóc Trăng
Kâmpóng Cham
Kâmpong Trâbêk
Kracheh
Srêng
Stoêng Treng
Phnom
Kâmpong Chhnang
Châu Đốc
Long Xuyên
Trà Vinh
Bạc Liêu
Mouths of the Mekong
Côn Đảo
Cân Thơ
Ràch Gia
Ca Mau
South China Sea

CAMBODIA
Suông
Mekong
Rach Gia
Kâmpông Sâom
Vinh

Kepulauan Natuna
(to Indonesia)

Champasak
Pakxé
Thmar
Phum Dângrêk
Muang Khong
Phum
Sén
Supraong
Phum
Kralanh
Moung Roessei
Trâpeăng Vêng
Surin
KRUNG THEP
Chhlong
Ba'r Buri
Bàttambang
Poithisat
Krâkôr
Kâmpong Spoe
PHNUM PENH
Odong
Kâmpong Saom
Chóam Khsant
Kâmpót
Kâmpong Saom
Kâmpóng Chhnang

MALAYSIA
Narathiwat
Malay Peninsula
Strait of Malacca

KRUNG THEP
(BANGKOK)
Samut Prakan
Chon Buri
Pattaya
Ban Chang
Ko Chang
Chanthaburi
Ratchanaburi
Phetchaburi
Ao Krung
Thep
Ban Hua Hin
Chumphon
Lang Suan
Ko Phangan
Ko Samui
Surat Thani
Sichon
Nakhon Si Thammarat
Pak Phanang
Thung Song
Phatthalung
Thale Luang
Songkhla
Pattani
Yala
Hat Yai
Narathiwat
Trang
Ko Lanta
Ko Ta Ru Tao
Pulau Langkawi
Pulau Pinang

Gulf of Thailand

Bilauktaung Range

Tavoy
Mali Kyun
Kadan Kyun
Mergui
Daung Kyun
Letsok-aw Kyun
Lanbi Kyun
Zadetkyi Kyun
Ko Phra Thong
Phang-Nga
Ko Phuket
Phuket
Tenasserim
Ranong

Sumatera
(Sumatra)
INDONESIA
Pulau Simeulue

Mergui Archipelago

Andaman Sea

North Andaman
Andaman Islands
(to India)
Middle Andaman
South Andaman
Little Andaman

Car Nicobar
Katchall Island
Little Nicobar
Nicobar Islands
(to India)
Great Nicobar

INDIAN OCEAN

Andaman Sea

139
143
138
138
133

ELEVATION

| | | | | | Below sea level | 0 | 100m | 250m | 500m | 1000m | 2000m | 4000m |
| -2000m | -1000m | -500m | -250m | -100m | | | | | | | | |

| 328ft | 820ft | 1640ft | 3281ft | 6562ft | 13 124ft |

| -6562ft | -3281ft | -1640ft | -820ft | -328ft | -164ft/-50m | 0 |

137

MARITIME SOUTHEAST ASIA

SINGAPORE

0 km 10
0 miles 10

MALAYSIA

Johore Strait

Causeway

Pulau Ubin

Pulau Tekong

Lim Chu Kang

Hougang

New Town

Bukit Panjang New Town

Changi

Choa Chu Kang

Bukit Timah 176m

Bedok New Town

Queenstown

City

Jurong Industrial Estate

Tebok Blangah

Sentosa

Selat Pandan

Pulau Sudong

Pulau Pawai

Strait of Singapore

104°

103°50'

103°40'

Urban areas
Open areas
Nature reserves

MYANMAR (BURMA)

100°

137

LAOS

VIETNAM

THAILAND

Gulf of Tongking

110°

Hainan Dao
(to China)

PARACEL ISLANDS
(disputed by China, Taiwan and Vie

CAMBODIA

Mekong

120°

South Ch

Sea

SPRATLY ISLANDS
(disputed by China, Malaysia,
Philippines, Taiwan and Vietnam)

133

Andaman
Sea

Isthmus of Kra

Gulf of
Thailand

Mouths of
the Mekong

Nicobar Islands
(to India)

Bandaaceh

Sigli

George
Town

Kota Bharu

Butterworth

Kuala Terengganu

Gunun

Kota Kinabalu

BANDAR SERI
BEGAWAN

Meulaboh

Langsa

Pulau Pinang

Taiping

Ipoh

Dungun

Cukai

BRUNEI
Miri

Medan

Tebingtinggi

Klang

KUALA LUMPUR

Kuantan

Kepulauan
Natuna

Bintulu

Pulau Simeulue

Pematangsiantar

Seremban

MALAYSIA

Barisan

Kepulauan
Banyak

Sibolga

Dannu
Toba

Melaka

Muar

Keluang

Johor Bahru

Selat Serasan

Sibu

Batang Raja

Sarawak

Sri Aman

Kuching

Equator

Pulau Nias

Batu Pahat

SINGAPORE

Pekanbaru

Singkawang

Sidas

Borneo

Solok

Rengat

Kepulauan
Lingga

Pontianak

Sungai Kapuas

Kalimantan

Samar

Balikpa

Padang

Pulau Siberut

Batang Hari

Kualatungkal

Jambi

Selat Karimata

Sampit

Sungai Barito

Ak

Kepulauan
Mentawai

Sungaipenuh

Pangkalpinang

Bangka

Banjarm

Palembang

Lahat

Pulau
Belitung

INDIA

Bengkulu

Kotabumi

Cirebon

Tegal

Java Sea

Sumatera
(Sumatra)

Bandarlampung

Serang

JAKARTA

Pekalongan

Semarang

Pu

Selat Sunda

Bogor

Kudus

Pulau
Madura

Sukabumi

Bandung

Surabaya

Probolings

INDIAN

Tasikmalaya

Jember

Jawa
(Java)

Cilacap

Magelang

Yogyakarta

Malang

Kediri

Madiun

Bali
Lo

OCEAN

Surakarta

100°

141

110°

0 km 400
0 miles 400

POPULATION

● National capital

○ Less than 50,000   ○ 50,000 -100,000   ◉ 100,000 - 500,000   ◼ Over 500,000

ELEVATION

					Below sea level	0	100m	250m	500m	1000m	2000m	4000m
-4000m	-3000m	-2000m	-1000m	-500m								
-13 124ft	-9843ft	-6562ft	-3281ft	-1640ft	-820ft/-250m	0		328ft	820ft	1640ft	3281ft	6562ft	13 124ft

THE INDIAN OCEAN

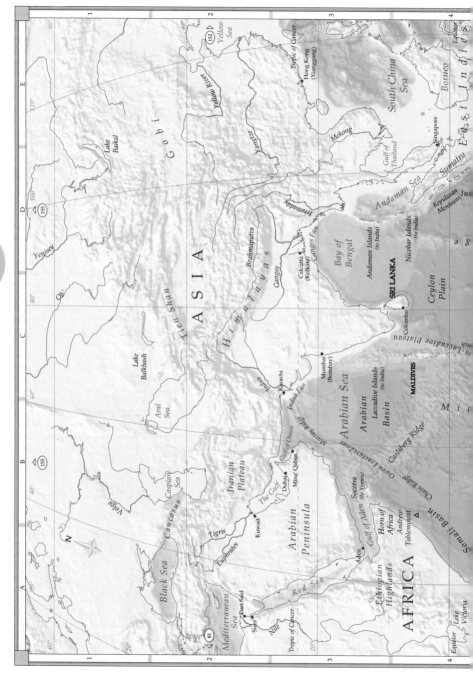

Major port

0 km · 1500
0 miles · 1500

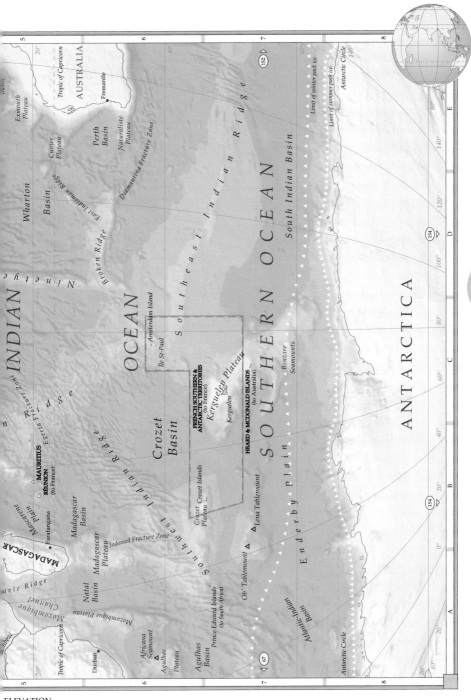

ELEVATION

-4000m	-3000m	-2000m	-1000m	-500m	-250m	0
-13 124ft	-9843ft	-6562ft	-3281ft	-1640ft	-820ft	0

141

AUSTRALASIA & OCEANIA

A

120°

152

140°

Philippine   Sea

20°

Philippine Basin

West
Mariana
Basin

Saipan

NORTHERN
MARIANA
ISLANDS
(to US)

160°

Mid-Pacific

WAKE ISLAND
(to US)

Mountai

MARSHALL ISLANDS

Kyushu-Palau Ridge

HAGÁTÑA
GUAM
(to US)

Mariana Trench

East
Mariana
Basin

M i c r o n

Ratak Chain

1

Philippine Trench

Philippines

Yap

Yap Trench

MICRONESIA

Hall
Islands

Chuuk
Islands

PALIKIR
Pohnpei

e s

Ralik Chain

MAJURO

*Sulu
Sea*

OREOR
Babeldaob

Mariana Rise

Caroline Islands

Kosrae

i

a

2

125

*Celebes
Sea*

Eauripik Rise

PALAU

M e l a n

Melanesian
Basin

Nauru·
NAURU

e

Tungaru

Tarawa
BAIRIKI

Banaba

Celebes

Equator

Bismarck Archipelago

Bismarck
Sea

New Britain

s

i

PAPUA NEW
GUINEA

Bougainville
Island

TUVALU

FONG

*Banda
Sea*

Mount Wilhelm
4509m▲

New Guinea

Solomon
Sea

Solomon Islands

HONIARA
Guadalcanal

SOLOMON
ISLANDS

Santa Cruz
Islands

a

Timor

Flores

PORT·MORESBY

3

*Arafura
Sea*

Torres Strait

*Coral
Sea*

VANUATU

Espíritu Santo

Malekula

*North Fiji
Basin*

Van

Viti L

*Timor
Sea*

Darwin

Arnhem
Land

*Gulf
of
Carpentaria*

Cape
York
Peninsula

CORAL SEA ISLANDS
(to Australia)

Efate
PORT-VILA

ASHMORE &
CARTIER ISLANDS
(to Australia)

Cairns

Townsville

Great Barrier Reef

NEW CALEDONIA
(to France)

New Caledonia
NOUMÉA

*Íles
Loyauté*

Mackay

So

Fiji

*INDIAN
OCEAN*

Broome

AUSTRALIA

Rockhampton

New Caledonia Ridge

Norfolk Ridge

NORFOLK ISLAN
(to Australia)

4

141

20°

*Great
Sandy
Desert*

Macdonnell
Ranges

Alice Springs

Simpson

Lord Howe Rise

Brisbane

Tropic of Capricorn

*Gibson
Desert*

Uluru
▲(Ayers Rock)
Lake Eyre North

Desert

Great Dividing   Range

Grey Range

Darling

Lord Howe
Island
(to Australia)

Lord Howe Basin

North N

Auckland

Geraldton

*Great
Victoria
Desert*

Lake Torrens
Lake Gairdner

Flinders Range

Newcastle

Sydney
Wollongong

Hamilton

**NEW
ZEALAND**

Kalgoorlie○

Nullarbor Plain

Adelaide

Bendigo○
Melbourne○

CANBERRA
Murray

▲Mount Kosciuszko
2228m

WELLINGTON

Perth◼

Great Australian Bight

Port Lincoln

Kangaroo
Island

Geelong

*Tasman
Sea*

South Island
Mount Cook
3744m▲

Ch

Esperance

*South
Australian
Basin*

*Bass
Strait*

Launceston

Hobart

Tasman Basin

Duned
Bo

5

Cape Leeuwin

Albany

Tasmania

Stewart Island

Antip

100°

40°

120°

154

*Tasman
Plateau*

140°

Auckland Islands
(to New Zealand)

160°

Camp
Plate

Campbell Island
(to New Zea

to New Zea

A

B

C

D

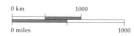

0 km _____ 1000

0 miles _____ 1000

POPULATION   ● National capital

○ Less than 50,000   ○ 50,000 -100,000   ◉ 100,000 - 500,000   ◼ Over 500,000

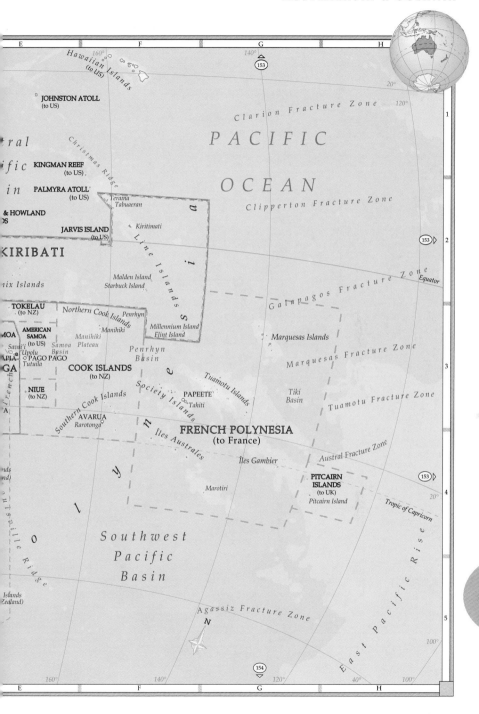

E   F   G   H

160°   140°   153

JOHNSTON ATOLL
(to US)

Hawaiian Islands
(to US)

Clarion Fracture Zone

PACIFIC

ral

ific   KINGMAN REEF
(to US)

Christmas Ridge

OCEAN

20°

120°

1

in   PALMYRA ATOLL
(to US)

Clipperton Fracture Zone

Teraina
Tabuaeran

& HOWLAND
OS

JARVIS ISLAND
(to US)

Kiritimati

Line Islands

153

2

KIRIBATI

nix Islands

Malden Island
Starbuck Island

Galapagos Fracture Zone   Equator

TOKELAU
(to NZ)

Northern Cook Islands   Penrhyn

Millennium Island
Flint Island

Marquesas Islands

Marquesas Fracture Zone

AMERICAN
SAMOA
(to US)

Manihiki

Manihiki
Plateau

Samoa
Basin

Penrhyn
Basin

3

MOA

Savai'i *Upolu*
PAGO PAGO
Tutuila

APIA

GA

COOK ISLANDS
(to NZ)

Tuamotu Islands

Tiki
Basin

Tuamotu Fracture Zone

NIUE
(to NZ)

Southern Cook Islands

AVARUA
Rarotonga

Society Islands

PAPEETE
Tahiti

FRENCH POLYNESIA
(to France)

Îles Australes

Îles Gambier

Austral Fracture Zone

20°

153

4

PITCAIRN
ISLANDS
(to UK)
Pitcairn Island

Tropic of Capricorn

Marotiri

ds
nd)

Southwest
Pacific
Basin

100°

Islands
Zealand)

Agassiz Fracture Zone

N

East Pacific Rise

5

160°   140°   120°   40°   100°

154

E   F   G   H

THE SOUTHWEST PACIFIC

GUAM
(to US)

Saipan
Tinian
Rota
HAGÁTÑA

NORTHERN MARIANA
ISLANDS
(to US)

MARSHA
ISLAND

Enewetak
Atoll
Bikini Atoll
Rongelap
Atoll

MICRONESIA

Yap

Ujelang Atoll
Kwajalein
Atoll
Namu Atoll
Ailinglaplap Atoll
Jaluit Atoll

Ratak Chain
Ralik Chain

Ai

Babeldaob
OREOR

Chuuk
Islands
PALIKIR
Pohnpei

Caroline Islands

Kosrae

Ebon Ato

PALAU

B

Equator

NAURU
Banaba

Admiralty
Islands
St.Matthias Group

New Guinea
Bismarck Archipelago
Bismarck Sea

New Ireland

Melan

Madang
PAPUA NEW GUINEA

Bougainville
Island

INDONESIA

Central Range
Mount Wilhelm
4509m
Lae
New
Britain

Choiseul
Santa Isabel
SOLOMON

Arafura Sea

Owen Stanley Range
Solomon Sea

New Georgia
Islands
HONIARA
Malaita

ISLANDS

Gulf of
Papua

D'Entrecasteaux
Islands

Guadalcanal
San Cristobal
Rennell

Santa Cruz
Islands

PORT MORESBY
Torres Strait

Louisiade
Archipelago

Coral Sea

VANUATU
Banks Island

Arnhem
Land
Groote
Eylandt
Cape
York
Peninsula

CORAL SEA ISLANDS
(to Australia)

Espiritu Santo
Malekula
Maéwo
Pentecost
Ambrym
Epi

Gulf of
Carpentaria
Barkly Tableland

Great Barrier Reef

Efate
PORT-V

NEW
CALEDONIA
(to France)

Erroma
Tannu
Ané

NORTHERN

Ouvéa
Lifou
Maré

TERRITORY

Tropic of Capricorn
Macdonnell

QUEENSLAND

Great Dividing Range

New
Caledonia
Îles Loyauté

NOUMÉA

Ranges

AUSTRALIA

0 km   750

POPULATION   ● National capital

0 miles   750

○ Less than 50,000   ○ 50,000 -100,000   ◉ 100,000 - 500,000   ◼ Over 500,000

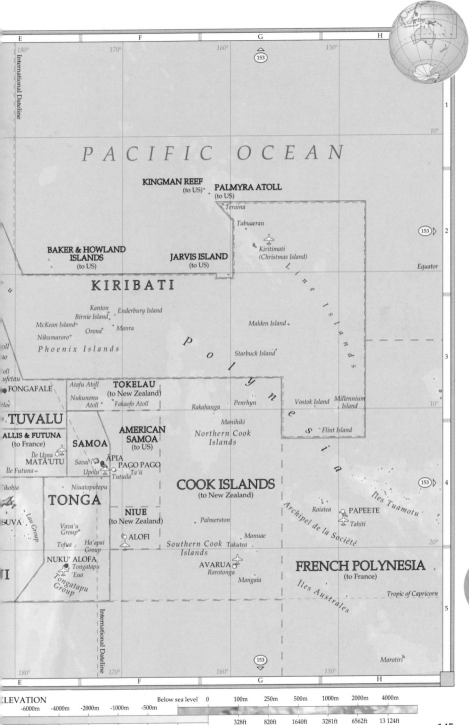

PACIFIC OCEAN

KINGMAN REEF
(to US)
PALMYRA ATOLL
(to US)

Teraina

Tabuaeran

BAKER & HOWLAND
ISLANDS
(to US)
JARVIS ISLAND
(to US)

Kiritimati
(Christmas Island)

Equator

KIRIBATI

Kanton
Birnie Island
Enderbury Island

Malden Island

McKean Island
Orona
Manra
Nikumaroro

P
o
l

Phoenix Islands

y

Starbuck Island

ufetau
FONGAFALE

Atafu Atoll
Nukunonu
Atoll
TOKELAU
(to New Zealand)
Fakaofo Atoll

n
e

Rakahanga
Penrhyn
Vostok Island
Millennium
Island

TUVALU
AMERICAN
SAMOA
(to US)
Manihiki
s
Flint Island

ALLIS & FUTUNA
(to France)
SAMOA
Northern Cook
Islands
i

Île Uvea
MATA'UTU
SAVAl'i
ÁPIA
PAGO PAGO
a

Île Futuna
Upolu
Ta'ū
Tutuila

ikobia
Niuatoputapu
COOK ISLANDS
(to New Zealand)
Îles Tuamotu

TONGA
Raiatea
PAPEETE

SUVA
NIUE
(to New Zealand)
Palmerston
Archipel de la Société
Tahiti

Vava'u
Group
ALOFI
Manuae

Tofua
Ha'apai
Group
Southern Cook
Takutea
Islands
FRENCH POLYNESIA
(to France)

NUKU' ALOFA
Tongatapu
'Eua
AVARUA
Rarotonga

Tongatapu
Group
Mangaia
Îles Australes

Tropic of Capricorn

Marotiri

ELEVATION

Below sea level	0	100m	250m	500m	1000m	2000m	4000m
-6000m	-4000m	-2000m	-1000m	-500m			

| | | | | 328ft | 820ft | 1640ft | 3281ft | 6562ft | 13 124ft |

-19 686ft -13 124ft -6562ft -3281ft -1640ft -820ft/-250m 0

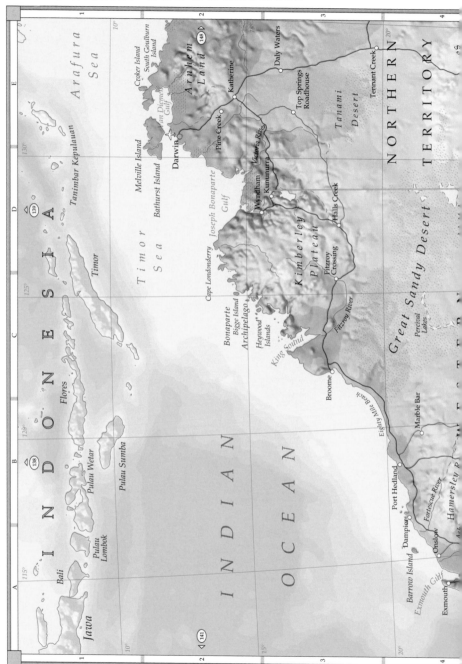

Arafura Sea

Croker Island

South Goulburn Island

Arnhem Land

Daly Waters

Tennant Creek

Katherine

Top Springs Roadhouse

Tanami Desert

NORTHERN TERRITORY

Pine Creek

Victoria River

Van Diemen Gulf

Darwin

Melville Island

Bathurst Island

Wyndham

Kununurra

Halls Creek

Joseph Bonaparte Gulf

Tanimbar Kepulauan

Timor

T i m o r   S e a

Cape Londonderry

Kimberley Plateau

Fitzroy Crossing

Pulau Wetar

I N D O N E S I A

Flores

Bonaparte Archipelago

Bigge Island

Heywood Islands

King Sound

Fitzroy River

Great Sandy Desert

Percival Lakes

Pulau Sumba

Broome

Eighty Mile Beach

Pulau Lombok

Bali

Jawa

I N D I A N   O C E A N

Marble Bar

Port Hedland

Fortescue River

Hamersley R

Barrow Island

Dampier

Onslow

Exmouth

Exmouth Gulf

0 km 400
0 miles 400

POPULATION

● National capital ◉ Internal administrative capital

○ Less than 50,000 ○ 50,000 -100,000 ◉ 100,000 - 500,000 ◼ Over 500,000

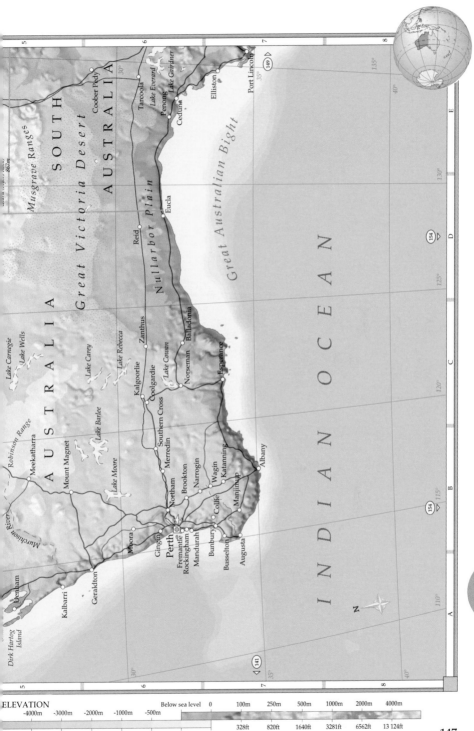

SOUTH AUSTRALIA

AUSTRALIA

Musgrave Range

Great Victoria Desert

Nullarbor Plain

Great Australian Bight

INDIAN OCEAN

Coober Pedy
Tarcoola
Lake Everard
Penong
Lake Gairdner
Ceduna
Elliston
Port Lincoln

Reid

Eucla

Zanthus
Balladonia
Kalgoorlie
Coolgardie
Norseman
Esperance
Lake Cowan

Lake Carnegie
Lake Wells
Lake Carey
Lake Rebecca
Lake Barlee
Lake Moore

Robinson Range

Meekatharra
Mount Magnet

Southern Cross
Merredin

Moora
Gingin
Northam
Brookton
Narrogin
Wagin
Katanning
Collie
Albany
Manjimup

Murchison River

Perth
Fremantle
Rockingham
Mandurah
Bunbury
Busselton
Augusta

Geraldton

Kalbarri
Denham

Dirk Hartog Island

N

ELEVATION

-4000m	-3000m	-2000m	-1000m	-500m	Below sea level 0		100m	250m	500m	1000m	2000m	4000m
-13 124ft	-9843ft	-6562ft	-3281ft	-1640ft	-820ft/-250m	0	328ft	820ft	1640ft	3281ft	6562ft	13 124ft

147

EASTERN AUSTRALIA

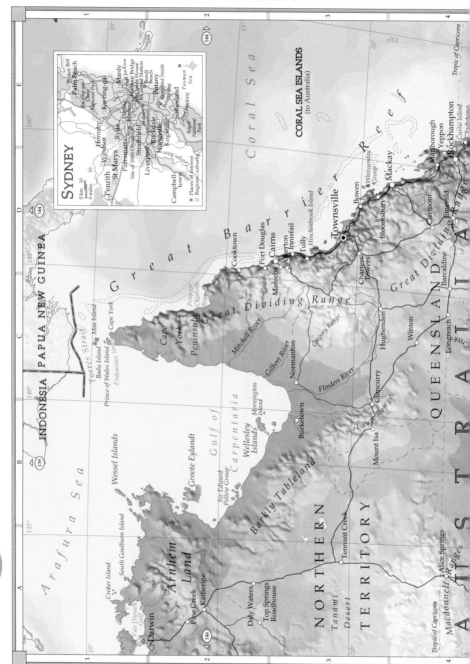

SYDNEY

Broken Bay
Palm Beach
Kuring-gai
Chase
National Park
Hornsby
Ku-ring-gai
Windsor
Manly
Ryde
Parramatta
Strathfield
Penrith
St Marys
Darling
Harbour Bridge
Opera House
Central Station
University
Liverpool
Rockdale
Hurstville
Kogarah
Campbell
town
Sutherland
Royal
National
Park
Bondi
Beach
Botany Bay
Bankstown Smith
Rushcutters
Bay
Hacking
Tasman
Sea

0 km   10
0 miles   10

■ Places of interest
▢ Regions/ suburbs

CORAL SEA ISLANDS
(to Australia)

Coral Sea

Great Barrier Reef

INDONESIA
PAPUA NEW GUINEA

Torres Strait

Cape York Peninsula

Great Dividing Range

Cooktown
Port Douglas
Cairns
Mareeba
Atherton
Innisfail
Tully
Hinchinbrook Island
Townsville
Bowen
Whitsunday
Group
Mackay
Bloomsbury
Clermont
Marlborough
Yeppon
Rockhampton
Emerald
Barcaldine
Longreach
Winton
Hughenden
Charters
Towers
Cloncurry
Mount Isa
Selwyn Range
Burketown
Normanton
Gilbert River
Flinders River
Mitchell River
Gregory Range

**Gulf of
Carpentaria**

Wellesley
Islands
Mornington
Island
Sir Edward
Pellew Group
Groote Eylandt

Wessel Islands

Arafura Sea

South Goulburn Island
Croker Island
Van Diemen
Gulf
Darwin
Pine Creek
Katherine
Daly Waters
Top Springs
Roadhouse
Tennant Creek
Alice Springs
Macdonnell Ranges

Tanami Desert

Barkly Tableland

**NORTHERN
TERRITORY**

QUEENSLAND

AUSTRALIA

Tropic of Capricorn

0 km   400
0 miles   400

POPULATION

● National capital   ◎ Internal administrative capital

○ Less than 50,000   ○ 50,000 -100,000   ◉ 100,000 - 500,000   ▣ Over 500,000

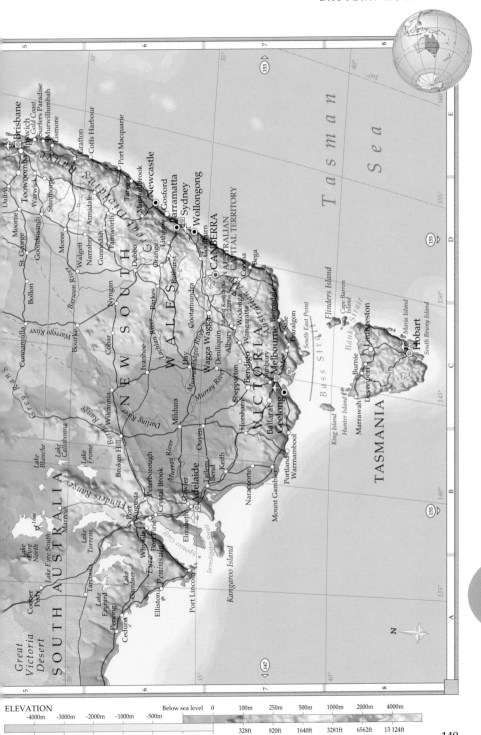

ELEVATION

					Below sea level	0	100m	250m	500m	1000m	2000m	4000m
-4000m	-3000m	-2000m	-1000m	-500m								
-13 124ft	-9843ft	-6562ft	-3281ft	-1640ft	-820ft/-250m	0	328ft	820ft	1640ft	3281ft	6562ft	13 124ft

NEW ZEALAND

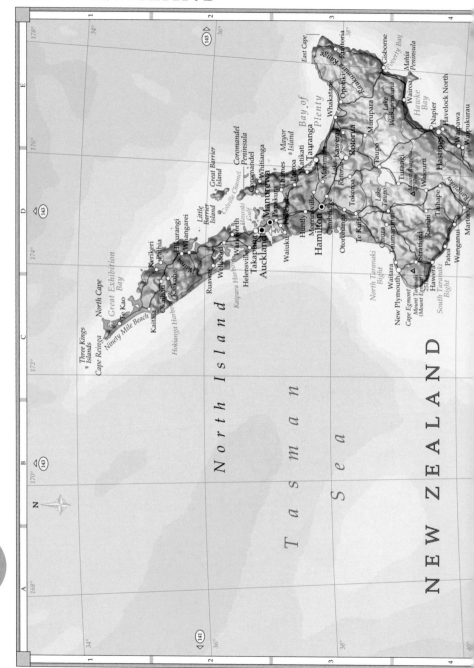

NEW ZEALAND

North Island

Tasman Sea

Three Kings Islands
Cape Reinga
North Cape
Great Exhibition Bay
Te Kao
Ninety Mile Beach
Kaitaia
Okaihau
Kaikohe
Hokianga Harbour
Kerikeri
Paihia
Waitangi
Kaikohe
Hikurangi
Whangarei
Dargaville
Ruawai
Kaipara Harbour
Welsford
Helensville
Warkworth
Takapuna
Auckland
Waiuku
Waitakere
Manukau Harbour
Hauraki Gulf
Little Barrier Island
Great Barrier Island
Colville Channel
Coromandel Peninsula
Coromandel
Whitianga
Mayor Island
Thames
Katikati
Papakura
Manurewa
Pokeno
Ngaruawahia
Morrinsville
Huntly
Cambridge
Hamilton
Otorohanga
Te Kuiti
Waitomo
Te Awamutu
Ohura
Matamata
Putaruru
Tokoroa
Lake Rotorua
Rotorua
Lake Kaveral
Mamaku
Tauranga
Bay of Plenty
Whakatane
Opotiki
Marupara
Raukumara Range
East Cape
Ruatoria
Gisborne
Poverty Bay
Mahia Peninsula
Wairoa
Lake Waikaremoana
Hawke Bay
Napier
Havelock North
Hastings
Waipawa
Waipukurau
Taupo
Lake Taupo
Turangi
Mount Ruapehu 2797m
Taumarunui
Raetihi
Waiouru
Taihape
Mangawai Range
Waitara
New Plymouth
Cape Egmont
Mount Taranaki (Mount Egmont) 2518m
North Taranaki Bight
Stratford
Hawera
South Taranaki Bight
Patea
Wanganui
Marton
Waiouru

POPULATION   ● National capital

○ Less than 50,000   ○ 50,000 -100,000   ◉ 100,000 - 500,000   ◼ Over 500,000

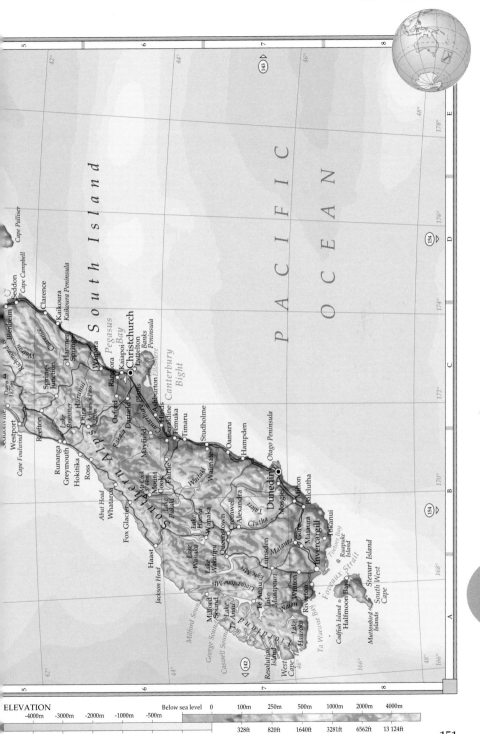

PACIFIC

OCEAN

South Island

143

154

154

142

South Island place names and features:

Cape Palliser

Cape Campbell
Clarence
Kaikoura
Kaikoura Peninsula
Seddon
Blenheim
Picton

Hanmer
Springs
Springs
Junction
Waipara
Rangiora
Pegasus Bay
Christchurch
Lyttelton
Kaiapoi Banks
Ellesmere Peninsula
Canterbury
Bight

Westport
Reefton
Runanga
Greymouth
Hokitika
Ross

Ben More
Tarn 1873m
Oxford
Darfield
Ashburton
Hinds
Geraldine
Temuka
Timaru
Studholme
Oamaru
Hampden

Lake
Brunner
Arthur's Pass
1220m
Mt Hutt
Hirunui
Rakaia
Mayfield
Canterbury Plains

About Head
Whataroa
Fox Glacier
Haast
Jackson Head

Mt Cook
3764m
Mount
Cook
Fairlie
Lake
Pukaki
Lake
Tekapo
Waitaki
Waimate

Southern Alps

Kä Tiritiri o te Moana

Otago Peninsula
Dunedin
Mosgiel
Milton
Balclutha

Lake
Hawea
Wanaka
Lake
Wanaka
Queenstown
Cromwell
Alexandra
Lake
Wakatipu

Eyre Mts
Lumsden
Lake
Manapouri
Te Anau
Lake
Te Anau
Livingstone Mts

Milford Sound
George Sound
Caswell Sound

Fiordland

Resolution
Island
West
Cape
South West
Cape

Codfish Island
Muttonbird
Islands

Stewart Island

Halfmoon Bay
Ruapuke
Island
Ruapuke Bay
Foveaux Strait

Te Wae Wae Bay
Riverton
Winton
Wairio
Invercargill
Gore
Mataura
Clutha
Mataura
Lake
Hauroko
Waiau

Cape Foulwind

Cape Campbell

Seddon

Richmond Range

Cape Brett

ELEVATION

| -4000m | -3000m | -2000m | -1000m | -500m | Below sea level | 0 | 100m | 250m | 500m | 1000m | 2000m | 4000m |

| -13 124ft | -9843ft | -6562ft | -3281ft | -1640ft | -820ft/-250m | 0 | 328ft | 820ft | 1640ft | 3281ft | 6562ft | 13 124ft |

151

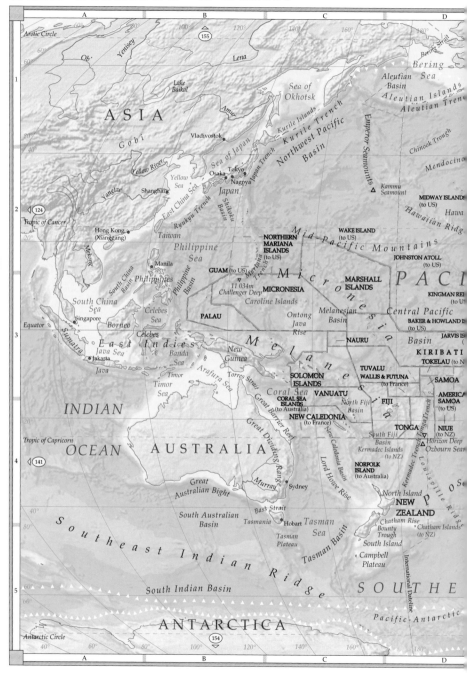

Major port

0 km · 2000

0 miles · 2000

152

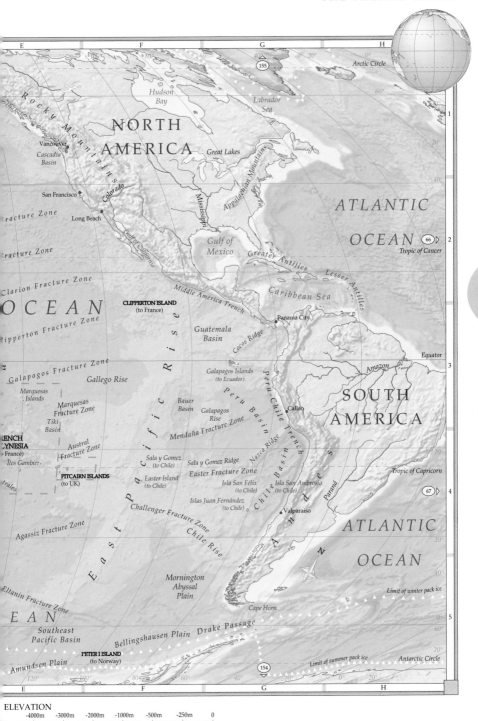

E F G H

Arctic Circle

Hudson Bay

NORTH AMERICA

Great Lakes

Labrador Sea

155

1

Vancouver

Cascadia Basin

Rocky Mountains

San Francisco

Colorado

Central California

Long Beach

Fracture Zone

Mississippi

Appalachian Mountains

ATLANTIC OCEAN

66

2

Tropic of Cancer

Fracture Zone

Clarion Fracture Zone

O C E A N

Clipperton Fracture Zone

Gulf of Mexico

Greater Antilles

Middle America Trench

Caribbean Sea

Lesser Antilles

CLIPPERTON ISLAND (to France)

East Pacific Rise

Guatemala Basin

Cocos Ridge

Panama City

Galapagos Fracture Zone

Gallego Rise

Galapagos Islands (to Ecuador)

Bauer Basin

Galapagos Rise

Peru Basin

Peru-Chile Trench

Amazon

Equator

3

Marquesas Islands

Marquesas Fracture Zone

Tiki Basin

SOUTH AMERICA

Callao

Mendaña Fracture Zone

Nazca Ridge

Sala y Gomez (to Chile)

Sala y Gomez Ridge

Andes

Chile Basin

FRENCH POLYNESIA (to France)

Îles Gambier

Austral Fracture Zone

Easter Fracture Zone

Easter Island (to Chile)

Isla San Félix (to Chile)

Isla San Ambrosio (to Chile)

Tropic of Capricorn

67

4

PITCAIRN ISLANDS (to UK)

Islas Juan Fernández (to Chile)

Valparaíso

Paraná

Challenger Fracture Zone

Chile Rise

ATLANTIC

Agassiz Fracture Zone

Mornington Abyssal Plain

OCEAN

Eltanin Fracture Zone

Limit of winter pack ice

Cape Horn

E A N

Southeast Pacific Basin

Bellingshausen Plain

Drake Passage

5

Amundsen Plain

PETER I ISLAND (to Norway)

Limit of summer pack ice

Antarctic Circle

154

E F G H

ELEVATION

-4000m	-3000m	-2000m	-1000m	-500m	-250m	0
-13 124ft	-9843ft	-6562ft	-3281ft	-1640ft	-820ft	0

ANTARCTICA

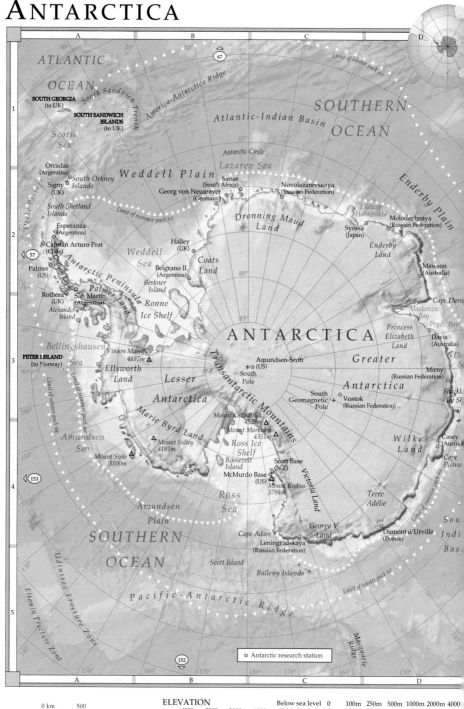

ATLANTIC

OCEAN

SOUTH GEORGIA
(to UK)

**SOUTH SANDWICH
ISLANDS**
(to UK)

*Scotia
Sea*

South Sandwich Trench

America-Antarctica Ridge

Limit of winter pack ice

SOUTHERN

Atlantic-Indian Basin

OCEAN

Enderby Plain

Antarctic Circle

Lazarev Sea

Orcadas
(Argentina)
Signy
(UK)

Weddell Plain

Sanae
(South Africa)
Georg von Neumayer
(Germany)

Novolazarevskaya
(Russian Federation)

South Orkney
Islands

*South Shetland
Islands*

Limit of summer pack ice

Dronning Maud
Land

Lützow
Holmbukta

Molodezhnaya
(Russian Federation)

Esperanza
(Argentina)

Capitán Arturo Prat
(Chile)

Palmer
(US)

Halley
(UK)

*Weddell
Sea*

Syowa
(Japan)

Enderby
Land

Mawson
(Australia)

Belgrano II
(Argentina)

Coats
Land

Rothera
(UK)

San Martín
(Argentina)

*Alexander
Island*

Berkner
Island

Ronne
Ice Shelf

Cape Darn

Mackenzie
Bay

Prydz Bay

Bellingshausen

Vinson Massif
4897m

Princess
Elizabeth
Land

Davis
(Australia)

PETER I ISLAND
(to Norway)

Sea

*Ellsworth
Land*

Amundsen-Scott
(US)
South
Pole

Greater

Mirny
(Russian Federation)

*Lesser
Antarctica*

South
Geomagnetic
Pole

Vostok
(Russian Federation)

Antarctica

Shackl
Ice Sh

*Amundsen
Sea*

Mount Kirkpatrick
4528m

Wilkes

Marie Byrd Land

Mount Markham
4351m

*Ross Ice
Shelf*

Land

Casey
(Austral

Mount Sidley
4181m

Mount Siple
3100m

Roosevelt
Island

Scott Base
(N.Z)

McMurdo Base
(US)

Mount Erebus
3794m

Victoria Land

Terre
Adélie

Cape
Poinse

*Ross
Sea*

*Amundsen
Plain*

SOUTHERN

OCEAN

George V
Land

Cape Adare
Leningradskaya
(Russian Federation)

Dumont d'Urville
(France)

*Sou
Indi
Bas*

Scott Island

Balleny Islands

Limit of winter pack ice

Pacific-Antarctic Ridge

Macquarie
Ridge

● Antarctic research station

ANTARCTICA

Transantarctic Mountains

Palmer Land

Antarctic Peninsula

Drake Passage

Elltanin Fracture Zone

Udintsev Fracture Zone

0 km   500

0 miles   500

ELEVATION
-4000m -3000m -2000m -1000m -500m

Below sea level 0   100m 250m 500m 1000m 2000m 4000

-13 124ft -9843ft -6562ft -3281ft -1640ft -820ft/-250m

328ft 820ft 1640ft 3281ft 6562ft 13 12

RCTIC OCEAN

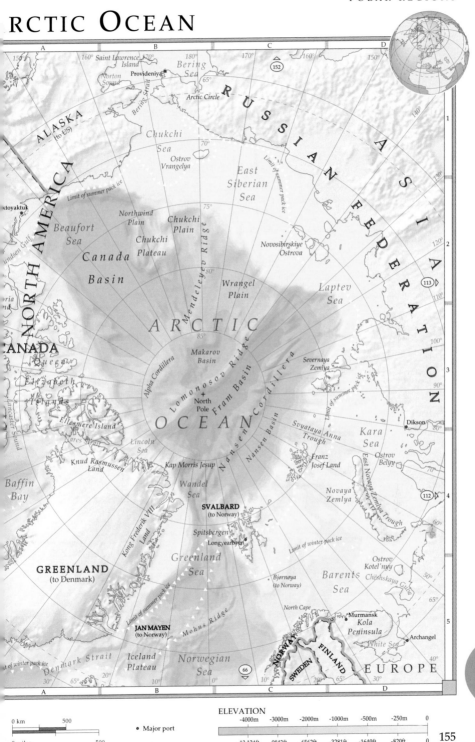

ELEVATION

	-4000m	-3000m	-2000m	-1000m	-500m	-250m	0
	-13 124ft	-9843ft	-6562ft	-3281ft	-1640ft	-820ft	0

0 km 500

0 miles 500

• Major port

OVERSEAS TERRITORIES & DEPENDENCIE

DESPITE THE RAPID process of global decolonization since the Second World War, around 10 million people in more than 50 territories around the world continue to live under the protection of France, Australia, the Netherlands, Denmark, Norway, New Zealand, the UK, or the USA. These remnants of former colonial empires may have persisted for economic, strategic or political reasons and are administered in a variety of ways.

AUSTRALIA

AUSTRALIA'S OVERSEAS TERRITORIES have not been an issue since Papua New Guinea became independent in 1975. Consequently there is no overriding policy toward them. Norfolk Island is inhabited by descendants of the H.M.S Bounty mutineers and more recent Australian migrants.

ASHMORE & CARTIER ISLANDS
Indian Ocean
STATUS: External territory
CLAIMED: 1978
CAPITAL: Not applicable
POPULATION: None
AREA: 5.2 sq km
(2 sq miles)

CHRISTMAS ISLAND
Indian Ocean
STATUS: External territory
CLAIMED: 1958
CAPITAL: Flying Fish Cove
POPULATION: 1,275
AREA: 134.6 sq km
(52 sq miles)

COCOS ISLANDS
Indian Ocean
STATUS: External territory
CLAIMED: 1955
CAPITAL: No official capital
POPULATION: 670
AREA: 14.24 sq km
(5.5 sq miles)

CORAL SEA ISLANDS
South Pacific
STATUS: External territory
CLAIMED: 1969
CAPITAL: None
POPULATION: 8 (meteorologists)
AREA: Less than 3 sq km
(1.16 sq miles)

HEARD & MCDONALD IS.
Indian Ocean
STATUS: External territory
CLAIMED: 1947
CAPITAL: Not applicable
POPULATION: None
AREA: 417 sq km
(161 sq miles)

NORFOLK ISLAND
South Pacific
STATUS: External territory
CLAIMED: 1774
CAPITAL: Kingston
POPULATION: 2,181
AREA: 34.4 sq km
(13.3 sq miles)

DENMARK

THE FAEROE ISLANDS have been under Danish administration since Queen Margreth I of Denmark inherited Norway in 1380. The Home Rule Act of 1948 gave the Faeroese control over all their internal affairs. Greenland first came under Danish rule in 1380. Today, Denmark is responsible for the island's foreign affairs and defense.

FAEROE ISLANDS
North Atlantic
STATUS: External territory
CLAIMED: 1380
CAPITAL: Tórshavn
POPULATION: 43,382
AREA: 1,399 sq km
(540 sq miles)

GREENLAND
North Atlantic
STATUS: External territory
CLAIMED: 1380
CAPITAL: Nuuk
POPULATION: 56,076
AREA: 2,175,516 sq km
(840,000 sq miles)

FRANCE

FRANCE HAS DEVELOPED economic ties with its overseas territories, thereby stressing interdependence over independence. Overseas *départements*, officially part of France, have their own governments. Territorial *collectivit.* and overseas *territoires* have varying degrees of autonomy.

CLIPPERTON ISLAND
East Pacific
STATUS: Dependency of French Polynesia
CLAIMED: 1930
CAPITAL: Not applicable
POPULATION: None
AREA: 7 sq km
(2.7 sq miles)

FRENCH GUIANA
South America
STATUS: Overseas department
CLAIMED: 1817
CAPITAL: Cayenne
POPULATION: 152,300
AREA: 90,996 sq km
(35,135 sq miles)

FRENCH POLYNESIA
South Pacific
STATUS: Overseas territory
CLAIMED: 1843
CAPITAL: Papeete
POPULATION: 219,521
AREA: 4,165 sq km
(1,608 sq miles)

GUADELOUPE
West Indies
STATUS: Overseas department
CLAIMED: 1635
CAPITAL: Basse-Terre
POPULATION: 419,500
AREA: 1,780 sq km
(687 sq miles)

MARTINIQUE
West Indies
STATUS: Overseas
department
CLAIMED: 1635
CAPITAL: Fort-de-France
POPULATION: 381,200
AREA: 1,100 sq km
(425 sq miles)

MAYOTTE
Indian Ocean
STATUS: Territorial
collectivity
CLAIMED: 1843
CAPITAL: Mamoudzou
POPULATION: 131,320
AREA: 374 sq km
(144 sq miles)

NEW CALEDONIA
South Pacific
STATUS: Overseas territory
CLAIMED: 1853
CAPITAL: Nouméa
POPULATION: 196,836
AREA: 19,103 sq km
(7,374 sq miles)

RÉUNION
Indian Ocean
STATUS: Overseas
department
CLAIMED: 1638
CAPITAL: Saint-Denis
POPULATION: 632,000
AREA: 2,512 sq km
(970 sq miles)

ST. PIERRE
& MIQUELON
North America
STATUS: Territorial collectivity
CLAIMED: 1604
CAPITAL: Saint-Pierre
POPULATION: 6,600
AREA: 242 sq km
(93.4 sq miles)

WALLIS & FUTUNA
South Pacific
STATUS: Overseas territory
CLAIMED: 1842
CAPITAL: Matā'Utu
POPULATION: 15,000
AREA: 274 sq km
(106 sq miles)

NETHERLANDS

THE COUNTRY'S TWO REMAINING overseas territories were formerly part of the Dutch West Indies. Both are now self-governing, but the Netherlands remains responsible for their defense.

ARUBA
West Indies
STATUS: Autonomous
part of the Netherlands
CLAIMED: 1643
CAPITAL: Oranjestad
POPULATION: 88,000
AREA: 194 sq km (75 sq miles)

NETHERLANDS ANTILLES
West Indies
STATUS: Autonomous
part of the Netherlands
CLAIMED: 1816
CAPITAL: Willemstad
POPULATION: 207,175
AREA: 800 sq km (308 sq miles)

NEW ZEALAND

NEW ZEALAND'S GOVERNMENT has no desire to retain any overseas territories. However, the economic weakness of its dependent territory Tokelau and its freely associated states, Niue and the Cook Islands, has forced New Zealand to remain responsible for their foreign policy and defense.

COOK ISLANDS
South Pacific
STATUS: Associated territory
CLAIMED: 1901
CAPITAL: Avarua
POPULATION: 20,200
AREA: 293 sq km
(113 sq miles)

NIUE
South Pacific
STATUS: Associated territory
CLAIMED: 1901
CAPITAL: Alofi
POPULATION: 2,080
AREA: 264 sq km
(102 sq miles)

TOKELAU
South Pacific
STATUS: Dependent territory
CLAIMED: 1926
CAPITAL: Not applicable
POPULATION: 1,577
AREA: 10.4 sq km (4 sq miles)

NORWAY

IN 1920, 41 nations signed the Spitsbergen Treaty recognizing Norwegian sovereignty over Svalbard. There is a NATO base on Jan Mayen. Bouvet Island is a nature reserve.

BOUVET ISLAND
South Atlantic
STATUS: Dependency
CLAIMED: 1928
CAPITAL: Not applicable
POPULATION: None
AREA: 58 sq km (22 sq miles)

JAN MAYEN
North Atlantic
STATUS: Dependency
CLAIMED: 1929
CAPITAL: Not applicable
POPULATION: None
AREA: 381 sq km (147 sq miles)

PETER I. ISLAND
Southern Ocean
STATUS: Dependency
CLAIMED: 1931
CAPITAL: Not applicable
POPULATION: None
AREA: 180 sq km (69 sq miles)

SVALBARD
Arctic Ocean
STATUS: Dependency
CLAIMED: 1920
CAPITAL: Longyearbyen
POPULATION: 3,231
AREA: 62,906 sq km
(24,289 sq miles)

Continued on p.158

UNITED KINGDOM

THE UK STILL has the largest number of overseas territories. These are locally-governed by a mixture of elected representatives and appointed officials, and they all enjoy a large measure of internal self-government, but certain powers, such as foreign affairs and defense, are reserved for Governors of the British Crown.

ANGUILLA
West Indies
STATUS: Dependent territory
CLAIMED: 1650
CAPITAL: The Valley
POPULATION: 10,300
AREA: 96 sq km
(37 sq miles)

ASCENSION ISLAND
South Atlantic
STATUS: Dependency of St. Helena
CLAIMED: 1673
CAPITAL: Georgetown
POPULATION: 1,099
AREA: 88 sq km
(34 sq miles)

BERMUDA
North Atlantic
STATUS: Crown colony
CLAIMED: 1612
CAPITAL: Hamilton
POPULATION: 60,144
AREA: 53 sq km
(20.5 sq miles)

BRITISH INDIAN OCEAN TERRITORY
STATUS: Dependent territory
CLAIMED: 1814
CAPITAL: Diego Garcia
POPULATION: 930
AREA: 60 sq km
(23 sq miles)

BRITISH VIRGIN ISLANDS
West Indies
STATUS: Dependent territory
CLAIMED: 1672
CAPITAL: Road Town
POPULATION: 17,896
AREA: 153 sq km
(59 sq miles)

CAYMAN ISLANDS
West Indies
STATUS: Dependent territory
CLAIMED: 1670
CAPITAL: George Town
POPULATION: 35,000
AREA: 259 sq km (100 sq miles)

FALKLAND ISLANDS
South Atlantic
STATUS: Dependent territory
CLAIMED: 1832
CAPITAL: Stanley
POPULATION: 2,564
AREA: 12,173 sq km
(4,699 sq miles)

GIBRALTAR
Southwest Europe
STATUS: Crown colony
CLAIMED: 1713
CAPITAL: Gibraltar
POPULATION: 27,086
AREA: 6.5 sq km (2.5 sq miles)

GUERNSEY
Channel Islands
STATUS: Crown dependency
CLAIMED: 1066
CAPITAL: St. Peter Port
POPULATION: 56,681
AREA: 65 sq km (25 sq miles)

ISLE OF MAN
British Isles
STATUS: Crown dependency
CLAIMED: 1765
CAPITAL: Douglas
POPULATION: 71,714
AREA: 572 sq km (221 sq miles)

JERSEY
Channel Islands
STATUS: Crown dependency
CLAIMED: 1066
CAPITAL: St. Helier
POPULATION: 85,150
AREA: 116 sq km (45 sq miles)

MONTSERRAT
West Indies
STATUS: Dependent territory
CLAIMED: 1632
CAPITAL: Plymouth
(currently uninhabitable)
POPULATION: 2,850
AREA: 102 sq km (40 sq miles)

PITCAIRN ISLANDS
South Pacific
STATUS: Dependent territory
CLAIMED: 1887
CAPITAL: Adamstown
POPULATION: 55
AREA: 3.5 sq km (1.35 sq miles)

ST. HELENA
South Atlantic
STATUS: Dependent territory
CLAIMED: 1673
CAPITAL: Jamestown
POPULATION: 6,472
AREA: 122 sq km (47 sq miles)

SOUTH GEORGIA & THE SOUTH SANDWICH ISLANDS
South Atlantic
STATUS: Dependent territory
CLAIMED: 1775
CAPITAL: Not applicable
POPULATION: No permanent residents
AREA: 3,592 sq km (1,387 sq miles)

TRISTAN DA CUNHA
South Atlantic
STATUS: Dependency of St. Helena
CLAIMED: 1612
CAPITAL: Edinburgh
POPULATION: 297
AREA: 98 sq km (38 sq miles)

TURKS & CAICOS ISLANDS
West Indies
STATUS: Dependent territory
CLAIMED: 1766
CAPITAL: Cockburn Town
POPULATION: 13,800
AREA: 430 sq km (166 sq miles)

UNITED STATES OF AMERICA

AMERICA'S OVERSEAS TERRITORIES have been seen as strategically useful, if expensive, links with its backyards." The US has, in most cases, given the local population a say in deciding their own status. A US Commonwealth territory, such as Puerto Rico, has a greater level of independence than that of a US unincorporated or external territory.

AMERICAN SAMOA
South Pacific
STATUS: Unincorporated territory
CLAIMED: 1900
CAPITAL: Pago Pago
POPULATION: 60,000
AREA: 195 sq km (75 sq miles)

BAKER & HOWLAND ISLANDS
South Pacific
STATUS: Unincorporated territory
CLAIMED: 1856
CAPITAL: Not applicable
POPULATION: None
AREA: 1.4 sq km (0.54 sq miles)

GUAM
West Pacific
STATUS: Unincorporated territory
CLAIMED: 1898
CAPITAL: Hagåtña
POPULATION: 149,249
AREA: 549 sq km (212 sq miles)

JARVIS ISLAND
South Pacific
STATUS: Unincorporated territory
CLAIMED: 1856
CAPITAL: Not applicable
POPULATION: None
AREA: 4.5 sq km (1.7 sq miles)

JOHNSTON ATOLL
Central Pacific
STATUS: Unincorporated territory
CLAIMED: 1858
CAPITAL: Not applicable
POPULATION: 327
AREA: 2.8 sq km (1 sq mile)

KINGMAN REEF
Central Pacific
STATUS: Administered territory
CLAIMED: 1856
CAPITAL: Not applicable
POPULATION: None
AREA: 1 sq km (0.4 sq miles)

MIDWAY ISLANDS
Central Pacific
STATUS: Administered territory
CLAIMED: 1867
CAPITAL: Not applicable
POPULATION: 453
AREA: 5.2 sq km (2 sq miles)

NAVASSA ISLAND
West Indies
STATUS: Unincorporated territory
CLAIMED: 1856
CAPITAL: Not applicable
POPULATION: None
AREA: 5.2 sq km (2 sq miles)

NORTHERN MARIANA ISLANDS
West Pacific
STATUS: Commonwealth territory
CLAIMED: 1947
CAPITAL: Saipan
POPULATION: 58,846
AREA: 457 sq km (177 sq miles)

PALMYRA ATOLL
Central Pacific
STATUS: Unincorporated territory
CLAIMED: 1898
CAPITAL: Not applicable
POPULATION: None
AREA: 12 sq km (5 sq miles)

PUERTO RICO
West Indies
STATUS: Commonwealth territory
CLAIMED: 1898
CAPITAL: San Juan
POPULATION: 3.8 million
AREA: 8,959 sq km (3,458 sq miles)

VIRGIN ISLANDS
West Indies
STATUS: Unincorporated territory
CLAIMED: 1917
CAPITAL: Charlotte Amalie
POPULATION: 101,809
AREA: 355 sq km (137 sq miles)

WAKE ISLAND
Central Pacific
STATUS: Unincorporated territory
CLAIMED: 1898
CAPITAL: Not applicable
POPULATION: 302
AREA: 6.5 sq km (2.5 sq miles)

GLOSSARY OF GEOGRAPHICAL TERMS

THE FOLLOWING GLOSSARY lists all geographical terms occuring on the maps and in the main-entry names in the Index–Gazetteer. These terms may precede, follow or be run together with the proper elements of the name; where they precede it the term is reversed for indexing purposes – thus Poluostov Yamal is indexed as Yamal, Poluostrov.

A

Å *Danish, Norwegian,* River
Alpen *German,* Alps
Altiplanicie *Spanish,* Plateau
Älv(en) *Swedish,* River
Anse *French,* Bay
Archipiélago *Spanish,* Archipelago
Arcipelago *Italian,* Archipelago
Arquipélago *Portuguese,* Archipelago
Aukštuma *Lithuanian,* Upland

B

Bahía *Spanish,* Bay
Baía *Portuguese,* Bay
Baḥr *Arabic,* River
Baie *French,* Bay
Bandao *Chinese,* Peninsula
Banjaran *Malay,* Mountain range
Batang *Malay,* Stream
-berg *Afrikaans, Norwegian,* Mountain
Birket *Arabic ,* Lake
Boğazı *Turkish,* Strait
Bucht *German,* Bay
Bugten *Danish,* Bay
Buḥayrat *Arabic,* Lake, reservoir
Buḥeiret *Arabic,* Lake
Bukit *Malay,* Mountain
-bukta *Norwegian,* Bay
bukten *Swedish,* Bay
Burnu *Turkish,* Cape, point
Buuraha *Somali,* Mountains

C

Cabo *Portuguese,* Cape
Cap *French,* Cape
Cascada *Portuguese,* Waterfall
Cerro *Spanish,* Mountain
Chaîne *French,* Mountain range
Chau *Cantonese,* Island
Chāy *Turkish,* Stream
Chhâk *Cambodian,* Bay
Chhu *Tibetan,* River
-chôsuji *Korean,* Reservoir

Chott *Arabic,* Salt lake, depression
Ch'ün-tao *Chinese,* Island group
Cordillera *Spanish,* Mountain range
Costa *Spanish,* Coast
Côte *French,* Coast
Cuchilla *Spanish,* Mountains

D

Dağı *Azerbaijani, Turkish,* Mountain
Dağları *Azerbaijani, Turkish,* Mountains
-dake *Japanese,* Peak
Danau *Indonesian,* Lake
Đao *Vietnamese,* Island
Daryā *Persian,* River
Daryācheh *Persian,* Lake
Dasht *Persian,* Plain, desert
Dawḥat *Arabic,* Bay
Dere *Turkish,* Stream
Dili *Azerbaijani,* Spit
-do *Korean,* Island
Dooxo *Somali,* Valley
Düzü *Azerbaijani,* Steppe
-dwīp *Bengali,* Island

E

Embalse *Spanish,* Reservoir
Erg *Arabic,* Dunes
Estany *Catalan,* Lake
Estrecho *Spanish,* Strait
-ey *Icelandic,* Island
Ezero *Bulgarian, Macedonian,* Lake

F

Fjord *Danish,* Fjord
-fjorden *Norwegian,* Fjord
-fjørdhur *Faeroese,* Fjord
Fleuve *French,* River
Fliegu *Maltese,* Channel
-fljór *Icelandic,* River

G

-gang *Korean,* River
Ganga *Nepali, Sinhala,* River
Gaoyuan *Chinese,* Plateau
-gawa *Japanese,* River
Gebel *Arabic,* Mountain

-gebirge *German,* Mountains
Ghubbat *Arabic,* Bay
Gjiri *Albanian,* Bay
Gol *Mongolian,* River
Golfe *French,* Gulf
Golfo *Italian, Spanish,* Gulf
Gora *Russian, Serbian,* Mountain
Gory *Russian,* Mountains
Guba *Russian,* Bay
Gunung *Malay,* Mountain

H

Ḥadd *Arabic,* Spit
-haehyŏp *Korean,* Strait
Haff *German,* Lagoon
Hai *Chinese,* Sea, bay
Ḥammādat *Arabic,* Plateau
Hāmūn *Persian,* Lake
Hawr *Arabic,* Lake
Hāyk' *Amharic,* Lake
He *Chinese,* River
Helodrano *Malagasy,* Bay
-hegység *Hungarian,* Mountain range
Hka *Burmese,* River
-ho *Korean,* Lake
Hô *Korean,* Reservoir
Holot *Hebrew,* Dunes
Hora *Belorussian,* Mountain
Hrada *Belorussian,* Mountains, ridge
Hsi *Chinese,* River
Hu *Chinese,* Lake

I

Île(s) *French,* Island(s)
Ilha(s) *Portuguese,* Island(s)
Ilhéu(s) *Portuguese,* Islet(s)
Irmak *Turkish,* River
Isla(s) *Spanish,* Island(s)
Isola (Isole) *Italian,* Island(s)

J

Jabal *Arabic,* Mountain
Jāl *Arabic,* Ridge
-järvi *Finnish,* Lake
Jazīrat *Arabic,* Island
Jazīreh *Persian,* Island
Jebel *Arabic,* Mountain

Jezero *Serbian/Croatian,* Lake
Jiang *Chinese,* River
-joki *Finnish,* River
-jökull *Icelandic,* Glacier
Juzur *Arabic,* Islands

K

Kaikyō *Japanese,* Strait
-kaise *Lappish,* Mountain
Kali *Nepali,* River
Kalnas *Lithuanian,* Mountain
Kalns *Latvian,* Mountain
Kang *Chinese,* Harbor
Kangri *Tibetan,* Mountain(s)
Kaôh *Cambodian,* Islan[d]
Kapp *Norwegian,* Cape
Kavīr *Persian,* Desert
K'edi *Georgian,* Mountain range
Kediet *Arabic,* Mountain
Kepulauan *Indonesian, Malay,* Island group
Khalîg, Khalīj *Arabic,* Gulf
Khawr *Arabic,* Inlet
Khola *Nepali,* River
Khrebet *Russian,* Mountain range
Ko *Thai,* Island
Kolpos *Greek,* Bay
-kopf *German,* Peak
Körfäzi *Azerbaijani,* Ba[y]
Körfezi *Turkish,* Bay
Kõrgustik *Estonian,* Upland
Koshi *Nepali,* River
Kowtal *Persian,* Pass
Kūh(hā) *Persian,* Mountain(s)
-kundo *Korean,* Island group
-kysten *Norwegian,* Coast
Kyun *Burmese,* Island

L

Laaq *Somali,* Watercourse
Lac *French,* Lake
Lacul *Romanian,* Lake
Lago *Italian, Portuguese, Spanish,* Lake
Laguna *Spanish,* Lagoon, Lake

Laht *Estonian,* Bay
Laut *Indonesian,* Sea
Lembalemba *Malagasy,*
  Plateau
Lerr *Armenian,*
  Mountain
Lerrnashght'a *Armenian,*
  Mountain range
Les *Czech,* Forest
Lich *Armenian,* Lake
Liqeni *Albanian,* Lake
Lumi *Albanian,* River
Lyman *Ukrainian,*
  Estuary

M

Mae Nam *Thai,* River
-mägi *Estonian,* Hill
Maja *Albanian,*
  Mountain
-man *Korean,* Bay
Marios *Lithuanian,*
  Lake
meer *Dutch,* Lake
Melkosopochnik
  Russian, Plain
meri *Estonian,* Sea
Mifraz *Hebrew,* Bay
Monkhafad *Arabic,*
  Depression
Mont(s) *French,*
  Mountain(s)
Monte *Italian,*
  Portuguese, Mountain
More *Russian,* Sea
Mörön *Mongolian,* River

N

Nagor'ye *Russian,*
  Upland
Nahal *Hebrew,* River
Nahr *Arabic,* River
Nam *Laotian,* River
Nehri *Turkish,* River
Nevado *Spanish,*
  Mountain (snow-
  capped)
Nisoi *Greek,* Islands
Nizmennost' *Russian,*
  Lowland, plain
Nosy *Malagasy,* Island
Nur *Mongolian,* Lake
Nuruu *Mongolian,*
  Mountains
Nuur *Mongolian,* Lake
Nyzovyna *Ukrainian,*
  Lowland, plain

O

Ostrov(a) *Russian,*
  Island(s)
Oued *Arabic,*
  Watercourse
oy *Faeroese,* Island
oy(a) *Norwegian,*
  Island
Oya *Sinhala,* River
Ozero *Russian,*
  Ukrainian, Lake

P

Passo *Italian,* Pass
Pegunungan *Indonesian,*
  Malay, Mountain range
Pelagos *Greek,* Sea
Penisola *Italian,*
  Peninsula
Peski *Russian,* Sands
Phanom *Thai,*
  Mountain
Phou *Laotian,*
  Mountain
Pic *Catalan,* Peak
Pico *Portuguese,*
  Spanish, Peak
Pik *Russian,* Peak
Planalto *Portuguese,*
  Plateau
Planina, Planini
  Bulgarian, Macedonian,
  Serbian, Croatian,
  Mountain range
Ploskogor'ye *Russian,*
  Upland
Poluostrov *Russian,*
  Peninsula
Potamos *Greek,* River
Proliv *Russian,* Strait
Pulau *Indonesian,*
  Malay, Island
Pulu *Malay,* Island
Punta *Portuguese,*
  Spanish, Point

Q

Qā' *Arabic,* Depression
Qolleh *Persian,*
  Mountain

R

Raas *Somali,* Cape
-rags *Latvian,* Cape
Ramlat *Arabic,* Sands
Ra's *Arabic,* Cape,
  point, headland
Ravnina *Bulgarian,*
  Russian, Plain
Récif *French,* Reef
Represa (Rep.) *Spanish,*
  Portuguese, Reservoir
-rettō *Japanese,* Island
  chain
Riacho *Spanish,*
  Stream
Riban' *Malagasy,*
  Mountains
Rio *Portuguese,* River
Río *Spanish,* River
Riu *Catalan,* River
Rivier *Dutch,* River
Rivière *French,* River
Rowd *Pashtu,* River
Rūd *Persian,* River
Rudohorie *Slovak,*
  Mountains
Ruisseau *French,*
  Stream

S

Sabkhat *Arabic,* Salt
  marsh
Şaḥrā' *Arabic,* Desert
Samudra *Sinhala,*
  Reservoir
-san *Japanese, Korean,*
  Mountain
-sanchi *Japanese,*
  Mountains
-sanmaek *Korean,*
  Mountain
Sarīr *Arabic,* Desert
Sebkha, Sebkhet *Arabic,*
  Salt marsh, depression
See *German,* Lake
Selat *Indonesian,* Strait
-selkä *Finnish,* Ridge
Selseleh *Persian,*
  Mountain range
Serra *Portuguese,*
  Mountain
Serranía *Spanish,*
  Mountain
Sha'īb *Arabic,*
  Watercourse
Shamo *Chinese,* Desert
Shan *Chinese,*
  Mountain(s)
Shan-mo *Chinese,*
  Mountain range
Shaṭṭ *Arabic,*
  Distributary
-shima *Japanese,* Island
Shui-tao *Chinese,*
  Channel
Sierra *Spanish,*
  Mountains
Son *Vietnamese,*
  Mountain
Sông *Vietnamese,* River
-spitze *German,* Peak
Štít *Slovak,* Peak
Stoeng *Cambodian,*
  River
Stretto *Italian,* Strait
Su Anbarı *Azerbaijani,*
  Reservoir
Sungai *Indonesian,*
  Malay, River
Suu *Turkish,* River

T

Tal *Mongolian,* Plain
Tandavan' *Malagasy,*
  Mountain range
Tangorombohitr'
  Malagasy, Mountain
  massif
Tao *Chinese,* Island
Tassili *Berber,* Plateau,
  mountain
Tau *Russian,*
  Mountain(s)
Taungdan *Burmese,*
  Mountain range
Teluk *Indonesian,*
  Malay, Bay

Terara *Amharic,*
  Mountain
Tog *Somali,* Valley
Tônlé *Cambodian,*
  Lake
Top *Dutch,* Peak
-tunturi *Finnish,*
  Mountain
Tur'at *Arabic,*
  Channel

V

Väin *Estonian,* Strait
-vatn *Icelandic,* Lake
-vesi *Finnish,* Lake
Vinh *Vietnamese,* Bay
Vodokhranilishche
  (Vdkhr.) *Russian,*
  Reservoir
Vodoskhovyshche
  (Vdskh.) *Ukrainian,* Reservoir
Volcán *Spanish,*
  Volcano
Vozvyshennost'
  Russian, Upland,
  plateau
Vrh *Macedonian,*
  Peak
Vysochyna *Ukrainian,*
  Upland
Vysočina *Czech,*
  Upland

W

Waadi *Somali,*
  Watercourse
Wādī *Arabic,*
  Watercourse
Wāḥat, Wâhat *Arabic,*
  Oasis
Wald *German,* Forest
Wan *Chinese,* Bay
Wyżyna *Polish,*
  Upland

X

Xé *Laotian,* River

Y

Yarımadası *Azerbaijani,*
  Peninsula
Yazovir *Bulgarian,*
  Reservoir
Yoma *Burmese,*
  Mountains
Yü *Chinese,* Island

Z

Zaliv *Bulgarian,*
  Russian, Bay
Zatoka *Ukrainian,* Bay
Zemlya *Russian,* Land

CONTINENTAL FACTFILES

NORTH & CENTRAL AMERICA

POLITICAL FEATURES

TOTAL AREA:
9,400,000 sq miles
(24,346,000 sq km)

TOTAL NUMBER OF COUNTRIES: 23

TOTAL POPULATION:
466.2 million

LARGEST CITY WITH POPULATION: Mexico City, Mexico 18 million

COUNTRY WITH HIGHEST POPULATION DENSITY: Barbados 1,614 people per sq mile (623 people per sq km)

LARGEST COUNTRY:
Canada 3,851,788 sq miles
(9,976,140 sq km)

SMALLEST COUNTRY:
Grenada 131 sq miles
(340 sq km)

PHYSICAL FEATURES

LARGEST LAKE: Lake Superior, Canada/ USA 32,150 sq miles (83,270 sq km)

LONGEST RIVER: Mississippi-Missouri, USA 3,740 miles (6,019 km)

HIGHEST POINT: Mt. McKinley (Denali), Alaska, USA 20,322 ft (6,194 m)

LOWEST POINT: Death Valley, California, USA 282 ft (86 m) below sea level

SOUTH AMERICA

POLITICAL FEATURES

TOTAL AREA:
6,880,000 sq miles
(17,819,000 sq km)

TOTAL NUMBER OF COUNTRIES: 12

TOTAL POPULATION:
332.3 million

LARGEST CITY WITH POPULATION: São Paulo, Brazil 10.1 million

COUNTRY WITH HIGHEST POPULATION DENSITY: Ecuador 118 people per sq mile (45 people per sq km)

LARGEST COUNTRY:
Brazil 3,286,469 sq miles
(8,511,965 sq km)

SMALLEST COUNTRY:
Suriname 63,039 sq miles
(163,270 sq km)

PHYSICAL FEATURES

LARGEST LAKE: Lake Titicaca, Bolivia/Peru 3,220 sq miles (8,340 sq km)

LONGEST RIVER: Amazon, Brazil 4,050 miles (6,516 km)

HIGHEST POINT: Cerro Aconcagua, Argentina 22,833 ft (6,959 m)

LOWEST POINT: Peninsula Valdés, Argentina 131 ft (40 m) below sea level

AFRICA

POLITICAL FEATURES

TOTAL AREA:
11,677,250 sq miles
(30,244,050 sq km)

TOTAL NUMBER OF COUNTRIES: 53

TOTAL POPULATION:
776.5 million

LARGEST CITY WITH POPULATION: Cairo, Egypt 6.4 million

COUNTRY WITH HIGHEST POPULATION DENSITY: Mauritius 1,671 people per sq mile (645 people per sq km)

LARGEST COUNTRY:
Sudan 967,493 sq miles
(2,505,810 sq km)

SMALLEST COUNTRY:
Seychelles 176 sq miles
(455 sq km)

PHYSICAL FEATURES

LARGEST LAKE: Lake Victoria, Uganda, Kenya, Tanzania, 26,828 sq miles (69,484 sq km)

LONGEST RIVER: Nile, Uganda/Sudan/Egypt 4,160 miles (6,695 km)

HIGHEST POINT: Kilimanjaro, Tanzania 19,341 ft (5,895 m)

LOWEST POINT: Lac', Assal, Djibouti 512 ft (156 m) below sea level

EUROPE

POLITICAL FEATURES

TOTAL AREA:
4,809,200 sq miles
(12,456,000 sq km)

TOTAL NUMBER OF COUNTRIES: 43

TOTAL POPULATION:
582.5 million

LARGEST CITY WITH POPULATION: Moscow, European Russia 9 million

COUNTRY WITH HIGHEST POPULATION DENSITY: Monaco 42,104 people per sq mile (16,256 people per sq km)

LARGEST COUNTRY: European Russia 1,527,341 sq miles (3,955,818 sq km)

SMALLEST COUNTRY:
Vatican City, Italy 0.17 sq miles (0.44 sq km)

PHYSICAL FEATURES

LARGEST LAKE: Ladoga, European Russia 7,100 sq miles (18,390 sq km)

LONGEST RIVER: Volga, European Russia 2,290 miles (3,688 km)

HIGHEST POINT: El' brus, Caucasus Mts, European Russia 18,510 ft (5,642 m)

LOWEST POINT: Volga Delta, Caspian Sea, European Russia 92 ft (28 m) below sea level

NORTH & WEST ASIA

POLITICAL FEATURES

 TOTAL AREA:
9,585,550 sq miles
(24,826,600 sq km)

TOTAL NUMBER OF COUNTRIES: 24

TOTAL POPULATION:
478.6 million

LARGEST CITY WITH POPULATION: Istanbul, Turkey 6.5 million

COUNTRY WITH HIGHEST POPULATION DENSITY: Bahrain 2,724 people per sq mile (1,052 people per sq km)

LARGEST COUNTRY: Asiatic Russia 5,065,471 square miles (13,119,582 sq km)

SMALLEST COUNTRY: Bahrain 239 sq miles (620 sq km)

PHYSICAL FEATURES

LARGEST LAKE: Caspian Sea 142,243 sq miles (371,000 sq km)

LONGEST RIVER: Ob'-Irtysh, Asiatic Russia 3,461 miles (5,570 km)

HIGHEST POINT: Pik Pobedy, Kyrgyzstan/China 24,408 ft (7,439 m)

LOWEST POINT: Dead Sea, Israel/Jordan 1,286 ft (392 m) below sea level

SOUTH & EAST ASIA

POLITICAL FEATURES

TOTAL AREA:
7,936,200 sq miles
(20,554,700 sq km)

TOTAL NUMBER OF COUNTRIES: 24

TOTAL POPULATION:
3,300 million

LARGEST CITY WITH POPULATION: Tokyo, Japan 18.1 million

 COUNTRY WITH HIGHEST POPULATION DENSITY: Singapore 16,400 people per sq mile (6,332 people per sq km)

LARGEST COUNTRY: China 3,705,386 sq miles (9,596,960 sq km)

SMALLEST COUNTRY: Maldives 116 sq miles (300 sq km)

PHYSICAL FEATURES

 LARGEST LAKE: Tônlé Sap, Cambodia 100 sq miles (2,850 sq km)

 LONGEST RIVER: Chang Jiang (Yangtze), China 3,965 miles (6,380 km)

 HIGHEST POINT: Mount Everest, Nepal 29,030 ft (8,848 m)

LOWEST POINT: Turpan Hami (Turfan Basin), China 505 ft (154 m) below sea level

AUSTRALASIA & OCEANIA

POLITICAL FEATURES

TOTAL AREA:
3,376,700 sq miles
(8,745,750 sq km)

TOTAL NUMBER OF COUNTRIES: 14

TOTAL POPULATION:
28.6 million

LARGEST CITY WITH POPULATION: Sydney, Australia 3.7 million

COUNTRY WITH HIGHEST POPULATION DENSITY: Nauru 1,455 people per sq mile (562 people per sq km)

LARGEST COUNTRY: Australia 2,967,892 sq miles (7,686,850 sq km)

SMALLEST COUNTRY: Nauru 8 sq miles (21 sq km)

PHYSICAL FEATURES

LARGEST LAKE: Lake Eyre, Australia 3,430 sq miles (8,884 sq km)

LONGEST RIVER: Murray-Darling, Australia 2,330 miles (3,750 km)

HIGHEST POINT: Mt. Wilhelm Papua New Guinea 14,794 ft (4,509 m)

LOWEST POINT: Lake Eyre, Australia 52 ft (16 m) below sea level

ANTARCTICA

POLITICAL FEATURES

TOTAL AREA: 5,405,500 sq miles (14,000,000 sq km) of which approx. 324,300 sq miles (840,000 sq km) is ice-free

TOTAL NUMBER OF COUNTRIES: The Antarctic Treaty has 30 participating nations and 14 with observer status. Claims by Australia, France, New Zealand, Norway, Argentina, Chile and the UK are not recognized by other member states.

TOTAL POPULATION: No indigenous population. 74 research stations, (42 are staffed all year-round). Population varies between about 1,000 (winter) and 4,000 (summer).

PHYSICAL FEATURES

TOTAL VOLUME OF ICE: 7,200,000 cu miles (30,000,000 cu km): contains 90% of the Earth's fresh water

 SEA ICE: 1,158,300 sq miles (3,000,000 sq km) in February. 7,722,000 sq miles (20,000,000 sq km) in October

 LOWEST TEMPERATURE: Vostok Station -89.5°C (-129°F)

 HIGHEST POINT: Vinson Massif 16,072 ft (4,897 m)

LOWEST POINT: Coastline 0ft/m

GEOGRAPHICAL COMPARISONS

LARGEST COUNTRIES

Russ. Fed. . . . . .6,592,735 sq miles . .(17,075,200 sq km)
Canada . . . . .3,851,788 sq miles . . .(9,976,140 sq km)
USA . . . . .3,717,792 sq miles . . .(9,629,091 sq km)
China . . . . .3,705,386 sq miles . . .(9,596,960 sq km)
Brazil . . . . .3,286,470 sq miles . . .(8,511,965 sq km)
Australia . . . . . .2,967,893 sq miles . . .(7,686,893 sq km)
India . . . . .1,269,339 sq miles . . .(3,287,590 sq km)
Argentina . . . . .1,068,296 sq miles . . .(2,766,890 sq km)
Kazakhstan . . . .1,049,150 sq miles . . .(2,717,300 sq km)
Sudan . . . . .967,493 sq miles . . .(2,505,810 sq km)

SMALLEST COUNTRIES

Vatican City . . . . .0.17 sq miles . . . .(0.44 sq km)
Monaco . . . . .0.75 sq miles . . . . . .(1.95 sq km)
Nauru . . . . .8 sq miles . . . .(21 sq km)
Tuvalu . . . . .10 sq miles . . . .(26 sq km)
San Marino . . . . .24 sq miles . . . .(61 sq km)
Liechtenstein . . . . .62 sq miles . . . .(160 sq km)
Marshall Islands . . . . .70 sq miles . . . .(181 sq km)
St. Kitts & Nevis . . . . .101 sq miles . . . .(261 sq km)
Maldives . . . . .116 sq miles . . . .(300 sq km)
Malta . . . . .122 sq miles . . . .(316 sq km)

LARGEST ISLANDS

(TO THE NEAREST 1,000 - OR 100,000 FOR THE LARGEST)
Greenland . . . . .849,400 sq miles . . .(2,200,000 sq km)
New Guinea . . .312,000 sq miles . . . .(808,000 sq km)
Borneo . . . . .292,222 sq miles . . . .(757,050 sq km)
Madagascar . . . .229,300 sq miles . . . .(594,000 sq km)
Sumatra . . . . .202,300 sq miles . . . .(524,000 sq km)
Baffin Island . . . .183,800 sq miles . . . .(476,000 sq km)
Honshu . . . . .88,800 sq miles . . . .(230,000 sq km)
Britain . . . . .88,700 sq miles . . . .(229,800 sq km)
Victoria Island . . . .81,900 sq miles . . . .(212,000 sq km)
Ellesmere Island . .75,700 sq miles . . . . .(196,000 sq km)

RICHEST COUNTRIES

(GNP PER CAPITA, IN US$)
Luxembourg 42.930
Liechtenstein 40,000
Switzerland 38,380
Norway 33,470
Denamrk 32,050
Japan 32,030
USA 31,910
Germany 25,620
Austria 25,430
Singapore 24,150

POOREST COUNTRIES

(GNP PER CAPITA, IN US$)
Somalia 10
Ethiopia 10
Congo, Dem. Rep. 11
Sierra Leone 13
Malawi 18
Niger 19
Mozambique 22
Burundi 24
Rwanda 25
Tanzania 26

MOST POPULOUS COUNTRIES

China 1,290,000,00
India 1,030,000,00
USA 281,400,00
Indonesia 214,000,00
Brazil 172,600,00
Pakistan 145,000,00
Russian Federation 144,700,00
Bangladesh 140,400,00
Japan 127,300,00
Nigeria 116,900,00

LEAST POPULOUS COUNTRIES

Vatican City 52
Tuvalu 10,80
Nauru 11,80
Palau 19,10
San Marino 26,90
Liechtenstein 32,20
Monaco 31,70
St. Kitts & Nevis .41,00
Antigua & Barbuda 66,40
Andorra 66,80

MOST DENSELY POPULATED COUNTRIES

Monaco . . . .42,104 people per sq mile . .(16,256 per sq k
Singapore . .16,400 people per sq mile . . .(6,332 per sq k
Malta . . . . . .3,213 people per sq mile . . .(2,241 per sq k
Vatican City 3,084 people per sq mile . .(1,191 per sq k
Bahrain . . . .2,724 people per sq mile . . .(1,052 per sq k
Maldives . .2,590 people per sq mile . .(1,000 per sq k
Bangladesh 2,525 people per sq mile . . . .(975 per sq k
Mauritius . .1,671 people per sq mile . . . .(645 per sq k
Barbados . .1,614 people per sq mile . . . .(623 per sq k
Taiwan . . . .1,598 people per sq mile . . . .(617 per sq k

Most Sparsely Populated Countries

Mongolia . . . . .4 people per sq mile . . . . .(2 per sq km)
Namibia . . . . . .6 people per sq mile . . . . .(2 per sq km)
Australia . . . . .7 people per sq mile . . . . .(3 per sq km)
Mauritania . . . .7 people per sq mile . . . . .(3 per sq km)
Suriname . . . . .7 people per sq mile . . . . .(3 per sq km)
Botswana . . . . .7 people per sq mile . . . . .(3 per sq km)
Iceland . . . . . . .7 people per sq mile . . . . .(3 per sq km)
Libya . . . . .8 people per sq mile . . . . .(3 per sq km)
Canada . . . . . . .8 people per sq mile . . . . .(3 per sq km)
Guyana . . . . . . .9 people per sq mile . . . . .(4 per sq km)

Most Widely Spoken Languages

1. Chinese (Mandarin)   6. Arabic
2. English   7. Bengali
3. Hindi   8. Portuguese
4. Spanish   9. Malay-Indonesian
5. Russian   10. French

Countries With The Most Land Borders

14: China *(Afghanistan, Bhutan, Myanmar, India,
    Kazakhstan, Kyrgyzstan, Laos, Mongolia,
    Nepal, North Korea, Pakistan, Russian
    Federation, Tajikistan, Vietnam)*

14: Russian Federation *(Azerbaijan, Belarus,
    China, Estonia, Finland, Georgia, Kazakhstan,
    Latvia, Lithuania, Mongolia, North Korea,
    Norway, Poland, Ukraine)*

10: Brazil *(Argentina, Bolivia, Colombia, French
    Guiana, Guyana, Paraguay, Peru, Suriname,
    Uruguay, Venezuela)*

9: Congo, Dem. Rep. *(Angola, Burundi,
    Central African Republic, Congo, Rwanda,
    Sudan, Tanzania, Uganda, Zambia)*

9: Germany *(Austria, Belgium, Czech Republic,
    Denmark, France, Luxembourg,
    Netherlands, Poland, Switzerland)*

9: Sudan *(Central African Republic, Chad,
    Congo, Dem. Rep., Egypt, Eritrea, Ethiopia,
    Kenya, Libya, Uganda)*

8: Austria *(Czech Republic, Germany, Hungary, Italy,
    Liechtenstein, Slovakia, Slovenia, Switzerland)*

8: France *(Andorra, Belgium, Germany, Italy,
    Luxembourg, Monaco, Spain, Switzerland)*

8: Tanzania *(Burundi, Congo, Dem. Rep.,
    Kenya, Malawi, Mozambique, Rwanda,
    Uganda, Zambia)*

8: Turkey *(Armenia, Azerbaijan, Bulgaria, Georgia,
    Greece, Iran, Iraq, Syria)*

8: Zambia *(Angola, Botswana, Congo, Dem. Rep.,
    Malawi, Mozambique, Namibia,
    Tanzania, Zimbabwe)*

Longest Rivers

Nile (NE Africa) . . . . .4,160 miles . . . .(6,695 km)
Amazon (South America) . .4,049 miles . . . .(6,516 km)
Yangtze (China) . . . . .3,915 miles . . . .(6,299 km)
Mississippi/Missouri (US) .3,710 miles . . . .(5,969 km)
Ob'-Irtysh (Russ. Fed.) . . .3,461 miles . . . .(5,570 km)
Yellow River (China) . . . .3,395 miles . . . .(5,464 km)
Congo (Central Africa) . . . .2,900 miles . . . .(4,667 km)
Mekong (Southeast Asia) . .2,749 miles . . . .(4,425 km)
Lena (Russian Federation) . .2,734 miles . . . .(4,400 km)
Mackenzie (Canada) . . . . .2,640 miles . . . .(4,250 km)
Yenisey (Russ. Federation) .2,541 miles . . . .(4,090 km)

Highest Mountains

(HEIGHT ABOVE SEA LEVEL)

Everest . . . . .29,030 ft . . . .(8,848 m)
K2 . . . . .28,253 ft . . . .(8,611 m)
Kanchenjunga I . . . . .28,210 ft . . . .(8,598 m)
Makalu I . . . . .27,767 ft . . . .(8,463 m)
Cho Oyu . . . . .26,907 ft . . . .(8,201 m)
Dhaulagiri I . . . . .26,796 ft . . . .(8,167 m)
Manaslu I . . . . .26,783 ft . . . .(8,163 m)
Nanga Parbat I . . . . .26,661 ft . . . .(8,126 m)
Annapurna I . . . . .26,547 ft . . . .(8,091 m)
Gasherbrum I . . . . .26,471 ft . . . .(8,068 m)

Largest Bodies Of Inland Water

(WITH AREA AND DEPTH)

Caspian Sea
143,243 sq miles (371,000 sq km) . . .3,215 ft (980 m)
Lake Superior
32,150 sq miles (83,270 sq km) . . . . .1,289 ft (393 m)
Lake Victoria
26,828 sq miles (69,484 sq km) . . . . . .328 ft (100 m)
Lake Huron
23,436 sq miles (60,700 sq km) . . . . . .751 ft (229 m)
Lake Michigan
22,402 sq miles (58,020 sq km) . . . . . .922 ft (281 m)
Lake Tanganyika
12,703 sq miles (32,900 sq km) . . . .4,700 ft (1,435 m)
Great Bear Lake
12,274 sq miles (31,790 sq km) . . . . .1,047 ft (319 m)
Lake Baikal
11,776 sq miles (30,500 sq km) . . . .5,712 ft (1,741 m)
Great Slave Lake
10,981 sq miles (28,440 sq km) . . . . . .459 ft (140 m)
Lake Erie
9,915 sq miles (25,680 sq km) . . . . .197 ft (60 m)

......*continued on p.166*

Adige 96 C2 Ger. Etsch. River
N Italy
Adirondack Mountains 41 F2
mountain range New York,
NE USA
Ādīs Ābeba 73 C5 Eng. Addis
Ababa. Country capital (Ethiopia)
C Ethiopia
Adıyaman 117 E4 Adıyaman,
SE Turkey
Adjud 108 C4 Vrancea, E Romania
Admiralty Islands 144 B3 island
group N PNG
Adra 93 E5 Andalucía, S Spain
Adrar 70 D3 C Algeria
Adrar des Iforas see Ifôghas, Adrar
des
Adrian 40 C3 Michigan, N USA
Adriatic Sea 103 E2 Alb. Deti
Adriatik, It. Mare Adriatico, SCr.
Jadransko More, Slvn. Jadransko
Morje. Sea N Mediterranean Sea
Adycha 115 F2 river NE Russian
Federation
Aegean Sea 105 C5 Gk. Aigaíon
Pélagos, Aigaío Pélagos, Turk. Ege
Denizi. Sea NE Mediterranean Sea
Aegviidu 106 D2 Ger.
Charlottenhof. Harjumaa,
NW Estonia
Aelana see Al 'Aqabah
Aelok see Ailuk Atoll
Aelōnlaplap see Ailinglaplap Atoll
Aeolian Islands see Eolie, Isole
Afar Depression see Danakil
Desert
Afghanistan 122 C4 Per. Dowlat-e
Eslāmī-ye Afghānestān; prev.
Republic of Afghanistan. Country
C Asia

Afghanistan 122

Official Name
Islamic State of Afghanistan
Formation 1919
Capital Kabul
Population 22.5 million / 90 people
per sq mile (35 people per sq km)
Total area 250,000 sq miles
(647,500 sq km)
Languages Pashtu, Tajik, Dari,
Farsi
Religions Sunni Muslim 84%, Shi'a
Muslim 15%, other 1%
Ethnic mix Pashtun 38%, Tajik 25%,
Hazara 19%, other 18%
Government Transitional regime
Currency Afghani = 100 puls
Literacy rate 37.3%
Calorie consumption 1,539
kilocalories

Afmadow 73 D6 Jubbada Hoose,
S Somalia
Africa 68 continent
Africa, Horn of 68 E4 physical region
Ethiopia /Somalia
Africana Seamount 141 A6 undersea
feature SW Indian Ocean
'Afrīn 118 B2 Ḥalab, N Syria
Afyon 116 B3 prev. Afyonkarahisar.
Áfyon, W Turkey
Agadez 75 G3 prev. Agadès.
Agadez, C Niger
Agadir 70 B3 SW Morocco
Agana/Agaña see Hagåtña
Agaro 73 C5 C Ethiopia
Agassiz Fracture Zone 143 G5
tectonic feature S Pacific Ocean
Agathónisi 105 D6 island
Dodekánisos, Greece,
Aegean Sea
Agde 91 C6 anc. Agatha. Hérault,
S France
Agedabia see Ajdābiyā
Agen 91 B5 anc. Aginnum. Lot-et-
Garonne, SW France
Aghri Dagh see Büyükağrı Dağı
Agiá 104 B4 var. Ayiá. Thessalía,
C Greece
Agialoúsa 102 D4 var. Yenierenköy.
NE Cyprus
Agía Marína 105 E6 Léros,
Dodekánisos, Greece,
Aegean Sea

Ágios Nikólaos 105 D8 var. Áyios
Nikólaos. Kríti, Greece,
E Mediterranean Sea
Āgra 134 D3 Uttar Pradesh, N India
Agram see Zagreb
Ağrı 117 F3 var. Karaköse; prev.
Karakılısse. Ağrı, NE Turkey
Agri **Dagi** see Büyükağrı Dağı
Agrigento 97 C7 Gk. Akragas; prev.
Girgenti. Sicilia, Italy,
C Mediterranean Sea
Agriovótano 105 C5 Évvoia,
C Greece
Agropoli 97 D5 Campania, S Italy
Aguachica 58 B2 Cesar, N Colombia
Aguadulce 53 F5 Coclé, S Panama
Agua Prieta 50 B1 Sonora,
NW Mexico
Aguascalientes 50 D4
Aguascalientes, C Mexico
Aguaytía 60 C3 Ucayali, C Peru
Aguilas 93 E4 Murcia, SE Spain
Aguililla 50 D4 Michoacán de
Ocampo, SW Mexico
Agulhas Basin 69 D8 undersea
feature SW Indian Ocean
Agulhas Plateau 67 D6 undersea
feature SW Indian Ocean
Ahaggar 75 F2 high plateau region
SE Algeria
Ahlen 94 B4 Nordrhein-Westfalen,
W Germany
Ahmadābād 134 C4 var.
Ahmedabad. Gujarāt, W India
Ahmadnagar 134 C5 var.
Ahmednagar. Mahārāshtra,
W India
Ahmedabad see Ahmadābād
Ahmednagar see Ahmadnagar
Ahuachapán 52 B3 Ahuachapán,
W El Salvador
Ahvāz 120 C3 var. Ahwāz; prev.
Nāsiri. Khūzestān, SW Iran
Ahvenanmaa see Åland
Ahwāz see Ahvāz
Aïdin see Aydın
Aígina 105 C6 var. Aíyina, Egina.
Aígina, C Greece
Aígio 105 B5 var. Egio; prev. Aíyion.
Dytikí Ellás, S Greece
Aiken 43 E2 South Carolina, SE USA
Ailigandí 53 G4 San Blas,
NE Panama
Ailinglaplap Atoll 144 D2 var.
Aelōnlaplap. Atoll Ralik Chain,
S Marshall Islands
Ailuk Atoll 144 D1 var. Aelok. Atoll
Ratak Chain, NE Marshall Islands
Ainaži 106 D3 Est. Heinaste, Ger.
Hainasch. Limbaži, N Latvia
'Aïn Ben Tili 74 D1 Tiris Zemmour,
N Mauritania
Aintab see Gaziantep
Aïoun el Atrous see 'Ayoûn
el 'Atroûs
Aïoun el Atroûss see 'Ayoûn
el 'Atroûs
Aiquile 61 F4 Cochabamba,
C Bolivia
Aïr see Aïr, Massif de l'
Air du Azbine see Aïr, Massif de l'
Aïr, Massif de l' 75 G2 var. Aïr, Air
du Azbine, Asben. Mountain range
NC Niger
Aiud 108 B4 Ger. Strassburg, Hung.
Nagyenyed; prev. Engeten. Alba,
SW Romania
Aix see Aix-en-Provence
Aix-en-Provence 91 D6 var. Aix;
anc. Aquae Sextiae. Bouches-du-
Rhône, SE France
Aíyina see Aígina
Aíyion see Aígio
Aizkraukle 106 C4 Aizkraukle,
S Latvia
Ajaccio 91 E7 Corse, France,
C Mediterranean Sea
Ajaria 117 F2 autonomous republic
SW Georgia
Aj Bogd Uul 126 D2 mountain
SW Mongolia
Ajdābiyā 71 G2 var. Agedabia,
Ajdābīyah. NE Libya
Ajdābīyah see Ajdābiyā
Ajjinena see El Geneina
Ajmer 134 D3 var. Ajmere.
Rājasthān, N India

Ajmere see Ajmer
Ajo 48 A3 Arizona, SW USA
Akaba see Al 'Aqabah
Akamagaseki see Shimonoseki
Akasha 72 B3 Northern, N Sudan
Akchâr 74 C2 desert W Mauritania
Akhalts'ikhe 117 F2 SW Georgia
Akhisar 116 A3 Manisa, W Turkey
Akhmīm 72 B2 anc. Panopolis.
C Egypt
Akhtubinsk 111 C7
Astrakhanskaya Oblast',
SW Russian Federation
Akimiski Island 38 C3 island
Northwest Territories, C Canada
Akinovka 109 F4 Zaporiz'ka
Oblast', S Ukraine
Akita 130 D4 Akita, Honshū,
C Japan
Akjoujt 74 C2 prev. Fort-Repoux.
Inchiri, W Mauritania
Akkeshi 130 E2 Hokkaidō,
NE Japan
Aklavik 36 D3 Northwest
Territories, NW Canada
Akmola see Astana
Akpatok Island 39 E1 island
Northwest Territories, C Canada
Akra Dhrepanon see Drépano,
Akrotírio
Akra Kanestron see Palioúri,
Akrotírio
Akron 40 D4 Ohio, N USA
Akrotiri see Akrotírion
Akrotírion 102 C5 var. Akrotiri. UK
air base S Cyprus
Aksai Chin 124 B2 Chin. Aksayqin.
Disputed region China /India
Aksaray 116 C4 Aksaray, C Turkey
Akşehir 116 B3 Konya, W Turkey
Aktau 114 A4 Kaz. Aqtaū; prev.
Shevchenko. Mangistau,
W Kazakhstan
Aktobe 92 B4 Kaz. Aqtöbe; prev.
Aktyubinsk. Aktyubinsk,
NW Kazakhstan
Aktsyabrski 107 C7 Rus.
Oktyabr'skiy; prev. Karpilovka.
Homyel'skaya Voblasts',
SE Belarus
Aktyubinsk see Aktobe
Akula 77 C5 Equateur, NW Dem.
Rep. Congo
Akureyri 83 E4 Nordhurland
Eystra, N Iceland
Akyab see Sittwe
Alabama 51 G1 off. State of Alabama;
also known as Camellia State,
Heart of Dixie, The Cotton State,
Yellowhammer State. State S USA
Alabama River 42 C3 river
Alabama, S USA
Alaca 116 C3 Çorum, N Turkey
Alagoas 63 G2 off. Estado de
Alagoas. State E Brazil
Alajuela 53 E4 Alajuela,
C Costa Rica
Alakanuk 36 C2 Alaska, USA
Al 'Alamayn see El 'Alamein
Al 'Amārah 120 C3 var. Amara.
E Iraq
Alamo 47 D6 Nevada, W USA
Alamogordo 48 D3 New Mexico,
SW USA
Alamosa 44 C5 Colorado, C USA
Åland 85 C6 var. Åland Islands, Fin.
Ahvenanmaa. Island group
SW Finland
Aland Islands see Åland
Åland Sea see Ålands Hav
Ålands Hav 85 C6 var. Aland Sea.
Strait Baltic Sea / Gulf of Bothnia
Alanya 116 C4 Antalya, S Turkey
Alappuzha see Alleppey
Al 'Aqabah 119 B8 var. Akaba,
Aqaba, 'Aqaba; anc. Aelana, Elath.
Ma'ān, SW Jordan
Alaska, Golfo de see Alaska,
Gulf of
Alaşehir 116 A4 Manisa, W Turkey
Al 'Ashārah 118 E3 var. Ashara.
Dayr az Zawr, E Syria
Alaska 36 C3 off. State of Alaska;
also known as Land of the
Midnight Sun, The Last Frontier,
Seward's Folly; prev. Russian
America. State NW USA
Alaska, Gulf of 36 C4 var. Golfo de
Alasca. Gulf Canada /USA

Alaska Peninsula 36 C3 peninsula
Alaska, USA
Alaska Range 34 B2 mountain range
Alaska, USA
Al-Asnam see Chlef
Al Awaynāt see Al 'Uwaynāt
Al 'Aynā 119 B7 Al Karak,
W Jordan
Alazeya 115 G2 river NE Russian
Federation
Al Bāb 118 B2 Ḥalab, N Syria
Albacete 93 E3 Castilla-La Mancha,
C Spain
Al Baghdādī 120 B3 var. Khān
al Baghdādī. SW Iraq
Al Bāha see Al Bāḥah
Al Bāḥah 121 B5 var. Al Bāha.
Al Bāḥah, SW Saudi Arabia
Al Baḥr al Mayyit see Dead Sea
Alba Iulia 108 B4 Ger. Weissenburg,
Hung. Gyulafehérvár; prev.
Bălgrad, Karlsburg, Károly-
Fehérvár. Alba, W Romania
Albania 101 C7 Alb. Republika e
Shqipërisë, Shqipëria; prev.
People's Socialist Republic of
Albania. Country SE Europe

Albania 101

Official name Republic of Albania
Formation 1912
Capital Tiranë
Population 3.1 million /279 people
per sq mile (108 people per sq km)
Total area 11,100 sq miles
(28,748 sq km) sq miles
Languages Albanian, Greek
Religions Sunni Muslim 70%,
Orthodox Christian 20%, Roman
Catholic 10%
Ethnic mix Albanian 86%,
Greek 12%, other 2%
Government Multiparty republic
Currency Lek = 100 qindars
Literacy rate 84.7%
Calorie consumption 2,864
kilocalories

Albany 38 C3 river Ontario,
S Canada
Albany 41 F3 state capital New York,
NE USA
Albany 42 D3 Georgia, SE USA
Albany 46 B3 Oregon, NW USA
Albany 147 B7 Western Australia
Al Bāridah 118 C4 var. Bāridah.
Ḥimş, C Syria
Al Başrah 120 C3 Eng. Basra; hist.
Busra, Bussora. SE Iraq
Al Batrūn see Batroûn
Al Baydā' 71 G2 var. Beida. NE Libya
Albemarle Island see Isabela, Isla
Albemarle Sound 43 G1 inlet
W Atlantic Ocean
Albergaria-a-Velha 92 B2 Aveiro,
N Portugal
Albert 90 C3 Somme, N France
Alberta 37 E4 province SW Canada
Albert Edward Nyanza see
Edward, Lake
Albert, Lake 73 B6 var. Albert
Nyanza, Lac Mobutu Sese Seko.
Lake Uganda /Dem. Rep. Congo
Albert Lea 45 F3 Minnesota, N USA
Albert Nyanza see Albert, Lake
Albi 91 C6 anc. Albiga. Tarn,
S France
Ålborg 80 D3 var. Aalborg, Ålborg-
Nørresundby; anc. Alburgum.
Nordjylland, N Denmark
Ålborg-Nørresundby see Ålborg
Alborz, Reshteh-ye Kūhhā-ye 120
C2 Eng. Elburz Mountains.
Mountain range N Iran
Albuquerque 48 D2 New Mexico,
SW USA
Al Burayqah see Marsá al Burayqah
Alburgum see Ålborg
Albury 149 C7 New South Wales,
SE Australia
Alcácer do Sal 92 B4 Setúbal,
W Portugal
Alcalá de Henares 93 E3 Ar.
Alkal'a; anc. Complutum. Madrid,
C Spain

Alcamo 97 C7 Sicilia, Italy,
C Mediterranean Sea
Alcañiz 93 F2 Aragón, NE Spain
Alcántara, Embalse de 92 C3
reservoir W Spain
Alcaudete 92 D4 Andalucía,
S Spain
Alcázar *see* Ksar-el-Kebir
Alcoi *see* Alcoy
Alcoy 93 F4 *var.* Alcoi. País
Valenciano, E Spain
Aldabra Group 79 G2 *island group*
SW Seychelles
Aldan 115 F3 *river* NE Russian
Federation
al Dar al Baida *see* Rabat
Alderney 90 A2 *island* Channel
Islands
Aleg 74 C3 Brakna, SW Mauritania
Aleksandropol' *see* Gyumri
Aleksin 111 B5 Tul'skaya Oblast',
W Russian Federation
Aleksinac 100 E4 Serbia, SE Serbia
and Montenegro (Yugo.)
Alençon 90 B3 Orne, N France
Alenquer 63 E2 Pará, NE Brazil
Aleppo *see* Ḥalab
Alert 37 F1 Ellesmere Island,
Nunavut, N Canada
Alès 91 C6 *prev.* Alais. Gard,
S France
Aleşd 108 B3 Hung. Élesd. Bihor,
SW Romania
Alessandria 96 B2 Fr. Alexandrie.
Piemonte, N Italy
Ålesund 85 A5 Møre og Romsdal,
S Norway
Aleutian Basin 113 G3 *undersea
feature* Bering Sea
Aleutian Islands 36 A3 *island group*
Alaska, USA
Aleutian Range 34 A2 *mountain
range* Alaska, USA
Aleutian Trench 113 H3 *undersea
feature* S Bering Sea
Alexander Archipelago 36 D4 *island
group* Alaska, USA
Alexander City 42 D2 Alabama,
S USA
Alexander Island 154 A3 *island*
Antarctica
Alexandra 151 B7 Otago, South
Island, NZ
Alexándreia 104 B4 *var.* Alexándria.
Kentrikí Makedonía, N Greece
Alexandria 72 B1 Ar.
Al Iskandarīyah. N Egypt
Alexándria *see* Alexándreia
Alexandria 42 B3 Louisiana, S USA
Alexandria 45 F2 Minnesota,
N USA
Alexandria 108 C5 Teleorman,
S Romania
Alexandroúpoli 104 D3 *var.*
Alexandroúpolis, *Turk.* Dedeagaç,
Dedeagach. Anatolikí Makedonía
kai Thráki, NE Greece
Alexandroúpolis *see*
Alexandroúpoli
Al Fāshir *see* El Fasher
Alfatar 104 E1 Silistra, NE Bulgaria
Alfeiós 105 B6 *prev.* Alfiós, *anc.*
Alpheius, Alpheus. *River* S Greece
Alföld *see* Great Hungarian Plain
Alga 114 B4 *Kaz.* Algha.
Aktyubinsk, NW Kazakhstan
Algarve 92 B4 *cultural region*
S Portugal
Algeciras 92 C5 Andalucía,
SW Spain
Algemesí 93 F3 País Valenciano,
E Spain
Al-Genain *see* El Geneina
Alger 71 E1 *var.* Algiers, El Djazaïr,
Al Jazair. *Country capital* (Algeria)
N Algeria
Algeria 70 C3 *Country* N Africa

Algeria 70

Official name People's Democratic
Republic of Algeria
Formation 1962
Capital Algiers
Population 30.8 million / 33 people
per sq mile (13 people per sq km)

Algeria (continued)

Total area 919,590 sq miles
(2,381,740 sq km)
Languages Arabic, Tamazight,
French
Religions Sunni Muslim 99%,
other 1%
Ethnic mix Arab 75%, Berber 24%,
European 1%
Government Multiparty republic
Currency Algerian dinar =
100 centimes
Literacy rate 67.8%
Calorie consumption 2,944
kilocalories

Algerian Basin 80 C5 *var.* Balearic
Plain *undersea feature*
W Mediterranean Sea
Al Ghābah 121 E5 *var.* Ghaba.
C Oman
Alghero 97 A5 Sardegna, Italy,
C Mediterranean Sea
Al Ghurdaqah *see* Hurghada
Algiers *see* Alger
Algona 45 F3 Iowa, C USA
Al Ḥajār al Gharbī 121 D5 *mountain
range* N Oman
Al Ḥasakah 118 D2 *var.* Al Hasijah,
El Haseke, Fr. Hassetché.
Al Ḥasakah, NE Syria
Al Hasijah *see* Al Ḥasakah
Al Ḥillah 120 B3 *var.* Hilla. C Iraq
Al Ḥiṣā 119 B7 Aṭ Ṭafīlah,
W Jordan
Al Ḥudaydah 121 B6 Eng. Hodeida.
W Yemen
Al Ḥufūf 120 C4 *var.* Hofuf. Ash
Sharqīyah, NE Saudi Arabia
Aliákmonas 104 B4 *prev.* Aliákmon,
anc. Haliacmon. *River* N Greece
Alíartos 105 C5 Stereá Ellás,
C Greece
Alicante 93 F4 *Cat.* Alacant. País
Valenciano, SE Spain
Alice 49 G5 Texas, SW USA
Alice Springs 148 A4 Northern
Territory, C Australia
Aliki *see* Alykí
Alima 77 B6 *river* C Congo
Alindao 76 C4 Basse-Kotto,
S Central African Republic
Aliquippa 40 D4 Pennsylvania,
NE USA
Alistráti 104 C3 Kentrikí
Makedonía, NE Greece
Alivéri 105 C5 *var.* Alivérion.
Évvoia, C Greece
Alivérion *see* Alivéri
Al Jabal al Akhḍar 71 G2 *mountain
range* NE Libya
Al Jabal ash Sharqī *see* Anti-
Lebanon
Al Jafr 119 B7 Ma'ān,
S Jordan
Al Jaghbūb 71 H3 NE Libya
Al Jahrā' 120 C4 *var.* Al Jahrah,
Jahra. C Kuwait
Al Jahrah *see* Al Jahrā'
Al Jawf 120 B4 *var.* Jauf. Al Jawf,
NW Saudi Arabia
Al Jazair *see* Alger
Al Jazīrah 118 E2 *physical region*
Iraq/Syria
Al Jīzah *see* El Gîza
Al Junaynah *see* El Geneina
Al Karak 119 B7 *var.* El Kerak,
Karak, Kerak; *anc.* Kir Moab, Kir
of Moab. Al Karak, W Jordan
Al-Kasr al-Kebir *see* Ksar-el-Kebir
Al Khalīl *see* Hebron
Al Khārijah *see* El Khârga
Al Khufrah 71 H4 SE Libya
Al Khums 71 F2 *var.* Homs, Khoms,
Khums. NW Libya
Alkmaar 86 C2 Noord-Holland,
NW Netherlands
Al Kūt 120 C3 *var.* Kūt al 'Amārah,
Kut al Imara. E Iraq
Al-Kuwait *see* Al Kuwayt
Al Kuwayt 120 C4 *var.* Al-Kuwait,
Eng. Kuwait, Kuwait City; *prev.*
Qurein. *Country capital* (Kuwait)
E Kuwait

Al Lādhiqīyah 118 A3 Eng. Latakia,
Fr. Lattaquié; *anc.* Laodicea,
Laodicea ad Mare. Al Lādhiqīyah,
W Syria
Allahābād 135 E3 Uttar Pradesh,
N India
Allanmyo 136 B4 Magwe,
C Myanmar
Allegheny Plateau 41 E3 *mountain
range* New York/Pennsylvania,
NE USA
Allentown 41 F4 Pennsylvania,
NE USA
Alleppey 132 C3 *var.* Alappuzha;
prev. Alleppi. Kerala, SW India
Alleppi *see* Alleppey
Alliance 44 D3 Nebraska, C USA
Al Līth 121 B5 Makkah, SW Saudi
Arabia
Alma-Ata *see* Almaty
Almada 92 B4 Setúbal, W Portugal
Al Madīnah 121 A5 Eng. Medina.
Al Madīnah, W Saudi Arabia
Al Mafraq 119 B6 *var.* Mafraq.
Al Mafraq, N Jordan
Al Mahdīyah *see* Mahdia
Al Mahrah 121 C6 *mountain range*
E Yemen
Al Majma'ah 120 B4 Ar Riyāḍ,
C Saudi Arabia
Al Mālikīyah 118 E1 Al Ḥasakah,
NE Syria
Al Manāmah 120 C4 Eng. Manama.
Country capital (Bahrain)
N Bahrain
Al Manāşir 118 E3 *mountain range*
E Syria
Almansa 93 F4 Castilla-La Mancha,
C Spain
Al Marj 71 G2 *var.* Barka, *It.* Barce.
NE Libya
Almaty 114 C5 *var.* Alma-Ata.
Almaty, SE Kazakhstan
Al Mawşil 120 B2 Eng. Mosul.
N Iraq
Al Mayādīn 118 D3 *var.* Mayadin,
Fr. Meyadine. Dayr az Zawr,
E Syria
Al Mazra' *see* Al Mazra'ah
Al Mazra'ah 119 B6 *var.* Al Mazra',
Mazra'a. Al Karak, W Jordan
Almelo 86 E3 Overijssel,
E Netherlands
Almendra, Embalse de 92 C2
reservoir Castilla-León, NW Spain
Almendralejo 92 C4 Extremadura,
W Spain
Almere 86 C3 *var.* Almere-stad.
Flevoland, C Netherlands
Almere-stad *see* Almere
Almería 93 E5 Ar. Al-Mariyya; *anc.*
Unci, Lat. Portus Magnus.
Andalucía, S Spain
Al'met'yevsk 111 D5 Respublika
Tatarstan, W Russian Federation
Al Mīnā' *see* El Mîna
Al Minyā *see* El Minya
Almirante 53 E4 Bocas del Toro,
NW Panama
Al Mudawwarah 119 B8 Ma'ān,
SW Jordan
Al Mukallā 121 C6 *var.* Mukalla.
SE Yemen
Al Obayyid *see* El Obeid
Alofi 145 F4 *dependent territory
capital* (Niue) W Niue
Aloja 106 D3 Limbaži, N Latvia
Alónnisos 105 C5 *island* Vóreioi
Sporádes, Greece, Aegean Sea
Álora 92 D5 Andalucía, S Spain
Alor, Kepulauan 139 E5 *island group*
E Indonesia
Al Oued *see* El Oued
Alpen *see* Alps
Alpena 40 D2 Michigan, N USA
Alpes *see* Alps
Alpha Cordillera 155 B3 *var.* Alpha
Ridge. *Undersea feature* Arctic
Ocean
Alpha Ridge *see* Alpha Cordillera
Alphen *see* Alphen aan den Rijn
Alphen aan den Rijn 86 C3 *var.*
Alphen. Zuid-Holland,
C Netherlands
Alpi *see* Alps
Alpine 49 F4 Texas, SW USA
Alpi Transilvaniei *see* Carpaţii
Meridionali
Alps 102 C1 Fr. Alpes, Ger.
Alpen, *It.* Alpi. *Mountain range*
C Europe

Al Qaḍārif *see* Gedaref
Al Qāmishlī 118 E1 *var.* Kamishli,
Qamishly. Al Ḥasakah, NE Syria
Al Qaşrayn *see* Kasserine
Al Qayrawān *see* Kairouan
Al-Qsar *see* Ksar-el-Kebir
Al Qubayyāt *see* Qoubaïyât
Al Qunayţirah 119 B5 *var.*
El Kuneitra, El Quneitra,
Kuneitra, Qunaytra.
Al Qunayţirah, SW Syria
Al Quşayr 118 B4 *var.* El Quseir,
Quşayr, Fr. Kousseir. Ḥimş,
W Syria
Al Quwayrah 119 B8 *var.*
El Quweira. Ma'ān, SW Jordan
Alsace 90 E3 *cultural region*
NE France
Alsdorf 94 A4 Nordrhein-Westfalen,
W Germany
Alt *see* Olt
Alta 84 D2 Fin. Alattio. Finnmark,
N Norway
Altai *see* Altai Mountains
Altai Mountains 126 C2 *var.* Altai,
Chin. Altay Shan, Rus. Altay.
Mountain range Asia/Europe
Altamaha River 43 E3 *river* Georgia,
SE USA
Altamira 63 E2 Pará, NE Brazil
Altamura 97 E5 *anc.* Lupatia.
Puglia, SE Italy
Altar, Desierto de 50 A1 *var.*
Sonoran Desert. *Desert*
Mexico/USA *see also* Sonoran
Desert
Altay 126 C2 Chin. A-le-t'ai, Mong.
Sharasume; *prev.* Ch'eng-hua,
Chenghwa. Xinjiang Uygur
Zizhiqu, NW China
Altay *see* Altai Mountains
Altay 126 D2 Govĭ-Altay,
W Mongolia
Altay Shan *see* Altai Mountains
Altin Köprü 120 B3 *var.* Altun
Kupri. N Iraq
Altiplano 61 F4 *physical region*
W South America
Alton 40 B5 Illinois, N USA
Alton 40 B4 Missouri, C USA
Altoona 41 E4 Pennsylvania,
NE USA
Alto Paraná *see* Paraná
Altun Kupri *see* Altin Köprü
Altun Shan 126 C3 *var.* Altyn Tagh.
Mountain range NW China
Altus 49 F2 Oklahoma, C USA
Altyn Tagh *see* Altun Shan
Al Ubayyiḍ *see* El Obeid
Alūksne 106 D3 Ger. Marienburg.
Alūksne, NE Latvia
Al 'Ulā 120 A4 Al Madīnah,
NW Saudi Arabia
Al 'Umarī 119 C6 'Ammān,
E Jordan
Alupka 109 F5 Respublika Krym,
S Ukraine
Alushta 109 F5 Respublika Krym,
S Ukraine
Al 'Uwaynāt 71 F4 *var.* Al Awaynāt.
SW Libya
Alva 49 F1 Oklahoma, C USA
Alvarado 51 F4 Veracruz-Llave,
E Mexico
Alvin 49 H4 Texas, SW USA
Al Wajh 120 A4 Tabūk, NW Saudi
Arabia
Alwar 134 D3 Rājasthān, N India
Al Wari'ah 120 C4 Ash Sharqīyah,
N Saudi Arabia
Alykí 104 C4 *var.* Aliki. Thásos,
N Greece
Alytus 107 B5 Pol. Olita. Alytus,
S Lithuania
Alzette 87 D8 *river* S Luxembourg
Amadeus, Lake 147 D5 *seasonal lake*
Northern Territory, C Australia
Amadi 73 B5 Western Equatoria,
SW Sudan
Amadjuak Lake 37 G3 *lake* Baffin
Island, Nunavut, N Canada
Amakusa-nada 131 A7 *gulf* Kyūshū,
SW Japan
Åmål 85 B6 Västra Götaland,
S Sweden
Amami-guntō 130 A3 *island group*
SW Japan

Amami-ō-shima *130 A3 island*
S Japan
Amantea *97 D6* Calabria, SW Italy
Amapá *63 E1* Amapá, NE Brazil
Amara *see* Al 'Amārah
Amarapura *136 B3* Mandalay,
C Myanmar
Amarillo *49 E2* Texas, SW USA
Amay *87 C6* Liège, E Belgium
Amazon *63 E1 Sp.* Amazonas. *River*
Brazil/Peru
Amazon Basin *62 D2 basin* N South
America
Amazon, Mouths of the *63 F1 delta*
NE Brazil
Ambam *77 B5* Sud, S Cameroon
Ambanja *79 G2* Antsiraňana,
N Madagascar
Ambarchik *115 G2* Respublika
Sakha (Yakutiya), NE Russian
Federation
Ambato *60 B1* Tungurahua,
C Ecuador
Ambérieu-en-Bugey *91 D5* Ain,
E France
Amboasary *79 F4* Toliara,
S Madagascar
Ambon *139 F4 prev.* Amboina,
Amboyna. Pulau Ambon,
E Indonesia
Ambositra *79 G3* Fianarantsoa,
SE Madagascar
Ambrim *see* Ambrym
Ambriz *78 A1* Bengo, NW Angola
Ambrym *144 D4 var.* Ambrim.
Island C Vanuatu
Amchitka Island *36 A2 island*
Aleutian Islands, Alaska, USA
Amdo *126 C5* Xizang Zizhiqu,
W China
Ameland *86 D1 Fris.* It Amelân.
Island Waddeneilanden,
N Netherlands
America-Antarctica Ridge *67 C7*
undersea feature S Atlantic Ocean
American Falls Reservoir *46 E4*
reservoir Idaho, NW USA
American Samoa *145 E4 US*
unincorporated territory
W Polynesia
Amersfoort *86 D3* Utrecht,
C Netherlands
Ames *45 F3* Iowa, C USA
Amfilochía *105 A5 var.* Amfilokhía.
Dytikí Ellás, C Greece
Amfilokhía *see* Amfilochía
Amga *115 F3 river* NE Russian
Federation
Amherst *39 F4* Nova Scotia,
SE Canada
Amida *see* Diyarbakır
Amiens *90 C3 anc.* Ambianum,
Samarobriva. Somme, N France
Amíndaion *see* Amýntaio
Amindeo *see* Amýntaio
Amíndîvi Islands *132 A2 island*
group Lakshadweep, India,
N Indian Ocean
Amirante Islands *79 G1 var.*
Amirantes Group. *Island group*
C Seychelles
Amirantes Group *see* Amirante
Islands
Amistad Reservoir *49 F4 var.* Presa
de la Amistad. *Reservoir*
Mexico/USA
'Ammān *119 B6 var.* Amman; *anc.*
Philadelphia, *Bibl.* Rabbah
Ammon, Rabbath Ammon.
Country capital (Jordan) 'Ammān,
NW Jordan
Amman *see* 'Ammān
Ammassalik *82 D4 var.*
Angmagssalik. S Greenland
Ammóchostos *102 D5 var.*
Famagusta, Gazimağusa.
E Cyprus
Âmol *120 D2 var.* Amul.
Māzandarān, N Iran
Amorgós *105 D6 island* Kykládes,
Greece, Aegean Sea
Amorgós *105 D6* Amorgós,
Kykládes, Greece, Aegean Sea
Amos *38 D4* Quebec, SE Canada
Amourj *74 D3* Hodh ech Chargui,
SE Mauritania
Amoy *see* Xiamen

Ampato, Nevado *61 E4 mountain*
S Peru
Amposta *93 F2* Cataluña,
NE Spain
Amrāvati *134 D4 prev.* Amraoti.
Mahārāshtra, C India
Amritsar *134 D2* Punjab, N India
Amstelveen *86 C3* Noord-Holland,
C Netherlands
Amsterdam *86 C3 country capital*
(Netherlands) Noord-Holland,
C Netherlands
Amsterdam Island *141 C6 island*
NE French Southern and
Antarctic Territories
Am Timan *76 C3* Salamat,
SE Chad
Amu Darya *122 D2 Rus.*
Amudar'ya, *Taj.* Dar''yoi Amu,
Turkm. Amyderya, *Uzb.*
Amudaryo; *anc.* Oxus. *River*
C Asia
Amu-Dar'ya *123 E3* Lebapskiy
Velayat, NE Turkmenistan
Amul *see* Âmol
Amund Ringnes Island *37 F2 island*
Nunavut, N Canada
Amundsen Basin *see* Fram Basin
Amundsen Gulf *37 E2 gulf*
Northwest Territories, N Canada
Amundsen Plain *154 A4 undersea*
feature S Pacific Ocean
Amundsen-Scott *154 B3 US research*
station Antarctica
Amundsen Sea *154 A4 sea* S Pacific
Ocean
Amuntai *138 D4 prev.* Amoentai.
Borneo, C Indonesia
Amur *115 G4 Chin.* Heilong Jiang.
River China/Russian Federation
Amvrosiyivka *109 H3 Rus.*
Amvrosiyevka. Donets'ka Oblast',
SE Ukraine
Amýntaio *104 B4 var.* Amindeo;
prev. Amíndaion. Dytikí
Makedonía, N Greece
Anabar *115 E2 river* NE Russian
Federation
An Abhainn Mhór *see* Blackwater
Anaco *59 E2* Anzoátegui,
NE Venezuela
Anaconda *44 B2* Montana, NW USA
Anacortes *46 B1* Washington,
NW USA
Anadolu Dağları *see* Doğu
Karadeniz Dağları
Anadyr' *115 G1 river* NE Russian
Federation
Anadyr' *115 H1* Chukotskiy
Avtonomnyy Okrug, NE Russian
Federation
Anadyr, Gulf of *see* Anadyrskiy
Zaliv
Anadyrskiy Zaliv *115 H1 Eng.* Gulf
of Anadyr. *Gulf* NE Russian
Federation
Anáfi *105 D7 anc.* Anaphe. *Island*
Kykládes, Greece, Aegean Sea
'Ânah *see* 'Annah
Anaheim *46 E2* California, W USA
Anaiza *see* 'Unayzah
Analalava *79 G2* Mahajanga,
NW Madagascar
Anamur *116 C5* İçel, S Turkey
Anantapur *132 C2* Andhra Pradesh,
S India
Anápolis *63 F3* Goiás, C Brazil
Anār *120 D3* Kermān, C Iran
Anatolia *116 C4 plateau* C Turkey
Anatom *see* Aneityum
Añatuya *64 C3* Santiago del Estero,
N Argentina
An Bhearú *see* Barrow
Anchorage *36 C3* Alaska, USA
Ancona *96 C3* Marche, C Italy
Ancud *65 B6 prev.* San Carlos de
Ancud. Los Lagos, S Chile
Ândalsnes *85 A5* Møre og Romsdal,
S Norway
Andalucía *92 D4 cultural region*
S Spain
Andalusia *42 C3* Alabama, S USA
Andaman Islands *124 B4 island*
group India, NE Indian Ocean
Andaman Sea *124 C4 sea* NE Indian
Ocean
Andenne *87 C6* Namur, SE Belgium

Anderlues *87 B7* Hainaut,
S Belgium
Anderson *40 C4* Indiana, N USA
Andes *64 B3 mountain range*
W South America
Andhra Pradesh *135 E5 state*
E India
Andijon *123 F2 Rus.* Andizhan.
Andijon Wiloyati, E Uzbekistan
Andikíthira *see* Antikýthira
Andipaxi *see* Antípaxoi
Andípsara *see* Antípsara
Ándissa *see* Ántissa
Andkhvoy *122 D3* Fāryāb,
N Afghanistan
Andorra *91 A7 Cat.* Valls
d'Andorra, *Fr.* Vallée d'Andorre.
Country SW Europe

Andorra 91

Official name Principality of
Andorra
Formation 1278
Capital Andorra la Vella
Population 66,800 / 370 people
per sq mile (143 people per sq km)
Total area 181 sq miles (468 sq km)
Languages Catalan, Spanish,
French, Portuguese
Religions Roman Catholic 94%,
other 6%
Ethnic mix Spanish 46%, Andorrian
28%, other 18%, French 8%
Government Parliamentary
democracy
Currency Euro (French franc and
Spanish peseta until 2002)
Literacy rate 99%
Calorie consumption not available

Andorra *see* Andorra la Vella
Andorra la Vella *91 A8 var.*
Andorra, *Fr.* Andorre la Vielle, *Sp.*
Andorra la Vieja. *Country capital*
(Andorra) C Andorra
Andorra la Vieja *see* Andorra la
Vella
Andorre la Vielle *see* Andorra la
Vella
Andover *89 D7* S England, UK
Andøya *84 C2 island* C Norway
Andreanof Islands *36 A3 island*
group Aleutian Islands, Alaska,
USA
Andrews *49 E3* Texas, SW USA
Andrew Tablemount *140 A4 var.*
Gora Andryu. *Undersea feature*
W Indian Ocean
Andria *97 D5* Puglia, SE Italy
An Droichead Nua *see* Newbridge
Ándros *105 C6 island* Kykládes,
Greece, Aegean Sea
Ándros *105 D6* Ándros, Kykládes,
Greece, Aegean Sea
Andros Island *54 B2 island*
NW Bahamas
Andros Town *54 C1* Andros Island,
NW Bahamas
Aneityum *144 D5 var.* Anatom; *prev.*
Kéamu. *Island* S Vanuatu
Ánewetak *see* Enewetak Atoll
Angara *115 E4 river* C Russian
Federation
Angarsk *115 E4* Irkutskaya Oblast',
S Russian Federation
Ånge *85 C5* Västernorrland,
C Sweden
Ángel de la Guarda, Isla *50 B2*
island NW Mexico
Angeles *139 E1 off.* Angeles City.
Luzon, N Philippines
Angel Falls *see* Ángel, Salto
Ángel, Salto *59 E3 Eng.* Angel Falls.
Waterfall E Venezuela
Ångermanälven *84 C4 river*
N Sweden
Angermünde *94 D3* Brandenburg,
NE Germany
Angers *90 B4 anc.* Juliomagus.
Maine-et-Loire, NW France
Anglesey *89 C5 island*
NW Wales, UK
Anglet *91 A6* Pyrénées-Atlantiques,
SW France
Angleton *49 H4* Texas, SW USA

Angmagssalik *see* Ammassalik
Ang Nam Ngum *136 C4 lake* C Laos
Angola *78 B2 prev.* People's
Republic of Angola, Portuguese
West Africa. *Country* SW Africa

Angola 78

Official name Republic of Angola
Formation 1975
Capital Luanda
Population 13.5 million /28 people
per sq mile (11 people per sq km)
Total area 481,351 sq miles
(1,246,700 sq km)
Languages Portuguese, Umbundu,
Kimbundu, Kikongo
Religions Roman Catholic 50%,
other 30%, Protestant 20%
Ethnic mix Ovimbundu 37%, other
25%, Kimbundu 25%, Bakongo 13%
Government Presidential regime
Currency Readjusted kwanza =
100 lwei
Literacy rate 40%
Calorie consumption 1,903
kilocalories

Angola Basin *69 B5 undersea feature*
E Atlantic Ocean
Angostura, Presa de la *51 G5*
reservoir SE Mexico
Angoulême *91 B5 anc.* Iculisma.
Charente, W France
Angoumois *91 B5 cultural region*
W France
Angren *123 F2* Toshkent Wiloyati,
E Uzbekistan
Anguilla *55 G3 UK dependent*
territory E West Indies
Anguilla Cays *54 B2 islets*
SW Bahamas
Anhui *128 C5 var.* Anhui Sheng,
Anhwei, Wan. Admin. region
province E China
Anhui Sheng *see* Anhui
Anhwei *see* Anhui
Anina *108 A4 Ger.* Steierdorf, *Hung.*
Stájerlakanina; *prev.* Ştaierdorf-
Anina, Steierdorf-Anina,
Steyerlak-Anina. Caraş-Severin,
SW Romania
Anjou *90 B4 cultural region*
NW France
Anjouan *79 F2 var.* Nzwani,
Johanna Island. *Island*
SE Comoros
Ankara *116 C3 prev.* Angora, *anc.*
Ancyra. *Country capital* (Turkey)
Ankara, C Turkey
Ankeny *45 F3* Iowa, C USA
Anklam *94 D2* Mecklenburg-
Vorpommern, NE Germany
Ankober *see* Anbā Longfort
An Longfort *see* Longford
An Mhuir Cheilteach *see* Celtic Sea
Annaba *71 E1 prev.* Bône. NE Algeria
An Nafūd *120 B4 desert* NW Saudi
Arabia
'Annah *120 B3 var.* 'Ânah. NW Iraq
An Najaf *120 B3 var.* Najaf. S Iraq
Annamitique, Chaîne *136 D4*
mountain range C Laos
Annapolis *41 F4 state capital*
Maryland, NE USA
Annapurna *135 E3 mountain*
C Nepal
An Nāqūrah *see* En Nâqoûra
Ann Arbor *40 C3* Michigan, N USA
An Nāşiriyah *120 C3 var.* Nasiriya.
SE Iraq
Annecy *91 D5 anc.* Anneciacum.
Haute-Savoie, E France
An Nīl al Azraq *see* Blue Nile
Anniston *42 D2* Alabama, S USA
Annotto Bay *54 B4* C Jamaica
An Ómaigh *see* Omagh
Anqing *128 D5* Anhui, E China
Anse La Raye *55 F1* NW Saint
Lucia
Anshun *128 B6* Guizhou, S China
Ansongo *75 E3* Gao, E Mali
An Srath Bán *see* Strabane
Antakya *116 D4 anc.* Antioch,
Antiochia. Hatay, S Turkey

Antalaha 79 G2 Antsirañana, NE Madagascar
Antalya 116 B4 prev. Adalia, anc. Attaleia, Bibl. Attalia. Antalya, SW Turkey
Antalya, Gulf of see Antalya Körfezi
Antalya Körfezi 116 B4 var. Gulf of Adalia, Eng. Gulf of Antalya. Gulf SW Turkey
Antananarivo 79 G3 prev. Tananarive. Country capital (Madagascar) Antananarivo, C Madagascar
Antarctica 154 B3 continent
Antarctic Peninsula 154 A2 peninsula Antarctica
Antep see Gaziantep
Antequera 92 D5 anc. Anticaria, Antiquaria. Andalucía, S Spain
Antequera see Oaxaca
Antibes 91 D6 anc. Antipolis. Alpes-Maritimes, SE France
Anticosti, Île d' 39 F3 Eng. Anticosti Island. Island Quebec, E Canada
Antigua 55 G3 island S Antigua and Barbuda, Leeward Islands
Antigua and Barbuda 55 G3 country E West Indies

Antigua and Barbuda 55

Official name Antigua and Barbuda
Formation 1981
Capital St. John's
Population 66,400 / 389 people per sq mile (150 people per sq km)
Total area 171 sq miles (442 sq km)
Languages English, English patois
Religions Anglican 45%, other Protestant 42%, Roman Catholic 10%, Rastafarian 1%, other 2%
Ethnic mix Black African 95%, other 5%
Government Parliamentary democracy
Currency Eastern Caribbean dollar = 100 cents
Literacy rate 95%
Calorie consumption 2,396 kilocalories

Antikýthira 105 B7 var. Andikíthira. Island S Greece
Anti-Lebanon 118 B4 var. Jebel esh Sharqi, Ar. Al Jabal ash Sharqī, Fr. Anti-Liban. Mountain range Lebanon/Syria
Anti-Liban see Anti-Lebanon
Antípaxoi 105 A5 var. Andipaxi. Island Iónioi Nísoi, Greece, C Mediterranean Sea
Antipodes Islands 142 D5 island group, S NZ
Antípsara 105 C6 var. Andípsara. Island E Greece
Ántissa 105 D5 var. Ándissa. Lésvos, E Greece
An tIúr see Newry
Antofagasta 64 B2 Antofagasta, N Chile
Antony 90 E2 Hauts-de-Seine, N France
Antserana see Antsirañana
An tSionainn see Shannon
Antsirañana 79 G2 var. Antserana; prev. Antsirane, Diégo-Suarez. Antsirañana, N Madagascar
Antsirane see Antsirañana
Antsohihy 79 G2 Mahajanga, NW Madagascar
An-tung see Dandong
Antwerp see Antwerpen
Antwerpen 87 C5 Eng. Antwerp, Fr. Anvers. Antwerpen, N Belgium
Anuradhapura 132 D3 North Central Province, C Sri Lanka
Anyang 128 C3 Henan, C China
A'nyêmaqên Shan 126 D4 mountain range C China
Anzio 97 C5 Lazio, C Italy
Aomen see Macao

Aomori 130 D3 Aomori, Honshū, C Japan
Aóos see Vjosës, Lumi i
Aosta 96 A1 anc. Augusta Praetoria. Valle d'Aosta, NW Italy
Ao Thai see Thailand, Gulf of
Aoukâr 74 D3 var. Aouker. Plateau C Mauritania
Aouk, Bahr 76 C4 river Central African Republic/Chad
Aouker see Aoukâr
Aozou 76 C1 Borkou-Ennedi-Tibesti, N Chad
Apalachee Bay 42 D3 bay Florida, SE USA
Apalachicola River 42 D3 river Florida, SE USA
Apamama see Abemama
Apaporis, Río 58 C4 river Brazil/Colombia
Apatity 110 C2 Murmanskaya Oblast', NW Russian Federation
Ape 106 D3 Alūksne, NE Latvia
Apeldoorn 86 D3 Gelderland, E Netherlands
Apennines see Appennino
Āpia 145 F4 country capital (Samoa) Upolu, SE Samoa
Apoera 59 G3 Sipaliwini, NW Suriname
Apostle Islands 40 B1 island group Wisconsin, N USA
Appalachian Mountains 35 D5 mountain range E USA
Appennino 96 E2 Eng. Apennines. Mountain range Italy/San Marino
Appingedam 86 E1 Groningen, NE Netherlands
Appleton 40 B2 Wisconsin, N USA
Apure, Río 58 C2 river W Venezuela
Apurímac, Río 60 D3 river S Peru
Apuseni, Munţii 108 A4 mountain range W Romania
'Aqaba see Al 'Aqabah
Aqaba, Gulf of 120 A4 var. Gulf of Elat, Ar. Khalīj al 'Aqabah; anc. Sinus Aelaniticus. Gulf NE Red Sea
Āqchah 123 E3 var. Āqcheh. Jowzjān, N Afghanistan
Āqcheh see Āqchah
Aquae Augustae see Dax
Aquae Sextiae see Aix-en-Provence
Aquae Tarbelicae see Dax
Aquidauana 63 E4 Mato Grosso do Sul, S Brazil
Aquila see L'Aquila
Aquila degli Abruzzo see L'Aquila
Aquitaine 91 B6 cultural region SW France
'Arabah, Wādī al 135 B7 Heb. Ha'Arava. Dry watercourse Israel/Jordan
Arabian Basin 124 A4 undersea feature N Arabian Sea
Arabian Desert see Eastern Desert
Arabian Peninsula 121 B5 peninsula SW Asia
Arabian Sea 124 A3 sea NW Indian Ocean
Aracaju 63 G3 state capital Sergipe, E Brazil
Araçuaí 63 F3 Minas Gerais, SE Brazil
Arad 108 A4 Arad, W Romania
'Arad 119 B7 Southern, S Israel
Arafura Sea 142 A3 Ind. Laut Arafuru. Sea W Pacific Ocean
Aragón 93 E2 cultural region E Spain
Araguaia, Río 63 E3 var. Araguaya. River C Brazil
Araguari 63 F3 Minas Gerais, SE Brazil
Araguaya see Araguaia, Río
Arāk 120 C3 prev. Sultānābād. Markazī, W Iran
Arakan Yoma 136 A3 mountain range W Myanmar
Aral Sea 122 C1 Kaz. Aral Tengizi, Rus. Aral'skoye More, Uzb. Orol Dengizi. Inland sea Kazakhstan/Uzbekistan
Aral'sk 114 B4 Kaz. Aral. Kyzylorda, SW Kazakhstan
Aranda de Duero 92 D2 Castilla-León, N Spain

Arandelovac 100 D4 prev. Arandjelovac. Serbia, C Serbia and Montenegro (Yugo.)
Aranjuez 92 D3 anc. Ara Jovis. Madrid, C Spain
Araouane 75 E2 Tombouctou, N Mali
'Ar'ar 120 B3 Al Ḥudūd ash Shamālīyah, NW Saudi Arabia
Aras 117 G3 Arm. Arak's, Az. Araz Nehri, Per. Rūd-e Aras, Rus. Araks; prev. Araxes. River SW Asia
Arauca 58 C2 Arauca, NE Colombia
Arauca, Río 58 C2 river Colombia/Venezuela
Arbela see Arbīl
Arbīl 120 B2 var. Erbil, Irbīl, Kurd. Hawlēr; anc. Arbela. N Iraq
Arbroath 88 D3 anc. Aberbrothock. E Scotland, UK
Arbyzynka 109 E3 Rus. Arbuzinka. Mykolayivs'ka Oblast', S Ukraine
Arcachon 91 B5 Gironde, SW France
Arcata 46 A4 California, W USA
Archangel see Arkhangel'sk
Archangel Bay see Chëshskaya Guba
Archidona 92 D5 Andalucía, S Spain
Archipel des Australes see Australes, Îles
Archipel des Tuamotu see Tuamotu, Îles
Archipel de Tahiti see Société, Archipel de la
Arco 96 C2 Trentino-Alto Adige, N Italy
Arctic-Mid Oceanic Ridge see Nansen Cordillera
Arctic Ocean 172 B3 ocean
Arda 104 C3 var. Ardhas, Gk. Ardas. River Bulgaria/Greece see also Ardas
Arda see Ardas
Ardabīl 120 C2 var. Ardebil. Ardabīl, NW Iran
Ardakān 120 D3 Yazd, C Iran
Ardas 104 D3 var. Ardhas, Bul. Arda. River Bulgaria/Greece see also Arda
Ardas see Arda
Arḍ aş Şawwān 119 C7 var. Ardh es Suwwān. Plain S Jordan
Ardebil see Ardabīl
Ardèche 91 C5 cultural region E France
Ardennes 87 C8 plateau W Europe
Ardhas see Ardas
Ardh es Suwwān see Arḍ aş Şawwān
Ardino 104 D3 Kŭrdzhali, S Bulgaria
Ard Mhacha see Armagh
Ardmore 49 G2 Oklahoma, C USA
Arelas see Arles
Arelate see Arles
Arendal 85 A6 Aust-Agder, S Norway
Arenys de Mar 93 G2 Cataluña, NE Spain
Areópoli 105 B7 prev. Areópolis. Pelopónnisos, S Greece
Arequipa 61 E4 Arequipa, SE Peru
Arezzo 96 C3 anc. Arretium. Toscana, C Italy
Argalasti 105 C5 Thessalía, C Greece
Argenteuil 90 D1 Val-d'Oise, N France
Argentina 65 B5 Country S South America

Argentina 65

Official name Republic of Argentina
Formation 1816
Capital Buenos Aires
Population 37.5 million / 35 people per sq mile (14 people per sq km)
Total area 1,068,296 sq miles (2,766,890 sq km)
Languages Spanish, Italian, Amerindian languages
Religions Roman Catholic 90%, Jewish 2%, Protestant 2%, other 6%

Argentina (continued)

Ethnic mix Indo European 85%, Mestizo 14%, Amerindian 1%
Government Presidential democracy
Currency Peso = 100 centavos
Literacy rate 96.8%
Calorie consumption 3,181 kilocalories

Argentina Basin see Argentine Basin
Argentine Basin 57 C7 var. Argentina Basin. Undersea feature SW Atlantic Ocean
Argentine Rise see Falkland Plateau
Arghandāb, Daryā-ye 123 E5 river SE Afghanistan
Argirocastro see Gjirokastër
Argo 72 B3 Northern, N Sudan
Argo Fracture Zone 141 C5 tectonic feature C Indian Ocean
Árgos 105 B6 Pelopónnisos, S Greece
Argostóli 105 A5 var. Argostólion. Kefallinía, Iónioi Nísoi, Greece, C Mediterranean Sea
Argostólion see Argostóli
Argun 125 E1 Chin. Ergun He, Rus. Argun'. River China/Russian Federation
Argyrokastron see Gjirokastër
Århus 85 B7 var. Aarhus. Århus, C Denmark
Aria see Herāt
Ari Atoll 132 A4 atoll C Maldives
Arica 64 B1 hist. San Marcos de Arica. Tarapacá, N Chile
Aridaía 104 B3 var. Aridea, Aridhaía. Dytikí Makedonía, N Greece
Aridea see Aridaía
Aridhaía see Aridaía
Arīḥā 118 B3 var. Arīḥā. Idlib, W Syria
Arīḥā see Jericho
Arinsal 91 A7 NW Andorra
Arizona 42 A4 off. State of Arizona; also known as Copper State, Grand Canyon State. Admin. region state SW USA
Arkansas 42 A1 off. State of Arkansas; also known as The Land of Opportunity. State S USA
Arkansas City 45 F5 Kansas, C USA
Arkansas River 49 G1 river C USA
Arkhangel'sk 114 B2 Eng. Archangel. Arkhangel'skaya Oblast', NW Russian Federation
Arkoi 105 E6 island Dodekánisos, Greece, Aegean Sea
Arles 91 D6 var. Arles-sur-Rhône; anc. Arelas, Arelate. Bouches-du-Rhône, SE France
Arles-sur-Rhône see Arles
Arlington 49 G2 Texas, SW USA
Arlington 41 E4 Virginia, NE USA
Arlon 87 D8 Dut. Aarlen, Ger. Arel; Lat. Orolaunum. Luxembourg, SE Belgium
Armagh 89 B5 Ir. Ard Mhacha. S Northern Ireland, UK
Armagnac 91 B6 cultural region S France
Armenia 117 F3 var. Ajastan, Arm. Hayastani Hanrapetut'yun; prev. Armenian Soviet Socialist Republic. Country SW Asia

Armenia 117

Official name Republic of Armenia
Formation 1991
Capital Yerevan
Population 3.8 million / 330 people per sq mile (128 people per sq km)
Total area 11,506 sq miles (29,800 sq km)
Languages Armenian, Russian
Religions The Armenian Apostolic Church 94%, other 6%

Armenia (continued)

Ethnic mix Armenian 93%,
Azeri 3%, Russian 2%, other 2%
Government Multiparty republic
Currency Dram = 100 louma
Literacy rate 98.4%
Calorie consumption 1,944
kilocalories

Armenia 58 B3 Quindío,
W Colombia
Armidale 149 D6 New South Wales,
SE Australia
Armstrong 38 B3 Ontario, S Canada
Armyans'k 109 F4 Rus. Armyansk.
Respublika Krym, S Ukraine
Arnaía 104 C4 var. Arnea. Kentrikí
Makedonía, N Greece
Arnaud 82 A3 river Quebec,
E Canada
Arnea see Arnaía
Arnedo 93 E2 La Rioja, N Spain
Arnhem 86 D4 Gelderland,
SE Netherlands
Arnhem Land 148 A2 physical region
Northern Territory, N Australia
Arno 96 B3 river C Italy
Arnold 45 G4 Missouri, C USA
Arorae 145 E3 atoll Tungaru,
W Kiribati
Arquipélago da Madeira see
Madeira
Arquipélago dos Açores see Azores
Ar Rahad see Er Rahad
Ar Ramādī 120 B3 var. Ramadi,
Rumadiya. SW Iraq
Ar Rāmī 118 C4 Ḩimş, C Syria
Ar Ramthā 119 B5 var. Ramtha.
Irbid, N Jordan
Arran, Isle of 88 C4 island
SW Scotland, UK
Ar Raqqah 118 C2 var. Rakka; anc.
Nicephorium. Ar Raqqah, N Syria
Arras 90 C2 anc. Nemetocenna. Pas-
de-Calais, N France
Ar Rawḍatayn 120 C4 var.
Raudhatain. N Kuwait
Arriaga 51 G5 Chiapas, SE Mexico
Ar Riyāḍ 121 C5 Eng. Riyadh.
Country capital (Saudi Arabia) Ar
Riyāḍ, C Saudi Arabia
Ar Rub 'al Khālī 121 C6 Eng.
Empty Quarter, Great Sandy
Desert. Desert SW Asia
Ar Rustāq 121 E5 var. Rostak,
Rustaq. N Oman
Ar Ruţbah 120 B3 var. Rutba.
SW Iraq
Árta 105 A5 anc. Ambracia. Ípeiros,
W Greece
Artashat 117 F3 S Armenia
Artemisa 54 B2 La Habana, W Cuba
Artesia 48 D3 New Mexico, SW USA
Arthur's Pass 151 C6 pass South
Island, NZ
Artigas 64 D3 prev. San Eugenio,
San Eugenio del Cuareim.
Artigas, N Uruguay
Art'ik 117 F2 W Armenia
Artois 90 C2 cultural region
N France
Artsyz 108 D4 Rus. Artsiz. Odes'ka
Oblast', SW Ukraine
Artvin 117 F2 Artvin, NE Turkey
Arua 73 B6 NW Uganda
Aruángua see Luangwa
Aruba 58 C1 var. Oruba. Dutch
autonomous region S West Indies
Aru, Kepulauan 139 G4 Eng. Aru
Islands; prev. Aroe Islands. Island
group E Indonesia
Arunáchal Pradesh 135 G3 cultural
region NE India
Arusha 73 C7 Arusha, N Tanzania
Arviat 37 G4 prev. Eskimo Point.
Nunavut, C Canada
Arvidsjaur 84 C4 Norrbotten,
N Sweden
Arys' 114 B5 Kaz. Arys. Yuzhnyy
Kazakhstan, S Kazakhstan
Asadābād 123 F4 var. Asadabad;
prev. Chaghasarāy. Kunar,
E Afghanistan
Asad, Buḩayrat al 134 C2 Eng. Lake
Assad. Lake N Syria

Asahi-dake 130 D2 mountain
Hokkaidō, N Japan
Asahikawa 130 D2 Hokkaidō,
N Japan
Asamankese 75 E5 SE Ghana
Āsānsol 135 F4 West Bengal,
NE India
Asben see Aïr, Massif de l'
Ascension Fracture Zone 69 A5
tectonic feature C Atlantic Ocean
Ascension Island 85 A5 dependency
of St. Helena C Atlantic Ocean
Ascoli Piceno 96 C4 anc. Asculum
Picenum. Marche, C Italy
Aseb 72 D4 var. Assab, Amh. Āseb.
SE Eritrea
Ashara see Al 'Ashārah
Ashburton 151 C6 Canterbury,
South Island, NZ
Ashburton River 146 A4 river
Western Australia
Ashdod 119 A6 anc. Azotus, Lat.
Azotus. Central, W Israel
Asheville 43 E1 North Carolina,
SE USA
Ashgabat 122 C3 prev. Ashkhabad,
Poltoratsk. Country capital
(Turkmenistan) Akhalskiy
Velayat, C Turkmenistan
Ashkelon see Ashqelon
Ashland 46 B4 Oregon, NW USA
Ashland 40 B1 Wisconsin, N USA
Ashmore and Cartier Islands 142
A3 Australian external territory
E Indian Ocean
Ashmyany 107 C5 Rus. Oshmyany.
Hrodzyenskaya Voblasts',
W Belarus
Ashqelon 119 A6 var. Ashkelon.
Southern, C Israel
Ash Shaddādah 118 D2 var. Ash
Shaddādah, Jisr ash Shadadi,
Shaddādī, Shedadi, Tell Shedadi.
Al Ḩasakah, NE Syria
Ash Shaddādah see Ash Shaddādah
Ash Shām see Dimashq
Ash Sharāh 119 B7 var. Esh Sharā.
Mountain range W Jordan
Ash Shāriqah 120 D4 Eng. Sharjah.
Ash Shāriqah, NE UAE
Ash Shawbak 119 B7 Ma'ān,
W Jordan
Ash Shiḩr 121 C6 SE Yemen
Asia 25 C2 continent
Asinara, Isola 96 A4 island W Italy
Asipovichy 107 D6 Rus. Osipovichi.
Mahilyowskaya Voblasts',
C Belarus
Aşkale 117 E3 Erzurum, NE Turkey
Askersund 85 C6 Örebro, C Sweden
Asmara 72 C4 Amh. Āsmera.
Country capital (Eritrea) C Eritrea
Assab see Aseb
As Sabkhah 118 D2 var. Sabkha. Ar
Raqqah, NE Syria
Aş Şafāwī 119 C6 Al Mafraq,
N Jordan
Aş Şaḩrā' al Gharbīyah see Sahara
el Gharbīya
Aş Şaḩrā' al Lībīyah see Libyan
Desert
Aş Şaḩrā' ash Sharqīyah see
Eastern Desert
As Salamīyah see Salamīyah
As Salţ 119 B6 var. Salt. Al Balqā',
NW Jordan
Assamaka see Assamakka
Assamakka 75 F2 var. Assamaka.
Agadez, NW Niger
As Samāwah 120 B3 var. Samawa.
S Iraq
Assen 86 E2 Drenthe,
NE Netherlands
Assenede 87 B5 Oost-Vlaanderen,
NW Belgium
Assiout see Asyūţ
Assiut see Asyūţ
Assouan see Aswān
Assu see Açu
Assuan see Aswān
As Sukhnah 118 C3 var. Sukhne, Fr.
Soukhné. Ḩimş, C Syria
As Sulaymānīyah 120 C3 var.
Sulaimaniya, Kurd. Slēmānī.
NE Iraq
As Sulayyil 121 B5 Ar Riyāḍ,
S Saudi Arabia

Aş Şuwār 118 D2 var. Şuwār. Dayr
az Zawr, E Syria
As Suwaydā' 119 B5 var.
El Suweida, Es Suweida,
Suweida, Fr. Soueida. As
Suwaydā', SW Syria
Astacus see Izmit
Astana 114 C4 prev. Akmola,
Akmolinsk, Tselinograd, Kaz.
Aqmola. country capital
(Kazakhstan) Akmola, N
Kazakhstan
Astarabad see Gorgān
Asterābād see Gorgān
Asti 96 A2 anc. Asta Colonia, Asta
Pompeia, Hasta Colonia, Hasta
Pompeia. Piemonte, NW Italy
Astipálaia see Astypálaia
Astorga 92 C1 anc. Asturica
Augusta. Castilla-León, N Spain
Astrabad see Gorgān
Astrakhan' 111 C7 Astrakhanskaya
Oblast', SW Russian Federation
Asturias 92 C1 cultural region
NW Spain
Astypálaia 105 D7 var. Astipálaia,
It. Stampalia. Island Kykládes,
Greece, Aegean Sea
Asunción 64 D2 country capital
(Paraguay) Central, S Paraguay
Aswān 72 B2 var. Assouan, Assuan;
anc. Syene. SE Egypt
Asyūţ 72 B2 var. Assiout, Assiut,
Siut; anc. Lycopolis. C Egypt
Atacama Desert see Atacama,
Desierto de
Atacama, Desierto de 64 B2 Eng.
Atacama Desert. Desert N Chile
Atafu Atoll 145 E3 island
NW Tokelau
Aṭār 74 C2 Adrar, W Mauritania
Atas Bogd 126 D3 mountain
SW Mongolia
Atascadero 47 B7 California,
W USA
Atatürk Barajı 117 E4 reservoir
S Turkey
Atbara 72 C3 var. 'Aṭbārah. River
Nile, NE Sudan
'Aṭbārah see Atbara
Atbasar 114 C4 Akmola,
N Kazakhstan
Atchison 45 F4 Kansas, C USA
Ath 87 B6 var. Aat. Hainaut,
SW Belgium
Athabasca 37 E5 var. Athabaska.
River Alberta, SW Canada
Athabasca 37 E5 var. Athabaska.
SW Canada
Athabasca, Lake 37 F4 lake
Alberta/Saskatchewan,
SW Canada
Athabaska see Athabasca
Athens see Athína
Athens 43 E2 Georgia, SE USA
Athens 40 D4 Ohio, N USA
Athens 49 G3 Texas, SW USA
Atherton 148 D3 Queensland,
NE Australia
Athína 105 C6 Eng. Athens; prev.
Athínai, anc. Athenae. Country
capital (Greece) Attikí, C Greece
Athlone 89 B5 Ir. Baile Átha Luain.
C Ireland
Ath Thawrah see Madīnat ath
Thawrah
Ati 76 C3 Batha, C Chad
Atikokan 38 B4 Ontario, S Canada
Atka 36 A3 Atka Island, Alaska,
USA
Atka 115 G3 Magadanskaya Oblast',
E Russian Federation
Atlanta 42 D2 state capital Georgia,
SE USA
Atlanta 49 H2 Texas, SW USA
Atlantic City 41 F4 New Jersey,
NE USA
Atlantic-Indian Basin 67 D7
undersea feature SW Indian Ocean
Atlantic-Indian Ridge 69 B8
undersea feature
SW Indian Ocean
Atlantic Ocean 66 B4 ocean
Atlas Mountains 70 C2 mountain
range NW Africa
Atlasovo 115 H3 Kamchatskaya
Oblast', E Russian Federation

Atlas Saharien 70 D2 var. Saharan
Atlas. Mountain range
Algeria/Morocco
Atlas Tellien 102 C3 Eng. Tell Atlas.
Mountain range N Algeria
Atlin 36 D4 British Columbia,
W Canada
Aţ Ţafīlah 119 B7 var. Et Tafila,
Tafila. Aţ Ţafīlah, W Jordan
Aţ Ţā'if 121 B5 Makkah, W Saudi
Arabia
At Tall al Abyaḍ 118 C2 var. Tall
al Abyaḍ, Tell Abyad, Fr. Tell
Abiad. Ar Raqqah, N Syria
Aţ Ţanf 118 D4 Ḩimş, S Syria
Attapu see Samakhixai
Attawapiskat 38 C3 river Ontario,
S Canada
Attawapiskat 38 C3 Ontario,
C Canada
At Tibnī 118 D2 var. Tibnī. Dayr az
Zawr, NE Syria
Attopeu see Samakhixai
Attu Island 36 A2 island Aleutian
Islands, Alaska, USA
Atyrau 114 B4 prev. Gur'yev.
Atyrau, W Kazakhstan
Aubagne 91 D6 anc. Albania.
Bouches-du-Rhône, SE France
Aubange 87 D8 Luxembourg,
SE Belgium
Aubervilliers 90 E1 Seine-St-Denis,
N France
Auburn 46 B2 Washington, NW USA
Auch 91 B6 Lat. Augusta Auscorum,
Elimberrum. Gers, S France
Auckland 150 D2 Auckland, North
Island, NZ
Auckland Islands 142 C5 island
group S NZ
Audincourt 90 E4 Doubs, E France
Audru 106 D2 Ger. Audern.
Pärnumaa, SW Estonia
Augathella 149 D5 Queensland,
E Australia
Augsburg 95 C6 Fr. Augsbourg; anc.
Augusta Vindelicorum. Bayern,
S Germany
Augusta 41 G2 state capital Maine,
NE USA
Augusta 43 E2 Georgia, SE USA
Augusta 147 A7 Western Australia
Augustów 98 E2 Rus. Avgustov.
Podlaskie, NE Poland
'Aujā et Tahtā see. Khirbet el 'Aujā
et Tahtā
Aulie Ata/Auliye-Ata see Taraz
Auob 78 B4 var. Oup. River
Namibia/South Africa
Aurangābād 134 D5 Mahārāshtra,
C India
Auray 90 A3 Morbihan, NW France
Aurès, Massif de l' 102 C4 mountain
range NE Algeria
Aurillac 91 C5 Cantal, C France
Aurora 44 D4 Colorado, C USA
Aurora 40 B3 Illinois, N USA
Aurora 45 G5 Missouri, C USA
Aurora 59 F2 NW Guyana
Aus 78 B4 Karas, SW Namibia
Ausa see Vic
Austin 49 G3 state capital Texas,
S USA
Austin 45 G3 Minnesota, N USA
Australes, Îles 143 F4 var. Archipel
des Australes, Îles Tubuai, Tubuai
Islands, Eng. Austral Islands.
Island group SW French Polynesia
Austral Fracture Zone 143 H4
tectonic feature S Pacific Ocean
Australia 142 A4 Country

Australia 142

Official name Commonwealth
of Australia
Formation 1901
Capital Canberra
Population 19.3 million / 7 people
per sq mile (3 people per sq km)
Total area 2,967,893 sq miles
(7,686,893 sq km)
Languages English, Vietnamese,
Greek, Arabic, Italian, Aboriginal
languages
Religions Christian 64%, other 34%

Australia (continued)

Ethnic mix European 95%, Asian 4%, Aboriginal and other 1%
Government Parliamentary democracy
Currency Australian dollar = 100 cents
Literacy rate 99%
Calorie consumption 3,176 kilocalories

Australian Alps 149 C7 *mountain range* SE Australia
Australian Capital Territory 149 D7 *prev.* Federal Capital Territory. *Territory* SE Australia
Austral Islands *see* Australes, Îles
Austria 95 D7 *Ger.* Österreich. *Country* C Europe

Austria 95

Official name Republic of Austria
Formation 1918
Capital Vienna
Population 8.1 million / 250 people per sq mile (97 people per sq km)
Total area 32,378 sq miles (83,858 sq km)
Languages German, Croatian, Slovenian
Religions Roman Catholic 78%, non-religious 9%, Protestant 5%, other (including Muslim and Jewish) 8%
Ethnic mix German 93%, Croat, Slovene, Hungarian 6%, other 1%
Government Parliamentary democracy
Currency Euro (Austrian schilling until 2002)
Literacy rate 99%
Calorie consumption 3,757 kilocalories

Auvergne 91 C5 *cultural region* C France
Auxerre 90 C4 *anc.* Autesiodorum, Autissiodorum. Yonne, C France
Avarua 145 G5 *dependent territory capital* (Cook Islands) Rarotonga, S Cook Islands
Ávdira 104 C3 Anatolikí Makedonía kai Thráki, NE Greece
Aveiro 92 B2 *anc.* Talabriga. Aveiro, W Portugal
Avela *see* Ávila
Avellino 97 D5 *anc.* Abellinum. Campania, S Italy
Avesta 85 C6 Kopparberg, C Sweden
Aveyron 91 C6 *river* S France
Avezzano 96 C4 Abruzzo, C Italy
Aviemore 88 C3 N Scotland, UK
Avignon 91 D6 *anc.* Avenio. Vaucluse, SE France
Avila *see* Ávila
Ávila 92 D3 *var.* Avila; *anc.* Abela, Abula, Abyla, Avela. Castilla-León, C Spain
Avilés 92 C1 Asturias, NW Spain
Avranches 90 B3 Manche, N France
Awaji-shima 131 C6 *island* SW Japan
Āwash 73 D5 *var.* Hawash. *River* C Ethiopia
Awbārī 71 F3 SW Libya
Ax *see* Dax
Axel 87 B5 Zeeland, SW Netherlands
Axel Heiberg Island 37 E1 *var.* Axel Heiburg. *Island* Nunavut, N Canada
Axel Heiburg *see* Axel Heiberg Island
Ayacucho 60 D4 Ayacucho, S Peru
Ayagoz 130 C5 *var.* Ayaguz, *Kaz.* Ayaköz; *prev.* Sergiopol. Vostochnyy Kazakhstan, E Kazakhstan
Ayaguz *see* Ayagoz
Ayaköz *see* Ayagoz
Ayamonte 92 C4 Andalucía, S Spain

Ayaviri 61 E4 Puno, S Peru
Aydarkül 123 E2 *Rus.* Ozero Aydarkul'. *Lake* C Uzbekistan
Aydın 116 A4 *var.* Aïdin; *anc.* Tralles. Aydın, SW Turkey
Ayers Rock *see* Uluru
Ayeyarwady *see* Irrawaddy
Ayiá *see* Agiá
Ayios Evstratios *see* Efstrátios, Ágios
Áyios Nikólaos *see* Ágios Nikólaos
Ayorou 75 E3 Tillabéri, W Niger
'Ayoûn el 'Atroûs 74 D3 *var.* Aïoun el Atrous, Aïoun el Atroûss. Hodh el Gharbi, SE Mauritania
Ayr 88 C4 W Scotland, UK
Ayteke Bi 130 B4 . *Kaz.* Zhangaqazaly, *prev.* Novokazalinsk Kyzylorda, SW Kazakhstan
Aytos 104 E2 Burgas, E Bulgaria
Ayutthaya 137 C5 *var.* Phra Nakhon Si Ayutthaya. Phra Nakhon Si Ayutthaya, C Thailand
Ayvalık 116 A3 Balıkesir, W Turkey
Azahar, Costa del 93 F3 *coastal region* E Spain
Azaouâd 75 E3 *desert* C Mali
A'zāz 118 B2 Halab, NW Syria
Azerbaijan 117 G2 *Az.* Azärbaycan, Azärbaycan Respublikası; *prev.* Azerbaijan SSR. *Country* SE Asia

Azerbaijan 117

Official name Republic of Azerbaijan
Formation 1991
Capital Baku
Population 8.1 million / 242 people per sq mile (94 people per sq km)
Total area 33,436 sq miles (86,600 sq km)
Languages Azeri, Russian
Religions Shi'a ithna Muslims 61%, Sunni Muslims 26%, Armenian and Russian Orthodox 11%, other 2%
Ethnic mix Azeri 90%, Russian 3%, Daghestani 3%, Armenian 2%, other 2%
Government Multiparty republic
Currency Manat = 100 gopik
Literacy rate 96%
Calorie consumption 2,468 kilocalories

Azimabad *see* Patna
Azogues 60 B2 Cañar, S Ecuador
Azores 92 A4 *var.* Açores, Ilhas dos Açores, *Port.* Arquipélago dos Açores. *Island group* Portugal, NE Atlantic Ocean
Azores-Biscay Rise 80 A3 *undersea feature* E Atlantic Ocean
Azoum, Bahr 76 C3 *seasonal river* SE Chad
Azov, Sea of 103 H1 *Rus.* Azovskoye More, *Ukr.* Azovs'ke More. *Sea* NE Black Sea
Azraq, Wāḥat al 135 C6 *oasis* N Jordan
Aztec 48 C1 New Mexico, SW USA
Azuaga 92 C4 Extremadura, W Spain
Azuero, Península de 53 F5 *peninsula* S Panama
Azul 65 D5 Buenos Aires, E Argentina
Azur, Côte d' 107 E6 *Coastal region* SE France
Az Zaqāzīq *see* Zagazig
Az Zarqā' 119 B6 *var.* Zarqa. Az Zarqā', NW Jordan
Az Zāwiyah 71 F2 *var.* Zawia. NW Libya
Az Zilfī 120 B4 Ar Riyāḍ, N Saudi Arabia
Æsernia *see* Isernia

B

Ba 100 D3 *prev.* Mba. Viti Levu, W Fiji
Baalbek 118 B4 *var.* Ba'labakk; *anc.* Heliopolis. E Lebanon
Bá an Daingin *see* Dingle Bay

Baardheere 73 D6 *var.* Bardere, *It.* Bardera. Gedo, SW Somalia
Baarle-Hertog 87 C5 Antwerpen, N Belgium
Baarn 86 C3 Utrecht, C Netherlands
Babadag 108 D5 Tulcea, SE Romania
Babahoyo 60 B2 *prev.* Bodegas. Los Ríos, C Ecuador
Bābā, Kūh-e 123 E4 *mountain range* C Afghanistan
Babayevo 110 B4 Vologodskaya Oblast', NW Russian Federation
Babeldaob 144 A1 *var.* Babeldaop, Babelthuap. *Island* N Palau
Babeldaop *see* Babeldaob
Bab el Mandeb 121 B7 *strait* Gulf of Aden/Red Sea
Babelthuap *see* Babeldaob
Bá Bheanntraí *see* Bantry Bay
Babruysk 107 D7 *Rus.* Bobruysk. Mahilyowskaya Voblasts', E Belarus
Babuyan Channel 139 E1 *channel* N Philippines
Babuyan Island 139 E1 *island* N Philippines
Bacabal 63 F2 Maranhão, E Brazil
Bacău 108 C4 *Hung.* Bákó. Bacău, NE Romania
Bắc Giang 136 D3 Ha Bắc, N Vietnam
Bacheykava 107 D5 *Rus.* Bocheykovo. Vitsyebskaya Voblasts', N Belarus
Back 37 F3 *river* Nunavut, N Canada
Bačka Palanka 100 D3 *prev.* Palanka. Serbia, NW Serbia and Montenegro (Yugo.)
Bačka Topola 100 D3 *Hung.* Topolya; *prev. Hung.* Bácstopolya. Serbia, N Serbia and Montenegro (Yugo.)
Bạc Liêu 137 D6 *var.* Vinh Loi. Minh Hai, S Vietnam
Bacolod 125 E4 *off.* Bacolod City. Negros, C Philippines
Bacolod City *see* Bacolod
Bácsszenttamás *see* Srbobran
Badajoz 92 C4 *anc.* Pax Augusta. Extremadura, W Spain
Baden-Baden 95 B6 *anc.* Aurelia Aquensis. Baden-Württemberg, SW Germany
Bad Freienwalde 94 D3 Brandenburg, NE Germany
Bad Hersfeld 94 B4 Hessen, C Germany
Bad Homburg *see* Bad Homburg vor der Höhe
Bad Homburg vor der Höhe 95 B5 *var.* Bad Homburg. Hessen, W Germany
Bá Dhún na nGall *see* Donegal Bay
Bad Ischl 95 D7 Oberösterreich, N Austria
Bad Krozingen 95 A6 Baden-Württemberg, SW Germany
Badlands 44 D2 *physical region* North Dakota, N USA
Badu Island 148 C1 *island* Queensland, NE Australia
Bad Vöslau 95 E6 Niederösterreich, NE Austria
Baetic Cordillera *see* Béticos, Sistemas
Baetic Mountains *see* Béticos, Sistemas
Bafatá 74 C4 C Guinea-Bissau
Baffin Bay 37 G2 *bay* Canada/Greenland
Baffin Island 37 G2 *island* Nunavut, NE Canada
Bafing 74 C3 *river* W Africa
Bafoussam 76 A4 Ouest, W Cameroon
Bafra 116 D2 Samsun, N Turkey
Bāft 120 D4 Kermān, S Iran
Bagaces 52 D4 Guanacaste, NW Costa Rica
Bagdad *see* Baghdād
Bagé 63 E5 Rio Grande do Sul, S Brazil
Baghdād 120 B3 *var.* Bagdad, *Eng.* Baghdad. *Country capital* (Iraq) C Iraq

Baghlān 123 E3 Baghlān, NE Afghanistan
Bago *see* Pegu
Bagoé 74 D4 *river* Côte d'Ivoire/Mali
Bagrationovsk 106 A4 *Ger.* Preussisch Eylau. Kaliningradskaya Oblast', W Russian Federation
Bagrax Hu *see* Bosten Hu
Baguio 139 E1 *off.* Baguio City. Luzon, N Philippines
Bagzane, Monts 75 F3 *mountain* N Niger
Bahama Islands *see* Bahamas

Bahamas 54

Official name Commonwealth of the Bahamas
Formation 1973
Capital Nassau
Population 308,000 / 57 people per sq mile (22 people per sq km)
Total area 5,382 sq miles (13,940 sq km)
Languages English, English Creole, French Creole
Religions Baptist 32%, Anglican 20%, Roman Catholic 19%, Church of God 6%, Methodist 6%, other 17%
Ethnic mix Black African 85%, Other 15%
Government Parliamentary democracy
Currency Bahamian dollar = 100 cents
Literacy rate 95.7%
Calorie consumption 2,443 kilocalories

Bahamas 54 C2 *Country* N West Indies
Bahamas 35 D6 *var.* Bahama Islands. *Island group* N West Indies
Bahāwalpur 134 C2 Punjab, E Pakistan
Bahía 63 F3 *off.* Estado da Bahia. *State* E Brazil
Bahía Blanca 65 C5 Buenos Aires, E Argentina
Bahía, Islas de la 52 C1 *Eng.* Bay Islands. *Island group* N Honduras
Bahir Dar 72 C4 *var.* Bahr Dar, Bahrdar Giyorgis. NW Ethiopia
Bahraich 135 E3 Uttar Pradesh, N India

Bahrain 120

Official name State of Bahrain
Formation 1971
Capital Manama
Population 652,000 / 2,724 people per sq mile (1,052 people per sq km)
Total area 239 sq miles (620 sq km)
Languages Arabic
Religions Muslim (mainly Shi'a) 99%, other 1%
Ethnic mix Bahraini 70%, Iranian, Indian, Pakistani 24%, other Arab 4%, European 2%
Government Constitutional monarchy
Currency Bahraini dinar = 1,000 fils
Literacy rate 87.6%
Calorie consumption not available

Bahrain 120 C4 *Ar.* Al Baḥrayn; *prev.* Bahrein, *anc.* Tylos or Tyros. *Country* SW Asia
Baḥr al Milḥ *see* Razāzah, Buḥayrat ar
Baḥrat Lūt *see* Dead Sea
Bahrat Tabariya *see* Tiberias, Lake
Bahr Dar *see* Bahir Dar
Bahrdar Giyorgis *see* Bahir Dar
Bahr el Azraq *see* Blue Nile
Bahr el Jebel *see* White Nile
Bahret Lut *see* Dead Sea
Bahr Tabariya, Sea of *see* Tiberias, Lake

Bahushewsk 107 E6 *Rus.*
Bogushëvsk. Vitsyebskaya
Voblasts', NE Belarus
Baia Mare 108 B3 *Ger.* Frauenbach,
Hung. Nagybánya; *prev.* Neustadt.
Maramureş, NW Romania
Baia Sprie 108 B3 *Ger.* Mittelstadt,
Hung. Felsőbánya. Maramureş,
NW Romania
Baïbokoum 76 B4 Logone-Oriental,
SW Chad
Baidoa *see* Baydhabo
Baie-Comeau 39 E3 Quebec,
SE Canada
Baikal, Lake *see* Baykal, Ozero
Baile Átha Luain *see* Athlone
Bailén 92 D4 Andalucía, S Spain
Baile na Mainistreach *see*
Newtownabbey
Băileşti 108 B5 Dolj, SW Romania
Ba Illi 76 B3 Chari-Baguirmi,
SW Chad
Bainbridge 42 D3 Georgia, SE USA
Bā'ir *see* Bāyir
Baireuth *see* Bayreuth
Bairiki 144 D2 *country capital*
(Kiribati) Tarawa, NW Kiribati
Bairnsdale 149 C7 Victoria,
SE Australia
Baishan 129 E3 *prev.* Hunjiang. Jilin,
NE China
Baiyin 128 B4 Gansu, C China
Baja 99 C7 Bács-Kiskun, S Hungary
Baja California 48 A4 *Eng.* Lower
California. *Peninsula* NW Mexico
Baja California 50 B2 state
NW Mexico
Bajo Boquete *see* Boquete
Bajram Curri 101 D5 Kukës,
N Albania
Bakala 76 C4 Ouaka, C Central
African Republic
Bakan *see* Shimonoseki
Baker 46 C3 Oregon, NW USA
Baker and Howland Islands 145 E2
US unincorporated territory
W Polynesia
Baker Lake 37 F3 Nunavut,
N Canada
Bakersfield 47 C7 California, W USA
Bakharden 122 C3 *Turkm.* Bäherden;
prev. Bakherden. Akhalskiy
Velayat, C Turkmenistan
Bakhchysaray 109 F5 *Rus.*
Bakhchisaray. Respublika Krym,
S Ukraine
Bakhmach 109 F1 Chernihivs'ka
Oblast', N Ukraine
Bākhtarān 120 C3 *prev.*
Kermānshāh, Qahremānshahr.
Kermānshāh. W Iran
Bakı 117 H2 *Eng.* Baku. *Country
capital* (Azerbaijan) E Azerbaijan
Bakony 99 C7 *Eng.* Bakony
Mountains, *Ger.* Bakonywald.
Mountain range W Hungary
Baku *see* Bakı
Balabac Island 129 C8 *island*
W Philippines
Balabac Strait 138 D2 *var.* Selat
Balabac. *Strait*
Malaysia/Philippines
Ba'labakk *see* Baalbek
Balaguer 93 F2 Cataluña,
NE Spain
Balakovo 111 C6 Saratovskaya
Oblast', W Russian Federation
Bālā Morghāb 122 D4 Laghmān,
NW Afghanistan
Balashov 111 B6 Saratovskaya
Oblast', W Russian Federation
Balaton C7 *var.* Lake Balaton, *Ger.*
Plattensee. *Lake* W Hungary
Balaton, Lake *see* Balaton
Balbina, Represa 62 D1 *reservoir*
NW Brazil
Balboa 53 G4 Panamá, C Panama
Balcarce 65 D5 Buenos Aires,
E Argentina
Balclutha 151 B7 Otago, South
Island, NZ
Baldy Mountain 44 C1 *mountain*
Montana, NW USA
Bâle *see* Basel
Baleares, Islas 93 G3 *Eng.* Balearic
Islands. *Island group* Spain,
W Mediterranean Sea

Balearic Islands *see* Baleares, Islas
Balearic Plain *see* Algerian Basin
Baleine, Rivière à la 39 E2 *river*
Quebec, E Canada
Balen 87 C5 Antwerpen, N Belgium
Băleshwar 135 F4 *prev.* Balasore.
Orissa, E India
Bali 138 D5 *island* C Indonesia
Balıkesir 116 A3 Balıkesir,
W Turkey
Balīkh, Nahr 118 C2 *river* N Syria
Balikpapan 138 D4 Borneo,
C Indonesia
Balkan Mountains 104 C2
Bul./Scr. Stara Planina. *Mountain
range* Bulgaria/Serbia and
Montenegro (Yugo.)
Balkh 123 E3 *anc.* Bactra. Balkh,
N Afghanistan
Balkhash 114 C5 *Kaz.* Balqash.
Karaganda, SE Kazakhstan
Balkhash, Lake *see* Balkhash,
Ozero
Balkhash, Ozero 114 C5 *Eng.* Lake
Balkhash, *Kaz.* Balqash. *Lake*
SE Kazakhstan
Balladonia 147 C6 Western
Australia
Ballarat 149 C7 Victoria,
SE Australia
Balleny Islands 154 B5 *island group*
Antarctica
Ballinger 49 F3 Texas, SW USA
Balochistan *see* Baluchistān
Balş 108 B5 Olt, S Romania
Balsas 63 F2 Maranhão, E Brazil
Balsas, Río 51 E5 *var.* Río Mexcala.
River S Mexico
Bal'shavik 107 D7 *Rus.* Bol'shevik.
Homyel'skaya Voblasts',
SE Belarus
Balta 108 D3 Odes'ka Oblast',
SW Ukraine
Bălţi 108 D3 *Rus.* Bel'tsy.
N Moldova
Baltic Sea 85 C7 *Ger.* Ostee, *Rus.*
Baltiskoye More. *Sea* N Europe
Baltimore 41 F4 Maryland, NE USA
Baltkrievija *see* Belarus
Baluchistān 134 B3 *var.* Balochistān,
Beluchistan. Admin. region
province SW Pakistan
Balvi 106 D4 Balvi, NE Latvia
Balykchy 123 G2 *Kir.* Ysyk-Köl;
prev. Issyk-Kul', Rybach'ye. Issyk-
Kul'skaya Oblast', NE Kyrgyzstan
Balzers 94 E2 S Liechtenstein
Bam 120 E4 Kermān, SE Iran
Bamako 74 D4 *country capital* (Mali)
Capital District, SW Mali
Bambari 76 C4 Ouaka, C Central
African Republic
Bamberg 95 C5 Bayern, SE Germany
Bamenda 76 A4 Nord-Ouest,
W Cameroon
Banaba 144 D2 *var.* Ocean Island.
Island Tungaru, W Kiribati
Bandaaceh 138 A3 *var.* Banda
Atjeh; *prev.* Koetaradja,
Kutaradja, Kutaraja. Sumatera,
W Indonesia
Banda Atjeh *see* Bandaaceh
Bandama 74 D5 *var.* Bandama
Fleuve. *River* S Côte d'Ivoire
Bandama Fleuve *see* Bandama
Bandar 'Abbās *see* Bandar-e 'Abbās
Bandarbeyla 73 E5 *var.* Bender
Beila, Bender Beyla. Bari,
NE Somalia
Bandar-e 'Abbās 120 D4 *var.*
Bandar 'Abbās; *prev.* Gombroon.
Hormozgān, S Iran
Bandar-e Büshehr 120 C4 *var.*
Büshehr, *Eng.* Bushire. Büshehr,
S Iran
Bandar-e Khamīr 120 D4
Hormozgān, S Iran
Bandar-e Langeh 120 D4 *var.*
Bandar-e Lengeh, Lingeh.
Hormozgān, S Iran
Bandar-e Lengeh *see* Bandar-e
Langeh
Bandar Kassim *see* Boosaaso
Bandarlampung 138 C4 *prev.*
Tanjungkarang, Teloekbetoeng,
Telukbetung. Sumatera,
W Indonesia

Bandar Maharani *see* Muar
Bandar Masulipatnam *see*
Machilīpatnam
Bandar Seri Begawan 138 D3 *prev.*
Brunei Town. *Country capital*
(Brunei) N Brunei
Bandar Sri Aman *see* Sri Aman
Banda Sea 139 F5 *var.* Laut Banda.
Sea E Indonesia
Bandiagara 75 E3 Mopti, C Mali
Bandırma 116 A3 *var.* Penderma.
Balıkesir, NW Turkey
Bandundu 77 C6 *prev.* Banningville.
Bandundu, W Dem. Rep. Congo
Bandung 138 C5 *prev.* Bandoeng.
Jawa, C Indonesia
Bangalore 132 C2 Karnātaka, S India
Bangassou 76 D4 Mbomou,
SE Central African Republic
Banggai, Kepulauan 139 E4 *island
group* C Indonesia
Banghāzī 71 G2 *Eng.* Bengazi,
Benghazi, *It.* Bengasi. NE Libya
Bangka, Pulau 138 C4 *island*
W Indonesia
Bangkok *see* Krung Thep
Bangkok, Bight of *see* Krung Thep,
Ao
Bangladesh 135 G3 *prev.* East
Pakistan. *Country* S Asia

Bangladesh 135

Official name People's Republic of
Bangladesh
Formation 1971
Capital Dhaka
Population 140.4 million /2,525
people per sq mile (975 people per
sq km)
Total area 55,598 sq miles
(144,000 sq km)
Languages Bengali, Urdu, Chakma,
Marma (Magh), Garo, Khasi,
Santhali, Tripuri, Mro
Religions Muslim (mainly Sunni)
87%, Hindu 12%, other 1%
Ethnic mix Bengali 98%, other 2%
Government Parliamentary
democracy
Currency Taka = 100 paisa
Literacy rate 41.4%
Calorie consumption 2,103
kilocalories

Bangor 89 B5 *Ir.* Beannchar.
E Northern Ireland, UK
Bangor 41 G2 Maine, NE USA
Bangor 89 C6 NW Wales, UK
Bangui 77 B5 *country capital*
(Central African Republic)
Ombella-Mpoko, SW Central
African Republic
Bangweulu, Lake 73 B8 *var.* Lake
Bengwelu. *Lake* N Zambia
Ban Hat Yai *see* Hat Yai
Ban Hin Heup 136 C4 Viangchan,
C Laos
Ban Houayxay *see* Houayxay
Ban Houei Sai *see* Houayxay
Ban Hua Hin 137 C6 *var.* Hua Hin.
Prachuap Khiri Khan,
SW Thailand
Bani 74 D3 *river* S Mali
Banias *see* Bāniyās
Banī Suwayf *see* Beni Suef
Bāniyās 118 A3 *var.* Banias, Baniyas,
Paneas. Tarţūs, W Syria
Baniyas *see* Bāniyās
Banja Luka 100 B3 Republika
Srpska, NW Bosnia and
Herzegovina
Banjarmasin 138 D4 *prev.*
Bandjarmasin. Borneo,
C Indonesia
Banjul 74 B3 *prev.* Bathurst. *Country
capital* (Gambia) W Gambia
Banks Island 37 E2 *island* Banks
Island, Northwest Territories,
NW Canada
Banks Islands 144 D4 *Fr.* Îles
Banks. *Island group* N Vanuatu
Banks Lake 46 B1 *reservoir*
Washington, NW USA
Banks Peninsula 151 C6 *peninsula*
South Island, NZ

Banks Strait 149 C8 *strait*
SW Tasman Sea
Bānkura 135 F4 West Bengal,
NE India
Ban Mak Khaeng *see* Udon Thani
Banmo *see* Bhamo
Bañolas *see* Banyoles
Ban Pak Phanang *see* Pak Phanang
Ban Sichon *see* Sichon
Banská Bystrica 99 C6 *Ger.*
Neusohl, *Hung.* Besztercebánya.
Banskobystrický Kraj, C Slovakia
Bantry Bay 89 A7 *Ir.* Bá Bheanntraí.
Bay SW Ireland
Banya 104 E2 Burgas, E Bulgaria
Banyak, Kepulauan 138 A3 *prev.*
Kepulauan Banjak. *Island group*
NW Indonesia
Banyo 76 B4 Adamaoua,
NW Cameroon
Banyoles 93 G2 *var.* Bañolas.
Cataluña, NE Spain
Banzare Seamounts 141 C7 *undersea
feature* S Indian Ocean
Baoji 128 B4 *var.* Pao-chi, Paoki.
Shaanxi, C China
Baoro 76 B4 Nana-Mambéré,
W Central African Republic
Baoshan 128 A6 *var.* Pao-shan.
Yunnan, SW China
Baotou 127 F3 *var.* Pao-t'ou,
Paotow. Nei Mongol Zizhiqu,
N China
Ba'qūbah 120 B3 *var.* Qubba. C Iraq
Baquerizo Moreno *see* Puerto
Baquerizo Moreno
Bar 101 C5 *It.* Antivari.
Montenegro, SW Serbia and
Montenegro (Yugo.)
Baraawe 73 D6 *It.* Brava.
Shabeellaha Hoose, S Somalia
Baraji, Hirfanli 116 C3 *lake*
C Turkey
Bārāmati 134 C5 Mahārāshtra, W India
Baranavichy 107 B6 *Pol.*
Baranowicze, *Rus.* Baranovichi.
Brestskaya Voblasts', SW Belarus
Barbados 55 G1 *country*
SE West Indies

Barbados 55

Official name Barbados
Formation 1966
Capital Bridgetown
Population 268,000 /1,614 people
per sq mile (623 people per sq km)
Total area 166 sq miles (430 sq km)
Languages English, Bajan
(Barbadian English)
Religions Anglican 40%, other 24%,
non-religious 17%, Pentecostal 8%,
Methodist 7%, Roman Catholic 4%
Ethnic mix Black African 90%,
other 10%
Government Parliamentary
democracy
Currency Barbados dollar = 100
cents
Literacy rate 98%
Calorie consumption 3,022
kilocalories

Barbastro 93 F2 Aragón, NE Spain
Barbate de Franco 92 C5 Andalucía,
S Spain
Barbuda 55 G3 *island* N Antigua
and Barbuda
Barcaldine 148 C4 Queensland,
E Australia
Barce *see* Al Marj
Barcelona 93 G2 *anc.* Barcino,
Barcinona. Cataluña, E Spain
Barcelona 59 E2 Anzoátegui,
NE Venezuela
Barcoo *see* Cooper Creek
Barcs 99 C7 Somogy, SW Hungary
Bardaï 76 C1 Borkou-Ennedi-
Tibesti, N Chad
Bardejov 99 D5 *Ger.* Bartfeld,
Hung. Bártfa. Prešovský Kraj,
E Slovakia
Bardera *see* Baardheere
Bardere *see* Baardheere
Bareilly 135 E3 *var.* Bareli. Uttar
Pradesh, N India

areli *see* Bareilly
arendrecht 86 C4 Zuid-Holland, SW Netherlands
arentin 90 C3 Seine-Maritime, N France
arentsberg 83 G2 Spitsbergen, N Svalbard
arentsøya 83 G2 *island* E Svalbard
arents Sea 110 C2 *Nor.* Barents Havet, *Rus.* Barentsevo More. *Sea* Arctic Ocean
arents Trough 81 E1 *undersea feature* SW Barents Sea
ar Harbor 41 H2 Mount Desert Island, Maine, NE USA
ari 97 E5 *var.* Bari delle Puglie; *anc.* Barium. Puglia, SE Italy
aridah *see* Al Bāridah
ari delle Puglie *see* Bari
arikot *see* Barīkowt
arīkowt 123 F4 *var.* Barikot. Kunar, NE Afghanistan
arillas 52 A2 *var.* Santa Cruz Barillas. Huehuetenango, NW Guatemala
arinas 58 C2 Barinas, W Venezuela
arisal 135 G4 Khulna, S Bangladesh
arisan, Pegunungan 138 B4 *mountain range* Sumatera, W Indonesia
arito, Sungai 138 D4 *river* Borneo, C Indonesia
arium *see* Bari
arka *see* Al Marj
arkly Tableland 148 B3 *plateau* Northern Territory/Queensland, N Australia
arlad 108 D4 *prev.* Bîrlad. Vaslui, E Romania
arlavento, Ilhas de 74 A2 *var.* Windward Islands. *Island group* N Cape Verde
ar-le-Duc 90 D3 *var.* Bar-sur-Ornain. Meuse, NE France
arlee, Lake 147 B6 *lake* Western Australia
arlee Range 146 A4 *mountain range* Western Australia
arletta 97 D5 *anc.* Barduli. Puglia, SE Italy
arlinek 98 B3 *Ger.* Berlinchen. Zachodniopomorskie, NW Poland
armouth 89 C6 NW Wales, UK
arnaul 114 D4 Altayskiy Kray, C Russian Federation
arnstaple 89 C7 SW England, UK
aroghil Pass 123 F3 *var.* Kowtal-e Barowghil. *Pass* Afghanistan/Pakistan
aron'ki 107 E7 *Rus.* Boron'ki. Mahilyowskaya Voblasts', E Belarus
arquisimeto 58 C2 Lara, NW Venezuela
arra 88 B3 *island* NW Scotland, UK
arra de Río Grande 53 E3 Región Autónoma Atlántico Sur, E Nicaragua
arragem de Sobradinho *see* Sobradinho, Represa de
arranca 60 C3 Lima, W Peru
arrancabermeja 58 B2 Santander, N Colombia
arranquilla 58 B1 Atlántico, N Colombia
arreiro 92 B4 Setúbal, W Portugal
arrier Range 149 C6 *hill range* New South Wales, SE Australia
arrow 89 B6 *Ir.* An Bhearú. *River* SE Ireland
arrow 36 D2 Alaska, USA
arrow-in-Furness 89 C5 NW England, UK
arrow Island 146 A4 *island* Western Australia
arstow 47 C7 California, W USA
ar-sur-Ornain *see* Bar-le-Duc
artang 123 F3 *river* SE Tajikistan
artica 59 F3 N Guyana
artın 116 C2 Bartın NW Turkey
artlesville 49 G1 Oklahoma, C USA
artoszyce 98 D2 *Ger.* Bartenstein. Warmińsko-Mazurskie, NE Poland

Baruun-Urt 127 F2 Sühbaatar, E Mongolia
Barú, Volcán 53 E5 *var.* Volcán de Chiriquí. *Volcano* W Panama
Barwon River 149 D5 *river* New South Wales, SE Australia
Barysaw 107 D6 *Rus.* Borisov. Minskaya Voblasts', NE Belarus
Basarabeasca 108 D4 *Rus.* Bessarabka. SE Moldova
Basel 95 A7 *Eng.* Basle, *Fr.* Bâle. Basel-Stadt, NW Switzerland
Basilan 139 E3 *island* SW Philippines
Basle *see* Basel
Basra *see* Al Başrah
Bassano del Grappa 96 C2 Veneto, NE Italy
Bassein 136 A4 *var.* Pathein. Irrawaddy, SW Myanmar
Basse-Terre 55 C4 *dependent territory capital* (Guadeloupe) Basse Terre, SW Guadeloupe
Basse Terre 55 C4 *island* W Guadeloupe
Basseterre 55 G3 *country capital* (Saint Kitts and Nevis) Saint Kitts, Saint Kitts and Nevis
Bassikounou 74 D3 Hodh ech Chargui, SE Mauritania
Bass Strait 149 C7 *strait* SE Australia
Bassum 94 B3 Niedersachsen, NW Germany
Bastia 91 E7 Corse, France, C Mediterranean Sea
Bastogne 87 D7 Luxembourg, SE Belgium
Bastrop 42 B2 Louisiana, S USA
Bastyn' 107 B7 *Rus.* Bostyn'. Brestskaya Voblasts', SW Belarus
Basuo *see* Dongfang
Bata 77 A5 NW Equatorial Guinea
Batabanó, Golfo de 54 A2 *gulf* W Cuba
Batajnica 100 D3 Serbia, N Serbia and Montenegro (Yugo.)
Batangas 139 E2 *off.* Batangas City. Luzon, N Philippines
Bătdâmbâng 137 C5 *prev.* Battambang. Bătdâmbâng, NW Cambodia
Batéké, Plateaux 77 B6 *plateau* S Congo
Bath 89 D7 *hist.* Akermanceaster, *anc.* Aquae Calidae, Aquae Solis. SW England, UK
Bathinda 134 D2 Punjab, NW India
Bathsheba 55 G1 E Barbados
Bathurst 39 F4 New Brunswick, SE Canada
Bathurst 149 D6 New South Wales, SE Australia
Bathurst Island 146 D2 *island* Northern Territory, N Australia
Bathurst Island 37 F2 *island* Parry Islands, Nunavut, N Canada
Bāţin, Wādī al 136 C4 *dry watercourse* SW Asia
Batman 117 E4 *var.* Iluh. Batman, SE Turkey
Batna 71 E2 NE Algeria
Baton Rouge 42 B3 *state capital* Louisiana, S USA
Batroûn 118 A4 *var.* Al Batrūn. N Lebanon
Batticaloa 132 D3 Eastern Province, E Sri Lanka
Battipaglia 97 D5 Campania, S Italy
Bat'umi 117 F2 W Georgia
Batu Pahat 138 B3 *prev.* Bandar Penggaram. Johor, Peninsular Malaysia
Bauchi 75 G4 Bauchi, NE Nigeria
Bauer Basin 153 F3 *undersea feature* E Pacific Ocean
Bauska 106 C3 *Ger.* Bauske. Bauska, S Latvia
Bautzen 94 D4 *Lus.* Budyšin. Sachsen, E Germany
Bavarian Alps 95 C7 *Ger.* Bayrische Alpen. *Mountain range* Austria/Germany
Bavispe, Río 50 C2 *river* NW Mexico
Bawīţi 72 B2 N Egypt
Bawku 75 E4 N Ghana

Bayamo 54 C3 Granma, E Cuba
Bayan Har Shan 126 D4 *var.* Bayan Khar. *Mountain range* C China
Bayanhongor 126 D2 Bayanhongor, C Mongolia
Bayan Khar *see* Bayan Har Shan
Bayano, Lago 53 G4 *lake* E Panama
Bay City 40 C3 Michigan, N USA
Bay City 49 G4 Texas, SW USA
Baydhabo 73 D6 *var.* Baydhowa, Isha Baydhabo, *It.* Baidoa. Bay, SW Somalia
Baydhowa *see* Baydhabo
Bayern 95 C6 *cultural region* SE Germany
Bayeux 90 B3 *anc.* Augustodurum. Calvados, N France
Bāyir 119 C7 *var.* Bā'ir. Ma'ān, S Jordan
Baykal, Ozero 115 E4 *Eng.* Lake Baikal. *Lake* S Russian Federation
Baymak 111 D6 Respublika Bashkortostan, W Russian Federation
Bayonne 91 A6 *anc.* Lapurdum. Pyrénées-Atlantiques, SW France
Bayramaly 122 D3 *prev.* Bayram-Ali. Maryyskiy Velayat, S Turkmenistan
Bayreuth 95 C5 *var.* Baireuth. Bayern, SE Germany
Bayrūt *see* Beyrouth
Baytown 49 H4 Texas, SW USA
Baza 93 E4 Andalucía, S Spain
Beagle Channel 65 C8 *channel* Argentina/Chile
Béal Feirste *see* Belfast
Beannchar *see* Bangor
Bear Lake 46 E4 *lake* Idaho/Utah, NW USA
Beas de Segura 93 E4 Andalucía, S Spain
Beata, Isla 55 E3 *island* SW Dominican Republic
Beatrice 45 F4 Nebraska, C USA
Beaufort Sea 36 D2 *sea* Arctic Ocean
Beaufort West 78 C5 *Afr.* Beaufort-Wes. Western Cape, SW South Africa
Beaumont 49 H3 Texas, SW USA
Beaune 90 D4 Côte d'Or, C France
Beauvais 90 C3 *anc.* Bellovacum, Caesaromagus. Oise, N France
Beaver Island 40 C2 *island* Michigan, N USA
Beaver Lake 49 H1 *reservoir* Arkansas, C USA
Beaver River 49 F1 *river* Oklahoma, C USA
Beāwar 134 C3 Rājasthān, N India
Bečej 100 D3 *Ger.* Altbetsche, *Hung.* Óbecse, Rácz-Becse; *prev.* Magyar-Becse, Stari Bečej. Serbia, N Serbia and Montenegro (Yugo.)
Béchar 70 D2 *prev.* Colomb-Béchar. W Algeria
Beckley 40 D5 West Virginia, NE USA
Bedford 89 D6 E England, UK
Bedum 86 E1 Groningen, NE Netherlands
Be'ér Menuḥa 119 B7 *var* Be'er Menukha. Southern, S Israel
Be'er Menukha *see* Be'ér Menuḥa
Beernem 87 A5 West-Vlaanderen, NW Belgium
Beersheba *see* Be'ér Sheva'
Be'ér Sheva' 119 A7 *var.* Beersheba, *Ar.* Bir es Saba. Southern, S Israel
Beesel 87 D5 Limburg, SE Netherlands
Beeville 49 G4 Texas, SW USA
Bega 149 D7 New South Wales, SE Australia
Beida *see* Al Bayḍā'
Beihai 128 B6 Guangxi Zhuangzu Zizhiqu, S China
Beijing 128 C3 *var.* Pei-ching, *Eng.* Peking; *prev.* Pei-p'ing. *Country/municipality capital* (China) Beijing Shi, E China
Beilen 86 E2 Drenthe, NE Netherlands
Beira 79 E3 Sofala, C Mozambique
Beirut *see* Beyrouth
Beit Leḥm *see* Bethlehem

Beiuş 108 B3 *Hung.* Belényes. Bihor, NW Romania
Beja 92 B4 *anc.* Pax Julia. Beja, SE Portugal
Béjar 92 C3 Castilla-León, N Spain
Bejraburi *see* Phetchaburi
Békéscsaba 99 D7 *Rom.* Bichiş-Ciaba. Békés, SE Hungary
Bekobod 123 E2 *Rus.* Bekabad; *prev.* Begovat. Toshkent Wiloyati, E Uzbekistan
Bela Crkva 100 E3 *Ger.* Weisskirchen, *Hung.* Fehértemplom. Serbia, W Serbia and Montenegro (Yugo.)
Belarus 107 B6 *prev.* Belorussia, *Latv.* Baltkrievija; *prev.* Belorussian SSR, *Rus.* Belorusskaya SSR. *Country* E Europe

Belarus 107

Official name Republic of Belarus
Formation 1991
Capital Minsk
Population 10.1 million / 126 people per sq mile (49 people per sq km)
Total area 80,154 sq miles (207,600 sq km)
Languages Belorussian, Russian
Religions Russian Orthodox 60%, other (including Muslim, Jews and Protestant) 32% Roman Catholic 8%
Ethnic mix Belorussian 78%, Russian 13%, Polish 4%, Ukrainian 3%, other 2%
Government Presidential regime
Currency Belorussian rouble = 100 kopeks
Literacy rate 99%
Calorie consumption 2,902 kilocalories

Belau *see* Palau
Belchatow *see* Bełchatów
Bełchatów 98 C4 *var.* Belchatow. Łódzkie, C Poland
Belcher Islands 38 C2 *Fr.* Îles Belcher. *Island group* Northwest Territories, SE Canada
Beledweyne 73 D5 *var.* Belet Huen, *It.* Belet Uen. Hiiraan, C Somalia
Belém 63 F1 *var.* Pará. *State capital* Pará, N Brazil
Belen 48 D2 New Mexico, SW USA
Belén 52 D4 Rivas, SW Nicaragua
Belet Huen *see* Beledweyne
Belet Uen *see* Beledweyne
Belfast 89 B5 *Ir.* Béal Feirste. *Admin capital* E Northern Ireland, UK
Belfield 44 D2 North Dakota, N USA
Belfort 90 E4 Territoire-de-Belfort, E France
Belgaum 132 B1 Karnātaka, W India
Belgium 87 B6 *Dut.* België, *Fr.* Belgique. *Country* NW Europe

Belgium 87

Official name Kingdom of Belgium
Formation 1830
Capital Brussels
Population 10.3 million / 874 people per sq mile (338 people per sq km)
Total area 11,780 sq miles (30,510 sq km)
Languages Dutch, French, German
Religions Roman Catholic 88%, Muslim 2%, other 10%
Ethnic mix Fleming 58%, Walloon 33%, Italian 2%, Moroccan 1%, other 6%
Government Parliamentary democracy
Currency Euro (Belgian franc until 2002)
Literacy rate 99%
Calorie consumption 3,701 kilocalories

Belgorod 111 A6 Belgorodskaya Oblast', W Russian Federation

Belgrade see Beograd
Belgrano II 154 A2 *Argentinian research station* Antarctica
Belice see Belize City
Beligrad see Berat
Beli Manastir 100 C3 Hung. Pélmonostor; prev. Monostor. Osijek-Baranja, NE Croatia
Bélinga 77 B5 Ogooué-Ivindo, NE Gabon
Belitung, Pulau 138 C4 island W Indonesia
Belize 52 B1 Sp. Belice; prev. British Honduras, Colony of Belize. *Country* Central America

Belize 52

Official name Belize
Formation 1981
Capital Belmopan
Population 200,000 /23 people per sq mile (9 people per sq km)
Total area 8,867 sq miles (22,966 sq km)
Languages English, English Creole, Spanish, Mayan, Garifuna (Carib)
Religions Roman Catholic 62%, Anglican 12%, Mennonite 4%, Methodist 6%, other 16%
Ethnic mix Mestizo 44%, Creole 30%, Maya 11%, Garifuna 7%, Asian Indian 4%, other 4%
Government Parliamentary democracy
Currency Belizean dollar = 100 cents
Literacy rate 93.2%
Calorie consumption 2,888 kilocalories

Belize 52 B1 *river* Belize/Guatemala
Belize see Belize City
Belize City 52 C1 var. Belize, Sp. Belice. Belize, NE Belize
Belkofski 36 B3 Alaska, USA
Belle Île 90 A4 island NW France
Belle Isle, Strait of 39 G3 strait Newfoundland and Labrador, E Canada
Belleville 40 B4 Illinois, N USA
Bellevue 45 F4 Iowa, C USA
Bellevue 46 B2 Washington, NW USA
Bellingham 46 B1 Washington, NW USA
Belling Hausen Mulde see Southeast Pacific Basin
Bellingshausen Abyssal Plain see Bellingshausen Plain
Bellingshausen Plain 153 F5 var. Bellingshausen Abyssal Plain. *Undersea feature* SE Pacific Ocean
Bellingshausen Sea 154 A3 sea Antarctica
Bellinzona 95 B8 Ger. Bellenz. Ticino, S Switzerland
Bello 58 B2 Antioquia, W Colombia
Bellville 78 B5 Western Cape, SW South Africa
Belmopan 52 C1 *country capital* (Belize) Cayo, C Belize
Belogradchik 104 B1 Vidin, NW Bulgaria
Belo Horizonte 63 F4 prev. Bello Horizonte. *State capital* Minas Gerais, SE Brazil
Belomorsk 110 B3 Respublika Kareliya, NW Russian Federation
Beloretsk 111 D6 Respublika Bashkortostan, W Russian Federation
Belorussia/Belorussian SSR see Belarus
Belorusskaya SSR see Belarus
Beloye More 110 C3 Eng. White Sea. *Sea* NW Russian Federation
Belozersk 110 B4 Vologodskaya Oblast', NW Russian Federation
Belton 49 G3 Texas, SW USA
Beluchistan see Baluchistān
Belukha, Gora 114 D5 mountain Kazakhstan/Russian Federation
Belyy, Ostrov 114 D2 island N Russian Federation

Bemaraha 79 F3 var. Plateau du Bemaraha. *Mountain range* W Madagascar
Bemidji 45 F1 Minnesota, N USA
Bemmel 86 D4 Gelderland, SE Netherlands
Benaco see Garda, Lago di
Benavente 92 D2 Castilla-León, N Spain
Bend 46 B3 Oregon, NW USA
Bender Beila see Bandarbeyla
Bender Beyla see Bandarbeyla
Bender Cassim see Boosaaso
Bendern 94 E1 NW Liechtenstein
Bender Qaasim see Boosaaso
Bendigo 149 C7 Victoria, SE Australia
Beneŝov 99 B5 Ger. Beneschau. Středočeský Kraj, W Czech Republic
Benevento 97 D5 anc. Beneventum, Malventum. Campania, S Italy
Bengal, Bay of 124 C4 bay N Indian Ocean
Bengbu 128 D5 var. Peng-pu. Anhui, E China
Benghazi see Banghāzī
Bengkulu 138 B4 prev. Bengkoeloe, Benkoelen, Benkulen. Sumatera, W Indonesia
Benguela 78 A2 var. Benguella. Benguela, W Angola
Benguella see Benguela
Bengweulu, Lake see Bangweulu, Lake
Ben Hope 88 B2 mountain N Scotland, UK
Beni 56 B4 var. El Beni. Admin. region *department* N Bolivia
Beni 77 E5 Nord Kivu, NE Dem. Rep. Congo
Benidorm 93 F4 País Valenciano, SE Spain
Beni-Mellal 70 C2 C Morocco
Benin 75 F4 prev. Dahomey. *Country* W Africa

Benin 75

Official name Republic of Benin
Formation 1960
Capital Porto-Novo
Population 6.4 million / 147 people per sq mile (57 people per sq km)
Total area 43,483 sq miles (112,620 sq km)
Languages French, Fon, Bariba, Yoruba, Adja, Houeda, Somba
Religions Indigenous beliefs 70%, Muslim 15%, Christian 15%
Ethnic mix Fon 47%, Baraba 10%, Adja 12%, other 31%
Government Presidential democracy
Currency CFA franc = 100 centimes
Literacy rate 40.3%
Calorie consumption 2,558 kilocalories

Benin, Bight of 75 F5 gulf W Africa
Benin City 75 F5 Edo, SW Nigeria
Beni, Río 61 E3 river N Bolivia
Beni Suef 72 B2 var. Banī Suwayf. N Egypt
Ben Nevis 88 C3 mountain N Scotland, UK
Benson 48 B3 Arizona, SW USA
Bent Jbaïl 119 A5 var. Bint Jubayl. S Lebanon
Benton 42 B1 Arkansas, C USA
Benue 76 B4 Fr. Bénoué. *River* Cameroon/Nigeria
Benue 75 G4 state SE Nigeria
Beograd 100 D3 Eng. Belgrade, Ger. Belgrad; anc. Singidunum. *Country capital* (Serbia, N Serbia and Montenegro (Yugo.)
Berane 101 D5 prev. Ivangrad. Montenegro, SW Serbia and Montenegro (Yugo.)
Berat 101 C6 var. Berati, SCr. Beligrad. Berat, C Albania
Berati see Berat
Berau, Teluk 139 G4 var. MacCluer Gulf. *Bay* Papua, E Indonesia
Berbera 72 D4 Woqooyi Galbeed, NW Somalia

Berbérati 77 B5 Mambéré-Kadéï, SW Central African Republic
Berck-Plage 90 C2 Pas-de-Calais, N France
Berdyans'k 109 G4 Rus. Berdyansk; prev. Osipenko. Zaporiz'ka Oblast', SE Ukraine
Berdychiv 108 D2 Rus. Berdichev. Zhytomyrs'ka Oblast', N Ukraine
Berehove 108 B3 Cz. Berehovo, Hung. Beregszász, Rus. Beregovo. Zakarpats'ka Oblast', W Ukraine
Berettyó 99 D7 Rom. Barcău; prev. Berătău, Beretău. *River* Hungary/Romania
Berettyóújfalu 99 D6 Hajdú-Bihar, E Hungary
Berezhany 108 C2 Pol. Brzeżany. Ternopil's'ka Oblast', W Ukraine
Berezniki 111 D5 Permskaya Oblast', NW Russian Federation
Berga 93 G2 Cataluña, NE Spain
Bergamo 96 B2 anc. Bergomum. Lombardia, N Italy
Bergara 93 E1 País Vasco, N Spain
Bergen 85 A5 Hordaland, S Norway
Bergen 94 D2 Mecklenburg-Vorpommern, NE Germany
Bergen 86 C2 Noord-Holland, NW Netherlands
Bergerac 91 B5 Dordogne, SW France
Bergeyk 87 C5 Noord-Brabant, S Netherlands
Bergse Maas 86 D4 river S Netherlands
Beringen 87 C5 Limburg, NE Belgium
Bering Sea 36 A2 sea N Pacific Ocean
Bering Strait 36 C2 Rus. Beringov Proliv. *Strait* Bering Sea/Chukchi Sea
Berja 93 E5 Andalucía, S Spain
Berkeley 47 B6 California, W USA
Berkner Island 154 A2 island Antarctica
Berkovitsa 104 C2 Montana, NW Bulgaria
Berlin 94 D3 *country capital* (Germany) Berlin, NE Germany
Berlin 41 G2 New Hampshire, NE USA
Bermejo, Río 64 C2 river N Argentina
Bermeo 93 E1 País Vasco, N Spain
Bermuda 35 D6 var. Bermuda Islands, Bermudas; prev. Somers Islands. *UK crown colony* NW Atlantic Ocean
Bermuda Islands see Bermuda
Bermuda Rise 35 E6 undersea feature C Sargasso Sea
Bermudas see Bermuda
Bern 95 A7 Fr. Berne. *Country capital* (Switzerland) Bern, W Switzerland
Bernau 94 D3 Brandenburg, NE Germany
Bernburg 94 C4 Sachsen-Anhalt, C Germany
Berne see Bern
Berner Alpen 95 A7 var. Berner Oberland, Eng. Bernese Oberland. *Mountain range* SW Switzerland
Berner Oberland see Berner Alpen
Bernese Oberland see Berner Alpen
Bernier Island 147 A5 island Western Australia
Berry 90 C4 cultural region C France
Berry Islands 54 C1 island group N Bahamas
Bertoua 77 B5 Est, E Cameroon
Beru 145 E2 var. Peru. Atoll Tungaru, W Kiribati
Berwick-upon-Tweed 88 D4 N England, UK
Berytus see Beyrouth
Besançon 90 D4 anc. Besontium, Vesontio. Doubs, E France
Beskra see Biskra
Betafo 79 G3 Antananarivo, C Madagascar
Betanzos 92 B1 Galicia, NW Spain

Bethlehem 119 B6 Ar. Beit Laḥm, Heb. Bet Lehem. C West Bank
Bethlehem 78 D4 Free State, C South Africa
Béticos, Sistemas 92 D4 var. Sistema Penibético, Eng. Baetic Cordillera, Baetic Mountains. *Mountain range* S Spain
Bet Lehem see Bethlehem
Bétou 77 C5 La Likouala, N Congo
Bette, Picco see Bette, Pic
Bette, Pic 71 G4 var. Bikkū Bittī, It. Picco Bette. *Mountain* S Libya
Bette, Picco see Bette, Pic
Beulah 40 C2 Michigan, N USA
Beuthen see Bytom
Beveren 87 B5 Oost-Vlaanderen, N Belgium
Beverley 89 D5 E England, UK
Bexley 89 B8 SE England, UK
Beyla 74 D4 Guinée-Forestière, SE Guinea
Beyrouth 118 A4 var. Bayrūt, Eng. Beirut; anc. Berytus. *Country capital* (Lebanon) W Lebanon
Beyşehir 116 B4 Konya, SW Turkey
Beyşehir Gölü 116 B4 lake C Turkey
Béziers 91 C6 anc. Baeterrae, Baeterrae Septimanorum, Julia Beterrae. Hérault, S France
Bhadrāvati 132 C2 Karnātaka, SW India
Bhāgalpur 135 F3 Bihār, NE India
Bhaktapur 135 F3 Central, C Nepal
Bhamo 136 B2 var. Banmo. Kachin State, N Myanmar
Bharūch 134 C4 Gujarāt, W India
Bhāvnagar 134 C4 prev. Bhaunagar. Gujarāt, W India
Bhopāl 134 D4 Madhya Pradesh, C India
Bhubaneshwar 135 F5 prev. Bhubaneswar, Bhuvaneshwar. Orissa, E India
Bhuket see Phuket
Bhusāwal 134 D4 prev. Bhusaval. Mahārāshtra, C India
Bhutan 135 G3 var. Druk-yul. *Country* S Asia

Bhutan 135

Official name Kingdom of Bhutan
Formation 1656
Capital Thimphu
Population 2.1 million / 116 people per sq mile (45 people per sq km)
Total area 18,147 sq miles (47,000 sq km)
Languages Dzongkha, Nepali, Assamese
Religions Mahayana Buddhist 70%, Hindu 24%, other 6%
Ethnic mix Bhote 50%, Nepalese 25%, other 25%
Government Monarchy
Currency Ngultrum = 100 chetrum
Literacy rate 47.3%
Calorie consumption not available

Biak, Pulau 139 G4 island E Indonesia
Biała Podlaska 98 E3 Lubelskie, E Poland
Białogard 98 B2 Ger. Belgard. Zachodniopomorskie, NW Poland
Białystok 98 E3 Rus. Belostok, Bielostok. Podlaskie, NE Poland
Biarritz 91 A6 Pyrénées-Atlantiques, SW France
Bicaz 108 C3 Hung. Békás. Neamţ, NE Romania
Biddeford 41 G2 Maine, NE USA
Bideford 89 C7 SW England, UK
Biel 95 A7 Fr. Bienne. Bern, W Switzerland
Bielefeld 94 B4 Nordrhein-Westfalen, NW Germany
Bielsko-Biała 99 C5 Ger. Bielitz, Bielitz-Biala. Śląskie, S Poland
Bielsk Podlaski 98 E3 Podlaskie, NE Poland
Bien Bien see Điện Biên
Biên Hoa 137 E6 Đông Nai, S Vietnam

Bienville, Lac *38 D2 lake* Quebec, C Canada

Bié, Planalto do *78 B2 var.* Bié Plateau. *Plateau* C Angola

Bié Plateau *see* Bié, Planalto do

Big Cypress Swamp *43 E5 wetland* Florida, SE USA

Bigge Island *146 C2 island* Western Australia

Bighorn Mountains *44 C2 mountain range* Wyoming, C USA

Bighorn River *44 C2 river* Montana/Wyoming, NW USA

Bignona *74 B3* SW Senegal

Big Sioux River *45 E2 river* Iowa/South Dakota, N USA

Big Spring *49 E3* Texas, SW USA

Bihać *100 B3* Federacija Bosna I Hercegovina, NW Bosnia and Herzegovina

Bihār *135 F4 prev.* Behar. Admin. region *state* N India

Biharamulo *73 B7* Kagera, NW Tanzania

Bihosava *107 D5 Rus.* Bigosovo. Vitsyebskaya Voblasts', NW Belarus

Bijeljina *100 C3* Republika Srpska, NE Bosnia and Herzegovina

Bijelo Polje *101 D5* Montenegro, SW Serbia and Montenegro (Yugo.)

Bīkāner *134 C3* Rājasthān, NW India

Bikin *115 G4* Khabarovskiy Kray, SE Russian Federation

Bikini Atoll *144 C1 var.* Pikinni. *Atoll* Ralik Chain, NW Marshall Islands

Bīkkū Bīttī *see* Bette, Pic

Bilāspur *135 E4* Madhya Pradesh, C India

Biläsuvar *117 H3 Rus.* Bilyasuvar; *prev.* Pushkino. SE Azerbaijan

Bila Tserkva *109 E2 Rus.* Belaya Tserkov'. Kyyivs'ka Oblast', N Ukraine

Bilauktaung Range *137 C6 var.* Thanintari Taungdan. *Mountain range* Myanmar/Thailand

Bilbao *93 E1 Basq.* Bilbo. País Vasco, N Spain

Bilecik *116 B3* Bilecik, NW Turkey

Billings *44 C2* Montana, NW USA

Bilma, Grand Erg de *75 H3 desert* NE Niger

Biloela *148 D4* Queensland, E Australia

Biloxi *42 C3* Mississippi, S USA

Biltine *76 C3* Biltine, E Chad

Bilwi *see* Puerto Cabezas

Bilzen *87 D6* Limburg, NE Belgium

Bimini Islands *54 C1 island group* W Bahamas

Binche *87 B7* Hainaut, S Belgium

Bindloe Island *see* Marchena, Isla

Binghamton *41 F3* New York, NE USA

Bingöl *117 E3* Bingöl, E Turkey

Bint Jubayl *see* Bent Jbaïl

Bintulu *138 D3* Sarawak, East Malaysia

Binzhou *128 D4* Shandong, E China

Bío Bío, Río *65 B5 river* C Chile

Bioco, Isla de *77 A5 var.* Bioko, *Eng.* Fernando Po, *Sp.* Fernando Póo; *prev.* Macías Nguema Biyogo. *Island* NW Equatorial Guinea

Bioko *see* Bioco, Isla de

Birāk *71 F3 var.* Brak. C Libya

Birao *76 D3* Vakaga, NE Central African Republic

Biratnagar *135 F3* Eastern, SE Nepal

Bir es Saba *see* Be'ér Sheva'

Birhār Sharīf *135 F3* Bihār, N India

Birjand *120 E3* Khorāsān, E Iran

Birkenfeld *95 A5* Rheinland-Pfalz, SW Germany

Birkenhead *89 C5* NW England, UK

Birmingham *42 C2* Alabama, S USA

Birmingham *89 C6* C England, UK

Bir Moghrein *see* Bîr Mogreïn

Bîr Mogreïn *74 C1 var.* Bir Moghrein; *prev.* Fort-Trinquet. Tiris Zemmour, N Mauritania

Birnie Island *145 E3 atoll* Phoenix Islands, C Kiribati

Birni-Nkonni *see* Birnin Konni

Birnin Konni *75 F3 var.* Birni-Nkonni. Tahoua, SW Niger

Birobidzhan *115 G4* Yevreyskaya Avtonomnaya Oblast', SE Russian Federation

Birsk *111 D5* Respublika Bashkortostan, W Russian Federation

Biržai *106 C4 Ger.* Birsen. Biržai, NE Lithuania

Birżebbuġa *102 B5* SE Malta

Bisbee *48 B3* Arizona, SW USA

Biscay, Bay of *80 B4 Sp.* Golfo de Vizcaya, *Port.* Baía de Biscaia. *Bay* France/Spain

Biscay Plain *80 B3 undersea feature* SE Bay of Biscay

Bīshah, Wādī *121 B5 dry watercourse* C Saudi Arabia

Bishkek *123 G2 var.* Pishpek; *prev.* Frunze. *Country capital* (Kyrgyzstan) Chuyskaya Oblast', N Kyrgyzstan

Bishop's Lynn *see* King's Lynn

Bishrī, Jabal *118 D3 mountain range* E Syria

Biskara *see* Biskra

Biskra *71 E2 var.* Beskra, Biskara. NE Algeria

Biskupiec *98 D2 Ger.* Bischofsburg. Warmińsko-Mazurskie, NE Poland

Bislig *139 F2* Mindanao, S Philippines

Bismarck *45 E2 state capital* North Dakota, N USA

Bismarck Archipelago *144 B3 island group* NE PNG

Bismarck Sea *144 B3 sea* W Pacific Ocean

Bisnulok *see* Phitsanulok

Bissau *74 B4 country capital* (Guinea-Bissau) W Guinea-Bissau

Bistriţa *108 B3 Ger.* Bistritz, *Hung.* Beszterce; *prev.* Nösen. Bistriţa-Năsăud, N Romania

Bitam *77 B5* Woleu-Ntem, N Gabon

Bitburg *95 A5* Rheinland-Pfalz, SW Germany

Bitlis *117 F3* Bitlis, SE Turkey

Bitola *101 D6 Turk.* Monastir; *prev.* Bitolj. S FYR Macedonia

Bitonto *97 D5 anc.* Butuntum. Puglia, SE Italy

Bitterroot Range *46 D2 mountain range* Idaho/Montana, NW USA

Bitung *139 F3 prev.* Bitoeng. Sulawesi, C Indonesia

Biu *75 H4* Borno, E Nigeria

Biwa-ko *131 C6 lake* Honshū, SW Japan

Bizerte *71 E1 Ar.* Banzart, *Eng.* Bizerta. N Tunisia

Bjelovar *100 B2 Hung.* Belovár. Bjelovar-Bilogora, N Croatia

Bjørnøya *83 E1 Eng.* Bear Island. *Island* N Norway

Blackall *148 C4* Queensland, E Australia

Black Drin *101 D6 Alb.* Lumi i Drinit të Zi, *SCr.* Crni Drim. *River* Albania/FYR Macedonia

Blackfoot *46 E4* Idaho, NW USA

Black Forest *see* Schwarzwald

Black Hills *44 D3 mountain range* South Dakota/Wyoming, N USA

Blackpool *89 C5* NW England, UK

Black Range *48 C2 mountain range* New Mexico, SW USA

Black River *136 C3 Chin.* Babian Jiang, Lixian Jiang, *Fr.* Rivière Noire, *Vtn.* Sông Đa. *River* China/Vietnam

Black River *54 B5* W Jamaica

Black Rock Desert *47 C5 desert* Nevada, W USA

Black Sand Desert *see* Garagumy

Black Sea *114 B1 var.* Euxine Sea, *Bul.* Cherno More, *Rom.* Marea Neagrǎ, *Rus.* Chernoye More, *Turk.* Karadeniz, *Ukr.* Chorne More. *Sea* Asia/Europe

Black Sea Lowland *109 E4 Ukr.* Prychornomors'ka Nyzovyna. *Depression* SE Europe

Black Volta *75 E4 var.* Borongo, Mouhoun, Moun Hou, *Fr.* Volta Noire. *River* W Africa

Blackwater *89 A6 Ir.* An Abhainn Mhór. *River* S Ireland

Blagoevgrad *104 C3 prev.* Gorna Dzhumaya. Blagoevgrad, SW Bulgaria

Blagoveshchensk *115 G4* Amurskaya Oblast', SE Russian Federation

Blake Plateau *35 D6 var.* Blake Terrace. *Undersea feature* W Atlantic Ocean

Blake Terrace *see* Blake Plateau

Blanca, Bahía *65 C5 bay* E Argentina

Blanca, Costa *93 F4 physical region* SE Spain

Blanche, Lake *149 B5 lake* South Australia

Blanc, Mont *91 D5 It.* Monte Bianco. *Mountain* France/Italy

Blanco, Cape *46 A4 headland* Oregon, NW USA

Blanes *93 G2* Cataluña, NE Spain

Blankenberge *87 A5* West-Vlaanderen, NW Belgium

Blankenheim *95 A5* Nordrhein-Westfalen, W Germany

Blanquilla, Isla *59 E1 var.* La Blanquilla. *Island* N Venezuela

Blantyre *79 E2 var.* Blantyre-Limbe. Southern, S Malawi

Blantyre-Limbe *see* Blantyre

Blaricum *86 C3* Noord-Holland, C Netherlands

Blenheim *151 C5* Marlborough, South Island, NZ

Blida *70 D2 var.* El Boulaida, El Boulaïda. N Algeria

Bloemfontein *78 C4 var.* Mangaung. *Country capital* (South Africa-judicial capital) Free State, C South Africa

Blois *90 C4 anc.* Blesae. Loir-et-Cher, C France

Bloomfield *48 C1* New Mexico, SW USA

Bloomington *40 B4* Illinois, N USA

Bloomington *40 C4* Indiana, N USA

Bloomington *45 F2* Minnesota, N USA

Bloomsbury *148 D3* Queensland, NE Australia

Bluefield *40 D5* West Virginia, NE USA

Bluefields *53 E3* Región Autónoma Atlántico Sur, SE Nicaragua

Blue Mountain Peak *54 B5 mountain* E Jamaica

Blue Mountains *46 C3 mountain range* Oregon/Washington, NW USA

Blue Nile *68 D4 var.* Abai, Bahr el Azraq, *Amh.* Ābay Wenz, *Ar.* An Nīl al Azraq. *River* Ethiopia/Sudan

Blue Nile *72 C4 var.* Blue Nile E Sudan

Blumenau *63 E5* Santa Catarina, S Brazil

Blythe *47 D8* California, W USA

Blytheville *42 C1* Arkansas, C USA

Bo *74 C4* S Sierra Leone

Boaco *52 D3* Boaco, S Nicaragua

Boa Vista *74 A3 island* Ilhas de Barlavento, E Cape Verde

Boa Vista *62 D1 state capital* Roraima, NW Brazil

Bobaomby, Tanjona *79 G2 Fr.* Cap d'Ambre. *Headland* N Madagascar

Bobigny *90 E1* Seine-St-Denis, N France

Bobo-Dioulasso *74 D4* SW Burkina Faso

Bobrynets' *109 E3 Rus.* Bobrinets. Kirovohrads'ka Oblast', C Ukraine

Boca Raton *43 F5* Florida, SE USA

Bocay *52 D2* Jinotega, N Nicaragua

Bocche del Po *see* Po, Foci del

Bocholt *94 A4* Nordrhein-Westfalen, W Germany

Bochum *94 A4* Nordrhein-Westfalen, W Germany

Bocşa *108 A4 Ger.* Bokschen, *Hung.* Boksánbánya. Caraş-Severin, SW Romania

Bodaybo *115 F4* Irkutskaya Oblast', E Russian Federation

Boden *84 D4* Norrbotten, N Sweden

Bodmin *89 C7* SW England, UK

Bodø *84 C3* Nordland, C Norway

Bodrum *116 A4* Muğla, SW Turkey

Boende *77 C5* Equateur, C Dem. Rep. Congo

Boetoeng *see* Buton, Pulau

Bogale *136 B4* Irrawaddy, SW Myanmar

Bogalusa *42 B3* Louisiana, S USA

Bogatynia *98 B4 Ger.* Reichenau. Dolnośląskie, SW Poland

Boğazlıyan *116 D3* Yozgat, C Turkey

Bogor *138 C5 Dut.* Buitenzorg. Jawa, C Indonesia

Bogotá *58 B3 prev.* Santa Fe, Santa Fe de Bogotá. *Country capital* (Colombia) Cundinamarca, C Colombia

Bo Hai *124 D4 var.* Gulf of Chihli. *Gulf* NE China

Bohemia *99 A5 Cz.* Čechy, *Ger.* Böhmen. *Cultural and historical region* W Czech Republic

Bohemian Forest *95 C5 Cz.* Ceský Les, Šumava, *Ger.* Böhmerwald. *Mountain range* C Europe

Böhmisch-Krumau *see* Český Krumlov

Bohol Sea *139 E2 var.* Mindanao Sea. *Sea* S Philippines

Bohoro Shan *126 B2 mountain range* NW China

Bohuslav *109 E2 Rus.* Boguslav. Kyyivs'ka Oblast', N Ukraine

Boise *46 D3 var.* Boise City. *State capital* Idaho, NW USA

Boise City *see* Boise

Boise City *49 E1* Oklahoma, C USA

Boizenburg *94 C3* Mecklenburg-Vorpommern, N Germany

Bojador *see* Boujdour

Bojnūrd *120 D2 var.* Bujnurd. Khorāsān, N Iran

Bokāro *135 F4* Bihār, N India

Boké *74 C4* Guinée-Maritime, W Guinea

Bokhara *see* Bukhoro

Boknafjorden *85 A6 fjord* S Norway

Bol *76 B3* Lac, W Chad

Bolgatanga *75 E4* N Ghana

Bolhrad *108 D4 Rus.* Bolgrad. Odes'ka Oblast', SW Ukraine

Bolívar, Pico *58 C2 mountain* W Venezuela

Bolivia *61 F3 Country* W South America

Bollène *91 D6* Vaucluse, SE France

Bolivia 61

Bollnäs *85 C5* Gävleborg, C Sweden

Bollon *149 D5* Queensland, C Australia

Bologna *96 C3* Emilia-Romagna, N Italy

Bol'shevik, Ostrov *115 E2 island* Severnaya Zemlya, N Russian Federation

Bol'shezemel'skaya Tundra 110 E3 *physical region* NW Russian Federation
Bol'shoy Lyakhovskiy, Ostrov 115 F2 *island* NE Russian Federation
Bolton 89 D5 *prev.* Bolton-le-Moors. NW England, UK
Bolu 116 B3 Bolu, NW Turkey
Bolungarvík 83 E4 Vestfirdhir, NW Iceland
Bolyarovo 104 D3 *prev.* Pashkeni. Yambol, E Bulgaria
Bolzano 96 C1 *Ger.* Bozen; *anc.* Bauzanum. Trentino-Alto Adige, N Italy
Boma 77 B6 Bas-Zaïre, W Dem. Rep. Dem. Rep. Congo
Bombay *see* Mumbai
Bomu 76 D4 *var.* Mbomou, Mbomu, M'Bomu. *River* Central African Republic/Dem. Rep. Congo
Bonaire 55 F5 *island* F. Netherlands Antilles
Bonanza 52 D2 Región Autónoma Atlántico Norte, NE Nicaragua
Bonaparte Archipelago 146 C2 *island group* Western Australia
Bon, Cap 102 D3 *headland* N Tunisia
Bonda 77 B6 Ogooué-Lolo, C Gabon
Bondoukou 75 E4 E Côte d'Ivoire
Bone *see* Watampone
Bone, Teluk 139 E4 *bay* Sulawesi, C Indonesia
Bongaigaon 135 G3 Assam, NE India
Bongo, Massif des 76 D4 *var.* Chaîne des Mongos. *Mountain range* NE Central African Republic
Bongor 76 B3 Mayo-Kébbi, SW Chad
Bonifacio 91 E7 Corse, France, C Mediterranean Sea
Bonifacio, Strait of 96 A4 *Fr.* Bouches de Bonifacio, *It.* Bocche de Bonifacio. *Strait* C Mediterranean Sea
Bonn 95 A5 Nordrhein-Westfalen, W Germany
Bononia *see* Boulogne-sur-Mer
Boosaaso 72 E4 *var.* Bandar Kassim, Bender Qaasim, Bosaso, *It.* Bender Cassim. Bari, N Somalia
Boothia, Gulf of 37 F2 *gulf* Nunavut, NE Canada
Boothia Peninsula 37 F2 *prev.* Boothia Felix. *Peninsula* Nunavut, NE Canada
Boppard 95 A5 Rheinland-Pfalz, W Germany
Boquete 53 E5 *var.* Bajo Boquete. Chiriquí, W Panama
Boquillas 50 D2 *var.* Boquillas del Carmen. Coahuila de Zaragoza, NE Mexico
Boquillas del Carmen *see* Boquillas
Bor 73 B5 Jonglei, S Sudan
Bor 100 E4 Serbia, E Serbia and Montenegro (Yugo.)
Borås 85 B7 Västra Götaland, S Sweden
Borborema, Planalto da 56 E3 *plateau* NE Brazil
Bordeaux 91 B5 *anc.* Burdigala. Gironde, SW France
Bordj Omar Driss 71 E3 E Algeria
Børgefjell 84 C4 *mountain range* C Norway
Borger 86 E2 Drenthe, NE Netherlands
Borger 49 E1 Texas, SW USA
Borgholm 85 C7 Kalmar, S Sweden
Borgo Maggiore 96 E1 NW San Marino
Borisoglebsk 111 B6 Voronezhskaya Oblast', W Russian Federation
Borlänge 85 C6 Kopparberg, C Sweden
Borne 86 E3 Overijssel, E Netherlands
Borneo 138 C4 *island* Brunei/Indonesia/Malaysia
Bornholm 85 B8 *island* E Denmark
Borohoro Shan 123 H1 *mountain range* NW China

Borongo *see* Black Volta
Borovan 104 C2 Vratsa, NW Bulgaria
Borovichi 110 B4 Novgorodskaya Oblast', W Russian Federation
Borovo 100 C3 Vukovar-Srijem, NE Croatia
Borşa 108 C3 Hung. Borsa. Maramureş, N Romania
Boryslaw 108 B2 Pol. Boryslaw, *Rus.* Borislav. L'vivs'ka Oblast', NW Ukraine
Bosanska Dubica 100 B3 *var.* Kozarska Dubica. Republika Srpska, NW Bosnia and Herzegovina
Bosanska Gradiška 100 B3 *var.* Gradiška. Republika Srpska, N Bosnia and Herzegovina
Bosanski Novi 100 B3 *var.* Novi Grad. Republika Srpska, NW Bosnia and Herzegovina
Bosanski Šamac 100 C3 *var.* Šamac. Republika Srpska, N Bosnia and Herzegovina
Bosaso *see* Boosaaso
Boskovice 99 B5 *Ger.* Boskowitz. Brněnský Kraj, SE Czech Republic
Bosna 100 C4 *river* N Bosnia and Herzegovina
Bosna I Hercegovina, Federacija Admin. region *republic* Bosnia and Herzegovina
Bosnia and Herzegovina 100 B3 *Country* SE Europe

Bosnia and Herzegovina 100

Official name Bosnia and Herzegovina
Formation 1992
Capital Sarajevo
Population 4.1 million /208 people per sq mile (80 people per sq km)
Total area 19,741 sq miles (51,129 sq km)
Languages Serbo-Croat
Religions Muslim (mainly Sunni) 40%, Serbian Orthodox 31%, Roman Catholic 15%, Protestant 4%, other 10%
Ethnic mix Bosniak 44%, Serb 31%, Croat 17%, other 8%
Government Multiparty republic
Currency Marka = 100 pfenniga
Literacy rate 93%
Calorie consumption 2,661 kilocalories

Bōsō-hantō 131 D6 *peninsula* Honshū, S Japan
Bosphorus *see* İstanbul Boğazı
Bosporus *see* İstanbul Boğazı
Bosporus Cimmerius *see* Kerch Strait
Bosporus Thracius *see* İstanbul Boğazı
Bossangoa 76 C4 Ouham, C Central African Republic
Bossembélé 76 C4 Ombella-Mpoko, C Central African Republic
Bossier City 42 A2 Louisiana, S USA
Bosten Hu 126 C3 *var.* Bagrax Hu. *Lake* NW China
Boston 89 E6 *prev.* St.Botolph's Town. E England, UK
Boston 41 G3 *state capital* Massachusetts, NE USA
Boston Mountains 42 B1 *mountain range* Arkansas, C USA
Botany 148 E2 New South Wales, SE Australia
Botany Bay 148 E2 *inlet* New South Wales, SE Australia
Boteti 78 C3 *var.* Botletle. *River* N Botswana
Bothnia, Gulf of 85 D5 Fin. Pohjanlahti, *Swe.* Bottniska Viken. *Gulf* N Baltic Sea
Botletle *see* Boteti

Botoşani 108 C3 Hung. Botosány. Botoşani, NE Romania
Botou 128 C4 *prev.* Bozhen. Hebei, E China
Botrange 87 D6 *mountain* E Belgium
Botswana 78 C3 *Country* S Africa

Botswana 78

Official name Republic of Botswana
Formation 1966
Capital Gaborone
Population 1.6 million /7 people per sq mile (3 people per sq km)
Total area 231,803 sq miles (600,370 sq km)
Languages English, Tswana, Shona, San, Khoikhoi, Ndebele
Religions Traditional beliefs 50%, Christian (mainly Protestant) 30%, other (including Muslim) 20%
Ethnic mix Tswana 98% other 2%
Government Presidential democracy
Currency Pula = 100 thebe
Literacy rate 77.2%
Calorie consumption 2,255 kilocalories

Bouar 76 B4 Nana-Mambéré, W Central African Republic
Bou Craa 70 B3 *var.* Bu Craa. NW Western Sahara
Bougainville Island 142 B3 *island* NE PNG
Bougaroun, Cap 102 C3 *headland* NE Algeria
Bougouni 74 D3 Sikasso, SW Mali
Boujdour 70 A3 *var.* Bojador. W Western Sahara
Boulder 44 C4 Colorado, C USA
Boulder 44 B2 Montana, NW USA
Boulogne *see* Boulogne-sur-Mer
Boulogne-Billancourt 90 D1 *prev.* Boulogne-sur-Seine. Hauts-de-Seine, N France
Boulogne-sur-Mer 90 C2 *var.* Boulogne; *anc.* Bononia, Gesoriacum, Gessoriacum. Pas-de-Calais, N France
Boûmdeïd 74 C3 *var.* Boumdeït.
Boumdeït *see* Boûmdeïd
Boundiali 74 D4 N Côte d'Ivoire
Bountiful 44 B4 Utah, W USA
Bounty Basin *see* Bounty Trough
Bounty Islands 142 D5 *island group* S NZ
Bounty Trough 152 C5 *var.* Bounty Basin. *Undersea feature* S Pacific Ocean
Bourbonnais 90 C4 Illinois, N USA
Bourg *see* Bourg-en-Bresse
Bourgas *see* Burgas
Bourge-en-Bresse *see* Bourg-en-Bresse
Bourg-en-Bresse 91 D5 *var.* Bourg, Bourge-en-Bresse. Ain, E France
Bourges 90 C4 *anc.* Avaricum. Cher, C France
Bourgogne 90 C4 *Eng.* Burgundy. *Cultural region* E France
Bourke 149 C5 New South Wales, SE Australia
Bournemouth 89 D7 S England, UK
Boutilimit 74 C3 Trarza, SW Mauritania
Bouvet Island 67 D7 *Norwegian dependency* S Atlantic Ocean
Bowen 148 D3 Queensland, NE Australia
Bowling Green 40 B5 Kentucky, S USA
Bowling Green 40 C3 Ohio, N USA
Boxmeer 86 D4 Noord-Brabant, SE Netherlands
Boyarka 109 E2 Kyyivs'ka Oblast', N Ukraine
Boysun 123 E3 *Rus.* Baysun. Surkhondaryo Wiloyati, S Uzbekistan

Bozeman 44 B2 Montana, NW USA
Bozüyük 116 B3 Bilecik, NW Turkey
Brač 100 B4 *var.* Brach, *It.* Brazza; *anc.* Brattia. *Island* S Croatia
Brach *see* Brač
Bradford 89 D5 N England, UK
Brady 49 F3 Texas, SW USA
Braga 92 B2 *anc.* Bracara Augusta. Braga, NW Portugal
Bragança 92 C2 *Eng.* Braganza; *anc.* Julio Briga. Bragança, NE Portuga
Brahmanbaria 135 G4 Chittagong, E Bangladesh
Brahmapur 135 F5 Orissa, E India
Brahmaputra 135 H3 *var.* Padma, Tsangpo, *Ben.* Jamuna, *Chin.* Yarlung Zangbo Jiang, *Ind.* Bramaputra, Dihang, Siang. *River* S Asia
Brăila 108 D4 Brăila, E Romania
Braine-le-Comte 87 B6 Hainaut, SW Belgium
Brainerd 45 F2 Minnesota, N USA
Brak *see* Birāk
Bramaputra *see* Brahmaputra
Brampton 38 D5 Ontario, S Canada
Branco, Rio 56 C3 *river* N Brazil
Brandberg 78 A3 *mountain* NW Namibia
Brandenburg 94 C3 *var.* Brandenburg an der Havel. Brandenburg, NE Germany
Brandenburg an der Havel *see* Brandenburg
Brandon 37 F5 Manitoba, S Canada
Braniewo 98 D2 *Ger.* Braunsberg. Warmińsko-Mazurskie, NE Polan
Brasília 63 F3 *country capital* (Brazi Distrito Federal, C Brazil
Braşov 108 C4 *Ger.* Kronstadt, *Hung* Brassó; *prev.* Oraşul Stalin. Braşov C Romania
Bratislava 99 C6 *Ger.* Pressburg, *Hung.* Pozsony. *Country capital* (Slovakia) Bratislavský Kraj, SW Slovakia
Bratsk 115 E4 Irkutskaya Oblast', C Russian Federation
Brattia *see* Brač
Braunschweig 94 C4 *Eng./Fr.* Brunswick. Niedersachsen, N Germany
Brava, Costa 93 H2 *coastal region* NE Spain
Bravo del Norte *see* Grande, Rio
Bravo del Norte, Río *see* Bravo, Rí
Bravo del Norte, Río *see* Grande, Rio
Bravo, Río 50 C1 *var.* Río Bravo del Norte, Rio Grande. *River* Mexico/USA
Bravo, Río *see* Grande, Rio
Brawley 47 D8 California, W USA
Brazil 62 C2 *Port.* República Federativa do Brasil, *Sp.* Brasil; *prev.* United States of Brazil. *Country* South America

Brazil 62

Official name Federative Republic of Brazil
Formation 1822
Capital Brasília
Population 172.6 million / 53 people per sq mile (20 people per sq km)
Total area 3,286,470 sq miles (8,511,965 sq km)
Languages Portuguese, German, Italian, Spanish, Polish, Japanese
Religions Roman Catholic 74%, Protestant 15%, Atheist 7%, other 4%
Ethnic mix Black 53%, Mixed 40%, White 6%, other 1%
Government Presidential democracy
Currency Real = 100 centavos
Literacy rate 85.2%
Calorie consumption 2,985 kilocalories

Brazil Basin 67 C5 *var.* Brazilian Basin, Brazil'skaya Kotlovina. *Undersea feature* W Atlantic Ocean

Brazilian Basin *see* Brazil Basin
Brazilian Highlands *see* Central, Planalto
razil'skaya Kotlovina *see* Brazil Basin
razos River 49 G3 *river* Texas, SW USA
razza *see* Brač
razzaville 77 B6 *country capital* (Congo) Capital District, S Congo
recht 87 C5 Antwerpen, N Belgium
recon Beacons 89 C6 *mountain range* S Wales, UK
reda 86 C4 Noord-Brabant, S Netherlands
ree 87 D5 Limburg, NE Belgium
regalnica 101 E6 *river* E FYR Macedonia
regenze 57 B7 *anc.* Brigantium. Vorarlberg, W Austria
regovo 104 B1 Vidin, NW Bulgaria
rčko 100 C3 Republika Srpska, NE Bosnia and Herzegovina
remen 94 B3 *Fr.* Brême. Bremen, NW Germany
remerhaven 94 B3 Bremen, NW Germany
remen 46 B2 Washington, NW USA
renham 49 G3 Texas, SW USA
renner Pass 96 C1 *var.* BrennerSattel, *Fr.* Col du Brenner, *Ger.* Brennerpass, *It.* Passo del Brennero. Pass Austria/Italy
rennerpass *see* Brenner Pass
renner Sattel *see* Brenner Pass
rescia 96 B2 *anc.* Brixia. Lombardia, N Italy
ressanone 96 C1 *Ger.* Brixen. Trentino-Alto Adige, N Italy
rest 107 A6 *Pol.* Brześć nad Bugiem, *Rus.* Brest-Litovsk; *prev.* Brześć Litewski. Brestskaya Voblasts', SW Belarus
rest 90 A3 Finistère, NW France
retagne 90 A3 *Eng.* Brittany; *Lat.* Britannia Minor. *Cultural region* NW France
rewton 42 C3 Alabama, S USA
rezovo 104 D2 *prev.* Abrashlare. Plovdiv, C Bulgaria
ria 76 D4 Haute-Kotto, C Central African Republic
riançon 91 D5 *anc.* Brigantio. Hautes-Alpes, SE France
ridgeport 41 F3 Connecticut, NE USA
ridgetown 55 G2 *country capital* (Barbados) SW Barbados
ridlington 89 D5 E England, UK
ridport 89 D7 S England, UK
rig 95 A7 *Fr.* Brigue, *It.* Briga. Valais, SW Switzerland
righam City 44 B3 Utah, W USA
righton 44 D4 Colorado, C USA
righton 89 E7 SE England, UK
rindisi 97 E5 *anc.* Brundisium, Brundusium. Puglia, SE Italy
risbane 149 E5 *state capital* Queensland, E Australia
ristol 89 D7 *anc.* Bricgstow. SW England, UK
ristol 41 F3 Connecticut, NE USA
ristol 40 D5 Virginia, NE USA
ristol Bay 36 B3 *bay* Alaska, USA
ristol Channel 89 C7 *inlet* England/Wales, UK
ristol 23 D2 *var.* Great Britain. *Island* UK
ritish Columbia 36 D4 *Fr.* Colombie-Britannique. *Province* SW Canada
ritish Indian Ocean Territory 141 B5 *UK dependent territory* C Indian Ocean
ritish Isles 89 *island group* NW Europe
ritish Virgin Islands 55 F3 *var.* Virgin Islands. *UK dependent territory* E West Indies
rive-la-Gaillarde 91 C5 *prev.* Brive, *anc.* Briva Curretia. Corrèze, C France
rno 99 B5 *Ger.* Brünn. Brněnský Kraj, SE Czech Republic
ročeni 106 B3 Saldus, SW Latvia

Brodeur Peninsula 37 F2 *peninsula* Baffin Island, Nunavut, NE Canada
Brodnica 98 C3 *Ger.* Buddenbrock. Kujawski-pomorskie, C Poland
Broek-in-Waterland 86 C3 Noord-Holland, C Netherlands
Broken Arrow 49 G1 Oklahoma, C USA
Broken Bay 148 E1 *bay* New South Wales, SE Australia
Broken Hill 149 B6 New South Wales, SE Australia
Broken Ridge 141 D6 *undersea feature* S Indian Ocean
Bromley 89 B8 SE England, UK
Brookhaven 42 B3 Mississippi, S USA
Brookings 45 F3 South Dakota, N USA
Brooks Range 36 D2 *mountain range* Alaska, USA
Brookton 147 B6 Western Australia
Broome 146 B3 Western Australia
Broomfield 44 D4 Colorado, C USA
Broucsella *see* Brussel
Brovary 109 E2 Kyyivs'ka Oblast', N Ukraine
Brownfield 49 E2 Texas, SW USA
Brownville 49 G5 Texas, SW USA
Brownwood 49 F3 Texas, SW USA
Brozha 107 D7 Mahilyowskaya Voblasts', E Belarus
Brugge 87 A5 *Fr.* Bruges. West-Vlaanderen, NW Belgium
Brummen 86 D3 Gelderland, E Netherlands
Brunei 138 D3*Mal.* Negara Brunei Darussalam. *Country* SE Asia

Brunei 138

Official name Sultanate of Brunei
Formation 1984
Capital Bandar Seri Begawan
Population 335,000 / 150 people per sq mile (58 people per sq km)
Total area 2,228 sq miles (5,770 sq km)
Languages Malay, English, Chinese
Religions Muslim 66%, Buddhist 14%, Christian 10%, other 10%
Ethnic mix Malay 67%, Chinese 16%, Indigenous 6%, other 11%
Government Monarchy
Currency Brunei dollar = 100 cents
Literacy rate 91.5%
Calorie consumption 2,832 kilocalories

Brunner, Lake 151 C5 *lake* South Island, NZ
Brunswick 43 E3 Georgia, SE USA
Brusa *see* Bursa
Brus Laguna 52 D2 Gracias a Dios, E Honduras
Brussa *see* Bursa
Brussel *var.* Brussels, *Fr.* Bruxelles, *Ger.* Brüssel; *anc.* Broucsella. *Country capital* (Belgium) Brussels, C Belgium *see also* Bruxelles
Brüssel *see* Brussel
Brussels *see* Brussel
Bruxelles *see* Brussels
Bryan 49 G3 Texas, SW USA
Bryansk 111 A5 Bryanskaya Oblast', W Russian Federation
Brzeg 98 C4 *Ger.* Brieg; *anc.* Civitas Altae Ripae. Opolskie, S Poland
Bucaramanga 58 B2 Santander, N Colombia
Buchanan 74 C5 *prev.* Grand Bassa. SW Liberia
Buchanan, Lake 49 F3 *reservoir* Texas, SW USA
Bucharest *see* București
Bu Craa *see* Bou Craa
București 108 C5 *Eng.* Bucharest, *Ger.* Bukarest; *prev.* Altenburg, *anc.* Cetatea Dâmboviței. *Country capital* (Romania) București, S Romania

Buda-Kashalyova 107 D7 *Rus.* Buda-Koshelëvo. Homyel'skaya Voblasts', SE Belarus
Budapest 99 C6 *off.* Budapest Fóváros, *SCr.* Budimpešta. *Country capital* (Hungary) Pest, N Hungary
Budaun 134 D3 Uttar Pradesh, N India
Buena Park 46 E2 California, W USA
Buenaventura 58 A3 Valle del Cauca, W Colombia
Buena Vista 39 H5 S Gibraltar
Buena Vista 61 G4 Santa Cruz, C Bolivia
Buenos Aires 64 D4 *hist.* Santa Maria del Buen Aire. *Country capital* (Argentina) Buenos Aires, E Argentina
Buenos Aires 53 E5 Puntarenas, SE Costa Rica
Buenos Aires, Lago 65 B6 *var.* Lago General Carrera. *Lake* Argentina/Chile
Buffalo 41 E3 New York, NE USA
Buffalo Narrows 37 F4 Saskatchewan, C Canada
Buff Bay 54 B5 E Jamaica
Buftea 108 C5 București, S Romania
Bug 81 E3 *Bel.* Zakhodni Buh, *Eng.* Western Bug, *Rus.* Zapadnyy Bug, *Ukr.* Zakhidnyy Buh. *River* E Europe
Buga 58 B3 Valle del Cauca, W Colombia
Bughotu *see* Santa Isabel
Buguruslan 111 D6 Orenburgskaya Oblast', W Russian Federation
Buhayrat Nāşir *see* Nasser, Lake
Buheiret Nāşir *see* Nasser, Lake
Bujalance 92 D4 Andalucía, S Spain
Bujanovac 101 E5 Serbia, SE Serbia and Montenegro (Yugo.)
Bujnurd *see* Bojnürd
Bujumbura 73 B7 *prev.* Usumbura. *Country capital* (Burundi) W Burundi
Bukavu 77 E6 *prev.* Costermansville. Sud Kivu, E Dem. Rep. Congo
Bukhara *see* Bukhoro
Bukhoro 122 D2 *var.* Bokhara, *Rus.* Bukhara. Bukhoro Wiloyati, C Uzbekistan
Bukoba 73 B6 Kagera, NW Tanzania
Bülach 95 B7 Zürich, NW Switzerland
Bulawayo 78 D3 *var.* Buluwayo. Matabeleland North, SW Zimbabwe
Buldur *see* Burdur
Bulgan 127 E2 Bulgan, N Mongolia
Bulgaria 104 C2 *Bul.* Bŭlgariya; *prev.* People's Republic of Bulgaria. *Country* SE Europe

Bulgaria 104

Official name Republic of Bulgaria
Formation 1908
Capital Sofia
Population 7.9 million / 184 people per sq mile (71 people per sq km)
Total area 42,822 sq miles (110,910 sq km)
Languages Bulgarian, Turkish, Macedonian, Romany
Religions Bulgarian Orthodox 84%, Muslim 13%, Jewish 1%, Roman Catholic 1%, other 1%
Ethnic mix Bulgarian 85%, Turkish 9%, Macedonian 3%, Romany 3%
Government Multiparty republic
Currency Lev = 100 stotinki
Literacy rate 98.4%
Calorie consumption 2,467 kilocalories

Bull Shoals Lake 42 B1 *reservoir* Arkansas/Missouri, C USA
Bulukumba 139 E4 *prev.* Boeloekoemba. Sulawesi, C Indonesia
Buluwayo *see* Bulawayo
Bumba 77 D5 Equateur, N Dem. Rep. Congo

Bunbury 147 A7 Western Australia
Bundaberg 148 F4 Queensland, E Australia
Bungo-suidō 131 B7 *strait* SW Japan
Bunia 77 E5 Orientale, NE Dem. Rep. Congo
Bünyan 116 D3 Kayseri, C Turkey
Buraida *see* Buraydah
Buraydah 120 B4 *var.* Buraida. Al Qaşīm, N Saudi Arabia
Burdur 116 B4 *var.* Buldur. Burdur, SW Turkey
Burdur Gölü 116 B4 *salt lake* SW Turkey
Burë 72 C4 C Ethiopia
Burgas 104 E2 *var.* Bourgas. Burgas, E Bulgaria
Burgaski Zaliv 104 E2 *gulf* E Bulgaria
Burgos 92 D2 Castilla-León, N Spain
Burhan Budai Shan 126 D4 *mountain range* C China
Buri Ram *see* Buriram
Buriram 137 D5 *var.* Buri Ram, Puriramya. Buri Ram, E Thailand
Burjassot 93 F3 País Valenciano, E Spain
Burkburnett 49 F2 Texas, SW USA
Burketown 148 B3 Queensland, NE Australia
Burkina *see* Burkina Faso
Burkina Faso 75 E4 *var.* Burkina; *prev.* Upper Volta. *Country* W Africa

Burkina Faso 75

Official name Burkina Faso
Formation 1960
Capital Ouagadougou
Population 11.9 million / 112 people per sq mile (43 people per sq km)
Total area 105,869 sq miles (274,200 sq km)
Languages French, Mossi, Fulani, Tuareg, Dyula, Songhai
Religions Traditional beliefs 55%, Muslim 35%, Roman Catholic 9%, other Christian 1%
Ethnic mix Mossi 50%, other 50%
Government Multiparty republic
Currency CFA franc = 100 centimes
Literacy rate 23.9%
Calorie consumption 2,293 kilocalories

Burley 46 D4 Idaho, NW USA
Burlington 45 G4 Iowa, C USA
Burlington 41 F2 Vermont, NE USA
Burma *see* Myanmar
Burnie 149 C8 Tasmania, SE Australia
Burns 46 C3 Oregon, NW USA
Burnside 37 F3 *river* Nunavut, NW Canada
Burnsville 45 F2 Minnesota, N USA
Burrel 101 D6 *var.* Burreli. Dibër, C Albania
Burreli *see* Burrel
Burriana 93 F3 País Valenciano, E Spain
Bursa 116 B3 *var.* Brussa; *prev.* Brusa, *anc.* Prusa. Bursa, NW Turkey
Burtnieks *see* Burtnieku Ezers
Burtnieku Ezers 106 C3 *var.* Burtnieks. *Lake* N Latvia
Burundi 73 B7 *prev.* Kingdom of Burundi, Urundi. *Country* C Africa

Burundi 73

Official name Republic of Burundi
Formation 1962
Capital Bujumbura
Population 6.5 million /605 people per sq mile (234 people per sq km)
Total area 10,745 sq miles (27,830 sq km)
Languages Kirundi, French, Kiswahili

179

Burundi (continued)

religions Christian 60%, Traditional beliefs 39%, Muslim 1%
Ethnic mix Hutu 85%, Tutsi 14%, Twa 1%
Government Transitional regime
Currency Burundi franc = 100 centimes
Literacy rate 48.3%
Calorie consumption 1,605 kilocalories

Buru, Pulau 139 F4 prev. Boeroe. Island E Indonesia
Buşayrah 118 D3 Dayr az Zawr, E Syria
Büshehr see Bandar-e Büshehr
Bushire see Bandar-e Büshehr
Busselton 147 A7 Western Australia
Buta 77 D5 Orientale, N Dem. Rep. Congo
Butembo 77 E5 Nord Kivu, NE Dem. Rep. Congo
Butler 41 E4 Pennsylvania, NE USA
Buton, Pulau 139 E4 var. Pulau Butung; prev. Boetoeng. Island C Indonesia
Butte 44 B2 Montana, NW USA
Butterworth 138 B3 Pinang, Peninsular Malaysia
Button Islands 39 E1 island group Northwest Territories, NE Canada
Butuan 139 F2 off. Butuan City. Mindanao, S Philippines
Buulobarde 73 D5 var. Buulo Berde. Hiiraan, C Somalia Africa
Buulo Berde see Buulobarde
Buur Gaabo 73 D6 Jubbada Hoose, S Somalia
Buynaksk 111 B8 Respublika Dagestan, SW Russian Federation
Büyükağrı Dağı 117 F3 var. Aghri Dagh, Agri Dagi, Koh I Noh, Masis, Eng. Great Ararat, Mount Ararat. Mountain E Turkey
Büyükmenderes Nehri 116 A4 river SW Turkey
Buzău 108 C4 Buzău, SE Romania
Buzuluk 111 D6 Akmola, C Kazakhstan
Byahoml' 107 D5 Rus. Begoml'. Vitsyebskaya Voblasts', N Belarus
Byalynichy 107 D6 Rus. Belynichi. Mahilyowskaya Voblasts', E Belarus
Bydgoszcz 98 C3 Ger. Bromberg. Kujawskie-pomorskie, C Poland
Byelaruskaya Hrada 107 B6 Rus. Belorusskaya Gryada. Ridge N Belarus
Byerezino 107 D6 Rus. Berezina. River C Belarus
Byron Island see Nikunau
Bytom 99 C5 Ger. Beuthen. Śląskie, S Poland
Bytča 99 C5 Žilinský Kraj, N Slovakia
Bytów 98 C2 Ger. Bütow. Pomorskie, N Poland
Byuzmeyin 122 C3 Turkm. Büzmeyin; prev. Bezmein. Akhalskiy Velayat, C Turkmenistan
Byval'ki 107 D8 Homyel'skaya Voblasts', SE Belarus
Byzantium see İstanbul

C

Caála 78 B2 var. Kaala, Robert Williams, Port. Vila Robert Williams. Huambo, C Angola
Caazapá 64 D3 Caazapá, S Paraguay
Caballo Reservoir 48 C3 reservoir New Mexico, SW USA
Cabañaquinta 92 D1 Asturias, N Spain
Cabanatuan 139 E1 off. Cabanatuan City. Luzon, N Philippines
Cabimas 58 C1 Zulia, NW Venezuela
Cabinda 78 A1 var. Kabinda. Cabinda, NW Angola
Cabinda 78 A1 var. Kabinda. Admin. region province NW Angola

Cabora Bassa, Lake see Cahora Bassa, Albufeira de
Caborca 50 B1 Sonora, NW Mexico
Cabot Strait 39 G4 strait E Canada
Cabras, Ilha das 76 E2 island S Sao Tome and Principe
Cabrera 93 G3 anc. Capraria. Island Islas Baleares, Spain, W Mediterranean Sea
Cáceres 92 C3 Ar. Qazris. Extremadura, W Spain
Cachimbo, Serra do 63 E2 mountain range C Brazil
Caconda 78 B2 Huíla, C Angola
Čadca 99 C5 Hung. Csaca. Žilinský Kraj, N Slovakia
Cadillac 40 C2 Michigan, N USA
Cadiz 139 E2 off. Cadiz City. Negros, C Philippines
Cádiz 92 C5 anc. Gades, Gadier, Gadir, Gadire. Andalucía, SW Spain
Cádiz, Golfo de 92 B5 Eng. Gulf of Cadiz. Gulf Portugal/Spain
Cadiz, Gulf of see Cádiz, Golfo de
Caen 90 B3 Calvados, N France
Caene see Qena
Caenepolis see Qena
Caerdydd see Cardiff
Caer Gybi see Holyhead
Caesarea Mazaca see Kayseri
Cafayate 64 C2 Salta, N Argentina
Cagayan de Oro 139 E2 off. Cagayan de Oro City. Mindanao, S Philippines
Cagliari 97 A6 anc. Caralis. Sardegna, Italy, C Mediterranean Sea
Caguas 55 F3 E Puerto Rico
Cahora Bassa, Albufeira de 78 D2 var. Lake Cabora Bassa. Reservoir NW Mozambique
Cahors 91 C5 anc. Cadurcum. Lot, S France
Cahul 108 D4 Rus. Kagul. S Moldova
Caicos Passage 54 D2 strait Bahamas/Turks and Caicos Islands
Caiffa see Hefa
Cailungo 96 E1 N San Marino
Caiphas see Hefa
Cairns 148 D3 Queensland, NE Australia
Cairo 72 B2 Ar. Al Qāhirah, var. El Qâhira. Country capital (Egypt) N Egypt
Caisleán an Bharraigh see Castlebar
Cajamarca 60 B3 prev. Caxamarca. Cajamarca, NW Peru
Čakovec 100 B2 Ger. Csakathurn, Hung. Csáktornya; prev. Ger. Tschakathurn. Medimurje, N Croatia
Calabar 75 G5 Cross River, S Nigeria
Calabozo 58 D2 Guárico, C Venezuela
Calafat 108 B5 Dolj, SW Romania
Calahorra 93 E2 La Rioja, N Spain
Calais 41 H2 Maine, NE USA
Calais 90 C2 Pas-de-Calais, N France
Calama 64 B2 Antofagasta, N Chile
Calamianes see Calamian Group
Calamian Group 129 C7 var. Calamianes. Island group W Philippines
Cǎlǎraşi see Cǎlǎraşi
Cǎlǎraşi 108 D3 var. Cǎlǎras, Rus. Kalarash. C Moldova
Cǎlǎraşi 108 C5 Cǎlǎraşi, SE Romania
Calatayud 93 E2 Aragón, NE Spain
Calbayog 139 E2 off. Calbayog City. Samar, C Philippines
Calcutta 135 G4 var. Kolkata. West Bengal, NE India
Caldas da Rainha 92 B3 Leiria, W Portugal
Caldera 64 B3 Atacama, N Chile
Caldwell 46 C3 Idaho, NW USA
Caledonia 52 C1 Corozal, N Belize
Caleta see Catalan Bay
Caleta Olivia 65 B6 Santa Cruz, SE Argentina

Calgary 37 E5 Alberta, SW Canada
Cali 58 B3 Valle del Cauca, W Colombia
Calicut 132 C2 var. Kozhikode. Kerala, SW India
California 47 B7 off. State of California; also known as El Dorado, The Golden State. State W USA
California, Golfo de 50 B2 Eng. Gulf of California; prev. Sea of Cortez. Gulf W Mexico
California, Gulf of see California, Golfo de
Cǎlimǎneşti 108 B4 Vâlcea, SW Romania
Callabonna, Lake 149 B5 lake South Australia
Callao 60 C4 Callao, W Peru
Callosa de Segura 93 F4 País Valenciano, E Spain
Calmar see Kalmar
Caloundra 149 E5 Queensland, E Australia
Caltanissetta 97 C7 Sicilia, Italy, C Mediterranean Sea
Caluula 72 E4 Bari, NE Somalia
Camabatela 78 B1 Cuanza Norte, NW Angola
Camacupa 78 B2 var. General Machado, Port. Vila General Machado. Bié, C Angola
Camagüey 54 C2 prev. Puerto Príncipe. Camagüey, C Cuba
Camagüey, Archipiélago de 54 C2 island group C Cuba
Camaná 61 E4 Arequipa, SW Peru
Camargue 91 D6 physical region SE France
Ca Mau 137 D6 prev. Quan Long. Minh Hai, S Vietnam
Cambodia 137 D5 var. Democratic Kampuchea, Roat Kampuchea, Cam. Kampuchea; prev. People's Democratic Republic of Kampuchea. Country SE Asia

Cambodia 137

Official name Kingdom of Cambodia
Formation 1953
Capital Phnom Penh
Population 13.4 million / 192 people per sq mile (74 people per sq km)
Total area 69,900 sq miles (181,040 sq km)
Languages Khmer, French, Chinese, Vietnamese, Cham
Religions Buddhist 93%, Muslim 6%, Christian 1%
Ethnic mix Khmer 90%, other 5% Vietnamese 4%, Chinese 1%,
Government Constitutional monarchy
Currency Riel = 100 sen
Literacy rate 37.4%
Calorie consumption 2,070 kilocalories

Cambrai 90 C2 Flem. Kambryk; prev. Cambray, anc. Cameracum. Nord, N France
Cambrian Mountains 89 C6 mountain range C Wales, UK
Cambridge 89 E6 Lat. Cantabrigia. E England, UK
Cambridge 41 F4 Maryland, NE USA
Cambridge 40 D4 Ohio, NE USA
Cambridge 54 A4 W Jamaica
Cambridge 150 D3 Waikato, North Island, NZ
Cambridge Bay 37 F3 district capital Victoria Island, Nunavut, NW Canada
Camden 42 B2 Arkansas, C USA
Cameroon 76 A4 Fr. Cameroun. Country W Africa

Cameroon

Official name Kingdom of Cambodia
Formation 1953

Cameroon (continued)

Capital Phnom Penh
Population 13.4 million / 192 people per sq mile (74 people per sq km)
Total area 69,900 sq miles (181,040 sq km)
Languages Khmer, French, Chinese, Vietnamese, Cham
Religions Buddhist 93%, Muslim 6%, Christian 1%
Ethnic mix Khmer 90%, other 5% Vietnamese 4%, Chinese 1%,
Government Constitutional monarchy
Currency Riel = 100 sen
Literacy rate 37.4%
Calorie consumption 2,070 kilocalories

Camocim 63 F2 Ceará, E Brazil
Camopi 59 H3 E French Guiana
Campamento 52 C2 Olancho, C Honduras
Campania 97 D5 cultural region SE Italy
Campbell, Cape 151 D5 headland South Island, NZ
Campbell Island 142 D5 island S NZ
Campbell Plateau 142 D5 undersea feature SW Pacific Ocean
Campbell River 36 D5 Vancouver Island, British Columbia, SW Canada
Campeche 51 G4 Campeche, SE Mexico
Campeche, Bahía de 51 F4 Eng. Bay of Campeche. Bay E Mexico
Câm Pha 136 E3 Quang Ninh, N Vietnam
Câmpina 108 C4 prev. Cîmpina. Prahova, SE Romania
Campina Grande 63 G2 Paraíba, E Brazil
Campinas 63 F4 São Paulo, S Brazil
Campobasso 97 D5 Molise, C Italy
Campo Criptana see Campo de Criptana
Campo de Criptana 93 E3 var. Campo Criptana. Castilla-La Mancha, C Spain
Campo dos Goitacazes see Campos
Campo Grande 63 E4 state capital Mato Grosso do Sul, SW Brazil
Campos 63 F4 var. Campo dos Goitacazes. Rio de Janeiro, SE Brazil
Câmpulung 108 B4 prev. Câmpulung-Muscel, Cîmpulung. Argeş, S Romania
Campus Stellae see Santiago
Cam Ranh 137 E6 Khanh Hoa, S Vietnam
Canada 34 B4 country N North America

Canada 34

Official name Canada
Formation 1867
Capital Ottawa
Population 31.1 million /8 people per sq mile (3 people per sq km)
Total area 3,851,788 sq miles (9,976,140 sq km)
Languages English, French, Chinese, Italian, German, Ukrainian, Inuktitul
Religions Roman Catholic 47%, Protestant 41%, non-religious 12%
Ethnic mix British origin 44%, French origin 25%, Other European 20%, other 11%
Government Parliamentary democracy
Currency Canadian dollar = 100 cents
Literacy rate 99%
Calorie consumption 3,174 kilocalories

Canada Basin 34 C2 *undersea feature*
Arctic Ocean
Canadian River 49 E2 *river*
SW USA
Çanakkale 116 A3 *var.* Dardanelli;
prev. Chanak, Kale Sultanie.
Çanakkale, W Turkey
Çanakkale Boğazı 116 A2 *Eng.*
Dardanelles. *Strait* NW Turkey
Cananea 50 B1 Sonora,
NW Mexico
Canarias, Islas 70 A2 *Eng.* Canary
Islands. *Island group* Spain,
NE Atlantic Ocean
Canarreos, Archipiélago de los 54
B2 *island group* W Cuba
Canary Islands *see* Canarias, Islas
Cañas 52 D4 Guanacaste,
NW Costa Rica
Canaveral, Cape 43 E4 *headland*
Florida, SE USA
Canavieiras 63 G3 Bahia, E Brazil
Canberra 142 C4 *country capital*
(Australia) Australian Capital
Territory, SE Australia
Cancún 51 H3 Quintana Roo,
SE Mexico
Candia *see* Irákleio
Canea *see* Chaniá
Cangzhou 128 D4 Hebei, E China
Caniapiscau 39 E2 *river* Quebec,
E Canada
Caniapiscau, Réservoir de 38 D3
reservoir Quebec, C Canada
Çanik Dağları 116 D2 *mountain
range* N Turkey
Canillo 91 A7 C Andorra
Çankırı 116 C3 *var.* Chankiri; *anc.*
Gangra, Germanicopolis. Çankırı,
N Turkey
Cannanore 132 B2 *var.* Kananur,
Kannur. Kerala, SW India
Cannes 91 D6 Alpes-Maritimes,
SE France
Canoas 63 E5 Rio Grande do Sul,
S Brazil
Canon City 44 C5 Colorado,
C USA
Cantabria 92 D1 *cultural region*
N Spain
Cantábrica, Cordillera 92 C1
mountain range N Spain
Cantaura 59 E2 Anzoátegui,
NE Venezuela
Canterbury 89 E7 *hist.*
Cantwaraburh, *anc.* Durovernum,
Lat. Cantuaria. SE England, UK
Canterbury Bight 151 C6 *bight*
South Island, NZ
Canterbury Plains 151 C6 *plain*
South Island, NZ
Cân Tho 137 E6 Cân Tho,
S Vietnam
Canton *see* Guangzhou
Canton 42 B2 Mississippi,
S USA
Canton 40 D4 Ohio, N USA
Canton Island *see* Kanton
Canyon 49 E2 Texas, SW USA
Cao Băng 136 D3 *var.* Caobang. Cao
Băng, N Vietnam
Caobang *see* Cao Băng
Cape Barren Island 149 C8 *island*
Furneaux Group, Tasmania,
SE Australia
Cape Basin 69 B7 *undersea feature*
S Atlantic Ocean
Cape Breton Island 39 G4 Fr. Île du
Cap-Breton. *Island* Nova Scotia,
SE Canada
Cape Charles 41 F5 Virginia,
NE USA
Cape Coast 75 E5 *prev.* Cape Coast
Castle. S Ghana
Cape Farewell *see*
Uummannarsuaq
Cape Girardeau 45 H5 Missouri,
C USA
Cape Horn *see* Hornos, Cabo de
Capelle aan den IJssel 86 C4 Zuid-
Holland, SW Netherlands
Cape Palmas *see* Harper
Cape Town 78 B5 *var.* Ekapa, *Afr.*
Kaapstad, Kapstad. *Country
capital* (South Africa-legislative
capital) Western Cape, SW South
Africa

Cape Verde 74 A2 *Port.* Cabo Verde,
Ilhas do Cabo Verde. *Country*
E Atlantic Ocean

Cape Verde 74

Official name Republic of Cape
Verde
Formation 1975
Capital Praia
Population 437,000/ 281 people
per sq mile (108 people per sq km)
Total area 1,557 sq miles
(4,033 sq km)
Languages Portuguese Creole,
Portuguese
Religions Roman Catholic 97%,
Protestant (Church of Nazarene) 1%,
other 2%
Ethnic mix Mestico 60%, African
30%, other 10%
Government Multiparty republic
Currency Cape Verde escudo =
100 centavos
Literacy rate 74.2%
Calorie consumption 3,278
kilocalories

Cape Verde Basin 66 C4 *undersea
feature* E Atlantic Ocean
Cape Verde Plain 66 C4 *undersea
feature* E Atlantic Ocean
Cape York Peninsula 148 C2
peninsula Queensland, N Australia
Cap-Haïtien 54 D3 *var.* Le Cap.
N Haiti
Capira 53 G5 Panamá, C Panama
Capitán Arturo Prat 154 A2 *Chilean
research station* South Shetland
Islands, Antarctica
Capitán Pablo Lagerenza 64 D1 *var.*
Mayor Pablo Lagerenza. Chaco,
N Paraguay
Capri, Isola di 97 C5 *island* S Italy
Caprivi Strip 78 C3 *Ger.*
Caprivizipfel; *prev.* Caprivi
Concession. *Cultural region*
NE Namibia
Caquetá 56 B3 *off.* Departamanto
del Caquetá. *Province* S Colombia
Caquetá, Río 58 C5 *var.* Rio Japurá,
Yapurá. *River* Brazil/Colombia *see
also* Japurá, Rio
CAR *see* Central African Republic
Caracal 108 B5 Olt, S Romania
Caracaraí 62 D1 Rondônia, W Brazil
Caracas 58 D1 *country capital*
(Venezuela) Distrito Federal,
N Venezuela
Caratasca, Laguna de 53 E2 *lagoon*
NE Honduras
Carballiño *see* O Carballiño
Carbondale 40 B5 Illinois, N USA
Carbonia 97 A6 *var.* Carbonia
Centro. Sardegna, Italy,
C Mediterranean Sea
Carbonia Centro *see* Carbonia
Carcassonne 91 C6 *anc.* Carcaso.
Aude, S France
Cárdenas 54 B2 Matanzas, W Cuba
Cardiff 89 C7 *Wel.* Caerdydd.
Admin capital S Wales, UK
Cardigan Bay 89 C6 *bay* W Wales,
UK
Carei 108 B3 *Ger.* Gross-Karol,
Karol, *Hung.* Nagykároly; *prev.*
Careii-Mari. Satu Mare,
NW Romania
Carey, Lake 147 B6 *lake* Western
Australia
Cariaco 59 E1 Sucre, NE Venezuela
Caribbean Sea 54 C4 *sea* W Atlantic
Ocean
Carlisle 88 C4 *anc.* Caer Luel,
Luguvallium, Luguvallum.
NW England, UK
Carlow 89 B6 *Ir.* Ceatharlach.
SE Ireland
Carlsbad 48 D3 New Mexico,
SW USA
Carlsberg Ridge 140 B4 *undersea
feature* S Arabian Sea
Carlsruhe *see* Karlsruhe
Carmana *see* Kermān
Carmarthen 89 C6 SW Wales, UK
Carmaux 91 C6 Tarn, S France

Carmel 40 C4 Indiana, N USA
Carmelita 52 B1 Petén, N Guatemala
Carmen 51 G4 *var.* Ciudad del
Carmen. Campeche, SE Mexico
Carmona 92 C4 Andalucía, S Spain
Carnaro *see* Kvarner
Carnarvon 147 A5 Western
Australia
Carnegie, Lake 147 B5 *salt lake*
Western Australia
Car Nicobar 133 F3 *island* Nicobar
Islands, India, NE Indian Ocean
Caroço, Ilha 76 E1 *island* N Sao
Tome and Principe
Carolina 63 F2 Maranhão, E Brazil
Caroline Island *see* Millennium
Island
Caroline Islands 106 C2 *island group*
C Micronesia
Caroní, Río 59 E3 *river* E Venezuela
Caronium *see* A Coruña
Carora 58 C1 Lara, N Venezuela
Carpathian Mountains 81 E4 *var.*
Carpathians, *Cz./Pol.* Karpaty, *Ger.*
Karpaten. *Mountain range*
E Europe
Carpathians *see* Carpathian
Mountains
Carpaţii Meridionali 108 B4 *var.*
Alpi Transilvaniei, Carpaţii
Sudici, *Eng.* South Carpathians,
Transylvanian Alps, *Ger.*
Südkarpaten, Transsylvanische
Alpen, *Hung.* Déli-Kárpátok,
Erdélyi-Havasok. *Mountain range*
C Romania
Carpaţii Occidentali 99 E7 *Eng.*
Western Carpathians. *Mountain
range* W Romania
Carpaţii Sudici *see* Carpaţii
Meridionali
Carpentaria, Gulf of 148 B2 *gulf*
N Australia
Carpi 96 C2 Emilia-Romagna,
N Italy
Carrara 96 B3 Toscana, C Italy
Carson City 47 C5 *state capital*
Nevada, W USA
Carson Sink 47 C5 *salt flat* Nevada,
W USA
Cartagena 93 F4 *anc.* Carthago
Nova. Murcia, SE Spain
Cartagena 58 B1 *var.* Cartagena de
los Indes. Bolívar, NW Colombia
Cartagena de los Indes *see*
Cartagena
Cartago 53 E4 Cartago, C Costa
Rica
Carthage 45 F5 Missouri, C USA
Cartwright 39 F2 Newfoundland
and Labrador, E Canada
Carúpano 59 E1 Sucre,
NE Venezuela
Caruthersville 45 H5 Missouri,
C USA
Cary 43 F1 North Carolina,
SE USA
Casablanca 70 C2 *Ar.* Dar-el-Beida.
NW Morocco
Casa Grande 48 B2 Arizona,
SW USA
Cascade Range 46 B3 *mountain
range* Oregon/Washington,
NW USA
Cascais 92 B4 Lisboa, C Portugal
Caserta 97 D5 Campania, S Italy
Casey 154 D4 *Australian research
station* Antarctica
Casino 91 C8 New South Wales,
SE Australia
Čáslav 95 B5 *Ger.* Tschaslau.
Středočesky Kraj, C Czech
Republic
Casper 44 C3 Wyoming, C USA
Caspian Depression 111 B7 *Kaz.*
Kaspiy Mangy Oypaty, *Rus.*
Prikaspiyskaya Nizmennost'.
Depression Kazakhstan/Russian
Federation
Caspian Sea 114 A4 *Az.* Xäzär
Dänizi, *Kaz.* Kaspiy Tengizi, *Per.*
Bahr-e Khazar, Daryā-ye Khazar,
Rus. Kaspiyskoye More. *Inland sea*
Asia/Europe
Cassai *see* Kasai
Castamoni *see* Kastamonu

Casteggio 96 B2 Lombardia,
N Italy
Castelló de la Plana 93 F3 *var.*
Castellón. País Valenciano,
E Spain
Castellón *see* Castelló de la Plana
Castelnaudary 91 C6 Aude,
S France
Castelo Branco 92 C3 Castelo
Branco, C Portugal
Castelsarrasin 91 B6 Tarn-et-
Garonne, S France
Castelvetrano 97 C7 Sicilia, Italy,
C Mediterranean Sea
Castilla-La Mancha 93 E3 *cultural
region* NE Spain
Castilla-León 92 C2 *cultural region*
NW Spain
Castlebar 89 A5 *Ir.* Caisleán an
Bharraigh. W Ireland
Castleford 89 D5 N England, UK
Castle Harbour 42 B5 *inlet*
Bermuda, NW Atlantic Ocean
Castricum 86 C3 Noord-Holland,
W Netherlands
Castries 55 F1 *country capital* (Saint
Lucia) N Saint Lucia
Castro 65 B6 Los Lagos, W Chile
Castrovillari 97 D6 Calabria,
SW Italy
Castuera 92 D4 Extremadura,
W Spain
Caswell Sound 151 A7 *sound* South
Island, NZ
Catacamas 52 D2 Olancho,
C Honduras
Catacaos 60 B3 Piura, NW Peru
Catalan Bay 93 H4 *var.* Caleta. *Bay*
E Gibraltar
Cataluña 93 G2 *cultural region*
N Spain
Catamarca *see* San Fernando del
Valle de Catamarca
Catania 97 D7 Sicilia, Italy,
C Mediterranean Sea
Catanzaro 97 D6 Calabria, SW Italy
Catarroja 93 F3 País Valenciano,
E Spain
Cat Island 54 C1 *island* C Bahamas
Catskill Mountains 41 F3 *mountain
range* New York, NE USA
Cauca, Río 58 B2 *river* N Colombia
Caucasia 58 B2 Antioquia,
NW Colombia
Caucasus 81 G4 *Rus.* Kavkaz.
Mountain range Georgia/Russian
Federation
Caura, Río 59 E3 *river* C Venezuela
Cavalla 74 D5 *var.* Cavally, Cavally
Fleuve. *River* Côte
d'Ivoire/Liberia
Cavally *see* Cavalla
Cavally Fleuve *see* Cavalla
Caviana de Fora, Ilha 63 E1 *var.*
Ilha Caviana. *Island* N Brazil
Caxito 78 B1 Bengo, NW Angola
Cayenne 59 H3 *dépendent territory
capital* (French Guiana) NE French
Guiana
Cayes 54 D3 *var.* Les Cayes.
SW Haiti
Cayman Brac 54 B3 *island*
E Cayman Islands
Cayman Islands 54 B3 UK *dependent
territory* W West Indies
Cay Sal 54 B3 *islet* SW Bahamas
Cazin 100 B3 Federacija Bosna I
Hercegovina, NW Bosnia and
Herzegovina
Cazorla 93 E4 Andalucía, S Spain
Ceadâr-Lunga *see* Ciadîr-Lunga
Ceará 63 F2 *off.* Estado do Ceará.
State C Brazil
Ceará Abyssal Plain *see* Ceará
Plain
Ceará Plain 56 E3 *var.* Ceara
Abyssal Plain. *Undersea feature*
W Atlantic Ocean
Ceatharlach *see* Carlow
Cébaco, Isla 53 F5 *island* SW Panama
Cebu 139 E2 *off.* Cebu City. Cebu,
C Philippines
Cecina 96 B3 Toscana, C Italy
Cedar City 44 A5 Utah, W USA
Cedar Falls 45 G3 Iowa, C USA
Cedar Lake 38 A2 *lake* Manitoba,
C Canada

Cedar Rapids 45 G3 Iowa, C USA
Cedros, Isla 50 A2 *island* W Mexico
Ceduna 149 A6 South Australia
Cefalu 97 C7 *anc.* Cephaloedium.
Sicilia, Italy, C Mediterranean Sea
Celebes *see* Sulawesi
Celebes Sea 139 E3 *Ind.* Laut
Sulawesi. *Sea*
Indonesia/Philippines
Celje 95 E7 *Ger.* Cilli. C Slovenia
Celldömölk 99 C6 Vas,
W Hungary
Celle 94 B3 *var.* Zelle.
Niedersachsen, N Germany
Celtic Sea 89 B7 *Ir.* An Mhuir
Cheilteach. *Sea* SW British Isles
Celtic Shelf 80 B3 *undersea feature*
E Atlantic Ocean
Cenderawasih, Teluk 139 G4 *var.*
Teluk Irian, Teluk Sarera. *Bay* W
Pacific Ocean
Cenon 91 B5 Gironde, SW France
Central African Republic 76 C4 *var.*
République Centrafricaine, *abbrev.*
CAR; *prev.* Ubangi-Shari, Oub
angui-Chari, Territoire de
l'Oubangui-Chari. *Country*
C Africa

Central African Republic 76

Official name Central African
Republic
Formation 1960
Capital Bangui
Population 3.8 million / 16 people
per sq mile (6 people per sq km)
Total area 240,534 sq miles
(622,984 sq km)
Languages French, Sango, Banda,
Gbaya
Religions Traditional beliefs 60%,
Christian 35%, Muslim 5%
Ethnic mix Baya 34%, Banda 27%,
Mandjia 21%, Sara 10%,
other 8%
Government Multiparty republic
Currency CFA franc = 100 centimes
Literacy rate 46.7%
Calorie consumption 1,946
kilocalories

Central, Cordillera 55 E3 *mountain
range* C Dominican Republic
Central, Cordillera 53 F5 *mountain
range* C Panama
Central, Cordillera 139 E1 *mountain
range* Luzon, N Philippines
Central, Cordillera 58 B3 *mountain
range* W Colombia
Central Group *see* Inner Islands
Centralia 46 B2 Washington,
NW USA
Central Indian Ridge *see* Mid-
Indian Ridge
Central Makrān Range 134 A3
mountain range W Pakistan
Central Pacific Basin 142 D1
undersea feature C Pacific Ocean
Central, Planalto 63 F3 *var.*
Brazilian Highlands. *Mountain
range* E Brazil
Central Range 144 B3 *mountain
range* NW PNG
Central Russian Upland *see*
Srednerusskaya Vozvyshennost'
Central Siberian Plateau *see*
Srednesibirskoye Ploskogor'ye
Central Siberian Uplands *see*
Srednesibirskoye Ploskogor'ye
Central, Sistema 92 D3 *mountain
range* C Spain
Central Valley 47 B6 *valley*
California, W USA
Cephaloedium *see* Cefalu
Ceram *see* Seram, Pulau
Ceram Sea 139 F4 *Ind.* Laut Seram.
Sea E Indonesia
Cerasus *see* Giresun
Cereté 58 B2 Córdoba,
NW Colombia
Cerignola 97 D5 Puglia, SE Italy
Cerigo *see* Kýthira
Çerkeş 116 C2 Çankın, N Turkey
Cernay 90 E4 Haut-Rhin,
NE France

Cerro Chirripó *see* Chirripó
Grande, Cerro
Cerro de Mulhacén *see*
Mulhacén
Cerro de Pasco 60 C3 Pasco,
C Peru
Cervera 93 F2 Cataluña, NE Spain
Cesena 96 C3 *anc.* Caesena. Emilia-
Romagna, N Italy
Cēsis 106 D3 *Ger.* Wenden. Cēsis,
C Latvia
České Budějovice 99 B5 *Ger.*
Budweis. Budějovický Kraj,
S Czech Republic
Český Krumlov 99 A5 *var.*
Böhmisch-Krumau, *Ger.*
Krummau. Budějovický Kraj,
S Czech Republic
Cetinje 101 C5 *It.* Cettigne.
Montenegro, SW Serbia and
Montenegro (Yugo.)
Ceuta 70 C2 *enclave* Spain, N Africa
Cévennes 91 C6 *mountain range*
S France
Ceyhan 116 D4 Adana, S Turkey
Ceylanpınar 117 E4 Şanlıurfa,
SE Turkey
Ceylon Plain 124 B4 *undersea feature*
N Indian Ocean
Ceyre to the Caribs *see* Marie-
Galante
Chachapoyas 60 B2 Amazonas,
NW Peru
Chachevichy 107 D6 *Rus.*
Chechevichi. Mahilyowskaya
Voblasts', E Belarus
Chaco *see* Gran Chaco
Chad 76 C3 *Fr.* Tchad. *Country*
C Africa

Chad 76

Official name Republic of Chad
Formation 1960
Capital N'Djamena
Population 8.1 million / 16 people
per sq mile (6 people per sq km)
Total area 495,752 sq miles
(1,284,000 sq km)
Languages French, Arabic, Sara,
Maba
Religions Muslim 50%, Traditional
beliefs 43%, Christian 7%
Ethnic mix Nomads (Tuareg and
Toubou) 38%, Sara 30, Arab 15%,
Other 17%
Government Presidential
democracy
Currency CFA franc = 100 centimes
Literacy rate 42.6%
Calorie consumption 2,046
kilocalories

Chad, Lake 76 B3 *Fr.* Lac Tchad.
Lake C Africa
Chadron 44 D3 Nebraska, C USA
Chadyr-Lunga *see* Ciadir-Lunga
Chāgai Hills 134 A2 *var.* Chāh Gay.
Mountain range
Afghanistan/Pakistan
Chaghasaráy *see* Asadābād
Chagos-Laccadive Plateau 124 B4
undersea feature N Indian Ocean
Chagos Trench 141 C5 *undersea
feature* N Indian Ocean
Chāh Gay *see* Chāgai Hills
Chaillu, Massif du 77 B6 *mountain
range* C Gabon
Chaîne des Dangrek *see* Dângrêk,
Chuŏr Phnum
Chaîne des Mitumba *see* Mitumba,
Monts
Chaîne des Mongos *see* Bongo,
Massif des
Chain Ridge 140 B4 *undersea feature*
N Indian Ocean
Chajul 52 B2 Quiché, W Guatemala
Chakhānsūr 122 D5 Nīmrūz,
SW Afghanistan
Chala 60 D4 Arequipa, SW Peru
Chalatenango 52 C3 Chalatenango,
N El Salvador
Chalcidice *see* Chalkidikí
Chalcis *see* Chalkída
Chálki 105 E7 *island* Dodekánisos,
Greece, Aegean Sea

Chalkída 105 C5 *var.* Halkida; *prev.*
Khalkís, *anc.* Chalcis. Evvoia,
E Greece
Chalkidikí 104 C4 *var.* Khalkidhikí;
anc. Chalcidice. *Peninsula*
NE Greece
Challans 90 B4 Vendée,
NW France
Challapata 61 F4 Oruro, SW Bolivia
Challenger Deep 152 B3 *undersea
feature* W Pacific Ocean
Challenger Fracture Zone 153 F4
tectonic feature SE Pacific Ocean
Châlons-en-Champagne 90 D3 *prev.*
Châlons-sur-Marne, *hist.* Arcae
Remorum, *anc.* Carolopois.
Marne, NE France
Chalon-sur-Saône 90 D4 *anc.*
Cabillonum. Saône-et-Loire,
C France
Cha Mai *see* Thung Song
Chaman 134 B2 Baluchistān,
SW Pakistan
Chambéry 91 D5 *anc.* Cambería.
Savoie, E France
Champagne 90 D3 Yukon Territory,
W Canada
Champaign 40 B4 Illinois, N USA
Champasak 137 D5 Champasak,
S Laos
Champlain, Lake 41 F2 *lake*
Canada/USA
Champotón 51 G4 Campeche,
SE Mexico
Chanak *see* Çanakkale
Chañaral 64 B3 Atacama, N Chile
Chanchiang *see* Zhanjiang
Chandeleur Islands 42 C3 *island
group* Louisiana, S USA
Chandigarh 134 D2 Punjab,
N India
Chandrapur 135 E5 Mahārāshtra,
C India
Changan *see* Xi'an
Changane 79 E3 *river*
S Mozambique
Changchun 128 D3 *var.*
Ch'angch'un, Ch'ang-ch'un; *prev.*
Hsinking. Jilin, NE China
Ch'angch'un *see* Changchun
Chang Jiang 128 B5 *var.* Yangtze
Kiang, *Eng.* Yangtze. *River*
C China
Changkiakow *see* Zhangjiakou
Chang, Ko 137 C6 *island* S Thailand
Changsha 128 C5 *var.* Ch'angsha,
Ch'ang-sha. Hunan, S China
Ch'angsha *see* Changsha
Changzhi 128 C4 Shanxi, C China
Chaniá 105 C7 *var.* Hania, Khaniá,
Eng. Canea; *anc.* Cydonia. Kríti,
Greece, E Mediterranean Sea
Chañi, Nevado de 64 B2 *mountain*
NW Argentina
Chankiri *see* Çankırı
Channel Islands 89 C8 *Fr.* Îles
Normandes. *Island group*
S English Channel
Channel Islands 47 B8 *island group*
California, W USA
Channel-Port aux Basques 39 G4
Newfoundland, Newfoundland
and Labrador, SE Canada
Channel, The *see* English Channel
Channel Tunnel 90 C2 *tunnel*
France/UK
Chantabun *see* Chanthaburi
Chantaburi *see* Chanthaburi
Chantada 92 C1 Galicia,
NW Spain
Chanthaburi 137 C6 *var.*
Chantabun, Chantaburi.
Chantaburi, S Thailand
Chanute 45 F5 Kansas, C USA
Chaouèn *see* Chefchaouen
Chaoyang 128 D3 Liaoning,
NE China
Chapala, Lago de 50 D4 *lake*
C Mexico
Chapan, Gora 122 B3 *mountain*
C Turkmenistan
Chapayevsk 111 C6 Samarskaya
Oblast', W Russian Federation
Chaplynka 109 F4 Khersons'ka
Oblast', S Ukraine
Charcot Seamounts 80 B3 *undersea
feature* E Atlantic Ocean

Chardzhev 122 D3 *prev.* Chardzhou
Chardzhui, Leninsk-Turkmenski,
Turkm. Chärjew. Lebapskiy
Velayat, E Turkmenistan
Charente 91 B5 *cultural region*
W France
Charente 91 B5 *river* W France
Chari 76 B3 *var.* Shari. *River* Central
African Republic/Chad
Chārīkār 123 E4 Parwān,
NE Afghanistan
Charity 59 F2 NW Guyana
Charkhlik *see* Ruoqiang
Charkhliq *see* Ruoqiang
Charleroi 87 C7 Hainaut,
S Belgium
Charlesbourg 39 E4 Quebec,
SE Canada
Charles de Gaulle 90 E1
international airport (Paris) Seine-
et-Marne, N France
Charles Island 38 D1 *island*
Northwest Territories, NE Canada
Charles Island *see* Santa María, Isla
Charleston 40 D5 *state capital* West
Virginia, NE USA
Charleston 43 F2 South Carolina,
SE USA
Charleville 149 D5 Queensland,
E Australia
Charleville-Mézières 90 D3
Ardennes, N France
Charlie-Gibbs Fracture Zone 66 B2
tectonic feature N Atlantic Ocean
Charlotte 43 E1 North Carolina,
SE USA
Charlotte Amalie 55 F3 *prev.* Saint
Thomas. *Dependent territory capital*
(Virgin Islands (US)) Saint
Thomas, N Virgin Islands (US)
Charlotte Harbor 43 E5 *inlet*
Florida, SE USA
Charlottesville 41 E5 Virginia,
NE USA
Charlottetown 39 F4 Prince Edward
Island, Prince Edward Island,
SE Canada
Charsk *see* Shar
Charters Towers 148 D3
Queensland, NE Australia
Chartres 90 C3 *anc.* Autricum,
Civitas Carnutum. Eure-et-Loir,
C France
Charus Nuur 126 C2 *lake*
NW Mongolia
Chashniki 107 D5 *Rus.* Chashniki.
Vitsyebskaya Voblasts', N Belarus
Châteaubriant 90 B4 Loire-
Atlantique, NW France
Châteaudun 90 C3 Eure-et-Loir,
C France
Châteauroux 90 C4 *prev.* Indreville.
Indre, C France
Château-Thierry 90 C3 Aisne,
N France
Châtelet 87 C7 Hainaut, S Belgium
Châtelherault *see* Châtellerault
Châtellerault 90 B4 *var.*
Châtelherault. Vienne, W France
Chatham Island *see* San Cristóbal,
Isla
Chatham Island Rise *see* Chatham
Rise
Chatham Islands 143 E5 *island
group* NZ, SW Pacific Ocean
Chatham Rise 142 D5 *var.* Chatham
Island Rise. *Undersea feature*
S Pacific Ocean
Chatkal Range 123 F2 *Rus.*
Chatkal'skiy Khrebet. *Mountain
range* Kyrgyzstan/Uzbekistan
Chattahoochee River 42 D3 *river*
SE USA
Chattanooga 42 D1 Tennessee,
S USA
Chatyr-Tash 123 G2 Narynskaya
Oblast', C Kyrgyzstan
Châu Đốc 137 D6 *var.* Chauphu,
Chau Phu. An Giang, S Vietnam
Chauk 136 A3 Magwe, W Myanmar
Chaumont 90 D4 *prev.* Chaumont-
en-Bassigny. Haute-Marne,
N France
Chau Phu *see* Châu Đốc
Chaves 92 C2 *anc.* Aquae Flaviae.
Vila Real, N Portugal
Chávez, Isla *see* Santa Cruz, Isla

Chavusy 107 E6 Rus. Chausy.
Mahilyowskaya Voblasts',
E Belarus
Chaykovskiy 111 D5 Permskaya
Oblast', NW Russian Federation
Cheb 99 A5 Ger. Eger. Karlovarský
Kraj, W Czech Republic
Cheboksary 111 C5 Chuvashskaya
Respublika, W Russian Federation
Cheboygan 40 C2 Michigan, N USA
Chechaouèn see Chefchaouen
Chech, Erg 74 D1 desert
Algeria/Mali
Che-chiang see Zhejiang
Cheduba Island 136 A4 island
W Myanmar
Chefchaouen 70 C2 var. Chaouèn,
Chechaouèn, Sp. Xauen.
N Morocco
Chefoo see Yantai
Cheju-do 129 E4 Jap. Saishū;
prev. Quelpart. Island S South
Korea
Cheju Strait 129 E4 strait S South
Korea
Chekiang see Zhejiang
Cheleken 122 B2 Balkanskiy
Velayat, W Turkmenistan
Chelkar 114 B4 Aktyubinsk,
W Kazakhstan
Chełm 98 E4 Rus. Kholm.
Lubelskie, E Poland
Chełmno 98 C3 Ger. Culm, Kulm.
Kujawski-pomorskie, C Poland
Chełmża 98 C3 Ger. Culmsee,
Kulmsee. Kujawski-pomorskie, C
Poland
Cheltenham 89 D6 C England, UK
Chelyabinsk 114 C3
Chelyabinskaya Oblast',
C Russian Federation
Chemnitz 94 D4 prev. Karl-Marx-
Stadt. Sachsen, E Germany
Chengchiatun see Liaoyuan
Ch'eng-chou see Zhengzhou
Chengchow see Zhengzhou
Chengde 128 D3 var. Jehol. Hebei,
E China
Chengdu 128 B5 var. Chengtu,
Ch'eng-tu. Sichuan, C China
Chenghsien see Zhengzhou
Ch'eng-tu see Chengdu
Chennai 132 D2 prev Madras. Tamil
Nādu, S India
Chenxian see Chenzhou
Chen Xian see Chenzhou
Chen Xiang see Chenzhou
Chenzhou 128 C6 var. Chenxian,
Chen Xian, Chen Xiang. Hunan,
S China
Chepelare 104 C3 Smolyan,
S Bulgaria
Chepén 60 B3 La Libertad, C Peru
Cher 90 C4 river C France
Cherbourg 90 B3 anc. Carusbur.
Manche, N France
Cherepovets 110 B4 Vologodskaya
Oblast', NW Russian Federation
Chergui, Chott ech 70 D2 salt lake
NW Algeria
Cherkasy 109 E2 Rus. Cherkassy.
Cherkas'ka Oblast', C Ukraine
Cherkessk 111 B7 Karachayevo-
Cherkesskaya Respublika,
SW Russian Federation
Chernihiv 109 E1 Rus. Chernigov,
Chernihivs'ka Oblast',
NE Ukraine
Chernivtsi 108 C3 Ger. Czernowitz,
Rom. Cernăuți, Rus. Chernovtsy.
Chernivets'ka Oblast', W Ukraine
Cherno More see Black Sea
Chernoye More see Black Sea
Chernyakhovsk 106 A4 Ger.
Insterburg. Kaliningradskaya
Oblast', W Russian Federation
Cherry Hill 41 F4 New Jersey,
NE USA
Cherski Range see Cherskogo,
Khrebet
Cherskiy 115 G2 Respublika Sakha
(Yakutiya), NE Russian
Federation
Cherskogo, Khrebet 115 F2 var.
Cherski Range. Mountain range
NE Russian Federation

Chervonohrad 108 C2 Rus.
Chervonograd. L'vivs'ka Oblast',
NW Ukraine
Chervyen' 107 D6 Rus. Cherven'.
Minskaya Voblasts', C Belarus
Cherykaw 107 E7 Rus. Cherikov.
Mahilyowskaya Voblasts',
E Belarus
Chesapeake Bay 41 F5 inlet
NE USA
Chesha Bay see Chëshskaya Guba
Chëshskaya Guba 172 D5 var.
Archangel Bay, Chesha Bay, Dvina
Bay. Bay NW Russian Federation
Chester 89 C6 Wel. Caerleon; hist.
Legaceaster, Lat. Deva, Devana
Castra. C England, UK
Chetumal 51 H4 var. Payo Obispo.
Quintana Roo, SE Mexico
Cheviot Hills 88 D4 hill range
England/Scotland, UK
Cheyenne 44 D4 state capital
Wyoming, C USA
Cheyenne River 44 D3 river South
Dakota/Wyoming, N USA
Chhapra 135 F3 prev. Chapra. Bihār,
N India
Chiai 128 D6 var. Chia-i, Chiayi,
Kiayi, Jiayi, Jap. Kagi. C Taiwan
Chia-i see Chiai
Chiang-hsi see Jiangxi
Chiang Mai 136 B4 var. Chiangmai,
Chiengmai, Kiangmai. Chiang
Mai, NW Thailand
Chiangmai see Chiang Mai
Chiang Rai 136 C3 var. Chianpai,
Chienrai, Muang Chiang Rai.
Chiang Rai, NW Thailand
Chiang-su see Jiangsu
Chian-ning see Nanjing
Chianpai see Chiang Rai
Chianti 96 C3 cultural region
C Italy
Chiapa see Chiapa de Corzo
Chiapa de Corzo 51 G5 var. Chiapa.
Chiapas, SE Mexico
Chiayi see Chiai
Chiba 130 B1 var. Tiba. Chiba,
Honshū, S Japan
Chibougamau 38 D3 Quebec,
SE Canada
Chicago 40 B3 Illinois, N USA
Ch'i-ch'i-ha-erh see Qiqihar
Chickasha 49 G2 Oklahoma, C USA
Chiclayo 60 B3 Lambayeque,
NW Peru
Chico 47 B5 California, W USA
Chico, Río 65 B6 river S Argentina
Chico, Río 65 B7 river SE Argentina
Chicoutimi 39 E4 Quebec,
SE Canada
Chiengmai see Chiang Mai
Chienrai see Chiang Rai
Chiesanuova 96 D2 SW San
Marino
Chieti 96 D4 var. Teate. Abruzzo,
C Italy
Chifeng 127 G2 var. Ulanhad. Nei
Mongol Zizhiqu, N China
Chih-fu see Yantai
Chihli see Hebei
Chihli, Gulf of see Bo Hai
Chihuahua 50 C2 Chihuahua,
NW Mexico
Childress 49 F2 Texas, SW USA
Chile 64 B3 Country SW South
America

Chile 64

Official name Republic of Chile
Formation 1818
Capital Santiago
Population 15.4 million / 53 people
per sq mile (20 people per sq km)
Total area 292,258 sq miles
(756,950 sq km)
Languages Spanish, Amerindian
languages
Religions Roman Catholic 80%,
other and non-religious 20%
Ethnic mix Mixed and European
90%, Amerindian 10%
Government Multiparty republic
Currency Chilean peso = 100
centavos

Chile (continued)

Literacy rate 95.7%
Calorie consumption 2,882
kilocalories

Chile Basin 57 A5 undersea feature
E Pacific Ocean
Chile Chico 65 B6 Aisén, W Chile
Chile Rise 57 A7 undersea feature
SE Pacific Ocean
Chililabombwe 78 D2 Copperbelt,
C Zambia
Chi-lin see Jilin
Chillán 65 B5 Bío Bío, C Chile
Chillicothe 40 D4 Ohio, N USA
Chiloé, Isla de 65 A6 var. Isla
Grande de Chiloé. Island
W Chile
Chilpancingo 51 E5 var.
Chilpancingo de los Bravos.
Guerrero, S Mexico
Chilpancingo de los Bravos see
Chilpancingo
Chilung 128 D6 var. Keelung, Jap.
Kirun, Kirun'; prev. Sp. Santissima
Trinidad. N Taiwan
Chimán 53 G5 Panamá, E Panama
Chimborazo 60 A1 volcano
C Ecuador
Chimbote 60 C3 Ancash, W Peru
Chimboy 122 D1 Rus. Chimbay.
Qoraqalpoghiston Respublikasi,
NW Uzbekistan
Chimoio 79 E3 Manica,
C Mozambique
China 124 C2 Chin. Chung-hua Jen-
min Kung-ho-kuo, Zhonghua
Renmin Gongheguo; prev. Chinese
Empire. Country E Asia

China 124

Official name People's Republic
of China
Formation 960
Capital Beijing
Population 1.29 billion /
348 people per sq mile (134 people
per sq km)
Total area 3,705,386 sq miles
(9,596,960 sq km)
Languages Mandarin, Wu,
Cantonese, Hsiang, Min,
Hakka, Kan
Religions Non-religious 59%,
Traditional beliefs 20%, other 21%
Ethnic mix Han 93%, other 7%
Government One-party state
Currency Yuan (Renminbi) = 10 jiao
Literacy rate 84.2%
Calorie consumption 3,029
kilocalories

Chi-nan see Jinan
Chinandega 52 C3 Chinandega,
NW Nicaragua
Chincha Alta 60 D4 Ica, SW Peru
Chin-chiang see Quanzhou
Chin-chou see Jinzhou
Chinchow see Jinzhou
Chindwin 136 B2 river
N Myanmar
Ch'ing Hai see Qinghai Hu
Chingola 78 D2 Copperbelt,
C Zambia
Ching-Tao see Qingdao
Chinguetti 74 C2 var. Chinguetti.
Adrar, C Mauritania
Chin Hills 136 A3 mountain range
W Myanmar
Chinhsien see Jinzhou
Chinnereth see Tiberias, Lake
Chinook Trough 113 H4 undersea
feature N Pacific Ocean
Chioggia 96 C2 anc. Fossa Claudia.
Veneto, NE Italy
Chíos 105 D5 var. Hios, Khíos, It.
Scio, Turk. Sakíz-Adasi. Chíos,
E Greece
Chíos 105 D5 var. Khíos. Island
E Greece
Chipata 78 D2 prev. Fort Jameson.
Eastern, E Zambia

Chiquián 60 C3 Ancash, W Peru
Chiquimula 52 B2 Chiquimula,
SE Guatemala
Chīrāla 132 D1 Andhra Pradesh,
E India
Chirchiq 123 E2 Rus. Chirchik.
Toshkent Wiloyati, E Uzbekistan
Chiriquí, Golfo de 53 E5 Eng.
Chiriquí Gulf. Gulf SW Panama
Chiriquí, Laguna de 53 E5 lagoon
NW Panama
Chirripó Grande, Cerro 52 D4 var.
Cerro Chirripó. Mountain
SE Costa Rica
Chisec 52 B2 Alta Verapaz,
C Guatemala
Chisholm 45 F1 Minnesota, N USA
Chisimaio see Kismaayo
Chisimayu see Kismaayo
Chişinău 108 D4 Rus. Kishinev.
Country capital (Moldova)
C Moldova
Chita 115 F4 Chitinskaya Oblast',
S Russian Federation
Chitato 78 C1 Lunda Norte,
NE Angola
Chitina 36 D3 Alaska, USA
Chitose 130 D2 var. Titose.
Hokkaidō, NE Japan
Chitré 53 F5 Herrera, S Panama
Chittagong 135 G4 Ben. Chāttāgām.
Chittagong, SE Bangladesh
Chitungwiza 78 D3 prev.
Chitangwiza. Mashonaland East,
NE Zimbabwe
Chlef 70 D2 var. Ech Cheliff, Ech
Chleff; prev. Al-Asnam, El Asnam,
Orléansville. NW Algeria
Chocolate Mountains 47 D8
mountain range California, W USA
Chodzież 98 C3 Wielkopolskie, C
Poland
Choele Choel 65 C5 Río Negro,
C Argentina
Choiseul 144 C3 var. Lauru. Island
NW Solomon Islands
Chojnice 98 C2 Ger. Knoitz.
Pomorskie, N Poland
Ch'ok'ē 72 C4 var. Choke
Mountains. Mountain range
NW Ethiopia
Choke Mountains see Ch'ok'ē
Cholet 90 B4 Maine-et-Loire,
NW France
Choluteca 52 C3 Choluteca,
S Honduras
Choluteca, Río 52 C3 river
SW Honduras
Choma 78 D2 Southern, S Zambia
Chomutov 98 A4 Ger. Komotau.
Ústecký Kraj, NW Czech Republic
Chona 113 E2 river C Russian
Federation
Chon Buri 137 C5 prev. Bang Pla
Soi. Chon Buri, S Thailand
Chone 60 A1 Manabí, W Ecuador
Ch'öngjin 129 E3 NE North Korea
Chongqing 128 B5 var. Ch'ung-
ching, Ch'ung-ch'ing, Chungking,
Pahsien, Tchongking, Yuzhou.
Chongqing, C China
Chongqing 128 B5 Admin. region
province C China
Chonos, Archipiélago de los 65 A6
island group S Chile
Chorne More see Black Sea
Chornomors'ke 109 E4 Rus.
Chernomorskoye. Respublika
Krym, S Ukraine
Chortkiv 108 C2 Rus. Chortkov.
Ternopil's'ka Oblast', W Ukraine
Chorum see Çorum
Chorzów 99 C5 Ger. Königshütte;
prev. Królewska Huta. Śląskie,
S Poland
Chōshi 131 D5 var. Tyōsi. Chiba,
Honshū, S Japan
Choszczno 98 B3 Ger. Arnswalde.
Zachodniopomorskie, NW Poland
Chota Nāgpur 135 E4 plateau
N India
Chott el-Hodna see Hodna, Chott El
Chott Melrhir see Melrhir, Chott
Choûm 74 C2 Adrar, C Mauritania
Choybalsan 127 F2 Dornod,
E Mongolia
Christchurch 151 C6 Canterbury,
South Island, NZ

Christiana *54 B5* C Jamaica
Christiansand *see* Kristiansand
Christianshåb *see* Qasigiannguit
Christiansund *see* Kristiansund
Christmas Island *141 D5 Australian external territory* E Indian Ocean
Christmas Ridge *143 E1 undersea feature* C Pacific Ocean
Chuan *see* Sichuan
Ch'uan-chou *see* Quanzhou
Chubut *57 B7 off.* Provincia de Chubut. Admin. *region province* S Argentina
Chubut, Río *65 B6 river* SE Argentina
Ch'u-chiang *see* Shaoguan
Chūgoku-sanchi *131 B6 mountain range* Honshū, SW Japan
Chuí *see* Chuy
Chukai *see* Cukai
Chukchi Plain *155 B2 undersea feature* Arctic Ocean
Chukchi Plateau *34 C2 undersea feature* Arctic Ocean
Chukchi Sea *34 B2 Rus.* Chukotskoye More. *Sea* Arctic Ocean
Chula Vista *47 C8* California, W USA
Chulucanas *60 B2* Piura, NW Peru
Chulym *114 D4 river* C Russian Federation
Chumphon *137 C6 var.* Jumporn. Chumphon, SW Thailand
Ch'unch'ŏn *129 E4 Jap.* Shunsen. N South Korea
Ch'ung-ching *see* Chongqing
Chungking *see* Chongqing
Chunya *115 E3 river* C Russian Federation
Chuquicamata *64 B2* Antofagasta, N Chile
Chur *95 B7 Fr.* Coire, *It.* Coira, *Rmsch.* Cuera, Quera; *anc.* Curia Rhaetorum. Graubünden, E Switzerland
Churchill *38 B2 river* Manitoba/Saskatchewan, C Canada
Churchill *39 F2 river* Newfoundland and Labrador, E Canada
Churchill *37 G4* Manitoba, C Canada
Chuska Mountains *48 C1 mountain range* Arizona/New Mexico, SW USA
Chusovoy *111 D5* Permskaya Oblast', NW Russian Federation
Chuuk Islands *144 B2 var.* Hogoley Islands; *prev.* Truk Islands. *Island group* Caroline Islands, C Micronesia
Chuy *64 E4 var.* Chuí. Rocha, E Uruguay
Chyhyryn *109 E2 Rus.* Chigirin. Cherkas'ka Oblast', N Ukraine
Ciadîr-Lunga *108 D4 var.* Ceadâr-Lunga, *Rus.* Chadyr-Lunga. S Moldova
Cide *116 C2* Kastamonu, N Turkey
Ciechanów *98 D3 prev.* Zichenau. Mazowieckie, C Poland
Ciego de Ávila *54 C2* Ciego de Ávila, C Cuba
Ciénaga *58 B1* Magdalena, N Colombia
Cienfuegos *54 B2* Cienfuegos, C Cuba
Cieza *93 E4* Murcia, SE Spain
Cihanbeyli *116 C3* Konya, C Turkey
Cikobia *145 E4 prev.* Thikombia. *Island* N Fiji
Cilacap *138 C5 prev.* Tjilatjap. Jawa, C Indonesia
Cill Airne *see* Killarney
Cill Chainnigh *see* Kilkenny
Cill Mhantáin *see* Wicklow
Cincinnati *40 C4* Ohio, N USA
Ciney *87 C7* Namur, SE Belgium
Cinto, Monte *91 E7 mountain* Corse, France, C Mediterranean Sea
Cipolletti *65 B5* Río Negro, C Argentina
Cirebon *138 C4 prev.* Tjirebon. Jawa, S Indonesia

Ciro Marino *97 E6* Calabria, S Italy
Cisnădie *108 B4 Ger.* Heltau, *Hung.* Nagydisznód. Sibiu, SW Romania
Citlaltépetl *see* Orizaba, Volcán Pico de
Citrus Heights *47 B5* California, W USA
Ciudad Bolívar *59 E2 prev.* Angostura. Bolívar, E Venezuela
Ciudad Acuña *see* Villa Acuña
Cuidad Camargo *50 D2* Chihuahua, N Mexico
Ciudad Cortés *see* Cortés
Ciudad Darío *52 D3 var.* Dario. Matagalpa, W Nicaragua
Ciudad de Dolores Hidalgo *see* Dolores Hidalgo
Ciudad de Guatemala *52 B2 var.* Gautemala City *Eng.* Guatemala City; *prev.* Santiago de los Caballeros. *Country capital* (Guatemala) Guatemala, C Guatemala
Ciudad del Carmen *see* Carmen
Ciudad del Este *64 E2 prev.* Cuidad Presidente Stroessner, Presidente Stroessner, Puerto Presidente Stroessner. Alto Paraná, SE Paraguay
Ciudad Delicias *see* Delicias
Ciudad de México *see* México
Ciudad de Panamá *see* Panamá
Ciudad Guayana *59 E2 prev.* San Tomé de Guayana, Santo Tomé de Guayana. Bolívar, NE Venezuela
Ciudad Guzmán *50 D4* Jalisco, SW Mexico
Ciudad Hidalgo *51 G5* Chiapas, SE Mexico
Ciudad Juárez *50 C1* Chihuahua, N Mexico
Ciudad Lerdo *50 D3* Durango, C Mexico
Ciudad Madero *51 E3 var.* Villa Cecilia. Tamaulipas, C Mexico
Ciudad Mante *51 E3* Tamaulipas, C Mexico
Ciudad Miguel Alemán *51 E2* Tamaulipas, C Mexico
Ciudad Obregón *50 B2* Sonora, NW Mexico
Ciudad Ojeda *58 C1* Zulia, NW Venezuela
Ciudad Porfirio Díaz *see* Piedras Negras
Ciudad Quesada *see* Quesada
Ciudad Real *92 D3* Castilla-La Mancha, C Spain
Ciudad-Rodrigo *92 C3* Castilla-León, N Spain
Ciudad Valles *51 E3* San Luis Potosí, C Mexico
Ciudad Victoria *51 E3* Tamaulipas, C Mexico
Ciutadella *see* Ciutadella de Menorca
Ciutadella de Menorca *93 H3 var.* Ciutadella. Menorca, Spain, W Mediterranean Sea
Civitanova Marche *96 D3* Marche, C Italy
Civitavecchia *96 C4 anc.* Centum Cellae, Trajani Portus. Lazio, C Italy
Claremore *49 G1* Oklahoma, C USA
Clarence *151 C5 river* South Island, NZ
Clarence *151 C5* Canterbury, South Island, NZ
Clarence Town *54 D2* Long Island, C Bahamas
Clarinda *45 F4* Iowa, C USA
Clarion Fracture Zone *153 E2 tectonic feature* NE Pacific Ocean
Clarión, Isla *50 A5 island* W Mexico
Clark Fork *44 A1 river* Idaho/Montana, NW USA
Clark Hill Lake *43 E2 var.* J.Storm Thurmond Reservoir. *Reservoir.* Georgia/South Carolina, SE USA
Clarksburg *40 D4* West Virginia, NE USA
Clarksdale *42 B2* Mississippi, S USA

Clarksville *42 C1* Tennessee, S USA
Clayton *49 E1* New Mexico, SW USA
Clearwater *43 E4* Florida, SE USA
Clearwater Mountains *46 D2 mountain range* Idaho, NW USA
Cleburne *49 G3* Texas, SW USA
Clermont *148 D4* Queensland, E Australia
Clermont-Ferrand *91 C5* Puy-de-Dôme, C France
Cleveland *40 D3* Ohio, N USA
Cleveland *42 D1* Tennessee, S USA
Clifton *48 C2* Arizona, SW USA
Clinton *42 B2* Mississippi, S USA
Clinton *49 F1* Oklahoma, C USA
Clipperton Fracture Zone *153 E3 tectonic feature* E Pacific Ocean
Clipperton Island *35 A7 French dependency of French Polynesia* E Pacific Ocean
Cloncurry *148 B3* Queensland, C Australia
Clonmel *89 B6 Ir.* Cluain Meala. S Ireland
Cloppenburg *94 B3* Niedersachsen, NW Germany
Cloquet *45 G2* Minnesota, N USA
Cloud Peak *44 C3 mountain* Wyoming, C USA
Clovis *49 E2* New Mexico, SW USA
Cluain Meala *see* Clonmel
Cluj-Napoca *108 B3 Ger.* Klausenburg, *Hung.* Kolozsvár; *prev.* Cluj, Cluj, NW Romania
Clutha *151 B7 river* South Island, NZ
Clyde *88 C4 river* W Scotland, UK
Coari *62 D2* Amazonas, N Brazil
Coast Mountains *36 D4 Fr.* Chaîne Côtière. *Mountain range* Canada/USA
Coast Ranges *46 A4 mountain range* W USA
Coats Island *37 G3 island* Nunavut, NE Canada
Coats Land *154 B2 physical region* Antarctica
Coatzacoalcos *51 G4 var.* Quetzalcoalco; *prev.* Puerto México. Veracruz-Llave, E Mexico
Cobán *52 B2* Alta Verapaz, C Guatemala
Cobar *149 C6* New South Wales, SE Australia
Cobija *61 E3* Pando, NW Bolivia
Coburg *95 C5* Bayern, SE Germany
Coca *see* Puerto Francisco de Orellana
Cochabamba *61 F4 hist.* Oropeza. Cochabamba, C Bolivia
Cochin *123 C7 var.* Kochi. Kerala, SW India
Cochinos, Bahía de *54 B2 Eng.* Bay of Pigs. *Bay* SE Cuba
Cochrane *42 B5* Aisén, S Chile
Cochrane *38 C4* Ontario, S Canada
Cocibolca *see* Nicaragua, Lago de
Cockburn Town *54 D2 var.* Grand Turk. *dependent territory capital* (Turks and Caicos Islands) Grand Turk Island, SE Turks and Caicos Islands
Cockpit Country, The *54 A4 physical region* W Jamaica
Cocobeach *77 A5* Estuaire, NW Gabon
Coconino Plateau *48 B1 plain* Arizona, SW USA
Coco, Río *53 E2 var.* Río Wanki, Segoviao Wangkí. *River* Honduras/Nicaragua
Cocos Basin *141 C5 undersea feature* E Indian Ocean
Cocos Island Ridge *see* Cocos Ridge
Cocos Islands *141 D5 island group* E Indian Ocean
Cocos Ridge *35 C8 var.* Cocos Island Ridge. *Undersea feature* E Pacific Ocean
Cod, Cape *41 G3 headland* Massachusetts, NE USA
Codfish Island *151 A8 island* SW NZ
Codlea *108 C4 Ger.* Zeiden, *Hung.* Feketehalom. Brașov, C Romania

Cody *44 C2* Wyoming, C USA
Coeur d'Alene *46 C2* Idaho, NW USA
Coevorden *86 E2* Drenthe, NE Netherlands
Coffs Harbour *149 E6* New South Wales, SE Australia
Cognac *91 B5 anc.* Compniacum. Charente, W France
Coiba, Isla de *53 E5 island* SW Panama
Coihaique *65 B6 var.* Coyhaique. Aisén, S Chile
Coimbatore *132 C3* Tamil Nādu, S India
Coimbra *92 B3 anc.* Conimbria, Conimbriga. Coimbra, W Portugal
Coín *92 D5* Andalucía, S Spain
Coirib, Loch *see* Corrib, Lough
Colby *45 E4* Kansas, C USA
Colchester *89 E6 hist.* Colneceaste, *anc.* Camulodunum. E England, UK
Col du Brenner *see* Brenner Pass
Coleman *49 F3* Texas, SW USA
Coleraine *88 B4 Ir.* Cúil Raithin. N Northern Ireland, UK
Colesberg *78 C5* Northern Cape, C South Africa
Colima *50 D4* Colima, S Mexico
Coll *88 B3 island* W Scotland, UK
College Station *49 G3* Texas, SW USA
Collie *147 A7* Western Australia
Colmar *90 E4 Ger.* Kolmar. Haut-Rhin, NE France
Cöln *see* Köln
Cologne *see* Köln
Colombia *58 B3 Country* N South America

Colombia 58

Official name Republic of Colombia
Formation 1819
Capital Bogotá
Population 42.8 million /97 people per sq mile (38 people per sq km)
Total area 439,733 sq miles (1,138,910 sq km)
Languages Spanish, Amerindian languages, English Creole
Religions Roman Catholic 95%, other 5%
Ethnic mix Mestizo 58%, White 20%, other 22%
Government Presidential democracy
Currency Colombian peso = 100 centavos
Literacy rate 91.8%
Calorie consumption 2,597 kilocalories

Colombian Basin *56 A1 undersea feature* SW Caribbean Sea
Colombo *132 C4 country capital* (Sri Lanka) Western Province, W Sri Lanka
Colón *53 G4 prev.* Aspinwall. Colón, C Panama
Colonia Agrippina *see* Köln
Colón Ridge *35 B8 undersea feature* E Pacific Ocean
Colorado *44 C4 off.* State of Colorado; also known as Centennial State, Silver State. *State* C USA
Colorado City *49 F3* Texas, SW USA
Colorado Plateau *48 B1 plateau* W USA
Colorado, Río *65 C5 river* E Argentina
Colorado, Río *see* Colorado River
Colorado River *35 B5 river.* Río Colorado. *River* Mexico/USA
Colorado River *49 G4 river* Texas, SW USA
Colorado Springs *44 D5* Colorado, C USA
Columbia *46 B3 river* Canada/USA

Columbia *43 E2 state capital* South Carolina, SE USA
Columbia *41 E4* Maryland, NE USA
Columbia *45 G4* Missouri, C USA
Columbia *42 C1* Tennessee, S USA
Columbia Plateau *46 C3 plateau* Idaho/Oregon, NW USA
Columbus *40 D4 state capital* Ohio, N USA
Columbus *42 D2* Georgia, SE USA
Columbus *40 C4* Indiana, N USA
Columbus *42 C2* Mississippi, S USA
Columbus *45 F4* Nebraska, C USA
Colville Channel *150 D2 channel* North Island, NZ
Colville River *36 D2 river* Alaska, USA
Comacchio *96 C3 var.* Commachio; *anc.* Comactium. Emilia-Romagna, N Italy
Comactium *see* Comacchio
Comalcalco *51 G4* Tabasco, SE Mexico
Coma Pedrosa, Pic de *91 A7 mountain* NW Andorra
Comarapa *61 F4* Santa Cruz, C Bolivia
Comayagua *52 C2* Comayagua, W Honduras
Comer See *see* Como, Lago di
Comilla *131 G4* Chittagong, E Bangladesh
Comino *102 A5 Malt.* Kemmuna. *Island* C Malta
Comitán *51 G5 var.* Comitán de Domínguez. Chiapas, SE Mexico
Comitán de Domínguez *see* Comitán
Commachio *see* Comacchio
Commissioner's Point *42 A5 headland* W Bermuda
Communism Peak *see* Kommunizm, Qullai
Como *96 B2 anc.* Comum. Lombardia, N Italy
Comodoro Rivadavia *65 B6* Chubut, SE Argentina
Como, Lago di *B2 var.* Lario, *Eng.* Lake Como, *Ger.* Comer See. *Lake* N Italy
Como, Lake *see* Como, Lago di
Comoros *79 F2 Fr.* République Fédérale Islamique des Comores. *Country* W Indian Ocean

Comoros 79

Official name Federal Islamic Republic of the Comoros
Formation 1975
Capital Moroni
Population 727,000 / 868 people per sq mile (335 people per sq km)
Total area 838 sq miles (2,170 sq km)
Languages Arabic, French, Comoran
Religions Muslim (mainly Sunni) 98%, Roman Catholic 1%, other 1%
Ethnic mix Comorian 97%, other 3%
Government Presidential democracy
Currency Comoros franc = 100 centimes
Literacy rate 59.6%
Calorie consumption 1,753 kilocalories

Compiègne *90 C3* Oise, N France
Compostella *see* Santiago
Comrat *108 D4 Rus.* Komrat. S Moldova
Conakry *74 C4 country capital* (Guinea) Conakry, SW Guinea
Concarneau *90 A3* Finistère, NW France
Concepción *64 D2 var.* Villa Concepción. Concepción, C Paraguay
Concepción *see* La Concepción
Concepción *65 B5* Bío Bío, C Chile
Concepción *61 G3* Santa Cruz, E Bolivia

Concepción de la Vega *see* La Vega
Conchos, Río *50 D2 river* C Mexico
Conchos, Río *48 D4 river* NW Mexico
Concord *41 G3 state capital* New Hampshire, NE USA
Concordia *64 D4* Entre Ríos, E Argentina
Concordia *45 E4* Kansas, C USA
Côn Đao *137 E7 var.* Con Son. *Island* S Vietnam
Condate *see* Cosne-Cours-sur-Loire
Condega *52 D3* Estelí, NW Nicaragua
Congo *77 D5 Fr.* Moyen-Congo; *prev.* Middle Congo. *Country* C Africa

Congo 77

Official name Republic of the Congo
Formation 1960
Capital Brazzaville
Population 3.1 million / 23 people per sq mile (9 people per sq km)
Total area 132,046 sq miles (342,000 sq km)
Languages French, Kongo, Teke, Lingala
Religions Traditional beliefs 50%, Christian 48%, Muslim 2%
Ethnic mix Bakongo 48%, Sangha 20%, Teke 17%, Mbochi 12%, other 3%
Government Presidential democracy
Currency CFA franc = 100 centimes
Literacy rate 80.7%
Calorie consumption 2,223 kilocalories

Congo, Dem. Rep. *77 C6 prev.* Zaire, Belgian Congo, Congo (Kinshasa). *Country* C Africa

Congo, Dem. Rep. 77

Official name Democratic Republic of the Congo
Formation 1960
Capital Kinshasa
Population 52.5 million / 58 people per sq mile (22 people per sq km)
Total area 905,563 sq miles (2,345,410 sq km)
Languages French, Kiswahili, Tshiluba
Religions Traditional beliefs 50%, Roman Catholic 37%, Protestant 13%
Ethnic mix Bantu and Hamitic 45%, other 55%
Government Military-based regime
Currency franc = 100 centimes
Literacy rate 61.4%
Calorie consumption 1,514 kilocalories

Congo *77 C6 var.* Kongo, *Fr.* Zaire. *River* C Africa
Congo Basin *77 C6 drainage basin* W Dem. Rep. Congo
Connacht *see* Connaught
Connaught *89 A5 var.* Connacht, *Ir.* Chonnacht, Cúige. *Cultural region* W Ireland
Connecticut *41 F3 off.* State of Connecticut; also known as Blue Law State, Constitution State, Land of Steady Habits, Nutmeg State. *State* NE USA
Connecticut *41 G3 river* Canada/USA
Conroe *49 G3* Texas, SW USA
Consolación del Sur *54 A2* Pinar del Río, W Cuba
Con Son *see* Côn Đao
Constance *see* Konstanz
Constance, Lake *B7 Ger.* Bodensee. *Lake* C Europe
Constanța *108 D5 var.* Küstendje, *Eng.* Constanza, *Ger.* Konstanza, *Turk.* Küstence. Constanța, SE Romania
Constantia *see* Konstanz

Constantine *71 E2 var.* Qacentina, *Ar.* Qoussantina. NE Algeria
Constantinople *see* İstanbul
Constanz *see* Konstanz
Constanza *see* Constanța
Coober Pedy *149 A5* South Australia
Cookeville *42 D1* Tennessee, S USA
Cook Islands *145 F4 territory in free association with NZ* S Pacific Ocean
Cook, Mount *151 B6 prev.* Aoraki, Aorangi. *Mountain* South Island, NZ
Cook Strait *151 D5 var.* Raukawa. *Strait* NZ
Cooktown *148 D2* Queensland, NE Australia
Coolgardie *147 B6* Western Australia
Cooma *149 D7* New South Wales, SE Australia
Coon Rapids *45 F2* Minnesota, N USA
Cooper Creek *148 C3 var.* Barcoo, Cooper's Creek. *Seasonal river* Queensland/South Australia
Cooper's Creek *see* Cooper Creek
Coos Bay *46 A3* Oregon, NW USA
Cootamundra *149 D6* New South Wales, SE Australia
Copacabana *61 E4* La Paz, W Bolivia
Copenhagen *see* København
Copiapó *64 B3* Atacama, N Chile
Copperas Cove *49 G3* Texas, SW USA
Coppermine *see* Kugluktuk
Coquimbo *64 B3* Coquimbo, N Chile
Corabia *108 B5* Olt, S Romania
Coral Harbour *37 G3* Southampton Island, Nunavut, NE Canada
Coral Sea *142 B3 sea* NW Pacific Ocean
Coral Sea Islands *144 B4 Australian external territory* SW Pacific Ocean
Corantijn Rivier *see* Courantyne River
Corcaigh *see* Cork
Corcovado, Golfo *65 B6 gulf* S Chile
Cordele *42 D3* Georgia, SE USA
Cordillera Ibérica *see* Ibérico, Sistema
Cordoba *see* Córdoba
Córdoba *62 D4 var.* Cordoba, *Eng.* Cordova; *anc.* Corduba. Andalucía, SW Spain
Córdoba *64 C3* Córdoba, C Argentina
Córdoba *51 F4* Veracruz-Llave, E Mexico
Cordova *see* Córdoba
Cordova *36 C3* Alaska, USA
Corduba *see* Córdoba
Corentyne River *see* Courantyne River
Corfu *see* Kérkyra
Coria *92 C3* Extremadura, W Spain
Corinth *see* Kórinthos
Corinth *42 C1* Mississippi, S USA
Corinth, Gulf of *see* Korinthiakós Kólpos
Corinthiacus Sinus *see* Korinthiakós Kólpos
Corinto *52 C3* Chinandega, NW Nicaragua
Cork *89 A6 Ir.* Corcaigh. S Ireland
Çorlu *116 A2* Tekirdağ, NW Turkey
Corner Brook *39 G3* Newfoundland, Newfoundland and Labrador, E Canada
Corn Islands *see* Maíz, Islas del
Cornwallis Island *37 F2 island* Nunavut, N Canada
Coro *58 C1 prev.* Santa Ana de Coro. Falcón, NW Venezuela
Corocoro *61 F4* La Paz, W Bolivia
Coromandel *150 D2* Waikato, North Island, NZ
Coromandel Coast *132 D2 coast* E India
Coromandel Peninsula *150 D2 peninsula* North Island, NZ
Coronado, Bahía de *52 D5 bay* S Costa Rica
Coronel Dorrego *65 C5* Buenos Aires, E Argentina

Coronel Oviedo *64 D2* Caaguazú, SE Paraguay
Corozal *52 C1* Corozal, N Belize
Corpus Christi *49 G4* Texas, SW USA
Corrales *48 D2* New Mexico, SW USA
Corrib, Lough *89 A5 Ir.* Loch Coirib. *Lake* W Ireland
Corrientes *64 D3* Corrientes, NE Argentina
Corriza *see* Korçë
Corse *91 E7 Eng.* Corsica. *Island* France, C Mediterranean Sea
Corsica *see* Corse
Corsicana *49 G3* Texas, SW USA
Cortegana *92 C4* Andalucía, S Spain
Cortés *53 E5 var.* Ciudad Cortés. Puntarenas, SE Costa Rica
Cortina d'Ampezzo *96 C1* Veneto, NE Italy
Coruche *92 B3* Santarém, C Portugal
Çoruh Nehri *117 E3 Geor.* Chorokhi, *Rus.* Chorokh. *River* Georgia/Turkey
Çorum *116 D3 var.* Chorum. Çorum, N Turkey
Corunna *see* A Coruña
Corvallis *46 B3* Oregon, NW USA
Corvo *92 A5 var.* Ilha do Corvo. *Island* Azores, Portugal, NE Atlantic Ocean
Cosenza *97 D6 anc.* Consentia. Calabria, SW Italy
Cosne-Cours-sur-Loire *90 C4 var.* Cosne-sur-Loire; *anc.* Condate. Nièvre, C France
Cosne-sur-Loire *see* Cosne-Cours-sur-Loire
Costa Mesa *46 D2* California, W USA
Costa Rica *53 E4 Country* Central America

Costa Rica 53

Official name Republic of Costa Rica
Formation 1838
Capital San José
Population 4.1 million / 208 people per sq mile (80 people per sq km)
Total area 19,730 sq miles (51,100 sq km)
Languages Spanish, English Creole, Bribri, Cabecar
Religions Roman Catholic 76%, other (including Protestant) 24%
Ethnic mix Mesitzo and European 96%, Black 2%, Indian 1%, Chinese 1%
Government Presidential democracy
Currency Costa Rican colón = 100 centimes
Literacy rate 95.6%
Calorie consumption 2,783 kilocalories

Cotagaita *61 F5* Potosí, S Bolivia
Côte d'Ivoire *74 D4 Eng.* Ivory Coast, Republic of the Ivory Coast. *Country* W Africa

Côte d'Ivoire 74

Official name Republic of Côte d'Ivoire
Formation 1960
Capital Yamoussoukro
Population 16.3 million / 131 people per sq mile (51 people per sq km)
Total area 124,502 sq miles (322,460 sq km)
Languages French, Akan, Kru, Voltaic
Religions Traditional beliefs 23%, Muslim 25%, Roman Catholic 23%, Protestant 6%, other 23%
Ethnic mix Baoule 23%, Bete 18%, Senufo 15% Agni-Ashanti 14%, Mandinka 11%, other 19%

185

Côte d'Ivoire (continued)

Government Multiparty republic
Currency CFA franc = 100 centimes
Literacy rate 47.1%
Calorie consumption 2,590 kilocalories

Côte d'Or 90 D4 *cultural region* C France
Cotonou 75 F5 *var.* Kotonu. S Benin
Cotrone *see* Crotone
Cotswold Hills 89 D6 *var.* Cotswolds. *Hill range* S England, UK
Cotswolds *see* Cotswold Hills
Cottbus 94 D4 *prev.* Kottbus. Brandenburg, E Germany
Council Bluffs 45 F4 Iowa, C USA
Courantyne River 59 G4 *var.* Corantijn Rivier, Corentyne River. *River* Guyana/Suriname
Courland Lagoon 106 A4 *Ger.* Kurisches Haff, *Rus.* Kurskiy Zaliv. *Lagoon* Lithuania/Russian Federation
Coutances 90 B3 *anc.* Constantia. Manche, N France
Couvin 87 C7 Namur, S Belgium
Coventry 89 D6 *anc.* Couentrey. C England, UK
Covilhã 92 C3 Castelo Branco, E Portugal
Cowan, Lake 147 B6 *lake* Western Australia
Coxen Hole *see* Roatán
Coxin Hole *see* Roatán
Coyhaique *see* Coihaique
Cozumel, Isla 51 H3 *island* SE Mexico
Cradock 78 C5 Eastern Cape, S South Africa
Craig 44 C4 Colorado, C USA
Craiova 108 B5 Dolj, SW Romania
Cranbrook 37 E5 British Columbia, SW Canada
Crane *see* The Crane
Crawley 89 E7 SE England, UK
Cremona 96 B2 Lombardia, N Italy
Cres 100 A3 *It.* Cherso; *anc.* Crexa. *Island* W Croatia
Crescent City 46 A4 California, W USA
Crescent Group 128 C7 *island group* C Paracel Islands
Creston 45 F4 Iowa, C USA
Crestview 42 D3 Florida, SE USA
Crete *see* Kríti
Créteil 90 E2 Val-de-Marne, N France
Crete, Sea of *see* Kritikó Pélagos
Creuse 90 B4 *river* C France
Crewe 89 D6 C England, UK
Crikvenica 100 A3 *It.* Cirquenizza; *prev.* Cirkvenica, Crjkvenica. Primorje-Gorski Kotar, NW Croatia
Crimea 81 F4 *var.* Krym, *Eng.* Crimea, Crimean Oblast; *prev.* Rus. Krymskaya ASSR, Krymskaya Oblast'. Admin. region *province* SE Ukraine
Crimean Oblast *see* Crimea
Cristóbal 52 A4 Colón, C Panama
Cristóbal Colón, Pico 58 B1 *mountain* N Colombia
Cristuru Secuiesc 108 C4 *prev.* Cristur, Cristuru Săcuiesc, Sitaş Cristuru, *Ger.* Kreutz, *Hung.* Székelykeresztúr, Szitás-Keresztúr. Harghita, C Romania
Crna Reka 101 D6 *river* S FYR Macedonia
Croatia 100 *Ger.* Kroatien, *SCr.* Hrvatska. *Country* SE Europe

Croatia 100

Official name Republic of Croatia
Formation 1991
Capital Zagreb
Population 4.7 million /215 people per sq mile (83 people per sq km)
Total area 21,831 sq miles (56,542 sq km)

Croatia 100

Languages Croatian
Religions Roman Catholic 76%, Orthodox 11%, Muslim 1%, other 12%
Ethnic mix Croat 78%, Serb 12%, Yugoslav 2%, other 8%
Government Parliamentary democracy
Currency Kuna = 100 lipa
Literacy rate 98.3%
Calorie consumption 2,843 kilocalories

Crocodile *see* Limpopo
Croia *see* Krujë
Croker Island 146 E2 *island* Northern Territory, N Australia
Cromwell 151 B7 Otago, South Island, NZ
Crooked Island 54 D2 *island* SE Bahamas
Crooked Island Passage 54 D2 *channel* SE Bahamas
Crookston 45 F1 Minnesota, N USA
Croton *see* Crotone
Crotona *see* Crotone
Crotone 97 E6 *var.* Cotrone; *anc.* Croton, Crotona. Calabria, SW Italy
Croydon 89 A8 SE England, UK
Crozet Basin 141 B6 *undersea feature* S Indian Ocean
Crozet Islands 141 B7 *island group* French Southern and Antarctic Territories
Crozet Plateau 141 B7 *var.* Crozet Plateaus. *Undersea feature* SW Indian Ocean
Crozet Plateaus *see* Crozet Plateau
Crystal Brook 149 B6 South Australia
Csorna 99 C6 Győr-Moson-Sopron, NW Hungary
Csurgó 99 C7 Somogy, SW Hungary
Cuando 78 C2 *var.* Kwando. *River* S Africa
Cuango 78 B1 *var.* Kwango. *River* Angola/Dem. Rep. Congo *see also* Kwango
Cuan na Gaillimhe *see* Galway Bay
Cuanza 78 B1 *var.* Kwanza. *River* C Angola
Cuauhtémoc 50 C2 Chihuahua, N Mexico
Cuautla 51 E4 Morelos, S Mexico
Cuba 54 B2 *Country* W West Indies

Cuba 54

Official name Republic of Cuba
Formation 1902
Capital Havana
Population 11.2 million /262 people per sq mile (101 people per sq km)
Total area 42,803 sq miles (110,860 sq km)
Languages Spanish
Religions Non-religious 49%, Roman Catholic 40%, Atheist 6%, Protestant 1%, other 4%
Ethnic mix White 66%, European-African 22%, Black 12%
Government One-party state
Currency Cuban peso = 100 centavos
Literacy rate 96.7%
Calorie consumption 2,564 kilocalories

Cubal 78 B2 Benguela, W Angola
Cubango 78 B2 *var.* Kavango, Kavengo, Kubango, Okavango, Okavongo. *River* S Africa *see also* Okavango
Cubango 78 B2 *var.* Kuvango, Port. Vila Artur de Paiva, Vila da Ponte. Huíla, SW Angola
Cúcuta 58 C2 *var.* San José de Cúcuta. Norte de Santander, N Colombia

Cuddapah 132 C2 Andhra Pradesh, S India
Cuenca 93 E3 *anc.* Conca. Castilla-La Mancha, C Spain
Cuenca 60 B2 Azuay, S Ecuador
Cuernavaca 51 E4 Morelos, S Mexico
Cuiabá 63 E3 *prev.* Cuyabá. *State capital* Mato Grosso, SW Brazil
Cúige *see* Connaught
Cúige Laighean *see* Leinster
Cúige Mumhan *see* Munster
Cuijck 86 D4 Noord-Brabant, SE Netherlands
Cúil Raithin *see* Coleraine
Cuito 78 B2 *var.* Kwito. *River* SE Angola
Cukai 138 B3 *var.* Chukai, Kemaman. Terengganu, Peninsular Malaysia
Culiacán 50 C3 *var.* Culiacán Rosales, Culiacán-Rosales. Sinaloa, C Mexico
Culiacán-Rosales *see* Culiacán
Cullera 93 F3 País Valenciano, E Spain
Cullman 42 C2 Alabama, S USA
Culmsee *see* Chełmża
Culpepper Island *see* Darwin, Isla
Cumaná 59 E1 Sucre, NE Venezuela
Cumbal, Nevada de 58 A4 *mountain* SW Colombia
Cumberland 41 E4 Maryland, NE USA
Cumberland Plateau 42 D1 *plateau* E USA
Cumberland Sound 37 H3 *inlet* Baffin Island, Nunavut, NE Canada
Cumpas 50 B2 Sonora, NW Mexico
Cunene 69 C6 *var.* Kunene. *River* Angola/Namibia *see also* Kunene
Cunene 78 A3 *province* S Angola
Cuneo 96 A2 *Fr.* Coni. Piemonte, NW Italy
Cunnamulla 149 C5 Queensland, E Australia
Ćuprija 100 E4 Serbia, E Serbia and Montenegro (Yugo.)
Curaçao 55 E5 *island* Netherlands Antilles
Curicó 64 B4 Maule, C Chile
Curitiba 63 E4 *prev.* Curytiba. *State capital* Paraná, S Brazil
Curtea de Argeş 108 C4 *var.* Curtea-de-Arges. Argeş, S Romania
Curtea-de-Arges *see* Curtea de Argeş
Curtici 108 A4 *Ger.* Kurtitsch, *Hung.* Kürtös. Arad, W Romania
Curtis Island 148 E4 *island* Queensland, SE Australia
Cusco 61 E4 *var.* Cuzco. Cusco, C Peru
Cusset 91 C5 Allier, C France
Cutch, Gulf of *see* Kachchh, Gulf of
Cuttack 135 F4 Orissa, E India
Cuvier Plateau 141 E6 *undersea feature* E Indian Ocean
Cuxhaven 94 B3 Niedersachsen, NW Germany
Cuyuni, Río *see* Cuyuni River
Cuyuni River 59 F3 *var.* Río Cuyuni. *River* Guyana/Venezuela
Cuzco *see* Cusco
Cyclades *see* Kykládes
Cydonia *see* Chaniá
Cymru *see* Wales
Cyprus 102 C4 *Gk.* Kypros, *Turk.* Kıbrıs, Kıbrıs Cumhuriyeti. *Country* E Mediterranean Sea

Cyprus 102

Official name Republic of Cyprus
Formation 1960
Capital Nicosia
Population 790,000 / 221 people per sq mile (85 people per sq km)
Total area 3,571 sq miles (9,250 sq km)
Languages Greek, Turkish, English
Religions Greek Orthodox 73%, Muslim 23%, other 4%
Ethnic mix Greek 77%, Turkish 18%, other (mainly British) 5%

Cyprus (continued)

Government Presidential democracy
Currency Cyprus pound/Turkish lira
Literacy rate 97.1%
Calorie consumption 3,259 kilocalories

Cythera *see* Kýthira
Cythnos *see* Kýthnos
Czech Republic 89 A5 *Cz.* Česká Republika. *Country* C Europe

Czech Republic 99

Official name Czech Republic
Formation 1993
Capital Prague
Population 10.3 million / 338 people per sq mile (131 people per sq km)
Total area 30,450 sq miles (78,866 sq km)
Languages Czech, Slovak, Hungarian
Religions Atheist 38%, Roman Catholic 39%, Protestant 3%, Hussites 2%, other 18%
Ethnic mix Czech 81%, Moravian 13%, Slovak 6%
Government Parliamentary democracy
Currency Czech koruna = 100 halura
Literacy rate 99%
Calorie consumption 3,104 kilocalories

Częstochowa 98 C4 *Ger.* Czenstochau, Tschenstochau, *Rus.* Chenstokhov. Śląskie, S Poland
Człuchów 98 C3 *Ger.* Schlochau. Pomorskie, N Poland

D

Dabajuro 58 C1 Falcón, NW Venezuela
Dabeiba 58 B2 Antioquia, NW Colombia
Dąbrowa Tarnowska 99 D5 Małopolskie, S Poland
Dabryn' 107 C8 *Rus.* Dobryn'. Homyel'skaya Voblasts', SE Belarus
Dagana 74 B3 N Senegal
Dagda 106 D4 Krāslava, SE Latvia
Dagenham 89 B8 SE England, UK
Dağlıq Qarabağ *see* Nagornyy Karabakh
Dagupan 139 E1 *off.* Dagupan City. Luzon, N Philippines
Da Hinggan Ling 127 G1 *Eng.* Great Khingan Range. *Mountain range* NE China
Dahm, Ramlat 121 B6 *desert* NW Yemen
Daimiel 92 D3 Castilla-La Mancha, C Spain
Daimoniá 105 B7 Pelopónnisos, S Greece
Dairen *see* Dalian
Dakar 74 B3 *country capital* (Senegal) W Senegal
Dakhla *see* Ad Dakhla
Dakoro 75 G3 Maradi, S Niger
Đakovica 101 D5 *var.* Djakovica, *Alb.* Gjakovë. Serbia, S Serbia and Montenegro (Yugo.)
Đakovo 100 C3 *var.* Djakovo, *Hung.* Diakovár. Osijek-Baranja, E Croatia
Dalai *see* Hulun Nur
Dalain Hob *see* Ejin Qi
Dalaman 116 A4 Muğla, SW Turkey
Dalandzadgad 127 E3 Ömnögovĭ, S Mongolia
Da Lat 137 E6 Lâm Đồng, S Vietnam
Dalby 149 D5 Queensland, E Australia

Dale City *41 E4* Virginia, NE USA
Dalhart *49 E1* Texas, SW USA
Dali *128 A6 var.* Xiaguan. Yunnan,
SW China
Dalian *128 D4 var.* Dairen, Dalien,
Lüda, Ta-lien, *Rus.* Dalny.
Liaoning, NE China
Dalien *see* Dalian
Dallas *49 G2* Texas, SW USA
Dalmacija *100 A4 Eng.* Dalmatia,
Ger. Dalmatien, *It.* Dalmazia.
Cultural region S Croatia
Dalny *see* Dalian
Dalton *42 D1* Georgia, SE USA
Daly Waters *148 A2* Northern
Territory, N Australia
Damachava *107 A6 var.*
Damachowa, *Pol.* Domaczewo,
Rus. Domachëvo. Brestskaya
Voblasts', SW Belarus
Damachowa *see* Damachava
Damān *134 C4* Damān and Diu,
W India
Damara *76 C4* Ombella-Mpoko,
S Central African Republic
Damas *see* Dimashq
Damasco *see* Dimashq
Damascus *see* Dimashq
Damāvand, Qolleh-ye *120 D3*
mountain N Iran
Dammām *see* Ad Dammām
Damoûr *119 A5 var.* Ad Dāmūr.
W Lebanon
Dampier *146 A4* Western Australia
Dampier, Selat *139 F4 strait* Papua,
E Indonesia
Damqawt *121 D6 var.* Damqut.
E Yemen
Damqut *see* Damqawt
Damxung *126 C5* Xizang Zizhiqu,
W China
Danakil Desert *72 D4 var.* Afar
Depression, Danakil Plain. *Desert*
E Africa
Danakil Plain *see* Danakil Desert
Danané *74 D5* W Côte d'Ivoire
Đà Năng *137 E5 prev.* Tourane.
Quang Nam-Đa Năng, C Vietnam
Danborg *see* Daneborg
Dandong *128 D3 var.* Tan-tung; *prev.*
An-tung. Liaoning, NE China
Daneborg *83 E3 var.* Danborg.
N Greenland
Dänew *see* Deynau
Dangerous Archipelago *see*
Tuamotu, Îles
Danghara *123 E3 Rus.* Dangara.
SW Tajikistan
Danghe Nanshan *126 D3 mountain*
range W China
Dangla *see* Tanggula Shan
Đângrêk, Chuŏr Phnum *137 D5 var.*
Phanom Dang Raek, Phanom
Dong Rak, *Fr.* Chaîne des
Dangrek. *Mountain range*
Cambodia/Thailand
Dangriga *52 C1 prev.* Stann Creek.
Stann Creek, E Belize
Danish West Indies *see* Virgin
Islands (US)
Danlí *52 D2* El Paraíso, S Honduras
Danmarksstraedet *see* Denmark
Strait
Dannenberg *94 C3* Niedersachsen,
N Germany
Dannevirke *150 D4* Manawatu-
Wanganui, North Island, NZ
Danube *81 E4* Bul. Dunav, *Cz.*
Dunaj, *Ger.* Donau, *Hung.* Duna,
Rom. Dunărea. *River* C Europe
Danville *41 E5* Virginia, NE USA
Dan Xian *see* Danzhou
Danxian/Dan Xian *see* Danzhou
Danzhou *128 C7 prev.* Dan Xian,
Danxian, Nada. Hainan, S China
Danziger Bucht *see* Danzig, Gulf of
Danzig, Gulf of *98 C2 var.* Gulf of
Pomorskie, *Ger.* Danziger Bucht,
Pol. Zakota Pomorskiea, *Rus.*
Gdan'skaya Bukhta. *Gulf*
N Poland
Daqm *see* Duqm
Dar'ā *119 B5 var.* Der'a, *Fr.* Déraa.
Dar'ā, SW Syria
Darabani *108 C3* Botoşani,
NW Romania
Daraut-Kurgan *see* Daroot-Korgon

Dardanelli *see* Çanakkale
Dar es Salaam *73 C7* Dar es Salaam,
E Tanzania
Darfield *151 C6* Canterbury, South
Island, NZ
Darfur *72 A4 var.* Darfur Massif.
Cultural region W Sudan
Darfur Massif *see* Darfur
Darhan *127 E2* Selenge, N Mongolia
Darién, Gulf of *58 A2 Sp.* Golfo del
Darién. *Gulf* S Caribbean Sea
Darién, Serranía del *53 H5*
mountain range Colombia/Panama
Dario *see* Ciudad Darío
Darjeeling *see* Darjiling
Darjiling *135 F3 prev.* Darjeeling.
West Bengal, NE India
Darling River *149 C6 river* New
South Wales, SE Australia
Darlington *89 D5* N England, UK
Darmstadt *95 B5* Hessen,
SW Germany
Darnah *71 G2 var.* Dérna. NE Libya
Darnley, Cape *154 D2 headland*
Antarctica
Daroca *93 E2* Aragón, NE Spain
Daroot-Korgon *123 F3 var.* Daraut-
Kurgan. Oshskaya Oblast',
SW Kyrgyzstan
Dartford *89 B8* SE England, UK
Dartmoor *89 C7 moorland*
SW England, UK
Dartmouth *39 F4* Nova Scotia,
SE Canada
Darvaza *122 C2 Turkm.* Derweze.
Akhalskiy Velayat,
C Turkmenistan
Darwin *146 D2 prev.* Palmerston,
Port Darwin. *Territory capital*
Northern Territory, N Australia
Darwin, Isla *60 A4 var.* Culpepper
Island. *Island* W Ecuador
Daryācheh-ye Hāmūn *see* Şāberī,
Hāmūn-e
Daryācheh-ye Sīstān *see* Şāberī,
Hāmūn-e
Darya-ye Morghāb *see* Murgab
Daryā-ye Pāmir *see* Pamir
Daryoi Pomir *see* Pamir
Dashkawka *107 D6 Rus.*
Dashkovka. Mahilyowskaya
Voblasts', E Belarus
Dashkhovuz *122 C2 Turkm.*
Dashhowuz; *prev.* Tashauz.
Dashkhovuzskiy Velayat,
N Turkmenistan
Datong *128 C3 var.* Tatung,
Ta-t'ung. Shanxi, C China
Daugavpils *106 D4 Ger.* Dünaburg;
prev. Rus. Dvinsk. *Municipality*
Daugvapils, SE Latvia
Daung Kyun *137 B6 island*
S Myanmar
Dauphiné *91 D5 cultural region*
E France
Dāvangere *132 C2* Karnātaka,
W India
Davao *139 F3 off.* Davao City.
Mindanao, S Philippines
Davao Gulf *139 F3 gulf* Mindanao,
S Philippines
Davenport *45 G3* Iowa, C USA
David *53 E5* Chiriquí, W Panama
Davie Ridge *141 A5 undersea feature*
W Indian Ocean
Davis *154 D3 Australian research*
station Antarctica
Davis Sea *154 D3 sea* Antarctica
Davis Strait *82 B3 strait* Baffin
Bay/Labrador Sea
Dawei *see* Tavoy
Dax *91 B6 var.* Ax; *anc.* Aquae
Augustae, Aquae Tarbelicae.
Landes, SW France
Dayr az Zawr *118 D3 var.* Deir ez
Zor. Dayr az Zawr, E Syria
Dayton *40 C4* Ohio, N USA
Daytona Beach *43 E4* Florida, SE USA
De Aar *78 C5* Northern Cape,
C South Africa
Dead Sea *119 B6 var.* Bahret Lut,
Lacus Asphaltites, *Ar.* Al Bahr
al Mayyit, Bahret Lut, *Heb.* Yam
HaMelah. *Salt lake* Israel/Jordan
Dealnu *see* Tana
Deán Funes *64 C3* Córdoba,
C Argentina

Death Valley *47 C7 valley*
California, W USA
Debar *101 D6 Ger.* Dibra, *Turk.*
Debre. W FYR Macedonia
Debica *99 D5* Podkarpackie, SE
Poland
De Bildt *see* De Bilt
De Bilt *86 C3 var.* De Bildt. Utrecht,
C Netherlands
Dębno *98 B3* Zachodniopomorskie,
NW Poland
Debrecen *99 D6 Ger.* Debreczin,
Rom. Debreţin; *prev.* Debreczen.
Hajdú-Bihar, E Hungary
Decatur *42 C1* Alabama, S USA
Decatur *40 B4* Illinois, N USA
Deccan *134 D5 Hind.* Dakshin.
Plateau C India
Děčín *98 B4 Ger.* Tetschen. Ústecký
Kraj, NW Czech Republic
Dedeagač *see* Alexandroúpoli
Dedeagach *see* Alexandroúpoli
Dedemsvaart *86 E3* Overijssel,
E Netherlands
Dee *88 C1 river* NE Scotland, UK
Deering *36 C2* Alaska, USA
Deggendorf *95 D6* Bayern,
SE Germany
Değirmenlik *102 C5* N Cyprus
Deh Bīd *120 D3* Fārs, C Iran
Dehli *see* Delhi
Deh Shū *122 D5 var.* Deshu.
Helmand, S Afghanistan
Deinze *87 B5* Oost-Vlaanderen,
NW Belgium
Deir ez Zor *see* Dayr az Zawr
Deirgeirt, Loch *see* Derg, Lough
Dej *108 B3 Hung.* Dés; *prev.* Deés.
Cluj, NW Romania
Dékoa *76 C4* Kémo, 188C Central
African Republic
De Land *43 E4* Florida, SE USA
Delano *47 C7* California, W USA
Delārām *122 D5* Farāh,
SW Afghanistan
Delaware *41 F4 off.* State of
Delaware; also known as Blue
Hen State, Diamond State, First
State. *State* NE USA
Delaware *40 D4* Ohio, N USA
Delft *86 B4* Zuid-Holland,
W Netherlands
Delfzijl *86 E1* Groningen,
NE Netherlands
Delgo *72 B3* Northern, N Sudan
Delhi *134 D3 var.* Dehli, *Hind.* Dilli;
hist. Shahjahanabad. Delhi, N India
Delicias *50 D2 var.* Ciudad Delicias.
Chihuahua, N Mexico
Déli-Kárpátok *see* Carpaţii
Meridionali
Delmenhorst *94 B3* Niedersachsen,
NW Germany
Del Rio *49 F4* Texas, SW USA
Deltona *43 E4* Florida, SE USA
Demba *77 D6* Kasai Occidental,
C Dem. Rep. Congo
Dembia *74 D4* Mbomou, SE Central
African Republic
Demchok *var.* Dêmqog. *Disputed*
region China/India *see also*
Dêmqog
Demchok *126 A4 var.* Dêmqog.
China/India *see also* Dêmqog
Demerara Plain *56 C2 undersea*
feature W Atlantic Ocean
Deming *48 C3* New Mexico,
SW USA
Demmin *94 C2* Mecklenburg-
Vorpommern, NE Germany
Demopolis *42 C2* Alabama, S USA
Dêmqog *var.* Demchok. *Disputed*
region China/India *see also*
Demchok
Denali *see* McKinley, Mount
Dender *87 B6 Fr.* Dendre. *River*
W Belgium
Denekamp *86 E3* Overijssel,
E Netherlands
Den Haag *see* 's-Gravenhage
Den Ham *86 E3* Overijssel,
E Netherlands
Denham *147 A5* Western Australia
Den Helder *86 C2* Noord-Holland,
NW Netherlands
Denia *93 F4* País Valenciano,
E Spain

Deniliquin *149 C7* New South
Wales, SE Australia
Denison *45 F3* Iowa, C USA
Denison *49 G2* Texas, SW USA
Denizli *116 B4* Denizli,
SW Turkey
Denmark *85 A7 Dan.* Danmark; *anc.*
Hafnia. *Country* N Europe

Denmark 85

Official name Kingdom of
Denmark
Formation AD 950
Capital Copenhagen (Koebenhavn)
Population 5.3 million / 319 people
per sq mile (123 people per sq km)
Total area 16,639 sq miles
(43,094 sq km)
Languages Danish
Religions Evangelical Lutheran
89%, Roman Catholic 1%, other 10%
Ethnic mix Danish 96%, Faeroe and
Inuit 1%, other (including
Scandinavian) 3%
Government Parliamentary
democracy
Currency Danish krone = 100 ore
Literacy rate 99%
Calorie consumption 3,396
kilocalories

Denmark Strait *82 D4 var.*
Danmarksstraedet. *Strait*
Greenland/Iceland
Dennery *55 F1* E Saint Lucia
Denow *123 E3 Rus.* Denau.
Surkhondaryo Wiloyati,
S Uzbekistan
Denpasar *138 D5 prev.* Paloe. Bali,
C Indonesia
Denton *49 G2* Texas, SW USA
D'Entrecasteaux Islands *144 B3*
island group SE PNG
Denver *44 D4 state capital* Colorado,
C USA
Der'a *see* Dar'ā
Déraa *see* Dar'ā
Dera Ghāzi Khān *134 C2 var.* Dera
Ghāzīkhān. Punjab, C Pakistan
Dera Ghāzīkhān *see* Dera Ghāzi
Khān
Deravica *101 D5 mountain* S Serbia
and Montenegro (Yugo.)
Derbent *111 B8* Respublika
Dagestan, SW Russian Federation
Derby *89 D6* C England, UK
Derelí *see* Gönnoi
Derg, Lough *89 A6 Ir.* Loch
Deirgeirt. *Lake* W Ireland
Derhachi *109 G2 Rus.* Dergachi.
Kharkivs'ka Oblast', E Ukraine
De Ridder *42 A3* Louisiana,
S USA
Dérna *see* Darnah
Derry *see* Londonderry
Derventa *100 B3* Republika Srpska,
N Bosnia and Herzegovina
Deschutes River *46 B3 river*
Oregon, NW USA
Desē *72 C4 var.* Desse, It. Dessie.
N Ethiopia
Deseado, Río *65 B7 river*
S Argentina
Desertas, Ilhas *70 A2 island group*
Madeira, Portugal, NE Atlantic
Ocean
Deshu *see* Deh Shū
Desierto de Altar *see* Sonoran
Desert
Des Moines *45 F3 state capital* Iowa,
C USA
Desna *109 E2 river* Russian
Federation/Ukraine
Dessau *94 C4* Sachsen-Anhalt,
E Germany
Desse *see* Desē
Dessie *see* Desē
Detroit *40 D3* Michigan, N USA
Detroit Lakes *45 F2* Minnesota,
N USA
Deurne *87 D5* Noord-Brabant,
SE Netherlands
Deva *108 B4 Ger.* Diemrich, *Hung.*
Déva. Hunedoara, W Romania
Đevđelija *see* Gevgelija

Deventer 86 D3 Overijssel, E Netherlands
Devils Lake 45 E1 North Dakota, N USA
Devoll see Devollit, Lumi i
Devollit, Lumi i 101 D6 var. Devoll. River SE Albania
Devon Island 37 F2 prev. North Devon Island. Island Parry Islands, Nunavut, NE Canada
Devonport 149 C8 Tasmania, SE Australia
Devrek 116 C2 Zonguldak, N Turkey
Dexter 45 H5 Missouri, C USA
Deynau 122 D3 var. Dyanev, Turkm. Dänew. Lebapskiy Velayat, NE Turkmenistan
Dezful 120 C3 var. Dizful. Khūzestān, SW Iran
Dezhou 128 D4 Shandong, E China
Dhaka 135 G4 prev. Dacca. Country capital (Bangladesh) Dhaka, C Bangladesh
Dhanbād 135 F4 Bihār, NE India
Dhekélia 102 C5 Eng. Dhekelia. Gk. Dekéleia. UK air base SE Cyprus
Dhidhimótikhon see Didymóteicho
Dhíkti Ori see Díkti
Dhodhekánisos see Dodekánisos
Dhomokós see Domokós
Dhráma see Dráma
Dhrepanon, Akrotírio see Drépano Akrotírio
Dhuusa Marreeb 73 E5 var. Dusa Marreb, It. Dusa Mareb. Galguduud, C Somalia
Diakovár see Đakovo
Diamantina, Chapada 63 F3 mountain range E Brazil
Diamantina Fracture Zone 141 E6 tectonic feature E Indian Ocean
Diarbekr see Diyarbakır
Dibrugarh 135 H3 Assam, NE India
Dickinson 44 D2 North Dakota, N USA
Didimotico see Didymóteicho
Didymóteicho 104 D3 var. Dhidhimótikhon, Didimotiho. Anatolikí Makedonía kai Thráki, NE Greece
Diégo-Suarez see Antsirañana
Diekirch 87 D7 Diekirch, C Luxembourg
Điện Biên 136 D3 var. Bien Bien, Dien Bien Phu. Lai Châu, N Vietnam
Dien Bien Phu see Điện Biên
Diepenbeek 87 D6 Limburg, NE Belgium
Diepholz 94 B3 Niedersachsen, NW Germany
Dieppe 90 C2 Seine-Maritime, N France
Dieren 86 D4 Gelderland, E Netherlands
Differdange 87 D8 Luxembourg, SW Luxembourg
Digne 91 D6 var. Digne-les-Bains. Alpes-de-Haute-Provence, SE France
Digne-les-Bains see Digne
Digoin 90 C4 Saône-et-Loire, C France
Digul, Sungai 139 H5 prev. Digoel. River Papua, E Indonesia
Dihang see Brahmaputra
Dijon 90 D4 anc. Dibio. Côte d'Or, C France
Dikhil 72 D4 SW Djibouti
Dikson 114 D2 Taymyrskiy (Dolgano-Nenetskiy) Avtonomnyy Okrug, N Russian Federation
Díkti 105 D8 var. Dhíkti Ori. Mountain range Kríti, Greece, E Mediterranean Sea
Dili 139 F5 var. Dilli, Dilly. Country capital (East Timor), N East Timor
Dilia 75 G3 var. Dillia. River SE Niger
Di Linh 137 E6 Lâm Đồng, S Vietnam
Dilli see Delhi
Dilli see Dili
Dillia see Dilia
Dilling 72 B4 var. Ad Dalanj. Southern Kordofan, C Sudan

Dillon 44 B2 Montana, NW USA
Dilly see Dili
Dilolo 77 D7 Ngounié, S Gabon
Dimashq 119 B5 var. Ash Shām, Esh Sham, Eng. Damascus, Fr. Damas, It. Damasco. Country capital (Syria) Dimashq, SW Syria
Dimitrovgrad 104 D3 Khaskovo, S Bulgaria
Dimitrovgrad 111 C6 Ul'yanovskaya Oblast', W Russian Federation
Dimovo 104 B1 Vidin, NW Bulgaria
Dinajpur 135 F3 Rajshahi, NW Bangladesh
Dinan 90 B3 Côtes d'Armor, NW France
Dinant 87 C7 Namur, S Belgium
Dinar 116 B4 Afyon, SW Turkey
Dinara see Dinaric Alps
Dinaric Alps 100 C4 var. Dinara. Mountain range Bosnia and Herzegovina / Croatia
Dindigul 132 C3 Tamil Nādu, SE India
Dingle Bay 89 A6 Ir. Bá an Daingin. Bay SW Ireland
Dinguiraye 74 C4 Haute-Guinée, N Guinea
Diourbel 74 B3 W Senegal
Dirê Dawa 73 D5 E Ethiopia
Dirk Hartog Island 147 A5 island Western Australia
Disappointment, Lake 146 C4 salt lake Western Australia
Dispur 135 G3 Assam, NE India
Divinópolis 63 F4 Minas Gerais, SE Brazil
Divo 74 D5 S Côte d'Ivoire
Diyarbakır 117 F4 var. Diarbekr; anc. Amida. Diyarbakır, SE Turkey
Dizful see Dezful
Djajapura see Jayapura
Djakovica see Đakovica
Djakovo see Đakovo
Djambala 77 B6 Plateaux, C Congo
Djanet 71 E4 prev. Fort Charlet. SE Algeria
Djéblé see Jablah
Djelfa 70 D2 var. El Djelfa. N Algeria
Djéma 76 D4 Haut-Mbomou, E Central African Republic
Djérablous see Jarāblus
Djerba see Jerba, Île de
Djérem 76 B4 river C Cameroon
Djevdjelija see Gevgelija
Djibouti 72 D4 var. Jibuti; prev. French Somaliland, French Territory of the Afars and Issas, Fr. Côte Française des Somalis, Territoire Français des Afars et des Issas. Country E Africa

Djibouti 72

Official name Republic of Djibouti
Formation 1977
Capital Djibouti
Population 644,000 / 76 people per sq mile (29 people per sq km)
Total area 8,490 sq miles (22,000 sq km)
Languages French, Arabic, Somali, Afar
Religions Muslim 94%, Christian 6%
Ethnic mix Issa 60%, Afar 35%, other 5%
Government Presidential democracy
Currency Djibouti franc = 100 centimes
Literacy rate 64.6%
Calorie consumption 2,050 kilocalories

Djibouti 72 D4 var. Jibuti. Country capital (Djibouti) E Djibouti
Djourab, Erg du 76 C2 dunes N Chad
Djúpivogur 83 E5 Austurland, SE Iceland
Dnepr see Dnieper
Dnieper 81 F4 Bel. Dnyapro, Rus. Dnepr, Ukr. Dnipro. River E Europe

Dnieper Lowland 109 E2 Bel. Prydnyaprowskaya Nizina, Ukr. Prydniprovs'ka Nyzovyna.
Lowlands Belarus / Ukraine
Dniester 81 E4 Rom. Nistru, Rus. Dnestr, Ukr. Dnister; anc. Tyras. River Moldova / Ukraine
Dnipro see Dnieper
Dniprodzerzhyns'k 109 F3 Rus. Dneprodzerzhinsk; prev. Kamenskoye. Dnipropetrovs'ka Oblast', E Ukraine
Dniprodzerzhyns'ke Vodoskhovyshche 109 F3 Rus. Dneprodzerzhinskoye Vodokhranilishche. Reservoir C Ukraine
Dnipropetrovs'k 109 F3 Rus. Dnepropetrovsk; prev. Yekaterinoslav. Dnipropetrovs'ka Oblast', E Ukraine
Dniprodrudne 109 F3 Rus. Dneprorudnoye. Zaporiz'ka Oblast', SE Ukraine
Doba 76 C4 Logone-Oriental, S Chad
Döbeln 94 D4 Sachsen, E Germany
Doberai, Jazirah 139 G4 Dut. Vogelkop. Peninsula Papua, E Indonesia
Doboj 100 C3 Republika Srpska, N Bosnia and Herzegovina
Dobre Miasto 98 D2 Ger. Guttstadt. Warmińsko-Mazurskie, N Poland
Dobrich 104 E1 Rom. Bazargic; prev. Tolbukhin. Dobrich, NE Bulgaria
Dobrush 107 D7 Homyel'skaya Voblasts', SE Belarus
Dodecánese see Dodekánisos
Dodekánisos 105 D6 var. Nóties Sporádes, Eng. Dodecanese; prev. Dhodhekánisos. Island group SE Greece
Dodge City 45 E5 Kansas, C USA
Dodoma 69 D5 country capital (Tanzania) Dodoma, C Tanzania
Dodoma 73 C7 region C Tanzania
Dogana 96 E1 NE San Marino
Dōgo 131 B6 island Oki-shotō, SW Japan
Dogondoutchi 75 F3 Dosso, SW Niger
Doğubayazıt 117 F3 Ağrı, E Turkey
Doğu Karadeniz Dağları 117 E3 var. Anadolu Dağları. Mountain range NE Turkey
Doha see Ad Dawhah
Doire see Londonderry
Dokkum 86 D1 Friesland, N Netherlands
Dokuchayevs'k 109 G3 var. Dokuchayevsk. Donets'ka Oblast', SE Ukraine
Dokuchayevsk see Dokuchayevs'k
Doldrums Fracture Zone 66 C4 tectonic feature W Atlantic Ocean
Dôle 90 D4 Jura, E France
Dolisie 77 B6 prev. Loubomo. Le Niari, S Congo
Dolomites see Dolomitiche, Alpi
Dolomiti see Dolomitiche, Alpi
Dolomitiche, Alpi 96 C1 var. Dolomiti, Eng. Dolomites, It. Dolomiti. Mountain range NE Italy
Dolores 64 D4 Buenos Aires, E Argentina
Dolores 52 B1 Petén, N Guatemala
Dolores 64 D4 Soriano, SW Uruguay
Dolores Hidalgo 51 E4 var. Ciudad de Dolores Hidalgo. Guanajuato, C Mexico
Dolyna 108 B2 Rus. Dolina. Ivano-Frankivs'ka Oblast', W Ukraine
Dolyns'ka 109 F3 Rus. Dolinskaya. Kirovohrads'ka Oblast', S Ukraine
Domachevo see Damachava
Domaczewo see Damachava
Dombås 85 B5 Oppland, S Norway
Domel Island see Letsôk-aw Kyun
Domeyko 64 B3 Atacama, N Chile

Dominica 55 H4 Country E West Indies

Dominica 55

Official name Commonwealth of Dominica
Formation 1978
Capital Roseau
Population 73,000 / 251 people per sq mile (97 people per sq km)
Total area 291 sq miles (754 sq km)
Languages English, French Creole
Religions Roman Catholic 77%, Protestant 15%, other 8%
Ethnic mix Black 91%, Mixed 6%, Indian 2%, other 1%
Government Parliamentary democracy
Currency East Caribbean dollar = 100 cents
Literacy rate 94%
Calorie consumption 2,994 kilocalories

Dominica Channel see Martinique Passage
Dominican Republic 55 E2 country C West Indies

Dominican Republic 55

Official name Dominican Republic
Formation 1865
Capital Santo Domingo
Population 8.5 million / 452 people per sq mile (174 people per sq km)
Total area 18,815 sq miles (48,730 sq km)
Languages Spanish, French Creole
Religions Roman Catholic 92%, other and non-religious 8%
Ethnic mix Mixed 75%, White 15%, Black 10%
Government Presidential democracy **Currency** Dominican Republic peso = 100 centavos
Literacy rate 83.6%
Calorie consumption 2,325 kilocalories

Domokós 105 B5 var. Dhomokós. Stereá Ellás, C Greece
Don 111 B6 var. Duna, Tanais. River SW Russian Federation
Donau see Danube
Donauwörth 95 C6 Bayern, S Germany
Don Benito 92 C3 Extremadura, W Spain
Doncaster 89 D5 anc. Danum. N England, UK
Dondo 78 B1 Cuanza Norte, NW Angola
Donegal 89 B5 Ir. Dún na nGall. NW Ireland
Donegal Bay 89 A5 Ir. Bá Dhún na nGall. Bay NW Ireland
Donets 109 G2 var. Sivers's'kyy Donets', Rus. Severskiy Donets. Serra Acaraí. river Russian Federation / Ukraine
Donets'k 109 G3 Rus. Donetsk; prev. Stalino. Donets'ka Oblast', E Ukraine
Dongfang 128 B7 var. Basuo. Hainan, S China
Dongguan 128 C6 Guangdong, S China
Đông Ha 136 E4 Quang Tri, C Vietnam
Đông Hôi 136 D4 Quang Binh, C Vietnam
Dongliao see Liaoyuan
Dongola 72 B3 var. Donqola, Dunqulah. Northern, N Sudan
Dongou 77 C5 La Likouala, NE Congo
Dongting Hu 128 C5 var. Tung-t'ing Hu. Lake S China
Donji Vakuf var. Srbobran, Federacija Bosna I Hercegovina, N Serbia and Montenegro (Yugo.)
Donostia-San Sebastián 93 E1 Vasco, N Spain

Donqola see Dongola
Doolow 73 D5 E Ethiopia
Doornik see Tournai
Door Peninsula 40 C2 peninsula
Wisconsin, N USA
Dooxo Nugaaleed 73 E5 var. Nogal
Valley. Valley E Somalia
Dordogne 91 B5 cultural region
SW France
Dordogne 91 B5 river W France
Dordrecht 86 C4 var. Dordt, Dort.
Zuid-Holland, SW Netherlands
Dordt see Dordrecht
Dorohoi 108 C3 Botoşani,
NE Romania
Dorotea 84 C4 Västerbotten,
N Sweden
Dorre Island 147 A5 island Western
Australia
Dort see Dordrecht
Dortmund 94 A4 Nordrhein-
Westfalen, W Germany
Dos Hermanas 92 C4 Andalucía,
S Spain
Dospad Dagh see Rhodope
Mountains
Dospat 104 C3 Smolyan,
S Bulgaria
Dothan 42 D3 Alabama, S USA
Dotnuva 106 B4 Kėdainiai,
C Lithuania
Douai 90 C2 prev. Douay, anc.
Duacum. Nord, N France
Douala 77 A5 var. Duala. Littoral,
W Cameroon
Douglas 89 C5 dependent territory
capital (Isle of Man) E Isle of Man
Douglas 48 C3 Arizona, SW USA
Douglas 44 D3 Wyoming, C USA
Douro 92 B2 Sp. Duero. River
Portugal/Spain see also Duero
Dover 89 E7 Fr. Douvres; Lat.
Dubris Portus. SE England, UK
Dover 41 F4 state capital Delaware,
NE USA
Dover, Strait of 90 C2 var. Straits of
Dover, Fr. Pas de Calais. Strait
England, UK/France
Dover, Straits of see Dover, Strait
of
Dovrefjell 85 B5 plateau S Norway
Downpatrick 89 B5 Ir. Dún Pádraig.
SE Northern Ireland, UK
Dōzen 131 B6 island Oki-shotō,
SW Japan
Drač see Durrës
Drachten 86 D2 Friesland,
N Netherlands
Drăgăşani 108 B5 Vâlcea,
SW Romania
Dragoman 104 B2 Sofiya,
W Bulgaria
Dra, Hamada du 70 C3 var.
Hammada du Drâa, Haut Plateau
du Dra. Plateau W Algeria
Drahichyn 107 B6 Pol. Drohiczyn
Poleski, Rus. Drogichin.
Brestskaya Voblasts', SW Belarus
Drakensberg 78 D5 mountain range
Lesotho/South Africa
Drake Passage 57 B8 passage
Atlantic Ocean/Pacific Ocean
Dralfa 104 D2 Tŭrgovishte,
N Bulgaria
Dráma 104 C3 var. Dhráma.
Anatolikí Makedonía kai Thráki,
NE Greece
Drammen 85 B6 Buskerud,
S Norway
Drau see Drava
Drava 100 C3 var. Drau, Eng. Drave,
Hung. Dráva. River C Europe see
also Drau
Dráva see Drava
Drave see Drava
Drawsko Pomorskie 98 B3 Ger.
Dramburg. Zachodniopomorskie,
NW Poland
Drépano, Akrotírio 104 C4 var.
Akra Dhrepanon. Headland
N Greece
Dresden 94 D4 Sachsen,
E Germany
Drin see Drinit, Lumi i
Drina 100 C3 river Bosnia and
Herzegovina/Serbia and
Montenegro (Yugo.)

Drinit, Lumi i 101 D5 var. Drin.
River NW Albania
Drobeta-Turnu Severin 108 B5 prev.
Turnu Severin. Mehedinţi,
SW Romania
Drogheda 89 B5 Ir. Droichead Átha.
NE Ireland
Drohobych 108 B2 Pol. Drohobycz,
Rus. Drogobych. L'vivs'ka Oblast',
NW Ukraine
Droichead Átha see Drogheda
Drôme 91 D5 cultural region
SE France
Dronning Maud Land 154 B2
physical region Antarctica
Drummondville 39 E4 Quebec,
SE Canada
Druskininkai 107 B5 Pol.
Druskienniki. Druskininkai,
S Lithuania
Dryden 38 B3 Ontario, C Canada
Drysa 107 D5 Rus. Drissa. River
N Belarus
Duala see Douala
Dubai see Dubayy
Dubăsari 108 D3 Rus. Dubossary.
NE Moldova
Dubawnt 37 F4 river Northwest
Territories/Nunavut, NW Canada
Dubayy 120 D4 Eng. Dubai.
Dubayy, NE UAE
Dubbo 149 D6 New South Wales,
SE Australia
Dublin 89 B5 Ir. Baile Átha Cliath;
anc. Eblana. Country capital
(Ireland), E Ireland
Dublin 43 E2 Georgia, SE USA
Dubno 108 C2 Rivnens'ka Oblast',
NW Ukraine
Dubrovnik 101 B5 It. Ragusa.
Dubrovnik-Neretva, SE Croatia
Dubuque 45 G3 Iowa, C USA
Dudelange 87 D8 var. Forge du
Sud, Ger. Dudelingen.
Luxembourg, S Luxembourg
Dudelingen see Dudelange
Duero 92 D2 Port. Douro. River
Portugal/Spain see also Douro
Duesseldorf see Düsseldorf
Duffel 87 C5 Antwerpen,
C Belgium
Dugi Otok 100 A4 var. Isola Grossa,
It. Isola Lunga. Island W Croatia
Duisburg 94 A4 prev. Duisburg-
Hamborn. Nordrhein-Westfalen,
W Germany
Duiven 86 D4 Gelderland,
E Netherlands
Duk Faiwil 73 B5 Jonglei, SE Sudan
Dulan 126 D4 var. Qagan Us.
Qinghai, C China
Dulce, Golfo 53 E5 gulf S Costa
Rica
Dülmen 94 A4 Nordrhein-
Westfalen, W Germany
Dulovo 104 E1 Silistra, NE Bulgaria
Duluth 45 G2 Minnesota, N USA
Dūmā 119 B5 Fr. Douma. Dimashq,
SW Syria
Dumas 49 E1 Texas, SW USA
Dumfries 88 C4 S Scotland, UK
Dumont d'Urville 154 C4 French
research station Antarctica
Dumyât 72 B1 Eng. Damietta.
N Egypt
Duna see Danube
Duna see Don
Dunaj see Danube
Dunaújváros 99 C7 prev.
Dunapentele, Sztálinváros. Fejér,
C Hungary
Dunav see Danube
Dunavska Ravnina 104 C2 Eng.
Danubian Plain. Plain N Bulgaria
Duncan 49 G2 Oklahoma, C USA
Dundalk 89 B5 Ir. Dún Dealgan.
NE Ireland
Dún Dealgan see Dundalk
Dundee 88 C4 E Scotland, UK
Dundee 78 D4 KwaZulu/Natal,
E South Africa
Dunedin 151 B7 Otago, South
Island, NZ
Dunfermline 88 C4 C Scotland,
UK
Dungu 77 E5 Orientale, NE Dem.
Rep. Congo

Dungun 138 B3 var. Kuala Dungun.
Terengganu, Peninsular Malaysia
Dunkerque 90 C2 Eng. Dunkirk,
Flem. Duinekerke; prev.
Dunquerque. Nord, N France
Dún Laoghaire 89 B6 Eng.
Dunleary; prev. Kingstown.
E Ireland
Dún na nGall see Donegal
Dún Pádraig see Downpatrick
Dunqulah see Dongola
Dunărea see Danube
Dupnitsa 104 C2 prev. Marek,
Stanke Dimitrov. Kyustendil,
W Bulgaria
Duqm 121 E5 var. Daqm. E Oman
Durance 91 D6 river SE France
Durango 50 D3 var. Victoria de
Durango. Durango, W Mexico
Durango 44 C5 Colorado, C USA
Durankulak 104 E1 Rom. Răcari;
prev. Blatnitsa, Duranulac.
Dobrich, NE Bulgaria
Durant 49 G2 Oklahoma, C USA
Durazzo see Durrës
Durban 78 D4 var. Port Natal.
KwaZulu/Natal, E South Africa
Durbe 106 B3 Ger. Durben. Liepāja,
W Latvia
Durg 135 E4 prev. Drug. Madhya
Pradesh, C India
Durham 89 D5 hist. Dunholme.
N England, UK
Durham 43 F1 North Carolina,
SE USA
Durostorum see Silistra
Durrës 101 C6 var. Durrësi, Dursi,
It. Durazzo, SCr. Drač, Turk. Draç.
Durrës, W Albania
Durrësi see Durrës
Dursi see Durrës
Durūz, Jabal ad 119 C5 mountain
SW Syria
D'Urville Island 150 C4 island C NZ
Dusa Mareb see Dhuusa Marreeb
Dusa Marreb see Dhuusa Marreeb
Dushanbe 123 E3 var. Dyushambe;
prev. Stalinabad, Taj. Dushanbe.
Country capital (Tajikistan)
W Tajikistan
Düsseldorf 94 A4 var. Duesseldorf.
Nordrhein-Westfalen, W Germany
Dūstī 123 E3 Rus. Dusti.
SW Tajikistan
Dutch Harbor 36 B3 Unalaska
Island, Alaska, USA
Dutch New Guinea see Papua
Duzdab see Zāhedān
Dvina see Severnaya Dvina
Dvina Bay see Chëshskaya Guba
Dyanev see Deynau
Dyersburg 42 C1 Tennessee,
S USA
Dyushambe see Dushanbe
Dza Chu see Mekong
Dzerzhinsk 111 C5
Nizhegorodskaya Oblast',
W Russian Federation
Dzhalal-Abad 123 F2 Kir. Jalal-
Abad. Dzhalal-Abadskaya
Oblast', W Kyrgyzstan
Dzhambul see Taraz
Dzhankoy 109 F4 Respublika
Krym, S Ukraine
Dzhelandy 123 F3 SE Tajikistan
Dzhergalan 123 G2 Kir. Jyrgalan.
Issyk-Kul'skaya Oblast',
NE Kyrgyzstan
Dzhizak see Jizzax
Dzhugdzhur, Khrebet 115 G3
mountain range E Russian
Federation
Dzhusaly 114 B4 Kaz. Zholsaly.
Kyzylorda, SW Kazakhstan
Działdowo 98 D3 Warmińsko-
Mazurskie, NE Poland
Dzuunmod 127 E2 Töv,
C Mongolia

E

Eagle Pass 49 F4 Texas, SW USA
East Azores Fracture Zone see East
Azores Fracture Zone
East Antarctica see Greater
Antarctica
East Australian Basin see Tasman
Basin

East Azores Fracture Zone 66 C3
var. East Açores Fracture Zone.
Tectonic feature E Atlantic Ocean
Eastbourne 89 E7 SE England, UK
East Cape 150 E3 headland North
Island, NZ
East China Sea 125 E2 Chin. Dong
Hai. Sea W Pacific Ocean
Easter Fracture Zone 153 G4 tectonic
feature E Pacific Ocean
Easter Island 153 F4 var. Rapa Nui,
island E Pacific Ocean
Eastern Desert 68 D3 var. Aş Şaḥrā'
ash Sharqīyah, Eng. Arabian
Desert, Eastern Desert. Desert
E Egypt
Eastern Ghats 124 B3 mountain
range SE India
Eastern Sayans 115 E4 Mong.
Dzüün Soyonī Nuruu, Rus.
Vostochnyy Sayan. Mountain range
Mongolia/Russian Federation
East Falkland 65 D8 var. Isla
Soledad. Island E Falkland Islands
East Grand Forks 45 E1 Minnesota,
N USA
East Indiaman Ridge 141 D6
undersea feature E Indian Ocean
East Indies 152 A3 island group
SE Asia
East Kilbride 88 C4 S Scotland, UK
East Korea Bay 129 E3 bay E North
Korea
Eastleigh 89 D7 S England, UK
East London 78 D5 Afr. Oos-
Londen; prev. Emonti, Port Rex.
Eastern Cape, S South Africa
Eastmain 38 D3 river Quebec,
C Canada
East Mariana Basin 142 B1 undersea
feature W Pacific Ocean
East Novaya Zemlya Trench 112 C1
var. Novaya Zemlya Trench.
Undersea feature W Kara Sea
East Pacific Rise 153 F4 undersea
feature E Pacific Ocean
East Saint Louis 40 B4 Illinois,
N USA
East Scotia Basin 67 C7 undersea
feature SE Scotia Sea
East Sea see Japan, Sea of
East Siberian Sea see Vostochno-
Sibirskoye More
East Timor 139 F5 var. Loro Sae
prev. Portuguese Timor, Timor
Timur. Country, SE Asia

East Timor 139

Official name East Timor
Formation 2002
Capital Dili
Population 737,811 /196 people per
sq mile (49 per sq km)
Total area 3,756 sq miles
(14, 874 sq km)
Languages Tetum (Portuguese/
Austronesian), Bahasa Indonesia,
Portuguese
Religions Roman Catholic 93%,
other 7%
Ethnic mix Various Papuan groups;
2% Chinese. In the 1990's
Indonesian settlers became
numerous, accounting for 20% of the
population by 1999.
Government Multiparty republic
Currency US dollar
Literacy rate 41 %
Calorie consumption not available

Eau Claire 40 A2 Wisconsin, N USA
Eauripik Rise 142 B2 undersea
feature W Pacific Ocean
Ebensee 95 D6 Oberösterreich,
N Austria
Eberswalde-Finow 94 D3
Brandenburg, E Germany
Ebetsu 130 D2 var. Ebetu.
Hokkaidō, NE Japan
Ebetu see Ebetsu
Ebolowa 77 A5 Sud, S Cameroon
Ebon Atoll 144 D2 var. Epoon. Atoll
Ralik Chain, S Marshall Islands
Ebro 93 E2 river NE Spain
Ebusus see Eivissa

Ech Cheliff *see* Chlef
Ech Chleff *see* Chlef
Echo Bay 37 *E3* Northwest Territories, NW Canada
Echt 87 *D5* Limburg, SE Netherlands
Ecija 92 *D4 anc.* Astigi. Andalucía, SW Spain
Ecuador 60 *B1 Country* NW South America

Ecuador 60

Official name Republic of Ecuador
Formation 1830
Capital Quito
Population 12.9 million /118 people per sq mile (45 people per sq km)
Total area 109,483 sq miles (283,560 sq km)
Languages Spanish, Quechua, other Amerindian languages
Religions Roman Catholic 93%, Protestant, Jewish and other 7%
Ethnic mix Mestizo 55%, Indian 25%, Black 10%, White 10%
Government Presidential democracy
Currency US dollar
Literacy rate 91.3%
Calorie consumption 2,693 kilocalories

Ed Da'ein 72 *A4* Southern Darfur, W Sudan
Ed Damazin 72 *C4 var.* Ad Damazīn. Blue Nile, E Sudan
Ed Damer 72 *C3 var.* Ad Damar, Ad Dāmir. River Nile, NE Sudan
Ed Debba 72 *B3* Northern, N Sudan
Ede 86 *D4* Gelderland, C Netherlands
Ede 75 *F5* Osun, SW Nigeria
Edéa 77 *A5* Littoral, SW Cameroon
Edeyin Murzuq *see* Murzuq, Idhān
Edfu *see* Idfu
Edgeoya 83 *G2 island* S Svalbard
Edgware 89 *A7* SE England, UK
Edinburg 49 *G5* Texas, SW USA
Edinburgh 88 *C4 admin capital* S Scotland, UK
Edirne 116 *A2 Eng.* Adrianople; *anc.* Adrianopolis, Hadrianopolis. Edirne, NW Turkey
Edmonds 46 *B2* Washington, NW USA
Edmonton 37 *E5* Alberta, SW Canada
Edmundston 39 *E4* New Brunswick, SE Canada
Edna 49 *G4* Texas, SW USA
Edolo 96 *B1* Lombardia, N Italy
Edremit 116 *A3* Balıkesir, NW Turkey
Edward, Lake 77 *E5 var.* Albert Edward Nyanza, Edward Nyanza, Lac Idi Amin, Lake Rutanzige. *Lake* Uganda/Zaire
Edward Nyanza *see* Edward, Lake
Edwards Plateau 49 *F3 plain* Texas, SW USA
Eeklo 87 *B5 var.* Eekloo. Oost-Vlaanderen, NW Belgium
Edzo 53 *E4 prev.* Rae-Edzo. Northwest Territories, NW Canada
Eekloo *see* Eeklo
Eersel 87 *C5* Noord-Brabant, S Netherlands
Efate 144 *D4 var.* Éfaté *Fr.* Vaté; *prev.* Sandwich Island. *Island* C Vanuatu
Effingham 40 *B4* Illinois, N USA
Eforie Sud 108 *D5* Constanţa, E Romania
Efstrátios, Ágios 104 *D4 var.* Ayios Evstratios. *Island* E Greece
Egadi, Isole 97 *B7 island group* S Italy
Eger 99 *D6 Ger.* Erlau. Heves, NE Hungary
Egeria Fracture Zone 141 *C5 tectonic feature* W Indian Ocean
Éghezée 87 *C6* Namur, C Belgium
Egina *see* Aígina
Egio *see* Aígio

Egmont, Mount *see* Taranaki, Mount
Egmont, Cape 150 *C4 headland* North Island, NZ
Egoli *see* Johannesburg
Egypt 72 *B2 Ar.* Jumhūrīyah Miṣr al 'Arabīyah; *prev.* United Arab Republic, *anc.* Aegyptus. *Country* NE Africa

Egypt 72

Official name Arab Republic of Egypt
Formation 1936
Capital Cairo
Population 69.1 million / 179 people per sq mile (69 people per sq km)
Total area 386,660 sq miles (1,001,450 sq km)
Languages Arabic, French, English, Berber
Religions Muslim (mainly Sunni) 94%, Coptic Christian and other 6%
Ethnic mix Eastern Hamitic 90%, other (Nubian, Armenian, Greek) 10%
Government Presidential democracy
Currency Egyptian pound = 100 piastres
Literacy rate 55.4%
Calorie consumption 3,346 kilocalories

Eibar 93 *E1* País Vasco, N Spain
Eibergen 86 *E3* Gelderland, E Netherlands
Eidfjord 85 *A5* Hordaland, S Norway
Eier-Berg *see* Suur Munamägi
Eifel 95 *A5 plateau* W Germany
Eiger 95 *B7 mountain* C Switzerland
Eigg 88 *B3 island* W Scotland, UK
Eight Degree Channel 132 *B3 channel* India/Maldives
Eighty Mile Beach 146 *B4 beach* Western Australia
Eijsden 87 *D6* Limburg, SE Netherlands
Eilat *see* Elat
Eindhoven 87 *D5* Noord-Brabant, S Netherlands
Eipel *see* Ipel'
Eipel *see* Ipoly
Eisenhüttenstadt 94 *D4* Brandenburg, E Germany
Eisenstadt 95 *E6* Burgenland, E Austria
Eisleben 94 *C4* Sachsen-Anhalt, C Germany
Eivissa 93 *G3 var.* Iviza, *Cast.* Ibiza; *anc.* Ebusus. *Island* Islas Baleares, Spain, W Mediterranean Sea
Eivissa 93 *G3 var.* Iviza, *Cast.* Ibiza; *anc.* Ebusus. Eivissa, Spain, W Mediterranean Sea
Ejea de los Caballeros 93 *E2* Aragón, NE Spain
Ejin Qi 126 *D3 var.* Dalain Hob. Nei Mongol Zizhiqu, N China
Ekapa *see* Cape Town
Ekiatapskiy Khrebet 115 *G1 mountain range* NE Russian Federation
El 'Alamein 72 *B1 var.* Al 'Alamayn. N Egypt
El Asnam *see* Chlef
Elat 119 *B8 var.* Eilat, Elath. Southern, S Israel
Elat, Gulf of *see* Aqaba, Gulf of
Elath *see* Al 'Aqabah
Elath *see* Elat
El'Atrun 72 *B3* Northern Darfur, NW Sudan
Elâzığ 117 *E3 var.* Elâziz. Elâzığ, E Turkey
Elâziz *see* Elâzığ
Elba, Isola d' 96 *B4 island* Archipelago Toscano, C Italy
Elbasan 101 *D6 var.* Elbasani. Elbasan, C Albania
Elbasani *see* Elbasan

Elbe 80 *D3 Cz.* Labe. *River* Czech Republic/Germany
El Beni *see* Beni
Elbert, Mount 44 *C4 mountain* Colorado, C USA
Elbing *see* Elblag
Elblag 98 *C2 var.* Elbląg, *Ger.* Elbing. Warmińsko-Mazurskie, NE Poland
El Boulaida *see* Blida
El'brus 111 *A8 var.* Gora El'brus. *Mountain* SW Russian Federation
El Burgo de Osma 93 *E2* Castilla-León, C Spain
El Cajon 47 *C8* California, W USA
El Calafate 65 *B7 var.* Calafate. Santa Cruz, S Argentina
El Callao 59 *E2* Bolívar, E Venezuela
El Campo 49 *G4* Texas, SW USA
El Carmen de Bolívar 58 *B2* Bolívar, NW Colombia
El Centro 47 *D8* California, W USA
Elche 93 *F4 var.* Elx-Elche; *anc.* Ilici, *Lat.* Illicis. País Valenciano, E Spain
Elda 93 *F4* País Valenciano, E Spain
El Djazaïr *see* Alger
El Djelfa *see* Djelfa
El Dorado 42 *B2* Arkansas, C USA
El Dorado 59 *F2* Bolívar, E Venezuela
El Dorado 45 *F5* Kansas, C USA
El Dorado 50 *C3* Sinaloa, C Mexico
Eldorado 64 *E3* Misiones, NE Argentina
Eldoret 73 *C6* Rift Valley, W Kenya
Elektrostal' 111 *B5* Moskovskaya Oblast', W Russian Federation
Elemi Triangle 73 *B5 disputed region* Kenya/Sudan
Elephant Butte Reservoir 48 *C2 reservoir* New Mexico, SW USA
Eleuthera Island 54 *C1 island* N Bahamas
El Fasher 72 *A4 var.* Al Fāshir. Northern Darfur, W Sudan
El Ferrol *see* Ferrol
El Ferrol del Caudillo *see* Ferrol
El Gedaref *see* Gedaref
El Geneina 72 *A4 var.* Ajjinena, Al-Genain, Al Junaynah. Western Darfur, W Sudan
Elgin 40 *B3* Illinois, N USA
Elgin 88 *C3* NE Scotland, UK
El Gïza 72 *B1 var.* Al Jīzah, Gîza, Gizeh. N Egypt
El Goléa 70 *D3 var.* Al Golea. C Algeria
El Hank 74 *D1 cliff* N Mauritania
El Haseke *see* Al Ḩasakah
Elista 111 *B7* Respublika Kalmykiya, SW Russian Federation
Elizabeth 149 *B6* South Australia
Elizabeth City 43 *G1* North Carolina, SE USA
Elizabethtown 40 *C5* Kentucky, S USA
El-Jadida 70 *C2 prev.* Mazagan. W Morocco
Elk 98 *E2 Ger.* Lyck. Warmińsko-Mazurskie, NE Poland
Elk City 49 *F1* Oklahoma, C USA
El Kerak *see* Al Karak
El Khalil *see* Hebron
El Khârga 72 *B2 var.* Al Khārijah. C Egypt
Elkhart 40 *C3* Indiana, N USA
El Khartûm *see* Khartoum
Elk River 45 *F2* Minnesota, N USA
El Kuneitra *see* Al Qunayţirah
Ellef Ringnes Island 37 *E1 island* Nunavut, N Canada
Ellen, Mount 44 *B5 mountain* Utah, W USA
Ellensburg 46 *B2* Washington, NW USA
Ellesmere Island 37 *F1 island* Queen Elizabeth Islands, Nunavut, N Canada
Ellesmere, Lake 151 *C6 lake* South Island, NZ
Elliston 149 *A6* South Australia
Ellsworth Land 154 *A3 physical region* Antarctica

El Mahbas 70 *B3 var.* Mahbés. SW Western Sahara
El Mina 118 *B4 var.* Al Mīnā'. N Lebanon
El Minya 72 *B2 var.* Al Minyā, Minya. C Egypt
Elmira 41 *E3* New York, NE USA
El Mreyyé 74 *D2 desert* E Mauritania
Elmshorn 94 *B3* Schleswig-Holstein, N Germany
El Muglad 72 *B4* Western Kordofan, C Sudan
El Obeid 72 *B4 var.* Al Obayyid, Al Ubayyiḑ. Northern Kordofan, C Sudan
El Ouâdi *see* El Oued
El Oued 71 *E2 var.* Al Oued, El Ouâdi, El Wad. NE Algeria
Eloy 48 *B2* Arizona, SW USA
El Paso 48 *D3* Texas, SW USA
El Porvenir 53 *G4* San Blas, N Panama
El Progreso 52 *C2* Yoro, NW Honduras
El Puerto de Santa María 92 *C5* Andalucía, S Spain
El Quds *see* Jerusalem
El Quneitra *see* Al Qunayţirah
El Quseir *see* Al Quşayr
El Quweira *see* Al Quwayrah
El Rama 53 *E3* Región Autónoma Atlántico Sur, SE Nicaragua
El Real 53 *H5 var.* El Real de Santa María. Darién, SE Panama
El Real de Santa María *see* El Real
El Reno 49 *F1* Oklahoma, C USA
El Salvador 52 *B3 Country* Central America

El Salvador 52

Official name Republic of El Salvador
Formation 1841
Capital San Salvador
Population 6.4 million /788 people per sq mile (304 people per sq km)
Total area 8,124 sq miles (21,040 sq km)
Languages Spanish
Religions Roman Catholic 80%, Evangelical 18%, other 2%
Ethnic mix Mestizo 94%, Indian 5%, White 1%
Government Presidential democracy
Currency Salvadorean colón = 100 centavos
Literacy rate 78.8%
Calorie consumption 2,503 kilocalories

El Sáuz 50 *C2* Chihuahua, N Mexico
El Serrat 91 *A7* N Andorra
Elst 86 *D4* Gelderland, E Netherlands
El Sueco 50 *C2* Chihuahua, N Mexico
El Suweida *see* As Suwaydā'
Eltanin Fracture Zone 153 *E5 tectonic feature* SE Pacific Ocean
El Tigre 59 *E2* Anzoátegui, NE Venezuela
Elvas 92 *C4* Portalegre, C Portugal
El Vendrell 93 *G2* Cataluña, NE Spain
El Vigía 58 *C2* Mérida, NW Venezuela
El Wad *see* El Oued
Elwell, Lake 44 *B1 reservoir* Montana, NW USA
Elx-Elche *see* Elche
Ely 47 *D5* Nevada, W USA
El Yopal *see* Yopal
Emajõgi 106 *D3 Ger.* Embach. *River* SE Estonia
Emba 114 *B4 Kaz.* Embi. Aktyubinsk, W Kazakhstan
Emden 94 *A3* Niedersachsen, NW Germany
Emerald 148 *D4* Queensland, E Australia
Emerald Isle *see* Montserrat

Emesa *see* Ḥimṣ
Emmaste 106 C2 Hiiumaa,
W Estonia
Emmeloord 86 D2 Flevoland,
N Netherlands
Emmen 86 E2 Drenthe,
NE Netherlands
Emmendingen 95 A6 Baden-
Württemberg, SW Germany
Emory Peak 49 E4 mountain Texas,
SW USA
Empalme 50 B2 Sonora,
NW Mexico
Emperor Seamounts 113 G3
undersea feature NW Pacific Ocean
Emporia 45 F5 Kansas, C USA
Empty Quarter *see* Ar Rub 'al Khālī
Ems 94 A3 *Dut.* Eems. *River*
NW Germany
Encamp 91 A8 C Andorra
Encarnación 64 D3 Itapúa,
S Paraguay
Encinitas 47 C8 California, W USA
Encs 99 D6 Borsod-Abaúj-Zemplén,
NE Hungary
Endeavour Strait 148 C1 *strait*
Queensland, NE Australia
Enderbury Island 145 F3 *atoll*
Phoenix Islands, C Kiribati
Enderby Land 154 C2 *physical region*
Antarctica
Enderby Plain 154 D2 *undersea
feature* S Indian Ocean
Enewetak Atoll 144 C1 *var.*
Änewetak, Eniwetok. *Atoll* Ralik
Chain, W Marshall Islands
Enfield 89 A7 SE England, UK
Engannim *see* Jenīn
Enghien 87 B6 *Dut.* Edingen.
Hainaut, SW Belgium
England 89 D5 *Lat.* Anglia. *National
region* UK
Englewood 44 D4 Colorado, C USA
English Channel 89 D8 *var.* The
Channel, Fr. la Manche. *Channel*
NW Europe
Engure 106 C3 Tukums, W Latvia
Engures Ezers 106 B3 *lake*
NW Latvia
Enguri 117 F1 *Rus.* Inguri. *River*
NW Georgia
Enid 49 F1 Oklahoma, C USA
Enikale Strait *see* Kerch Strait
Eniwetok *see* Enewetak Atoll
En Nâqoûra 119 A5 *var.* An
Nâqûrah. SW Lebanon
Ennedi 76 D2 *plateau* E Chad
Ennis 89 A6 *Ir.* Inis. W Ireland
Ennis 49 G3 Texas, SW USA
Enniskillen 89 B5 *var.* Inniskilling,
Ir. Inis Ceithleann. SW Northern
Ireland, UK
Enns 95 D6 *river* C Austria
Enschede 86 E3 Overijssel,
E Netherlands
Ensenada 50 A1 Baja California,
NW Mexico
Entebbe 73 B6 S Uganda
Entroncamento 92 B3 Santarém,
C Portugal
Enugu 75 G5 Enugu, S Nigeria
Eolie, Isole 97 C6 *var.* Isole Lipari,
Eng. Aeolian Islands, Lipari
Islands. *Island group* S Italy
Epanomí 104 B4 Kentrikí
Makedonía, N Greece
Epéna 77 B5 La Likouala, NE Congo
Eperies *see* Prešov
Eperjes *see* Prešov
Epi 144 D4 *var.* Epi. *Island*
C Vanuatu
Epi *see* Epi
Epinal 90 D4 Vosges, NE France
Epiphania *see* Ḥamāh
Epitoli *see* Pretoria
Epoon *see* Ebon Atoll
Epsom 89 A8 SE England, UK
Equatorial Guinea 77 A5 *Country*
C Africa

Equatorial Guinea 77

Official name Republic of
Equatorial Guinea
Formation 1968
Capital Malabo

Equatorial Guinea (continued)

Population 470,000 /43 people per
sq mile (17 people per sq km)
Total area 10,830 sq miles
(28,051 sq km)
Languages Spanish, Fang, Bubi
Religions Roman Catholic 90%,
other 10%
Ethnic mix Fang 85%, Bubi 4%,
other 11%
Government Presidential regime
Currency CFA franc = 100 centimes
Literacy rate 83.2%
Calorie consumption not available

Erautini *see* Johannesburg
Erbil *see* Arbīl
Erciş 117 F3 Van, F. Turkey
Erdélyi-Havasok *see* Carpaţii
Meridionali
Erdenet 127 E2 Bulgan,
N Mongolia
Erdi 76 C2 *plateau* NE Chad
Erdi Ma 76 D2 *desert* NE Chad
Erebus, Mount 154 B4 *mountain*
Ross Island, Antarctica
Ereğli 116 C4 Konya, S Turkey
Erenhot 127 F2 *var.* Erlian. Nei
Mongol Zizhiqu, NE China
Erevan *see* Yerevan
Erfurt 94 C4 Thüringen, C Germany
Ergene Irmağı 116 A2 *var.* Ergene
Irmağı. *River* NW Turkey
Erg Iguid *see* Iguîdi, 'Erg
Ergun He *see* Argun
Ergun Zuoqi 127 F1 Nei Mongol
Zizhiqu, N China
Erie 40 D3 Pennsylvania, NE USA
Erie, Lake 40 D3 *Fr.* Lac Érié. *Lake*
Canada/USA
Eritrea 72 C4 *Tig.* Ērtra. *Country*
E Africa

Eritrea 72

Official name State of Eritrea
Formation 1993
Capital Asmara
Population 3.8 million / 81 people
per sq mile (31 people per sq km)
Total area 46,842 sq miles
(121,320 sq km)
Languages Tigrinya, English, Tigre,
Afar, Arabic, Bilen, Kunama,
Nara, Saho, Hadareb
Religions Christian 45%, Muslim
45%, other 10%
Ethnic mix Tigray and Kunama
40%, Tigray 50%, Afar 4%,
Saho 3%, other 4%
Government Transitional regime
Currency Nakfa = 100 cents
Literacy rate 55.7%
Calorie consumption 1,665
kilocalories

Erivan *see* Yerevan
Erlangen 95 C5 Bayern, S Germany
Erlian *see* Erenhot
Ermelo 86 D3 Gelderland,
C Netherlands
Ermióni 105 C6 Pelopónnisos,
S Greece
Ermoúpoli 105 D6 *var.* Hermoupolis;
prev. Ermoúpolis. Sýros, Kykládes,
Greece, Aegean Sea
Ermoúpolis *see* Ermoúpoli
Ernākulam 132 C3 Kerala, SW India
Erode 132 C2 Tamil Nādu, SE India
Erquelinnes 87 B7 Hainaut,
S Belgium
Er-Rachidia 70 C2 *var.* Ksar
al Soule. E Morocco
Er Rahad 72 B4 *var.* Ar Rahad.
Northern Kordofan, C Sudan
Erromango 144 D4 *island* S Vanuatu
Ertis *see* Irtysh
Erzgebirge 95 C5 Cz. Krušné Hory,
Eng. Ore Mountains. *Mountain
range* Czech Republic/Germany
see also Krušné Hory
Erzincan 117 E3 *var.* Erzinjan.
Erzincan, E Turkey

Erzinjan *see* Erzincan
Erzurum 117 E3 *prev.* Erzurum.
Erzurum, NE Turkey
Esbjerg 85 A7 Ribe, W Denmark
Escaldes 91 A8 C Andorra
Escanaba 40 C2 Michigan, N USA
Esch-sur-Alzette 87 D8
Luxembourg, S Luxembourg
Escondido 47 C8 California, W USA
Escuinapa 50 D3 *var.* Escuinapa de
Hidalgo. Sinaloa, C Mexico
Escuinapa de Hidalgo *see*
Escuinapa
Escuintla 51 G5 Chiapas, SE Mexico
Escuintla 52 B2 Escuintla,
S Guatemala
Eşfahān 120 C3 *Eng.* Isfahan; *anc.*
Aspadana. Eşfahān, C Iran
Esh Sham *see* Dimashq
Esh Sharā *see* Ash Sharāh
Eskişehir 116 B3 *var.* Eskishehr.
Eskişehir, W Turkey
Eskishehr *see* Eskişehir
Eslāmābād 120 C3 *var.* Eslāmābād-e
Gharb; *prev.* Harunabad,
Shāhābād. Kermānshāhān, W Iran
Eslāmābād-e Gharb *see* Eslāmābād
Esmeraldas 60 A1 Esmeraldas,
N Ecuador
Esna *see* Isna
Espanola 48 D1 New Mexico,
SW USA
Esperance 147 B7 Western Australia
Esperanza 154 A2 *Argentinian
research station* Antarctica
Esperanza 50 B2 Sonora,
NW Mexico
Espinal 58 B3 Tolima, C Colombia
Espinhaço, Serra do 56 D4 *mountain
range* SE Brazil
Espírito Santo 63 F4 *off.* Estado do
Espírito Santo. *State* E Brazil
Espíritu Santo 144 C4 *var.* Santo.
Island W Vanuatu
Espoo 85 D6 *Swe.* Esbo. Etelä-
Suomi, S Finland
Esquel 65 B6 Chubut, SW Argentina
Essaouira 70 B2 *prev.* Mogador.
W Morocco
Es Semara *see* Smara
Essen 94 A4 *var.* Essen an der Ruhr.
Nordrhein-Westfalen, W Germany
Essen 87 C5 Antwerpen, N Belgium
Essen an der Ruhr *see* Essen
Essequibo River 59 F3 *river*
C Guyana
Es Suweida *see* As Suwaydā'
Estacado, Llano 49 E2 *plain* New
Mexico/Texas, SW USA
Estados, Isla de los 65 C8 *prev. Eng.*
Staten Island. *Island* S Argentina
Estância 63 G3 Sergipe, E Brazil
Estelí 52 D3 Estelí, NW Nicaragua
Estella *see* Estella-Lizarra
Estella-Lizarra 93 E1 *Bas.* Lizarra
var. Estella. Navarra, N Spain
Estepona 92 D5 Andalucía,
S Spain
Estevan 37 F5 Saskatchewan,
S Canada
Estonia 106 D2*Est.* Eesti Vabariik,
Ger. Estland, *Latv.* Igaunija; *prev.*
Estonian SSR, *Rus.* Estonskaya
SSR. *Country* NE Europe

Estonia 106

Official name Republic of Estonia
Formation 1991
Capital Tallinn
Population 1.4 million / 80 people
per sq mile (31 people per sq km)
Total area 17,462 sq miles
(45,226 sq km)
Languages Estonian, Russian
Religions Evangelical Lutheran
56%, Russian Orthodox 25%,
Other 19%
Ethnic mix Estonian 62%, Russian
30%, other 8%
Government Parliamentary
democracy
Currency Kroon = 100 cents
Literacy rate 99%
Calorie consumption 3 376
kilocalories

Estrela, Serra da 92 C3 *mountain
range* C Portugal
Estremoz 92 C4 Évora, S Portugal
Esztergom 99 C6 Ger. Gran; *anc.*
Strigonium. Komárom-Esztergom,
N Hungary
Étalle 87 D8 Luxembourg,
SE Belgium
Etāwah 134 D3 Uttar Pradesh,
N India
Ethiopia 73 C5 *prev.* Abyssinia,
People's Democratic Republic of
Ethiopia. *Country* E Africa

Ethiopia 73

Official name Federal Democratic
Republic of Ethiopia
Formation 1896
Capital Addis Ababa
Population 64.5 million / 148
people per sq mile (57 people per sq
km)
Total area 435,184 sq miles
(1,127,127 sq km)
Languages Amharic, Tigrinya, Galla
Religions Muslim 40%, Ethopian
Orthodox 40%, other 20%
Ethnic mix Oromo 40%, Amhara
25%, Sidamo 9%, Somali 6%, Berta
6%, other 14%
Government Multiparty republic
Currency Ethopian birr = 100 cents
Literacy rate 38.4%
Calorie consumption 2,023
kilocalories

Ethiopian Highlands 73 C5 *var.*
Ethiopian Plateau. *Plateau*
N Ethiopia
Ethiopian Plateau *see* Ethiopian
Highlands
Etna, Monte 97 C7 *Eng.* Mount
Etna. *Volcano* Sicilia, Italy,
C Mediterranean Sea
Etna, Mount *see* Etna, Monte
Etosha Pan 78 B3 *salt lake*
N Namibia
Etoumbi 77 B5 Cuvette, NW Congo
Et Tafila *see* Aţ Ţafilah
Ettelbrück 87 D8 Diekirch,
C Luxembourg
'Eua 144 E5 *prev.* Middlebury
Island. *Island* Tongatapu Group,
SE Tonga
Euboea *see* Évvoia
Eucla 147 D6 Western Australia
Euclid 40 D3 Ohio, N USA
Eufaula Lake 49 G1 *var.* Eufaula
Reservoir. *Reservoir* Oklahoma,
C USA
Eufaula Reservoir *see* Eufaula Lake
Eugene 46 B3 Oregon, NW USA
Eupen 87 D6 Liège, E Belgium
Euphrates 112 B4 *Ar.* Al Furāt, *Turk.*
Fırat Nehri. *River* SW Asia
Eureka 47 A5 California, W USA
Eureka 44 A1 Montana, NW USA
Europa Point 93 H5 *headland*
S Gibraltar
Europe 34 E1 *continent*
Eutin 94 C2 Schleswig-Holstein,
N Germany
Euxine Sea *see* Black Sea
Evansdale 45 G3 Iowa, C USA
Evanston 40 B3 Illinois, N USA
Evanston 44 B4 Wyoming, C USA
Evansville 40 B5 Indiana, N USA
Eveleth 45 G1 Minnesota, N USA
Everard, Lake 149 A6 *salt lake* South
Australia
Everest, Mount 126 B5 *Chin.*
Qomolangma Feng, *Nep.*
Sagarmatha. *Mountain*
China/Nepal
Everett 46 B2 Washington,
NW USA
Everglades, The 43 F5 *wetland*
Florida, SE USA
Evje 85 A6 Aust-Agder, S Norway
Évora 92 B4 *anc.* Ebora, *Lat.*
Liberalitas Julia.Évora, C Portugal
Évreux 90 C3 *anc.* Civitas
Eburovicum. Eure, N France
Évros *see* Maritsa
Évry 90 E2 Essonne, N France

Évvoia 101 E8 Lat. Euboea. Island
C Greece
Ewarton 54 B5 C Jamaica
Excelsior Springs 45 F4 Missouri,
C USA
Exe 89 C7 river SW England, UK
Exeter 89 C7 anc. Isca
Damnoniorum. SW England, UK
Exmoor 89 C7 moorland
SW England, UK
Exmouth 89 C7 SW England, UK
Exmouth 146 A4 Western Australia
Exmouth Gulf 146 A4 gulf Western
Australia
Exmouth Plateau 141 E5 undersea
feature E Indian Ocean
Extremadura 92 C3 cultural region
W Spain
Exuma Cays 54 C1 islets C Bahamas
Exuma Sound 54 C1 sound
C Bahamas
Eyre Mountains 151 A7 mountain
range South Island, NZ
Eyre North, Lake 149 A5 salt lake
South Australia
Eyre Peninsula 149 A6 peninsula
South Australia
Eyre South, Lake 149 A5 salt lake
South Australia

F

Faadhippolhu Atoll 132 B4 var.
Fadiffolu, Lhaviyani Atoll. Atoll
N Maldives
Fabens 48 D3 Texas, SW USA
Fada 76 C2 Borkou-Ennedi-Tibesti,
E Chad
Fada-Ngourma 75 E4 E Burkina
faso
Fadiffolu see Faadhippolhu Atoll
Faenza 96 C3 anc. Faventia. Emilia-
Romagna, N Italy
Faeroe-Iceland Ridge 80 C1
undersea feature NW Norwegian
Sea
Faeroe-Shetland Trough 80 C2
undersea feature NE Atlantic Ocean
Faeroes Islands 83 E5 Dan.
Færoerne, Faer. Føroyar. Danish
external territory N Atlantic
Ocean
Faetano 96 E2 E San Marino
Făgăraş 108 C4 Ger. Fogarasch,
Hung. Fogaras. Braşov,
C Romania
Fagibina, Lake see Faguibine, Lac
Fagne 87 C7 hill range S Belgium
Faguibine, Lac 75 E3 var. Lake
Fagibina. Lake NW Mali
Fahlun see Falun
Fahraj 120 D4 Kermān, SE Iran
Faial 92 A5 var. Ilha do Faial. Island
Azores, Portugal, NE Atlantic
Ocean
Fairbanks 36 D3 Alaska, USA
Fairfield 47 B6 California, W USA
Fair Isle 88 D2 island NE Scotland,
UK
Fairlie 151 B6 Canterbury, South
Island, NZ
Fairmont 45 F3 Minnesota, N USA
Faisalābād 134 C2 prev. Lyallpur.
Punjab, NE Pakistan
Faizābād see Feyzābād
Faizābād 135 E3 Uttar Pradesh,
N India
Fakaofo Atoll 145 F3 island
SE Tokelau
Falam 136 A3 Chin State,
W Myanmar
Falconara Marittima 96 C3 Marche,
C Italy
Falkland Islands 65 D7 var.
Falklands, Islas Malvinas. UK
dependent territory SW Atlantic
Ocean
Falkland Plateau 57 D7 var.
Argentine Rise. Undersea feature
SW Atlantic Ocean
Falklands see Falkland Islands
Fallbrook 47 C8 California, W USA
Falmouth 89 C7 SW England, UK
Falmouth 54 A4 W Jamaica
Falster 85 B8 island SE Denmark
Fălticeni 108 C3 Hung. Falticsén.
Suceava, NE Romania

Falun 85 C6 var. Fahlun.
Kopparberg, C Sweden
Famagusta see Ammóchostos
Famagusta Bay see Kólpos
Ammóchostos
Famenne 87 C7 physical region
SE Belgium
Fang 136 C3 Chiang Mai,
NW Thailand
Fano 96 C3 anc. Colonia Julia
Fanestris, Fanum Fortunae.
Marche, C Italy
Farafangana 79 G4 Fianarantsoa,
SE Madagascar
Farāh 122 D4 var. Farah, Fararud.
Farāh, W Afghanistan
Farāh Rūd 122 D4 river
W Afghanistan
Faranah 74 C4 Haute-Guinée,
S Guinea
Fararud see Farāh
Farasān, Jazā'ir 121 A6 island group
SW Saudi Arabia
Farewell, Cape 150 C4 headland
South Island, NZ
Farewell, Cape see Nunap Isua
Farghona 123 F2 Rus. Fergana; prev.
Novyy Margilan. Farghona
Wiloyati, E Uzbekistan
Fargo 45 F2 North Dakota, N USA
Faribault 45 F2 Minnesota,
N USA
Farīdābād 134 D3 Haryāna, N India
Farkhor 123 E3 Rus. Parkhar.
SW Tajikistan
Farmington 45 G5 Missouri, C USA
Farmington 48 C1 New Mexico,
SW USA
Faro 92 B5 Faro, S Portugal
Farquhar Group 79 G2 island group
S Seychelles
Farvel, Kap see Nunap Isua
Fastiv 109 E2 Rus. Fastov. Kyyivs'ka
Oblast', NW Ukraine
Fauske 84 C3 Nordland,
C Norway
Faxaflói 82 D5 Eng. Faxa Bay. Bay
W Iceland
Faya 76 C2 prev. Faya-Largeau,
Largeau. Borkou-Ennedi-Tibesti,
N Chad
Fayetteville 42 A1 Arkansas,
C USA
Fayetteville 43 F1 North Carolina,
SE USA
Fdérick see Fdérik
Fdérik 74 C2 var. Fdérick, Fr. Fort
Gouraud. Tiris Zemmour,
NW Mauritania
Fear, Cape 43 F2 headland Bald
Head Island, North Carolina,
SE USA
Fécamp 90 B3 Seine-Maritime,
N France
**Federation of the separate
territories of** see Malaysia
Fehérgyarmat 99 E6 Szabolcs-
Szatmár-Bereg, E Hungary
Fehmarn 94 C2 island N Germany
Fehmarn Belt 94 C2 Ger.
Fehmarnbelt. Strait
Denmark/Germany
Feijó 62 C2 Acre, W Brazil
Feilding 150 D4 Manawatu-
Wanganui, North Island, NZ
Feira see Feira de Santana
Feira de Santana 63 G3 var. Feira.
Bahia, E Brazil
Felanitx 93 G3 anc. Canati,
Felaniche. Mallorca, Spain,
W Mediterranean Sea
Felidhu Atoll 132 B4 atoll
C Maldives
Felipe Carrillo Puerto 51 H4
Quintana Roo, SE Mexico
Felixstowe 89 E6 E England, UK
Femunden 85 B5 lake S Norway
Fengcheng 128 D3 var. Feng-cheng,
Fenghwangcheng. Liaoning,
NE China
Feng-cheng see Fengcheng
Fenghwangcheng see Fengcheng
Fengtien see Liaoning
Fenoarivo 79 G3 Toamasina,
E Madagascar
Fens, The 89 E6 wetland E England,
UK

Feodosiya 109 F5 var. Kefe, It. Kaffa;
anc. Theodosia. Respublika Krym,
S Ukraine
Féres 104 D3 Anatolikí Makedonía
kai Thráki, NE Greece
Fergus Falls 45 F2 Minnesota,
N USA
Ferkessédougou 74 D4 N Côte
d'Ivoire
Fermo 96 C4 anc. Firmum Picenum.
Marche, C Italy
Fernandina, Isla 60 A5 var.
Narborough Island. Island
Galapagos Islands, Ecuador,
E Pacific Ocean
Fernando de Noronha 63 H2 island
E Brazil
Fernando Po see Bioco, Isla de
Fernando Póo see Bioco, Isla de
Ferrara 96 C2 anc. Forum Alieni.
Emilia-Romagna, N Italy
Ferreñafe 60 B3 Lambayeque,
W Peru
Ferro see Hierro
Ferrol 92 B1 var. El Ferrol; prev.
El Ferrol del Caudillo. Galicia,
NW Spain
Ferwerd 86 D1 Fris. Ferwert.
Friesland, N Netherlands
Fès 70 C2 Eng. Fez. N Morocco
Feteşti 108 D5 Ialomița,
SE Romania
Fethiye 116 B4 Muğla, SW Turkey
Fetlar 88 D1 island NE Scotland, UK
Feyzābād 123 F3 var. Faizabad,
Faizābād, Feyzābād, Fyzabad.
Badakhshān, NE Afghanistan
Fianarantsoa 79 F3 Fianarantsoa,
C Madagascar
Fianga 76 B4 Mayo-Kébbi,
SW Chad
Fier 101 C6 var. Fieri. Fier,
SW Albania
Fieri see Fier
Figeac 91 C5 Lot, S France
Figig see Figuig
Figueira da Foz 92 B3 Coimbra,
W Portugal
Figueres 93 G2 Cataluña, E Spain
Figuig 70 D2 var. Figig. E Morocco
Fiji 145 E5 Fij. Viti. Country
SW Pacific Ocean

Fiji 145

Official name Republic of the Fiji
Islands
Formation 1970
Capital Suva
Population 823,000 / 117 people
per sq mile (45 people per sq km)
Total area 7,054 sq miles
(18,270 sq km)
Languages Fijian, English, Hindi,
Urdu, Tamil, Telegu
Religions Hindu 38%, Methodist
37%, Roman Catholic 9%, other 16%
Ethnic mix Melanesian 48%,
Indian 46%, other 6%
Government Multiparty republic
Currency Fiji dollar = 100 cents
Literacy rate 92.9%
Calorie consumption 2,861
kilocalories

Filadelfia 52 D4 Guanacaste,
W Costa Rica
Filiaşi 108 B5 Dolj, SW Romania
Filipstad 85 B6 Värmland,
C Sweden
Finale Ligure 96 A3 Liguria,
NW Italy
Finchley 89 A7 SE England, UK
Findlay 40 C4 Ohio, N USA
Finike 116 B4 Antalya,
SW Turkey
Finland 84 D4 Fin. Suomen
Tasavalta, Suomi. Country
N Europe

Finland 84

Official name Republic of Finland
Formation 1917
Capital Helsinki

Finland (continued)

Population 5.2 million / 40 people
per sq mile (15 people per sq km)
Total area 130,127 sq miles
(337,030 sq km)
Languages Finnish, Swedish, Sami
Religions Evangelical Lutheran
89%, Finnish Orthodox 1%, Roman
Catholic 1%, other 9%
Ethnic mix Finnish 93%,
other (including Sami) 7%
Government Paliamentary
democracy
Currency Euro (Markka until 2002)
Literacy rate 99%
Calorie consumption 3,227
kilocalories

Finland, Gulf of 85 D6 Est. Soome
Laht, Fin. Suomenlahti, Ger.
Finnischer Meerbusen, Rus.
Finskiy Zaliv, Swe. Finska Viken.
Gulf E Baltic Sea
Finnmarksvidda 84 D2 physical
region N Norway
Finsterwalde 94 D4 Brandenburg,
E Germany
Fiordland 151 A7 physical region
South Island, NZ
Fiorina 96 E1 NE San Marino
Firenze 96 C3 Eng. Florence; anc.
Florentia. Toscana, C Italy
Fischbacher Alpen 95 E7 mountain
range E Austria
Fish 78 B4 var. Vis. River S Namibia
Fishguard 89 C6 Wel. Abergwaun.
SW Wales, UK
Fisterra, Cabo 92 B1 headland
NW Spain
Fitzroy Crossing 146 C3 Western
Australia
Fitzroy River 146 C3 river Western
Australia
Flagstaff 48 B2 Arizona, SW USA
Flanders 87 A6 Dut. Vlaanderen, Fr.
Flandre. Cultural region
Belgium/France
Flathead Lake 44 B1 lake Montana,
NW USA
Flat Island 128 C8 island NE Spratly
Islands
Flatts Village 42 B5 var. The Flatts
Village. C Bermuda
Flensburg 94 B2 Schleswig-
Holstein, N Germany
Flinders Island 149 C8 island
Furneaux Group, Tasmania,
SE Australia
Flinders Ranges 149 B6 mountain
range South Australia
Flinders River 148 C3 river
Queensland, NE Australia
Flin Flon 37 F5 Manitoba, C Canada
Flint 40 C3 Michigan, N USA
Flint Island 145 G4 island Line
Islands, E Kiribati
Floreana, Isla see Santa María, Isla
Florence see Firenze
Florence 42 C1 Alabama, S USA
Florence 43 F2 South Carolina,
SE USA
Florencia 58 B4 Caquetá, S Colombia
Florentia see Firenze
Flores 92 A5 island Azores,
Portugal, NE Atlantic Ocean
Flores 139 E5 island Nusa Tenggara,
C Indonesia
Flores 52 B1 Petén, N Guatemala
Flores Sea 138 D5 Ind. Laut Flores.
Sea C Indonesia
Floriano 63 F2 Piauí, E Brazil
Florianópolis 63 F5 prev. Destêrro.
State capital Santa Catarina,
S Brazil
Florida 43 E4 off. State of Florida;
also known as Peninsular State,
Sunshine State. State SE USA
Florida 64 D4 Florida, S Uruguay
Florida Bay 43 E5 bay Florida,
SE USA
Florida Keys 43 E5 island group
Florida, SE USA
Florida, Straits of 54 B1 strait
Atlantic Ocean/Gulf of Mexico

lórina 104 B4 var. Phlórina. Dytikí
Makedonía, N Greece
lorissant 45 G4 Missouri, C USA
lóuba, Akrotírio 105 D7 headland
Astypálaia, Kykládes, Greece,
Aegean Sea
'oča 100 C4 var. Srbinje, Republika
Srpska, SE Bosnia and
Herzegovina
ocşani 108 C4 Vrancea, E Romania
oggia 97 D5 Puglia, SE Italy
ogo 74 A3 island Ilhas de
Sotavento, SW Cape Verde
oix 91 B6 Ariège, S France
olégandros 105 C7 island
Kykládes, Greece, Aegean Sea
oleyet 38 C4 Ontario, S Canada
oligno 96 C4 Umbria, C Italy
olkestone 89 E7 SE England, UK
ond du Lac 40 B2 Wisconsin,
N USA
ongafale 145 E3 var. Funafuti.
Country capital (Tuvalu) Funafuti
Atoll, SE Tuvalu
onseca, Gulf of 52 C3 Sp. Golfo de
Fonseca. Gulf Central America
ontainebleau 90 C3 Seine-et-
Marne, N France
ontenay-le-Comte 90 B4 Vendée,
NW France
ontvieille 91 B8 SW Monaco
onyód 99 C7 Somogy, W Hungary
oochow see Fuzhou
orchheim 95 C5 Bayern,
SE Germany
orel, Mont 82 D4 mountain
SE Greenland
orfar 88 C3 E Scotland, UK
orge du Sud see Dudelange
orlì 96 C3 anc. Forum Livii. Emilia-
Romagna, N Italy
ormentera 93 G4 anc. Ophiusa,
Lat. Frumentum. Island Islas
Baleares, Spain,
W Mediterranean Sea
ormosa 64 D2 Formosa,
NE Argentina
ormosa, Serra 63 E3 mountain
range C Brazil
ormosa Strait see Taiwan Strait
orrest City 42 B1 Arkansas, C USA
ort Albany 38 C3 Ontario,
C Canada
ort-Bayard see Zhanjiang
ort Collins 44 D4 Colorado,
C USA
ort Davis 49 E3 Texas, SW USA
ort-de-France 55 H4 prev. Fort-
Royal. Dependent territory capital
(Martinique) W Martinique
ort Dodge 45 F3 Iowa, C USA
ortescue River 146 A4 river
Western Australia
ort Frances 38 B4 Ontario,
S Canada
ort Good Hope 37 E3 var. Good
Hope. Northwest Territories,
NW Canada
ort Gouraud see Fdérik
orth 88 C4 river C Scotland, UK
orth, Firth of 88 C4 estuary
E Scotland, UK
ort-Lamy see Ndjamena
ort Lauderdale 43 F5 Florida,
SE USA
ort Liard 37 E4 var. Liard.
Northwest Territories, W Canada
ort Madison 45 G4 Iowa, C USA
ort McMurray 37 E4 Alberta,
C Canada
ort McPherson 36 D3 var.
McPherson. Northwest
Territories, NW Canada
ort Morgan 44 D4 Colorado, C USA
ort Myers 43 E5 Florida, SE USA
ort Nelson 37 E4 British Columbia,
W Canada
ort Peck Lake 44 C1 reservoir
Montana, NW USA
ort Pierce 43 F4 Florida, SE USA
ort Providence 37 E4 var.
Providence. Northwest
Territories, W Canada

Fort St.John 37 E4 British
Columbia, W Canada
Fort Scott 45 F5 Kansas, C USA
Fort Severn 38 C2 Ontario,
C Canada
Fort-Shevchenko 114 A4
Mangistau, W Kazakhstan
Fort Simpson 37 E4 var. Simpson.
Northwest Territories, W Canada
Fort Smith 37 E4 district capital
Northwest Territories, W Canada
Fort Smith 42 B1 Arkansas, C USA
Fort Stockton 49 E3 Texas, SW USA
Fort-Trinquet see Bîr Mogreïn
Fort Vermilion 37 E4 Alberta,
W Canada
Fort Walton Beach 42 C3 Florida,
SE USA
Fort Wayne 40 C4 Indiana, N USA
Fort William 88 C3 N Scotland, UK
Fort Worth 49 G2 Texas, SW USA
Fort Yukon 36 D3 Alaska, USA
Fougamou 77 A6 Ngounié,
C Gabon
Fougères 90 B3 Ille-et-Vilaine,
NW France
Fou-hsin see Fuxin
Foulwind, Cape 151 B5 headland
South Island, NZ
Foumban 76 A4 Ouest,
NW Cameroon
Fou-shan see Fushun
Foveaux Strait 151 A8 strait S NZ
Foxe Basin 37 G3 sea Nunavut,
N Canada
Fox Glacier 151 B6 West Coast,
South Island, NZ
Fox Mine 37 F4 Manitoba,
C Canada
Fraga 93 F2 Aragón, NE Spain
Fram Basin 155 C3 var. Amundsen
Basin. Undersea feature Arctic
Ocean
France 90 B4 It./Sp. Francia; prev.
Gaul, Gaule, Lat. Gallia. Country
W Europe

France 90

Official name French Republic
Formation 987
Capital Paris
Population 59.5 million / 282 people
per sq mile (109 people per sq km)
Total area 211,208 sq miles
(547,030 sq km)
Languages French, Provenial,
German, Breton, Catalan, Basque
Religions Roman Catholic 88%,
Muslim 8%, Protestant 2%, other 2%
Ethnic mix French 90%, North
African 6%, German 2%, other 2%
Government Multiparty republic
Currency Euro (French franc until
2002)
Literacy rate 99%
Calorie consumption 3,591
kilocalories

Franceville 77 B6 var. Massoukou,
Masuku. Haut-Ogooué, E Gabon
Francfort prev see Frankfurt am
Main
Franche-Comté 90 D4 cultural region
E France
Francis Case, Lake 45 E3 reservoir
South Dakota, N USA
Francisco Escárcega 51 G4
Campeche, SE Mexico
Francistown 78 D3 North East,
NE Botswana
Franconian Jura see Fränkische Alb
Frankenalb see Fränkische Alb
Frankenstein see Zabkowice
Śląskie
Frankenstein in Schlesien see
Ząbkowice Śląskie
Frankfort 40 C5 state capital
Kentucky, S USA
Frankfort on the Main see
Frankfurt am Main
Frankfurt see Frankfurt am Main
Frankfurt am Main 95 B5 var.
Frankfurt, Fr. Francfort; prev. Eng.
Frankfort on the Main. Hessen,
SW Germany

Frankfurt an der Oder 94 D3
Brandenburg, E Germany
Fränkische Alb 95 C6 var.
Frankenalb, Eng. Franconian Jura.
Mountain range S Germany
Franklin 42 C1 Tennessee, S USA
Franklin D.Roosevelt Lake 46 C1
reservoir Washington, NW USA
Frantsa-Iosifa, Zemlya 114 D1 Eng.
Franz Josef Land. Island group
N Russian Federation
Franz Josef Land see Frantsa-Iosifa,
Zemlya
Fraserburgh 88 D3 NE Scotland, UK
Fraser Island 148 E4 var. Great
Sandy Island. Island Queensland,
E Australia
Fredericksburg 41 E5 Virginia,
NE USA
Fredericton 39 F4 New Brunswick,
SE Canada
Frederikshåb see Paamiut
Fredrikstad 85 B6 Østfold,
S Norway
Freeport 54 C1 Grand Bahama
Island, N Bahamas
Freeport 49 H4 Texas, SW USA
Freetown 74 C4 country capital
(Sierra Leone) W Sierra Leone
Freiburg see Freiburg im Breisgau
Freiburg im Breisgau 95 A6 var.
Freiburg, Fr. Fribourg-en-Brisgau.
Baden-Württemberg,
SW Germany
Fremantle 147 A6 Western Australia
Fremont 45 F4 Nebraska, C USA
French Guiana 59 H3 var. Guiana,
Guyane. French overseas department
N South America
French Polynesia 143 F4 French
overseas territory C Polynesia
**French Southern and Antarctic
Territories** 141 B7 Fr. Terres
Australes et Antarctiques
Françaises. French overseas territory
S Indian Ocean
Fresnillo 50 D3 var. Fresnillo de
González Echeverría. Zacatecas,
C Mexico
Fresnillo de González Echeverría
see Fresnillo
Fresno 47 C6 California, W USA
Frías 64 C3 Catamarca, N Argentina
Fribourg-en-Brisgau see Freiburg
im Breisgau
Friedrichshafen 95 B7 Baden-
Württemberg, S Germany
Frobisher Bay 82 B3 inlet Baffin
Island, Northwest Territories,
NE Canada
Frohavet 84 B4 sound C Norway
Frome 149 B6 salt lake South
Australia
Frontera 51 G4 Tabasco, SE Mexico
Frontignan 91 C6 Hérault,
S France
Frostviken see Kvarnbergsvattnet
Frøya 84 A4 island W Norway
Frunze see Bishkek
Frýdek-Místek 99 C5 Ger. Friedek-
Mistek. Ostravský Kraj, E Czech
Republic
Fu-chien see Fujian
Fu-chou see Fuzhou
Fuengirola 92 D5 Andalucía,
S Spain
Fuerte Olimpo 64 D2 var. Olimpo.
Alto Paraguay, NE Paraguay
Fuerte, Río 48 C5 river C Mexico
Fuerteventura 70 B3 island Islas
Canarias, Spain, NE Atlantic
Ocean
Fuhkien see Fujian
Fu-hsin see Fuxin
Fuji 131 D6 var. Huzi. Shizuoka,
Honshū, S Japan
Fujian 128 D6 var. Fu-chien,
Fuhkien, Fujian Sheng, Fukien,
Min. Admin. region province
SE China
Fujian Sheng see Fujian
Fuji-san 131 C6 var. Fujiyama, Eng.
Mount Fuji. Mountain Honshū,
SE Japan
Fujiyama see Fuji-san
Fukang 126 C2 Xinjiang Uygur
Zizhiqu, W China

Fukien see Fujian
Fukui 131 C6 var. Hukui. Fukui,
Honshū, SW Japan
Fukuoka 131 A7 var. Hukuoka; hist.
Najima. Fukuoka, Kyūshū,
SW Japan
Fukushima 130 D4 var. Hukusima.
Fukushima, Honshū, C Japan
Fulda 95 B5 Hessen, C Germany
Funafuti see Fongafale
Funafuti Atoll 145 E3 atoll C Tuvalu
Funchal 70 A2 Madeira, Portugal,
NE Atlantic Ocean
Fundy, Bay of 39 F5 bay
Canada/USA
Furnes see Veurne
Fürth 95 C5 Bayern, S Germany
Furukawa 130 D4 var. Hukukawa.
Miyagi, Honshū, C Japan
Fushun 128 D3 var. Fou-shan, Fu-
shun. Liaoning, NE China
Fu-shun see Fushun
Fusin see Fuxin
Füssen 95 C7 Bayern, S Germany
Futog 100 D3 Serbia, NW Serbia
and Montenegro (Yugo.)
Futuna, Île 145 E4 island S Wallis
and Futuna
Fuxin 128 D3 var. Fou-hsin, Fu-hsin,
Fusin. Liaoning, NE China
Fuzhou 128 D6 var. Foochow, Fu-
chou. Fujian, SE China
Fuzhou see Linchuan
Fyn 85 B8 Ger. Fünen. Island
C Denmark
Fyzabad see Feyzābād

G

Gaafu Alifu Atoll see North
Huvadhu Atoll
Gaafu Dhaalu Atoll see South
Huvadhu Atoll
Gaalkacyo 73 E5 var. Galka'yo, It.
Galcaio. Mudug, C Somalia
Gabela 78 B2 Cuanza Sul,
W Angola
Gabès 71 E2 var. Qābis. E Tunisia
Gabès, Golfe de 71 F2 Ar. Khalīj
Qābis. Gulf E Tunisia
Gabon 77 B6 Country C Africa

Gabon 77

Official name Gabonese Republic
Formation 1960
Capital Libreville
Population 1.3 million / 13 people
per sq mile (5 people per sq km)
Total area 103,346 sq miles
(267,667 sq km)
Languages French, Fang, Punu,
Sira, Nzebi, Mpongwe
Religions Christian 55%,
Traditional beliefs 40%, Muslim 1%,
other 4%
Ethnic mix Fang 35%, Eshira 25%,
other Bantu 29%, other 11%
Government Multiparty republic
Currency CFA franc = 100 centimes
Literacy rate 70.8%
Calorie consumption 2,564
kilocalories

Gaborone 78 C4 prev. Gaberones.
Country capital (Botswana) South
East, SE Botswana
Gabrovo 104 D2 Gabrovo,
N Bulgaria
Gadag 132 C1 Karnātaka, W India
Gadsden 42 D2 Alabama, S USA
Gaeta 97 C5 Lazio, C Italy
Gaeta, Golfo di 97 C5 var. Gulf of
Gaeta. Gulf C Italy
Gaeta, Gulf of see Gaeta, Golfo di
Gäfle see Gävle
Gafsa 71 E2 var. Qafşah. W Tunisia
Gagnoa 74 D5 C Côte d'Ivoire
Gagra 117 E1 NW Georgia
Gaillac 91 C6 var. Gaillac-sur-Tarn.
Tarn, S France
Gaillac-sur-Tarn see Gaillac
Gaillimh see Galway
Gainesville 43 E3 Florida, SE USA
Gainesville 42 D2 Georgia, SE USA
Gainesville 49 G2 Texas, SW USA

Gairdner, Lake 149 A6 salt lake South Australia
Gaizin see Gaizina Kalns
Gaizina Kalns 106 C3 var. Gaiziņ. Mountain E Latvia
Galán, Cerro 64 B3 mountain NW Argentina
Galanta 99 C6 Hung. Galánta. Trnavský Kraj, W Slovakia
Galapagos Fracture Zone 153 E3 tectonic feature E Pacific Ocean
Galapagos Islands 153 F3 var. Islas de los Galápagos,Tortoise Islands. Island group Ecuador, E Pacific Ocean
Galapagos Rise 153 F3 undersea feature E Pacific Ocean
Galashiels 88 C4 SE Scotland, UK
Galaţi 108 D4 Ger. Galatz. Galaţi, E Romania
Galcaio see Gaalkacyo
Galesburg 40 B3 Illinois, N USA
Galicia 92 B1 cultural region NW Spain
Galicia Bank 80 B4 undersea feature E Atlantic Ocean
Galilee, Sea of see Tiberias, Lake
Galka'yo see Gaalkacyo
Galle 132 D4 prev. Point de Galle. Southern Province, SW Sri Lanka
Gallego Rise 153 F3 undersea feature E Pacific Ocean
Gallegos see Río Gallegos
Gallipoli 97 E6 Puglia, SE Italy
Gällivare 84 C3 Norrbotten, N Sweden
Gallup 48 C1 New Mexico, SW USA
Galtat-Zemmour 70 B3 C Western Sahara
Galveston 49 H4 Texas, SW USA
Galway 89 A5 Ir. Gaillimh. W Ireland
Galway Bay 89 A6 Ir. Cuan na Gaillimhe. Bay W Ireland
Gambell 36 C2 Saint Lawrence Island, Alaska, USA
Gambia 74 C3 Fr. Gambie. River W Africa
Gambia 74 B3 Country W Africa

Gambia 74

Official name Republic of The Gambia
Formation 1965
Capital Banjul
Population 1.34 million / 307 people per sq mile (119 people per sq km)
Total area 4,363 sq miles (11,300 sq km)
Languages English, Mandinka, Fulani, Wolof, Jola, Soninke
Religions Sunni Muslim 90%, Christian 9%, Indigenous beliefs 1%
Ethnic mix Mandinka 42%, Fulani 18%, Wolof 16%, Jola 10%, Serahuli 9%, other 5%
Government Multiparty republic
Currency Dalasi = 100 butut
Literacy rate 36.6%
Calorie consumption 2,474 kilocalories

Gambier, Îles 143 G4 island group E French Polynesia
Gamboma 77 B6 Plateaux, E Congo
Gan see Gansu
Gan see Jiangxi
Gan 132 B5 Addu Atoll, C Maldives
Gäncä 117 G2 Rus. Gyandzha; prev. Kirovabad, Yelisavetpol. W Azerbaijan
Gandajika 77 D7 Kasai Oriental, S Dem. Rep. Congo
Gander 39 G3 Newfoundland, Newfoundland and Labrador, SE Canada
Gāndhīdhām 134 C4 Gujarāt, W India
Gandía 93 F3 País Valenciano, E Spain
Ganges 135 F3 Ben. Padma. River Bangladesh/India see also Padma
Ganges Cone see Ganges Fan

Ganges Fan 140 D3 var. Ganges Cone. Undersea feature N Bay of Bengal
Ganges, Mouths of the 135 G4 delta Bangladesh/India
Gangra see Çankırı
Gangtok 135 F3 Sikkim, N India
Gansu 128 B4 var. Gan, Gansu Sheng, Kansu. Admin. region province N China
Gansu Sheng see Gansu
Ganzhou 128 D6 Jiangxi, S China
Gao 75 E3 Gao, E Mali
Gaoual 74 C4 Moyenne-Guinée, N Guinea
Gaoxiong see Kaohsiung
Gap 91 D5 anc. Vapincum. Hautes-Alpes, SE France
Gar 126 A4 var. Gar Xincun. Xizang Zizhiqu, W China
Garachiné 53 G5 Darién, SE Panama
Garagum see Garagumy
Garagum Kanaly see Garagumskiy Kanal
Garagumskiy Kanal 122 D3 var. Kara Kum Canal, Karakumskiy Kanal, Turkm. Garagum Kanaly. Canal C Turkmenistan
Garagumy 122 C3 var. Qara Qum, Eng. Black Sand Desert, Kara Kum, Turkm. Garagum; prev. Peski Karakumy. Desert C Turkmenistan
Gara Khitrino 104 D2 Shumen, NE Bulgaria
Garda, Lago di 72 var. Benaco, Eng. Lake Garda, Ger. Gardasee. Lake NE Italy
Garda, Lake see Garda, Lago di
Gardasee see Garda, Lago di
Garden City 45 E5 Kansas, C USA
Gardeyz see Gardēz
Gardēz 123 E4 var. Gardeyz, Gordiaz. Paktiā, E Afghanistan
Gargždai 106 B3 Gargždai, W Lithuania
Garissa 73 D6 Coast, E Kenya
Garland 49 G2 Texas, SW USA
Garman, Loch see Wexford
Garoe see Garoowe
Garonne 91 B5 anc. Garumna. River S France
Garoowe 73 E5 var. Garoe. Nugaal, N Somalia
Garoua 76 B4 var. Garua. Nord, N Cameroon
Garrygala see Kara-Kala
Garry Lake 37 F3 lake Nunavut, N Canada
Garsen 73 D6 Coast, S Kenya
Garua see Garoua
Garwolin 98 D4 Mazowieckie, C Poland
Gar Xincun see Gar
Gary 40 B3 Indiana, N USA
Garzón 58 B4 Huila, S Colombia
Gascogne 91 B6 Eng. Gascony. Cultural region S France
Gascoyne River 147 A5 river Western Australia
Gaspé 39 F3 Quebec, SE Canada
Gaspé, Péninsule de 39 E4 var. Péninsule de la Gaspésie. Peninsula Quebec, SE Canada
Gastonia 43 E1 North Carolina, SE USA
Gastoúni 105 B6 Dytikí Ellás, S Greece
Gatchina 110 B4 Leningradskaya Oblast', NW Russian Federation
Gatineau 38 D4 Quebec, SE Canada
Gatún, Lago 53 F4 reservoir C Panama
Gauja 106 D3 Ger. Aa. River Estonia/Latvia
Gauteng see Johannesburg
Gāvbandī 120 D4 Hormozgān, S Iran
Gávdos 105 C8 island SE Greece
Gavere 87 B6 Oost-Vlaanderen, NW Belgium
Gävle 85 C6 var. Gäfle; prev. Gefle. Gävleborg, C Sweden
Gawler 149 B6 South Australia
Gaya 135 F3 Bihār, N India
Gayndah 149 E5 Queensland, E Australia

Gaza 119 A6 Ar. Ghazzah, Heb. 'Azza. NE Gaza Strip
Gaz-Achak 122 D2 Turkm. Gazojak. Lebapskiy Velayat, NE Turkmenistan
Gazandzhyk 122 B2 Turkm. Gazanjyk; prev. Kazandzhik. Balkanskiy Velayat, W Turkmenistan
Gaza Strip 119 A7 Ar. Qiṭā' Ghazzah. Disputed region SW Asia
Gazi Antep see Gaziantep
Gaziantep 116 D4 var. Gazi Antep; prev. Aintab, Antep. Gaziantep, S Turkey
Gazimağusa see Ammóchostos
Gazimağusa Körfezi see Kólpos Ammóchostos
Gazli 122 D2 Bukhoro Wiloyati, C Uzbekistan
Gbanga 74 D5 var. Gbarnga. N Liberia
Gbarnga see Gbanga
Gdańsk 98 C2 Fr. Dantzig, Ger. Danzig. Pomorskie, N Poland
Gdan'skaya Bukhta see Danzig, Gulf of
Pomorskie, Gulf of see Danzig, Gulf of
Gdynia 98 C2 Ger. Gdingen. Pomorskie, N Poland
Gedaref 72 C4 var. Al Qaḍārif, El Gedaref, Gedaref, E Sudan
Gediz 116 B3 Kütahya, W Turkey
Gediz Nehri 116 A3 river W Turkey
Geel 87 C5 var. Gheel. Antwerpen, N Belgium
Geelong 149 C7 Victoria, SE Australia
Ge'e'mu see Golmud
Gefle see Gävle
Geilo 85 A5 Buskerud, S Norway
Gejiu 128 B6 var. Kochiu. Yunnan, S China
Gëkdepe see Geok-Tepe
Gela 97 C7 prev. Terranova di Sicilia. Sicilia, Italy, C Mediterranean Sea
Geldermalsen 86 C4 Gelderland, C Netherlands
Geleen 87 D6 Limburg, SE Netherlands
Gelinsoor see Gellinsoor
Gellinsoor 73 E5 var. Gelinsoor. Mudug, NE Somalia
Gembloux 87 C6 Namur, Belgium
Gemena 77 C5 Equateur, NW Dem. Rep. Congo
Gemona del Friuli 96 D2 Friuli-Venezia Giulia, NE Italy
Genck see Genk
General Alvear 64 B4 Mendoza, W Argentina
General Eugenio A.Garay 64 C1 Guairá, S Paraguay
General Machado see Camacupa
General Santos 139 F3 off. General Santos City. Mindanao, S Philippines
Geneva see Genève
Geneva, Lake 74 Fr. Lac de Genève, Lac Léman, le Léman, Ger. Genfer See. Lake France/Switzerland
Genève 95 A7 Eng. Geneva, Ger. Genf, It. Ginevra. Genève, SW Switzerland
Genf see Genève
Genk 87 D6 var. Genck. Limburg, NE Belgium
Gennep 86 D4 Limburg, SE Netherlands
Genoa see Genova
Genova 102 D1 Eng. Genoa, Fr. Gênes; anc. Genua. Liguria, NW Italy
Genova, Golfo di 96 A3 Eng. Gulf of Genoa. Gulf NW Italy
Genovesa, Isla 60 B5 var. Tower Island. Island Galapagos Islands, Ecuador, E Pacific Ocean
Gent 87 B5 Eng. Ghent, Fr. Gand. Oost-Vlaanderen, NW Belgium
Geok-Tepe 122 C3 var. Gëkdepe, Turkm. Gökdepe. Akhalskiy Velayat, C Turkmenistan

George 82 A4 river Newfoundland and Labrador/Quebec, E Canada
George 78 C5 Western Cape, S South Africa
George, Lake 43 E3 lake Florida, SE USA
Georges Bank 35 D5 undersea feature W Atlantic Ocean
George Sound 151 A7 sound South Island, NZ
Georges River 148 D2 river New South Wales, SE Australia
George Town 54 B3 var. Georgetown. Dependent territory capital (Cayman Islands) Grand Cayman, SW Cayman Islands
George Town 138 B3 var. Penang, Pinang. Pinang, Peninsular Malaysia
George Town 54 C2 Great Exuma Island, C Bahamas
Georgetown 59 F2 country capital (Guyana) N Guyana
Georgetown 43 F2 South Carolina, SE USA
George V Land 154 C4 physical region Antarctica
Georgia 117 F2 Geor. Sak'art'velo, Rus. Gruzinskaya SSR, Gruziya; prev. Georgian SSR. Country SW Asia

Georgia 117

Official name Georgia
Formation 1991
Capital Tbilisi
Population 5.2 million /193 people per sq mile (75 people per sq km)
Total area 26,911 sq miles (69,700 sq km)
Languages Georgian, Russian
Religions Georgian Orthodox 65%, Muslim 11%, Russian Orthodox 10%, Armenian Orthodox 8%, Unknown 6%
Ethnic mix Georgian 70%, Armenian 8%, Russian 6%, Azeri 6%, Ossetian 3%, other 7%
Government Presidential democracy
Currency Lari = 100 tetri
Literacy rate 99%
Calorie consumption 2,412 kilocalories

Georgia 42 D2 off. State of Georgia; also known as Empire State of the South, Peach State. State SE USA
Georgian Bay 40 D2 lake bay Ontario, S Canada
Georgia, Strait of 46 A1 strait British Columbia, W Canada
Georg von Neumayer 154 A2 German research station Antarctica
Gera 94 C4 Thüringen, E Germany
Geráki 105 B6 Pelopónnisos, S Greece
Geraldine 151 B6 Canterbury, South Island, NZ
Geraldton 147 A6 Western Australia
Geral, Serra 57 D5 mountain range S Brazil
Gerede 116 C2 Bolu, N Turkey
Gereshk 122 D5 Helmand, SW Afghanistan
Gering 44 D3 Nebraska, C USA
Germanicopolis see Çankırı
Germany 94 B4 var. Bundesrepublik Deutschland, Deutschland. Country N Europe

Germany 94

Official name Federal Republic of Germany
Formation 1871
Capital Berlin
Population 82 million / 595 people per sq mile (230 people per sq km)
Total area 137,846 sq miles (357,021 sq km)
Languages German, Turkish
Religions Protestant 34%, Roman Catholic 33%, Muslim 3%, other 30

Germany (continued)

Ethnic mix German 92%, other 8%
Government Parliamentary
democracy
Currency Euro (Deutsche Mark
until 2002)
Literacy rate 99%
Calorie consumption 3,451
kilocalories

Geroliménas 105 B7 Pelopónnisos,
S Greece
Gerona see Girona
Gerpinnes 87 C7 Hainaut,
S Belgium
Gerunda see Girona
Gerze 116 D2 Sinop, N Turkey
Gesoriacum see Boulogne-sur-Mer
Gessoriacum see Boulogne-sur-Mer
Getafe 92 D3 Madrid, C Spain
Gevaş 117 F3 Van, SE Turkey
Gevgeli see Gevgelija
Gevgelija 101 E6 var. Đevđelija,
Djevdjelija, Turk. Gevgeli. SE FYR
Macedonia
Ghaba see Al Ghābah
Ghana 75 E5 Country W Africa

Ghana 75

Official name Republic of Ghana
Formation 1957
Capital Accra
Population 19.7 million / 214
people per sq mile (83 people per sq
km)
Total area 92,100 sq miles
238,540 sq km)
Languages English, Twi, Fanti, Ewe,
Ga, Adangbe, Gurma, Dagomba
Religions Christian 43%,
Traditional beliefs 38%, Muslim 11%,
other 8%
Ethnic mix Ashanti and Fanti 52%,
Moshi-Dagomba 16%, Ewe 12%,
Ga 8%, Yoruba 1%, other 11%
Government Presidential
democracy
Currency Cedi = 100 pesewas
Literacy rate 71.5%
Calorie consumption 2,699
kilocalories

Ghanzi 78 C3 var. Khanzi. Ghanzi,
W Botswana
Gharandal 119 B7 Ma'ān,
SW Jordan
Ghardaïa 70 D2 N Algeria
Gharvān see Gharyān
Gharyān 71 F2 var. Gharvān.
NW Libya
Ghazni 123 E4 var. Ghazni. Ghaznī,
E Afghanistan
Ghazni see Ghaznī
Gheel see Geel
Gheorgheni 108 C4 prev.
Gheorghieni, Sint-Miclǎuş, Ger.
Niklasmarkt, Hung.
Gyergyószentmiklós. Harghita,
C Romania
Ghijduwon 122 D2 Rus.
Gizhduvan. Bukhoro Wiloyati,
C Uzbekistan
Ghūdara 123 F3 var. Gudara, Rus.
Kudara. SE Tajikistan
Ghurdaqah see Hurghada
Ghūrīān 122 D4 Herāt,
W Afghanistan
Giannitsá 104 B4 var. Yiannitsá.
Kentrikí Makedonía,
N Greece
Gibraltar 93 G4 UK dependent
territory SW Europe
Gibraltar, Bay of 93 G5 bay
Gibraltar/Spain
Gibraltar, Strait of 92 C5 Fr.
Détroit de Gibraltar, Sp.
Estrecho de Gibraltar. Strait
Atlantic Ocean
Mediterranean Sea
Gibson Desert 147 B5 desert
Western Australia
Giedraičiai 107 C5 Molėtai,
E Lithuania

Giessen 95 B5 Hessen,
W Germany
Gifu 131 C6 var. Gihu. Gifu,
Honshū, SW Japan
Giganta, Sierra de la 50 B3
mountain range W Mexico
Gihu see Gifu
Gijón 92 D1 var. Xixón. Asturias,
NW Spain
Gilani see Gnjilane
Gila River 48 A2 river Arizona,
SW USA
Gilbert River 148 C3 river
Queensland, NE Australia
Gilf Kebir Plateau 72 A2 Ar.
Haḍabat al Jilf al Kabīr. Plateau
SW Egypt
Gillette 44 D3 Wyoming, C USA
Gilroy 47 B6 California, W USA
Gimie, Mount 55 F1 mountain
C Saint Lucia
Gimma see Jīma
Ginevra see Genève
Gingin 147 A6 Western Australia
Giohar see Jawhar
Girardot 58 B3 Cundinamarca,
C Colombia
Giresun 117 E2 var. Kerasunt; anc.
Cerasus, Pharnacia. Giresun,
NE Turkey
Girin see Jilin
Girne see Kyrenia
Girona 93 G2 var. Gerona; anc.
Gerunda. Cataluña, NE Spain
Gisborne 150 E3 Gisborne, North
Island, NZ
Gissar Range 123 E3 Rus.
Gissarskiy Khrebet. Mountain
range Tajikistan/Uzbekistan
Githio see Gýtheio
Giulianova 96 D4 Abruzzo, C Italy
Giumri see Gyumri
Giurgiu 108 C5 Giurgiu, S Romania
Gîza see El Gîza
Gizeh see El Gîza
Giżyko 98 D2 Warmińsko-
Mazurskie, NE Poland
Gjakovë see Đakovica
Gjilan see Gnjilane
Gjinokastër see Gjirokastër
Gjirokastër 101 C7 var. Gjirokastra;
prev. Gjinokastër, Gk.
Argyrokastron, It. Argirocastro.
Gjirokastër, S Albania
Gjirokastra see Gjirokastër
Gjoa Haven 37 F3 King William
Island, Nunavut, NW Canada
Gjøvik 85 B5 Oppland, S Norway
Glace Bay 39 G4 Cape Breton
Island, Nova Scotia, SE Canada
Gladstone 148 E4 Queensland,
E Australia
Glåma 85 B5 river SE Norway
Glasgow 88 C4 S Scotland, UK
Glavn'a Morava see Velika Morava
Glazov 111 D5 Udmurtskaya
Respublika, NW Russian
Federation
Glendale 48 B2 Arizona, SW USA
Glendive 44 D2 Montana, NW USA
Glens Falls 41 F3 New York,
NE USA
Glina 100 B3 Sisak-Moslavina,
NE Croatia
Glittertind 85 A5 mountain
S Norway
Gliwice 99 C5 Ger. Gleiwitz.
Śląskie, S Poland
Globe 48 B2 Arizona, SW USA
Głogów 98 B4 Ger. Glogau, Glogow.
Dolnośląskie
Gloucester 89 D6 hist. Caer Glou,
Lat. Glevum. C England, UK
Głowno 98 D4 Łódź, C Poland
Gniezno 98 C3 Ger. Gnesen.
Wielkopolskie, C Poland
Gnjilane 101 D5 var. Gilani, Alb.
Gjilan. Serbia, S Serbia and
Montenegro (Yugo.)
Goa see Panaji
Gobabis 78 B3 Omaheke,
E Namibia
Gobi 126 D3 desert China/Mongolia
Gobō 131 C6 Wakayama, Honshū,
SW Japan
Godāvari 124 B3 var. Godavari.
River C India

Godhavn see Qeqertarsuaq
Godhra 134 C4 Gujarāt, W India
Godoy Cruz 64 B4 Mendoza,
W Argentina
Godthaab see Nuuk
Godthåb see Nuuk
Goeree 86 B4 island
SW Netherlands
Goes 87 B5 Zeeland,
SW Netherlands
Goettingen see Göttingen
Gogebic Range 40 B1 hill range
Michigan/Wisconsin, N USA
Goiânia 63 E3 prev. Goyania. State
capital Goiás, C Brazil
Goiás 63 E3 Goiás, C Brazil
Gojôme 130 D4 Akita, Honshū,
NW Japan
Gökçeada 104 D4 var. Imroz Adası,
Gk. Imbros. Island NW Turkey
Gökdepe see Geok-Tepe
Göksun 116 D4 Kahramanmaraş,
C Turkey
Gol 85 A5 Buskerud, S Norway
Golan Heights 119 B5 Ar.
Al Jawlān, Heb. HaGolan.
Mountain range NW Syria
Goldap 98 E2 Ger. Goldap.
Warmińsko-Mazurskie,
NE Poland
Gold Coast 149 E5 cultural region
Queensland, E Australia
Golden Bay 150 C4 bay South
Island, NZ
Goldsboro 43 F1 North Carolina,
SE USA
Goleniów 98 B3 Ger. Gollnow.
Zachodniopomorskie, NW Poland
Golmo see Golmud
Golub-Dobrzyń 98 C3 Kujawski-
pomorskie, C Poland
Golmud 126 D4 var. Ge'e'mu,
Golmo, Chin. Ko-erh-mu. Qinghai,
C China
Goma 77 E6 Nord Kivu, NE Dem.
Rep. Congo
Gombi 75 H4 Adamawa, E Nigeria
Gombroon see Bandar-e 'Abbās
Gomera 70 A3 island Islas Canarias,
Spain, NE Atlantic Ocean
Gómez Palacio 50 D3 Durango,
C Mexico
Gonaïves 54 D3 var. Les Gonaïves.
N Haiti
Gonâve, Île de la 54 D3 island
C Haiti
Gondar see Gonder
Gonder 72 C4 var. Gondar.
N Ethiopia
Gondia 135 E4 Mahārāshtra,
C India
Gonggar 126 C5 Xizang Zizhiqu,
W China
Gonni see Gónnoi
Gónnoi 104 B4 var. Gonni, Gónnos;
prev. Dereli. Thessalía, C Greece
Gónnos see Gónnoi
Good Hope see Fort Good Hope
Good Hope, Cape of 78 B5 Afr.
Kaap de Goede Hoop, Kaap die
Goeie Hoop. Headland SW South
Africa
Goodland 44 D4 Kansas, C USA
Goondiwindi 149 D5 Queensland,
E Australia
Goor 86 E3 Overijssel,
E Netherlands
Goose Green 65 D7 var. Prado del
Ganso. East Falkland, Falkland
Islands
Goose Lake 46 B4 var. Lago dos
Gansos. Lake California/Oregon,
W USA
Göppingen 95 B6 Baden-
Württemberg, SW Germany
Gora Andryu see Andrew
Tablemount
Gora El'brus see El'brus
Góra Kalwaria 114 D4
Mazowieckie, C Poland
Gorakhpur 135 E3 Uttar Pradesh,
N India
Goražde 100 C4 Federacija Bosna I
Hercegovina, SE Bosnia and
Herzegovina
Gordiaz see Gardēz

Gore 151 B7 Southland, South
Island, NZ
Gorē 73 C5 C Ethiopia
Goré 76 C4 Logone-Oriental,
S Chad
Gorgān 120 D2 var. Astarabad,
Astrabad, Gurgan; prev.
Asterābād, anc. Hyrcania.
Golestān, N Iran
Gori 117 F2 C Georgia
Gorinchem 86 C4 var. Gorkum.
Zuid-Holland, C Netherlands
Goris 117 G3 SE Armenia
Gorkum see Gorinchem
Görlitz 94 D4 Sachsen, E Germany
Gornji Milanovac 100 C4 Serbia,
C Serbia and Montenegro (Yugo.)
Gorontalo 139 E4 Sulawesi,
C Indonesia
Gorontalo, Teluk see Tomini, Gulf
of
Gorssel 86 D3 Gelderland,
E Netherlands
Gory Putorana see Putorana, Plato
Gorzów Wielkopolski 98 B3 Ger.
Landsberg, Landsberg an der
Warthe. Lubuskie, W Poland
Gosford 149 D6 New South Wales,
SE Australia
Goshogawara 130 D3 var.
Gosyogawara. Aomori, Honshū,
C Japan
Gospić 100 A3 Lika-Senj, C Croatia
Gostivar 101 D6 W FYR Macedonia
Gosyogawara see Goshogawara
Göteborg 85 B7 Eng. Gothenburg.
Västra Götaland, S Sweden
Gotel Mountains 75 G5 mountain
range E Nigeria
Gotha 94 C4 Thüringen,
C Germany
Gothenburg see Göteborg
Gothenburg 80 D3 Nebraska,
C USA
Gotland 85 C7 island SE Sweden
Gotō-rettō 131 A7 island group
SW Japan
Gotska Sandön 106 B1 island
SE Sweden
Gōtsu 131 B6 var. Gôtu. Shimane,
Honshū, SW Japan
Göttingen 94 B4 var. Goettingen.
Niedersachsen, C Germany
Gôtu see Gōtsu
Gouda 86 C4 Zuid-Holland,
C Netherlands
Gough Fracture Zone 67 C6 tectonic
feature S Atlantic Ocean
Gough Island 69 B8 island Tristan
da Cunha, S Atlantic Ocean
Gouin, Réservoir 38 D4 reservoir
Quebec, SE Canada
Goulburn 149 D6 New South
Wales, SE Australia
Goundam 75 E3 Tombouctou,
NW Mali
Gouré 75 G3 Zinder, SE Niger
Governador Valadares 63 F4 Minas
Gerais, SE Brazil
Govĭ Altayn Nuruu 127 E3
mountain range S Mongolia
Goya 64 D3 Corrientes,
NE Argentina
Goz Beïda 76 C3 Ouaddaï, SE Chad
Gozo 97 C8 Malt. Ghawdex. Island
N Malta
Graciosa 92 A5 var. Ilha Graciosa.
Island Azores, Portugal,
NE Atlantic Ocean
Gradačac 100 C3 Federacija Bosna I
Hercegovina, N Bosnia and
Herzegovina
Gradaús, Serra dos 63 E3 mountain
range C Brazil
Gradiška see Bosanska Gradiška
Grafton 149 E5 New South Wales,
SE Australia
Grafton 45 E1 North Dakota, N USA
Graham Land 154 A2 physical region
Antarctica
Grajewo 98 E3 Podlaskie,
NE Poland
Grampian Mountains 88 C3
mountain range C Scotland, UK
Granada 92 D5 Andalucía, S Spain
Granada 52 D3 Granada,
SW Nicaragua

Gran Canaria 70 A3 *var.* Grand Canary. *Island* Islas Canarias, Spain, NE Atlantic Ocean
Gran Chaco 64 D2 *var.* Chaco. *Lowland plain* South America
Grand *see* Cockburn Town
Grand Bahama Island 54 B1 *island* N Bahamas
Grand Banks of Newfoundland 34 E4 *undersea feature* NW Atlantic Ocean
Grand Canary *see* Gran Canaria
Grand Canyon 48 A1 *canyon* Arizona, SW USA
Grand Cayman 54 B3 *island* SW Cayman Islands
Grande, Bahía 65 B7 *bay* S Argentina
Grande Comore 79 F2 *var.* Njazidja, Great Comoro. *Island* NW Comoros
Grande de Chiloé, Isla *see* Chiloé, Isla de
Grande Prairie 37 E4 Alberta, W Canada
Grand Erg Occidental 70 D3 *desert* W Algeria
Grand Erg Oriental 71 E3 *desert* Algeria/Tunisia
Grande, Rio 35 B6 *var.* Río Bravo, Sp. Río Bravo del Norte, Bravo del Norte. *River* Mexico/USA
Grande, Rio 49 F4 *river* Texas, SW USA
Grande, Rio *see* Bravo, Río
Grande, Río 51 E2 *river* S Mexico
Grande Terre 55 G3 *island* E West Indies
Grand Falls 39 G3 Newfoundland, Newfoundland and Labrador, SE Canada
Grand Forks 45 E1 North Dakota, N USA
Grand Island 45 E4 Nebraska, C USA
Grand Junction 44 C4 Colorado, C USA
Grand Rapids 40 C3 Michigan, N USA
Grand Rapids 45 F1 Minnesota, N USA
Grand-Santi 59 G3 W French Guiana
Gran Lago *see* Nicaragua, Lago de
Gran Malvina, Isla *see* West Falkland
Gran Paradiso 96 A2 Fr. Grand Paradis. *Mountain* NW Italy
Gran Santiago *see* Santiago
Grants 48 C2 New Mexico, SW USA
Grants Pass 46 B4 Oregon, NW USA
Granville 90 B3 Manche, N France
Graulhet 91 C6 Tarn, S France
Grave 86 D4 Noord-Brabant, SE Netherlands
Grayling 36 C2 Alaska, USA
Graz 95 E7 *prev.* Gratz. Steiermark, SE Austria
Great Abaco 54 C1 *var.* Abaco Island. *Island* N Bahamas
Great Alföld *see* Great Hungarian Plain
Great Ararat *see* Büyükağrı Dağı
Great Australian Bight 147 D7 *bight* S Australia
Great Barrier Island 150 D2 *island* N NZ
Great Barrier Reef 148 D2 *reef* Queensland, NE Australia
Great Basin 47 C5 *basin* W USA
Great Bear Lake 37 E3 Fr. Grand Lac de l'Ours. *Lake* Northwest Territories, NW Canada
Great Belt *see* Storebælt
Great Bend 45 E5 Kansas, C USA
Great Bermuda *see* Bermuda
Great Britain *see* Britain
Great Comoro *see* Grande Comore
Great Dividing Range 148 D4 *mountain range* NE Australia
Greater Antarctica 154 C3 *var.* East Antarctica. *Physical region* Antarctica
Greater Antilles 54 D3 *island group* West Indies

Greater Caucasus 117 G2 *Az.* Bas Qafqaz Silsiläsi, *Geor.* Kavkasioni, *Rus.* Bol'shoy Kavkaz. *Mountain range* Asia/Europe
Greater Sunda Islands 124 D5 *var.* Sunda Islands. *Island group* Indonesia
Great Exhibition Bay 150 C1 *inlet* North Island, NZ
Great Exuma Island 54 C2 *island* C Bahamas
Great Falls 44 B1 Montana, NW USA
Great Hungarian Plain 99 C7 *var.* Great Alföld, Plain of Hungary, *Hung.* Alföld. *Plain* SE Europe
Great Inagua 54 D2 *var.* Inagua Islands. *Island* S Bahamas
Great Indian Desert *see* Thar Desert
Great Karroo *see* Great Karoo
Great Lakes 35 C5 *lakes* Ontario, Canada/USA
Great Meteor Seamount *see* Great Meteor Tablemount
Great Meteor Tablemount 66 B3 *var.* Great Meteor Seamount. *Undersea feature* E Atlantic Ocean
Great Nicobar 133 G3 *island* Nicobar Islands, India, NE Indian Ocean
Great Plain of China 125 E2 *plain* E China
Great Plains 45 E3 *var.* High Plains. *Plains* Canada/USA
Great Rift Valley 73 C5 *var.* Rift Valley. *Depression* Asia/Africa
Great Ruaha 73 C7 *river* S Tanzania
Great Saint Bernard Pass 96 A1 *Fr.* Col du Grand-Saint-Bernard, *It.* Passo di Gran San Bernardo. *Pass* Italy/Switzerland
Great Salt Lake 44 A3 *salt lake* Utah, W USA
Great Salt Lake Desert 44 A4 *plain* Utah, W USA
Great Sand Sea 71 H3 *desert* Egypt/Libya
Great Sandy Desert 146 C4 *desert* Western Australia
Great Sandy Island *see* Fraser Island
Great Slave Lake 37 E4 *Fr.* Grand Lac des Esclaves. *Lake* Northwest Territories, NW Canada
Great Sound 42 A5 *bay* Bermuda, NW Atlantic Ocean
Great Victoria Desert 147 C5 *desert* South Australia/Western Australia
Great Wall of China 128 C4 *ancient monument* N China
Great Yarmouth 89 E6 *var.* Yarmouth. E England, UK
Gredos, Sierra de 92 D3 *mountain range* W Spain
Greece 105 A5 Gk. Ellás; *anc.* Hellas. *Country* SE Europe

Greece 105

Official name Hellenic Republic
Formation 1829
Capital Athens
Population 10.6 million / 208 people per sq mile (80 people per sq km)
Total area 50,942 sq miles (131,940 sq km)
Languages Greek, Turkish, Macedonian, Albanian
Religions Greek Orthodox 98%, Muslim 1%, other 1%
Ethnic mix Greek 98%, other 2%
Government Presidential democracy
Currency Euro (Drachma until 2002)
Literacy rate 97.3%
Calorie consumption 3,705 kilocalories

Greece 81 E5 New York, NE USA
Greeley 44 D4 Colorado, C USA

Green Bay 40 B2 *lake bay* Michigan/Wisconsin, N USA
Green Bay 40 B2 Wisconsin, N USA
Greeneville 43 E1 Tennessee, S USA
Greenland 82 D3 Dan. Grønland, Inuit Kalaallit Nunaat. Danish external territory NE North America
Greenland Sea 83 F2 *sea* Arctic Ocean
Green Mountains 41 G2 *mountain range* Vermont, NE USA
Greenock 88 C4 W Scotland, UK
Green River 40 C5 *river* Kentucky, C USA
Green River 44 B4 *river* Utah, W USA
Green River 44 B3 Wyoming, C USA
Greensboro 43 F1 North Carolina, SE USA
Greenville 42 B2 Mississippi, S USA
Greenville 43 F1 North Carolina, SE USA
Greenville 43 E1 South Carolina, SE USA
Greenville 49 G2 Texas, SW USA
Greenwich 89 B8 SE England, UK
Greenwood 42 B2 Mississippi, S USA
Greenwood 43 E2 South Carolina, SE USA
Gregory Range 148 C3 *mountain range* Queensland, E Australia
Greifswald 94 D2 Mecklenburg-Vorpommern, NE Germany
Grenada 55 G5 *country* SE West Indies

Grenada 55

Official name Grenada
Formation 1974
Capital St. George's
Population 98,000 /747 people per sq mile (288 people per sq km)
Total area 131 sq miles (340 sq km)
Languages English, English Creole
Religions Roman Catholic 68%, Anglican 17%, other 15%
Ethnic mix Black 82%, Mulatto 13%, Indian 3%, other 2%
Government Parliamentary democracy
Currency East Caribbean dollar = 100 cents
Literacy rate 96%
Calorie consumption 2,764 kilocalorie

Grenada 42 C2 Mississippi, S USA
Grenadines, The 55 H4 *island group* Grenada/St Vincent and the Grenadines
Grenoble 91 D5 *anc.* Cularo, Gratianopolis. Isère, E France
Gresham 46 B3 Oregon, NW USA
Grevená 104 B4 Dytikí Makedonía, N Greece
Grevenmacher 87 E8 Grevenmacher, E Luxembourg
Greymouth 151 B5 West Coast, South Island, NZ
Grey Range 149 C5 *mountain range* New South Wales/Queensland, E Australia
Greytown *see* San Juan del Norte
Griffin 42 D2 Georgia, SE USA
Grimari 76 C4 Ouaka, C Central African Republic
Grimsby 89 E5 *prev.* Great Grimsby. E England, UK
Grobiņa 106 B3 Ger. Grobin. Liepāja, W Latvia
Grodzisk Wielkopolski 98 B3 Wielkopolskie, C Poland
Groesbeek 86 D4 Gelderland, SE Netherlands
Grójec 98 D3 Mazowieckie, C Poland
Groningen 86 E1 Groningen, NE Netherlands
Groote Eylandt 148 B2 *island* Northern Territory, N Australia

Grootfontein 78 B3 Otjozondjupa, N Namibia
Groot Karasberge 78 B4 *mountain range* S Namibia
Groot Karoo *see* Great Karoo
Gros Islet 55 F1 N Saint Lucia
Grosse Morava *see* Velika Morava
Grosseto 96 B4 Toscana, C Italy
Grossglockner 95 C7 *mountain* W Austria
Groznyy 111 B8 Chechenskaya Respublika, SW Russian Federation
Grudziądz 98 C3 Ger. Graudenz. Kujawski-pomorskie, C Poland
Grums 85 B6 Värmland, C Sweden
Gryazi 111 B6 Lipetskaya Oblast', W Russian Federation
Gryfice 98 B2 Ger. Greifenberg, Greifenberg in Pommern. Zachodniopomorskie, NW Poland
Guabito 53 E4 Bocas del Toro, NW Panama
Guadalajara 93 E3 Ar. Wad Al-Hajarah; *anc.* Arriaca. Castilla-La Mancha, C Spain
Guadalajara 50 D4 Jalisco, C Mexico
Guadalcanal 144 C3 *island* C Solomon Islands
Guadalquivir 92 D4 *river* W Spain
Guadalupe 50 D3 Zacatecas, C Mexico
Guadalupe Peak 48 D3 *mountain* Texas, SW USA
Guadalupe River 49 G4 *river* SW USA
Guadarrama, Sierra de 93 E2 *mountain range* C Spain
Guadeloupe 55 H3 French *overseas department* E West Indies
Guadiana 92 C4 *river* Portugal/Spain
Guadix 93 E4 Andalucía, S Spain
Guaimaca 52 C2 Francisco Morazán, C Honduras
Guajira, Península de la 58 B1 *peninsula* N Colombia
Gualaco 52 D2 Olancho, C Honduras
Gualán 52 B2 Zacapa, C Guatemala
Gualdicciolo 96 D1 NW San Marino
Gualeguaychú 64 D4 Entre Ríos, E Argentina
Guam 144 B1 US *unincorporated territory* W Pacific Ocean
Guamúchil 50 C3 Sinaloa, C Mexico
Guanabacoa 54 B2 La Habana, W Cuba
Guanajuato 51 E4 Guanajuato, C Mexico
Guanare 58 C2 Portuguesa, N Venezuela
Guanare, Río 58 D2 *river* W Venezuela
Guangdong 128 C6 *var.* Guangdong Sheng, Kuang-tung, Kwangtung, Yue. Admin. region *province* S China
Guangdong Sheng *see* Guangdong
Guangxi *see* Guangxi Zhuangzu Zizhiqu
Guangxi Zhuangzu Zizhiqu 128 C6 *var.* Guangxi, Gui, Kuang-hsi, Kwangsi, *Eng.* Kwangsi Chuang Autonomous Region. Admin. region *autonomous region* S China
Guangyuan 128 B5 *var.* Kuang-yuan, Kwangyuan. Sichuan, C China
Guangzhou 128 C6 *var.* Kuang-chou, Kwangchow, *Eng.* Canton. Guangdong, S China
Guantánamo 54 D3 Guantánamo, SE Cuba
Guantánamo Bay 54 D3 US *military installation*, SE Cuba
Guaporé, Rio 63 F3 *var.* Río Iténez. *River* Bolivia/Brazil *see also* Iténez, Río
Guarda 92 C3 Guarda, N Portugal
Guarumal 53 F5 Veraguas, S Panama
Guasave 50 C3 Sinaloa, C Mexico

Guatemala 52 A2 *Country* Central America

Guatemala 52

Official name Republic of Guatemala
Formation 1838
Capital Guatemala City
Population 11.7 million / 278 people per sq mile (107 people per sq km)
Total area 42,042 sq miles (108,890 sq km)
Languages Spanish, Quiché, Mam, Cakchiquel, Kekchí
Religions Roman Catholic 65%, Protestant 33%, other 2%
Ethnic mix Amerindian 60%, Mestizo 30%, other 10%
Government Presidential democracy
Currency Quetzal = 100 centavos
Literacy rate 68.8%
Calorie consumption 2,171 kilocalories

Guatemala Basin 35 B7 *undersea feature* E Pacific Ocean
Guatemala City *see* Ciudad de Guatemala
Guaviare 56 B2 *off.* Comisaría Guaviare. *Province* S Colombia
Guaviare, Río 58 D3 *river* E Colombia
Guayaquil 60 A2 *var.* Santiago de Guayaquil. Guayas, SW Ecuador
Guayaquil, Golfo de 60 A2 *var.* Gulf of Guayaquil. *Gulf* SW Ecuador
Guayaquil, Gulf of *see* Guayaquil, Golfo de
Guaymas 50 B2 Sonora, NW Mexico
Gubadag 122 C2 *Turkm.* Tel'man; *prev.* Tel'mansk. Dashkhovuzskiy Velayat, N Turkmenistan
Guben 94 D4 *var.* Wilhelm-Pieck-Stadt. Brandenburg, E Germany
Gudara *see* Ghūdara
Gudaut'a 117 E1 NW Georgia
Guéret 90 C4 Creuse, C France
Guernsey 89 D8 UK *dependent territory* NW Europe
Guerrero Negro 50 A2 Baja California Sur, NW Mexico
Gui *see* Guangxi Zhuangzu Zizhiqu
Guiana *see* French Guiana
Guiana Highlands 62 D1 *var.* Macizo de las Guayanas. *Mountain range* N South America
Guidder *see* Guider
Guider 76 B4 *var.* Guidder. Nord, N Cameroon
Guidimouni 75 G3 Zinder, S Niger
Guildford 89 D7 SE England, UK
Guilin 128 C6 *var.* Kuei-lin, Kweilin. Guangxi Zhuangzu Zizhiqu, S China
Guimarães 92 B2 *var.* Guimarães. Braga, N Portugal
Guinea 74 C4 *var.* Guinée; *prev.* French Guinea, People's Revolutionary Republic of Guinea. *Country* W Africa

Guinea 74

Official name Republic of Guinea
Formation 1958
Capital Conakry
Population 8.3 million / 87 people per sq mile (34 people per sq km)
Total area 94,925 sq miles (245,857 sq km)
Languages French, Fulani, Malinke, Soussou
Religions Muslim 65%, Traditional beliefs 33%, Christian 2%
Ethnic mix Fula (Fulani) 30%, Malinke 30%, Soussou 15%, Kissi 10%, other tribes 10%, other 25%
Government Multiparty republic
Currency Guinea franc = 100 centimes
Literacy rate 41.1%
Calorie consumption 2,353 kilocalories

Guinea Basin 69 A5 *undersea feature* E Atlantic Ocean
Guinea-Bissau 74 B4 *Fr.* Guinée-Bissau, *Port.* Guiné-Bissau; *prev.* Portuguese Guinea. *Country* W Africa

Guinea-Bissau 74

Official name Republic of Guinea-Bissau
Formation 1974
Capital Bissau
Population 1.2 million / 86 people per sq mile (33 people per sq km)
Total area 13,946 sq miles (36,120 sq km)
Languages Portuguese Creole, Fulani Balante, Malinke, Portuguese
Religions Indigenous beliefs 52%, Muslim 40%, Christian 8%
Ethnic mix Balante 25%, Madinka 12%, Fila 20%, Mandyako 11%, other 32%
Government Presidential democracy
Currency CFA franc = 100 centimes
Literacy rate 38.8%
Calorie consumption 2,333 kilocalories

Guinea, Gulf of 68 B4 *Fr.* Golfe de Guinée. *Gulf* E Atlantic Ocean
Güiria 59 E1 Sucre, NE Venezuela
Guiyang 128 B6 *var.* Kuei-Yang, Kuei-yang, Kueyang, Kweiyang; *prev.* Kweichu. Guizhou, S China
Guizhou 128 B6 *var.* Guizhou Sheng, Kuei-chou, Kweichow, Qian. Admin. region *province* S China
Guizhou Sheng *see* Guizhou
Gujarāt 134 C4 *var.* Gujerat. Admin. region *state* W India
Gujerat *see* Gujarāt
Gujrānwāla 134 D2 Punjab, NE Pakistan
Gujrāt 134 D2 Punjab, E Pakistan
Gulbarga 132 C1 Karnātaka, C India
Gulbene 106 D3 Ger. Alt-Schwanenburg. Gulbene, NE Latvia
Gulfport 42 C3 Mississippi, S USA
Gulf, The 120 C4 *var.* Persian Gulf, *Ar.* Khalīj al 'Arabī, *Per.* Khalīj-e Fars. *Gulf* SE Asia
Guliston 123 E2 Rus. Gulistan. Sirdaryo Wiloyati, E Uzbekistan
Gulja *see* Yining
Gulkana 36 D3 Alaska, USA
Gulu 73 B6 N Uganda
Gulyantsi 104 C1 Pleven, N Bulgaria
Guma *see* Pishan
Gümülcine *see* Komotiní
Gümüljina *see* Komotiní
Gümüşane *see* Gümüşhane
Gümüşhane 117 E3 *var.* Gümüşane, Gumushkhane. Gümüşhane, NE Turkey
Gumushkhane *see* Gümüşhane
Güney Doğu Toroslar 117 E4 *mountain range* SE Turkey
Gunnbjørn Fjeld 82 D4 *var.* Gunnbjörns Bjerge. *Mountain* C Greenland
Gunnbjörns Bjerge *see* Gunnbjørn Fjeld
Gunnedah 149 D6 New South Wales, SE Australia
Gunnison 44 C5 Colorado, C USA
Gurbantünggüt Shamo 126 B2 *desert* W China
Gurgan *see* Gorgān
Guri, Embalse de 59 E2 *reservoir* E Venezuela
Gurktaler Alpen 95 D7 *mountain range* S Austria
Gürün 116 D3 Sivas, C Turkey
Gusau 75 G4 Zamfara, NW Nigeria
Gusev 106 B4 Ger. Gumbinnen. Kaliningradskaya Oblast', W Russian Federation
Gushgy 122 D4 *prev.* Kushka. Maryyskiy Velayat, S Turkmenistan

Gustavus 36 D4 Alaska, USA
Güstrow 94 C3 Mecklenburg-Vorpommern, NE Germany
Gütersloh 94 B4 Nordrhein-Westfalen, W Germany
Guwāhāti 135 G3 *prev.* Gauhāti. Assam, NE India
Guyana 59 F3 *prev.* British Guiana. *Country* N South America

Guyana 59

Official name Cooperative Republic of Guyana
Formation 1966
Capital Georgetown
Population 763,000 / 9 people per sq mile (4 people per sq km)
Total area 83,000 sq miles (214,970 sq km)
Languages English, English Creole, Hindi, Tamil, Amerindian languages
Religions Christian 57%, Hindu 33%, Muslim 9%, other 1%
Ethnic mix East Indian 52%, Black African 38%, other 10%
Government Presidential democracy
Currency Guyana dollar = 100 cents
Literacy rate 98.5%
Calorie consumption 2,582 kilocalories

Guyane *see* French Guiana
Guymon 49 E1 Oklahoma, C USA
Güzelyurt *see* Mórfou
Gvardeysk 106 A4 Ger. Tapaiu. Kaliningradskaya Oblast', W Russian Federation
Gwādar 134 A3 *var.* Gwadur. Baluchistān, SW Pakistan
Gwadur *see* Gwādar
Gwalior 134 D3 Madhya Pradesh, C India
Gwanda 78 D3 Matabeleland South, SW Zimbabwe
Gwy *see* Wye
Gyangzê 126 C5 Xizang Zizhiqu, W China
Gyaring Co 126 C5 *lake* W China
Gympie 149 E5 Queensland, E Australia
Gyomaendrőd 99 D7 Békés, SE Hungary
Gyöngyös 99 D6 Heves, NE Hungary
Győr 99 C6 Ger. Raab; *Lat.* Arrabona. Győr-Moson-Sopron, NW Hungary
Gýtheio 105 B6 *var.* Githio; *prev.* Yíthion. Pelopónnisos, S Greece
Gyumri 117 F2 *var.* Giumri, *Rus.* Kumayri; *prev.* Aleksandropol', Leninakan. W Armenia
Gyzylarbat 122 C2 *prev.* Kizyl-Arvat. Balkanskiy Velayat, W Turkmenistan

H

Haabai *see* Ha'apai Group
Haacht 87 C6 Vlaams Brabant, C Belgium
Haaksbergen 86 E3 Overijssel, E Netherlands
Ha'apai Group 145 F4 *var.* Haabai. *Island group* C Tonga
Haapsalu 106 D2 Ger. Hapsal. Läänemaa, W Estonia
Haarlem 86 C3 *prev.* Harlem. Noord-Holland, W Netherlands
Haast 151 B6 West Coast, South Island, NZ
Hachijō-jima 131 D6 *var.* Hatizyō Zima. *Island* Izu-shotō, SE Japan
Hachinohe 130 D3 Aomori, Honshū, C Japan
Hadama *see* Nazrēt
Haddummati Atoll *see* Hadhdhunmathi Atoll
Hadejia 75 G3 *river* N Nigeria
Hadejia 75 G4 Jigawa, N Nigeria
Hadera 119 A6 *var.* Khadera. Haifa, C Israel

Hadhdhunmathi Atoll 132 A5 *var.* Haddummati Atoll, Laamu Atoll. *Atoll* S Maldives
Ha Đông 136 D3 *var.* Hadong. Ha Tây, N Vietnam
Hadong *see* Ha Đông
Hạdramawt 121 C6 *Eng.* Hadhramaut. *Mountain range* S Yemen
Haerbin *see* Harbin
Haerhpin *see* Harbin
Hafren *see* Severn
Hagåtña 160 B1 *var.* Agana / Agaña. *Dependent territory capital* (Guam), NW Guam
Hagerstown 41 E4 Maryland, NE USA
Ha Giang 136 D3 Ha Giang, N Vietnam
Hagondange 90 D3 Moselle, NE France
Haguenau 90 E3 Bas-Rhin, NE France
Haicheng 128 D3 Liaoning, NE China
Haidarabad *see* Hyderābād
Haifa *see* Ḥefa
Haifong *see* Hai Phong
Haikou 128 C7 *var.* Hai-k'ou, Hoihow, *Fr.* Hoï-Hao. Hainan, S China
Hai-k'ou *see* Haikou
Ḥā'il 120 B4 *off.* Minṭaqah Ḥā'il. *Province* N Saudi Arabia
Hai-la-erh *see* Hailar
Hailar 127 F1 *var.* Hai-la-erh; *prev.* Hulun. Nei Mongol Zizhiqu, N China
Hailuoto 84 D4 Swe. Karlö. *Island* W Finland
Hainan 128 B7 *var.* Hainan Sheng, Qiong. Admin. region *province* S China
Hainan Dao 128 C7 *island* S China
Hainan Sheng *see* Hainan
Haines 36 D4 Alaska, USA
Hainichen 94 D4 Sachsen, E Germany
Hai Phong 136 D3 *var.* Haifong, Haiphong. N Vietnam
Haiphong *see* Hai Phong
Haiti 54 D3 C West Indies

Haiti 54

Official name Republic of Haiti
Formation 1804
Capital Port-au-Prince
Population 8.3 million / 775 people per sq mile (299 people per sq km)
Total area 10,714 sq miles (27,750 sq km)
Languages English, French Creole
Religions Roman Catholic 80%, Protestant 16%, non-religious 1%, other 3%
Ethnic mix Black African 95%, Mulatto and European 5%
Government Multiparty republic
Currency Gourde = 100 centimes
Literacy rate 49.8%
Calorie consumption 2,056 kilocalories

Haiya 72 C3 Red Sea, NE Sudan
Hajdúhadház 99 D6 Hajdú-Bihar, E Hungary
Hajine *see* Abū Ḥardān
Hajnówka 98 E3 Ger. Hermhausen. Podlaskie, NE Poland
Hakodate 130 D3 Hokkaidō, NE Japan
Ḥalab 118 B2 *Eng.* Aleppo, *Fr.* Alep; *anc.* Beroea. Ḥalab, NW Syria
Ḥalāniyāt, Juzur al 137 D6 *var.* Jazā'ir Bin Ghalfān, *Eng.* Kuria Muria Islands. *Island group* S Oman
Halberstadt 94 C4 Sachsen-Anhalt, C Germany
Halden 85 B6 *prev.* Fredrikshald. Østfold, S Norway
Halfmoon Bay 151 D4 *var.* Oban. Stewart Island, Southland, NZ
Halifax 39 F4 Nova Scotia, SE Canada

197

Halkida *see* Chalkída
Halle *87 B6 Fr.* Hal. Vlaams
 Brabant, C Belgium
Halle *94 C4 var.* Halle an der Saale.
 Sachsen-Anhalt, C Germany
Halle an der Saale *see* Halle
Halle-Neustadt *94 C4* Sachsen-
 Anhalt, C Germany
Halley *154 B2 UK research station*
 Antarctica
Hall Islands *142 B2 island group*
 C Micronesia
Halls Creek *146 C3* Western
 Australia
Halmahera, Pulau *139 F3 prev.*
 Djailolo, Gilolo, Jailolo. *Island*
 E Indonesia
Halmahera Sea *139 F4 Ind.* Laut
 Halmahera. *Sea* E Indonesia
Halmstad *85 B7* Halland, S Sweden
Hama *see* Ḥamāh
Hamada *131 B6* Shimane, Honshū,
 SW Japan
Hamadān *120 C3 anc.* Ecbatana.
 Hamadān, W Iran
Ḥamāh *118 B3 var.* Hama; *anc.*
 Epiphania, *Bibl.* Hamath. Ḥamāh,
 W Syria
Hamamatsu *131 D6 var.*
 Hamamatu. Shizuoka, Honshū,
 S Japan
Hamamatu *see* Hamamatsu
Hamar *85 B5 prev.* Storhammer.
 Hedmark, S Norway
Hamath *see* Ḥamāh
Hamburg *94 B3* Hamburg,
 N Germany
Ḥamḍ, Wādī al *136 A4 dry
 watercourse* W Saudi Arabia
Hämeenlinna *85 D5 Swe.*
 Tavastehus. Etelä-Suomi,
 S Finland
Hamersley Range *146 A4 mountain
 range* Western Australia
Hamhŭng *129 E3* C North Korea
Hami *126 C3 var.* Ha-mi, Uigh.
 Kumul, Qomul. Xinjiang Uygur
 Zizhiqu, NW China
Ha-mi *see* Hami
Hamilton *42 C2* Alabama, S USA
Hamilton *38 D5* Ontario, S Canada
Hamilton *88 C4* S Scotland, UK
Hamilton *150 D3* Waikato, North
 Island, NZ
Ḥamīm, Wādī al *87 G2 river*
 NE Libya
Hamiton *42 A5 dependent territory
 capital* (Bermuda) C Bermuda
Hamm *94 B4 var.* Hamm in
 Westfalen. Nordrhein-Westfalen,
 W Germany
Hamma du Drâa *see* Dra,
 Hamada du
Hammamet, Golfe de *102 D3 Ar.*
 Khalīj al Ḥammāmāt. *Gulf*
 NE Tunisia
Ḥammār, Hawr al *136 C3 lake*
 SE Iraq
Hamm in Westfalen *see* Hamm
Hampden *151 B7* Otago, South
 Island, NZ
Hamrun *102 B5* C Malta
Hâncești *see* Hîncești
Handan *128 C4 var.* Han-tan. Hebei,
 E China
Haneda *130 A2 international airport*
 (Tōkyō) Tōkyō, Honshū, S Japan
HaNegev *119 A7 Eng.* Negev. *Desert*
 S Israel
Hanford *47 C6* California, W USA
Hangayn Nuruu *126 D2 mountain
 range* C Mongolia
Hang-chou *see* Hangzhou
Hangchow *see* Hangzhou
Hangō *see* Hanko
Hangzhou *128 D5 var.* Hang-chou,
 Hangchow. Zhejiang, SE China
Hania *see* Chaniá
Hanka, Lake *see* Khanka, Lake
Hanko *85 D6 Swe.* Hangō. Etelä-
 Suomi, SW Finland
Han-k'ou *see* Wuhan
Hankow *see* Wuhan
Hanmer Springs *151 C5*
 Canterbury, South Island, NZ

Hannibal *45 G4* Missouri, C USA
Hannover *94 B3 Eng.* Hanover.
 Niedersachsen, NW Germany
Hanöbukten *85 B7 bay* S Sweden
Ha Nôi *136 D3 Eng.* Hanoi, *Fr.* Ha
 noï. *Country capital* (Vietnam)
 N Vietnam
Hanoi *see* Ha Nôi
Han Shui *127 E4 river* C China
Han-tan *see* Handan
Hantsavichy *107 B6 Pol.*
 Hancewicze, *Rus.* Gantsevichi.
 Brestskaya Voblasts', SW Belarus
Hanyang *see* Wuhan
Hanzhong *128 B5* Shaanxi, C China
Hāora *135 F4 prev.* Howrah. West
 Bengal, NE India
Haparanda *84 D4* Norrbotten,
 N Sweden
Haradok *107 E5 Rus.* Gorodok.
 Vitsyebskaya Voblasts', N Belarus
Haradzyets *107 B6 Rus.* Gorodets.
 Brestskaya Voblasts', SW Belarus
Haramachi *131 D4* Fukushima,
 Honshū, E Japan
Harany *107 D5 Rus.* Gorany.
 Vitsyebskaya Voblasts', N Belarus
Harare *78 D3 prev.* Salisbury.
 Country capital (Zimbabwe)
 Mashonaland East, NE Zimbabwe
Harbavichy *107 E6 Rus.* Gorbovichi.
 Mahilyowskaya Voblasts',
 E Belarus
Harbel *74 C5* W Liberia
Harbin *129 E2 var.* Haerbin, Ha-erh-
 pin, Kharbin; *prev.* Haerhpin,
 Pingkiang, Pinkiang.
 Heilongjiang, NE China
Hardangerfjorden *85 A6 fjord*
 S Norway
Hardangervidda *85 A6 plateau*
 S Norway
Hardenberg *86 E3* Overijssel,
 E Netherlands
Harelbeke *85 A6 var.* Harlebeke.
 West-Vlaanderen, W Belgium
Harem *see* Ḥārim
Haren *86 E2* Groningen,
 NE Netherlands
Hārer *73 D5* E Ethiopia
Hargeisa *see* Hargeysa
Hargeysa *73 D5 var.* Hargeisa.
 Woqooyi Galbeed, NW Somalia
Hariana *see* Haryāna
Hari, Batang *138 B4 prev.* Djambi.
 River Sumatera, W Indonesia
Ḥārim *118 B2 var.* Harem. Idlib,
 W Syria
Harima-nada *131 B6 sea* S Japan
Harīrūd *var.* Tedzhen, *Turkm.* Tejen.
 River Afghanistan/Iran *see also*
 Tedzhen
Harlan *45 F3* Iowa, C USA
Harlebeke *see* Harelbeke
Harlingen *86 D2 Fris.* Harns.
 Friesland, N Netherlands
Harlingen *49 G5* Texas, SW USA
Harlow *89 E6* E England, UK
Harney Basin *46 B4 basin* Oregon,
 NW USA
Härnösand *85 C5 var.* Hernösand.
 Västernorrland, C Sweden
Har Nuur *126 C2 lake*
 NW Mongolia
Harper *74 D5 var.* Cape Palmas.
 NE Liberia
Harricana *38 D3 river* Quebec,
 SE Canada
Harris *88 B3 physical region*
 NW Scotland, UK
Harrisburg *41 F4 state capital*
 Pennsylvania, NE USA
Harrisonburg *41 F4* Virginia,
 NE USA
Harrison, Cape *39 F2 headland*
 Newfoundland and Labrador,
 E Canada
Harris Ridge *see* Lomonosov Ridge
Harrogate *89 D5* N England, UK
Hârșova *108 D5 prev.* Hîrșova.
 Constanța, SE Romania
Harstad *84 C2* Troms, N Norway
Hartford *41 G3 state capital*
 Connecticut, NE USA
Hartlepool *89 D5* N England, UK
Harunabad *see* Eslāmābād
Harwich *89 E6* E England, UK

Haryāna *134 D2 var.* Hariana.
 Admin. region *state* N India
Hasselt *87 C6* Limburg, NE Belgium
Hassetché *see* Al Ḥasakah
Hastings *150 E4* Hawke's Bay,
 North Island, NZ
Hastings *45 E4* Nebraska, C USA
Hastings *89 E7* SE England, UK
Hațeg *108 B4 Ger.* Wallenthal, *Hung.*
 Hátszeg; *prev.* Hatzog, Hötzing.
 Hunedoara, SW Romania
Hatizyô Zima *see* Hachijō-jima
Hattem *86 D3* Gelderland,
 E Netherlands
Hatteras, Cape *43 G1 headland*
 North Carolina, SE USA
Hatteras Plain *35 D6 undersea
 feature* W Atlantic Ocean
Hattiesburg *42 C3* Mississippi, S USA
Hatton Bank *see* Hatton Ridge
Hatton Ridge *80 B2 var.* Hatton
 Bank. *Undersea feature* N Atlantic
 Ocean
Hat Yai *137 C7 var.* Ban Hat Yai.
 Songkhla, SW Thailand
Haugesund *85 A6* Rogaland,
 S Norway
Haukeligrend *85 A6* Telemark,
 S Norway
Haukivesi *85 E5 lake* SE Finland
Hauraki Gulf *150 D2 gulf* North
 Island, NZ
Hauroko, Lake *151 A7 lake* South
 Island, NZ
Haut Atlas *70 B3 Eng.* High Atlas.
 Mountain range C Morocco
Hautes Fagnes *87 D6 Ger.* Hohes
 Venn. *Mountain range* E Belgium
Haut Plateau du Dra *see* Dra,
 Hamada du
Hauts Plateaux *70 D2 plateau*
 Algeria/Morocco
Hauzenberg *95 D6* Bayern,
 SE Germany
Havana *see* La Habana
Havana *35 D6* Illinois, N USA
Havant *89 D7* S England, UK
Havelock *43 F1* North Carolina,
 SE USA
Havelock North *150 E4* Hawke's
 Bay, North Island, NZ
Haverfordwest *89 C6* SW Wales, UK
Havířov *95 C5* Ostravský Kraj,
 E Czech Republic
Havre *44 C1* Montana, NW USA
Havre-St-Pierre *39 F3* Quebec,
 E Canada
Hawai'i *87 B8 Haw.* Hawai'i. *Island*
 Hawaiian Islands, USA, C Pacific
 Ocean
Hawaii *47 A8 off.* State of Hawaii;
 also known as Aloha State,
 Paradise of the Pacific. *State* USA,
 C Pacific Ocean
Hawaiian Islands *152 D2 prev.*
 Sandwich Islands. *Island group*
 Hawaii, USA, C Pacific Ocean
Hawaiian Ridge *113 H4 undersea
 feature* N Pacific Ocean
Hawash *see* Āwash
Hawea, Lake *151 B6 lake* South
 Island, NZ
Hawera *150 D4* Taranaki, North
 Island, NZ
Hawick *88 C4* SE Scotland, UK
Hawke Bay *150 E4 bay* North
 Island, NZ
Hawler *see* Arbil
Hawthorne *47 C6* Nevada, W USA
Hay *149 C6* New South Wales,
 SE Australia
Hayes *38 B2 river* Manitoba,
 C Canada
Hay River *37 E4* Northwest
 Territories, W Canada
Hays *45 E5* Kansas, C USA
Haysyn *108 D3 Rus.* Gaysin.
 Vinnyts'ka Oblast', C Ukraine
Heard and McDonald Islands *141
 B7 Australian external territory*
 S Indian Ocean
Hearst *38 C4* Ontario, S Canada
Heathrow *89 A8 international airport*
 (London)SE England, UK
Hebei *128 C4 var.* Hebei Sheng,
 Hopeh, Hopei, Ji; *prev.* Chihli.
 Admin. region *province* E China

Hebei Sheng *see* Hebei
Hebron *119 A6 var.* Al Khalīl,
 El Khalil, *Heb.* Hevron; *anc.*
 Kiriath-Arba. S West Bank
Hebrus *see* Maritsa
Heemskerk *86 C3* Noord-Holland,
 W Netherlands
Heerde *86 D3* Gelderland,
 E Netherlands
Heerenveen *86 D2 Fris.* It
 Hearrenfean. Friesland,
 N Netherlands
Heerhugowaard *86 C2* Noord-
 Holland, NW Netherlands
Heerlen *87 D6* Limburg,
 SE Netherlands
Heerwegen *see* Polkowice
Hefa *119 A5 var.* Haifa; *hist.* Caiffa,
 Caiphas, *anc.* Sycaminum. Haifa,
 N Israel
Hefa, Mifraz *119 A5 Eng.* Bay of
 Haifa. *Bay* N Israel
Hefei *128 D5 var.* Hofei; *hist.*
 Luchow. Anhui, E China
Hegang *129 E2* Heilongjiang,
 NE China
Hei *see* Heilongjiang
Heide *94 B2* Schleswig-Holstein,
 N Germany
Heidelberg *95 B5* Baden-
 Württemberg, SW Germany
Heidenheim *see* Heidenheim an
 der Brenz
Heidenheim an der Brenz *95 B6
 var.* Heidenheim. Baden-
 Württemberg, S Germany
Heilbronn *95 B6* Baden-
 Württemberg, SW Germany
Heilongjiang *128 D2 var.* Hei,
 Heilongjiang Sheng, Hei-lung-
 chiang, Heilungkiang. Admin.
 region *province* NE China
Heilongjiang Sheng *see*
 Heilongjiang
Heiloo *86 C3* Noord-Holland,
 NW Netherlands
Hei-lung-chiang *see* Heilongjiang
Heilungkiang *see* Heilongjiang
Heimdal *85 B5* Sør-Trøndelag,
 S Norway
Hekimhan *116 D3* Malatya,
 C Turkey
Helena *44 B2 state capital* Montana,
 NW USA
Helensville *150 D2* Auckland,
 North Island, NZ
Helgoland Bay *see* Helgoländer
 Bucht
Helgoländer Bucht *94 A2 var.*
 Helgoland Bay, Heligoland Bight.
 Bay NW Germany
Heligoland Bight *see* Helgoländer
 Bucht
Heliopolis *see* Baalbek
Hellevoetsluis *86 B4* Zuid-Holland,
 SW Netherlands
Hellín *93 E4* Castilla-La Mancha,
 C Spain
Helmand, Daryā-ye *var.* Rūd-e
 Hīrmand. *River* Afghanistan/Iran
 see also Hīrmand, Rūd-e
Helmond *87 D5* Noord-Brabant,
 S Netherlands
Helsingborg *85 B7 prev.*
 Hälsingborg. Skåne, S Sweden
Helsinki *85 D6 Swe.* Helsingfors.
 Country capital (Finland) Etelä-
 Suomi, S Finland
Henan *128 C5 var.* Henan Sheng,
 Honan, Yu. Admin. region
 province C China
Henan Sheng *see* Henan
Henderson *40 B5* Kentucky, S USA
Henderson *47 D7* Nevada, W USA
Henderson *49 H3* Texas, SW USA
Hengchow *see* Hengyang
Hengduan Shan *128 A5 mountain
 range* SW China
Hengelo *86 E3* Overijssel,
 E Netherlands
Hengnan *see* Hengyang
Hengyang *128 C6 var.* Hengnan,
 Heng-yang; *prev.* Hengchow.
 Hunan, S China
Heng-yang *see* Hengyang
Heniches'k *109 F4 Rus.* Genichesk.
 Khersons'ka Oblast', S Ukraine

Hennebont 90 A3 Morbihan, NW France

Henzada 136 B4 Irrawaddy, SW Myanmar

Herakleion see Irákleio

Herāt 122 D4 var. Herat; anc. Aria. Herāt, W Afghanistan

Herat see Herāt

Heredia 53 E4 Heredia, C Costa Rica

Hereford 49 E2 Texas, SW USA

Herford 94 B4 Nordrhein-Westfalen, NW Germany

Herk-de-Stad 87 C6 Limburg, NE Belgium

Hermansverk 85 A5 Sogn Og Fjordane, S Norway

Hermhausen see Hajnówka

Hermiston 46 C2 Oregon, NW USA

Hermon, Mount 119 B5 Ar. Jabal ash Shaykh. Mountain S Syria

Hermosillo 50 B2 Sonora, NW Mexico

Hermoupolis see Ermoúpoli

Hernösand see Härnösand

Herrera del Duque 92 D3 Extremadura, W Spain

Herselt 87 C5 Antwerpen, C Belgium

Herstal 87 D6 Fr. Héristal. Liège, E Belgium

Hessen 95 B5 cultural region C Germany

Hevron see Hebron

Heydebrech see Kędzierzyn-Kole

Heywood Islands 146 C3 island group Western Australia

Hibbing 45 F1 Minnesota, N USA

Hidalgo del Parral 50 C2 var. Parral. Chihuahua, N Mexico

Hida-sanmyaku 131 C5 mountain range Honshū, S Japan

Hierro 70 A3 var. Ferro. Island Islas Canarias, Spain, NE Atlantic Ocean

High Plains see Great Plains

High Point 43 E1 North Carolina, SE USA

High Veld see Great Karoo

Hiiumaa 106 C2 Ger. Dagden, Swe. Dagö. Island W Estonia

Hikurangi 150 D2 Northland, North Island, NZ

Hildesheim 94 B4 Niedersachsen, N Germany

Hilla see Al Ḥillah

Hillaby, Mount 55 G1 mountain N Barbados

Hill Bank 52 C1 Orange Walk, N Belize

Hillegom 86 C3 Zuid-Holland, W Netherlands

Hilo 47 B8 Hawaii, USA, C Pacific Ocean

Hilton Head Island 43 E2 South Carolina, SE USA

Hilversum 86 C3 Noord-Holland, C Netherlands

Himalaya see Himalayas

Himalayas 135 E2 var. Himalaya, Chin. Himalaya Shan. Mountain range S Asia

Himalaya Shan see Himalayas

Himeji 131 C6 var. Himezi. Hyōgo, Honshū, SW Japan

Himezi see Himeji

Ḥimṣ 118 B4 var. Homs; anc. Emesa. Ḥimṣ, C Syria

Hînceşti 108 D4 var. Hâncești; prev. Kotovsk. C Moldova

Hinchinbrook Island 148 D3 island Queensland, NE Australia

Hinds 151 C6 Canterbury, South Island, NZ

Hindu Kush 123 F4 Per. Hendū Kosh. Mountain range Afghanistan/Pakistan

Hinesville 43 E3 Georgia, SE USA

Hinnøya 84 C3 island C Norway

Hinson Bay 42 A5 bay W Bermuda

Hios see Chíos

Hirosaki 130 D3 Aomori, Honshū, C Japan

Hiroshima 131 B6 var. Hirosima. Hiroshima, Honshū, SW Japan

Hirosima see Hiroshima

Hirson 90 D3 Aisne, N France

Hispaniola 56 B1 island Dominion Republic/Haiti

Hitachi 131 D5 var. Hitati. Ibaraki, Honshū, S Japan

Hitati see Hitachi

Hitra 84 A4 prev. Hitteren. Island S Norway

Hjälmaren 85 C6 Eng. Lake Hjalmar. Lake C Sweden

Hjørring 85 B7 Nordjylland, N Denmark

Hkakabo Razi 136 B1 mountain Myanmar/China

Hlobyne 109 F2 Rus. Globino. Poltavs'ka Oblast', NE Ukraine

Hlukhiv 109 F1 Rus. Glukhov. Sums'ka Oblast', NE Ukraine

Hlybokaye 107 D5 Rus. Glubokoye. Vitsyebskaya Voblasts', N Belarus

Hoa Binh 136 D3 Hoa Binh, N Vietnam

Hoang Liên Son 136 D3 mountain range N Vietnam

Hobart 149 C8 prev. Hobarton, Hobart Town. State capital Tasmania, SE Australia

Hobbs 49 E3 New Mexico, SW USA

Hobro 85 A7 Nordjylland, N Denmark

Hô Chi Minh 137 E6 var. Ho Chi Minh City; prev. Saigon. S Vietnam

Ho Chi Minh City see Hô Chi Minh

Hódmezővásárhely 99 D7 Csongrád, SE Hungary

Hodna, Chott El 118 C4 var. Chott el-Hodna, Ar. Shatt al-Hodna. Salt lake N Algeria

Hodonín 99 C5 Ger. Göding. Brněnský Kraj, SE Czech Republic

Hoë Karoo see Great Karoo

Hof 95 C5 Bayern, SE Germany

Hofei see Hefei

Hōfu 131 B7 Yamaguchi, Honshū, SW Japan

Hofuf see Al Hufūf

Hogoley Islands see Chuuk Islands

Hohe Tauern 95 C7 mountain range W Austria

Hohhot 127 F3 var. Huhehot, Huhuohaote, Mong. Kukukhoto; prev. Kweisui, Kwesui. Nei Mongol Zizhiqu, N China

Hôi An 137 E5 prev. Faifo. Quang Nam-Đa Nãng, C Vietnam

Hoï-Hao see Haikou

Hoihow see Haikou

Hokianga Harbour 150 C2 inlet SE Tasman Sea

Hokitika 151 B5 West Coast, South Island, NZ

Hokkaidō 130 C2 prev. Ezo, Yeso, Yezo. Island NE Japan

Hola Prystan' 109 E4 Rus. Golaya Pristan. Khersons'ka Oblast', S Ukraine

Holbrook 48 B2 Arizona, SW USA

Holetown 55 G1 prev. Jamestown. W Barbados

Holguín 54 C2 Holguín, SE Cuba

Hollabrunn 95 E6 Niederösterreich, NE Austria

Hollandia see Jayapura

Holly Springs 42 C1 Mississippi, S USA

Holman 37 E3 Victoria Island, Northwest Territories, N Canada

Holmsund 84 D4 Västerbotten, N Sweden

Holon 119 A6 var. Kholon. Tel Aviv, C Israel

Holovanivs'k 109 E3 Rus. Golovanevsk. Kirovohrads'ka Oblast', C Ukraine

Holstebro 85 A7 Ringkøbing, W Denmark

Holsteinborg see Sisimiut

Holsteinsborg see Sisimiut

Holstenborg see Sisimiut

Holstensborg see Sisimiut

Holyhead 89 C5 Wel. Caer Gybi. NW Wales, UK

Hombori 75 E3 Mopti, S Mali

Homs see Al Khums

Homs see Ḥimṣ

Homyel' 107 D7 Rus. Gomel'. Homyel'skaya Voblasts', SE Belarus

Honan see Henan

Honan see Luoyang

Hondo see Honshū

Hondo 49 F4 Texas, SW USA

Honduras 52 C2 Country Central America

Honduras 52

Official name Republic of Honduras
Formation 1838
Capital Tegucigalpa
Population 6.6 million / 153 people per sq mile (59 people per sq km)
Total area 43,278 sq miles (112,090 sq km)
Languages Spanish, Black Carib, English Creole
Religions Roman Catholic 97%, Protestant minority 3%
Ethnic mix Mestizo 90%, Black African 5%, Amerindian 4%, White 1%
Government Presidential democracy
Currency Lempira = 100 centavos
Literacy rate 74.6%
Calorie consumption 2,395 kilocalories

Honduras, Gulf of 52 C2 Sp. Golfo de Honduras. Gulf W Caribbean Sea

Honefoss 85 B6 Buskerud, S Norway

Honey Lake 47 B5 lake California, W USA

Hon Gai see Hông Gai

Hongay see Hông Gai

Hông Gai 136 E3 var. Hon Gai, Hongay. Quang Ninh, N Vietnam

Hong Kong 128 A1 China. Xianggang, S China

Hong Kong Island 128 B2 Chin. Xianggang. Island S China

Honiara 144 C3 country capital (Solomon Islands) Guadalcanal, C Solomon Islands

Honjō 130 D4 var. Honzyô. Akita, Honshū, C Japan

Honolulu 47 A8 admin capital Oahu, Hawaii, USA, C Pacific Ocean

Honshū 131 E5 var. Hondo, Honsyû. Island SW Japan

Honsyû see Honshū

Honzyô see Honjō

Hoogeveen 86 E2 Drenthe, NE Netherlands

Hoogezand-Sappemeer 86 E2 Groningen, NE Netherlands

Hoorn 86 C2 Noord-Holland, NW Netherlands

Hopa 117 E2 Artvin, NE Turkey

Hope 36 C3 British Columbia, SW Canada

Hopedale 39 F2 Newfoundland and Labrador, NE Canada

Hopeh see Hebei

Hopei see Hebei

Hopkinsville 40 B5 Kentucky, S USA

Horasan 117 F3 Erzurum, NE Turkey

Horizon Deep 152 D4 undersea feature W Pacific Ocean

Horki 107 E6 Rus. Gorki. Mahilyowskaya Voblasts', E Belarus

Horlivka 109 G3 Rom. Adâncata, Rus. Gorlovka. Donets'ka Oblast', E Ukraine

Hormuz, Strait of 120 D4 var. Strait of Ormuz, Per. Tangeh-ye Hormoz. Strait Iran/Oman

Hornos, Cabo de 65 C8 Eng. Cape Horn. Headland S Chile

Hornsby 148 E1 New South Wales, SE Australia

Horodnya 109 E1 Rus. Gorodnya. Chernihivs'ka Oblast', NE Ukraine

Horodyshche 109 E2 Rus. Gorodishche. Cherkas'ka Oblast', C Ukraine

Horokhiv 108 B2 Pol. Gródek Jagielloński, Rus. Gorodok, Gorodok Yagellonski. L'vivs'ka Oblast', NW Ukraine

Horoshiri-dake 130 D2 var. Horosiri Dake. Mountain Hokkaidō, N Japan

Horosiri Dake see Horoshiri-dake

Horsburgh Atoll 132 A4 atoll N Maldives

Horseshoe Bay 42 A5 bay W Bermuda

Horseshoe Seamounts 80 A4 undersea feature E Atlantic Ocean

Horsham 149 B7 Victoria, SE Australia

Horst 87 D5 Limburg, SE Netherlands

Horten 85 B6 Vestfold, S Norway

Horyn' 107 B7 Rus. Goryn. River NW Ukraine

Hosingen 87 D7 Diekirch, NE Luxembourg

Hospitalet see L'Hospitalet de Llobregat

Hotan 126 B4 var. Khotan, Chin. Ho-t'ien. Xinjiang Uygur Zizhiqu, NW China

Ho-t'ien see Hotan

Hoting 84 C4 Jämtland, C Sweden

Hot Springs 42 B1 Arkansas, C USA

Houayxay 136 C3 var. Ban Houayxay, Ban Houei Sai. Bokèo, N Laos

Houghton 40 B1 Michigan, N USA

Houilles 91 B5 Yvelines, N France

Houlton 41 H1 Maine, NE USA

Houma 42 B3 Louisiana, S USA

Houston 49 H4 Texas, SW USA

Hovd 126 C2 var. Khovd. Hovd, W Mongolia

Hove 89 E7 SE England, UK

Hoverla, Hora 108 C3 Rus. Gora Goverla. Mountain W Ukraine

Hovsgol, Lake see Hövsgöl Nuur

Hövsgöl Nuur 126 D1 var. Lake Hovsgol. Lake N Mongolia

Howar, Wādi 72 A3 var. Ouadi Howa. River Chad/Sudan see also Howa, Ouadi

Hoy 88 C2 island N Scotland, UK

Hoyerswerda 94 D4 Sachsen, E Germany

Hradec Králové 99 B5 Ger. Königgrätz. Hradecký Kraj, N Czech Republic

Hrandzichy 107 B5 Rus. Grandichi. Hrodzyenskaya Voblasts', W Belarus

Hranice 99 C5 Ger. Mährisch-Weisskirchen. Olomoucký Kraj, E Czech Republic

Hrebinka 109 E2 Rus. Grebenka. Poltavs'ka Oblast', NE Ukraine

Hrodna 107 B5 Pol. Grodno. Hrodzyenskaya Voblasts', W Belarus

Hsia-men see Xiamen

Hsiang-t'an see Xiangtan

Hsi Chiang see Xi Jiang

Hsing-k'ai Hu see Khanka, Lake

Hsining see Xining

Hsinking see Changchun

Hsin-yang see Xinyang

Hsu-chou see Xuzhou

Huacho 60 C4 Lima, W Peru

Hua Hin see Ban Hua Hin

Huaihua 128 C5 Hunan, S China

Huailai 128 C3 prev. Shacheng. Hebei, E China

Huainan 128 D5 var. Huai-nan, Hwainan. Anhui, E China

Huai-nan see Huainan

Huajuapan 51 F5 var. Huajuapan de León. Oaxaca, SE Mexico

Huajuapan de León see Huajuapan

Hualapai Peak 48 A2 mountain Arizona, SW USA

Huallaga, Río 60 C2 river N Peru

Huambo 78 B2 Port. Nova Lisboa. Huambo, C Angola

Huancavelica 60 D4 Huancavelica, SW Peru

Huancayo 60 D3 Junín, C Peru

Huang He 128 C4 var. Yellow River. River C China

Huangshan 128 C5 var. Huang-shih, Hwangshih. Hubei, C China

Huang-shih see Huangshi

Huanta 60 D4 Ayacucho, C Peru

Huánuco 60 C3 Huánuco, C Peru
Huanuni 61 F4 Oruro, W Bolivia
Huaral 60 C4 Lima, W Peru
Huarás see Huaraz
Huaraz 60 C3 var. Huarás. Ancash,
W Peru
Huarmey 60 C3 Ancash, W Peru
Huatabampo 50 C2 Sonora,
NW Mexico
Hubli 124 B3 Karnātaka, SW India
Huddersfield 89 D5 N England,
UK
Hudiksvall 85 C5 Gävleborg,
C Sweden
Hudson Bay 37 G4 bay NE Canada
Hudson Strait 37 H3 Fr. Détroit
d'Hudson. Strait
Nunavut/Quebec, NE Canada
Hudur see Xuddur
Huê 136 E4 Thua Thiên-Huê,
C Vietnam
Huehuetenango 52 A2
Huehuetenango, W Guatemala
Huelva 92 C4 anc. Onuba.
Andalucía, SW Spain
Huesca 93 F2 anc. Osca. Aragón,
NE Spain
Huéscar 93 E4 Andalucía, S Spain
Hughenden 148 C3 Queensland,
NE Australia
Hugo 49 G2 Oklahoma, C USA
Huhehot see Hohhot
Huhuohaote see Hohhot
Huíla Plateau 78 B2 plateau
S Angola
Huixtla 51 G5 Chiapas, SE Mexico
Hukui see Fukui
Hukuoka see Fukuoka
Hukusima see Fukushima
Hulingol 127 G2 prev. Huolin Gol.
Nei Mongol Zizhiqu, N China
Hull see Kingston upon Hull
Hull 38 D4 Quebec, SE Canada
Hulst 87 B5 Zeeland,
SW Netherlands
Hulun see Hailar
Hu-lun Ch'ih see Hulun Nur
Hulun Nur 127 F1 var. Hu-lun Ch'ih;
prev. Dalai Nor. lake NE China
Humaitá 62 D2 Amazonas, N Brazil
Humboldt River 47 C5 river
Nevada, W USA
Humphreys Peak 48 B1 mountain
Arizona, SW USA
Humpolec 99 B5 Ger. Gumpolds,
Humpoletz. Jihlavský Kraj,
C Czech Republic
Hunan 128 C6 var. Hunan Sheng,
Xiang. Admin. region province
S China
Hunan ShEng see Xiang
Hunedoara 108 B4 Ger. Eisenmarkt,
Hung. Vajdahunyad. Hunedoara,
SW Romania
Hünfeld 95 B5 Hessen, C Germany
Hungary 99 C6 Ger. Ungarn, Hung.
Magyarország, Rom. Ungaria, SCr.
Mađarska, Ukr. Uhorshchyna;
prev. Hungarian People's
Republic. Country C Europe

Hungary 99

Official name Republic of Hungary
Formation 1918
Capital Budapest
Population 9.9 million / 276 people
per sq mile (106 people per sq km)
Total area 35,919 sq miles
(93,030 sq km)
Languages Hungarian
Religions Roman Catholic 64%,
Calvinist 20%, non-religious 7%,
Lutheran 4%, other 5%
Ethnic mix Magyar 90%, German
2%, Romany 1%, Slovak 1%,
other 6%
Government Parliamentary
democracy
Currency Forint = 100 filler
Literacy rate 99%
Calorie consumption 3,458
kilocaloriesi

Hungary, Plain of see Great
Hungarian Plain

Hunter Island 149 B8 island
Tasmania, SE Australia
Huntington 40 D4 West Virginia,
NE USA
Huntington Beach 47 B8 California,
W USA
Huntly 150 D3 Waikato, North
Island, NZ
Huntsville 42 D1 Alabama, S USA
Huntsville 49 G3 Texas, SW USA
Hurghada 72 C2 var. Al Ghurdaqah,
Ghurdaqah. E Egypt
Huron 45 E3 South Dakota, N USA
Huron, Lake 40 D2 lake
Canada/USA
Hurukawa see Furukawa
Hurunui 151 C5 river South Island,
NZ
Húsavík 83 E4 Nordhurland Eystra,
NE Iceland
Husum 94 B2 Schleswig-Holstein,
N Germany
Hutchinson 45 E5 Kansas, C USA
Hutchinson Island 43 F4 island
Florida, SE USA
Huy 87 C6 Dut. Hoei, Hoey. Liège,
E Belgium
Huzi see Fuji
Hvannadalshnúkur 83 E5 mountain
S Iceland
Hvar 100 B4 It. Lesina; anc. Pharus.
Island S Croatia
Hwainan see Huainan
Hwange 78 D3 prev. Wankie.
Matabeleland North,
W Zimbabwe
Hwangshih see Huangshi
Hyargas Nuur 126 C2 lake
NW Mongolia
Hyderābād 134 D5 var. Haidarabad.
Andhra Pradesh, C India
Hyderābād 134 B3 var. Haidarabad.
Sind, SE Pakistan
Hyères 91 D6 Var, SE France
Hyères, Îles d' 91 D6 island group
S France
Hypanis see Kuban'
Hyrcania see Gorgān
Hyvinkää 85 D5 Swe. Hyvinge.
Etelä-Suomi, S Finland

I

Ialomiţa 108 C5 river SE Romania
Iaşi 108 D3 Ger. Jassy. Iaşi,
NE Romania
Ibadan 75 F5 Oyo, SW Nigeria
Ibagué 58 B3 Tolima, C Colombia
Ibar 100 D4 Alb. Ibër. River C Serbia
and Montenegro (Yugo.)
Ibarra 60 B1 var. San Miguel de
Ibarra. Imbabura, N Ecuador
Iberian Mountains see Ibérico,
Sistema
Iberian Peninsula 80 B4 physical
region Portugal/Spain
Iberian Plain 80 B4 undersea feature
E Atlantic Ocean
Ibérico, Sistema 93 E2 var.
Cordillera Ibérica, Eng. Iberian
Mountains. Mountain range
NE Spain
Ibiza see Eivissa
Ibo see Sassandra
Ica 60 D4 Ica, SW Peru
Içá see Putumayo, Río
Icaria see Ikaría
Içá, Rio 62 C2 var. Río Putumayo.
River NW South America see also
Putumayo, Río
Iceland 83 E4 Dan. Island, Icel.
Ísland. Country N Atlantic Ocean

Iceland 83

Official name Republic of Iceland
Formation 1944
Capital Reykjavík
Population 281,000 /7 people per
sq mile (3 people per sq km)
Total area 39,768 sq miles
(103,000 sq km)
Languages Icelandic
Religions Evangelical Lutheran
93%, non-religious 6%, other
Christian 1%

Iceland (continued)

Ethnic mix Icelandic 94%, Danish
1%, other 5%
Government Parliamentary
democracy
Currency Icelandic króna = 100
aurar
Literacy rate 99%
Calorie consumption 3,342
kilocalories

Iceland Basin 80 B1 undersea feature
N Atlantic Ocean
Icelandic Plateau see Iceland
Plateau
Iceland Plateau 172 B5 var.
Icelandic Plateau. Undersea feature
S Greenland Sea
Iconium see Konya
Idabel 49 H2 Oklahoma, C USA
Idaho 46 D3 off. State of Idaho; also
known as Gem of the Mountains,
Gem State. State NW USA
Idaho Falls 46 E3 Idaho, NW USA
Idensalmi see Iisalmi
Idfu 72 B2 var. Edfu. SE Egypt
Ídhra see Ýdra
Idi Amin, Lac see Edward, Lake
Idini 74 B2 Trarza, W Mauritania
Idlib 118 B3 Idlib, NW Syria
Idre 85 B5 Kopparberg, C Sweden
Iecava 106 C3 Bauska, S Latvia
Ieper 87 A6 Fr. Ypres. West-
Vlaanderen, W Belgium
Ierápetra 105 D8 Kriti, Greece,
E Mediterranean Sea
Ierisós see Ierissós
Ierissós 104 C4 var. Ierisós. Kentrikí
Makedonía, N Greece
Iferouâne 75 G2 Agadez, N Niger
Ifôghas, Adrar des 75 E2 var. Adrar
des Iforas. Mountain range NE Mali
Igarka 114 D3 Krasnoyarskiy Kray,
N Russian Federation
Iglesias 97 A5 Sardegna, Italy,
C Mediterranean Sea
Igloolik 37 G2 Nunavut,
N Canada
Igoumenítsa 104 A4 Ípeiros,
W Greece
Iguaçu, Rio 63 E4 Sp. Río Iguazú.
River Argentina/Brazil see also
Iguazú, Río
Iguaçu, Salto do 63 E4 Sp. Cataratas
del Iguazú; prev. Victoria Falls.
Waterfall Argentina/Brazil see also
Iguazú, Cataratas del
Iguala 51 E4 var. Iguala de la
Independencia. Guerrero, S Mexico
Iguala de la Independencia see
Iguala
Iguïdi, 'Erg 70 C3 var. Erg Iguid.
Desert Algeria/Mauritania
Ihavandiffulu Atoll see
Ihavandippolhu Atoll
Ihavandippolhu Atoll 132 A3 var.
Ihavandiffulu Atoll. Atoll
N Maldives
Ihosy 79 F4 Fianarantsoa,
S Madagascar
IJmuiden 86 C3 Noord-Holland, W
Netherlands
Iisalmi 84 E4 var. Idensalmi. Itä-
Suomi, C Finland
IJssel 86 D3 var. Yssel. River
Netherlands/Germany
IJsselmeer 86 C2 prev. Zuider Zee.
Lake N Netherlands
IJsselmuiden 86 D3 Overijssel,
E Netherlands
Ijzer 87 A6 river W Belgium
Ikaría 105 D6 var. Kariot, Nicaria,
Nikaria; anc. Icaria. Island
Dodekánisos, Greece, Aegean Sea
Ikela 77 D6 Equateur, C Dem. Rep.
Congo
Iki 131 A7 island SW Japan
Ilagan 139 E1 Luzon, N Philippines
Ilave 61 E4 Puno, S Peru
Iława 98 D3 Ger. Deutsch-Eylau.
Warmińsko-Mazurskie, NE
Poland
Ilebo 77 C6 prev. Port-Francqui.
Kasai Occidental, W Dem. Rep.
Congo

Île-de-France 90 C3 cultural region
N France
Îles de la Société see Société,
Archipel de la
Îles Tubuai see Australes, Îles
Ilfracombe 89 C7 SW England, UK
Ilha Caviana see Caviana de Fora,
Ilha
Ilha de Madeira see Madeira
Ilha do Corvo see Corvo
Ilha do Faial see Faial
Ilha do Pico see Pico
Ilha do Porto Santo see Porto Santo
Ilha Graciosa see Graciosa
Ilhas dos Açores see Azores
Ilha Terceira see Terceira
Ílhavo 92 B2 Aveiro, N Portugal
Ili 112 C3 Kaz. Ile, Rus. Reka Ili.
River China/Kazakhstan
Iliamna Lake 36 C3 lake Alaska,
USA
Ilici see Elche
Iligan 139 E2 off. Iligan City.
Mindanao, S Philippines
Illapel 64 B4 Coquimbo, C Chile
Illichivs'k 109 E4 Rus. Il'ichevsk.
Odes'ka Oblast', SW Ukraine
Illicis see Elche
Illinois 40 A4 off. State of Illinois;
also known as Prairie State,
Sucker State. State C USA
Illinois River 40 B4 river Illinois,
C USA
Ilo 61 E4 Moquegua, SW Peru
Iloilo 139 E2 off. Iloilo City. Panay
Island, C Philippines
Ilorin 75 F4 Kwara, W Nigeria
Îlots de Bass see Marotiri
Ilovlya 111 B6 Volgogradskaya
Oblast', SW Russian Federation
Iluh see Batman
Il'yaly 122 C2 var. Yylanly.
Dashkhovuzskiy Velayat,
N Turkmenistan
Imatra 85 E5 Etelä-Suomi,
S Finland
Imbros see Gökçeada
Imişli 117 H3 Rus. Imishli.
C Azerbaijan
Imola 96 C3 Emilia-Romagna,
N Italy
Imperatriz 63 F2 Maranhão,
NE Brazil
Imperia 96 A3 Liguria, NW Italy
Impfondo 77 C5 La Likouala,
NE Congo
Imphāl 135 H3 Manipur, NE India
Imroz Adası see Gökçeada
Inagua Islands see Great Inagua
Inagua Islands see Little Inagua
Inarijärvi 84 D2 Lapp. Aanaarjävri,
Swe. Enareträsk. Lake N Finland
Inawashiro-ko 131 D5 var.
Inawasiro Ko. Lake Honshū,
C Japan
Inawasiro Ko see Inawashiro-ko
Íncesu 116 D3 Kayseri, C Turkey
Inch'ŏn 129 E4 off. Inch'ŏn-
gwangyŏksi, Jap. Jinsen; prev.
Chemulpo. NW South Korea
Incudine, Monte 91 E7 mountain
Corse, France, C Mediterranean
Sea
Indefatigable Island see Santa
Cruz, Isla
Independence 45 F4 Missouri,
C USA
Independence Fjord 83 E1 fjord
N Greenland
Independence Mountains 46 C4
mountain range Nevada, NW USA
India 124 B3 var. Indian Union,
Union of India, Hind. Bhārat.
Country S Asia

India 124

Official name Republic of India
Formation 1947
Capital New Delhi
Population 1.03 billion / 790 people
per sq mile (305 people per sq km)
Total area 1,269,339 sq miles
(3,287,590 sq km)
Languages Hindi, English, and 16
regional languages

India (continued)

Religions Hindu 83%, Muslim 11%, Christian 2%, Sikh 2%, other 2%
Ethnic mix Indo-Aryan 72%, Dravidian 25%, Mongoloid and other 3%
Government Parliamentary democracy
Currency Indian rupee = 100 paisa
Literacy rate 57.2%
Calorie consumption 2,428 kilocalories

Indiana 40 B4 *off.* State of Indiana; also known as The Hoosier State. *State* N USA
Indianapolis 40 C4 *state capital* Indiana, N USA
Indian Church 52 C1 Orange Walk, N Belize
Indian Desert *see* Thar Desert
Indianola 45 F4 Iowa, C USA
Indigirka 115 F2 *river* NE Russian Federation
Indija 100 D3 Hung. India; *prev.* Indjija. Serbia, N Serbia and Montenegro (Yugo.)
Indira Point 132 G3 *headland* Andaman and Nicobar Islands, India, NE Indian Ocean
Indomed Fracture Zone 141 B6 *tectonic feature* SW Indian Ocean
Indonesia 138 B4 *Ind.* Republik Indonesia; *prev.* Dutch East Indies, Netherlands East Indies, United States of Indonesia. *Country* SE Asia

Indonesia 138

Official name Republic of Indonesia
Formation 1949
Capital Jakarta
Population 214 million / 289 people per sq mile (111 people per sq km)
Total area 741,096 sq miles (1,919,440 sq km)
Languages Bahasa Indonesia, Javanese, Madurese, Sundanese, Dutch
Religions Muslim 87%, Protestant 6%, Roman Catholic 3%, other 4%
Ethnic mix Javanese 45%, Sundanese 14%, Coastal Malays 8%, Madurese 8%, other 25%
Government Multiparty republic
Currency Rupiah = 100 sen
Literacy rate 86.9%
Calorie consumption 2,902 kilocalories

Indore 134 D4 Madhya Pradesh, C India
Indus 134 C2 Chin. Yindu He; *prev.* Yin-tu Ho. *River* S Asia
Indus Cone *see* Indus Fan
Indus Fan 112 C5 *var.* Indus Cone. *Undersea feature* N Arabian Sea
Indus, Mouths of the 134 B4 *delta* S Pakistan
Inebolu 116 C2 Kastamonu, N Turkey
Ineu 108 A4 Hung. Borosjenő; *prev.* Ináu. Arad, W Romania
Infiernillo, Presa del 51 E4 *reservoir* S Mexico
Inglewood 46 D2 California, W USA
Ingolstadt 95 C6 Bayern, S Germany
Inhambane 79 E4 Inhambane, SE Mozambique
Inhulets' 109 F3 Rus. Ingulets. Dnipropetrovs'ka Oblast', E Ukraine
I-ning *see* Yining
Inis *see* Ennis
Inis Ceithleann *see* Enniskillen
Inn 95 C6 *river* C Europe
Innaanganeq 82 C1 *var.* Kap York. *Headland* NW Greenland

Inner Hebrides 88 B4 *island group* W Scotland, UK
Inner Islands 79 H1 *var.* Central Group. *Island group* NE Seychelles
Inner Mongolia 127 F3 *var.* Nei Mongol, *Eng.* Inner Mongolia, Inner Mongolian Autonomous Region; *prev.* Nei Monggol Zizhiqu. Admin. region *autonomous region* N China
Inner Mongolian Autonomous Region *see* Inner Mongolia
Innisfail 148 D3 Queensland, NE Australia
Inniskilling *see* Enniskillen
Innsbruck *see* Innsbruck
Innsbruck 95 C7 *var.* Innsbruck. Tirol, W Austria
Inoucdjouac *see* Inukjuak
Inowrocław 98 C3 Ger. Hohensalza; *prev.* Inowrazlaw. Kujawski-pomorskie, C Poland
I-n-Salah 70 D3 *var.* In Salah. C Algeria
In Salah *see* I-n-Salah
Insula *see* Lille
Inta 110 E3 Respublika Komi, NW Russian Federation
International Falls 45 F1 Minnesota, N USA
Inukjuak 38 D2 *var.* Inoucdjouac; *prev.* Port Harrison. Quebec, NE Canada
Inuuvik *see* Inuvik
Inuvik 36 D3 *var.* Inuuvik. *District capital* Northwest Territories, NW Canada
Invercargill 151 A7 Southland, South Island, NZ
Inverness 88 C3 N Scotland, UK
Investigator Ridge 141 D5 *undersea feature* E Indian Ocean
Investigator Strait 149 B7 *strait* South Australia
Inyangani 78 D3 *mountain* NE Zimbabwe
Ioánnina 104 A4 *var.* Janina, Yannina. Ípeiros, W Greece
Iola 45 F5 Kansas, C USA
Ionia Basin *see* Ionian Basin
Ionian Basin 80 D5 *var.* Ionia Basin. *Undersea feature* Ionian Sea, C Mediterranean Sea
Ionian Islands *see* Iónioi Nísoi
Ionian Sea 103 E3 Gk. Iónio Pélagos, It. Mar Ionio. *Sea* C Mediterranean Sea
Iónioi Nísoi 105 A5 Eng. Ionian Islands. *Island group* W Greece
Íos 105 D6 *var.* Nio. Island Kykládes, Greece, Aegean Sea
Íos 105 D6 Íos, Kykládes, Greece, Aegean Sea
Iowa 45 F3 *off.* State of Iowa; also known as The Hawkeye State. *State* C USA
Iowa City 45 G3 Iowa, C USA
Iowa Falls 45 G3 Iowa, C USA
Ipel' 99 C6 *var.* Ipoly, Ger. Eipel. *River* Hungary/Slovakia
Ipiales 58 A4 Nariño, SW Colombia
Ipoh 138 B3 Perak, Peninsular Malaysia
Ipoly 99 C6 *var.* Ipel', Ger. Eipel. *River* Hungary/Slovakia
Ippy 76 C4 Ouaka, C Central African Republic
Ipswich 89 E6 hist. Gipeswic. E England, UK
Ipswich 149 E5 Queensland, E Australia
Iqaluit 37 H3 prev. Frobisher Bay. Baffin Island, Nunavut, NE Canada
Iquique 64 B1 Tarapacá, N Chile
Iquitos 60 C1 Loreto, N Peru
Irákleio 105 D7 *var.* Herakleion, Eng. Candia; *prev.* Iráklion. Kríti, Greece, E Mediterranean Sea
Iráklion *see* Irákleio
Iran 120 C3 *prev.* Persia. *Country* SW Asia

Iran 120

Official name Islamic Republic of Iran
Formation 1502
Capital Tehran
Population 71.4 million / 112 people per sq mile (43 people per sq km)
Total area 636,406 sq miles (1,648,293 sq km)
Languages Farsi, Azeri, Gilaki, Baluchi, Mazanderani, Kurdish, Arabic
Religions Shi'a Muslim 95%, Sunni Muslim 4%, other 1%
Ethnic mix Persian 50%, Azeri 24%, Lur and Bakhtiari 8%, Kurd 8%, other 10%
Government Islamic theocracy
Currency Iranian rial = 100 dinars
Literacy rate 76.8%
Calorie consumption 2,913 kilocalories

Iranian Plateau 120 D3 *var.* Plateau of Iran. *plateau* N Iran
Iran, Plateau of *see* Iranian Plateau
Irapuato 51 E4 Guanajuato, C Mexico
Iraq 120 B3 Ar. 'Irāq. *Country* SW Asia

Iraq 120

Official name Republic of Iraq
Formation 1932
Capital Baghdad
Population 23.6 million / 140 people per sq mile (54 people per sq km)
Total area 168,753 sq miles (437,072 sq km)
Languages Arabic, Kurdish, Armenian, Assyrian, Turkic languages
Religions Shi'a ithna Muslim 62%, Sunni Muslim 33%, other 5%
Ethnic mix Arab 79%, Kurdish 16%, Persian 3%, Turkman 2%
Government One-party republic
Currency Iraqi dinar = 1,000 fils
Literacy rate 55.9%
Calorie consumption 2,197 kilocalories

Irbid 119 B5 Irbid, N Jordan
Irbil *see* Arbil
Ireland 80 C3 Lat. Hibernia. *Island* Ireland/UK
Ireland, Republic of 89 A5 *var.* Ireland, *Ir.* Éire. *Country* NW Europe

Ireland 89

Official name Ireland
Formation 1922
Capital Dublin
Population 3.8 million / 140 people per sq mile (54 people per sq km)
Total area 27,135 sq miles (70,280 sq km)
Languages English, Irish Gaelic
Religions Roman Catholic 88%, Anglican 3%, other and non-religious 9%
Ethnic mix Irish 95%, other 5%
Government Parliamentary democracy
Currency Euro (Punt until 2002)
Literacy rate 99%
Calorie consumption 3,613 kilocalories

Irian Barat *see* Papua
Irian Jaya *see* Papua
Irian, Teluk *see* Cenderawasih, Teluk
Iringa 73 C7 Iringa, C Tanzania
Iriomote-jima 130 A4 *island* Sakishima-shotō, SW Japan
Iriona 52 D2 Colón, NE Honduras

Irish Sea 89 C5 Ir. Muir Éireann. *Sea* C British Isles
Irkutsk 115 E4 Irkutskaya Oblast', S Russian Federation
Irminger Basin *see* Reykjanes Basin
Iroise 90 A3 *sea* NW France
Iron Mountain 40 B2 Michigan, N USA
Ironwood 40 B1 Michigan, N USA
Irrawaddy 136 B2 *var.* Ayeyarwady. *River* W Myanmar
Irrawaddy, Mouths of the 137 A5 *delta* SW Myanmar
Irtish *see* Irtysh
Irtysh 114 C4 *var.* Irtish, *Kaz.* Ertis. *River* C Asia
Irún 93 E1 País Vasco, N Spain
Iruña *see* Pamplona
Isabela, Isla 60 A5 *var.* Albemarle Island. *Island* Galapagos Islands, Ecuador, E Pacific Ocean
Isaccea 108 D4 Tulcea, E Romania
Isachsen 37 F1 Ellef Ringnes Island, Nunavut, N Canada
Isafjördhur 83 E4 Vestfirdhir, NW Iceland
Isbarta *see* Isparta
Ise 131 C6 Mie, Honshū, SW Japan
Isère 91 D5 *river* E France
Isernia 97 D5 *var.* Æsernia. Molise, C Italy
Ise-wan 131 C6 *bay* S Japan
Isha Baydhabo *see* Baydhabo
Ishigaki-jima 130 A4 *var.* Isigaki Zima. *Island* Sakishima-shotō, SW Japan
Ishikari-wan 130 C2 *bay* Hokkaidō, NE Japan
Ishim 114 C4 Kaz. Esil. *River* Kazakhstan/Russian Federation
Ishim 114 C4 Tyumenskaya Oblast', C Russian Federation
Ishinomaki 130 D4 *var.* Isinomaki. Miyagi, Honshū, C Japan
Ishkoshim 123 F3 Rus. Ishkashim. S Tajikistan
Isigaki Zima *see* Ishigaki-jima
Isinomaki *see* Ishinomaki
Isiro 77 E5 Orientale, NE Dem. Rep. Congo
Iskãr *see* Iskŭr
İskenderun 116 D4 Eng. Alexandretta. Hatay, S Turkey
İskenderun Körfezi 118 A2 Eng. Gulf of Alexandretta. *Gulf* S Turkey
Iskŭr 104 C2 *var.* Iskãr. *River* NW Bulgaria
Iskŭr, Yazovir 104 B2 prev. Yazovir Stalin. *Reservoir* W Bulgaria
Isla Cristina 92 C4 Andalucía, S Spain
Isla Gran Malvina *see* West Falkland
Islāmābād 134 C1 *country capital* (Pakistan) Federal Capital Territory Islāmābād, NE Pakistan
I-n-Sâkâne, 'Erg 75 E2 desert N Mali
Islas de los Galápagos *see* Galapagos Islands
Islas Malvinas *see* Falkland Islands
Islay 88 B4 island SW Scotland, UK
Isle 91 B5 river W France
Isle of Man 89 B5 UK crown dependency NW Europe
Ismailia *see* Ismâ'ilîya
Ismâ'ilîya 72 B1 var. Ismailia. N Egypt
Ismid *see* İzmit
Isna 72 B2 var. Esna. SE Egypt
Isoka 78 D1 Northern, NE Zambia
Isola Grossa *see* Dugi Otok
Isola Lunga *see* Dugi Otok
Isole Lipari *see* Eolie, Isole
Isparta 116 B4 var. Isbarta. Isparta, SW Turkey
İspir 117 E3 Erzurum, NE Turkey
Israel 119 A7 var. Medinat Israel, *Heb.* Yisrael, Yisra'el. *Country* SW Asia

Israel 119

Official name State of Israel
Formation 1948
Capital Jerusalem

Israel (continued)

Population 6.2 million / 773 people per sq mile (305 people per sq km)
Total area 8,019 sq miles (20,770 sq km)
Languages Hebrew, Arabic, Yiddish, German, Russian, Polish, Romanian, Persian
Religions Jewish 82%, Muslim (mainly Sunni) 14%, other (including Druze) 4%
Ethnic mix Jewish 82%, other (mostly Arab) 18%
Government Parliamentary democracy
Currency Shekel = 100 agorot
Literacy rate 96%
Calorie consumption 3,562 kilocalories

Issiq Köl *see* Issyk-Kul', Ozero
Issoire *91 C5* Puy-de-Dôme, C France
Issyk-Kul', Ozero *123 G2 var.* Issiq Köl, *Kir.* Ysyk-Köl. *Lake* E Kyrgyzstan
İstanbul *116 B2 Bul.* Tsarigrad, *Eng.* Istanbul; *prev.* Constantinople, *anc.* Byzantium. Istanbul, NW Turkey
İstanbul Boğazı *116 B2 var.* Bosporus Thracius, *Eng.* Bosphorus, Bosporus, *Turk.* Karadeniz Boğazı. *Strait* NW Turkey
Istra *100 A3 Eng.* Istria, *Ger.* Istrien. *Cultural region* NW Croatia
Istra *96 D2 Eng.* Istria. *Peninsula* NW Croatia
Itabuna *63 G3* Bahia, E Brazil
Itagüí *58 B3* Antioquia, W Colombia
Itaipú, Represa de *63 E4 reservoir* Brazil/Paraguay
Itaituba *63 E2* Pará, NE Brazil**Italy** *96 C3 It.* Italia, Republica Italiana. *Country* S Europe
Italy *96 C3 It.* Italia, Republica Italiana. *Country* S Europe

Italy 96

Official name Italian Republic
Formation 1861
Capital Rome
Population 57.5 million /494 people per sq mile (191 people per sq km)
Total area 116,305 sq miles (301,230 sq km)
Languages Italian, German, French, Rhaeto-Romanic, Sardinian
Religions Roman Catholic 83%, other and non-religious 17%
Ethnic mix Italian 94%, Sardinian 2%, other 4%
Government Parliamentary democracy
Currency Euro (Italian lira until 2002)
Literacy rate 98.4%
Calorie consumption 3,661 kilocalories

Italy *80 D4* Texas, SW USA
Iténez, Río *see* Guaporé, Rio
Ithaca *41 E3* New York, NE USA
Itoigawa *131 C5* Niigata, Honshū, C Japan
Itseqqortoormiit *see* Ittoqqortoormiit
Ittoqqortoormiit *83 E3 var.* Itseqqortoormiit, *Dan.* Scoresbysund, *Eng.* Scoresby Sound. C Greenland
Iturup, Ostrov *130 E1 island* Kuril'skiye Ostrova, SE Russian Federation
Itzehoe *94 B2* Schleswig-Holstein, N Germany
Ivalo *84 D2 Lapp.* Avveel, Avvil. Lappi, N Finland
Ivanava *107 B7* Pol. Janów, Janów Poleski, *Rus.* Ivanovo. Brestskaya Voblasts', SW Belarus

Ivanhoe *149 C6* New South Wales, SE Australia
Ivano-Frankivs'k *108 C2 Ger.* Stanislau, *Pol.* Stanisławów, *Rus.* Ivano-Frankovsk; *prev.* Stanislav. Ivano-Frankivs'ka Oblast', W Ukraine
Ivanovo *111 B5* Ivanovskaya Oblast', W Russian Federation
Ivatsevichy *107 B6 Pol.* Iwacewicze, *Rus.* Ivantsevichi, Ivatsevichi. Brestskaya Voblasts', SW Belarus
Ivigtut *see* Ivittuut
Ivittuut *82 B4 var.* Ivigtut. S Greenland
Iviza *see* Eivissa
Ivory Coast *see* Côte d'Ivoire
Ivujivik *38 D1* Quebec, NE Canada
Iwaki *131 D5* Fukushima, Honshū, N Japan
Iwakuni *131 B7* Yamaguchi, Honshū, SW Japan
Iwanai *130 C2* Hokkaidō, NE Japan
Iwate *130 D3* Iwate, Honshū, N Japan
Ixtapa *51 E5* Guerrero, S Mexico
Ixtepec *51 F5* Oaxaca, SE Mexico
Iyo-nada *131 B7 sea* S Japan
Izabal, Lago de *52 B2 prev.* Golfo Dulce. *Lake* E Guatemala
İzad Khvāst *120 D3* Fārs, C Iran
Izegem *87 A6 prev.* Iseghem. West-Vlaanderen, W Belgium
Izhevsk *111 D5 prev.* Ustinov. Udmurtskaya Respublika, NW Russian Federation
Izmail *108 D4 Rus.* Izmail. Odes'ka Oblast', SW Ukraine
İzmir *116 A3 prev.* Smyrna. İzmir, W Turkey
İzmit *116 B2 var.* Ismid; *anc.* Astacus. Kocaeli, NW Turkey
İznik Gölü *116 B3 lake* NW Turkey
Izu-hantō *131 D6 peninsula* Honshū, S Japan
Izu Shichito *see* Izu-shotō
Izu-shotō *131 D6 var.* Izu Shichito. *Island group* S Japan
Izvor *104 B2* Pernik, W Bulgaria
Izyaslav *108 C2* Khmel'nyts'ka Oblast', W Ukraine
Izyum *109 G2* Kharkivs'ka Oblast', E Ukraine

J

Jabal ash Shifā *120 A4 desert* NW Saudi Arabia
Jabalpur *135 E4 prev.* Jubbulpore. Madhya Pradesh, C India
Jabbūl, Sabkhat al *134 B2 salt flat* NW Syria
Jablah *118 A3 var.* Jeble, *Fr.* Djéblé. Al Lādhiqīyah, W Syria
Jaca *93 F1* Aragón, NE Spain
Jacaltenango *52 A2* Huehuetenango, W Guatemala
Jackson *42 B2 state capital* Mississippi, S USA
Jackson *45 H5* Missouri, C USA
Jackson *42 C1* Tennessee, S USA
Jackson Head *151 A6 headland* South Island, NZ
Jacksonville *43 E3* Florida, SE USA
Jacksonville *40 B4* Illinois, N USA
Jacksonville *43 F1* North Carolina, SE USA
Jacksonville *49 G3* Texas, SW USA
Jacmel *54 D3 var.* Jaquemel. S Haiti
Jacobābād *134 B3* Sind, SE Pakistan
Jaén *92 D4* Andalucía, SW Spain
Jaén *60 B2* Cajamarca, N Peru
Jaffna *132 D3* Northern Province, N Sri Lanka
Jagannath *see* Puri
Jagdalpur *135 E5* Madhya Pradesh, C India
Jagdaqi *127 G1* Nei Mongol Zizhiqu, N China
Jagodina *100 D4 prev.* Svetozarevo. Serbia, C Serbia and Montenegro (Yugo.)
Jahra *see* Al Jahrā'
Jaipur *134 D3 prev.* Jeypore. Rājasthān, N India
Jaisalmer *134 C3* Rājasthān, NW India

Jajce *100 B3* Federacija Bosna I Hercegovina, W Bosnia and Herzegovina
Jakarta *138 C5 prev.* Djakarta, *Dut.* Batavia. *Country capital* (Indonesia) Jawa, C Indonesia
Jakobstad *84 D4 Fin.* Pietarsaari. Länsi-Suomi, W Finland
Jalālābād *123 F4 var.* Jalalabad, Jelalabad. Nangarhār, E Afghanistan
Jalandhar *134 D2 prev.* Jullundur. Punjab, N India
Jalapa *see* Xalapa
Jalapa *52 D3* Nueva Segovia, NW Nicaragua
Jalapa Enríquez *see* Xalapa
Jalpa *50 D4* Zacatecas, C Mexico
Jālū *71 G3 var.* Jūlā. NE Libya
Jaluit Atoll *144 D2 var.* Jālwōj. *Atoll* Ralik Chain, S Marshall Islands
Jālwōj *see* Jaluit Atoll
Jamaame *73 D6 It.* Giamame; *prev.* Margherita. Jubbada Hoose, S Somalia
Jamaica *54 A4 country* W West Indies

Jamaica 54

Official name Jamaica
Formation 1962
Capital Kingston
Population 2.6 million / 613 people per sq mile (237 people per sq km)
Total area 4,243 sq miles (10,990 sq km)
Languages English, English Creole
Religions Christian (Church of God, Baptist, Anglican, other Protestant) 55%, other and non-religious 45%
Ethnic mix Black African 75%, Mulatto 13%, European and Chinese 11%, Indian 1%
Government Parliamentary democracy
Currency Jamaican dollar = 100 cents
Literacy rate 86.8%
Calorie consumption 2,693 kilocalories

Jamaica *56 A1 island* W West Indies
Jamaica Channel *54 D3 channel* Haiti/Jamaica
Jamālpur *135 F3* Bihār, NE India
Jambi *138 B4 var.* Telanaipura; *prev.* Djambi. Sumatera, W Indonesia
James Bay *38 C3 bay* Ontario/Quebec, E Canada
James River *45 E2 river* North Dakota/South Dakota, N USA
James River *41 E5 river* Virginia, NE USA
Jamestown *41 E3* New York, NE USA
Jamestown *45 E2* North Dakota, N USA
Jammu *134 D2 prev.* Jummoo. Jammu and Kashmir, NW India
Jammu and Kashmīr *134 D1 disputed region* India/Pakistan
Jämnagar *134 C4 prev.* Navanagar. Gujarāt, W India
Jamshedpur *135 F4* Bihār, NE India
Jamuna *see* Brahmaputra
Janaúba *63 F3* Minas Gerais, SE Brazil
Janesville *40 B3* Wisconsin, N USA
Janīn *see* Jenīn
Janina *see* Ioánnina
Jan Mayen *83 F4 Norwegian dependency* N Atlantic Ocean
Jánoshalma *99 C7 SCr.* Jankovac. Bács-Kiskun, S Hungary
Japan *130 C4 var.* Nippon, *Jap.* Nihon. *Country* E Asia

Japan 130

Official name Japan
Formation 1590
Capital Tokyo
Population 127.3 million / 873

Japan (continued)

people per sq mile (337 people per sq km)
Total area 145,882 sq miles (377,835 sq km)
Languages Japanese, Korean, Chinese
Religions Shinto and Buddhist 76%, Buddhist 16%, other (including Christian) 8%
Ethnic mix Japanese 99%, other (mainly Korean) 1%
Government Parliamentary democracy
Currency Yen = 100 sen
Literacy rate 99%
Calorie consumption 2,762 kilocalories

Japan, Sea of *130 A4 var.* East Sea, *Rus.* Yapanskoye More. *Sea* NW Pacific Ocean
Japan Trench *125 F1 undersea feature* NW Pacific Ocean
Japiim *62 C2 var.* Máncio Lima. Acre, W Brazil
Japurá, Rio *62 C2 var.* Rio Caquetá, Yapurá. *River* Brazil/Colombia *see also* Caquetá, Río
Jaqué *53 G5* Darién, SE Panama
Jaquemel *see* Jacmel
Jarablos *see* Jarābulus
Jarābulus *118 C2 var.* Jarablos, Jerablus, *Fr.* Djérablous. Ḥalab, N Syria
Jardines de la Reina, Archipiélago de los *54 B2 island group* C Cuba
Jarocin *98 C4* Wielkopolskie, C Poland
Jarosław *99 E5 Ger.* Jaroslau, *Rus.* Yaroslav. Podkarpackie, SE Poland
Jarqūrghon *123 E3 Rus.* Dzharkurgan. Surkhondaryo Wiloyati, S Uzbekistan
Jarvis Island *145 G2 US unincorporated territory* C Pacific Ocean
Jasło *99 D5* Podkarpackie, SE Poland
Jastrzębie-Zdrój *99 C5* Śląskie, S Poland
Jataí *63 E3* Goiás, C Brazil
Jativa *see* Xátiva
Jauf *see* Al Jawf
Jaunpiebalga *106 D3* Gulbene, NE Latvia
Jaunpur *135 E3* Uttar Pradesh, N India
Java *152 A3 prev.* Djawa. *Island* C Indonesia
Javalambre *93 E3 mountain* E Spain
Javari, Rio *62 C2 var.* Yavarí. *River* Brazil/Peru
Java Sea *138 D4 Ind.* Laut Jawa. *Sea* W Indonesia
Java Trench *124 D5 var.* Sunda Trench. *Undersea feature* E Indian Ocean
Jawhar *73 D6 var.* Jowhar, *It.* Giohar. Shabeellaha Dhexe, S Somalia
Jaya, Puncak *139 G4 prev.* Puntjak Carstensz, Puntjak Sukarno. *Mountain* Papua, E Indonesia
Jayapura *139 H4 var.* Djajapura, *Dut.* Hollandia; *prev.* Kotabaru, Sukarnapura. Papua, E Indonesia
Jazā'ir Bin Ghalfān *see* Ḥalāniyāt, Juzur al
Jazīrat Jarbah *see* Jerba, Île de
Jazīreh-ye Qeshm *see* Qeshm
Jaz Mūrīān, Hāmūn-e *120 E4 lake* SE Iran
Jebba *75 F4* Kwara, W Nigeria
Jebel esh Sharqi *see* Anti-Lebanon
Jebel Uweinat *see* 'Uwaynāt, Jabal al
Jeble *see* Jablah
Jędrzejów *98 D4 Ger.* Endersdorf. Świętokrzyskie, C Poland

Jefferson City *45 G5 state capital*
Missouri, C USA
Jega *75 F4* Kebbi, NW Nigeria
Jehol *see* Chengde
Jēkabpils *106 C4 Ger.* Jakobstadt.
Jēkabpils, S Latvia
Jelalabad *see* Jalālābād
Jelenia Góra *98 B4 Ger.* Hirschberg,
Hirschberg im Riesengebirge,
Hirschberg in Riesengebirge,
Hirschberg in Schlesien.
Dolnośląskie, SW Poland
Jelgava *106 C3 Ger.* Mitau. Jelgava,
C Latvia
Jemappes *87 B6* Hainaut,
C Belgium
Jember *138 D5 prev.* Djember. Jawa,
C Indonesia
Jena *94 C4* Thüringen, C Germany
Jenīn *119 A6 var.* Janīn, Jinīn; *anc.*
Engannim. N West Bank
Jerablus *see* Jarābulus
Jerada *70 D2* NE Morocco
Jerba, Île de *71 F2 var.* Djerba,
Jazīrat Jarbah. *Island* E Tunisia
Jérémie *54 D3* SW Haiti
Jerez *see* Jeréz de la Frontera
Jeréz de la Frontera *92 C5 var.*
Jerez; *prev.* Xeres. Andalucía,
SW Spain
Jeréz de los Caballeros *92 C4*
Extremadura, W Spain
Jericho *119 B6 Ar.* Arīḥā, *Heb.*
Yeriḥo. E West Bank
Jerid, Chott el *87 E2 var.* Shaṭṭ
al Jarīd. *Salt lake* SW Tunisia
Jersey *89 D8 UK dependent territory*
NW Europe
Jerusalem *103 H4 Ar.* El Quds, *Heb.*
Yerushalayim; *anc.* Hierosolyma.
Country capital (Israel) Jerusalem,
NE Israel
Jerusalem *112 A4* Admin. region
district E Israel
Jesenice *95 D7 Ger.* Assling.
NW Slovenia
Jessore *135 G4* Khulna,
W Bangladesh
Jesús María *64 C3* Córdoba,
C Argentina
Jhānsi *134 D3* Uttar Pradesh,
N India
Jhelum *134 C2* Punjab, NE Pakistan
Ji *see* Hebei
Ji *see* Jilin
Jiangmen *128 C6* Guangdong,
S China
Jiangsu *128 D4 var.* Chiang-su,
Jiangsu Sheng, Kiangsu, Su.
Admin. region *province* E China
Jiangsu Sheng *see* Jiangsu
Jiangxi *128 C6 var.* Chiang-hsi, Gan,
Jiangxi Sheng, Kiangsi. Admin.
region *province* S China
Jiangxi Sheng *see* Jiangxi
Jiaxing *128 D5* Zhejiang, SE China
Jiayi *see* Chiai
Jibuti *see* Djibouti
Jiddah *121 A5 Eng.* Jedda. Makkah,
W Saudi Arabia
Jih-k'a-tse *see* Xigazê
Jihlava *99 B5 Ger.* Iglau, *Pol.*
Igława. Jihlavský Kraj, C Czech
Republic
Jilib *73 D6 It.* Gelib. Jubbada
Dhexe, S Somalia
Jilin *128 D3 var.* Chi-lin, Girin, Ji,
Jilin Sheng, Kirin. Admin. region
province NE China
Jilin *129 E3 var.* Chi-lin, Girin,
Kirin; *prev.* Yungki, Yunki. Jilin,
NE China
Jilin Sheng *see* Jilin
Jīma *73 C5 var.* Jimma, *It.* Gimma.
C Ethiopia
Jimbolia *108 A4 Ger.* Hatzfeld,
Hung. Zsombolya. Timiş,
W Romania
Jiménez *50 D2* Chihuahua,
N Mexico
Jimma *see* Jīma
Jimsar *126 C3* Xinjiang Uygur
Zizhiqu, NW China
Jin *see* Shanxi
Jin *see* Tianjin Shi
Jinan *128 C4 var.* Chinan, Chi-nan,
Tsinan. Shandong, E China

Jingdezhen *128 C5* Jiangxi, S China
Jinghong *128 A6 var.* Yunjinghong.
Yunnan, SW China
Jinhua *128 D5* Zhejiang, SE China
Jinīn *see* Jenīn
Jining *127 F3* Shandong, E China
Jinja *73 C6* S Uganda
Jinotega *52 D3* Jinotega,
NW Nicaragua
Jinotepe *52 D3* Carazo,
SW Nicaragua
Jinsha Jiang *128 A5 river* SW China
Jinzhou *128 D3 var.* Chin-chou,
Chinchow; *prev.* Chinhsien.
Liaoning, NE China
Jisr ash Shadadi *see* Ash Shadādah
Jiu *108 B5 Ger.* Schil, Schyl, *Hung.*
Zsil, Zsily. *River* S Romania
Jiujiang *128 C5* Jiangxi, S China
Jixi *129 E2* Heilongjiang, NE China
Jīzān *121 B6 var.* Qīzān. Jīzān,
SW Saudi Arabia
Jizzakh *123 E2 Rus.* Dzhizak.
Jizzakh Wiloyati, C Uzbekistan
João Pessoa *63 G2 prev.* Paraíba.
State capital Paraíba, E Brazil
Jo'burg *see* Johannesburg
Jo-ch'iang *see* Ruoqiang
Jodhpur *134 C3* Rājasthān,
NW India
Joensuu *85 E5* Itä-Suomi,
E Finland
Jõetsu *131 C5 var.* Zyõetu. Niigata,
Honshū, C Japan
Johanna Island *see* Anjouan
Johannesburg *78 D4 var.* Egoli,
Erautini, Gauteng, *abbrev.* Jo'burg.
Gauteng, NE South Africa
John Day River *46 C3 river* Oregon,
NW USA
John o'Groats *88 C2* N Scotland,
UK
Johnston Atoll *143 E1 US*
unincorporated territory C Pacific
Ocean
Johor Baharu *see* Johor Bahru
Johor Bahru *138 B3 var.* Johor
Baharu, Johore Bahru. Johor,
Peninsular Malaysia
Johore Bahru *see* Johor Bahru
Johore Strait *138 A1 Mal.* Selat
Johor. *Strait* Malaysia/Singapore
Joinville *see* Joinville
Joinville *63 E4 var.* Joinvile. Santa
Catarina, S Brazil
Jokkmokk *84 C3* Norrbotten,
N Sweden
Joliet *40 B3* Illinois, N USA
Jonava *106 B4 Ger.* Janow, *Pol.*
Janów. Jonava, C Lithuania
Jonesboro *42 B1* Arkansas, C USA
Joniškis *106 C3 Ger.* Janischken.
Joniškis, N Lithuania
Jönköping *85 B7* Jönköping,
S Sweden
Jonquière *39 E4* Quebec, SE Canada
Joplin *45 F5* Missouri, C USA
Jordan *119 B5 Ar.* Urdunn, *Heb.*
HaYarden. *River* SW Asia
Jordan *119 B6 Ar.* Al Mamlakah
al Urdunīyah al Hāshimīyah,
Al Urdunn; *prev.* Transjordan.
Country SW Asia

Jordan 119

Official name Hashemite Kingdom
of Jordan
Formation 1946
Capital Amman
Population 5.1 million /143 people
per sq mile (55 people per sq km)
Total area 35,637 sq miles
(92,300 sq km)
Languages Arabic
Religions Muslim (mainly Sunni)
92%, other (mostly Christian) 8%
Ethnic mix Arab 98% (Palestinian
40%), Armenian 1%, Circassian 1%
Government Constitutional
monarchy
Currency Jordanian dinar = 1,000
fils
Literacy rate 89.2%
Calorie consumption 2,749
kilocalories

Jorhāt *135 H3* Assam, NE India
Jos *75 G4* Plateau, C Nigeria
Joseph Bonaparte Gulf *146 D2 gulf*
N Australia
Jos Plateau *75 G4 plateau* C Nigeria
Jotunheimen *85 A5 mountain range*
S Norway
Joûnié *118 A4 var.* Junīyah.
W Lebanon
Joure *86 D2* Fris. De Jouwer.
Friesland, N Netherlands
Joutseno *85 E5* Etelä-Suomi, S
Finland
Jowhar *see* Jawhar
JStorm Thurmond Reservoir *see*
Clark Hill Lake
Juan Aldama *50 D3* Zacatecas,
C Mexico
Juan de Fuca, Strait of *46 A1 strait*
Canada/USA
Juan Fernández, Islas *57 A6 Eng.*
Juan Fernandez Islands. *Island*
group W Chile
Juazeiro *63 G2 prev.* Joazeiro. Bahia,
E Brazil
Juazeiro do Norte *63 G2* Ceará,
E Brazil
Juba *73 D6 Amh.* Genalē Wenz, *It.*
Guiba, Som. Ganaane, Webi Jubba.
River Ethiopia/Somalia
Juba *73 B5 var.* Jūbā. Bahr el Gabel,
S Sudan
Júcar *93 E3 var.* Jucar. *River* C Spain
Juchitán *51 F5 var.* Juchitán de
Zaragosa. Oaxaca, SE Mexico
Juchitán de Zaragosa *see* Juchitán
Judayyidat Hāmīr *120 B3* S Iraq
Judenburg *95 D7* Steiermark,
C Austria
Juigalpa *52 D3* Chontales,
S Nicaragua
Juiz de Fora *63 F4* Minas Gerais,
SE Brazil
Jujuy *see* San Salvador de Jujuy
Jūlā *see* Jālū
Juliaca *61 E4* Puno, SE Peru
Juliana Top *59 G3 mountain*
C Suriname
Jumilla *93 E4* Murcia, SE Spain
Jumporn *see* Chumphon
Junction City *45 F4* Kansas, C USA
Juneau *36 D4 state capital* Alaska,
USA
Junín *64 C4* Buenos Aires,
E Argentina
Junīyah *see* Joûnié
Junkseylon *see* Phuket
Jur *73 B5 river* C Sudan
Jura *88 B4 island* SW Scotland, UK
Jura *95 A7 canton* NW Switzerland
Jura *90 D4 department* E France
Jurbarkas *106 B4 Ger.* Georgenburg,
Jurburg. Jurbarkas, W Lithuania
Jūrmala *106 C3* Rīga, C Latvia
Juruá, Rio *62 C2 var.* Río Yuruá.
River Brazil/Peru
Juruena, Rio *62 D3 river* W Brazil
Jutiapa *52 B2* Jutiapa, S Guatemala
Juticalpa *52 D2* Olancho,
C Honduras
Juventud, Isla de la *54 A2 var.* Isla
de Pinos, *Eng.* Isle of Youth; *prev.*
The Isle of the Pines. *Island*
W Cuba
Južna Morava *101 E5 Ger.* Südliche
Morava. *River* SE Serbia and
Montenegro (Yugo.)
Juzur Qarqannah *see* Kerkenah,
Îles de
Jwaneng *78 C4* Southern,
SE Botswana
Jylland *85 A7 Eng.* Jutland.
Peninsula W Denmark
Jyväskylä *85 D5* Länsi-Suomi,
W Finland

K

K2 *126 A4 Chin.* Qogir Feng, *Eng.*
Mount Godwin Austen. *Mountain*
China/Pakistan
Kaafu Atoll *see* Male' Atoll
Kaaimanston *59 G3* Sipaliwini,
N Suriname
Kaakhka *122 C3 var.* Kaka.
Akhalskiy Velayat,
S Turkmenistan

Kaala *see* Caála
Kaamanen *84 D2 Lapp.* Gámas.
Lappi, N Finland
Kaapstad *see* Cape Town
Kaaresuvanto *84 C3 Lapp.*
Gárassavon. Lappi, N Finland
Kabale *73 B6* SW Uganda
Kabinda *see* Cabinda
Kabinda *77 D7* Kasai Oriental,
SE Dem. Rep. Congo
Kābol *see* Kābul
Kabompo *78 C2 river* W Zambia
Kābul *123 E4 var.* Kabul, *Per.* Kābol.
Country capital (Afghanistan)
Kābul, E Afghanistan
Kabul *see* Kābul
Kabwe *78 D2* Central, C Zambia
Kachchh, Gulf of *134 B4 var.* Gulf
of Cutch, Gulf of Kutch. *Gulf*
W India
Kachchh, Rann of *134 B4 var.* Rann
of Kachh, Rann of Kutch. *Salt*
marsh India/Pakistan
Kachh, Rann of *see* Kachchh,
Rann of
Kadan Kyun *137 B5 prev.* King
Island. *Island* Mergui Archipelago,
S Myanmar
Kadavu *145 E4 prev.* Kandavu.
Island S Fiji
Kadoma *78 D3 prev.* Gatooma.
Mashonaland West, C Zimbabwe
Kadugli *72 B4* Southern Kordofan,
S Sudan
Kaduna *75 G4* Kaduna,
C Nigeria
Kadzhi-Say *123 G2 Kir.* Kajisay.
Issyk-Kul'skaya Oblast',
NE Kyrgyzstan
Kaédi *74 C3* Gorgol,
S Mauritania
Kaffa *see* Feodosiya
Kafue *78 C2 river* C Zambia
Kafue *78 D2* Lusaka, SE Zambia
Kaga Bandoro *76 C4 prev.* Fort-
Crampel. Nana-Grébizi, C Central
African Republic
Kâghet *74 D1 var.* Karet. *Physical*
region N Mauritania
Kagi *see* Chiai
Kagoshima *131 B8 var.* Kagosima.
Kagoshima, Kyūshū,
SW Japan
Kagoshima-wan *131 A8 bay*
SW Japan
Kagosima *see* Kagoshima
Kahmard, Daryā-ye *123 E4 prev.*
Darya-i-Surkhab. *River*
NE Afghanistan
Kahramanmaraş *see*
Kahramanmaraş
Kahramanmaraş *116 D4 var.*
Kahraman Maraş, Maraş, Marash.
Kahramanmaraş, S Turkey
Kaiapoi *151 C6* Canterbury, South
Island, NZ
Kaifeng *128 C4* Henan, C China
Kai, Kepulauan *139 F4 prev.* Kei
Islands. *Island group* Maluku,
SE Indonesia
Kaikohe *150 C2* Northland, North
Island, NZ
Kaikoura *151 C5* Canterbury, South
Island, NZ
Kaikoura Peninsula *151 C5*
peninsula South Island, NZ
Kainji Lake *see* Kainji Reservoir
Kainji Reservoir *75 F4 var.* Kainji
Lake. *Reservoir* W Nigeria
Kaipara Harbour *150 C2 harbour*
North Island, NZ
Kairouan *71 E2 var.* Al Qayrawān.
E Tunisia
Kaisaria *see* Kayseri
Kaiserlautern *95 A5* Rheinland-
Pfalz, SW Germany
Kaišiadorys *107 B5* Kaišiadorys,
S Lithuania
Kaitaia *150 C2* Northland, North
Island, NZ
Kajaani *84 E4 Swe.* Kajana. Oulu,
C Finland
Kaka *see* Kaakhka
Kake *36 D4* Kupreanof Island,
Alaska, USA
Kakhovka *109 F4* Khersons'ka
Oblast', S Ukraine

Kakhovs'ka Vodoskhovyshche 109 F4 *Rus.* Kakhovskoye Vodokhranilishche. *Reservoir* SE Ukraine

Kākināda 132 D1 *prev.* Cocanada. Andhra Pradesh, E India

Kaktovik 36 D2 Alaska, USA

Kalahari Desert 78 B4 *desert* Southern Africa

Kalamariá 104 B4 Kentrikí Makedonía, N Greece

Kalámata 105 B6 *prev.* Kalámai. Pelopónnisos, S Greece

Kalamazoo 40 C3 Michigan, N USA

Kalambaka *see* Kalampáka

Kálamos 105 C5 Attikí, C Greece

Kalampáka 104 B4 *var.* Kalambaka. Thessalía, C Greece

Kalanchak 109 F4 Khersons'ka Oblast', S Ukraine

Kalarash *see* Călăraşi

Kalasin 136 D4 *var.* Muang Kalasin. Kalasin, E Thailand

Kalāt 123 E5 *Per.* Qalāt. Zābul, S Afghanistan

Kālat 134 B2 *var.* Kelat, Khelat. Baluchistān, SW Pakistan

Kalbarri 147 A5 Western Australia

Kalecik 116 C3 Ankara, N Turkey

Kalemie 77 E6 *prev.* Albertville. Shaba, SE Dem. Rep. Congo

Kale Sultanie *see* Çanakkale

Kalgan *see* Zhangjiakou

Kalgoorlie 147 B6 Western Australia

Kalima 77 D6 Maniema, E Dem. Rep. Congo

Kalimantan 138 D4 *Eng.* Indonesian Borneo. *Geopolitical region* Borneo, C Indonesia

Kálimnos *see* Kálymnos

Kaliningrad *see* Kaliningradskaya Oblast'

Kaliningrad 106 A4 Kaliningradskaya Oblast', W Russian Federation

Kaliningradskaya Oblast' 106 B4 *var.* Kaliningrad. Admin. region *province and enclave* W Russian Federation

Kalinkavichy 107 C7 *Rus.* Kalinkovichi. Homyel'skaya Voblasts', SE Belarus

Kalispell 44 B1 Montana, NW USA

Kalisz 98 C4 *Ger.* Kalisch, *Rus.* Kalish; *anc.* Calisia. Wielkopolskie, C Poland

Kalix 84 D4 Norrbotten, N Sweden

Kalixälven 84 D3 *river* N Sweden

Kallaste 106 E3 *Ger.* Krasnogor. Tartumaa, SE Estonia

Kallavesi 85 E5 *lake* SE Finland

Kalloní 105 D5 Lésvos, E Greece

Kalmar 85 C7 *var.* Calmar. Kalmar, S Sweden

Kalmthout 87 C5 Antwerpen, N Belgium

Kalpáki 104 A4 Ípeiros, W Greece

Kalpeni Island 132 B3 *island* Lakshadweep, India, N Indian Ocean

Kaluga 111 B5 Kaluzhskaya Oblast', W Russian Federation

Kalush 108 C2 *Pol.* Kałusz. Ivano-Frankivs'ka Oblast', W Ukraine

Kalutara 132 D4 Western Province, SW Sri Lanka

Kalvarija 107 B5 *Pol.* Kalwaria. Marijampolė, S Lithuania

Kalyān 134 C5 Mahārāshtra, W India

Kálymnos 105 D6 *var.* Kálimnos. *Island* Dodekánisos, Greece, Aegean Sea

Kama 110 D4 *river* NW Russian Federation

Kamarang 59 F3 W Guyana

Kamchatka *see* Kamchatka, Poluostrov

Kamchatka, Poluostrov 115 G3 *Eng.* Kamchatka. *Peninsula* E Russian Federation

Kamensk-Shakhtinskiy 111 B6 Rostovskaya Oblast', SW Russian Federation

Kamina 77 D7 Shaba, S Dem. Rep. Congo

Kamishli *see* Al Qāmishlī

Kamloops 37 E5 British Columbia, SW Canada

Kammu Seamount 152 C2 *undersea feature* N Pacific Ocean

Kampala 73 B6 *country capital* (Uganda) S Uganda

Kâmpóng Cham 137 D6 *prev.* Kompong Cham. Kâmpóng Cham, C Cambodia

Kâmpóng Chhnăng 137 D6 *prev.* Kompong. Kâmpóng Chhnăng, C Cambodia

Kâmpóng Saôm 137 D6 *prev.* Kompong Som, Sihanoukville. Kâmpóng Saôm, SW Cambodia

Kâmpóng Spoe 137 D6 *prev.* Kompong Speu. Kâmpóng Spœ, S Cambodia

Kâmpôt 137 D6 Kâmpôt, SW Cambodia

Kam"yanets'-Podil's'kyy 108 C3 *Rus.* Kamenets-Podol'skiy. Khmel'nyts'ka Oblast', W Ukraine

Kam"yanka-Dniprovs'ka 109 F3 *Rus.* Kamenka Dneprovskaya. Zaporiz'ka Oblast', SE Ukraine

Kamyshin 111 B6 Volgogradskaya Oblast', SW Russian Federation

Kanaky *see* New Caledonia

Kananga 77 D6 *prev.* Luluabourg. Kasai Occidental, S Dem. Rep. Congo

Kananur *see* Cannanore

Kanara *see* Karnātaka

Kanash 111 C5 Chuvashskaya Respublika, W Russian Federation

Kanazawa 131 C5 Ishikawa, Honshū, SW Japan

Kanbe 136 B4 Yangon, SW Myanmar

Kānchīpuram 132 C2 *prev.* Conjeeveram. Tamil Nādu, SE India

Kandahār 123 E5 *Per.* Qandahār. Kandahār, S Afghanistan

Kandalakša *see* Kandalaksha

Kandalaksha 110 B2 *var.* Kandalakša, *Fin.* Kantalahti. Murmanskaya Oblast', NW Russian Federation

Kandangan 138 D4 Borneo, C Indonesia

Kandava 106 C3 *Ger.* Kandau. Tukums, W Latvia

Kandi 75 F4 N Benin

Kandy 132 D3 Central Province, C Sri Lanka

Kane Fracture Zone 66 B4 *tectonic feature* NW Atlantic Ocean

Kaneohe 47 A8 *Haw.* Kāne'ohe. Oahu, Hawaii, USA, C Pacific Ocean

Kangān 120 D4 Būshehr, S Iran

Kangaroo Island 149 A7 *island* South Australia

Kangertittivaq 83 E4 *Dan.* Scoresby Sund. *Fjord* E Greenland

Kangikajik 83 E4 *var.* Kap Brewster. *Headland* E Greenland

Kaniv 109 E2 *Rus.* Kanëv. Cherkas'ka Oblast', C Ukraine

Kanivs'ke Vodoskhovyshche 109 E2 *Rus.* Kanevskoye Vodokhranilishche. *Reservoir* C Ukraine

Kanjiža 100 D2 *Ger.* Altkanischa, *Hung.* Magyarkanizsa, Ókanizsa; *prev.* Stara Kanjiža. Serbia, N Serbia and Montenegro (Yugo.)

Kankaanpää 85 D5 Länsi-Suomi, W Finland

Kankakee 40 B3 Illinois, N USA

Kankan 74 D4 Haute-Guinée, E Guinea

Kannur *see* Cannanore

Kano 75 G4 Kano, N Nigeria

Kānpur 135 E3 *Eng.* Cawnpore. Uttar Pradesh, N India

Kansas 49 F1 *off.* State of Kansas; also known as Jayhawker State, Sunflower State. *State* C USA

Kansas 45 F5 Kansas, C USA

Kansas City 45 F4 Kansas, C USA

Kansas City 45 F4 Missouri, C USA

Kansas River 45 F5 *river* Kansas, C USA

Kansk 115 E4 Krasnoyarskiy Kray, S Russian Federation

Kansu *see* Gansu

Kantalahti *see* Kandalaksha

Kántanos 105 C7 Kríti, Greece, E Mediterranean Sea

Kantemirovka 111 B6 Voronezhskaya Oblast', W Russian Federation

Kanton 145 F3 *var.* Abariringa, Canton Island; *prev.* Mary Island. *Atoll* Phoenix Islands, C Kiribati

Kanye 78 C4 Southern, SE Botswana

Kaohsiung 128 D6 *var.* Gaoxiong, *Jap.* Takao, Takow. S Taiwan

Kaolack 74 B3 *var.* Kaolak. W Senegal

Kaolak *see* Kaolack

Kaolan *see* Lanzhou

Kaoma 78 C2 Western, W Zambia

Kap Brewster *see* Kangikajik

Kapelle 87 B5 Zeeland, SW Netherlands

Kapellen 87 C5 Antwerpen, N Belgium

Kap Farvel *see* Uummannarsuaq

Kapka, Massif du 76 C2 *mountain range* E Chad

Kaplangky, Plato 122 C2 *ridge* Turkmenistan/Uzbekistan

Kapoeta 73 C5 Eastern Equatoria, SE Sudan

Kaposvár 99 C7 Somogy, SW Hungary

Kappeln 94 B2 Schleswig-Holstein, N Germany

Kapstad *see* Cape Town

Kaptsevichy 107 C7 *Rus.* Koptsevichi. Homyel'skaya Voblasts', SE Belarus

Kapuas, Sungai 138 C4 *prev.* Kapoeas. *River* Borneo, C Indonesia

Kapuskasing 38 C4 Ontario, S Canada

Kapyl' 107 C6 *Rus.* Kopyl'. Minskaya Voblasts', C Belarus

Kap York *see* Innaanganeq

Kara-Balta 123 F2 Chuyskaya Oblast', N Kyrgyzstan

Karabil', Vozvyshennost' 122 D3 *mountain range* S Turkmenistan

Karabük 116 C2 Karabük, NW Turkey

Karāchi 134 B3 Sind, SE Pakistan

Karadeniz *see* Black Sea

Karadeniz Boğazı *see* İstanbul Boğazı

Karaferiye *see* Véroia

Karaganda 114 C4 *Kaz.* Qaraghandy. Karaganda, C Kazakhstan

Karaginskiy, Ostrov 115 H2 *island* E Russian Federation

Karak *see* Al Karak

Kara-Kala 122 C3 *var.* Garrygala. Balkanskiy Velayat, W Turkmenistan

Karakax *see* Moyu

Karakılısse *see* Ağrı

Karakol 123 G2 *prev.* Przheval'sk. Issyk-Kul'skaya Oblast', NE Kyrgyzstan

Karakol 123 G2 *var.* Karakolka. Issyk-Kul'skaya Oblast', NE Kyrgyzstan

Karakolka *see* Karakol

Karakoram Range 134 D1 *mountain range* C Asia

Karaköse *see* Ağrı

Kara Kum *see* Garagumy

Kara Kum Canal *see* Garagumskiy Kanal

Karakumskiy Kanal *see* Garagumskiy Kanal

Karamai *see* Karamay

Karaman 116 C4 Karaman, S Turkey

Karamay 126 B2 *var.* Karamai, Kelamayi; *prev.* Chin. K'o-la-ma-i. Xinjiang Uygur Zizhiqu, NW China

Karamea Bight 151 B5 *gulf* South Island, NZ

Karapelit 104 E1 *Rom.* Stejarul. Dobrich, NE Bulgaria

Kara-Say 123 G2 Issyk-Kul'skaya Oblast', NE Kyrgyzstan

Karasburg 78 B4 Karas, S Namibia

Kara Sea *see* Karskoye More

Karatau 114 C5 *Kaz.* Qarataū. Zhambyl, S Kazakhstan

Karavás 105 B7 Kýthira, S Greece

Karbalā' 120 B3 *var.* Kerbala, Kerbela. S Iraq

Kardhítsa *see* Kardítsa

Karditsa 105 B5 *var.* Kardhítsa. Thessalía, C Greece

Kärdla 106 C2 *Ger.* Kertel. Hiiumaa, W Estonia

Karet *see* Kâghet

Kargı 116 C2 Çorum, N Turkey

Kargilik *see* Yecheng

Kariba 78 D2 Mashonaland West, N Zimbabwe

Kariba, Lake 78 D3 *reservoir* Zambia/Zimbabwe

Karibib 78 B3 Erongo, C Namibia

Karies *see* Karyés

Karigasniemi 84 D2 *Lapp.* Garegegasnjárga. Lappi, N Finland

Karimata, Selat 138 C4 *strait* W Indonesia

Karīmnagar 134 D5 Andhra Pradesh, C India

Karin 72 D4 Woqooyi Galbeed, N Somalia

Kariot *see* Ikaría

Káristos *see* Kárystos

Karkiníts'ka Zatoka 109 E4 *Rus.* Karkinitskiy Zaliv. *Gulf* S Ukraine

Karkük *see* Kirkūk

Karlovac 100 B3 *Ger.* Karlstadt, *Hung.* Károlyváros. Karlovac, C Croatia

Karlovy Vary 99 A5 *Ger.* Karlsbad; *prev. Eng.* Carlsbad. Karlovarský Kraj, W Czech Republic

Karlskrona 85 C7 Blekinge, S Sweden

Karlsruhe 95 B6 *var.* Carlsruhe. Baden-Württemberg, SW Germany

Karlstad 85 B6 Värmland, C Sweden

Karnāl 134 D2 Haryāna, N India

Karnātaka 132 C1 *var.* Kanara; *prev.* Maisur, Mysore. Admin. region *state* W India

Karnobat 104 D2 Burgas, E Bulgaria

Karnul *see* Kurnool

Karpaten *see* Carpathian Mountains

Kárpathos 105 E7 *It.* Scarpanto; *anc.* Carpathos, Carpathus. *Island* SE Greece

Kárpathos 105 E7 Kárpathos, SE Greece

Karpaty *see* Carpathian Mountains

Karpenísi 105 B5 *prev.* Karpenísion. Stereá Ellás, C Greece

Kars 117 F2 *var.* Qars. Kars, NE Turkey

Kārsava 106 D4 *Ger.* Karsau; *prev. Rus.* Korsovka. Ludza, E Latvia

Karskiye Vorota, Proliv 110 E2 *Eng.* Kara Strait. *Strait* N Russian Federation

Karskoye More 114 D2 *Eng.* Kara Sea. *Sea* Arctic Ocean

Karyés 104 C4 *var.* Karies. *Ágion* Óros, N Greece

Kárystos 105 C6 *var.* Káristos. Évvoia, C Greece

Kasai 77 C6 *var.* Cassai, Kassai. *River* Angola/Dem. Rep. Congo

Kasaji 77 D7 Shaba, S Dem. Rep. Congo

Kasama 78 D1 Northern, N Zambia

Kāsaragod 132 B2 Kerala, SW India

Kāshān 120 C3 Eşfahān, C Iran

Kashi 126 A3 *Chin.* Kaxgar, K'o-shih, *Uigh.* Kashgar. Xinjiang Uygur Zizhiqu, NW China

Kasongo 77 D6 Maniema, E Dem. Rep. Congo

Kasongo-Lunda 77 C7 Bandundu, SW Dem. Rep. Congo

Kásos 105 D7 *island* SE Greece

Kaspiysk 111 B8 Respublika Dagestan, SW Russian Federation

Kassai *see* Kasai
Kassala 72 C4 Kassala, E Sudan
Kassel 94 B4 *prev.* Cassel. Hessen, C Germany
Kasserine 71 E2 *var.* Al Qaşrayn. W Tunisia
Kastamonu 116 C2 *var.* Castamoni, Kastamuni. Kastamonu, N Turkey
Kastamuni *see* Kastamonu
Kastaneá 104 B4 Kentrikí Makedonía, N Greece
Kastélli 105 C7 Kríti, Greece, E Mediterranean Sea
Kastoría 104 B4 Dytikí Makedonía, N Greece
Kástro 105 C6 Sífnos, Kykládes, Greece, Aegean Sea
Kastsyukovichy 107 E7 *Rus.* Kostyukovichi. Mahilyowskaya Voblasts', E Belarus
Kastsyukowka 107 D7 *Rus.* Kostyukovka. Homyel'skaya Voblasts', SE Belarus
Kasulu 73 B7 Kigoma, W Tanzania
Kasumiga-ura 131 D5 *lake* Honshū, S Japan
Katahdin, Mount 41 G1*mountain* Maine, NE USA
Katalla 36 C3 Alaska, USA
Katana *see* Qaţanā
Katanning 147 B7 Western Australia
Katawaz *see* Zarghūn Shahr
Katchall Island 133 F3 *island* Nicobar Islands, India, NE Indian Ocean
Kateríni 104 B4 Kentrikí Makedonía, N Greece
Katha 136 B2 Sagaing, N Myanmar
Katherine 148 A2 Northern Territory, N Australia
Kathmandu 124 C3 *prev.* Kantipur. *Country capital* (Nepal) Central, C Nepal
Katikati 150 D3 Bay of Plenty, North Island, NZ
Katima Mulilo 78 C3 Caprivi, NE Namibia
Katiola 74 D4 C Côte d'Ivoire
Káto Achaḯa 105 B5 *var.* Kato Ahaia, Káto Akhaḯa. Dytikí Ellás, S Greece
Kato Ahaia *see* Káto Achaḯa
Káto Akhaḯa *see* Káto Achaḯa
Katoúna 105 A5 Dytikí Ellás, C Greece
Katowice 99 C5 *Ger.* Kattowitz. Śląskie, S Poland
Katsina 75 G3 Katsina, N Nigeria
Kattaqŭrghon 123 E2 *Rus.* Kattakurgan. Samarqand Wiloyati, C Uzbekistan
Kattavía 105 E7 Ródos, Dodekánisos, Greece, Aegean Sea
Kattegat 85 B7 *Dan.* Kattegatt. *Strait* N Europe
Kauai 47 A7 *Haw.* Kaua'i. *Island* Hawaiian Islands, Hawaii, USA, C Pacific Ocean
Kaufbeuren 95 C6 Bayern, S Germany
Kaunas 106 B4 *Ger.* Kauen, *Pol.* Kowno; *prev. Rus.* Kovno. Kaunas, C Lithuania
Kavadarci 101 E6 *Turk.* Kavadar. C FYR Macedonia
Kavajë 101 C6 *It.* Cavaia, Kavaja. Tiranë, W Albania
Kavála 104 C3 *prev.* Kaválla. Anatolikí Makedonía kai Thráki, NE Greece
Kávali 132 D2 Andhra Pradesh, E India
Kavango *see* Cubango
Kavaratti Island 132 A3 *island* Lakshadweep, India, N Indian Ocean
Kavarna 104 E2 Dobrich, NE Bulgaria
Kavengo *see* Cubango
Kavīr, Dasht-e 120 D3 *var.* Great Salt Desert. *Salt pan* N Iran
Kavīr-e Lūt *see* Lūt, Dasht-e
Kawagoe 131 D5 Saitama, Honshū, S Japan
Kawasaki 130 A2 Kanagawa, Honshū, S Japan
Kawerau 150 E3 Bay of Plenty, North Island, NZ

Kaya 75 E3 C Burkina faso
Kayan 136 B4 Yangon, SW Myanmar
Kayan, Sungai 138 D3 *prev.* Kajan. *River* Borneo, C Indonesia
Kayes 74 C3 Kayes, W Mali
Kayseri 116 D3 *var.* Kaisaria; *anc.* Caesarea Mazaca, Mazaca. Kayseri, C Turkey
Kazach'ye 115 F2 Respublika Sakha (Yakutiya), NE Russian Federation
Kazakhskiy Melkosopochnik 114 C4 *Eng.* Kazakh Uplands, Kirghiz Steppe, *Kaz.* Saryarqa. *Uplands* C Kazakhstan
Kazakhstan 114 B4 *var.* Kazakstan, *Kaz.* Qazaqstan, Qazaqstan Respublikasy; *prev.* Kazakh Soviet Socialist Republic, *Rus.* Kazakhskaya SSR. *Country* C Asia

Kazakhstan 114

Official name Republic of Kazakhstan
Formation 1991
Capital Astana
Population 16.1 million / 15 people per sq mile (6 people per sq km)
Total area 1,049,150 sq miles (2,717,300 sq km)
Languages Kazakh, Russian, German, Uighur, Korean
Religions Muslim (mainly Sunni) 50%, Russian Orthodox 13%, other 37%
Ethnic mix Kazakh 53%, Russian 30%, Ukranian 4%, German 2%, Tartar 2%, other 9%
Government Presidential democracy
Currency Tenge = 100 tein
Literacy rate 99%
Calorie consumption 2,991 kilocalories

Kazakh Uplands *see* Kazakhskiy Melkosopochnik
Kazan' 111 C5 Respublika Tatarstan, W Russian Federation
Kazanlŭk 104 D2 *prev.* Kazanlik. Stara Zagora, C Bulgaria
Kazbegi *see* Kazbek
Kazbek 117 F1 *var.* Kazbegi, *Geor.* Mqinvartsveri. *Mountain* N Georgia
Kāzerūn 120 D4 Fārs, S Iran
Kazvin *see* Qazvīn
Kéa 105 C6 *prev.* Kéos, *anc.* Ceos. *Island* Kykládes, Greece, Aegean Sea
Kéa 105 C6 Kéa, Kykládes, Greece, Aegean Sea
Kea, Mauna 47 B8 *mountain* Hawaii, USA, C Pacific Ocean
Kéamu *see* Aneityum
Kearney 45 E4 Nebraska, C USA
Keban Barajı 117 E3 *reservoir* C Turkey
Kebkabiya 72 A4 Northern Darfur, W Sudan
Kebnekaise 84 C3 *mountain* N Sweden
Kecskemét 99 D7 Bács-Kiskun, C Hungary
Kediri 138 D5 Jawa, C Indonesia
Kędzierzyn-Kole 99 C5 *Ger.* Heydebrech. Opolskie, S Poland
Keelung *see* Chilung
Keetmanshoop 78 B4 Karas, S Namibia
Kefallinía 105 A5 *var.* Kefallonía. *Island* Iónioi Nísoi, Greece, C Mediterranean Sea
Kefallonía *see* Kefallinía
Kefe *see* Feodosiya
Kehl 95 A6 Baden-Württemberg, SW Germany
Keila 106 D2 *Ger.* Kegel. Harjumaa, NW Estonia
Keïta 75 F3 Tahoua, C Niger
Keitele 84 D4 *lake* C Finland
Keith 149 B7 South Australia
Kēk-Art 123 G2 *prev.* Alaykel', Alay-Kuu. Oshskaya Oblast', SW Kyrgyzstan
Kékes 99 C6 *mountain* N Hungary

Kelamayi *see* Karamay
Kelang *see* Klang
Kelat *see* Kālat
Kelifskiy Uzboy 122 D3 *salt marsh* E Turkmenistan
Kelkit Çayı 117 E3 *river* N Turkey
Kelmė 106 B4 Kelmė, C Lithuania
Kélo 76 B4 Tandjilé, SW Chad
Kelowna 37 E5 British Columbia, SW Canada
Kelso 46 B2 Washington, NW USA
Keluang 138 B3 *var.* Kluang. Johor, Peninsular Malaysia
Kem' 110 B3 Respublika Kareliya, NW Russian Federation
Kemah 117 E3 Erzincan, E Turkey
Kemaman *see* Cukai
Kemerovo 114 D4 *prev.* Shcheglovsk. Kemerovskaya Oblast', C Russian Federation
Kemi 84 D4 Lappi, NW Finland
Kemijärvi 84 D3 *Swe.* Kemiträsk. Lappi, N Finland
Kemijoki 84 D3 *river* NW Finland
Kemin 123 G2 *prev.* Bystrovka. Chuyskaya Oblast', N Kyrgyzstan
Kempele 84 D4 Oulu, C Finland
Kempten 95 B7 Bayern, S Germany
Kendal 89 D5 NW England, UK
Kendari 139 E4 Sulawesi, C Indonesia
Kenedy 49 G4 Texas, SW USA
Kenema 74 C4 SE Sierra Leone
Këneurgench 122 C2 *Turkm.* Köneürgench; *prev.* Kunya-Urgench. Dashkhovuzskiy Velayat, N Turkmenistan
Kenge 77 C6 Bandundu, SW Dem. Rep. Congo
Keng Tung 136 C3 *var.* Kentung. Shan State, E Myanmar
Kénitra 70 C2 *prev.* Port-Lyautey. NW Morocco
Kennett 45 H5 Missouri, C USA
Kennewick 46 C2 Washington, NW USA
Kenora 38 A3 Ontario, S Canada
Kenosha 40 B3 Wisconsin, N USA
Kentau 114 B5 Yuzhnyy Kazakhstan, S Kazakhstan
Kentucky 40 C5 *off.* Commonwealth of Kentucky; *also known as* The Bluegrass State. *State* C USA
Kentucky Lake 40 B5 *reservoir* Kentucky/Tennessee, S USA
Kentung *see* Keng Tung
Kenya 73 C6 *Country* E Africa

Kenya 73

Official name Republic of Kenya
Formation 1963
Capital Nairobi
Population 31.3 million / 139 people per sq mile (54 people per sq km)
Total area 224,961 sq miles (582,650 sq km)
Languages Kiswahili, English, Kikuyu, Luo, Kamba
Religions Christian 60%, Traditional beliefs 25%, Muslim 6%, other 9%
Ethnic mix Kikuyu 21%, Luhya 14%, Luo 13%, Kamba 11%, Kalenjin 11%, other 30%
Government Presidential democracy
Currency Kenya shilling = 100 cents
Literacy rate 82.4%
Calorie consumption 1,965 kilocalories

Keokuk 45 G4 Iowa, C USA
Kępno 98 C4 Wielkopolskie, C Poland
Keppel Island *see* Niuatoputapu
Kepulauan Sangihe *see* Sangir, Kepulauan
Kerak *see* Al Karak
Kerala 132 C2 *state* S India
Kerasunt *see* Giresun
Keratéa *see* Keratéa
Keratéa 105 C6 *var.* Keratea. Attikí, C Greece
Kerbala *see* Karbalā'

Kerbela *see* Karbalā'
Kerch 109 G5 *Rus.* Kerch'. Respublika Krym, SE Ukraine
Kerchens'ka Protska *see* Kerch Strait
Kerchenskiy Proliv *see* Kerch Strait
Kerch Strait 109 G4 *var.* Bosporus Cimmerius, Enikale Strait, *Rus.* Kerchenskiy Proliv, *Ukr.* Kerchens'ka Protska. *Strait* Black Sea/Sea of Azov
Kerguelen 141 C7 *island* C French Southern and Antarctic Territories
Kerguelen Plateau 141 C7 *undersea feature* S Indian Ocean
Kerí 105 A6 Zákynthos, Iónioi Nísoi, Greece, C Mediterranean Sea
Kerikeri 150 D2 Northland, North Island, NZ
Kerkenah 122 *var.* 102 D4 *var.* Kerkenna Islands, *Ar.* Juzur Qarqannah. *Island group* E Tunisia
Kerkenna Islands *see* Kerkenah, Îles de
Kerki 122 D3 Lebapskiy Velayat, E Turkmenistan
Kérkira *see* Kérkyra
Kerkrade 87 D6 Limburg, SE Netherlands
Kerkuk *see* Kirkūk
Kérkyra 104 A4 *var.* Kérkira, *Eng.* Corfu. *Island* Iónioi Nísoi, Greece, C Mediterranean Sea
Kermadec Islands 152 C4 *island group* NZ, SW Pacific Ocean
Kermadec Trench 143 E4 *undersea feature* SW Pacific Ocean
Kermān 120 D3 *var.* Kirman; *anc.* Carmana. Kermān, C Iran
Kermānshāh *see* Bākhtarān
Kerrville 49 F4 Texas, SW USA
Kerulen 127 E2 *Chin.* Herlen He, *Mong.* Herlen Gol. *River* China/Mongolia
Kerýneia 102 C5 *var.* Girne, Kyrenia. N Cyprus
Kesennuma 130 D4 Miyagi, Honshū, C Japan
Keszthely 99 C7 Zala, SW Hungary
Ketchikan 36 D4 Revillagigedo Island, Alaska, USA
Kętrzyn 98 D2 *Ger.* Rastenburg. Warmiusko-Mazurskie, NE Poland
Kettering 89 D6 C England, UK
Kettering 40 C4 Ohio, N USA
Keuruu 85 D5 Länsi-Suomi, W Finland
Keweenaw Peninsula 40 B1 *peninsula* Michigan, N USA
Key Largo 43 F5 Key Largo, Florida, SE USA
Key West 43 E5 Florida Keys, Florida, SE USA
Khabarovsk 115 G4 Khabarovskiy Kray, SE Russian Federation
Khadera *see* Ḥadera
Khairpur 134 B3 Sind, SE Pakistan
Khalīj al 'Aqabah *see* Aqaba, Gulf of
Khalīj al 'Arabī *see* Gulf, The
Khalīj-e Fars *see* Gulf, The
Khalkidhikí *see* Chalkidikí
Khalkís *see* Chalkída
Khambhāt, Gulf of 134 C4 *Eng.* Gulf of Cambay. *Gulf* W India
Khamīs Mushayt 121 B6 *var.* Hamis Musait. 'Asīr, SW Saudi Arabia
Khānābād 123 E3 Kunduz, NE Afghanistan
Khān al Baghdādī *see* Al Baghdādī
Khandwa 134 D4 Madhya Pradesh, C India
Khanh *see* Soc Trăng
Khaniá *see* Chaniá
Khanka, Lake 129 E2 *var.* Hsingk'ai Hu, Lake Hanka, *Chin.* Xingkai Hu, *Rus.* Ozero Khanka. *Lake* China/Russian Federation
Khanthabouli 136 D4 *prev.* Savannakhét. Savannakhét, S Laos
Khanty-Mansiysk 114 C3 *prev.* Ostyako-Voguls'k. Khanty-Mansiyskiy Avtonomnyy Okrug, C Russian Federation

Khān Yūnis *119 A7 var.* Khān Yūnus. S Gaza Strip
Khān Yūnus *see* Khān Yūnis
Khanzi *see* Ghanzi
Kharagpur *135 F4* West Bengal, NE India
Kharbin *see* Harbin
Kharkiv *109 G2 Rus.* Khar'kov. Kharkivs'ka Oblast', NE Ukraine
Kharmanli *104 D3* Khaskovo, S Bulgaria
Khartoum *72 B4 var.* El Khartûm, Khartum. *Country capital* (Sudan) Khartoum, C Sudan
Khartum *see* Khartoum
Khasavyurt *111 B8* Respublika Dagestan, SW Russian Federation
Khâsh, Dasht-e *122 D5 Eng.* Khash Desert. *Desert* SW Afghanistan
Khashim Al Qirba *see* Khashm el Girba
Khashm al Qirbah *see* Khashm el Girba
Khashm el Girba *72 C4 var.* Khashim Al Qirba, Khashm al Qirbah. Kassala, E Sudan
Khaskovo *104 D3* Khaskovo, S Bulgaria
Khaydarkan *123 F2 var.* Khaydarken. Oshskaya Oblast', SW Kyrgyzstan
Khaydarken *see* Khaydarkan
Khelat *see* Kālat
Kherson *109 E4* Khersons'ka Oblast', S Ukraine
Kheta *115 E2 river* N Russian Federation
Khíos *see* Chíos
Khirbet el 'Aujā et Tahtā *119 E7 var.* 'Aujā et Tahtā. E West Bank
Khiwa *122 D2 Rus.* Khiva. Khorazm Wiloyati, W Uzbekistan
Khmel'nyts'kyy *108 C2 Rus.* Khmel'nitskiy; *prev.* Proskurov. Khmel'nyts'ka Oblast', W Ukraine
Khodasy *107 E6 Rus.* Khodosy. Mahilyowskaya Voblasts', E Belarus
Khodoriv *108 C2 Pol.* Chodorów, *Rus.* Khodorov. L'vivs'ka Oblast', NW Ukraine
Khodzhent *see* Khŭjand
Khoi *see* Khvoy
Khojend *see* Khŭjand
Khokand *see* Qŭqon
Kholm *123 E3 var.* Tashqurghan, *Pash.* Khulm. Balkh, N Afghanistan
Kholon *see* Holon
Khoms *see* Al Khums
Khong Sedone *see* Muang Khôngxédôn
Khon Kaen *136 D4 var.* Muang Khon Kaen. Khon Kaen, E Thailand
Khor *115 G4* Khabarovskiy Kray, SE Russian Federation
Khorat *see* Nakhon Ratchasima
Khorugh *123 F3 Rus.* Khorog. S Tajikistan
Khotan *see* Hotan
Khouribga *70 B2* C Morocco
Khovd *see* Hovd
Khowst *123 F4* Paktiā, E Afghanistan
Khoy *see* Khvoy
Khoyniki *107 D8 Rus.* Khoyniki. Homyel'skaya Voblasts', SE Belarus
Khrebet Kolymskiy *see* Kolyma Range
Khrebet Kopetdag *see* Koppeh Dāgh
Khrebet Lomonosova *see* Lomonosov Ridge
Khudzhand *see* Khŭjand
Khŭjand *123 E2 var.* Khodzhent, Khojend, *Rus.* Khudzhand; *prev.* Leninabad, *Taj.* Leninobod. N Tajikistan
Khulm *see* Kholm
Khulna *135 G4* Khulna, SW Bangladesh
Khums *see* Al Khums
Khust *108 B3 Cz.* Chust, Husté, *Hung.* Huszt. Zakarpats'ka Oblast', W Ukraine

Khvoy *120 C2 var.* Khoi, Khoy. Āzarbāyjān-e Bākhtarī, NW Iran
Khyber Pass *134 C1 var.* Kowtal-e Khaybar. *Pass* Afghanistan/Pakistan
Kiangmai *see* Chiang Mai
Kiang-ning *see* Nanjing
Kiangsi *see* Jiangxi
Kiangsu *see* Jiangsu
Kiáto *105 B6 prev.* Kiáton. Pelopónnisos, S Greece
Kiayi *see* Chiai
Kibangou *77 B6* Le Niari, SW Congo
Kibombo *77 D6* Maniema, E Dem. Rep. Congo
Kičevo *101 D6* SW FYR Macedonia
Kidderminster *89 D6* C England, UK
Kiel *94 B2* Schleswig-Holstein, N Germany
Kielce *98 D4 Rus.* Keltsy. Świętokrzyskie, C Poland
Kieler Bucht *94 B2 bay* N Germany
Kiev *see* Kyyiv
Kiffa *74 C3* Assaba, S Mauritania
Kigali *73 B6 country capital* (Rwanda) C Rwanda
Kigoma *73 B7* Kigoma, W Tanzania
Kihnu *106 C2 var.* Kihnu Saar, *Ger.* Kühnö. *Island* SW Estonia
Kihnu Saar *see* Kihnu
Kii-suidō *131 C7 strait* S Japan
Kikinda *100 D3 Ger.* Grosskikinda, *Hung.* Nagykikinda; *prev.* Velika Kikinda. Serbia, N Serbia and Montenegro (Yugo.)
Kikládhes *see* Kykládes
Kikwit *77 C6* Bandundu, W Dem. Rep. Congo
Kilien Mountains *see* Qilian Shan
Kilimane *see* Quelimane
Kilimanjaro *73 C7 var.* Uhuru Peak. *Mountain* NE Tanzania
Kilimanjaro *69 E5 region* E Tanzania
Kilingi-Nõmme *106 D3 Ger.* Kurkund. Pärnumaa, SW Estonia
Kilis *116 D4* Kilis S Turkey
Kiliya *108 D4 Rom.* Chilia-Nouă. Odes'ka Oblast', SW Ukraine
Kilkenny *89 B6 Ir.* Cill Chainnigh. S Ireland
Kilkís *104 B3* Kentrikí Makedonía, N Greece
Killarney *89 A6 Ir.* Cill Airne. SW Ireland
Killeen *49 G3* Texas, SW USA
Kilmain *see* Quelimane
Kilmarnock *88 C4* W Scotland, UK
Kilwa *see* Kilwa Kivinje
Kilwa Kivinje *73 C7 var.* Kilwa. Lindi, SE Tanzania
Kimberley *78 C4* Northern Cape, C South Africa
Kimberley Plateau *146 C3 plateau* Western Australia
Kimch'aek *129 E3 prev.* Sŏngjin. E North Korea
Kinabalu, Gunung *138 D3 mountain* East Malaysia
Kindersley *37 F5* Saskatchewan, S Canada
Kindia *74 C4* Guinée-Maritime, SW Guinea
Kindley Field *42 A4 air base* E Bermuda
Kindu *77 D6 prev.* Kindu-Port-Empain. Maniema, C Dem. Rep. Congo
Kineshma *111 C5* Ivanovskaya Oblast', W Russian Federation
King Island *149 B8 island* Tasmania, SE Australia
Kingman *48 A1* Arizona, SW USA
Kingman Reef *145 E2 US territory* C Pacific Ocean
Kingsford Smith *148 E2 international airport* (Sydney) New South Wales, SE Australia
King's Lynn *89 E6 var.* Bishop's Lynn, Kings Lynn, Lynn, Lynn Regis. E England, UK
King Sound *146 B3 sound* Western Australia
Kingsport *43 E1* Tennessee, S USA
Kingston *54 B5 country capital* (Jamaica) E Jamaica
Kingston *41 F3* New York, NE USA

Kingston *38 D5* Ontario, SE Canada
Kingston upon Hull *89 D5 var.* Hull. E England, UK
Kingston upon Thames *89 A8* SE England, UK
Kingstown *55 H4 country capital* (Saint Vincent and the Grenadines) Saint Vincent, Saint Vincent and the Grenadines
Kingsville *49 G5* Texas, SW USA
King William Island *37 F3 island* Nunavut, N Canada Arctic Ocean
Kinrooi *87 D5* Limburg, NE Belgium
Kinshasa *77 B6 prev.* Léopoldville. *Country capital* (Congo (Zaire)) Kinshasa, W Dem. Rep. Congo
Kintyre *88 B4 peninsula* W Scotland, UK
Kinyeti *73 B5 mountain* S Sudan
Kiparissía *see* Kyparissía
Kipili *73 B7* Rukwa, W Tanzania
Kipushi *77 D8* Shaba, SE Dem. Rep. Congo
Kirdzhali *see* Kŭrdzhali
Kirghiz Range *123 F2 Rus.* Kirgizskiy Khrebet; *prev.* Alexander Range. *Mountain range* Kazakhstan/Kyrgyzstan
Kirghiz Steppe *see* Kazakhskiy Melkosopochnik
Kiriath-Arba *see* Hebron
Kiribati *145 F2 Country* C Pacific Ocean

Kiribati 145

Official name Republic of Kiribati
Formation 1979
Capital Bairiki (Tarawa Atoll)
Population 92,000 / 332 people per sq mile (128 people per sq km)
Total area 277 sq miles (717 sq km)
Languages English, Micronesian dialect
Religions Roman Catholic 53%,Kiribati Protestant Church 39%, other 8%
Ethnic mix Micronesian 96%, other 4%
Government Non-party democracy
Currency Australian dollar = 100 cents
Literacy rate 98%
Calorie consumption 2,957 kilocalories

Kırıkhan *116 D4* Hatay, S Turkey
Kırıkkale *116 C3* Kırıkkale, C Turkey
Kirin *see* Jilin
Kirinyaga *73 C6 prev.* Mount Kenya. *Volcano* C Kenya
Kirishi *110 B4 var.* Kirisi. Leningradskaya Oblast', NW Russian Federation
Kirisi *see* Kirishi
Kiritimati *145 G2 prev.* Christmas Island. *Atoll* Line Islands, E Kiribati
Kirkenes *84 E2 var.* Kirkkoniemi. Finnmark, N Norway
Kirkkoniemi *see* Kirkenes
Kirkland Lake *38 D4* Ontario, S Canada
Kırklareli *116 A2 prev.* Kirk-Kilissa. Kırklareli, NW Turkey
Kirkpatrick, Mount *154 B3 mountain* Antarctica
Kirksville *45 G4* Missouri, C USA
Kirkūk *120 B3 var.* Karkūk, Kerkuk. N Iraq
Kirkwall *88 C2* NE Scotland, UK
Kirkwood *45 G4* Missouri, C USA
Kirman *see* Kermān
Kir Moab *see* Al Karak
Kirov *111 C5 prev.* Vyatka. Kirovskaya Oblast', NW Russian Federation
Kirovabad *see* Gäncä
Kirovo-Chepetsk *111 D5* Kirovskaya Oblast', NW Russian Federation
Kirovohrad *109 E3 Rus.* Kirovograd; *prev.* Kirovo, Yelizavetgrad, Zinov'yevsk. Kirovohrads'ka Oblast', C Ukraine

Kīrthar Range *134 B3 mountain range* S Pakistan
Kirun' *see* Chilung
Kiruna *84 C3* Norrbotten, N Sweden
Kisangani *77 D5 prev.* Stanleyville. Orientale, NE Dem. Rep. Congo
Kislovodsk *111 B7* Stavropol'skiy Kray, SW Russian Federation
Kismaayo *73 D6 var.* Chisimayu, Kismayu, *It.* Chisimaio. Jubbada Hoose, S Somalia
Kismayu *see* Kismaayo
Kissidougou *74 C4* Guinée-Forestière, S Guinea
Kissimmee, Lake *43 E4 lake* Florida, SE USA
Kisumu *73 C6 prev.* Port Florence. Nyanza, W Kenya
Kisvárda *99 E6 Ger.* Kleinwardein. Szabolcs-Szatmár-Bereg, E Hungary
Kita *74 D3* Kayes, W Mali
Kitakyūshū *131 A7 var.* Kitakyūsyū. Fukuoka, Kyūshū, SW Japan
Kitakyūsyū *see* Kitakyūshū
Kitami *130 D2* Hokkaidō, NE Japan
Kitchener *38 C5* Ontario, S Canada
Kíthira *see* Kýthira
Kíthnos *see* Kýthnos
Kitimat *36 D4* British Columbia, SW Canada
Kitinen *84 D3 river* N Finland
Kitob *123 E3 Rus.* Kitab. Qashqadaryo Wiloyati, S Uzbekistan
Kitwe *78 D2 var.* Kitwe-Nkana. Copperbelt, C Zambia
Kitwe-Nkana *see* Kitwe
Kitzbühler Alpen *95 C7 mountain range* W Austria
Kivalina *36 C2* Alaska, USA
Kivalo *84 D3 ridge* C Finland
Kivertsi *108 C1 Pol.* Kiwerce, *Rus.* Kivertsy. Volyns'ka Oblast', NW Ukraine
Kivu, Lake *77 E6 Fr.* Lac Kivu. *Lake* Rwanda/Dem. Rep. Congo
Kızıl Irmak *116 C3 river* C Turkey
Kizil Kum *see* Kyzyl Kum
Kladno *99 A5* Středočeský Kraj, NW Czech Republic
Klagenfurt *95 D7 Slvn.* Celovec. Kärnten, S Austria
Klaipėda *106 B3 Ger.* Memel. Klaipėda, NW Lithuania
Klamath Falls *46 B4* Oregon, NW USA
Klamath Mountains *46 A4 mountain range* California/Oregon, W USA
Klang *138 B3 var.* Kelang; *prev.* Port Swettenham. Selangor, Peninsular Malaysia
Klarälven *85 B6 river* Norway/Sweden
Klatovy *99 A5 Ger.* Klattau. Plzeňský Kraj, W Czech Republic
Klazienaveen *86 E2* Drenthe, NE Netherlands
Klein Karas *78 B4* Karas, S Namibia
Kleisoúra *105 A5* Ípeiros, W Greece
Klerksdorp *78 D4* North-West, N South Africa
Klimavichy *107 E7 Rus.* Klimovichi. Mahilyowskaya Voblasts', E Belarus
Klintsy *111 A5* Bryanskaya Oblast', W Russian Federation
Klisura *104 C2* Plovdiv, C Bulgaria
Ključ *100 B3* Federacija Bosna I Hercegovina, NW Bosnia and Herzegovina
Kłobuck *98 C4* Śląskie, S Poland
Klosters *95 B7* Graubünden, SE Switzerland
Kluang *see* Keluang
Kluczbork *98 C4 Ger.* Kreuzburg, Kreuzburg in Oberschlesien. Opolskie, S Poland
Klyuchevskaya Sopka, Vulkan *115 H3 volcano* E Russian Federation
Knin *100 B4* Šibenik-Knin, S Croatia
Knjaževac *100 E4* Serbia, E Serbia and Montenegro (Yugo.)
Knokke-Heist *87 A5* West-Vlaanderen, NW Belgium
Knoxville *42 D1* Tennessee, S USA

Knud Rasmussen Land 82 D1
physical region N Greenland
Kōbe 131 C6 Hyōgo, Honshū,
SW Japan
København 85 B7 *Eng.*
Copenhagen; *anc.* Hafnia. *Country
capital* (Denmark) Sjælland,
København, E Denmark
Kobenni 74 D3 Hodh el Gharbi,
S Mauritania
Koblenz 95 A5 *prev.* Coblenz, *Fr.*
Coblence, *anc.* Confluentes.
Rheinland-Pfalz, W Germany
Kobryn 107 A6 *Pol.* Kobryn, *Rus.*
Kobrin. Brestskaya Voblasts',
SW Belarus
K'obulet'i 117 F2 W Georgia
Kočani 101 E6 NE FYR Macedonia
Kočevje 95 D8 *Ger.* Gottschee.
S Slovenia
Koch Bihār 135 G3 West Bengal,
NE India
Kōchi 131 B7 *var.* Kôti. Kōchi,
Shikoku, SW Japan
Kochi *see* Cochin
Kochiu *see* Gejiu
Kodiak 36 C3 Kodiak Island,
Alaska, USA
Kodiak Island 36 C3 *island* Alaska,
USA
Koeln *see* Köln
Ko-erh-mu *see* Golmud
Koetai *see* Mahakam, Sungai
Koetaradja *see* Bandaaceh
Kōfu 131 D5 *var.* Kôhu. Yamanashi,
Honshū, S Japan
Kogarah 148 E2 New South Wales,
SE Australia
Kogon 122 D2 *Rus.* Kagan. Bukhoro
Wiloyati, C Uzbekistan
Kohīma 135 H3 Nāgāland,
E India
Koh I Noh *see* Golmud
Kohtla-Järve 106 E2 Ida-Virumaa,
NE Estonia
Kōhu *see* Kōfu
Kokand *see* Qŭqon
Kokkola 84 D4 *Swe.* Karleby; *prev.*
Swe. Gamlakarleby. Länsi-Suomi,
W Finland
Koko *see* Qinghai Hu
Koko 75 H4 Kebbi, W Nigeria
Kokomo 40 C4 Indiana, N USA
Koko Nor *see* Qinghai
Kokrines 36 C2 Alaska, USA
Kokshaal-Tau 123 G2 *Rus.* Khrebet
Kakshaal-Too. *Mountain range*
China/Kyrgyzstan
Kokshetau 114 C4 *Kaz.* Kökshetaü;
prev. Kokchetav. Severnyy
Kazakhstan, N Kazakhstan
Koksijde 87 A5 West-Vlaanderen,
W Belgium
Koksoak 38 D2 *river* Quebec,
E Canada
Kokstad 78 D5 KwaZulu/Natal,
E South Africa
Kola *see* Kol'skiy Poluostrov
Kolaka 139 E4 Sulawesi,
C Indonesia
Kolam *see* Quilon
K'o-la-ma-i *see* Karamay
Kola Peninsula *see* Kol'skiy
Poluostrov
Kolari 84 D3 Lappi, NW Finland
Kolárovo 99 C6 *Ger.* Gutta; *prev.*
Guta, *Hung.* Gúta. Nitriansky
Kraj, SW Slovakia
Kolda 74 C3 S Senegal
Kolding 85 A7 Vejle, C Denmark
Kölen 81 E1 *Nor.* Kjølen. *Mountain
range* Norway/Sweden
Kolguyev, Ostrov 110 C2 *island*
NW Russian Federation
Kolhāpur 132 B1 Mahārāshtra,
SW India
Kolhumadulu Atoll 132 A5 *var.*
Kolumadulu Atoll, Thaa Atoll.
Atoll S Maldives
Kolín 99 B5 *Ger.* Kolin. Středočeský
Kraj, C Czech Republic
Kolka 106 C2 Talsi, NW Latvia
Kolkasrags 106 C2 *prev. Eng.* Cape
Domesnes. *Headland*
NW Latvia
Kolkata *see* Calcutta
Kollam *see* Quilon

Köln 94 A4 *var.* Koeln, *Eng./Fr.*
Cologne; *prev.* Cöln, *anc.* Colonia
Agrippina, Oppidum Ubiorum.
Nordrhein-Westfalen, W Germany
Koło 98 C3 Wielkopolskie, C Poland
Kołobrzeg 98 B2 *Ger.* Kolberg.
Zachodniopomorskie,
NW Poland
Kolokani 74 D3 Koulikoro,
W Mali
Kolomna 111 B5 Moskovskaya
Oblast', W Russian Federation
Kolomyya 108 C3 *Ger.* Kolomea.
Ivano-Frankivs'ka Oblast',
W Ukraine
Kolpa 100 A2 *Ger.* Kulpa, *SCr.*
Kupa. *River* Croatia/Slovenia
Kolpino 110 B4 Leningradskaya
Oblast', NW Russian Federation
Kólpos Ammóchostos 102 C5 *var.*
Famagusta Bay, *bay* E Cyprus
Kol'skiy Poluostrov 110 C2 *Eng.*
Kola Peninsula. *Peninsula*
NW Russian Federation
Kolyma 115 G2 *river* NE Russian
Federation
Kolyma Range 113 G2 *var.* Khrebet
Kolymskiy, *Eng.* Kolyma Range.
Mountain range E Russian
Federation
Komatsu 131 C5 *var.* Komatu.
Ishikawa, Honshū, SW Japan
Komatu *see* Komatsu
Kommunizma Pik *see*
Kommunizm, Qullai
Kommunizm, Qullai 123 F3 *var.*
Qullai Garmo, *Eng.* Communism
Peak, *Rus.* Kommunizma Pik;
prev. Stalin Peak. *Mountain*
E Tajikistan
Komoé 75 E4 *var.* Komoé Fleuve.
River E Côte d'Ivoire
Komoé Fleuve *see* Komoé
Komotiní 104 D3 *var.* Gümüljina,
Turk. Gümülcine. Anatolikí
Makedonía kai Thráki, NE Greece
Komsomolets, Ostrov 115 E1 *island*
Severnaya Zemlya, N Russian
Federation
Komsomol'sk-na-Amure 115 G4
Khabarovskiy Kray, SE Russian
Federation
Kondolovo 104 E3 Burgas, E Bulgaria
Kondopoga 110 B3 Respublika
Kareliya, NW Russian Federation
Kondoz *see* Kunduz
Kondūz *see* Kunduz
Kong Christian IX Land 82 D4 *Eng.*
King Christian IX Land. *Physical
region* SE Greenland
Kong Frederik IX Land 82 C3 *Eng.*
King Frederik IX Land. *Physical
region* SW Greenland
Kong Frederik VIII Land 83 E2
Eng. King Frederik VIII Land.
Physical region
NE Greenland
Kong Frederik VI Kyst 82 C4 *Eng.*
King Frederik VI Coast. *Physical
region* SE Greenland
Kong Karls Land 83 G2 *Eng.* King
Charles Islands. *Island group*
SE Svalbard
Kongo *see* Congo
Kongolo 77 D6 Shaba, E Dem. Rep.
Congo
Kongor 73 B5 Jonglei, SE Sudan
Kong Oscar Fjord 83 E3 *fjord*
E Greenland
Kongsberg 85 B6 Buskerud,
S Norway
Kông, Tônle 137 E5 *Lao.* Xê Kong.
River Cambodia/Laos
Konia *see* Konya
Konieh *see* Konya
Konin 98 C3 *Ger.* Kuhnau.
Wielkopolskie, C Poland
Konispol 101 C7 *var.* Konispoli.
Vlorë, S Albania
Konispoli *see* Konispol
Kónitsa 104 A4 Ípeiros,
W Greece
Konitz *see* Chojnice

Konjic 100 C4 Federacija Bosna I
Hercegovina, S Bosnia and
Herzegovina
Konosha 110 C4 Arkhangel'skaya
Oblast', NW Russian Federation
Konotop 109 F1 Sums'ka Oblast',
NE Ukraine
Konstanz 95 B7 *var.* Constanz, *Eng.*
Constance; *hist.* Kostnitz, *anc.*
Constantia. Baden-Württemberg,
S Germany
Konstanza *see* Constanţa
Konya 116 C4 *var.* Konieh; *prev.*
Konia, *anc.* Iconium. Konya,
C Turkey
Kopaonik 101 D5 *mountain range*
S Serbia and Montenegro (Yugo.)
Koper 95 D8 *It.* Capodistria; *prev.*
Kopar. SW Slovenia
Kopetdag Range 122 C3 *mountain
range* Iran/Turkmenistan
Koppeh Dāgh 120 D2 *var.* Khrebet
Kopetdag. *Mountain range*
Iran/Turkmenistan
Koprivnica 100 B2 *Ger.* Kopreinitz,
Hung. Kaproncza. Koprivnica-
Križevci, N Croatia
Korat *see* Nakhon Ratchasima
Korat Plateau 136 D4 *plateau*
E Thailand
Korba 135 E4 Madhya Pradesh,
C India
Korça *see* Korçë
Korçë 101 D6 *var.* Korça, *Gk.*
Korytsa, *It.* Corriza; *prev.* Koritsa.
Korçë, SE Albania
Korčula 100 B4 *It.* Curzola; *anc.*
Corcyra Nigra. *Island* S Croatia
Korea Bay 127 G3 *bay* China/North
Korea
Korea Strait 131 A7 *Jap.* Chōsen-
kaikyō, *Kor.* Taehan-haehyŏp.
Channel Japan/South Korea
Korhogo 74 D4 N Côte d'Ivoire
Korinthiakós Kólpos 105 B5 *Eng.*
Gulf of Corinth; *anc.* Corinthiacus
Sinus. *Gulf* C Greece
Koritsa *see* Korçë
Kōriyama 131 D5 Fukushima,
Honshū, C Japan
Korla 126 C3 *Chin.* K'u-erh-lo.
Xinjiang Uygur Zizhiqu, NW China
Körmend 99 B7 Vas, W Hungary
Koróni 105 B6 Pelopónnisos, S Greece
Koror *see* Oreor
Korosten' 108 D1 Zhytomyrs'ka
Oblast', NW Ukraine
Koro Toro 76 C2 Borkou-Ennedi-
Tibesti, N Chad
Kortrijk 87 A6 Fr. Courtrai. West-
Vlaanderen, W Belgium
Koryak Range *see* Koryakskoye
Nagor'ye
Koryakskiy Khrebet *see*
Koryakskoye Nagor'ye
Koryakskoye Nagor'ye 115 H2 *var.*
Koryakskiy Khrebet, *Eng.* Koryak
Range. *Mountain range*
NE Russian Federation
Koryazhma 110 C4 Arkhangel'skaya
Oblast', NW Russian Federation
Korytsa *see* Korçë
Kos 105 E6 *It.* Coo; *anc.* Cos. *Island*
Dodekánisos, Greece, Aegean Sea
Kos 105 E6 Kos, Dodekánisos,
Greece, Aegean Sea
Kō-saki 131 A7 *headland* Nagasaki,
Tsushima, SW Japan
Kościan 98 B4 *Ger.* Kosten.
Wielkopolskie, C Poland
Koscian *see* Lubań
Kościerzyna 98 C2 Pomorskie,
NW Poland
Kosciusko, Mount *see* Kosciuszko,
Mount
Kosciuszko, Mount 149 C7 *prev.*
Mount Kosciusko. *Mountain* New
South Wales, SE Australia
Koshikijima-rettō 131 A8 *var.*
Kosikizima Rettō. *Island group*
SW Japan
Košice 99 D6 *Ger.* Kaschau, *Hung.*
Kassa. Košický Kraj, E Slovakia
Kosikizima Rettō *see*
Koshikijima-rettō

Koson 123 E3 *Rus.* Kasan.
Qashqadaryo Wiloyati,
S Uzbekistan
Kosovo 101 D5 *prev.* Autonomous
Province of Kosovo and Metohija.
Region S Serbia and Montenegro
(Yugo.)
Kosovo Polje 101 D5 Serbia,
S Serbia and Montenegro (Yugo.)
Kosovska Mitrovica 101 D5 Alb.
Mitrovicë; *prev.* Mitrovica, Titova
Mitrovica. Serbia, S Serbia and
Montenegro (Yugo.)
Kosrae 144 C2 *prev.* Kusaie. *Island*
Caroline Islands,
E Micronesia
Kossou, Lac de 74 D5 *lake* C Côte
d'Ivoire
Kostanay 130 C4 *var.* Kustanay, *Kaz.*
Qostanay. Kostanay, N
Kazakhstan
Kosten *see* Lubań
Kostenets 104 C2 *prev.* Georgi
Dimitrov. Sofiya, W Bulgaria
Kostnitz *see* Konstanz
Kostroma 110 B4 Kostromskaya
Oblast', NW Russian
Federation
Kostyantynivka 109 G3 *Rus.*
Konstantinovka. Donets'ka
Oblast', SE Ukraine
Koszalin 98 B2 *Ger.* Köslin.
Zachodniopomorskie, NW Poland
Kota 134 D3 *prev.* Kotah. Rājasthān,
N India
Kota Baharu *see* Kota Bharu
Kota Bahru *see* Kota Bharu
Kotabaru *see* Jayapura
Kota Bharu 138 B3 *var.* Kota
Baharu, Kota Bahru. Kelantan,
Peninsular Malaysia
Kotabumi 138 B4 *prev.* Kotaboemi.
Sumatera, W Indonesia
Kota Kinabalu 138 D3 *prev.*
Jesselton. Sabah, East Malaysia
Kotel'nyy, Ostrov 115 E2 *island*
Novosibirskiye Ostrova,
N Russian Federation
Kôti *see* Kōchi
Kotka 85 E5 Kymi, S Finland
Kotlas 110 C4 Arkhangel'skaya
Oblast', NW Russian Federation
Kotonu *see* Cotonou
Kotor 101 C5 *It.* Cattaro.
Montenegro, SW Serbia and
Montenegro (Yugo.)
Kotovs'k 108 D3 *Rus.* Kotovsk.
Odes'ka Oblast', SW Ukraine
Kotovsk *see* Hîncești
Kotte *see* Sri Jayawardanapura
Kotto 76 D4 *river* Central African
Republic/Dem. Rep. Congo
Kotuy 115 E2 *river* N Russian
Federation
Koudougou 75 E4 C Burkina faso
Koulamoutou 77 B6 Ogooué-Lolo,
C Gabon
Koulikoro 74 D3 Koulikoro,
SW Mali
Koumra 76 C4 Moyen-Chari, S Chad
Kourou 59 H3 N French Guiana
Kousseir *see* Al Quşayr
Kousséri 76 B3 *prev.* Fort-Foureau.
Extrême-Nord, NE Cameroon
Koutiala 74 D4 Sikasso, S Mali
Kouvola 85 E5 Kymi, S Finland
Kovel' 108 C1 Pol. Kowel. Volyns'ka
Oblast', NW Ukraine
Kowloon 128 A2 *Chin.* Jiulong.
Hong Kong, S China
Kowtal-e Barowghīl *see* Baroghil
Pass
Kowtal-e Khaybar *see* Khyber Pass
Kozáni 104 B4 Dytikí Makedonía,
N Greece
Kozara 100 B3 *mountain range*
NW Bosnia and Herzegovina
Kozarska Dubica *see* Bosanska
Dubica
Kozhikode *see* Calicut
Kōzu-shima 131 D6 *island* E Japan
Kozyatyn 108 D2 *Rus.* Kazatin.
Vinnyts'ka Oblast', C Ukraine
Kpalimé 75 E5 *var.* Palimé.
SW Togo
Krâchéh 137 D6 *prev.* Kratie.
Krâchéh, E Cambodia

Kragujevac 100 D4 Serbia, C Serbia and Montenegro (Yugo.)
Kra, Isthmus of 137 B6 isthmus Malaysia/Thailand
Kraków 99 D5 Eng. Cracow, Ger. Krakau; anc. Cracovia. Małopolskie, S Poland
Krălänh 137 D5 Siĕmréab, NW Cambodia
Kraljevo 100 D4 prev. Rankovićevo. Serbia, C Serbia and Montenegro (Yugo.)
Kramators'k 109 G3 Rus. Kramatorsk. Donets'ka Oblast', SE Ukraine
Kramfors 85 C5 Västernorrland, C Sweden
Kranéa 104 B4 Dytikí Makedonía, N Greece
Kranj 95 D7 Ger. Krainburg. NW Slovenia
Krāslava 106 D4 Krāslava, SE Latvia
Krasnaye 107 C5 Rus. Krasnoye. Minskaya Voblasts', C Belarus
Krasnoarmeysk 111 C6 Saratovskaya Oblast', W Russian Federation
Krasnodar 111 A7 prev. Ekaterinodar, Yekaterinodar. Krasnodarskiy Kray, SW Russian Federation
Krasnodon 109 H3 Luhans'ka Oblast', E Ukraine
Krasnohvardiys'ke 109 F4 Rus. Krasnogvardeyskoye. Respublika Krym, S Ukraine
Krasnokamensk 115 F4 Chitinskaya Oblast', S Russian Federation
Krasnokamsk 111 D5 Permskaya Oblast', W Russian Federation
Krasnoperekops'k 109 F4 Rus. Krasnoperekopsk. Respublika Krym, S Ukraine
Krasnovodskiy Zaliv 122 A2 Turkm. Krasnowodsk Aylagy. Lake gulf W Turkmenistan
Krasnoyarsk 114 D4 Krasnoyarskiy Kray, S Russian Federation
Krasnystaw 98 E4 Rus. Krasnostav. Lubelskie, E Poland
Krasnyy Kut 111 C6 Saratovskaya Oblast', W Russian Federation
Krasnyy Luch 109 H3 prev. Krindachevka. Luhans'ka Oblast', E Ukraine
Krâvanh, Chuŏr Phnum 137 C6 Eng. Cardamom Mountains, Fr. Chaîne des Cardamomes. Mountain range W Cambodia
Krefeld 94 A4 Nordrhein-Westfalen, W Germany
Kremenchug 109 F2 Rus. Kremenchug. Poltavs'ka Oblast', NE Ukraine
Kremenchuts'ke Vodoskhovyshche 109 F2 Eng. Kremenchuk Reservoir, Rus. Kremenchugskoye Vodokhranilishche. Reservoir C Ukraine
Kremenets' 108 C2 Pol. Krzemieniec, Rus. Kremenets. Ternopil's'ka Oblast', W Ukraine
Kreminna 109 G2 Rus. Kremennaya. Luhans'ka Oblast', E Ukraine
Kresena see Kresna
Kresna 104 C3 var. Kresena. Blagoevgrad, SW Bulgaria
Kretikon Delagos see Kritikó Pélagos
Kretinga 106 B3 Ger. Krottingen. Kretinga, NW Lithuania
Krishna 132 C1 prev. Kistna. River C India
Krishnagiri 132 C2 Tamil Nādu, SE India
Kristiansand 85 A6 var. Christiansand. Vest-Agder, S Norway
Kristianstad 85 B7 Skåne, S Sweden
Kristiansund 84 A4 var. Christiansund. Møre og Romsdal, S Norway
Kríti 105 C7 Eng. Crete. Island Greece, Aegean Sea

Kritikó Pélagos 105 D7 var. Kretikon Delagos, Eng. Sea of Crete; anc. Mare Creticum. Sea Greece, Aegean Sea
Kríževci 100 B2 Ger. Kreuz, Hung. Kőrös. Varaždin, NE Croatia
Krk 100 A3 It. Veglia; anc. Curieta. Island NW Croatia
Krolevets' 109 F1 Rus. Krolevets. Sums'ka Oblast', NE Ukraine
Kronach 95 C5 Bayern, E Germany
Kroonstad 78 D4 Free State, C South Africa
Kropotkin 111 A7 Krasnodarskiy Kray, SW Russian Federation
Krosno 99 D5 Ger. Krossen. Podkarpackie, SE Poland
Krosno Odrzańskie 98 B3 Ger. Crossen, Kreisstadt. Lubuskie, W Poland
Krško 95 E8 Ger. Gurkfeld; prev. Videm-Krško. E Slovenia
Kruhlaye 107 D6 Rus. Krugloye. Mahilyowskaya Voblasts', E Belarus
Kruja see Krujë
Krujë 101 C6 var. Kruja, It. Croia. Durrës, C Albania
Krummau see Český Krumlov
Krung Thep 137 C5 var. Krung Thep Mahanakhon, Eng. Bangkok. Country capital (Thailand) Bangkok, C Thailand
Krung Thep, Ao 137 C5 var. Bight of Bangkok. Bay S Thailand
Krung Thep Mahanakhon see Krung Thep
Krupki 107 D6 Rus. Krupki. Minskaya Voblasts', C Belarus
Krychaw 107 E7 Rus. Krichëv. Mahilyowskaya Voblasts', E Belarus
Krym see Crimea
Krymskaya Oblast' See Crimea
Kryms'ki Hory 109 F5 mountain range S Ukraine
Kryms'kyy Pivostriv 109 F5 peninsula S Ukraine
Krynica 99 D5 Ger. Tannenhof. Małopolskie, S Poland
Kryve Ozero 109 E3 Odes'ka Oblast', SW Ukraine
Kryvyy Rih 109 F3 Rus. Krivoy Rog. Dnipropetrovs'ka Oblast', SE Ukraine
Ksar al Kabir see Ksar-el-Kebir
Ksar al Soule see Er-Rachidia
Ksar-el-Kebir 70 C2 var. Alcázar, Ksar al Kabir, Ksar-el-Kébir, Ar. Al-Kasr al-Kebir, Al-Qsar al-Kbir, Sp. Alcazarquivir. NW Morocco
Ksar-el-Kébir see Ksar-el-Kebir
Kuala Dungun see Dungun
Kuala Lumpur 138 B3 country capital (Malaysia) Kuala Lumpur, Peninsular Malaysia
Kuala Terengganu 138 B3 var. Kuala Trengganu. Terengganu, Peninsular Malaysia
Kuala Trengganu see Kuala Terengganu
Kualatungkal 138 B4 Sumatera, W Indonesia
Kuang-chou see Guangzhou
Kuang-hsi see Guangxi Zhuangzu Zizhiqu
Kuang-tung see Guangdong
Kuang-yuan see Guangyuan
Kuantan 138 B3 Pahang, Peninsular Malaysia
Kuban' 109 G5 var. Hypanis. River SW Russian Federation
Kubango see Cubango
Kuching 138 C3 prev. Sarawak. Sarawak, East Malaysia
Kūchnay Darweyshān 122 D5 Helmand, S Afghanistan
Kuçova see Kuçovë
Kuçovë 101 C6 var. Kuçova; prev. Qyteti Stalin. Berat, C Albania
Kudara see Ghūdara
Kudus 138 C5 prev. Koedoes. Jawa, C Indonesia
Kuei-chou see Guizhou
Kuei-lin see Guilin
Kuei-Yang see Guiyang
Kueyang see Guiyang

Kugluktuk 53 E3 var. Qurlurtuuq prev. Coppermine. Nunavut, NW Canada
Kuhmo 84 E4 Oulu, E Finland
Kühnö see Kihnu
Kuibyshev see Kuybyshevskoye Vodokhranilishche
Kuito 78 B2 Port. Silva Porto. Bié, C Angola
Kuji 130 D3 var. Kuzi. Iwate, Honshū, C Japan
Kukës 101 D5 var. Kukësi. Kukës, NE Albania
Kukësi see Kukës
Kukong see Shaoguan
Kukukhoto see Hohhot
Kula Kangri 135 G3 var. Kulhakangri. Mountain Bhutan/China
Kuldīga 106 B3 Ger. Goldingen. Kuldiga, W Latvia
Kuldja see Yining
Kulhakangri see Kula Kangri
Kullorsuaq 82 D2 var. Kuvdlorssuak. C Greenland
Kulmsee see Chełmża
Kūlob 123 F3 Rus. Kulyab. SW Tajikistan
Kulu 116 C3 Konya, W Turkey
Kulunda Steppe 114 C4 Kaz. Qulyndy Zhazyghy, Rus. Kulundinskaya Ravnina. Grassland Kazakhstan/Russian Federation
Kum see Qom
Kuma 111 B7 river SW Russian Federation
Kumamoto 131 A7 Kumamoto, Kyūshū, SW Japan
Kumanovo 101 E5 Turk. Kumanova. N FYR Macedonia
Kumasi 75 E5 prev. Coomassie. C Ghana
Kumayri see Gyumri
Kumba 77 A5 Sud-Ouest, W Cameroon
Kumertau 111 D6 Respublika Bashkortostan, W Russian Federation
Kumo 75 G4 Gombe, E Nigeria
Kumon Range 136 B2 mountain range N Myanmar
Kumul see Hami
Kunashiri see Kunashir, Ostrov
Kunashir, Ostrov 130 E1 var. Kunashiri. Island Kuril'skiye Ostrova, SE Russian Federation
Kunda 106 E2 Lääne-Virumaa, NE Estonia
Kunduz 123 E3 var. Kondoz, Kundūz, Qondūz, Per. Kondūz. Kunduz, NE Afghanistan
Kuneitra see Al Qunaytirah
Kunene see Cunene
Kungsbacka 85 B7 Halland, S Sweden
Kungur 111 D5 Permskaya Oblast', NW Russian Federation
Kunlun Mountains see Kunlun Shan
Kunlun Shan 126 B4 Eng. Kunlun Mountains. Mountain range NW China
Kunming 128 B6 var. K'un-ming; prev. Yunnan. Yunnan, SW China
K'un-ming see Kunming
Kununurra 146 D3 Western Australia
Kuopio 85 E5 Itä-Suomi, C Finland
Kupang 139 E5 prev. Koepang. Timor, C Indonesia
Kup"yans'k 109 G2 Rus. Kupyansk. Kharkivs'ka Oblast', E Ukraine
Kura 117 H3 Az. Kür, Geor. Mtkvari, Turk. Kura Nehri. River SW Asia
Kurashiki 131 B6 var. Kurasiki. Okayama, Honshū, SW Japan
Kurasiki see Kurashiki
Kurdistan 117 F4 cultural region SW Asia
Kŭrdzhali 104 D3 var. Kirdzhali. Kŭrdzhali, S Bulgaria
Kure 131 B7 Hiroshima, Honshū, SW Japan
Küre Dağları 116 C2 mountain range N Turkey
Kuressaare 106 C2 Ger. Arensburg; prev. Kingissepp. Saaremaa, W Estonia

Kureyka 112 D2 river N Russian Federation
Kuria Muria Islands see Ḩalāniyāt, Juzur al
Kurile Islands see Kuril'skiye Ostrova
Kurile-Kamchatka Depression see Kurile Trench
Kurile Trench 113 F3 var. Kurile-Kamchatka Depression. Undersea feature NW Pacific Ocean
Kuril'sk 130 E1 Kuril'skiye Ostrova, Sakhalinskaya Oblats', SE Russian Federation
Kuril'skiye Ostrova 115 H4 Eng. Kurile Islands. Island group SE Russian Federation
Ku-ring-gai 148 E1 New South Wales, SE Australia
Kurnool 132 C1 var. Karnul. Andhra Pradesh, S India
Kursk 111 A6 Kurskaya Oblast', W Russian Federation
Kuršumlija 101 D5 Serbia, S Serbia and Montenegro (Yugo.)
Kuruktag 126 C3 mountain range NW China
Kurume 131 A7 Fukuoka, Kyūshū, SW Japan
Kurupukari 59 F3 C Guyana
Kurzeme 106 B3 Eng. Courland, Ger. Kurland. Former province W Latvia
Kushiro 130 D2 var. Kusiro. Hokkaidō, NE Japan
Kusiro see Kushiro
Kuskokwim Mountains 36 C3 mountain range Alaska, USA
Kuźnica 98 E2 Podlaskie, NE Poland
Kustanay see Kostanay
Küstence see Constanța
Küstendje see Constanța
Kütahya 116 B3 prev. Kutaia. Kütahya, W Turkey
Kutai see Mahakam, Sungai
K'ut'aisi 117 F2 W Georgia
Kūt al 'Amārah see Al Kūt
Kut al Imara see Al Kūt
Kutaradja see Bandaaceh
Kutaraja see Bandaaceh
Kutch, Gulf of see Kachchh, Gulf of
Kutch, Rann of see Kachchh, Rann of
Kutina 100 B3 Sisak-Moslavina, NE Croatia
Kutno 98 C3 Łódzkie, C Poland
Kuujjuaq 39 E2 prev. Fort-Chimo. Quebec, E Canada
Kuusamo 84 E3 Oulu, Finland
Kuvango see Cubango
Kuvdlorssuak see Kullorsuaq
Kuwait 120 C4 var. Dawlat al Kuwait, Koweit, Kuwit. Country SW Asia

Kunlun Mountains see Kunlun Shan

Kuwait 120

Official name State of Kuwait
Formation 1961
Capital Kuwait City
Population 2 million / 291 people per sq mile (112 people per sq km)
Total area 6880 sq miles (17,820 sq km)
Languages Arabic, English
Religions Muslim (mainly Sunni) 85%, Christian, Hindu and other 15%
Ethnic mix Kuwaiti 45%, other Arab 35%, South Asian 9%, Iranian 4%, other 7%
Government Constitutional monarchy
Currency Kuwaiti dinar = 1,000 fils
Literacy rate 82.6%
Calorie consumption 3,132 kilocalories

Kuwait see Al Kuwayt
Kuwait City see Al Kuwayt
Kuwajleen see Kwajalein Atoll
Kuwayt 120 C3 E Iraq

Kuybyshev Reservoir *see*
Kuybyshevskoye
Vodokhranilishche
**Kuybyshevskoye
Vodokhranilishche** 111 C5 *var.*
Kuibyshev, *Eng.* Kuybyshev
Reservoir. *Reservoir* W Russian
Federation
Kuytun 126 B2 Xinjiang Uygur
Zizhiqu, NW China
Kuzi *see* Kuji
Kuznetsk 111 B6 Penzenskaya
Oblast', W Russian Federation
Kvaløya 84 C2 island N Norway
Kvarnbergsvattnet 84 B4 *var.*
Frostviken. *Lake* N Sweden
Kvarner 100 A3 *var.* Carnaro, *It.*
Quarnero. *Gulf* W Croatia
Kvitøya 83 G1 island NE Svalbard
Kwajalein Atoll 144 C1 *var.*
Kuwajleen. *Atoll* Ralik Chain,
C Marshall Islands
Kwando *see* Cuando
Kwangchow *see* Guangzhou
Kwangju 129 E4 *off.* Kwangju-
gwangyŏksi, *var.* Guangju,
Kwangchu, *Jap.* Kōshū. SW South
Korea
Kwango 77 C7 Port. Cuango. *River*
Angola/Dem. Rep. Congo *see also*
Cuango
Kwango *see* Cuango
Kwangsi *see* Guangxi Zhuangzu
Zizhiqu
**Kwangsi Chuang Autonomous
Region** *see* Guangxi Zhuangzu
Zizhiqu
Kwangtung *see* Guangdong
Kwangyuan *see* Guangyuan
Kwanza *see* Cuanza
Kweichow *see* Guizhou
Kweichu *see* Guiyang
Kweilin *see* Guilin
Kweisui *see* Hohhot
Kweiyang *see* Guiyang
Kwekwe 78 D3 *prev.* Que Que.
Midlands, C Zimbabwe
Kwesui *see* Hohhot
Kwidzyń 98 C2 Ger. Marienwerder.
Pomorskie, N Poland
Kwigillingok 36 C3 Alaska, USA
Kwilu 77 C6 *river* W Dem. Rep.
Congo
Kwito *see* Cuito
Kyabé 76 C4 Moyen-Chari, S Chad
Kyaikkami 137 B5 *prev.* Amherst.
Mon State, S Myanmar
Kyaiklat 136 B4 Irrawaddy,
SW Myanmar
Kyaikto 136 B4 Mon State,
S Myanmar
Kyakhta 115 E5 Respublika
Buryatiya, S Russian Federation
Kyaukse 136 B3 Mandalay,
C Myanmar
Kyjov 99 C5 Ger. Gaya. Brněnský
Kraj, SE Czech Republic
Kykládes 105 D6 *var.* Kikládhes,
Eng. Cyclades. *Island group*
SE Greece
Kými 105 C5 prev. Kími. Évvoia,
C Greece
Kyōto 131 C6 Kyōto, Honshū,
SW Japan
Kyparissía 105 B6 *var.* Kiparissía.
Pelopónnisos, S Greece
Kyrenia *see* Kerýneia
Kyrgyzstan 123 *var.* Kirghizia;
prev. Kirgizskaya SSR, Kirghiz
SSR, Republic of Kyrgyzstan.
Country C Asia

Kyrgyzstan 123

Official name Kyrgyz Republic
Formation 1991
Capital Bishkek
Population 5 million /65 people
per sq mile (25 people per sq km)
Total area 76,641 sq miles
98,500 sq km)
Languages Kyrgyz, Russian
Religions Muslim (mainly Sunni)
0%, Russian Orthodox 30%

Kyrgyzstan (continued)

Ethnic mix Kyrgyz 57%,
Russian 19%, Uzbek 13%,Tartar 2%,
Ukranian 2%, other 7%
Government Presidential
democracy
Currency Som = 100 teen
Literacy rate 97%
Calorie consumption 2,871
kilocalories

Kýthira 105 C7 *var.* Kíthira, *It.*
Cerigo; *Lat.* Cythera. *Island*
S Greece
Kýthnos 105 C6 *var.* Kíthnos,
Thermiá, *It.* Termia; *anc.* Cythnos.
Island Kykládes, Greece, Aegean
Sea
Kýthnos 105 C6 Kýthnos, Kykládes,
Greece, Aegean Sea
Kythréa 102 C5 N Cyprus
Kyūshū 131 B7 *var.* Kyûsyû. *Island*
SW Japan
Kyushu-Palau Ridge 125 F3 *var.*
Kyusyu-Palau Ridge. *Undersea
feature* W Pacific Ocean
Kyustendil 104 B2 *anc.* Pautalia.
Kyustendil, W Bulgaria
Kyûsyû *see* Kyūshū
Kyusyu-Palau Ridge *see* Kyushu-
Palau Ridge
Kyyiv 109 E2 *Eng.* Kiev, *Rus.* Kiyev.
Country capital (Ukraine)
Kyyivs'ka Oblast', N Ukraine
Kyyivs'ke Vodokhovyshche 109
E1 *Eng.* Kiev Reservoir, *Rus.*
Kiyevskoye Vodokhranilishche.
Reservoir N Ukraine
Kyzyl 114 D4 Respublika Tyva,
C Russian Federation
Kyzyl Kum 122 D2 *var.* Kizil Kum,
Qizil Qum, Qizilqum. *Desert*
Kazakhstan/Uzbekistan
Kyzylorda 114 B5 *var.* Kyzyl-orda,
Qizil Orda, *Kaz.* Kyzylorda; *prev.*
Perovsk. Kyzylorda, S Kazakhstan
Kyzyl-Suu 123 G2 *prev.* Pokrovka.
Issyk-Kul'skaya Oblast',
NE Kyrgyzstan
Kyzyl-orda *see* Kyzylorda

L

La Algaba 92 C4 Andalucía,
S Spain
Laamu Atoll *see* Hadhdhunmathi
Atoll
Laarne 87 B5 Oost-Vlaanderen,
NW Belgium
La Asunción 59 E1 Nueva Esparta,
NE Venezuela
Laâyoune 70 B3 *var.* Aaiún.
Dependent territory capital (Western
Sahara) NW Western Sahara
la Baule-Escoublac 90 A4 Loire-
Atlantique, NW France
Labé 74 C4 Moyenne-Guinée,
NW Guinea
La Blanquilla *see* Blanquilla, Isla
Laborec 99 E5 Hung. Laborca. *River*
E Slovakia
Labrador 39 F2 *cultural region*
Newfoundland and Labrador,
SW Canada
Labrador Basin 34 E3 *var.* Labrador
Sea Basin. *Undersea feature*
Labrador Basin
Labrador Sea 82 A4 *sea*
NW Atlantic Ocean
Labrador Sea Basin *see* Labrador
Basin
Labutta 137 A5 Irrawaddy,
SW Myanmar
Laç 101 C6 *var.* Laci. Lezhë,
C Albania
La Calera 64 B4 Valparaíso, C Chile
La Carolina 92 D4 Andalucía,
S Spain
Laccadive Islands *see* Lakshadweep
La Ceiba 52 D2 Atlántida,
N Honduras
Lachanás 104 B3 Kentrikí
Makedonía, N Greece
La Chaux-de-Fonds 95 A7
Neuchâtel, W Switzerland

Lachlan River 149 C6 *river* New
South Wales, SE Australia
Laci *see* Laç
la Ciotat 91 D6 *anc.* Citharista.
Bouches-du-Rhône, SE France
La Concepción 58 C1 Zulia,
NW Venezuela
La Concepción 53 E5 *var.*
Concepción. Chiriquí, W Panama
La Condamine 91 C8 NW Andorra
Laconia 41 G2 New Hampshire,
NE USA
La Crosse 40 A2 Wisconsin,
N USA
La Cruz 52 D4 Guanacaste,
NW Costa Rica
Lacus Asphaltites *see* Dead Sea
Ladoga, Lake *see* Ladozhskoye
Ozero
Ladozhskoye Ozero 110 B3 *Eng.*
Lake Ladoga, *Fin.* Laatokka. *Lake*
NW Russian Federation
Ladysmith 40 B2 Wisconsin, N USA
Lae 144 B3 Morobe, W PNG
La Esperanza 52 C2 Intibucá,
SW Honduras
Lafayette 40 C4 Indiana, N USA
Lafayette 42 B3 Louisiana, S USA
La Fé 54 A2 Pinar del Río, W Cuba
Lafia 75 G4 Nassarawa, C Nigeria
la Flèche 90 B4 Sarthe, NW France
Lagdo, Lac de 76 B4 *lake*
N Cameroon
Laghouat 70 D2 N Algeria
Lago dos Gansos *see* Goose Lake
Lago General Carrera *see* Buenos
Aires, Lago
Lago Nyassa *see* Nyasa, Lake
Lago Pampa Aullagas *see* Poopó,
Lago
Lagos 92 B5 *anc.* Lacobriga. Faro,
S Portugal
Lagos 75 F5 Lagos, SW Nigeria
Lagos de Moreno 51 E4 Jalisco,
SW Mexico
Lagouira 70 A4 SW Western Sahara
La Grande 46 C3 Oregon, NW USA
La Guaira 66 B4 Distrito Federal,
N Venezuela
Laguna Merín *see* Mirim Lagoon
Lagunas 64 B1 Tarapacá, N Chile
Lagunillas 61 G4 Santa Cruz,
SE Bolivia
La Habana 54 B2 *var.* Havana.
Country capital (Cuba) Ciudad de
La Habana, W Cuba
Lahat 138 B4 Sumatera,
W Indonesia
La Haye *see* 's-Gravenhage
Laholm 85 B7 Halland, S Sweden
Lahore 134 D2 Punjab, NE
Pakistan
Lahr 95 A6 Baden-Württemberg,
S Germany
Lahti 85 D5 Swe. Lahtis. Etelä-
Suomi, S Finland
Laï 76 B4 *prev.* Behagle, De Behagle.
Tandjilé, S Chad
Lai Châu 136 D3 Lai Châu,
N Vietnam
Laila *see* Laylá
La Junta 44 D5 Colorado, C USA
Lake Charles 42 A3 Louisiana,
S USA
Lake City 43 E3 Florida, SE USA
Lake District 89 C5 *physical region*
NW England, UK
Lake Havasu City 48 A2 Arizona,
SW USA
Lake Jackson 49 H4 Texas, SW USA
Lakeland 43 E4 Florida, SE USA
Lakeside 47 C8 California, W USA
Lakewood 44 D4 Colorado, C USA
Lakhnau *see* Lucknow
Lakonikós Kólpos 105 B7 *gulf*
S Greece
Lakselv 84 D2 Finnmark,
N Norway
Lakshadweep 132 A3 *Eng.*
Laccadive Islands. *Island group*
India, N Indian Ocean
la Laon *see* Laon
Lalibela 72 C4 N Ethiopia
La Libertad 52 B1 Petén,
N Guatemala
La Ligua 64 B4 Valparaíso, C Chile
Lalín 92 C1 Galicia, NW Spain

Lalitpur 135 F3 Central, C Nepal
La Louvière 87 B6 Hainaut,
S Belgium
La Maçana *see* La Massana
la Maddalena 96 A4 Sardegna, Italy,
C Mediterranean Sea
la Manche *see* English Channel
Lamar 44 D5 Colorado, C USA
La Marmora, Punta 97 A5 mountain
Sardegna, Italy, C Mediterranean
Sea
La Massana 91 A8 *var.* La Maçana.
W Andorra
Lambaréné 77 A6 Moyen-Ogooué,
W Gabon
Lamego 92 C2 Viseu, N Portugal
Lamesa 49 E3 Texas, SW USA
Lamezia 97 D6 Calabria, SE Italy
Lamía 105 B5 Stereá Ellás, C Greece
Lamoni 45 F4 Iowa, C USA
Lampang 136 C4 *var.* Muang
Lampang. Lampang,
NW Thailand
Lámpeia 105 B6 Dytikí Ellás,
S Greece
Lanbi Kyun 137 B6 *prev.* Sullivan
Island. *Island* Mergui Archipelago,
S Myanmar
Lancang Jiang *see* Mekong
Lancaster 47 C7 California, W USA
Lancaster 89 D5 NW England, UK
Lancaster 41 F4 Pennsylvania,
NE USA
Lancaster Sound 37 F2 *sound*
Nunavut, N Canada
Lan-chou *see* Lanzhou
Lan-chow *see* Lanzhou
Landen 87 C6 Vlaams Brabant,
C Belgium
Lander 44 C3 Wyoming, C USA
Landerneau 90 A3 Finistère,
NW France
Landes 91 B5 *department* SW France
Land's End 89 B8 *headland*
SW England, UK
Landshut 95 C6 Bayern,
SE Germany
Langar 123 E2 Rus. Lyangar.
Nawoiy Wiloyati, C Uzbekistan
Langfang 128 C4 Hebei, E China
Langkawi, Pulau 137 B7 *island*
Peninsular Malaysia
Langres 90 D4 Haute-Marne,
N France
Langsa 138 A3 Sumatera,
W Indonesia
Lang Shan 127 E3 *mountain range*
N China
Lang Son 136 D3 *var.* Langson.
Lang Sơn, N Vietnam
Langson *see* Lang Son
Lang Suan 137 B6 Chumphon,
SW Thailand
Languedoc 91 C6 *cultural region*
S France
Länkäran 117 H3 *Rus.* Lenkoran'.
S Azerbaijan
Lansing 40 C3 *state capital*
Michigan, N USA
Lanta, Ko 137 B7 *island* S Thailand
Lantau Island 128 A2 *Cant.* Tai Yue
Shan, *Chin.* Landao. *Island* Hong
Kong, S China
Lan-ts'ang Chiang *see* Mekong
Lanzarote 70 B3 *island* Islas Canarias,
Spain, NE Atlantic Ocean
Lanzhou 128 B4 *var.* Lan-chou,
Lanchow, Lan-chow; *prev.* Kaolan.
Gansu, C China
Lao Cai 136 D3 Lao Cai, N Vietnam
Laojunmiao *see* Yumen
Laon 90 D3 *var.* la Laon; *anc.*
Laudunum. Aisne, N France
La Orchila, Isla 58 D1 island
N Venezuela
La Oroya 60 C3 Junín, C Peru
Laos 136 D4 *Country* SE Asia

Laos 136

Official name Lao People's
Democratic Republic
Formation 1953
Capital Vientiane
Population 5.4 million / 59 people
per sq mile (23 people per sq km)

Laos (continued)

Total area 91,428 sq miles
(236,800 sq km)
Languages Lao, Mon-Khmer,
Chinese, Yao, Vietnamese, French
Religions Buddhist 85%, other
(including Animist) 15%
Ethnic mix Lao Loum 66%, Lao
Theung 30%, Lao Soung 2%,
other 2%
Government One-party republic
Currency New kip = 100 cents
Literacy rate 48.7%
Calorie consumption 2,266
kilocalories

La Palma 70 A3 island Islas
Canarias, Spain, NE Atlantic
Ocean
La Palma 53 G5 Darién,
SE Panama
La Paz 61 F4 var. La Paz de
Ayacucho. Country capital
(Bolivia-legislative and
administrative capital) La Paz,
W Bolivia
La Paz 50 B3 Baja California Sur,
NW Mexico
La Paz, Bahía de 50 B3 bay
W Mexico
La Paz de Ayacucho see La Paz
La Perouse Strait 130 D1 Jap. Sōya-
kaikyō, Rus. Proliv Laperuza.
Strait Japan/Russian Federation
Lápithos 102 C5 NW Cyprus
Lapland 84 D3 Fin. Lappi, Swe.
Lappland. Cultural region N Europe
La Plata 64 D4 Buenos Aires,
E Argentina
Lappeenranta 85 E5 Swe.
Villmanstrand. Etelä-Suomi, S
Finland
Lappi see Lapland
Lappland see Lapland
Lapta see Lápithos
Laptev Sea see Laptevykh, More
Laptevykh, More 115 E2 Eng.
Laptev Sea. Sea Arctic Ocean
Lapua 85 D5 Swe. Lappo. Länsi-
Suomi, W Finland
La Puebla see La Pobla
Łapy 98 E3 Podlaskie
N Argentina
L'Aquila 96 C4 var. Aquila, Aquila
degli Abruzzo. Abruzzo, C Italy
Laracha 92 B1 Galicia, NW Spain
Laramie 44 C4 Wyoming, C USA
Laramie Mountains 44 C3 mountain
range Wyoming, C USA
Laredo 93 E1 Cantabria, N Spain
Laredo 49 F5 Texas, SW USA
Largo 43 E4 Florida, SE USA
Largo, Cayo 54 B2 island W Cuba
Lario see Como, Lago di
La Rioja 93 E2 La Rioja,
NW Argentina
Lárisa 104 B4 var. Larissa. Thessalía,
C Greece
Larissa see Lárisa
Lārkāna 134 B3 var. Larkhana. Sind,
SE Pakistan
Larkhana see Lārkāna
Larnaca see Lárnaka
Lárnaka 102 C5 var. Larnaca,
Larnax. SE Cyprus
Larnax see Lárnaka
la Rochelle 90 B4 anc. Rupella.
Charente-Maritime, W France
la Roche-sur-Yon 90 B4 prev.
Bourbon Vendée, Napoléon-
Vendée. Vendée, NW France
La Roda 93 E3 Castilla-La Mancha,
C Spain
La Romana 55 E3 E Dominican
Republic
Larvotto 91 C8 N Monaco
La-sa see Lhasa
Las Cabezas de San Juan 92 C5
Andalucía, S Spain
Las Cruces 48 D3 New Mexico,
SW USA
La See d'Urgel 93 G1 var. La Seu
d'Urgell, Seo de Urgel. Cataluña,
NE Spain

La Serena 64 B3 Coquimbo, C Chile
La Seu d'Urgell see La See d'Urgel
la Seyne-sur-Mer 91 D6 Var,
SE France
Lashio 136 B3 Shan State,
E Myanmar
Lashkar Gāh 122 D5 var. Lash-Kar-
Gar'. Helmand, S Afghanistan
Lash-Kar-Gar' see Lashkar Gāh
La Sila 97 D6 mountain range
SW Italy
La Sirena 52 D3 Región Autónoma
Atlántico Sur, E Nicaragua
Łask 98 C4 Łódzkie, C Poland
Las Lomitas 64 D2 Formosa,
N Argentina
La Solana 93 E4 Castilla-La
Mancha, C Spain
Las Palmas de Gran Canaria 70 A3
Gran Canaria, Islas Canarias,
Spain, NE Atlantic Ocean
La Spezia 96 B3 Liguria, NW Italy
Lassa see Lhasa
Las Tablas 53 F5 Los Santos,
S Panama
Las Tunas 54 C2 var. Victoria de las
Tunas. Las Tunas, E Cuba
Las Vegas 47 D7 Nevada, W USA
Latacunga 60 B1 Cotopaxi,
C Ecuador
la Teste 91 B5 Gironde, SW France
Latina 97 C5 prev. Littoria. Lazio,
C Italy
La Tortuga, Isla 59 E1 var. Isla
Tortuga. Island N Venezuela
La Tuque 39 E4 Quebec, SE Canada
Latvia 106 C3 Ger. Lettland, Latv.
Latvija,Latvijas Republika; prev.
Latvian SSR, Rus. Latviyskaya
SSR. Country NE Europe

Latvia 106

Official name Republic of Latvia
Formation 1991
Capital Riga
Population 2.4 million / 96 people
per sq mile (37 people per sq km)
Total area 24,938 sq miles
(64,589 sq km)
Languages Latvian, Russian
Religions Lutheran 55%, Roman
Catholic 24%, Russian Orthodox 9%,
other 12%
Ethnic mix Latvian 57%,
Russian 32%, Belarussian 4%,
Ukranian 3%, Polish 2%, other 2%
Government Presidential democracy
Currency Lat = 100 santimi
Literacy rate 99%
Calorie consumption 2,855
kilocalories

Laudunum see Laon
Lauenburg see Lębork
Lauenburg in Pommern see Lębork
Lau Group 145 E4 island group E Fiji
Launceston 149 C8 Tasmania,
SE Australia
La Unión 93 F4 Murcia, SE Spain
La Unión 52 C2 Olancho,
C Honduras
Laurel 42 C3 Mississippi, S USA
Laurel 44 C2 Montana, NW USA
Laurentian Highlands see
Laurentian Mountains
Laurentian Mountains 39 E3 var.
Laurentian Highlands, Fr. Les
Laurentides. Plateau
Newfoundland and
Labrador/Quebec, Canada
Lauria 97 D6 Basilicata, S Italy
Laurinburg 43 F1 North Carolina,
SE USA
Lauru see Choiseul
Lausanne 95 A7 It. Losanna. Vaud,
SW Switzerland
Laut Banda see Banda Sea
Laut, Pulau 138 D4 prev. Laoet.
Island Borneo, C Indonesia
Laval 39 E3 Quebec, SE Canada
Laval 90 B3 Mayenne,
NW France
Laval 38 D4 Quebec, SE Canada
La Vega 55 E3 var. Concepción de
Vega. C Dominican Republic
La Vila Jojosa see Villajoyosa

Lávrio 105 C6 prev. Lávrion. Attikí,
C Greece
Lawrence 41 G3 Massachusetts,
NE USA
Lawrenceburg 42 C1 Tennessee,
S USA
Lawton 49 F2 Oklahoma, C USA
La Yarada 61 E4 Tacna, SW Peru
Laylá 121 C5 var. Laila. Ar Riyāḍ,
C Saudi Arabia
Lazarev Sea 154 B1 sea Antarctica
Lázaro Cárdenas 51 E5 Michoacán
de Ocampo, SW Mexico
Læsø 85 B7 island N Denmark
Leamhcán see Lucan
Leamington 38 C5 Ontario, S Canada
Lebak 139 E3 Mindanao,
S Philippines
Lebanon 118 A4 Ar. Al Lubnān, Fr.
Liban. Country SW Asia

Lebanon 118

Official name Republic of Lebanon
Formation 1941
Capital Beirut
Population 3.6 million / 897 people
per sq mile (346 people per sq km)
Total area 4,015 sq miles
(10,400 sq km)
Languages Arabic, French,
Armenian, Assyrian
Religions Muslim 70%,
Christian 30%
Ethnic mix Arab 94%, Armenian
4%, other 2%
Government Multiparty republic
Currency Lebanese pound =
100 piastres
Literacy rate 86%
Calorie consumption 3,155
kilocalories

Lebanon 45 G5 Missouri, C USA
Lebanon 41 G2 New Hampshire,
NE USA
Lebanon 46 B3 Oregon, NW USA
Lebap 122 D2 Lebapskiy Velayat,
NE Turkmenistan
Lebedyn 109 F2 Rus. Lebedin.
Sums'ka Oblast', NE Ukraine
Lębork 98 C2 var. Lębórk, Ger.
Lauenburg, Lauenburg in
Pommern. Pomorskie,
N Poland
Lebrija 92 C5 Andalucía, S Spain
Lebu 65 A5 Bío Bío, C Chile
le Cannet 91 D6 Alpes-Maritimes,
SE France
Le Cap see Cap-Haïtien
Lecce 97 E6 Puglia, SE Italy
Lechainá 105 B6 var. Lehena,
Lekhainá. Dytikí Ellás,
S Greece
Leduc 37 E5 Alberta, SW Canada
Leech Lake 45 F2 lake Minnesota,
N USA
Leeds 89 D5 N England, UK
Leek 86 E2 Groningen,
NE Netherlands
Leer 94 A3 Niedersachsen,
NW Germany
Leeuwarden 86 D1 Fris. Ljouwert.
Friesland, N Netherlands
Leeuwin, Cape 142 A5 headland
Western Australia
Leeward Islands 55 G3 island group
E West Indies
Leeward Islands see Sotavento,
Ilhas de
Lefkáda 105 A5 It. Santa Maura;
prev. Levkás, anc. Leucas. Island
Iónioi Nísoi, Greece,
C Mediterranean Sea
Lefkáda 105 A5 prev. Levkás.
Lefkáda, Iónioi Nísoi, Greece,
C Mediterranean Sea
Lefká Óri 105 C7 mountain range
Kríti, Greece, E Mediterranean Sea
Lefkímmi 105 A5 var. Levkímmi.
Kérkyra, Iónioi Nísoi, Greece,
C Mediterranean Sea
Legaspi 139 E2 off. Legaspi City.
Luzon, N Philippines
Legnica 98 B4 Ger. Liegnitz.
Dolnośląskie

le Havre 90 B3 Eng. Havre; prev.
Havre-de-Grâce. Seine-Maritime,
N France
Lehena see Lechainá
Leicester 89 D6 Lat. Batae
Coritanorum. C England, UK
Leiden 86 B3 prev. Leyden, anc.
Lugdunum Batavorum. Zuid-
Holland, W Netherlands
Leie 90 D2 Fr. Lys. River
Belgium/France
Leinster 89 B6 Ir. Cúige Laighean.
Cultural region E Ireland
Leipsoi 105 E6 island Dodekánisos,
Greece, Aegean Sea
Leipzig 94 C4 Pol. Lipsk; hist.
Leipsic, anc. Lipsia. Sachsen,
E Germany
Leiria 92 B3 anc. Collipo. Leiria,
C Portugal
Leirvik 85 A6 Hordaland,
S Norway
Lek 86 C4 river SW Netherlands
Lekhainá see Lechainá
Lekhchevo 104 C2 Montana,
NW Bulgaria
Leksand 85 C5 Kopparberg,
C Sweden
Lelystad 86 D3 Flevoland,
C Netherlands
le Mans 90 B3 Sarthe, NW France
Lemesós 102 C5 var. Limassol.
SW Cyprus
Lena 115 F3 river NE Russian
Federation
Lena Tablemount 141 B7 undersea
feature S Indian Ocean
Len Dao 128 C8 island S Spratly
Islands
Lengshuitan 128 C6 Hunan,
S China
Leninabad see Khūjand
Leninakan see Gyumri
Lenine 109 G5 Rus. Lenino.
Respublika Krym, S Ukraine
Leningorsk 114 D4 Kaz. Leningor.
Vostochnyy Kazakhstan,
E Kazakhstan
Leningrad see Sankt-Peterburg
Leningradskaya 154 B4 Russian
research station Antarctica
Leninobod see Khūjand
Leninpol' 123 F2 Talasskaya
Oblast', NW Kyrgyzstan
Lenti 99 B7 Zala, SW Hungary
Leoben 95 E7 Steiermark,
C Austria
León 51 E4 var. León de los
Aldamas. Guanajuato, C Mexico
León 92 D1 Castilla-León,
NW Spain
León 52 C3 León, NW Nicaragua
León de los Aldamas see León
Leonídi 105 B6 Pelopónnisos,
S Greece
Lepe 92 C4 Andalucía, S Spain
le Portel 90 C2 Pas-de-Calais,
N France
le Puy 91 C5 prev. le Puy-en-Velay,
hist. Anicium, Podium Anicensis.
Haute-Loire, C France
Léré 76 B4 Mayo-Kébbi, SW Chad
Lerma 92 D2 Castilla-León,
N Spain
Léros 105 D6 island Dodekánisos,
Greece, Aegean Sea
Lerrnayin Gharabakh see
Nagornyy Karabakh
Lerwick 88 D1 NE Scotland, UK
Lesbos see Lésvos
Les Cayes see Cayes
Les Gonaïves see Gonaïves
Lesh see Lezhë
Leshan 128 B5 Sichuan, C China
les Herbiers 90 B4 Vendée,
NW France
Leshi see Lezhë
Leskovac 101 E5 Serbia, SE Serbia
and Montenegro (Yugo.)
Les Laurentides see Laurentian
Highlands
Lesotho 78 D4 prev. Basutoland.
Country S Africa

Lesotho 78

Official name Kingdom of Lesotho

Lesotho (continued)

Formation 1966
Capital Maseru
Population 2.1 million / 179 people per sq mile (69 people per sq km)
Total area 11,720 sq miles (30,355 sq km)
Languages English, Sesotho, Zulu
Religions Traditional beliefs 10%, Christian 90%,
Ethnic mix Sotho 97%, European and Asian 3%
Government Constitutional monarchy
Currency Loti = 100 lisente
Literacy rate 83.3%
Calorie consumption 2,300 kilocalories

les Sables-d'Olonne 90 B4 Vendée, NW France
Lesser Antarctica 154 A3 var. West Antarctica. Physical region Antarctica
Lesser Antilles 55 G4 island group E West Indies
Lesser Caucasus 117 F2 Rus. Malyy Kavkaz. Mountain range SW Asia
Lesser Sunda Islands see Nusa Tenggara
Lésvos 116 A3 anc. Lesbos. Island E Greece
Leszno 98 B4 Ger. Lissa. Wielkopolskie, C Poland
Lethbridge 37 E5 Alberta, SW Canada
Lethem 59 F3 S Guyana
Leti, Kepulauan 139 F5 island group E Indonesia
Letpadan 136 B4 Pegu, SW Myanmar
Letsôk-aw Kyun 137 B6 var. Letsutan Island; prev. Domel Island. Island Mergui Archipelago, S Myanmar
Letsutan Island see Letsôk-aw Kyun
Leuven 87 C6 Fr. Louvain, Ger. Löwen. Vlaams Brabant, C Belgium
Leuze see Leuze-en-Hainaut
Leuze-en-Hainaut 87 B6 var. Leuze. Hainaut, SW Belgium
Levanger 84 B4 Nord-Trøndelag, C Norway
Levelland 49 E2 Texas, SW USA
Leverkusen 94 A4 Nordrhein-Westfalen, W Germany
Levice 99 C6 Ger. Lewentz, Lewenz, Hung. Léva. Nitriansky Kraj, SW Slovakia
Levin 150 D4 Manawatu-Wanganui, North Island, NZ
Levkímmi see Lefkímmi
Lewis, Isle of 88 B2 island NW Scotland, UK
Lewis Range 44 B1 mountain range Montana, NW USA
Lewiston 46 C2 Idaho, NW USA
Lewiston 41 G2 Maine, NE USA
Lewistown 44 C1 Montana, NW USA
Lexington 40 C5 Kentucky, S USA
Lexington 45 E4 Nebraska, C USA
Leyte 139 F2 island C Philippines
Leżajsk 99 E5 Podkarpackie, SE Poland
Lezha see Lezhë
Lezhë 101 C6 var. Lezha; prev. Lesh, Leshi. Lezhë, NW Albania
Lhasa 126 C5 var. La-sa, Lassa. Xizang Zizhiqu, W China
Lhaviyani Atoll see Faadhippolhu Atoll
Lhazê 126 C5 Xizang Zizhiqu, W China
L'Hospitalet de Llobregat 93 G2 var. Hospitalet. Cataluña, NE Spain
Liancourt Rocks 131 A5 Jap. Takeshima, Kor. Tok-Do. Island group Japan/South Korea
Lianyungang 128 C4 var. Xinpu. Jiangsu, E China

Liao see Liaoning
Liaodong Wan 127 G3 Eng. Gulf of Lantung, Gulf of Liaotung. Gulf NE China
Liao He 125 E1 river NE China
Liaoning 128 D3 var. Liao, Liaoning Sheng, Shengking; Hist. Fengtien, Shenking. Admin. region province NE China
Liaoyuan 129 E3 var. Dongliao, Shuang-liao, Jap. Chengchiatun. Jilin, NE China
Liard see Fort Liard
Liban, Jebel 118 B4 Ar. Jabal al Gharbî, Jabal Lubnân, Eng. Mount Lebanon. Mountain range C Lebanon
Libby 44 A1 Montana, NW USA
Liberal 45 E5 Kansas, C USA
Liberec 98 B4 Ger. Reichenberg. Liberecký Kraj, N Czech Republic
Liberia 74 C5 Country W Africa

Liberia 74

Official name Republic of Liberia
Formation 1847
Capital Monrovia
Population 3.1 million / 72 people per sq mile (28 people per sq km)
Total area 43,000 sq miles (111,370 sq km)
Languages English, Kpelle, Vai, Bassa, Kru, Grebo, Kissi, Gola, Loma
Religions Christian 68%, Traditional beliefs 18%, Muslim 14%
Ethnic mix Indigenous tribes (16 main groups) 95%, Americo-Liberians 5%
Government Multiparty republic
Currency Liberian dollar = 100 cents
Literacy rate 54%
Calorie consumption 2,076 kilocalories

Liberia 52 D4 Guanacaste, NW Costa Rica
Libian Desert see Libyan Desert
Libourne 91 B5 Gironde, SW France
Libreville 77 A5 country capital (Gabon) Estuaire, NW Gabon
Libya 71 F3 Ar. Al Jamāhīrīyah al 'Arabīyah al Lībīyah ash Sha'bīyah al Ishtirākīyah; prev. Libyan Arab Republic. Country N Africa

Libya 71

Official name Great Socialist People's Libyan Arab Jamahariyah
Formation 1951
Capital Tripoli
Population 5.4 million /8 people per sq mile (3 people per sq km)
Total area 679,358 sq miles (1,759,540 sq km)
Languages Arabic, Tuareg
Religions Muslim (mainly Sunni) 97%, other 3%
Ethnic mix Arab and Berber 95%, other 5%
Government One-party state
Currency Libyan dinar = 1,000 dirhams
Literacy rate 80.1%
Calorie consumption 3,305 kilocalories

Libyan Desert 71 H4 var. Libian Desert, Ar. Aş Şahrā' al Lībīyah. Desert N Africa
Libyan Plateau 103 F4 var. Aḍ Diffah. Plateau Egypt/Libya
Lichtenfels 95 C5 Bayern, SE Germany
Lichtenvoorde 86 E4 Gelderland, E Netherlands
Lichuan 128 C5 Hubei, C China
Lida 107 B5 Rus. Lida. Hrodzyenskaya Voblasts', W Belarus

Lidköping 85 B6 Västra Götaland, S Sweden
Lidoríki 105 B5 prev. Lidhorikón, Lidokhorikon. Stereá Ellás, C Greece
Lidzbark Warmiński 98 D2 Ger. Heilsberg. Warmińsko-Mazurskie, NE Poland
Liechtenstein 94 D1 Country C Europe

Liechtenstein 94

Official name Principality of Liechtenstein
Formation 1719
Capital Vaduz
Population 32,200/ 521 people per sq mile (201 people per sq km)
Total area 62 sq miles (160 sq km)
Languages German, Alemannish dialect, Italian
Religions Roman Catholic 81%, Protestant 7%, other 12%
Ethnic mix Liechtensteiner 63%, Foreign residents 37%
Government Parliamentary democracy
Currency Swiss franc = 100 centimes
Literacy rate 99%
Calorie consumption not available

Liège 87 D6 Dut. Luik, Ger. Lüttich. Liège, E Belgium
Lienz 95 D7 Tirol, W Austria
Liepāja 106 B3 Ger. Libau. Liepāja, W Latvia
Liezen 95 D7 Steiermark, C Austria
Liffey 89 B6 river E Ireland
Lifou 144 D5 island Îles Loyauté, E New Caledonia
Liger see Loire
Ligure, Appennino 96 A2 Eng. Ligurian Mountains. Mountain range NW Italy
Ligurian Sea 96 A3 Fr. Mer Ligurienne, It. Mar Ligure. Sea N Mediterranean Sea
Lihue 47 A7 Haw. Līhu'e. Kauai, Hawaii, USA, C Pacific Ocean
Lihula 106 D2 Ger. Leal. Läänemaa, W Estonia
Likasi 77 D7 prev. Jadotville. Shaba, SE Dem. Rep. Congo
Liknes 85 A6 Vest-Agder, S Norway
Lille 90 C2 var. l'Isle, Dut. Rijssel, Flem. Ryssel; prev. Lisle, anc. Insula. Nord, N France
Lillehammer 85 B5 Oppland, S Norway
Lillestrøm 85 B6 Akershus, S Norway
Lilongwe 79 E2 country capital (Malawi) Central, W Malawi
Lima 60 C4 country capital (Peru) Lima, W Peru
Limanowa 99 D5 Małopolskie, S Poland
Limassol see Lemesós
Limerick 89 A6 Ir. Luimneach. SW Ireland
Límnos 103 F3 anc. Lemnos. Island E Greece
Limoges 91 C5 anc. Augustoritum Lemovicensium, Lemovices. Haute-Vienne, C France
Limón 53 E4 var. Puerto Limón. Limón, E Costa Rica
Limón 52 D2 Colón, NE Honduras
Limousin 91 C5 cultural region C France
Limoux 91 C6 Aude, S France
Limpopo 78 D3 var. Crocodile. River S Africa
Linares 92 D4 Andalucía, S Spain
Linares 64 B4 Maule, C Chile
Linares 51 E3 Nuevo León, NE Mexico
Linchuan 128 C5 var. Fuzhou. Jiangxi, S China
Lincoln 89 D5 anc. Lindum, Lindum Colonia. E England, UK

Lincoln 45 F4 state capital Nebraska, C USA
Lincoln 41 H2 Maine, NE USA
Lincoln Sea 34 D2 sea Arctic Ocean
Linden 59 F3 E Guyana
Líndhos see Líndos
Lindi 73 D8 Lindi, SE Tanzania
Líndos 105 E7 var. Líndhos. Ródos, Dodekánisos, Greece, Aegean Sea
Line Islands 145 G3 island group E Kiribati
Lingeh see Bandar-e Langeh
Lingen 94 A3 var. Lingen an der Ems. Niedersachsen, NW Germany
Lingen an der Ems see Lingen
Lingga, Kepulauan 138 B4 island group W Indonesia
Linköping 85 C6 Östergötland, S Sweden
Linz 95 D6 anc. Lentia. Oberösterreich, N Austria
Lion, Golfe du 91 C7 Eng. Gulf of Lion, Gulf of Lions; anc. Sinus Gallicus. Gulf S France
Lipari Islands see Eolie, Isole
Lipari, Isola 97 D6 island Isole Eolie, S Italy
Lipetsk 111 B5 Lipetskaya Oblast', W Russian Federation
Lipno 98 C3 Kujawsko-pomorskie, C Poland
Lipova 108 A4 Hung. Lippa. Arad, W Romania
Liqeni i Ohrit see Ohrid, Lake
Lira 73 B6 N Uganda
Lisala 77 C5 Equateur, N Dem. Rep. Congo
Lisboa 92 B4 Eng. Lisbon; anc. Felicitas Julia, Olisipo. Country capital (Portugal) Lisboa, W Portugal
Lisbon see Lisboa
Lisieux 90 B3 anc. Noviomagus. Calvados, N France
Liski 111 B6 prev. Georgiu-Dezh. Voronezhskaya Oblast', W Russian Federation
Lisle see Lille
l'Isle see Lille
Lismore 149 E5 Victoria, SE Australia
Lisse 86 C3 Zuid-Holland, W Netherlands
Litang 128 A5 Sichuan, C China
Litani, Nahr el 135 B5 var. Nahr al Litant. River C Lebanon
Lithgow 149 D6 New South Wales, SE Australia
Lithuania 106 B4 Ger. Litauen, Lith. Lietuva, Pol. Litwa, Rus. Litva; prev. Lithuanian SSR, Rus. Litovskaya SSR. Country NE Europe

Lithuania 106

Official name Republic of Lithuania
Formation 1991
Capital Vilnius
Population 3.7 million / 147 people per sq mile (57 peopleper sq km)
Total area 25,174 sq miles (65,200 sq km)
Languages Lithuanian, Russian
Religions Roman Catholic 83%, Protestant 5%, other 12%
Ethnic mix Lithuanian 80%, Russian 9%, Polish 7%, Belarussian 2%, other 2%
Government Parliamentary democracy
Currency Litas = 100 centas
Literacy rate 99%
Calorie consumption 3,040 kilocalories

Litóchoro 104 B4 var. Litohoro, Litókhoron. Kentrikí Makedonía, N Greece
Litohoro see Litóchoro
Litókhoron see Litóchoro
Little Alföld 99 C6 Ger. Kleines Ungarisches Tiefland, Hung. Kisalföld, Slvk. Podunajská Rovina. Plain Hungary/Slovakia

Little Andaman 133 F2 island
Andaman Islands, India,
NE Indian Ocean
Little Barrier Island 150 D2 island
N NZ
Little Bay 93 H5 bay S Gibraltar
Little Cayman 54 B3 island
E Cayman Islands
Little Falls 45 F2 Minnesota, N USA
Littlefield 49 E2 Texas, SW USA
Little Inagua 54 D2 var. Inagua
Islands. Island S Bahamas
Little Minch, The 88 B3 strait
NW Scotland, UK
Little Missouri River 44 D2 river
NW USA
Little Nicobar 133 G3 island
Nicobar Islands, India, NE Indian
Ocean
Little Rock 42 B1 state capital
Arkansas, C USA
Little Saint Bernard Pass 91 D5 Fr.
Col du Petit St-Bernard, It. Colle
di Piccolo San Bernardo. Pass
France/Italy
Little Sound 42 A5 bay Bermuda,
NW Atlantic Ocean
Littleton 44 D4 Colorado, C USA
Liuchow see Liuzhou
Liuzhou 128 C6 var. Liu-chou,
Liuchow. Guangxi Zhuangzu
Zizhiqu, S China
Livanátes 105 B5 prev. Livanátai.
Stereá Ellás, C Greece
Līvāni 106 D4 Ger. Lievenhof. Preiļi,
SE Latvia
Liverpool 148 D2 New South
Wales, SE Australia
Liverpool 39 F5 Nova Scotia,
SE Canada
Liverpool 89 C5 NW England,
UK
Livingston 44 B2 Montana,
NW USA
Livingston 78 C3 var. Maramba.
Southern, S Zambia
Livingstone 49 H3 Texas, SW USA
Livingstone Mountains 151 A7
mountain range South Island, NZ
Livno 100 B4 Federacija Bosna I
Hercegovina, SW Bosnia and
Herzegovina
Livojoki 84 D4 river C Finland
Livonia 40 D3 Michigan, N USA
Livorno 96 B3 Eng. Leghorn.
Toscana, C Italy
Lixoúri 105 A5 prev. Lixoúrion.
Kefallinía, Iónioi Nísoi, Greece,
C Mediterranean Sea
Ljubljana 95 D7 Ger. Laibach, It.
Lubiana; anc. Aemona, Emona.
Country capital (Slovenia)
C Slovenia
Ljungby 85 B7 Kronoberg,
S Sweden
Ljusdal 85 C5 Gävleborg,
C Sweden
Ljusnan 85 C5 river C Sweden
Llanelli 89 C6 prev. Llanelly.
SW Wales, UK
Llanes 92 D1 Asturias, N Spain
Llanos 58 D2 physical region
Colombia/Venezuela
Lleida 93 F2 Cast. Lérida; anc.
Ilerda. Cataluña, NE Spain
Lluchmayor see Llucmajor
Llucmajor 93 G3 var. Lluchmayor.
Mallorca, Spain, W Mediterranean
Sea
Loaita Island 128 C8 island
W Spratly Islands
Loanda see Luanda
Lobatse 78 C4 var. Lobatsi.
Kgatleng, SE Botswana
Lobatsi see Lobatse
Löbau 94 D4 Sachsen, E Germany
Lobito 78 B2 Benguela, W Angola
Lob Nor see Lop Nur
Loburi see Lop Buri
Locarno 95 B8 Ger. Luggarus.
Ticino, S Switzerland
Lochem 86 E3 Gelderland,
E Netherlands
Lockport 41 E3 New York, NE USA
Lodja 77 D6 Kasai Oriental, C Dem.
Rep. Congo

Lodwar 73 C6 Rift Valley, NW Kenya
Łódź 98 D4 Rus. Lodz. Łódzkie,
C Poland
Loei 136 C4 var. Loey, Muang Loei.
Loei, C Thailand
Loey see Loei
Lofoten 84 B3 var. Lofoten Islands.
Island group C Norway
Lofoten Islands see Lofoten
Logan 44 B3 Utah, W USA
Logan, Mount 36 D3 mountain
Yukon Territory, W Canada
Logroño 93 E1 anc. Vareia, Lat.
Juliobriga. La Rioja, N Spain
Loibl Pass 95 D7 Ger. Loiblpass,
Slvn. Ljubelj. Pass
Austria/Slovenia
Loi-Kaw 136 B4 Kayah State,
C Myanmar
Loire 90 B4 var. Liger. River
C France
Loja 60 B2 Loja, S Ecuador
Lokitaung 73 C5 Rift Valley,
NW Kenya
Lokoja 75 G4 Kogi, C Nigeria
Loksa 106 E2 Ger. Loxa. Harjumaa,
NW Estonia
Lolland 85 B8 prev. Laaland. Island
S Denmark
Lom 104 C1 prev. Lom-Palanka.
Montana, NW Bulgaria
Lomami 77 D6 river C Dem. Rep.
Congo
Lomas 60 D4 Arequipa, SW Peru
Lomas de Zamora 64 D4 Buenos
Aires, E Argentina
Lombardia 96 B2 cultural region
N Italy
Lombok, Pulau 138 D5 island Nusa
Tenggara, C Indonesia
Lomé 75 F5 country capital (Togo)
S Togo
Lomela 77 D6 Kasai Oriental,
C Dem. Rep. Congo
Lommel 87 C5 Limburg,
N Belgium
Lomond, Loch 88 B4 lake
C Scotland, UK
Lomonosov Ridge 155 B3 var.
Harris Ridge, Rus. Khrebet
Lomnosova. Undersea feature
Arctic Ocean
Lompoc 47 B7 California,
W USA
Lom Sak 136 C4 var. Muang Lom
Sak. Phetchabun, C Thailand
Łomża 98 D3 off. Wojewódstwo
Łomżyńskie, Rus. Lomzha.
Podlaskie, NE Poland
Loncoche 65 B5 Araucanía, C Chile
London 89 A7 anc. Augusta, Lat.
Londinium. Country capital (UK)
SE England, UK
London 40 C5 Kentucky, S USA
London 38 C5 Ontario, S Canada
Londonderry 88 B4 var. Derry, Ir.
Doire. NW Northern Ireland, UK
Londonderry, Cape 146 C2 headland
Western Australia
Londrina 63 E4 Paraná, S Brazil
Longa, Proliv 115 G1 Eng. Long
Strait. Strait NE Russian
Federation
Long Bay 43 F2 bay North
Carolina/South Carolina, E USA
Long Beach 47 C7 California,
W USA
Longford 89 B5 Ir. An Longfort.
C Ireland
Long Island 54 D2 island
C Bahamas
Long Island 41 G4 island New York,
NE USA
Long Island see Bermuda
Longlac 38 C3 Ontario, S Canada
Longmont 44 D4 Colorado, C USA
Longreach 148 C4 Queensland,
E Australia
Long Strait see Longa, Proliv
Longview 49 H3 Texas, SW USA
Longview 46 B2 Washington,
NW USA
Long Xuyên 137 D6 var.
Longxuyen. An Giang, S Vietnam
Longxuyen see Long Xuyên
Longyan 128 D6 Fujian,
SE China

Longyearbyen 83 G2 dependent
territory capital (Svalbard)
Spitsbergen, W Svalbard
Lons-le-Saunier 90 D4 anc. Ledo
Salinarius. Jura, E France
Lop Buri 137 C5 var. Loburi. Lop
Buri, C Thailand
Lop Nor see Lop Nur
Lop Nur 126 C3 var. Lob Nor, Lop
Nor, Lo-pu Po. Seasonal lake
NW China
Loppersum 86 E1 Groningen,
NE Netherlands
Lo-pu Po see Lop Nur
Lorca 93 E4 Ar. Lurka; anc.
Eliocroca, Lat. Illur co. Murcia,
S Spain
Lord Howe Island 142 C4 island
E Australia
Lord Howe Rise 142 C4 undersea
feature SW Pacific Ocean
Loreto 50 B3 Baja California Sur,
W Mexico
Lorient 90 A3 prev. l'Orient.
Morbihan, NW France
Lorn, Firth of 88 B4 inlet
W Scotland, UK
Loro Sae see East Timor
Lörrach 95 A7 Baden-Württemberg,
S Germany
Lorraine 90 D3 cultural region
NE France
Los Alamos 48 C1 New Mexico,
SW USA
Los Amates 52 B2 Izabal,
E Guatemala
Los Angeles 47 C7 California,
W USA
Los Ángeles 65 B5 Bío Bío, C Chile
Lošinj 100 A3 Ger. Lussin, It.
Lussino. Island W Croatia
Los Mochis 50 C3 Sinaloa,
C Mexico
Los Roques, Islas 58 D1 island group
N Venezuela
Los Testigos, Isla 55 G5 island
NE Venezuela
Lost River Range 46 D3 mountain
range Idaho, C USA
Lot 91 B5 cultural region C France
Lot 91 B5 river S France
Lotagipi Swamp 73 C5 wetland
Kenya/Sudan
Louangnamtha 136 C3 var. Luong
Nam Tha. Louang Namtha,
N Laos
Louangphabang 124 D3 var.
Louangphrabang, Luang Prabang.
Louangphabang, N Laos
Louangphrabang see
Louangphabang
Loudéac 90 A3 Côtes d'Armor,
NW France
Loudi 128 C3 Hunan, S China
Louga 74 B3 NW Senegal
Louisiade Archipelago 144 B4
island group SE PNG
Louisiana 42 A2 off. State of
Louisiana; also known as Creole
State, Pelican State. State S USA
Louisville 40 C5 Kentucky, S USA
Louisville Ridge 143 E4 undersea
feature S Pacific Ocean
Loup River 45 E4 river Nebraska,
C USA
Lourdes 91 B6 Hautes-Pyrénées,
S France
Louth 89 E5 E England, UK
Loutrá 104 C4 Kentriki Makedonía,
N Greece
Lóuva 78 C1 Lunda Norte,
NE Angola
Louvain-la-Neuve 87 C6 Wallon
Brabant, C Belgium
Louviers 90 C3 Eure, N France
Lovech 104 C2 Lovech, N Bulgaria
Loveland 44 D4 Colorado, C USA
Lovosice 98 A4 Ger. Lobositz.
Ústecký Kraj, NW Czech Republic
Lowell 41 G3 Massachusetts,
NE USA
Lower California see Baja
California
Lower Hutt 151 D5 Wellington,
North Island, NZ
Lower Lough Erne 89 A5 lake
SW Northern Ireland, UK

Lower Red Lake 45 F1 lake
Minnesota, N USA
Lower Tunguska see Nizhnyaya
Tunguska
Lowestoft 89 E6 E England, UK
Lo-yang see Luoyang
Loyauté, Îles 144 D5 island group
S New Caledonia
Loyew 107 D8 Rus. Loyev.
Homyel'skaya Voblasts',
SE Belarus
Loznica 100 C3 Serbia, W Serbia
and Montenegro (Yugo.)
Lu see Shandong
Lualaba 77 D6 Fr. Loualaba. River
SE Dem. Rep. Congo
Luanda 78 A1 var. Loanda, Port. São
Paulo de Loanda. Country capital
(Angola) Luanda, NW Angola
Luang Prabang see
Louangphabang
Luang, Thale 137 C7 lagoon
S Thailand
Luangua, Rio see Luangwa
Luangwa 73 B8 var. Aruângua, Rio
Luangua. River
Mozambique/Zambia
Luanshya 78 D2 Copperbelt,
C Zambia
Luarca 92 C1 Asturias, N Spain
Lubaczów 99 E5 var. Lúbaczów.
Podkarpackie, SE Poland
Lubań 98 B4 var. Koscian, Ger.
Kosten. Dolnośląskie,
SW Poland
Lubānas Ezers see Lubāns
Lubango 78 B2 Port. Sá da
Bandeira. Huíla, SW Angola
Lubāns 106 D4 var. Lubānas Ezers.
Lake E Latvia
Lubao 77 D6 Kasai Oriental,
C Dem. Rep. Congo
Lübben 94 D4 Brandenburg,
E Germany
Lübbenau 94 D4 Brandenburg,
E Germany
Lubbock 49 E2 Texas, SW USA
Lübeck 94 C2 Schleswig-Holstein,
N Germany
Lubelska, Wyżyna 98 E4 plateau
SE Poland
Lubin 98 B4 Ger. Lüben.
Dolnośląskie, SW Poland
Lublin 98 E4 Rus. Lyublin.
Lubelskie, E Poland
Lubliniec 98 C4 Śląskie, S Poland
Lubny 109 F2 Poltavs'ka Oblast',
NE Ukraine
Lubsko 98 B4 Ger. Sommerfeld.
Lubuskie, W Poland
Lubumbashi 77 E8 prev.
Élisabethville. Shaba, SE Dem.
Rep. Congo
Lubutu 77 D6 Maniema, E Dem.
Rep. Congo
Lucan 89 B5 Ir. Leamhcán.
E Ireland
Lucano, Appennino 97 D5 Eng.
Lucanian Mountains. Mountain
range S Italy
Lucapa 78 C1 var. Lukapa. Lunda
Norte, NE Angola
Lucca 96 B3 anc. Luca. Toscana,
C Italy
Lucea 54 A4 W Jamaica
Lucena 139 E1 off. Lucena City.
Luzon, N Philippines
Lucena 92 D4 Andalucía, S Spain
Lučenec 99 D6 Ger. Losontz, Hung.
Losonc. Banskobystrický Kraj,
C Slovakia
Luchow see Hefei
Lucknow 135 E3 var. Lakhnau.
Uttar Pradesh, N India
Lüda see Dalian
Luda Kamchiya 104 D2 river
E Bulgaria
Lüderitz 78 B4 prev. Angra
Pequena. Karas, SW Namibia
Ludhiāna 134 D2 Punjab, N India
Ludington 40 C2 Michigan, N USA
Ludus 108 B4 Ger. Ludasch, Hung.
Marosludas. Mureş, C Romania
Ludvika 85 C6 Kopparberg,
C Sweden
Ludwiglust 94 C3 Mecklenburg-
Vorpommern, N Germany

Ludwigsburg 95 B6 Baden-Württemberg, SW Germany
Ludwigsfelde 94 D3 Brandenburg, NE Germany
Ludwigshafen 95 B5 var. Ludwigshafen am Rhein. Rheinland-Pfalz, W Germany
Ludwigshafen am Rhein see Ludwigshafen
Ludza 106 D4 Ger. Ludsan. Ludza, E Latvia
Luebo 77 C6 Kasai Occidental, SW Dem. Rep. Congo
Luena 78 C2 var. Lwena, Port. Luso. Moxico, E Angola
Lufira 77 E7 river SE Dem. Rep. Congo
Lufkin 49 H3 Texas, SW USA
Luga 110 A4 Leningradskaya Oblast', NW Russian Federation
Lugano 95 B8 Ger. Lauis. Ticino, S Switzerland
Lugenda, Rio 79 E2 river N Mozambique
Lugo 92 C1 anc. Lugus Augusti. Galicia, NW Spain
Lugoj 108 A4 Ger. Lugosch, Hung. Lugos. Timiş, W Romania
Luhans'k 109 H3 Rus. Lugansk; prev. Voroshilovgrad. Luhans'ka Oblast', E Ukraine
Luimneach see Limerick
Lukapa see Lucapa
Lukenie 77 C6 river C Dem. Rep. Congo
Lukovit 104 C2 Lovech, N Bulgaria
Łuków 98 E4 Ger. Bogendorf. Lubelskie, E Poland
Lukuga 77 D7 river SE Dem. Rep. Congo
Luleå 84 D4 Norrbotten, N Sweden
Luleälven 84 C3 river N Sweden
Lulonga 77 C5 river NW Dem. Rep. Congo
Lulua 77 D7 river S Dem. Rep. Congo
Lumbo 79 F2 Nampula, NE Mozambique
Lumsden 151 A7 Southland, South Island, NZ
Lund 85 B7 Skåne, S Sweden
Lüneburg 94 C3 Niedersachsen, N Germany
Lungkiang see Qiqihar
Lungué-Bungo 78 C2 var. Lungwebungu. River Angola/Zambia see also Lungwebungu
Lungwebungu see Lungué-Bungo
Luninyets 107 B7 Pol. Luniniec, Rus. Luninets. Brestskaya Voblasts', SW Belarus
Lunteren 86 D4 Gelderland, C Netherlands
Luong Nam Tha see Louangnamtha
Luoyang 128 C4 var. Honan, Lo-yang. Henan, C China
Lúrio 79 F2 Nampula, NE Mozambique
Lúrio, Rio 79 E2 river NE Mozambique
Lusaka 78 D2 country capital (Zambia) Lusaka, SE Zambia
Lushnja see Lushnjë
Lushnjë 101 C6 var. Lushnja. Fier, C Albania
Luso see Luena
Lüt, Dasht-e 120 D3 var. Kavīr-e Lūt. Desert E Iran
Luton 89 D6 SE England, UK
Łutselk'e 37 F4 prev. Snowdrift. Northwest Territories, W Canada
Luts'k 108 C1 Pol. Łuck, Rus. Lutsk. Volyns'ka Oblast', NW Ukraine
Lutzow-Holm Bay see Lützow Holmbukta
Lützow Holmbukta 154 C2 var. Lutzow-Holm Bay. Bay Antarctica
Luuq 73 D6 It. Lugh Ganana. Gedo, SW Somalia
Luvua 77 D7 river SE Dem. Rep. Congo
Luwego 73 C8 river S Tanzania

Luxembourg 87 D8 var. Lëtzebuerg, Luxemburg. Country NW Europe

Luxembourg 87

Official name Grand Duchy of Luxembourg
Formation 1867
Capital Luxembourg
Population 442,000/ 433 people per sq mile (171 people per sq km)
Total area 998 sq miles (2,586 sq km)
Languages French, German, Luxembourgish
Religions Roman Catholic 97%, other 3%
Ethnic mix Luxembourger 73%, Foreign residents 27%
Government Parliamentary democracy
Currency Euro (Luxembourg and Belgian Franc until 2002)
Literacy rate 99%
Calorie consumption 3,701 kilocalories

Luxembourg 87 D8 country capital (Luxembourg) Luxembourg, S Luxembourg
Luxor 72 B2 Ar. Al Uqşur. E Egypt
Luza 110 C4 Kirovskaya Oblast', NW Russian Federation
Luz, Costa de la 92 C5 coastal region SW Spain
Luzern 95 B7 Fr. Lucerne, It. Lucerna. Luzern, C Switzerland
Luzon 139 E1 island N Philippines
Luzon Strait 125 E3 strait Philippines/Taiwan
L'viv 108 B2 Ger. Lemberg, Pol. Lwów, Rus. L'vov. L'vivs'ka Oblast', W Ukraine
Lwena see Luena
Lyakhavichy 107 B6 Rus. Lyakhovichi. Brestskaya Voblasts', SW Belarus
Lycksele 84 C4 Västerbotten, N Sweden
Lycopolis see Asyût
Lyel'chytsy 107 C7 Rus. Lel'chitsy. Homyel'skaya Voblasts', SE Belarus
Lyepyel' 107 D5 Rus. Lepel'. Vitsyebskaya Voblasts', N Belarus
Lyme Bay 89 C7 bay S England, UK
Lynchburg 41 E5 Virginia, NE USA
Lynn Regis see King's Lynn
Lyon 91 D5 Eng. Lyons; anc. Lugdunum. Rhône, E France
Lyozna 107 E6 Rus. Liozno. Vitsyebskaya Voblasts', NE Belarus
Lypovets' 108 D2 Rus. Lipovets. Vinnyts'ka Oblast', C Ukraine
Lysychans'k 109 H3 Rus. Lisichansk. Luhans'ka Oblast', E Ukraine
Lyttelton 151 C6 Canterbury, South Island, NZ
Lyubotyn 109 G2 Rus. Lyubotin. Kharkivs'ka Oblast', E Ukraine
Lyulyakovo 104 E2 prev. Keremitlik. Burgas, E Bulgaria
Lyusina 107 B6 Rus. Lyusino. Brestskaya Voblasts', SW Belarus

M

Ma'ān 119 B7 Ma'ān, SW Jordan
Maardu 106 D2 Ger. Maart. Harjumaa, NW Estonia
Ma'aret-en-Nu'man see Ma'arrat an Nu'mān
Ma'arrat an Nu'mān 118 B3 var. Ma'aret-en-Nu'man, Fr. Maarret enn Naamâne. Idlib, NW Syria
Maarret enn Naamâne see Ma'arrat an Nu'mān
Maaseik 87 D5 prev. Maeseyck. Limburg, NE Belgium
Maastricht 87 D6 var. Maestricht; anc. Traietum ad Mosam, Traiectum Tungorum. Limburg, SE Netherlands

Macao 129 C6 Chin. Aomen, Port. Macao. S China
Macapá 63 E1 state capital Amapá, N Brazil
Macassar see Ujungpandang
MacCluer Gulf see Berau, Teluk
Macdonnell Ranges 146 D4 mountain range Northern Territory, C Australia
Macedonia, FYR 101 D6 var. Macedonia, Mac. Makedonija, abbrev. FYR Macedonia, FYROM. Country SE Europe

Macedonia 101

Official name Former Yugoslav Republic of Macedonia
Formation 1991
Capital Skopje
Population 2 million / 204 people per sq mile (79 people per sq km)
Total area 9,781 sq miles (25,333 sq km)
Languages Macedonian, Albania, Serbo-Croat
Religions Christian 74%, Muslim 26%
Ethnic mix Macedonian 67%, Albanian 23%, Turkish 4%, other 6%
Government Multiparty republic
Currency Macedonian denar = 100 deni
Literacy rate 94%
Calorie consumption 3,006 kilocalories

Maceió 63 G3 state capital Alagoas, E Brazil
Machachi 60 B1 Pichincha, C Ecuador
Machala 60 B2 El Oro, SW Ecuador
Machanga 79 E3 Sofala, E Mozambique
Machilipatnam 132 D1 var. Bandar Masulipatnam. Andhra Pradesh, E India
Machiques 58 C2 Zulia, NW Venezuela
Macías Nguema Biyogo see Bioco, Isla de
Măcin 108 D5 Tulcea, SE Romania
Macizo de las Guayanas see Guiana Highlands
Mackay 148 D3 Queensland, NE Australia
Mackay, Lake 146 C4 salt lake Northern Territory/Western Australia
Mackenzie 37 E3 river Northwest Territories, NW Canada
Mackenzie Bay 154 D3 bay Antarctica
Mackenzie Mountains 36 D3 mountain range Northwest Territories, NW Canada
Macleod, Lake 146 A4 lake Western Australia
Macomb 40 A4 Illinois, N USA
Macomer 97 A5 Sardegna, Italy, C Mediterranean Sea
Macon 42 D2 Georgia, SE USA
Macon 45 G4 Missouri, C USA
Mâcon 91 D5 anc. Matisco, Matisco Ædourum. Saône-et-Loire, C France
Macquarie Ridge 154 C5 undersea feature SW Pacific Ocean
Macuspana 51 G4 Tabasco, SE Mexico
Ma'dabā 119 B6 var. Mādabā, Madeba; anc. Medeba. 'Ammān, NW Jordan
Madagascar 79 F3 Malg. Madagasikara; prev. Malagasy Republic. Country W Indian Ocean

Madagascar 79

Official name Republic of Madagascar
Formation 1960
Capital Antananarivo
Population 16.4 million /72 people per sq mile (28 people per sq km)

Madagascar (continued)

Total area 226,656 sq miles (587,040 sq km)
Languages French, Malagasy
Religions Traditional beliefs 52%, Christian 41%, Muslim 7%
Ethnic mix Merina 26%, Betsilio 12%, Betsimisaraka 15%, other 47%
Government Presidential democracy
Currency Malagasy franc = 100 centimes
Literacy rate 66.5%
Calorie consumption 2,007 kilocalories

Madagascar 79 F3 island W Indian Ocean
Madagascar Basin 69 E7 undersea feature W Indian Ocean
Madagascar Plateau 69 E7 var. Madagascar Ridge, Madagascar Rise, Rus. Madagaskarskiy Khrebet. Undersea feature W Indian Ocean
Madagascar Ridge see Madagascar Plateau
Madagascar Rise see Madagascar Plateau
Madagaskarskiy Khrebet see Madagascar Plateau
Madang 144 B3 Madang, N PNG
Madanīyīn see Médenine
Made 86 C4 Noord-Brabant, S Netherlands
Madeba see Ma'dabā
Madeira 70 A2 var. Ilha de Madeira. Island Portugal, NE Atlantic Ocean
Madeira 70 A2 var. Madeira, Port. Arquipélago da Madeira. Island group Portugal, NE Atlantic Ocean
Madeira Plain 66 C3 undersea feature E Atlantic Ocean
Madeira, Rio 62 D2 Sp. Río Madera. River Bolivia/Brazil see also Madera, Río
Madeleine, Îles de la 39 F4 Eng. Magdalen Islands. Island group Quebec, E Canada
Madera 47 B6 California, W USA
Madhya Pradesh 135 E4 prev. Central Provinces and Berar. Admin. region state C India
Madīnat ath Thawrah 118 C2 var. Ath Thawrah. Ar Raqqah, N Syria Asia
Madison 40 B3 state capital Wisconsin, N USA
Madison 45 F3 South Dakota, N USA
Madiun 138 D5 prev. Madioen. Jawa, C Indonesia
Madona 106 D4 Ger. Modohn. Madona, E Latvia
Madras see Tamil Nādu
Madras see Chennai
Madre de Dios 56 B4 off. Departamento de Madre de Dios. Department E Peru
Madre de Dios, Río 61 E3 river Bolivia/Peru
Madre del Sur, Sierra 51 E5 mountain range S Mexico
Madre, Laguna 51 F3 lagoon NE Mexico
Madre, Laguna 49 G5 lake Texas, SW USA
Madre Occidental, Sierra 50 C3 var. Western Sierra Madre. Mountain range C Mexico
Madre Oriental, Sierra 51 E3 var. Eastern Sierra Madre. Mountain range C Mexico
Madrid 92 D3 country capital (Spain) Madrid, C Spain
Madurai 132 C3 prev. Madura, Mathurai. Tamil Nādu, S India
Madura, Pulau 138 D5 prev. Madoera. Island C Indonesia
Maebashi 131 D5 var. Maebasi, Mayebashi. Gunma, Honshū, S Japan
Maebasi see Maebashi

Mae Nam Khong see Mekong
Mae Nam Nan 136 C4 river NW Thailand
Mae Nam Yom 136 C4 river W Thailand
Maestricht see Maastricht
Maéwo 144 D4 prev. Aurora. Island C Vanuatu
Mafia 73 D7 island E Tanzania
Mafraq see Al Mafraq
Magadan 115 G3 Magadanskaya Oblast', E Russian Federation
Magangué 58 B2 Bolívar, N Colombia
Magdalena 56 A2 off. Departamento del Magdalena. Province N Colombia
Magdalena 61 F3 Beni, N Bolivia
Magdalena 50 B1 Sonora, NW Mexico
Magdalena, Isla 50 B3 island W Mexico
Magdalena, Río 58 B2 river C Colombia
Magdeburg 94 C4 Sachsen-Anhalt, C Germany
Magelang 138 C5 Jawa, C Indonesia
Magellan, Strait of 65 B8 Sp. Estrecho de Magallanes. Strait Argentina/Chile
Mageroy see Magerøya
Magerøya 84 D1 var. Mageröy. Island N Norway
Maggiore, Lake 96 B1 It. Lago Maggiore. Lake Italy/Switzerland
Maglaj 100 C3 Federacija Bosna I Hercegovina, N Bosnia and Herzegovina
Maglie 97 E6 Puglia, SE Italy
Magna 44 B4 Utah, W USA
Magnesia see Manisa
Magnitogorsk 114 B4 Chelyabinskaya Oblast', C Russian Federation
Magta' Lahjar 74 C3 var. Magta Lahjar, Magta' Lahjar, Magtá Lahjar. Brakna, SW Mauritania
Magway see Magwe
Magwe 136 A3 var. Magway. Magwe, W Myanmar
Mahajanga 79 F2 var. Majunga. Mahajanga, NW Madagascar
Mahakam, Sungai 138 D4 var. Koetai, Kutai. River Borneo, C Indonesia
Mahalapye 78 D3 var. Mahalatswe. Central, SE Botswana
Mahalatswe see Mahalapye
Mahān 120 D3 Kermān, E Iran
Mahānadi 135 F4 river E India
Mahārāshtra 134 D5 state W India
Mahbés see El Mahbas
Mahbūbnagar 134 D5 Andhra Pradesh, C India
Mahdia 71 F2 var. Al Mahdīyah, Mehdia. NE Tunisia
Mahé 79 H1 island Inner Islands, NE Seychelles
Mahia Peninsula 150 E4 peninsula North Island, NZ
Mahilyow 107 D6 Rus. Mogilëv. Mahilyowskaya Voblasts', E Belarus
Mahmūd-e 'Erāqī see Maḥmūd-e Rāqī
Maḥmūd-e Rāqī 123 E4 var. Mahmūd-e 'Erāqī. Kāpīsā, NE Afghanistan
Mahón 93 H3 Cat. Maó, Eng. Port Mahon; anc. Portus Magonis. Menorca, Spain, W Mediterranean Sea
Maicao 58 C1 La Guajira, N Colombia
Mai Ceu see Maych'ew
Mai Chio see Maych'ew
Maidstone 89 E7 SE England, UK
Maiduguri 75 H4 Borno, NE Nigeria
Maimāna see Meymaneh
Main 95 B5 river C Germany
Mai-Ndombe, Lac 77 C6 prev. Lac Léopold II. Lake W Dem. Rep. Congo
Maine 41 G2 off. State of Maine; also known as Lumber State, Pine Tree State. State NE USA

Maine 90 B3 cultural region NW France
Maine, Gulf of 41 H2 gulf NE USA
Main Island see Bermuda
Mainland 88 C2 island Orkney, N Scotland, UK
Mainland 88 D1 island Shetland, NE Scotland, UK
Mainz 95 B5 Fr. Mayence. Rheinland-Pfalz, SW Germany
Maio 74 A3 var. Mayo. Island Ilhas de Sotavento, SE Cape Verde
Maisur see Karnātaka
Maisur see Mysore
Maizhokunggar 126 C5 Xizang Zizhiqu, W China
Maíz, Islas del 53 E3 var. Corn Islands. Island group SE Nicaragua
Mājro see Majuro Atoll
Majunga see Mahajanga
Majuro Atoll 144 D2 var. Mājro. Atoll Ratak Chain, SE Marshall Islands
Makale see Mek'elē
Makarov Basin 155 B3 undersea feature Arctic Ocean
Makarska 100 B4 It. Macarsca. Split-Dalmacija, SE Croatia
Makasar see Ujungpandang
Makassar see Ujungpandang
Makassar Strait 138 D4 Ind. Selat Makasar. Strait C Indonesia
Makay 79 F3 var. Massif du Makay. Mountain range SW Madagascar
Makeni 74 C4 C Sierra Leone
Makhachkala 114 A4 prev. Petrovsk-Port. Respublika Dagestan, SW Russian Federation
Makin 144 D2 prev. Pitt Island. Atoll Tungaru, W Kiribati
Makira see San Cristobal
Makiyivka 109 G3 Rus. Makeyevka; prev. Dmitriyevsk. Donets'ka Oblast', E Ukraine
Makkah 121 A5 Eng. Mecca. Makkah, W Saudi Arabia
Makkovik 39 F2 Newfoundland and Labrador, NE Canada
Makó 99 D7 Rom. Macău. Csongrád, SE Hungary
Makoua 77 B5 Cuvette, C Congo
Makran Coast 120 E4 coastal region SE Iran
Makrany 107 A6 Rus. Mokrany. Brestskaya Voblasts', SW Belarus
Mākū 120 B2 Āzarbāyjān-e Bākhtarī, NW Iran
Makurdi 75 G4 Benue, C Nigeria
Mala see Malaita
Malabār Coast 132 B3 coast SW India
Malabo 77 A5 prev. Santa Isabel. Country capital (Equatorial Guinea) Isla de Bioco, NW Equatorial Guinea
Malacca see Melaka
Malacca, Strait of 138 B3 Ind. Selat Malaka. Strait Indonesia/Malaysia
Malacky 99 C6 Hung. Malacka. Bratislavský Kraj, W Slovakia
Maladzyechna 107 C5 Pol. Molodeczno, Rus. Molodechno. Minskaya Voblasts', C Belarus
Málaga 92 D5 anc. Malaca. Andalucía, S Spain
Malagarasi River 73 B7 river W Tanzania
Malaita 144 C3 var. Mala. Island N Solomon Islands
Malakal 73 B5 Upper Nile, S Sudan
Malakula see Malekula
Malang 138 D5 Jawa, C Indonesia
Malange see Malanje
Malanje 78 B1 var. Malange. Malanje, NW Angola
Mälaren 85 C6 lake C Sweden
Malatya 117 E4 anc. Melitene. Malatya, SE Turkey
Mala Vyska 109 E3 Rus. Malaya Viska. Kirovohrads'ka Oblast', S Ukraine

Malawi 79 E1 prev. Nyasaland, Nyasaland Protectorate. Country S Africa

Malawi 79

Official name Republic of Malawi
Formation 1964
Capital Lilongwe
Population 11.6 million / 254 people per sq mile (98 people per sq km)
Total area 45,745 sq miles (118,480 sq km)
Languages English, Chewa, Lomwe, Yao, Ngoni
Religions Protestant 55%, Roman Catholic 20%, Muslim 20%, other 5%
Ethnic mix Bantu 99%, other 1%
Government Presidential democracy
Currency Malawi kwacha = 100 tambala
Literacy rate 60.1%
Calorie consumption 2,181 kilocalories

Malawi, Lake see Nyasa, Lake
Malay Peninsula 124 D4 peninsula Malaysia/Thailand
Malaysia 138 B3 var. Federation of Malaysia; prev. the separate territories of Federation of Malaya, Sarawak and Sabah (North Borneo) and Singapore. Country SE Asia

Malaysia 138

Official name Federation of Malaysia
Formation 1963
Capital Kuala Lumpur
Population 22.6 million / 178 people per sq mile (69 people per sq km)
Total area 127,316 sq miles (329,750 sq km)
Languages English, Bahasa Malaysia, Malay, Chinese, Tamil
Religions Muslim 53%, Buddhist 19%, Chinese faiths 12%, other 16%
Ethnic mix Malay 48%, Chinese 29%, Indigenous tribes 12%, other 11%
Government Presidential democracy
Currency Ringgit = 100 cents
Literacy rate 87.5%
Calorie consumption 2,919 kilocalories

Malaysia, Federation of see Malaysia
Malbork 98 C2 Ger. Marienburg, Marienburg in Westpreussen. Pomorskie, N Poland
Malchin 94 C3 Mecklenburg-Vorpommern, N Germany
Malden 45 H5 Missouri, C USA
Malden Island 145 G3 prev. Independence Island. Atoll E Kiribati
Maldives 132 A4 Country N Indian Ocean

Maldives 132

Official name Republic of Maldives
Formation 1965
Capital Malé
Population 300,000 / 2,590 people per sq mile (1000 people per sq km)
Total area 116 sq miles (300 sq km)
Languages Dhivehi (Maldivian)
Religions Sunni Muslim 100%
Ethnic mix Mixed Arab, Sinhalese, Malay 100%
Government Non-party democracy
Currency Rufiyaa (Maldivian rupee) = 100 laari
Literacy rate 96.4%
Calorie consumption 2,592 kilocalories

Male' 132 B4 Male' Atoll, C Maldives
Male' Atoll 132 B4 var. Kaafu Atoll. Atoll C Maldives
Malekula 144 D4 var. Malakula; prev. Mallicolo. Island W Vanuatu
Malesína 105 C5 SterEá Ellás, E Greece
Malheur Lake 46 C3 lake Oregon, NW USA
Mali 75 E3 Fr. République du Mali; prev. French Sudan, Sudanese Republic. Country W Africa

Mali 75

Official name Republic of Mali
Formation 1960
Capital Bamako
Population 11.7 million / 24 people per sq mile (9 people per sq km)
Total area 478,764 sq miles (1,240,000 sq km)
Languages French, Bambara, Fulani, Senufo, Soninké
Religions Muslim (mainly Sunni) 80%, Traditional beliefs 18%, other 2%
Ethnic mix Bambara 32%, Fula 14%, Senufu 12%, Soninka 9%, other 33%
Government Multiparty republic
Currency CFA franc = 100 centimes
Literacy rate 41.4%
Calorie consumption 2,403 kilocalories

Malik, Wadi al see Milk, Wadi el
Mali Kyun 137 B5 var. Tavoy Island. Island Mergui Archipelago, S Myanmar
Malindi 73 D7 Coast, SE Kenya
Malko Tŭrnovo 104 E3 Burgas, E Bulgaria
Mallaig 88 B3 N Scotland, UK
Mallicolo see Malekula
Mallorca 93 G3 Eng. Majorca; anc. Baleares Major. Island Islas Baleares, Spain, W Mediterranean Sea
Malmberget 84 C3 Norrbotten, N Sweden
Malmédy 87 D6 Liège, E Belgium
Malmö 85 B7 Skåne, S Sweden
Maloelap see Maloelap Atoll
Maloelap Atoll 144 D1 var. Maloelap. Atoll E Marshall Islands
Małopolska 98 D4 plateau S Poland
Malozemel'skaya Tundra 110 D3 physical region NW Russian Federation
Malta 97 C8 Country C Mediterranean Sea

Malta 97

Official name Republic of Malta
Formation 1964
Capital Valletta
Population 392,000 / 3,213 people per sq mile (1,241 people per sq km)
Total area 122 sq miles (316 sq km)
Languages Maltese, English
Religions Roman Catholic 98%, other and non-religious 2%
Ethnic mix Maltese (mixed Arab, Sicilian, Norman, Spanish, Italian, English) 96%, other 4%
Government Parliamentary democracy
Currency Maltese lira = 100 cents
Literacy rate 92.1%
Calorie consumption 3,543 kilocalories

Malta 97 C8 island Malta, C Mediterranean Sea
Malta 44 C1 Montana, NW USA
Malta 106 D4 Rēzekne, SE Latvia
Malta Channel 97 C8 It. Canale di Malta. Strait Italy/Malta
Maluku 139 F4 Dut. Molukken, Eng. Moluccas; prev. Spice Islands. Island group E Indonesia

Malung 85 B6 Kopparberg, C Sweden
Malyn 108 D2 *Rus.* Malin. Zhytomyrs'ka Oblast', N Ukraine
Mamberamo, Sungai 139 H4 *river* Papua, E Indonesia
Mambij *see* Manbij
Mamonovo 106 A4 *Ger.* Heiligenbeil. Kaliningradskaya Oblast', W Russian Federation
Mamoré, Rio 61 F3 *river* Bolivia/Brazil
Mamou 74 C4 Moyenne-Guinée, W Guinea
Mamoudzou 79 F2 *dependent territory capital* (Mayotte) C Mayotte
Mamuno 78 C3 Ghanzi, W Botswana
Manacor 93 G3 Mallorca, Spain, W Mediterranean Sea
Manado 139 F3 *prev.* Menado. Sulawesi, C Indonesia
Managua 52 D3 *country capital* (Nicaragua) Managua, W Nicaragua
Managua, Lago de 52 C3 *var.* Xolotlán. *Lake* W Nicaragua
Manakara 79 G4 Fianarantsoa, SE Madagascar
Manama *see* Al Manāmah
Mananjary 79 G3 Fianarantsoa, SE Madagascar
Manapouri, Lake 151 A7 *lake* South Island, NZ
Manar *see* Mannar
Manas, Gora 123 E2 *mountain* Kyrgyzstan/Uzbekistan
Manaus 62 D2 *prev.* Manáos. *State capital* Amazonas, NW Brazil
Manavgat 116 B4 Antalya, SW Turkey
Manbij 118 C2 *var.* Mambij, *Fr.* Membidj. Ḥalab, N Syria
Manchester 89 D5 *Lat.* Mancunium. NW England, UK
Manchester 41 G3 New Hampshire, NE USA
Man-chou-li *see* Manzhouli
Manchuria 125 E1 *cultural region* NE China
Máncio Lima *see* Japiim
Mand *see* Mand, Rūd-e
Mandalay 136 B3 Mandalay, C Myanmar
Mandan 45 E2 North Dakota, N USA
Mandeville 54 B5 C Jamaica
Mándra 105 C6 Attikí, C Greece
Mand, Rūd-e 120 D4 *var.* Mand. *River* S Iran
Mandurah 147 A6 Western Australia
Manduria 97 E5 Puglia, SE Italy
Mandya 132 C2 Karnātaka, C India
Manfredonia 97 D5 Puglia, SE Italy
Mangai 77 C6 Bandundu, W Dem. Rep. Congo
Mangaia 145 G5 *island group* S Cook Islands
Mangalia 108 D5 *anc.* Callatis. Constanța, SE Romania
Mangalmé 76 C3 Guéra, SE Chad
Mangalore 132 B2 Karnātaka, W India
Mangaung *see* Bloemfontein
Mango *see* Sansanné-Mango
Mangoky 79 F3 *river* W Madagascar
Manhattan 45 F4 Kansas, C USA
Manicouagan, Réservoir 38 D3 *lake* Quebec, E Canada
Manihiki 145 G4 *atoll* N Cook Islands
Manihiki Plateau 143 E3 *undersea feature* C Pacific Ocean
Maniitsoq 82 C3 *var.* Sukkertoppen, *Dan.* Sukkertoppen. S Greenland
Manila 139 E1 *off.* City of Manila. *Country capital* (Philippines) Luzon, N Philippines
Manisa 116 A3 *var.* Manissa; *prev.* Saruhan, *anc.* Magnesia. Manisa, W Turkey
Manissa *see* Manisa
Manitoba 37 F5 *province* S Canada

Manitoba, Lake 37 F5 *lake* Manitoba, S Canada
Manitoulin Island 38 C4 *island* Ontario, S Canada
Maniitsoq *see* Maniitsoq
Manizales 58 B3 Caldas, W Colombia
Manjimup 147 A7 Western Australia
Mankato 45 F3 Minnesota, N USA
Manlleu 93 G2 Cataluña, NE Spain
Manly 148 E1 New South Wales, SE Australia
Manmād 134 C5 Mahārāshtra, W India
Mannar 132 C3 *var.* Manar. Northern Province, NW Sri Lanka
Mannar, Gulf of 132 C3 *gulf* India/Sri Lanka
Mannheim 95 B5 Baden-Württemberg, SW Germany
Manono 77 E7 Shaba, SE Dem. Rep. Congo
Manosque 91 D6 Alpes-de-Haute-Provence, SE France
Manra 145 F3 *prev.* Sydney Island. *Atoll* Phoenix Islands, C Kiribati
Mansa 78 D2 *prev.* Fort Rosebery. Luapula, N Zambia
Mansel Island 37 G3 *island* Nunavut, NE Canada
Mansfield 40 D4 Ohio, N USA
Manta 60 A2 Manabí, W Ecuador
Manteca 47 B6 California, W USA
Mantova 96 B2 *Eng.* Mantua, *Fr.* Mantoue. Lombardia, NW Italy
Manuae 145 G4 *island* S Cook Islands
Manurewa 150 D3 *var.* Manukau. Auckland, North Island, NZ
Manzanares 93 E3 Castilla-La Mancha, C Spain
Manzanillo 50 D4 Colima, SW Mexico
Manzanillo 54 C3 Granma, E Cuba
Manzhouli 127 F1 *var.* Man-chou-li. Nei Mongol Zizhiqu, N China
Mao 76 B3 Kanem, W Chad
Maoke, Pegunungan 139 H4 *Dut.* Sneeuw-gebergte, *Eng.* Snow Mountains. *Mountain range* Papua, E Indonesia
Maoming 128 C6 Guangdong, S China
Mapmaker Seamounts 125 H2 *undersea feature* N Pacific Ocean
Maputo 78 D4 *prev.* Lourenço Marques. *Country capital* (Mozambique) Maputo, S Mozambique
Marabá 63 F2 Pará, NE Brazil
Maracaibo 58 C1 Zulia, NW Venezuela
Maracaibo, Lago de 58 C2 *var.* Lake Maracaibo. *Inlet* NW Venezuela
Maracaibo, Lake *see* Maracaibo, Lago de
Maracay 58 D2 Aragua, N Venezuela
Marada *see* Marādah
Marādah 71 G3 *var.* Marada. N Libya
Maradi 75 G3 Maradi, S Niger
Maragha *see* Marāgheh
Marāgheh 120 C2 *var.* Maragha. Āzarbāyjān-e Khāvarī, NW Iran
Marajó, Baía de 63 F1 *bay* N Brazil
Marajó, Ilha de 63 E1 *island* N Brazil
Marakesh *see* Marrakech
Maramba *see* Livingstone
Maranhão 63 F2 *off.* Estado do Maranhão. *State* E Brazil
Marañón, Río 60 B2 *river* N Peru
Maraş *see* Kahramanmaraş
Marash *see* Kahramanmaraş
Marathon 38 C4 Ontario, S Canada
Marathónas 105 C5 *prev.* Marathón. Attikí, C Greece
Marbella 92 D5 Andalucía, S Spain
Marble Bar 146 B4 Western Australia
Marburg an der Lahn 94 B4 *hist.* Marburg. Hessen, W Germany
March *see* Morava
Marche 91 C5 *cultural region* C France

Marche 96 C3 *cultural region* E Italy
Marche-en-Famenne 87 C7 Luxembourg, SE Belgium
Marchena, Isla 60 B5 *var.* Bindloe Island. *Island* Galapagos Islands, Ecuador, E Pacific Ocean
Mar Chiquita, Laguna 64 C3 *lake* C Argentina
Marcounda *see* Markounda
Mardān 134 C1 North-West Frontier Province, N Pakistan
Mar del Plata 65 D5 Buenos Aires, E Argentina
Mardin 117 E4 Mardin, SE Turkey
Maré 144 D5 *island* Îles Loyauté, E New Caledonia
Marea Neagră *see* Black Sea
Mare Creticum *see* Kritikó Pélagos
Mareeba 148 D3 Queensland, NE Australia
Margarita, Isla de 59 E1 *island* N Venezuela
Margate 89 E7 *prev.* Mergate. SE England, UK
Marghita 108 B3 Hung. Margitta. Bihor, NW Romania
Marhanets' 109 F3 *Rus.* Marganets. Dnipropetrovs'ka Oblast', E Ukraine
María Cleofas, Isla 50 C4 *island* C Mexico
Maria Island 149 C8 *island* Tasmania, SE Australia
María Madre, Isla 50 C4 *island* C Mexico
María Magdalena, Isla 50 C4 *island* C Mexico
Mariana Trench 125 G4 *undersea feature* W Pacific Ocean
Mariánské Lázně 99 A5 *Ger.* Marienbad. Karlovarský Kraj, W Czech Republic
Marías, Islas 50 C4 *island group* C Mexico
Maribor 95 E7 *Ger.* Marburg. NE Slovenia
Marica *see* Maritsa
Maridi 73 B5 Western Equatoria, SW Sudan
Marie Byrd Land 154 A3 *physical region* Antarctica
Marie-Galante 55 G4 *var.* Ceyre to the Caribs. *Island* SE Guadeloupe
Mariental 78 B4 Hardap, SW Namibia
Mariestad 85 B6 Västra Götaland, S Sweden
Marietta 42 D2 Georgia, SE USA
Marijampolė 106 B4 *prev.* Kapsukas. Marijampolė, S Lithuania
Marília 63 E4 São Paulo, S Brazil
Marín 92 B1 Galicia, NW Spain
Mar'ina Horka 107 C6 *Rus.* Mar'ina Gorka. Minskaya Voblasts', C Belarus
Maringá 63 E4 Paraná, S Brazil
Marion 45 G3 Iowa, C USA
Marion 40 D4 Ohio, N USA
Marion, Lake 43 E2 *reservoir* South Carolina, SE USA
Mariscal Estigarribia 64 D2 Boquerón, NW Paraguay
Maritsa 104 D3 *var.* Marica, *Gk.* Évros, *Turk.* Meriç; *anc.* Hebrus. *River* SW Europe *see also* Évros/Meriç
Maritzburg *see* Pietermaritzburg
Mariupol' 109 G4 *prev.* Zhdanov. Donets'ka Oblast', SE Ukraine
Marka 73 D6 *var.* Merca. Shabeellaha Hoose, S Somalia
Markham, Mount 154 B4 *mountain* Antarctica
Markounda 76 C4 *var.* Marcounda. Ouham, NW Central African Republic
Marktredwitz 95 C5 Bayern, E Germany
Marlborough 148 D4 Queensland, E Australia
Marmande 91 B5 *anc.* Marmanda. Lot-et-Garonne, SW France
Marmara Denizi 116 A2 *Eng.* Sea of Marmara. *Sea* NW Turkey

Marmara, Sea of *see* Marmara Denizi
Marmaris 116 A4 Muğla, SW Turkey
Marne 90 C3 *cultural region* N France
Marne 90 D3 *river* N France
Maro 76 C4 Moyen-Chari, S Chad
Maroantsetra 79 G2 Toamasina, NE Madagascar
Maromokotro 79 G2 *mountain* N Madagascar
Maroni River 59 G3 *Dut.* Marowijne. *River* French Guiana/Suriname
Maros *see* Mureş
Marosch *see* Mureş
Marotiri 143 F4 *var.* Îlots de Bass, Morotiri. *Island group* Îles Australes, SW French Polynesia
Maroua 76 B3 Extrême-Nord, N Cameroon
Marquesas Fracture Zone 153 E3 *tectonic feature* E Pacific Ocean
Marquesas Islands 153 E3 *island group* N French Polynesia
Marquette 40 B1 Michigan, N USA
Marrakech 70 C2 *var.* Marakesh, *Eng.* Marrakesh; *prev.* Morocco. W Morocco
Marrakesh *see* Marrakech
Marrawah 149 C8 Tasmania, SE Australia
Marree 149 B5 South Australia
Marsá al Burayqah 71 G3 *var.* Al Burayqah. N Libya
Marsabit 73 C6 Eastern, N Kenya
Marsala 97 B7 *anc.* Lilybaeum. Sicilia, Italy, C Mediterranean Sea
Marsberg 94 B4 Nordrhein-Westfalen, W Germany
Marseille 91 D6 *Eng.* Marseilles; *anc.* Massilia. Bouches-du-Rhône, SE France
Marshall 45 F2 Minnesota, N USA
Marshall 49 H2 Texas, SW USA
Marshall Islands 144 C1 *Country* W Pacific Ocean

Marshall Islands 144

Official name Republic of the Marshall Islands
Formation 1986
Capital Majuro
Population 68,100 / 973 people per sq mile (376 people per sq km)
Total area 70 sq miles (181 sq km)
Languages Marshallese, English, Japanese, German
Religions Protestant 90%, Roman Catholic 8%, other 2%
Ethnic mix Micronesian 97%, other 3%
Government Parliamentary democracy
Currency US dollar = 100 cents
Literacy rate 91%
Calorie consumption not available

Marshall Seamounts 125 H3 *undersea feature* SW Pacific Ocean
Marsh Harbour 54 C1 Great Abaco, W Bahamas
Martaban 136 B4 *var.* Moktama. Mon State, S Myanmar
Martha's Vineyard 41 G3 *island* Massachusetts, NE USA
Martigues 91 D6 Bouches-du-Rhône, SE France
Martin 99 C5 *Ger.* Sankt Martin, *Hung.* Turócszentmárton; *prev.* Turčiansky Svätý Martin. Žilinský Kraj, N Slovakia
Martinique 55 G4 *French overseas department* E West Indies
Martinique Channel *see* Martinique Passage
Martinique Passage 55 G4 *var.* Dominica Channel, Martinique Channel. *Channel* Dominica/Martinique
Marton 150 D4 Manawatu-Wanganui, North Island, NZ
Martos 92 D4 Andalucía, S Spain
Marungu 77 E7 *mountain range* SE Dem. Rep. Congo

Mary 122 D3 prev. Merv. Maryyskiy Velayat, S Turkmenistan
Maryborough see Portlaoise
Maryborough 149 D4 Queensland, E Australia
Mary Island see Kanton
Maryland 41 E5 off. State of Maryland; also known as America in Miniature, Cockade State, Free State, Old Line State. State NE USA
Maryland 42 D1 Tennessee, S USA
Maryville 45 F4 Missouri, C USA
Masai Steppe 73 C7 grassland NW Tanzania
Masaka 73 B6 SW Uganda
Masallı 117 H3 Rus. Masally. S Azerbaijan
Masasi 73 C8 Mtwara, SE Tanzania
Masawa see Massawa
Masaya 52 D3 Masaya, W Nicaragua
Mascarene Basin 141 B5 undersea feature W Indian Ocean
Mascarene Islands 79 H4 island group W Indian Ocean
Mascarene Plain 141 B5 undersea feature W Indian Ocean
Mascarene Plateau 141 B5 undersea feature W Indian Ocean
Maseru 78 D4 country capital (Lesotho) W Lesotho
Mashhad 120 E2 var. Meshed. Khorāsān, NE Iran
Mas-ha 119 D7 W Bank
Masindi 73 B6 W Uganda
Masīra see Maşīrah, Jazīrat
Masira, Gulf of see Maşīrah, Khalīj
Maşīrah, Jazīrat 121 E5 var. Masīra. Island E Oman
Maşīrah, Khalīj 121 E5 var. Gulf of Masira. Bay E Oman
Masis see Büyükağrı Dağı
Maskat see Masqaţ
Mason City 45 F3 Iowa, C USA
Masqaţ 121 E5 var. Maskat, Eng. Muscat. Country capital (Oman) NE Oman
Massa 96 B3 Toscana, C Italy
Massachusetts 41 G3 off. Commonwealth of Massachusetts; also known as Bay State, Old Bay State, Old Colony State. State NE USA
Massawa 72 C4 var. Masawa, Amh. Mits'iwa. E Eritrea
Massenya 76 B3 Chari-Baguirmi, SW Chad
Massif Central 91 C5 plateau C France
Massif du Makay see Makay
Massoukou see Franceville
Masterton 151 D5 Wellington, North Island, NZ
Masty 107 B5 Rus. Mosty. Hrodzyenskaya Voblasts', W Belarus
Masuda 131 B6 Shimane, Honshū, SW Japan
Masuku see Franceville
Masvingo 78 D3 prev. Fort Victoria, Nyanda, Victoria. Masvingo, SE Zimbabwe
Maşyāf 118 B3 Fr. Misiaf. Ḥamāh, C Syria
Matadi 77 B6 Bas-Zaïre, W Dem. Rep. Congo
Matagalpa 52 D3 Matagalpa, C Nicaragua
Matale 132 D3 Central Province, C Sri Lanka
Matam 74 C3 NE Senegal
Matamata 150 D3 Waikato, North Island, NZ
Matamoros 50 D3 Coahuila de Zaragoza, NE Mexico
Matamoros 51 E2 Tamaulipas, C Mexico
Matane 39 E4 Quebec, SE Canada
Matanzas 54 B2 Matanzas, NW Cuba
Matara 132 D4 Southern Province, S Sri Lanka
Mataram 138 D5 Pulau Lombok, C Indonesia
Mataró 93 G2 anc. Illuro. Cataluña, E Spain
Mataura 151 B7 river South Island, NZ

Mataura 151 B7 Southland, South Island, NZ
Mata Uta see Matā'utu
Matā'utu 145 E4 var. Mata Uta. Dependent territory capital (Wallis and Futuna) Île Uvea, Wallis and Futuna
Matera 97 E5 Basilicata, S Italy
Matías Romero 51 F5 Oaxaca, SE Mexico
Mato Grosso 63 E4 prev. Vila Bela da Santissima Trindade. Mato Grosso, W Brazil
Mato Grosso do Sul 63 E4 off. Estado de Mato Grosso do Sul. State S Brazil
Mato Grosso, Planalto de 56 C4 plateau C Brazil
Matosinhos 92 B2 prev. Matozinhos. Porto, NW Portugal
Matsue 131 B6 var. Matsuye, Matue. Shimane, Honshū, SW Japan
Matsumoto 131 C5 var. Matumoto. Nagano, Honshū, S Japan
Matsuyama 131 B7 var. Matuyama. Ehime, Shikoku, SW Japan
Matsuye see Matsue
Matterhorn 95 A8 It. Monte Cervino. Mountain Italy/Switzerland see also Cervino, Monte
Matthews Ridge 59 N Guyana
Matthew Town 54 D2 Great Inagua, S Bahamas
Matucana 60 C4 Lima, W Peru
Matue see Matsue
Matumoto see Matsumoto
Maturín 59 E2 Monagas, NE Venezuela
Matuyama see Matsuyama
Mau 135 E3 var. Maunāth Bhanjan. Uttar Pradesh, N India
Maui 47 B8 island Hawaii, USA, C Pacific Ocean
Maulmain see Moulmein
Maun 78 C3 Ngamiland, C Botswana
Maunāth Bhanjan see Mau
Mauren 94 E1 NE Liechtenstein
Mauritania 74 C2 Ar. Mūrītānīyah. Country W Africa

Mauritania 74

Official name Islamic Republic of Mauritania
Formation 1960
Capital Nouakchott
Population 2.7 million / 7 people per sq mile (3 people per sq km)
Total area 397,953 sq miles (1,030,700 sq km)
Languages Hassaniyah Arabic, French, Wolof
Religions Muslim (Sunni) 100%
Ethnic mix Maure 81%, Wolof 7%, Tukolor 5%, Soninka 3%, other 4%
Government Multiparty republic
Currency Ouguiya = 5 khoums
Literacy rate 42.3%
Calorie consumption 2,638 kilocalories

Mauritius 79 H3 Fr. Maurice. Country W Indian Ocean

Mauritius 79

Official name Mauritius
Formation 1968
Capital Port Louis
Population 1.2 million / 1,671 people per sq mile (645 people per sq km)
Total area 718 sq miles (1,860 sq km)
Languages English, French, French Creole, Hindi, Urdu, Tamil, Chinese
Religions Hindu 52%, Muslim 17%, Roman Catholic 26%, other 5%
Ethnic mix Indo-Mauritian 68%, Creole 27%, Sino-Mauritian 3%, Franco-Mauritian 2%
Government Parliamentary democracy

Mauritius (continued)

Currency Mauritian rupee = 100 cents
Literacy rate 84.6%
Calorie consumption 2,985 kilocalories

Mauritius 141 B5 island W Indian Ocean
Mawlamyine see Moulmein
Mawson 154 D2 Australian research station Antarctica
Maya 52 B1 river E Russian Federation
Mayadin see Al Mayādīn
Mayaguana 54 D2 island SE Bahamas
Mayaguana Passage 54 D2 passage SE Bahamas
Mayagüez 55 F3 W Puerto Rico
Mayamey 120 D2 Semnān, N Iran
Maya Mountains 52 B2 Sp. Montañas Mayas. Mountain range Belize/Guatemala
Maych'ew 72 C4 var. Mai Chio, It. Mai Ceu. N Ethiopia
Maydān Shahr 123 E4 Wardag, E Afghanistan
Mayebashi see Maebashi
Mayfield 151 B6 Canterbury, South Island, NZ
Maykop 111 A7 Respublika Adygeya, SW Russian Federation
Maymana see Meymaneh
Maymyo 136 B3 Mandalay, C Myanmar
Mayo see Maio
Mayor Island 150 D3 island NE NZ
Mayor Pablo Lagerenza see Capitán Pablo Lagerenza
Mayotte 79 F2 French territorial collectivity E Africa
May Pen 54 B5 C Jamaica
Mazabuka 78 D2 Southern, S Zambia
Mazaca see Kayseri
Mazār-e Sharīf 123 E3 var. Mazār-i Sharif. Balkh, N Afghanistan
Mazār-i Sharif see Mazār-e Sharīf
Mazatlán 50 C3 Sinaloa, C Mexico
Mažeikiai 106 B3 Mažeikiai, NW Lithuania
Mazirbe 106 C2 Talsi, NW Latvia
Mazra'a see Al Mazra'ah
Mazury 98 D3 physical region NE Poland
Mazyr 107 C7 Rus. Mozyr'. Homyel'skaya Voblasts', SE Belarus
Mbabane 78 D4 country capital (Swaziland) NW Swaziland
Mbacké see Mbaké
M'Baiki see Mbaïki
Mbaïki 77 C5 var. M'Baiki. Lobaye, SW Central African Republic
Mbaké 74 B3 var. Mbacké. W Senegal
Mbala 78 D1 prev. Abercorn. Northern, NE Zambia
Mbale 73 C6 E Uganda
Mbandaka 77 C5 prev. Coquilhatville. Équateur, NW Dem. Rep. Congo
M'Banza Congo 78 B1 var. Mbanza Congo; prev. São Salvador, São Salvador do Congo. Zaire, NW Angola
Mbanza-Ngungu 77 B6 Bas-Zaïre, W Dem. Rep. Congo
Mbarara 73 B6 SW Uganda
Mbé 76 B4 Nord, N Cameroon
Mbeya 73 C7 Mbeya, SW Tanzania
Mbomou see Bomu
M'Bomu see Bomu
Mbour 74 B3 W Senegal
Mbuji-Mayi 77 D7 prev. Bakwanga. Kasai Oriental, S Dem. Rep. Congo
McAlester 49 G2 Oklahoma, C USA
McAllen 49 G5 Texas, SW USA
McCamey 49 E3 Texas, SW USA
McClintock Channel 37 F2 channel Nunavut, N Canada
McComb 42 B3 Mississippi, S USA

McCook 45 E4 Nebraska, C USA
McKean Island 145 E3 island Phoenix Islands, C Kiribati
McKinley, Mount 36 C3 var. Denali. Mountain Alaska, USA
McKinley Park 36 C3 Alaska, USA
McMinnville 46 B3 Oregon, NW USA
McMurdo Base 154 B4 US research station Antarctica
McPherson see Fort McPherson
McPherson 45 E5 Kansas, C USA
Mdantsane 78 D5 Eastern Cape, SE South Africa
Mead, Lake 47 D6 reservoir Arizona/Nevada, W USA
Meghālaya 113 G3 state, NE India
Mecca see Makkah
Mechelen 87 C5 Eng. Mechlin, Fr. Malines. Antwerpen, C Belgium
Mecklenburger Bucht 94 C2 bay N Germany
Mecsek 99 C7 mountain range SW Hungary
Medan 138 B3 Sumatera, E Indonesia
Medeba see Ma'dabā
Medellín 58 B3 Antioquia, NW Colombia
Médenine 71 F2 var. Madanīyīn. SE Tunisia
Medford 46 B4 Oregon, NW USA
Medgidia 108 D5 Constanţa, SE Romania
Medias 108 B4 Ger. Mediasch, Hung. Medgyes. Sibiu, C Romania
Medicine Hat 37 F5 Alberta, SW Canada
Medinaceli 93 E2 Castilla-León, N Spain
Medina del Campo 92 D2 Castilla-León, N Spain
Mediterranean Sea 102 D3 Fr. Mer Méditerranée. Sea Africa/Asia/Europe
Médoc 91 B5 cultural region SW France
Medvezh'yegorsk 110 B3 Respublika Kareliya, NW Russian Federation
Meekatharra 147 B5 Western Australia
Meemu Atoll see Mulaku Atoll
Meerssen 87 D6 var. Mersen. Limburg, SE Netherlands
Meerut 134 D3 Uttar Pradesh, N India
Mehdia see Mahdia
Meheso see Mī'eso
Me Hka see Nmai Hka
Mehrīz 120 D3 Yazd, C Iran
Mehtar Lām see Mehtarlām
Mehtarlām 123 F4 var. Mehtar Lām, Meterlam, Metharlam, Metharlam. Laghmān, E Afghanistan
Meiktila 136 B3 Mandalay, C Myanmar
Mejillones 64 B2 Antofagasta, N Chile
Mek'elē 72 C4 var. Makale. N Ethiopia
Mékhé 74 B3 NW Senegal
Mekong 124 D3 var. Lan-ts'ang Chiang, Cam. Mékôngk, Chin. Lancang Jiang, Lao. Mènam Khong, Th. Mae Nam Khong, Tib. Dza Chu, Vtn. Sông Tiên Giang. River SE Asia
Mékôngk see Mekong
Mekong, Mouths of the 137 E6 delta S Vietnam
Melaka 138 B3 var. Malacca. Melaka, Peninsular Malaysia
Melanesia 144 D3 island group W Pacific Ocean
Melanesian Basin 142 C2 undersea feature W Pacific Ocean
Melbourne 149 C7 state capital Victoria, SE Australia
Melbourne 43 E4 Florida, SE USA
Melghir, Chott 71 E2 var. Chott Melrhir. Salt lake E Algeria
Melilla 80 B5 anc. Rusaddir, Russadir. Melilla, Spain, N Africa
Melilla 70 D2 enclave Spain, N Africa
Melita 37 F5 Manitoba, S Canada

216

Melitopol' 109 F4 Zaporiz'ka
Oblast', SE Ukraine
Melle 87 B5 Oost-Vlaanderen,
NW Belgium
Mellerud 85 B6 Västra Götaland,
S Sweden
Mellieha 102 B5 E Malta
Mellizo Sur, Cerro 65 A7 *mountain*
S Chile
Melo 64 E4 Cerro Largo,
NE Uruguay
Melsungen 94 B4 Hessen,
C Germany
Melun 90 C3 *anc.* Melodunum.
Seine-et-Marne, N France
Melville Island 146 D2 *island*
Northern Territory, N Australia
Melville Island 37 E2 *island* Parry
Islands, Northwest
Territories/Nunavut,
NW Canada
Melville, Lake 39 F2 *lake*
Newfoundland and Labrador,
E Canada
Melville Peninsula 37 G3 *peninsula*
Northwest Territories,
NE Canada
Membidj *see* Manbij
Memmingen 95 B6 Bayern,
S Germany
Memphis 42 C1 Tennessee, S USA
Ménaka 75 F3 Goa, E Mali
Menaldum 86 D1 Fris. Menaam.
Friesland, N Netherlands
Mènam Khong *see* Mekong
Mendaña Fracture Zone 153 F4
tectonic feature E Pacific Ocean
Mende 91 C5 *anc.* Mimatum.
Lozère, S France
Mendeleyev Ridge 155 B2 *undersea
feature* Arctic Ocean
Mendocino Fracture Zone 152 D2
tectonic feature NE Pacific Ocean
Mendoza 64 B4 Mendoza,
W Argentina
Menemen 116 A3 İzmir,
W Turkey
Menengiyn Tal 127 F2 *plain*
E Mongolia
Menongue 78 B2 *var.* Vila Serpa
Pinto, *Port.* Serpa Pinto. Cuando
Cubango, C Angola
Menorca 93 H3 *Eng.* Minorca; *anc.*
Balearis Minor. *Island* Islas
Baleares, Spain, W Mediterranean
Sea
Mentawai, Kepulauan 138 A4
island group W Indonesia
Meppel 86 D2 Drenthe,
NE Netherlands
Merano 96 C1 *Ger.* Meran. Trentino-
Alto Adige, N Italy
Merca *see* Marka
Mercedes *see* Villa Mercedes
Mercedes 64 D3 Corrientes,
NE Argentina
Mercedes 64 D4 Soriano,
SW Uruguay
Meredith, Lake 49 E1 *reservoir*
Texas, SW USA
Merefa 109 G2 Kharkivs'ka Oblast',
E Ukraine
Mergui 137 B6 Tenasserim,
S Myanmar
Mergui Archipelago 137 B6 *island
group* S Myanmar
Meriç *see* Maritsa
Mérida 92 C4 *anc.* Augusta Emerita.
Extremadura, W Spain
Mérida 58 C2 Mérida,
W Venezuela
Mérida 51 H3 Yucatán,
SW Mexico
Meridian 42 C2 Mississippi,
S USA
Mérignac 91 B5 Gironde,
SW France
Merkinė 107 B5 Varėna,
S Lithuania
Merowe 72 B3 *desert* W Sudan
Merredin 147 B6 Western Australia
Mersen *see* Meerssen
Mersey 89 D5 *river* NW England,
UK
Mersin 116 C4 İçel, S Turkey
Mērsrags 106 C3 Talsi,
NW Latvia

Meru 73 C6 Eastern, C Kenya
Merzifon 116 D2 Amasya,
N Turkey
Merzig 95 A5 Saarland,
SW Germany
Mesa 48 B2 Arizona, SW USA
Meshed *see* Mashhad
Mesopotamia 57 C5 *var.*
Mesopotamia Argentina. *Physical
region* NE Argentina
Mesopotamia Argentina *see*
Mesopotamia
Messalo, Rio 79 E2 *var.* Mualo.
River NE Mozambique
Messana *see* Messina
Messene *see* Messina
Messina 97 D7 *var.* Messana,
Messene; *anc.* Zancle. Sicilia, Italy,
C Mediterranean Sea
Messina 78 D3 Northern, NE South
Africa
Messina, Stretto di 97 D7 *Eng.*
Strait of Messina. *Strait* SW Italy
Messini 105 B6 Pelopónnisos,
S Greece
Mestghanem *see* Mostaganem
Mestia 117 F1 *var.* Mestiya.
N Georgia
Mestiya *see* Mestia
Mestre 96 C2 Veneto, NE Italy
Meta 56 B2 *off.* Departamento del
Meta. *Province* C Colombia
Metairie 42 B3 Louisiana, S USA
Metán 64 C2 Salta, N Argentina
Metapán 52 B2 Santa Ana,
NW El Salvador
Meta, Río 58 D3 *river*
Colombia/Venezuela
Meterlam *see* Mehtarlām
Methariam *see* Mehtarlām
Metharlam *see* Mehtarlām
Metković 100 B4 Dubrovnik-
Neretva, SE Croatia
Métsovo 104 B4 *prev.* Métsovon.
Ípeiros, C Greece
Metz 90 D3 *anc.* Divodurum
Mediomatricum, Mediomatrica,
Metis. Moselle, NE France
Meulaboh 138 A3 Sumatera,
W Indonesia
Meuse 87 C6 *Dut.* Maas. *River*
W Europe *see also* Maas
Meuse 90 D3 *department*
NE France
Mexcala, Río *see* Balsas, Río
Mexicali 50 A1 Baja California,
NW Mexico
Mexico 50 C3 *var.* Méjico, México,
Sp. Estados Unidos Mexicanos.
Country N Central America

Mexico 50

Official name United States of
Mexico
Formation 1836
Capital Mexico City
Population 100.4 million / 132
people per sq mile
(51 people per sq km)
Total area 761,602 sq miles
(1,972,550 sq km)
Languages Spanish, Nahuatl,
Mayan, Zapotec, Mixtec, Otomi,
Totonac, Tzotzil, Tzeltal
Religions Roman Catholic 95%,
Protestant 1%, other 4%
Ethnic mix Mestizo 55%,
Amerindian 20%, European 16%,
other 9%
Government Presidential
democracy
Currency Mexican peso = 100
centavos
Literacy rate 91.3%
Calorie consumption 3,165
kilocalories

Mexico 45 G4 Missouri, C USA
México 51 E4 *var.* Ciudad de
México, *Eng.* Mexico City.
Country capital (Mexico) México,
C Mexico
Mexico City *see* México
Mexico, Gulf of 51 F2 *Sp.* Golfo de
México. *Gulf* W Atlantic Ocean

Meyadine *see* Al Mayādīn
Meymaneh 122 D3 *var.* Maimāna,
Maymana. Fāryāb,
NW Afghanistan
Mezen' 110 D3 *river* NW Russian
Federation
Mezőtúr 99 D7 Jász-Nagykun-
Szolnok, E Hungary
Mgarr 102 A5 Gozo, N Malta
Miahuatlán 51 F5 *var.* Miahuatlán
de Porfirio Díaz. Oaxaca,
SE Mexico
Miahuatlán de Porfirio Díaz *see*
Miahuatlán
Miami 43 F5 Florida, SE USA
Miami 49 G1 Oklahoma, C USA
Miami Beach 43 F5 Florida,
SE USA
Miāneh 120 C2 *var.* Miyāneh.
Āzarbāyjān-e Khāvari, NW Iran
Mianyang 128 B5 Sichuan, C China
Miastko 98 C2 *Ger.* Rummelsburg
in Pommern. Pomorskie,
N Poland
Mi Chai *see* Nong Khai
Michalovce 99 E5 *Ger.* Grossmichel,
Hung. Nagymihály. Košický Kraj,
E Slovakia
Michigan 40 C1 *off.* State of
Michigan; also known as Great
Lakes State, Lake State, Wolverine
State. *State* N USA
Michigan, Lake 40 C2 *lake* N USA
Michurinsk 111 B5
Tambovskaya Oblast', W Russian
Federation
Micoud 55 F2 SE Saint Lucia
Micronesia 144 B1 *Country*
W Pacific Ocean

Micronesia 144

Official name Federated States of
Micronesia
Formation 1986
Capital Palikir (Pohnpei island)
Population 133,000 / 490 people per
sq mile (189 people per sq km)
Total area 271 sq miles (702 sq km)
Languages English, Trukese,
Pohnpeian, Mortlockese, Losrean
Religions Roman Catholic 50%,
Protestant 48%, other 2%
Ethnic mix Micronesian 100%
Government Non-party democracy
Currency US dollar = 100 cents
Literacy rate 89%
Calorie consumption not available

Micronesia 144 C1 *island group*
W Pacific Ocean
Mid-Atlantic Cordillera *see* Mid-
Atlantic Ridge
Mid-Atlantic Ridge 66 C3 *var.* Mid-
Atlantic Cordillera, Mid-Atlantic
Rise, Mid-Atlantic Swell. *Undersea
feature* Atlantic Ocean
Mid-Atlantic Rise *see* Mid-Atlantic
Ridge
Mid-Atlantic Swell *see* Mid-
Atlantic Ridge
Middelburg 87 B5 Zeeland,
SW Netherlands
Middelharnis 86 B4 Zuid-Holland,
SW Netherlands
Middelkerke 87 A5 West-
Vlaanderen, W Belgium
Middle America Trench 35 B7
undersea feature E Pacific Ocean
Middle Andaman 133 F2 *island*
Andaman Islands, India,
NE Indian Ocean
Middlesboro 40 C5 Kentucky, S USA
Middlesbrough 89 D5 N England,
UK
Middletown 41 F4 New Jersey,
NE USA
Middletown 41 F3 New York,
NE USA
Mid-Indian Basin 141 C5 *undersea
feature* N Indian Ocean
Mid-Indian Ridge 141 C5 *var.*
Central Indian Ridge. *Undersea
feature* C Indian Ocean
Midland 40 C3 Michigan, N USA
Midland 38 D5 Ontario, S Canada

Midland 49 E3 Texas, SW USA
Mid-Pacific Mountains 152 C2 *var.*
Mid-Pacific Seamounts. *Undersea
feature* NW Pacific Ocean
Mid-Pacific Seamounts *see* Mid-
Pacific Mountains
Midway Islands 152 D2 *US territory*
C Pacific Ocean
Miechów 99 D5 Małopolskie,
S Poland
Międzyrzec Podlaski 98 E3
Lubelskie, E Poland
Międzyrzecz 98 B3 *Ger.* Meseritz.
Lubuskie, W Poland
Mielec 99 D5 Podkarpackie,
SE Poland
Miercurea-Ciuc 108 C4 *Ger.*
Szeklerburg, *Hung.* Csíkszereda.
Harghita, C Romania
Mieres del Camín *see* Mieres del
Camino
Mieres del Camino 108 D1 *var.*
Mieres del Camín. Asturias,
NW Spain
Mieresch *see* Mureş
Mī'ēso 73 D5 *var.* Meheso, Miesso.
C Ethiopia
Miesso *see* Mī'ēso
Miguel Asua 50 D3 *var.* Miguel
Auza. Zacatecas, C Mexico
Miguel Auza *see* Miguel Asua
Mijdrecht 86 C3 Utrecht,
C Netherlands
Mikashevichy 107 C7 *Pol.*
Mikaszewicze, *Rus.* Mikashevichi.
Brestskaya Voblasts', SW Belarus
Mikhaylovka 111 B6 Volgogradskaya
Oblast', SW Russian Federation
Míkonos *see* Mýkonos
Mikre 104 C2 Lovech, N Bulgaria
Mikun' 110 D4 Respublika Komi,
NW Russian Federation
Mikuni-sanmyaku 131 D5 *mountain
range* Honshū, N Japan
Mikura-jima 131 D6 *island* E Japan
Milagro 60 B2 Guayas, SW Ecuador
Milan *see* Milano
Milange 79 E2 Zambézia,
NE Mozambique
Milano 96 B2 *Eng.* Milan, *Ger.*
Mailand; *anc.* Mediolanum.
Lombardia, N Italy
Milas 116 A4 Muğla, SW Turkey
Milashavichy 107 C7 *Rus.*
Milashevichi. Homyel'skaya
Voblasts', SE Belarus
Mildura 149 C6 Victoria,
SE Australia
Mile *see* Mili Atoll
Miles 149 D5 Queensland,
E Australia
Miles City 44 C2 Montana, NW USA
Milford Haven 89 C6 *prev.* Milford.
SW Wales, UK
Milford Sound 151 A6 *inlet* South
Island, NZ
Milford Sound 151 A6 Southland,
South Island, NZ
Mili Atoll 144 D2 *var.* Mile. *Atoll*
Ratak Chain, SE Marshall Islands
Mil'kovo 115 H3 Kamchatskaya
Oblast', E Russian Federation
Milk River 44 C1 *river* Montana,
NW USA
Milk River 37 E5 Alberta,
SW Canada
Milk, Wadi el 88 B4 *var.* Wadi
al Malik. *River* C Sudan
Milledgeville 43 E2 Georgia, SE USA
Mille Lacs Lake 45 F2 *lake*
Minnesota, N USA
Millennium Island 160 C8 *prev.*
Caroline Island, Thornton Island.
Atoll Line Islands, E Kiribati
Millerovo 111 B6 Rostovskaya
Oblast', SW Russian Federation
Mílos 105 C7 *island* Kykládes,
Greece, Aegean Sea
Mílos 105 C6 Mílos, Kykládes,
Greece, Aegean Sea
Milton 151 B7 Otago, South Island,
NZ
Milton Keynes 89 D6 SE England,
UK
Milwaukee 40 B3 Wisconsin, N USA
Min *see* Fujian
Mīnā' Qābūs 140 B3 NE Oman

Minas Gerais 63 *F3 off.* Estado de
Minas Gerais. *State* E Brazil
Minatitlán 51 *F4* Veracruz-Llave,
E Mexico
Minbu 136 *A3* Magwe,
W Myanmar
Minch, The 88 *B3 var.* North Minch.
Strait NW Scotland, UK
Mindanao 139 *F2 island*
S Philippines
Mindanao Sea *see* Bohol Sea
Mindelheim 95 *C6* Bayern,
S Germany
Mindello *see* Mindelo
Mindelo 74 *A2 var.* Mindello; *prev.*
Porto Grande. São Vicente,
N Cape Verde
Minden 94 *B4 anc.* Minthun.
Nordrhein-Westfalen,
NW Germany
Mindoro 139 *E2 island* N Philippines
Mindoro Strait 139 *E2 strait*
W Philippines
Mineral Wells 49 *F2* Texas, SW USA
Mingäçevir 117 *G2 Rus.*
Mingechaur, Mingechevir.
C Azerbaijan
Mingãora 134 *C1 var.* Mingora,
Mongora. North-West Frontier
Province, N Pakistan
Mingora *see* Mingãora
Minho 92 *B2 former province*
N Portugal
Minho, Rio 92 *B2 Sp.* Miño. *river*
Portugal/Spain *see also* Miño
Minicoy Island 132 *B3 island*
SW India
Minius *see* Miño
Minna 75 *G4* Niger, C Nigeria
Minneapolis 45 *F2* Minnesota,
N USA
Minnesota 45 *F2 off.* State of
Minnesota; also known as Gopher
State, New England of the West,
North Star State. *State* N USA
Miño 92 *B2 var.* Mino, Minius, *Port.*
Rio Minho. *River* Portugal/Spain
see also Minho, Rio
Mino *see* Miño
Minot 45 *E1* North Dakota, N USA
Minsk 107 *C6 country capital*
(Belarus) Minskaya Voblasts',
C Belarus
Minskaya Wzvyshsha 107 *C6*
mountain range C Belarus
Minsk Mazowiecki 98 *D3 var.*
Nowo-Minsk. Mazowieckie,
C Poland
Minto, Lac 38 *D2 lake* Quebec,
C Canada
Minya *see* El Minya
Miraflores 50 *C3* Baja California
Sur, W Mexico
Miranda de Ebro 93 *E1* La Rioja,
N Spain
Miri 138 *D3* Sarawak, East Malaysia
Mirim Lagoon 63 *E5 var.* Lake
Mirim, *Sp.* Laguna Merín. *Lagoon*
Brazil/Uruguay
Mirim, Lake *see* Mirim Lagoon
Mírina *see* Mýrina
Mīrjāveh 120 *E4* Sīstān va
Balūchestān, SE Iran
Mirny 154 *C3 Russian research
station* Antarctica
Mirnyy 115 *F3* Respublika Sakha
(Yakutiya), NE Russian
Federation
Mīrpur Khās 134 *B3* Sind,
SE Pakistan
Mirtóo Pélagos 105 *C6 Eng.*
Mirtoan Sea; *anc.* Myrtoum Mare.
Sea S Greece
Miskito Coast *see* Mosquito Coast
Miskitos, Cayos 53 *E2 island group*
NE Nicaragua
Miskolc 99 *D6* Borsod-Abaúj-
Zemplén, NE Hungary
Misool, Pulau 139 *F4 island*
Maluku, E Indonesia
Miṣrātah 71 *F2 var.* Misurata.
NW Libya
Mission 49 *G5* Texas, SW USA
Mississippi 42 *B2 off.* State of
Mississippi; also known as Bayou
State, Magnolia State. *State*
SE USA

Mississippi Delta 42 *B4 delta*
Louisiana, S USA
Mississippi River 35 *C6 river* C USA
Missoula 44 *B1* Montana, NW USA
Missouri 45 *F5 off.* State of
Missouri; also known as Bullion
State, Show Me State. *State* C USA
Missouri River 45 *E3 river* C USA
Mistassini, Lac 38 *D3 lake* Quebec,
SE Canada
Mistelbach an der Zaya 95 *E6*
Niederösterreich, NE Austria
Misurata *see* Miṣrātah
Misti, Volcán 61 *E4 mountain* S Peru
Mitchell 149 *D5* Queensland,
E Australia
Mitchell 45 *E3* South Dakota, N USA
Mitchell, Mount 43 *E1 mountain*
North Carolina, SE USA
Mitchell River 148 *C2 river*
Queensland, NE Australia
Mi Tho *see* My Tho
Mitilíni *see* Mytilíni
Mito 131 *D5* Ibaraki, Honshū,
S Japan
Mits'iwa *see* Massawa
Mitspe Ramon *see* Mizpé Ramon
Mitú 58 *C4* Vaupés, SE Colombia
Mitumba, Monts 77 *E7 var.* Chaîne
des Mitumba, Mitumba Range.
Mountain range E Dem. Rep.
Congo
Mitumba Range *see* Mitumba,
Monts
Miyako 130 *D4* Iwate, Honshū,
C Japan
Miyako-jima 131 *D6 island*
Sakishima-shotō, SW Japan
Miyakonojō 131 *B8 var.*
Miyakonzyô. Miyazaki, Kyūshū,
SW Japan
Miyakonzyô *see* Miyakonojō
Miyāneh *see* Mīāneh
Miyazaki 131 *B8* Miyazaki,
Kyūshū, SW Japan
Mizil 108 *C5* Prahova, SE Romania
Miziya 104 *C1* Vratsa, NW Bulgaria
Mizpé Ramon 119 *A7 var.* Mitspe
Ramon, Southern, S Israel
Mjøsa 85 *B6 var.* Mjøsen. *Lake*
S Norway
Mjøsen *see* Mjøsa
Mladenovac 100 *D4* Serbia,
C Serbia and Montenegro (Yugo.)
Mława 98 *D3* Mazowieckie,
C Poland
Mljet 101 *B5 It.* Meleda; *anc.* Melita.
Island S Croatia
Mmabatho 78 *C4* North-West,
N South Africa
Moab 44 *B5* Utah, W USA
Moab, Kir of *see* Al Karak
Moa Island 148 *C1 island*
Queensland, NE Australia
Moanda 77 *B6 var.* Mouanda. Haut-
Ogooué, SE Gabon
Moba 77 *E7* Shaba, E Dem. Rep.
Congo
Mobay *see* Montego Bay
Mobaye 77 *C5* Basse-Kotto,
S Central African Republic
Moberly 45 *G4* Missouri, C USA
Mobile 42 *C3* Alabama, S USA
Mobutu Sese Seko, Lac *see* Albert,
Lake
Mochudi 78 *C4* Kgatleng,
SE Botswana
Mocímboa da Praia 79 *F2 var.* Vila
de Mocímboa da Praia. Cabo
Delgado, N Mozambique
Môco 78 *B2 var.* Morro de Môco.
Mountain W Angola
Mocoa 58 *A4* Putumayo,
SW Colombia
Mocuba 79 *E3* Zambézia,
NE Mozambique
Modena 96 *B3 anc.* Mutina. Emilia-
Romagna, N Italy
Modesto 47 *B6* California, W USA
Modica 97 *C7 anc.* Motyca. Sicilia,
Italy, C Mediterranean Sea
Modimolle 56 *D4 var.* Nylstroom,
NE South Africa
Modriča 100 *C3* Republika Srpska,
N Bosnia and Herzegovina
Moe 149 *C7* Victoria, SE Australia
Moero, Lac *see* Mweru, Lake

Mogadishu *see* Muqdisho
Mogilno 98 *C3* Kujawski-
pomorskie, C Poland
Mohammedia 70 *C2 prev.* Fédala.
NW Morocco
Mohave, Lake 47 *D7 reservoir*
Arizona/Nevada, W USA
Mohawk River 41 *F3 river* New
York, NE USA
Mohéli 79 *F2 var.* Mwali, Mohilla,
Mohila, Fr. Moili. *Island* S Comoros
Mohila *see* Mohéli
Mohilla *see* Mohéli
Mohns Ridge 83 *F3 undersea feature*
Greenland Sea/Norwegian Sea
Moho 61 *E4* Puno, SW Peru
Mohoro 73 *C7* Pwani, E Tanzania
Mohyliv-Podil's'kyy 108 *D3 Rus.*
Mogilev-Podol'skiy. Vinnyts'ka
Oblast', C Ukraine
Moi 85 *A6* Rogaland, S Norway
Moili *see* Mohéli
Mo i Rana 84 *C3* Nordland,
C Norway
Möisaküla 106 *D3 Ger.* Moiseküll.
Viljandimaa, S Estonia
Moissac 91 *B6* Tarn-et-Garonne,
S France
Mojácar 93 *E5* Andalucía, S Spain
Mojave Desert 47 *D7 plain*
California, W USA
Moktama *see* Martaban
Mol 87 *C5 prev.* Moll. Antwerpen,
N Belgium
Moldavia *see* Moldova
Moldavian SSR/Moldavskaya SSR
see Moldova
Molde 85 *A5* Møre og Romsdal,
S Norway
Moldo-Too, Khrebet 123 *G2 prev.*
Khrebet Moldotau. *Mountain
range* C Kyrgyzstan
Moldova 108 *D3 var.* Moldavia; *prev.*
Moldavian SSR, *Rus.* Moldavskaya
SSR. *Country* SE Europe

Moldova Nouă 108 *A4 Ger.*
Neumoldowa, *Hung.* Újmoldova.
Caraş-Severin, SW Romania
Moldoveanul *see* Vârful
Moldoveanu
Molfetta 97 *E5* Puglia, SE Italy
Mollendo 61 *E4* Arequipa, SW Peru
Mölndal 85 *B7* Västra Götaland,
S Sweden
Molochans'k 109 *G4 Rus.*
Molochansk. Zaporiz'ka Oblast',
SE Ukraine
Molodezhnaya 154 *C2 Russian
research station* Antarctica
Molokai 47 *B8 Haw.* Moloka'i.
Island Hawaii, USA, C Pacific
Ocean
Molokai Fracture Zone 153 *E2*
tectonic feature NE Pacific Ocean
Molopo 78 *C4 seasonal river*
Botswana/South Africa
Mólos 105 *B5* Stereá Ellás, C Greece
Moluccas *see* Maluku
Molucca Sea 139 *F4 Ind.* Laut
Maluku. *Sea* E Indonesia
Mombasa 73 *D7 international airport*
Coast, SE Kenya

Mombasa 73 *D7* Coast, SE Kenya
Mombetsu *see* Monbetsu
Momchilgrad 104 *D3 prev.*
Mastanli. Kŭrdzhali, S Bulgaria
Møn 85 *B8 prev.* Møen. *Island*
SE Denmark
Monaco 91 *E6 Country* W Europe

Monaco 91

Official name Principality of
Monaco
Formation 1861
Capital Monaco
Population 31,700 / 42,104 people
per sq mile (16,256 people per sq km)
Total area 0.75 sq miles (1.95 sq km)
Languages French, Italian,
Monégasque, English
Religions Roman Catholic, 89%,
Protestant 6%, other 5%
Ethnic mix French 47%,
Monégasque 17%, Italian 16%,
other 20%
Government Constitutional
monarchy
Currency Euro (French franc until
2002)
Literacy rate 99%
Calorie consumption not available

Monaco 91 *C7 var.* Monaco-Ville;
anc. Monoecus. *Country capital*
(Monaco) S Monaco
Monaco, Port de 91 *C8 bay*
S Monaco
Monaco-Ville *see* Monaco
Monahans 49 *F3* Texas, SW USA
Mona, Isla 55 *E3 island* W Puerto
Rico
Mona Passage 55 *E3 Sp.* Canal de la
Mona. *Channel* Dominican
Republic/Puerto Rico
Monbetsu 130 *D2 var.* Mombetsu,
Monbetu. Hokkaidō, NE Japan
Monbetu *see* Monbetsu
Moncalieri 96 *A2* Piemonte,
NW Italy
Monchegorsk 110 *C2*
Murmanskaya Oblast',
NW Russian Federation
Monclova 50 *D2* Coahuila de
Zaragoza, NE Mexico
Moncton 39 *F4* New Brunswick,
SE Canada
Mondovì 96 *A2* Piemonte, NW Italy
Monfalcone 96 *D2* Friuli-Venezia
Giulia, NE Italy
Monforte 92 *C1* Galicia,
NW Spain
Mongo 76 *C3* Guéra, C Chad
Mongolia 126 *C2 Mong.* Mongol
Uls. *Country* E Asia

Mongolia 126

Official name Mongolia
Formation 1924
Capital Ulan Bator
Population 2.6 million / 4 people
per sq mile (2 people per sq km)
Total area 604,247 sq miles
(1,565,000 sq km)
Languages Khalkha Mongolian,
Kazakh, Chinese, Russian
Religions Tibetan Buddhist 96%,
Muslim 4%
Ethnic mix Mongol 90%, Kazakh
4%, Chinese 2%, Russian 2%,
other 2%
Government Multiparty republic
Currency Tugrik (togrog) = 100
möngös
Literacy rate 99%
Calorie consumption 1,981
kilocalories

Mongolia, Plateau of 124 *D1 plateau*
E Mongolia
Mongora *see* Mingãora
Mongu 78 *C2* Western, W Zambia
Monkchester *see* Newcastle upon
Tyne
Monkey Bay 79 *E2* Southern,
SE Malawi

Moldova 108

Official name Republic of Moldova
Formation 1991
Capital Chisinau
Population 4.3 million / 329 people
per sq mile (127 people per sq km)
Total area 13,067 sq miles
(33,843 sq km)
Languages Romanian, Moldovan,
Russian
Religions Eastern Orthodox 98%,
Jewish 2%
Ethnic mix Moldovan 65%,
Ukranian 14%, Russian 13%,
Gagauzi 4%, other 4%
Government Parliamentary
democracy
Currency Moldovan leu = 100 bani
Literacy rate 99%
Calorie consumption 2,764
kilocalories

Monkey River *see* Monkey River Town
Monkey River Town *52 C2 var.* Monkey River. Toledo, SE Belize
Monoecus *see* Monaco
Mono Lake *47 C6 lake* California, W USA
Monóvar *93 F4* País Valenciano, E Spain
Monroe *42 B2* Louisiana, S USA
Monrovia *74 C5 country capital* (Liberia) W Liberia
Mons *87 B6 Dut.* Bergen. Hainaut, S Belgium
Monselice *96 C2* Veneto, NE Italy
Montagnes Rocheuses *see* Rocky Mountains
Montana *44 B1 off.* State of Montana; also known as Mountain State, Treasure State. *State* NW USA
Montana *104 C2 prev.* Ferdinand, Mikhaylovgrad. Montana, NW Bulgaria
Montargis *90 C4* Loiret, C France
Montauban *91 B6* Tarn-et-Garonne, S France
Montbéliard *90 D4* Doubs, E France
Mont Cenis, Col du *91 D5 pass* E France
Mont-de-Marsan *91 B6* Landes, SW France
Monteagudo *61 G4* Chuquisaca, S Bolivia
Monte-Carlo *91 C8* NE Monaco
Monte Caseros *64 D3* Corrientes, NE Argentina
Monte Cristi *54 D3 var.* San Fernando de Monte Cristi. NW Dominican Republic
Montegiardino *96 E2* SE San Marino
Montego Bay *54 A4 var.* Mobay. W Jamaica
Montélimar *91 D5 anc.* Acunum Acusio, Montilium Adhemari. Drôme, E France
Montemorelos *51 E3* Nuevo León, NE Mexico
Montenegro *101 C5 Serb.* Crna Gora. Admin. region *republic* SW Serbia and Montenegro (Yugo.)
Monte Patria *64 B3* Coquimbo, C Chile
Monterey *see* Monterrey
Monterey *47 B6* California, W USA
Monterey Bay *47 A6 bay* California, W USA
Montería *58 B2* Córdoba, NW Colombia
Montero *61 G4* Santa Cruz, C Bolivia
Monterrey *51 E3 var.* Monterey. Nuevo León, NE Mexico
Montes Claros *63 F3* Minas Gerais, SE Brazil
Montevideo *64 D4 country capital* (Uruguay) Montevideo, S Uruguay
Montevideo *45 F2* Minnesota, N USA
Montgenèvre, Col de *91 D5 pass* France/Italy
Montgomery *42 D2 state capital* Alabama, S USA
Monthey *95 A7* Valais, SW Switzerland
Montluçon *90 C4* Allier, C France
Montoro *92 D4* Andalucía, S Spain
Montpelier *41 G2 state capital* Vermont, NE USA
Montpellier *91 C6* Hérault, S France
Montréal *39 F4 Eng.* Montreal. Quebec, SE Canada
Montrose *44 C5* Colorado, C USA
Montrose *88 D3* E Scotland, UK
Montserrat *55 G3 var.* Emerald Isle. *UK dependent territory* E West Indies
Monywa *136 B3* Sagaing, C Myanmar
Monza *96 B2* Lombardia, N Italy
Monze *78 D2* Southern, S Zambia

Monzón *93 F2* Aragón, NE Spain
Moonie *149 D5* Queensland, E Australia
Moora *147 A6* Western Australia
Moore *49 G1* Oklahoma, C USA
Moore, Lake *147 B6 lake* Western Australia
Moorhead *45 F2* Minnesota, N USA
Moose *38 C3 river* Ontario, S Canada
Moosehead Lake *41 G1 lake* Maine, NE USA
Moosonee *38 C3* Ontario, SE Canada
Mopti *75 E3* Mopti, C Mali
Moquegua *61 E4* Moquegua, SE Peru
Mora *85 C5* Kopparberg, C Sweden
Morales *52 C2* Izabal, E Guatemala
Morant Bay *54 B5* E Jamaica
Moratalla *93 E4* Murcia, SE Spain
Morava *99 C5 var.* March. *River* C Europe *see also* March
Morava *see* Velika Morava
Moravia *99 B5* Iowa, C USA
Moray Firth *88 C3 inlet* N Scotland, UK
Morea *see* Pelopónnisos
Moreau River *44 D2 river* South Dakota, N USA
Moree *149 D5* New South Wales, SE Australia
Morelia *51 E4* Michoacán de Ocampo, S Mexico
Morena, Sierra *92 C4 mountain range* S Spain
Moreni *108 C5* Dâmbovița, S Romania
Mórfou *102 C5* W Cyprus
Morgan City *42 B3* Louisiana, S USA
Morghāb, Daryā-ye *122 D3 var.* Murgab, Murghāb, *Turkm.* Murgap Deryasy. *River* Afghanistan/Turkmenistan *see also* Murgab
Morioka *130 D4* Iwate, Honshū, C Japan
Morlaix *90 A3* Finistère, NW France
Mornington Abyssal Plain *67 A7 undersea feature* SE Pacific Ocean
Mornington Island *148 B2 island* Wellesley Islands, Queensland, N Australia
Morocco *70 B3 Ar.* Al Mamlakah. *Country* N Africa

Morocco 70

Official name Kingdom of Morocco
Formation 1956
Capital Rabat
Population 30.4 million / 176 people per sq mile (68 people per sq km)
Total area 172,316 sq miles (446,300 sq km)
Languages Arabic, Berber (Shluh, Tamazight, Riffian), French, Spanish
Religions Muslim 99%, other 1%
Ethnic mix Arab 70%, Berber 29%, European 1%
Government Constitutional monarchy
Currency Moroccan dirham = 100 centimes
Literacy rate 48.9%
Calorie consumption 2,964 kilocalories

Morocco *see* Marrakech
Morogoro *73 C7* Morogoro, E Tanzania
Moro Gulf *139 E3 gulf* S Philippines
Morón *54 C2* Ciego de Ávila, C Cuba
Mörön *126 D2* Hövsgöl, N Mongolia
Morondava *79 F3* Toliara, W Madagascar
Moroni *79 F2 country capital* (Comoros) Grande Comore, NW Comoros
Morotai, Pulau *139 F3 island* Maluku, E Indonesia

Morotiri *see* Marotiri
Morrinsville *150 D3* Waikato, North Island, NZ
Morris *45 F2* Minnesota, N USA
Morris Jesup, Kap *83 E1 headland* N Greenland
Morro de Môco *see* Môco
Morvan *90 D4 physical region* C France
Moscow *see* Moskva
Moscow *46 C2* Idaho, NW USA
Mosel *95 A5 Fr.* Moselle. *River* W Europe *see also* Moselle
Moselle *87 E8 Ger.* Mosel. *River* W Europe *see also* Mosel
Moselle *90 D3 department* NE France
Mosgiel *151 B7* Otago, South Island, NZ
Moshi *73 C7* Kilimanjaro, NE Tanzania
Mosjøen *84 B4* Nordland, C Norway
Moskva *111 B5 Eng.* Moscow. *Country capital* (Russian Federation) Gorod Moskva, W Russian Federation
Moskva *123 E3 Rus.* Moskovskiy; *prev.* Chubek. SW Tajikistan
Mosonmagyaróvár *99 C6 Ger.* Wieselburg-Ungarisch-Altenburg; *prev.* Moson and Magyaróvár, *Ger.* Wieselburg and Ungarisch-Altenburg. Győr-Moson-Sopron, NW Hungary
Mosquito Coast *53 E3 var.* Miskito Coast. *Coastal region* E Nicaragua
Mosquitos, Golfo de los *53 F4 Eng.* Mosquito Gulf. Gulf N Panama
Moss *85 B6* Østfold, S Norway
Mosselbaai *78 C7 var.* Mosselbai, *Eng.* Mossel Bay. Western Cape, SW South Africa
Mossendjo *77 B6* Le Niari, SW Congo
Mossoró *63 G2* Rio Grande do Norte, NE Brazil
Most *98 A4 Ger.* Brüx. Ústecký Kraj, NW Czech Republic
Mosta *102 B5 var.* Musta. C Malta
Mostaganem *70 D2 var.* Mestghanem. NW Algeria
Mostar *100 C4* Federacija Bosna I Hercegovina, S Bosnia and Herzegovina
Mosul *see* Al Mawşil
Mota del Cuervo *93 E3* Castilla-La Mancha, C Spain
Motagua, Río *52 B2 river* Guatemala/Honduras
Motril *92 D5* Andalucía, S Spain
Motru *108 B4* Gorj, SW Romania
Motueka *151 C5* Tasman, South Island, NZ
Motul *51 H3 var.* Motul de Felipe Carrillo Puerto. Yucatán, SE Mexico
Motul de Felipe Carrillo Puerto *see* Motul
Mouanda *see* Moanda
Mouhoun *see* Black Volta
Mouila *77 A6* Ngounié, C Gabon
Mould Bay *37 E2* Prince Patrick Island, Northwest Territories/Nunavut, N Canada
Moulins *90 C4* Allier, C France
Moulmein *136 B4 var.* Maulmain. Mawlamyine. Mon State, S Myanmar
Moundou *76 B4* Logone-Occidental, SW Chad
Moŭng Roessei *137 D5* Bătdâmbâng, W Cambodia
Moun Hou *see* Black Volta
Mountain Home *42 B1* Arkansas, C USA
Mount Ara *see* Büyükağrı Dağı
Mount Cook *151 B6* Canterbury, South Island, NZ
Mount Desert Island *41 H2 island* Maine, NE USA
Mount Fuji *see* Fuji-san
Mount Gambier *149 B7* South Australia
Mount Isa *148 B3* Queensland, C Australia
Mount Magnet *147 B5* Western Australia

Mount Pleasant *45 G4* Iowa, C USA
Mount Pleasant *40 C3* Michigan, N USA
Mount Vernon *40 B5* Illinois, N USA
Mount Vernon *46 B1* Washington, NW USA
Mourdi, Dépression du *76 C2 desert lowland* Chad/Sudan
Mouscron *87 A6 Dut.* Moeskroen. Hainaut, W Belgium
Mouse River *see* Souris River
Moussoro *76 B3* Kanem, W Chad
Moyen Atlas *70 C2 Eng.* Middle Atlas. *Mountain range* N Morocco
Moyobamba *60 B2* San Martín, NW Peru
Moyu *126 B3 var.* Karakax. Xinjiang Uygur Zizhiqu, NW China
Moyynkum, Peski *123 F1 Kaz.* Moyynqum. *Desert* S Kazakhstan
Mozambique *79 E3 prev.* People's Republic of Mozambique, Portuguese East Africa. *Country* S Africa

Mozambique 79

Official name Republic of Mozambique
Formation 1975
Capital Maputo
Population 18.6 million / 60 people per sq mile (23 people per sq km)
Total area 309,494 sq miles (801,590 sq km)
Languages Portuguese, Makua, Tsonga, Sena, Lomwe
Religions Traditional beliefs 60%, Christian 30%, Muslim 10%
Ethnic mix Makua Lomwe 47%, Tsonga 23%, Malawi 12%, Shona 11%, Yao 4%, other 3%
Government Multiparty republic
Currency Metical = 100 centavos
Literacy rate 44%
Calorie consumption 1,927 kilocalories

Mozambique Basin *see* Natal Basin
Mozambique Channel *79 E3 Fr.* Canal de Mozambique, *Mal.* Lakandranon' i Mozambika. *Strait* W Indian Ocean
Mozambique Plateau *69 D7 var.* Mozambique Rise. *Undersea feature* SW Indian Ocean
Mozambique Rise *see* Mozambique Plateau
Mpama *77 B6 river* C Congo
Mpika *78 D2* Northern, NE Zambia
Mqinvartsveri *see* Kazbek
Mragowo *98 D2 Ger.* Sensburg. Olsztyn, NE Poland
Mtwara *73 D8* Mtwara, SE Tanzania
Mualo *see* Messalo, Rio
Muang Chiang Rai *see* Chiang Rai
Muang Kalasin *see* Kalasin
Muang Khôn *137 D5* Champasak, S Laos
Muang Khôngxédôn *137 D5 var.* Khong Sedone. Salavan, S Laos
Muang Khon Kaen *see* Khon Kaen
Muang Lampang *see* Lampang
Muang Loei *see* Loei
Muang Lom Sak *see* Lom Sak
Muang Nakhon Sawan *see* Nakhon Sawan
Muang Namo *136 C3* Oudômxai, N Laos
Muang Nan *see* Nan
Muang Phalan *136 D4 var.* Muang Phalane. Savannakhét, S Laos
Muang Phalane *see* Muang Phalan
Muang Phayao *see* Phayao
Muang Phitsanulok *see* Phitsanulok
Muang Phrae *see* Phrae
Muang Roi Et *see* Roi Et
Muang Sakon Nakhon *see* Sakon Nakhon
Muang Samut Prakan *see* Samut Prakan
Muang Sing *136 C3* Louang Namtha, N Laos

Muang Ubon *see* Ubon Ratchathani
Muar 138 *B3 var.* Bandar Maharani.
 Johor, Peninsular Malaysia
Mucojo 79 *F2* Cabo Delgado,
 N Mozambique
Mudanjiang 129 *E3 var.* Mu-tan-
 chiang. Heilongjiang, NE China
Mudon 137 *B5* Mon State,
 S Myanmar
Muenchen *see* Munich
Muenster *see* Münster
Mufulira 78 *D2* Copperbelt,
 C Zambia
Mughla *see* Muğla
Muğla 116 *A4 var.* Mughla. Muğla,
 SW Turkey
Mūḩ, Sabkhat al 134 *C3* lake
 C Syria
Muir Éireann *see* Irish Sea
Muisne 60 *A1* Esmeraldas,
 NW Ecuador
Mukacheve 108 *B3* Hung. Munkács,
 Rus. Mukachevo. Zakarpats'ka
 Oblast', W Ukraine
Mukalla *see* Al Mukallā
Mula 93 *E4* Murcia, SE Spain
Mulaku Atoll 132 *B4 var.* Meemu
 Atoll. *Atoll* C Maldives
Muleshoe 49 *E2* Texas, SW USA
Mulhacén 93 *E5 var.* Cerro de
 Mulhacén. *Mountain* S Spain
Mulhouse 90 *E4 Ger.* Mülhausen.
 Haut-Rhin, NE France
Muller, Pegunungan 138 *D4 Dut.*
 Müller-gerbergte. *Mountain range*
 Borneo, C Indonesia
Müllheim 95 *A6* Baden-
 Württemberg, SW Germany
Mull, Isle of 88 *B4 island*
 W Scotland, UK
Mulongo 77 *D7* Shaba, SE Dem.
 Rep. Congo
Multán 134 *C2* Punjab, E Pakistan
Mumbai 134 *C5 prev.* Bombay.
 Mahārāshtra, W India
Munamägi *see* Suur Munamägi
München 95 *C5* Bayern,
 E Germany
Muncie 40 *C4* Indiana, N USA
Mungbere 77 *E5* Orientale,
 NE Dem. Rep. Congo
Mu Nggava *see* Rennell
Munich 80 *D4 var.* Muenchen,
 Bayern, SE Germany
Munkhafaḑ al Qaṭṭārah *see*
 Qaṭṭāra, Monkhafad el
Munster 89 *A6 Ir.* Cúige Mumhan.
 Cultural region S Ireland
Münster 94 *A4 var.* Muenster,
 Münster in Westfalen. Nordrhein-
 Westfalen, W Germany
Münster in Westfalen *see* Münster
Muong Xiang Ngeun 136 *C4 var.*
 Xieng Ngeun. Louangphabang,
 N Laos
Muonio 84 *D3* Lappi,
 N Finland
Muonioälv 84 *D3 river*
 Finland/Sweden
Muqāṭ 119 *C5* Al Mafraq,
 E Jordan
Muqdisho 73 *D6 Eng.* Mogadishu,
 It. Mogadiscio. *Country capital*
 (Somalia) Banaadir, S Somalia
Mur 95 *E7 SCr.* Mura. *River*
 C Europe
Muradiye 117 *F3* Van, E Turkey
Murapara *see* Murupara
Murata 96 *E2* S San Marino
Murchison River 147 *A5 river*
 Western Australia
Murcia 93 *E4 cultural region*
 SE Spain
Murcia 93 *F4* Murcia, SE Spain
Mureş 108 *A4 var.* Maros, Mureşul,
 Ger. Marosch, Mieresch. *River*
 Hungary/Romania *see also* Maros
Mureşul *see* Mureş
Murfreesboro 42 *D1* Tennessee,
 S USA
Murgab 122 *D3 prev.* Murgap.
 Maryyskiy Velayat,
 S Turkmenistan
Murgab 122 *D3 var.* Murghab, Pash.
 Daryā-ye Morghāb, *Turkm.*
 Murgap Deryasy. *River*
 Afghanistan/Turkmenistan *see*
 also Morghāb, Daryā-ye

Murgap *see* Murgab
Murgap Deryasy *see* Morghāb,
 Daryā-ye/Murgab
Murghab *see* Morghāb, Daryá-
 ye/Murgab
Murghob 123 *F3 Rus.* Murgab.
 SE Tajikistan
Murgon 149 *E5* Queensland,
 E Australia
Müritz 94 *C3 var.* Müritzee. *Lake*
 NE Germany
Müritzee *see* Müritz
Murmansk 110 *C2* Murmanskaya
 Oblast', NW Russian Federation
Murmashi 110 *C2* Murmanskaya
 Oblast', NW Russian Federation
Murom 111 *B5* Vladimirskaya
 Oblast', W Russian Federation
Muroran 130 *D3* Hokkaidō,
 NE Japan
Muros 92 *B1* Galicia, NW Spain
Murray Fracture Zone 153 *E2*
 tectonic feature NE Pacific Ocean
Murray Range *see* Murray Ridge
Murray Ridge 112 *C5 var.* Murray
 Range. *Undersea feature* N Arabian
 Sea
Murray River 149 *B6 river*
 SE Australia
Murrumbidgee River 149 *C6 river*
 New South Wales, SE Australia
Murska Sobota 95 *E7 Ger.* Olsnitz.
 NE Slovenia
Murupara 150 *E3 var.* Murapara.
 Bay of Plenty, North Island, NZ
Murviedro *see* Sagunto
Murwāra 135 *E4* Madhya Pradesh,
 N India
Murwillumbah 149 *E5* New South
 Wales, SE Australia
Murzuq, Idhān 71 *F4 var.* Edeyin
 Murzuq. *Desert* SW Libya
Mürzzuschlag 95 *E7* Steiermark,
 E Austria
Muş 117 *F3 var.* Mush. Muş,
 E Turkey
Mūsa, Gebel 72 *C2 mountain*
 NE Egypt
Musala 104 *B3 mountain* W Bulgaria
Muscat *see* Masqaṭ
Muscatine 45 *G3* Iowa, C USA
Musgrave Ranges 147 *D5 mountain*
 range South Australia
Mush *see* Muş
Muskegon 40 *C3* Michigan,
 N USA
Muskogee 49 *G1* Oklahoma,
 C USA
Musoma 73 *C6* Mara, N Tanzania
Musta *see* Mosta
Musters, Lago 65 *B6 lake*
 S Argentina
Muswellbrook 149 *D6* New South
 Wales, SE Australia
Mut 116 *C4* İçel, S Turkey
Mu-tan-chiang *see* Mudanjiang
Mutare 78 *D3 var.* Mutari; *prev.*
 Umtali. Manicaland, E Zimbabwe
Mutari *see* Mutare
Mutsu-wan 130 *D3 bay* N Japan
Muttonbird Islands 151 *A8 island*
 group SW NZ
Mu Us Shamo 127 *E3 var.* Ordos
 Desert. *Desert* N China
Muy Muy 52 *D3* Matagalpa,
 C Nicaragua
Müynoq 122 *C1 Rus.* Muynak.
 Qoraqalpog'iston Respublikasi,
 NW Uzbekistan
Mužlja 100 *D3 Hung.* Felsőmuzslya;
 prev. Gornja Mužlja. Serbia,
 N Serbia and
 Montenegro (Yugo.)
Mwali *see* Mohéli
Mwanza 73 *B6* Mwanza,
 NW Tanzania
Mweka 77 *C6* Kasai Occidental,
 C Dem. Rep. Congo
Mwene-Ditu 77 *D7* Kasai Oriental,
 S Dem. Rep. Congo
Mweru, Lake 77 *D7 var.* Lac Moero.
 Lake Congo (Zaire)/Zambia
Mweru Wantipa, Lake 77 *E7 lake*
 N Zambia
Myadziel 107 *C5 Pol.* Miadzioł
 Nowy, *Rus.* Myadel'. Minskaya
 Voblasts', N Belarus

Myanmar 136 *A3 var.* Burma.
 Country SE Asia

Myanmar (Burma) 136

Official name	Union of Myanmar
Formation	1948
Capital	Rangoon (Yangoon)
Population	48.4 million / 185 people per sq mile (71 people per sq km)
Total area	261,969 sq miles (678,500 sq km)
Languages	Burmese, Karen, Shan, Chin, Kachin, Mon, Palaung, Wa
Religions	Buddhist 87%, Christian 6%, Muslim 4%, Hindu 1%, other 2%
Ethnic mix	Burman (Bamah) 68%, Shan 9%, Karen 6%, Rakhine 4%, other 13%
Government	Military-based regime
Currency	Kyat = 100 pyas
Literacy rate	84.7%
Calorie consumption	2,842 kilocalories

Myanaung 136 *B4* Irrawaddy,
 SW Myanmar
Myaungmya 136 *A4* Irrawaddy,
 SW Myanmar
Myerkulavichy 107 *D7 Rus.*
 Merkulovichi. Homyel'skaya
 Voblasts', SE Belarus
Myingyan 136 *B3* Mandalay,
 C Myanmar
Myitkyina 136 *B2* Kachin State,
 N Myanmar
Mykolayiv 109 *E4 Rus.* Nikolayev.
 Mykolayivs'ka Oblast', S Ukraine
Mýkonos 105 *D6 var.* Míkonos. *Island*
 Kykládes, Greece, Aegean Sea
Myrhorod 109 *F2 Rus.* Mirgorod.
 Poltavs'ka Oblast', NE Ukraine
Mýrina 104 *D4 var.* Mírina. Límnos,
 SE Greece
Myrtle Beach 43 *F2* South Carolina,
 SE USA
Mýrtos 105 *D8* Kríti, Greece,
 E Mediterranean Sea
Myślibórz 98 *B3*
 Zachodniopomorskie, NW Poland
Mysore 132 *C2 var.* Maisur.
 Karnātaka, W India
Mysore *see* Karnātaka
My Tho 137 *E6 var.* Mi Tho. Tiên
 Giang, S Vietnam
Mytilene *see* Mytilíni
Mytilíni 105 *D5 var.* Mitilíni; *anc.*
 Mytilene. Lésvos, E Greece
Mzuzu 79 *E2* Northern, N Malawi

N

Naberezhnyye Chelny 111 *D5 prev.*
 Brezhnev. Respublika Tatarstan,
 W Russian Federation
Nablus 119 *A6 var.* Nābulus, *Heb.*
 Shekhem; *anc.* Neapolis, *Bibl.*
 Shechem. N West Bank
Nābulus *see* Nablus
Nacala 79 *F2* Nampula,
 NE Mozambique
Nada *see* Danzhou
Nadi 145 *E4 prev.* Nandi. Viti Levu,
 W Fiji
Nadur 102 *A5* Gozo, N Malta
Nadvirna 108 *C3* Pol. Nadwórna,
 Rus. Nadvornaya. Ivano-
 Frankivs'ka Oblast', W Ukraine
Nadvoitsy 110 *B3* Respublika
 Kareliya, NW Russian Federation
Nadym 114 *C3* Yamalo-Nenetskiy
 Avtonomnyy Okrug, N Russian
 Federation
Náfpaktos 105 *B5 var.* Návpaktos.
 Dytikí Ellás, C Greece
Náfplio 105 *B6 prev.* Návplion.
 Pelopónnisos, S Greece
Naga 139 *E2 off.* Naga City; *prev.*
 Nueva Caceres. Luzon,
 N Philippines
Nagano 131 *C5* Nagano, Honshū,
 S Japan
Nagaoka 131 *D5* Niigata, Honshū,
 C Japan
Nagara Pathom *see* Nakhon
 Pathom

Murgap *see* Murgab
Nagara Sridharmaraj *see* Nakhon
 Si Thammarat
Nagara Svarga *see* Nakhon Sawan
Nagasaki 131 *A7* Nagasaki,
 Kyūshū, SW Japan
Nagato 131 *A7* Yamaguchi, Honshū,
 SW Japan
Nāgercoil 132 *C3* Tamil Nādu,
 SE India
Nagorno-Karabakhskaya
 Avtonomnaya Oblast *see*
 Nagornyy Karabakh
Nagornyy Karabakh 117 *G3 var.*
 Nagorno-Karabakhskaya
 Avtonomnaya Oblast, *Arm.*
 Lernnayin Gharabakh, *Az.* Dağlıq
 Qarabağ. *Former autonomous region*
 SW Azerbaijan
Nagoya 131 *C6* Aichi, Honshū,
 SW Japan
Nāgpur 134 *D4* Mahārāshtra,
 C India
Nagqu 126 *C5 Chin.* Na-ch'ii; *prev.*
 Hei-ho. Xizang Zizhiqu, W China
Nagykálló 99 *E6* Szabolcs-Szatmár-
 Bereg, E Hungary
Nagykanizsa 99 *C7 Ger.*
 Grosskanizsa. Zala, SW Hungary
Nagykőrös 99 *D7* Pest, C Hungary
Nagyszentmiklós *see* Sânnicolau
 Mare
Naha 130 *A3* Okinawa, Okinawa,
 SW Japan
Nahariya *see* Nahariyya
Nahariyya 119 *A5 var.* Nahariya.
 Northern, N Israel
Nahr al 'Aşi *see* Orantes
Nahr al Litant *see* Lītani, Nahr el
Nahr an Nīl *see* Nile
Nahr el Aassi *see* Orantes
Nahuel Huapi, Lago 65 *B5 lake*
 W Argentina
Nā'īn 120 *D3* Eşfahān, C Iran
Nain 39 *F2* Newfoundland and
 Labrador, NE Canada
Nairobi 69 *E5 country capital*
 (Kenya) Nairobi Area, S Kenya
Nairobi 73 *C6 international airport*
 Nairobi Area, S Kenya
Najaf *see* An Najaf
Najima *see* Fukuoka
Najin 129 *E3* NE North Korea
Najrān 121 *B6 var.* Abā as Su'ūd.
 Najrān, S Saudi Arabia
Nakambé *see* White Volta
Nakamura 131 *B7* Kōchi, Shikoku,
 SW Japan
Nakatsugawa 131 *C6 var.*
 Nakatugawa. Gifu, Honshū,
 SW Japan
Nakatugawa *see* Nakatsugawa
Nakhodka 115 *G5* Primorskiy Kray,
 SE Russian Federation
Nakhon Pathom 137 *C5 var.* Nagara
 Pathom, Nakorn Pathom. Nakhon
 Pathom, W Thailand
Nakhon Ratchasima 137 *C5 var.*
 Khorat, Korat. Nakhon
 Ratchasima, E Thailand
Nakhon Sawan 137 *C5 var.* Muang
 Nakhon Sawan, Nagara Svarga.
 Nakhon Sawan, W Thailand
Nakhon Si Thammarat 137 *C7 var.*
 Nagara Sridhārmaraj, *Mal.*
 Sithammaraj. Nakhon Si
 Thammarat, SW Thailand
Nakhon Sithammaraj *see* Nakhon
 Si Thammarat
Nakorn Pathom *see* Nakhon Pathom
Nakuru 73 *C6* Rift Valley, SW Kenya
Nal'chik 111 *B8* Kabardino-
 Balkarskaya Respublika,
 SW Russian Federation
Nālūt 71 *F2* NW Libya
Namakan Lake 40 *A1 lake*
 Canada/USA
Namangan 123 *F2* Namangan
 Wiloyati, E Uzbekistan
Nambala 78 *D2* Central, C Zambia
Nam Dinh 136 *D3* Nam Ha,
 N Vietnam
Namib Desert 78 *B3 desert*
 W Namibia
Namibe 78 *A2 Port.* Moçâmedes,
 Mossâmedes. Namibe,
 SW Angola

Namibia 78 B3 var. South West
Africa, Afr. Suidwes-Afrika, Ger.
Deutsch-Südwestafrika; prev.
German Southwest Africa, South-
West Africa. Country S Africa

Namibia 78

Official name Republic of Namibia
Formation 1990
Capital Windhoek
Population 1.8 million / 6 people
per sq mile (2 people per sq km)
Total area 318,694 sq miles
(825,418 sq km)
Languages English, Ovambo,
Kavango, Bergdama, German,
Afrikaans
Religions Christian 90%, other 10%
Ethnic mix Ovambo 50%, other
tribes 16%, Kavango 9%, Herero 8%,
Damara 8%, other 9%
Government Parliamentary
democracy
Currency Namibian dollar = 100
cents
Literacy rate 82%
Calorie consumption 2,649
kilocalories

Namo see Namu Atoll
Nam Ou 136 C3 river N Laos
Nampa 46 D3 Idaho, NW USA
Nampula 79 E2 Nampula,
NE Mozambique
Namsos 84 B4 Nord-Trøndelag,
C Norway
Nam Tha 136 C4 river N Laos
Namu Atoll 144 D2 var. Namo.
Atoll Ralik Chain, C Marshall
Islands
Namur 87 C6 Dut. Namen. Namur,
SE Belgium
Namyit Island 128 C8 island
S Spratly Islands
Nan 136 C4 var. Muang Nan. Nan,
NW Thailand
Nanaimo 36 D5 Vancouver Island,
British Columbia, SW Canada
Nanchang 128 C5 var. Nan-ch'ang,
Nanch'ang-hsien. Jiangxi, S China
Nanch'ang-hsien see Nanchang
Nan-ching see Nanjing
Nancy 90 D3 Meurthe-et-Moselle,
NE France
Nandaime 52 D3 Granada,
SW Nicaragua
Nänded 134 D5 Mahārāshtra,
C India
Nandyāl 132 C1 Andhra Pradesh,
E India
Nanjing 128 C5 var. Nan-ching,
Nanking; prev. Chianning, Chian-
ning, Kiang-ning. Jiangsu,
E China
Nanking see Nanjing
Nanning 128 B6 var. Nan-ning; prev.
Yung-ning. Guangxi Zhuangzu
Zizhiqu, S China
Nan-ning see Nanning
Nanortalik 82 C5 S Greenland
Nanpan Jiang 136 D2 river S China
Nanping 128 D6 var. Nan-p'ing;
prev. Yenping. Fujian, SE China
Nansei-Shotō 130 A2 var. Ryukyu
Islands. Island group SW Japan
Nansei Syotō Trench see Ryukyu
Trench
Nansen Basin 155 C4 undersea
feature Arctic Ocean
Nansen Cordillera 155 B3 var.
Arctic-Mid Oceanic Ridge,
Nansen Ridge. Undersea feature
Arctic Ocean
Nansen Ridge see Nansen
Cordillera
Nanterre 90 D1 Hauts-de-Seine,
N France
Nantes 90 B4 Bret. Naoned; anc.
Condivincum, Namnetes. Loire-
Atlantique, NW France
Nantucket Island 41 G3 island
Massachusetts, NE USA
Nanumaga 145 E3 var. Nanumanga.
Atoll NW Tuvalu
Nanumanga see Nanumaga

Nanumea Atoll 145 E3 atoll
NW Tuvalu
Nanyang 128 C5 var. Nan-yang.
Henan, C China
Napa 47 B6 California, W USA
Napier 150 E4 Hawke's Bay, North
Island, NZ
Naples 80 D5 anc. Neapolis.
Campania, S Italy
Naples 43 E5 Florida, SE USA
Napo 56 A3 province NE Ecuador
Napo, Río 60 C1 river
Ecuador/Peru
Naracoorte 149 B7 South Australia
Naradhivas see Narathiwat
Narathiwat 137 C7 var. Naradhivas.
Narathiwat, SW Thailand
Narbada see Narmada
Narbonne 91 C6 anc. Narbo
Martius. Aude, S France
Narborough Island see Fernandina,
Isla
Nares Abyssal Plain see Nares Plain
Nares Plain 35 E6 var. Nares
Abyssal Plain. Undersea feature
NW Atlantic Ocean
Nares Strait 82 D1 Dan. Nares
Stræde. Strait Canada/Greenland
Narew 98 E3 river E Poland
Narmada 124 B3 var. Narbada. River
C India
Narowlya 107 C8 Rus. Narovlya.
Homyel'skaya Voblasts',
SE Belarus
Närpes 85 D5 Fin. Närpiö. Länsi-
Suomi, W Finland
Narrabri 149 D6 New South Wales,
SE Australia
Narrogin 147 B6 Western Australia
Narva 106 E2 prev. Narova. River
Estonia/Russian Federation
Narva 106 E2 Ida-Virumaa,
NE Estonia
Narva Bay 106 E2 Est. Narva Laht,
Ger. Narwa-Bucht, Rus. Narvskiy
Zaliv. Bay Estonia/Russian
Federation
Narva Reservoir 106 E2 Est. Narva
Veehoidla, Rus. Narvskoye
Vodokhranilishche. Reservoir
Estonia/Russian Federation
Narvik 84 C3 Nordland, C Norway
Nar'yan-Mar 110 D3 prev.
Beloshchel'ye, Dzerzhinskiy.
Nenetskiy Avtonomnyy Okrug,
NW Russian Federation
Naryn 123 G2 Narynskaya Oblast',
C Kyrgyzstan
Năsăud 108 B3 Ger. Nussdorf,
Hung. Naszód. Bistriţa-Năsăud,
N Romania
Nase see Naze
Nāshik 134 C5 prev. Nāsik.
Mahārāshtra, W India
Nashua 41 G3 New Hampshire,
NE USA
Nashville 42 C1 state capital
Tennessee, S USA
Näsijärvi 85 D5 lake SW Finland
Nāsiri see Ahvāz
Nasiriya see An Nāşirīyah
Nassau 54 C1 country capital
(Bahamas) New Providence,
N Bahamas
Nasser, Lake 72 B3 var. Buhayrat
Nasir, Buḩayrat Nāşir, Buheiret
Nâşir. Lake Egypt/Sudan
Nata 78 C3 Central, NE Botswana
Natal 63 G2 Rio Grande do Norte,
E Brazil
Natal Basin 141 A6 var.
Mozambique Basin. Undersea
feature W Indian Ocean
Natanya see Netanya
Natchez 42 B3 Mississippi, S USA
Natchitoches 42 A2 Louisiana,
S USA
Nathanya see Netanya
Natitingou 75 F4 NW Benin
Natsrat see Nazerat
Natuna Islands 124 D4 island group
W Indonesia
Naturaliste Plateau 141 E6 undersea
feature E Indian Ocean
Naugard see Nowogard
Naujamiestis 106 C4 Panevėžys,
C Lithuania

Nauru 144 D2 prev. Pleasant Island.
Country W Pacific Ocean

Nauru 144

Official name Republic of Nauru
Formation 1968
Capital No official capital
Population 11,800 / 1,455 people
per sq mile (562 people per sq km)
Total area 9 sq miles (21 sq km)
Languages Nauruan, English,
Kiribati, Chinese, Tuvaluan
Religions Nauruan Congregational
Church 60%, Roman Catholic 35,
other 5%
Ethnic mix Nauruan 62%, other
Pacific islanders 25%, Chinese and
Vietnamese 8%, European 5%
Government Non-party democracy
Currency Australian dollar = 100
cents
Literacy rate 99%
Calorie consumption not available

Nauta 60 C2 Loreto, N Peru
Navahrudak 107 C6 Pol.
Nowogródek, Rus. Novogrudok.
Hrodzyenskaya Voblasts',
W Belarus
Navapolatsk 107 D5 Rus.
Novopolotsk. Vitsyebskaya
Voblasts', N Belarus
Navarra 93 E2 cultural region
N Spain
Navassa Island 54 C3 US
unincorporated territory C West
Indies
Navojoa 50 C2 Sonora, NW Mexico
Navolat see Navolato
Navolato 66 C3 var. Navolat.
Sinaloa, C Mexico
Návpaktos see Náfpaktos
Nawabashah see Nawābshāh
Nawābshāh 134 B3 var.
Nawabashah. Sind, S Pakistan
Nawoiy 123 E2 Rus. Navoi. Nawoiy
Wiloyati, C Uzbekistan
Naxçıvan 117 G3 Rus.
Nakhichevan'. SW Azerbaijan
Náxos 105 D6 var. Naxos. Náxos,
Kykládes, Greece, Aegean Sea
Náxos 105 D6 island Kykládes,
Greece, Aegean Sea
Nayoro 130 D2 Hokkaidō,
NE Japan
Nazca 60 D4 Ica, S Peru
Nazca Ridge 57 A5 undersea feature
E Pacific Ocean
Naze 130 B3 var. Nase. Kagoshima,
Amami-ōshima, SW Japan
Nazerat 119 A5 var. Natsrat, Ar. En
Nazira, Eng. Nazareth. Northern,
N Israel
Nazilli 116 A4 Aydın, SW Turkey
Nazrēt 73 C5 var. Adama, Hadama.
C Ethiopia
N'Dalatando 78 B1 Port. Salazar,
Vila Salazar. Cuanza Norte,
NW Angola
Ndélé 76 C4 Bamingui-Bangoran,
N Central African Republic
Ndendé 77 B6 Ngounié, S Gabon
Ndindi 77 A6 Nyanga, S Gabon
Ndjamena 76 B3 var. N'Djamena;
prev. Fort-Lamy. Country capital
(Chad) Chari-Baguirmi,
W Chad
Ndjolé 77 A5 Moyen-Ogooué,
W Gabon
Ndola 78 D2 Copperbelt, C Zambia
Neagh, Lough 89 B5 lake
E Northern Ireland, UK
Néa Moudanía 104 C4 var. Néa
Moudhaniá. Kentrikí Makedonía,
N Greece
Néa Moudhaniá see Néa Moudanía
Neápoli 104 B4 prev. Neápolis.
Dytikí Makedonía, N Greece
Neápoli 105 D8 Kríti, Greece,
E Mediterranean Sea
Neápoli 105 C7 Pelopónnisos,
S Greece
Neapolis see Nablus
Near Islands 36 A2 island group
Aleutian Islands, Alaska, USA

Néa Zíchni 104 C3 var. Néa Zíkhni;
prev. Néa Zíkhna. Kentrikí
Makedonía, NE Greece
Néa Zíkhna see Néa Zíchni
Néa Zíkhni see Néa Zíchni
Nebaj 52 B2 Quiché, W Guatemala
Nebitdag 122 B2 Balkanskiy
Velayat, W Turkmenistan
Neblina, Pico da 62 C1 mountain
NW Brazil
Nebraska 44 D4 off. State of
Nebraska; also known as
Blackwater State, Cornhusker
State, Tree Planters State. State
C USA
Nebraska City 45 F4 Nebraska,
C USA
Neches River 49 H3 river Texas,
SW USA
Neckar 95 B6 river SW Germany
Necochea 65 D5 Buenos Aires,
E Argentina
Neder Rijn 86 D4 Eng. Lower
Rhine. River C Netherlands
Nederweert 87 D5 Limburg,
SE Netherlands
Neede 86 E3 Gelderland,
E Netherlands
Neerpelt 87 D5 Limburg,
NE Belgium
Neftekamsk 111 D5 Respublika
Bashkortostan, W Russian
Federation
Negēlē 73 D5 var. Negelli, It.
Neghelli. C Ethiopia
Negelli see Negēlē
Neghelli see Negēlē
Negomane 79 E2 var. Negomano.
Cabo Delgado, N Mozambique
Negomano see Negomane
Negombo 132 C3 Western Province,
SW Sri Lanka
Negotin 100 E4 Serbia, E Serbia and
Montenegro (Yugo.)
Negra, Punta 60 A3 headland
NW Peru
Negreşti-Oaş 108 B3 Hung.
Avasfelsöfalu; prev. Negreşti. Satu
Mare, NE Romania
Negro, Río 65 C5 river E Argentina
Negro, Río 60 D1 river N South
America
Negro, Río 64 D4 river
Brazil/Uruguay
Negros 139 E2 island C Philippines
Nehbandān 120 E3 Khorāsān, E Iran
Neijiang 128 B5 Sichuan, C China
Nei Monggol Zizhiqu see Inner
Mongolia
Nei Mongol see Inner Mongolia
Neiva 58 B3 Huila, S Colombia
Nellore 132 D2 Andhra Pradesh,
E India
Nelson 37 G4 river Manitoba,
C Canada
Nelson 151 C5 Nelson, South
Island, NZ
Néma 74 D3 Hodh ech Chargui,
SE Mauritania
Neman 106 A4 Bel. Nyoman, Ger.
Memel, Lith. Nemunas, Pol.
Niemen, Rus. Neman. River
NE Europe
Neman 106 B4 Ger. Ragnit.
Kaliningradskaya Oblast',
W Russian Federation
Neméa 105 B6 Pelopónnisos,
S Greece
Nemours 90 C3 Seine-et-Marne,
N France
Nemuro 130 E2 Hokkaidō,
NE Japan
Neochóri 105 B5 Dytikí Ellás,
C Greece
Nepal 135 E3 Country S Asia

Nepal 135

Official name Kingdom of Nepal
Formation 1769
Capital Kathmandu
Population 23.6 million / 434
people per sq mile (168 people per
sq km)
Total area 54,363 sq miles
(140,800 sq km)

Nepal (continued)

Languages Nepali, Maithili,Bhojpuri
Religions Hindu 90%, Buddhist 5%, Muslim 3%, other 2%
Ethnic mix Nepalese 52%, Maithili 11%, Tibeto-Burmese 10%, Bhojpuri 8%, other 19%
Government Constitutional monarchy
Currency Nepalese rupee = 100 paisa
Literacy rate 41.5%
Calorie consumption 2,436 kilocalories

Nereta 106 C4 Aizkraukle, S Latvia
Neretva 100 C4 river Bosnia and Herzegovina/Croatia
Neringa 106 A3 Ger. Nidden; prev. Nida. Neringa, SW Lithuania
Neris 107 C5 Bel. Viliya, Pol. Wilia; prev. Pol. Wilja. River Belarus/Lithuania
Nerva 92 C4 Andalucía, S Spain
Neryungri 115 F4 Respublika Sakha (Yakutiya), NE Russian Federation
Neskaupstadhur 83 E5 Austurland, E Iceland
Ness, Loch 88 C3 lake N Scotland, UK
Néstos 104 C3 Bul. Mesta, Turk. Kara Su. River Bulgaria/Greece see also Mesta
Netanya 119 A6 var. Natanya, Nathanya. Central, C Israel
Netherlands 86 C3 var. Holland, Dut. Koninkrijk der Nederlanden, Nederland. Country NW Europe

Netherlands 86

Official name Kingdom of the Netherlands
Formation 1648
Capital Amsterdam, The Hague
Population 16.2 million / 1,010 people per sq mile (390 people per sq km)
Total area 16,033 sq miles (41,526 sq km)
Languages Dutch, Frisian
Religions Roman Catholic 36%, Protestant 27%, Muslim 3%, other 34%
Ethnic mix Dutch 82%, other 18%
Government Parliamentary democracy   **Currency** Euro (Netherlands guilder until 2002)
Literacy rate 99%
Calorie consumption 3,294 kilocalories

Netherlands Antilles 55 E5 prev. Dutch West Indies. Dutch autonomous region S Caribbean Sea
Netherlands New Guinea see Papua
Nettilling Lake 37 G3 lake Baffin Island, Nunavut, N Canada
Neubrandenburg 94 D3 Mecklenburg-Vorpommern, NE Germany
Neuchâtel 95 A7 Ger. Neuenburg. Neuchâtel, W Switzerland
Neuchâtel, Lac de A7 Ger. Neuenburger See. Lake W Switzerland
Neufchâteau 87 D8 Luxembourg, SE Belgium
Neumünster 94 B2 Schleswig-Holstein, N Germany
Neunkirchen 95 A5 Saarland, SW Germany
Neuquén 65 B5 Neuquén, SE Argentina
Neuruppin 94 C3 Brandenburg, NE Germany
Neusalz an der Oder see Nowa Sól
Neusiedler See 95 E6 Hung. Fertő. Lake Austria/Hungary

Neustadt an der Weinstrasse 95 B5 prev. Neustadt an der Haardt, hist. Niewenstat, anc. Nova Civitas. Rheinland-Pfalz, SW Germany
Neustrelitz 94 D3 Mecklenburg-Vorpommern, NE Germany
Neu-Ulm 95 B6 Bayern, S Germany
Neuwied 95 A5 Rheinland-Pfalz, W Germany
Neuzen see Terneuzen
Nevada 47 C5 off. State of Nevada; also known as Battle Born State, Sagebrush State, Silver State. State W USA
Nevada, Sierra 92 D5 mountain range S Spain
Nevers 90 C4 anc. Noviodunum. Nièvre, C France
Neves 76 E2 São Tomé, S Sao Tome and Principe
Nevinnomyssk 111 B7 Stavropol'skiy Kray, SW Russian Federation
Nevşehir 116 C3 var. Nevshehr. Nevşehir, C Turkey
Nevshehr see Nevşehir
Newala 73 C8 Mtwara, SE Tanzania
New Albany 40 C5 Indiana, N USA
New Amsterdam 59 G3 E Guyana
Newark 41 F4 New Jersey, NE USA
New Bedford 41 G3 Massachusetts, NE USA
Newberg 46 B3 Oregon, NW USA
New Bern 43 F1 North Carolina, SE USA
New Braunfels 49 G4 Texas, SW USA
Newbridge 89 B6 Ir. An Droichead Nua. C Ireland
New Britain 144 B3 island E PNG
New Brunswick 39 E4 Fr. Nouveau-Brunswick. Province SE Canada
New Caledonia 144 D4 var. Kanaky, Fr. Nouvelle-Calédonie. French overseas territory SW Pacific Ocean
New Caledonia 144 C5 island SW Pacific Ocean
New Caledonia Basin 142 C4 undersea feature W Pacific Ocean
Newcastle see Newcastle upon Tyne
Newcastle 149 D6 New South Wales, SE Australia
Newcastle upon Tyne 88 D4 var. Newcastle; hist. Monkchester, Lat. Pons Aelii. NE England, UK
New Delhi 134 D3 country capital (India) Delhi, N India
Newfoundland 39 G3 Fr. Terre-Neuve. Island Newfoundland, SE Canada
Newfoundland 39 F2 Fr. Terre Neuve. Province SE Canada
Newfoundland Basin 66 B3 undersea feature NW Atlantic Ocean
New Georgia Islands 144 C3 island group NW Solomon Islands
New Glasgow 39 F4 Nova Scotia, SE Canada
New Goa see Pānji
New Guinea 144 A3 Dut. Nieuw Guinea, Ind. Irian. Island Indonesia/PNG
New Hampshire 41 F2 off. State of New Hampshire; also known as The Granite State. State NE USA
New Haven 41 G3 Connecticut, NE USA
New Iberia 42 B3 Louisiana, S USA
New Ireland 144 C3 island NE PNG
New Jersey 41 F4 off. State of New Jersey; also known as The Garden State. State NE USA
Newman 146 B4 Western Australia
Newmarket 89 F6 E England, UK
New Mexico 48 C2 off. State of New Mexico; also known as Land of Enchantment, Sunshine State. State SW USA
New Orleans 42 B3 Louisiana, S USA
New Plymouth 150 C4 Taranaki, North Island, NZ
Newport 40 C4 Kentucky, S USA

Newport 89 D7 S England, UK
Newport 89 C7 SE Wales, UK
Newport 41 G2 Vermont, NE USA
Newport News 41 F5 Virginia, NE USA
New Providence 54 C1 island N Bahamas
Newquay 89 C7 SW England, UK
Newry 89 B5 Ir. An tIúr. SE Northern Ireland, UK
New Sarum see Salisbury
New Siberian Islands see Novosibirskiye Ostrova
New South Wales 149 C6 state SE Australia
Newton 45 G3 Iowa, C USA
Newtownabbey 89 B5 Ir. Baile na Mainistreach. E Northern Ireland, UK
New Ulm 45 F2 Minnesota, N USA
New York 41 F4 New York, NE USA
New York 41 F3 state NE USA
New Zealand 150 A4 abbrev. NZ. Country SW Pacific Ocean

New Zealand 150

Official name Dominion of New Zealand
Formation 1947
Capital Wellington
Population 3.8 million /37 people per sq mile (14 people per sq km)
Total area 103,737 sq miles (268,680 sqkm)
Languages English, Maori
Religions Methodist 24%, Presbyterian 18%, non-religious 16%, Roman Catholic 15%, Methodist 5%, other 22%
Ethnic mix European 77%, Maori 12%, Pacific Islanders 5%, other 6%
Government Parliamentary democracy
Currency New Zealand dollar = 100 cents
Literacy rate 99%
Calorie consumption 3252 kilocalories

Neyveli 132 C2 Tamil Nādu, SE India
Ngangzê Co 126 B5 lake W China
Ngaoundéré 76 B4 var. N'Gaoundéré. Adamaoua, N Cameroon
N'Giva 78 B3 var. Ondjiva, Port. Vila Pereira de Eça. Cunene, S Angola
Ngo 77 B6 Plateaux, SE Congo
Ngoko 77 B5 river Cameroon/Congo
Ngourti 75 H3 Diffa, E Niger
Nguigmi 75 H3 var. N'Guigmi. Diffa, SE Niger
Nguru 75 G3 Yobe, NE Nigeria
Nha Trang 137 E6 Khanh Hoa, S Vietnam
Niagara Falls 40 D3 waterfall Canada/USA
Niagara Falls 41 E3 New York, NE USA
Niagara Falls 38 D5 Ontario, S Canada
Niamey 75 F3 country capital (Niger) Niamey, SW Niger
Niangay, Lac 75 E3 lake E Mali
Nia-Nia 77 E5 Orientale, NE Dem. Rep. Congo
Nias 138 A3 island W Indonesia
Nicaragua 52 D3 Country Central America

Nicaragua 52

Official name Republic of Nicaragua
Formation 1838
Capital Managua
Population 5.2 million /104 people per sq mile (40 people per sq km)
Total area 49,998 sq miles (129,494 sq km)

Nicaragua 52

Languages Spanish, English Creole, 40%, Traditional beliefs 10%
Ethnic mix Hausa 21%, Yoruba 21%, Ibo 18%, Fulani 11%, other 29%
Government Multiparty republic
Currency Naira = 100 kobo
Literacy rate 63.9%
Calorie consumption 2,850 kilocalories

Nicaragua, Lago de 52 D4 var. Cocibolca, Gran Lago, Eng. Lake Nicaragua. Lake S Nicaragua
Nicaragua, Lake see Nicaragua, Lago de
Nicaria see Ikaria
Nice 91 D6 It. Nizza; anc. Nicaea. Alpes-Maritimes, SE France
Nicephorium see Ar Raqqah
Nicholas II Land see Severnaya Zemlya
Nicholls Town 54 C1 Andros Island, NW Bahamas
Nicobar Islands 124 B4 island group India, E Indian Ocean
Nicosia 102 C5 Gk. Lefkosía, Turk. Lefkoşa. Country capital (Cyprus) C Cyprus
Nicoya 52 D4 Guanacaste, W Costa Rica
Nicoya, Golfo de 52 D5 gulf W Costa Rica
Nicoya, Península de 52 D4 peninsula NW Costa Rica
Nidzica 98 D3 Ger. Niedenburg. Warmińsko-Mazurskie, NE Poland
Niedere Tauern 99 A6 mountain range C Austria
Nieuw Amsterdam 59 G3 Commewijne, NE Suriname
Nieuw-Bergen 86 D4 Limburg, SE Netherlands
Nieuwegein 86 C4 Utrecht, C Netherlands
Nieuw Nickerie 59 G3 Nickerie, NW Suriname
Niğde 116 C4 Niğde, C Turkey
Niger 75 F3 Country W Africa

Niger 75

Official name Republic of Niger
Formation 1960
Capital Niamey
Population 11.2 million / 23 people per sq mile (9 people per sq km)
Total area 489,189 sq miles (1,267,000 sq km)
Languages French, Hausa, Djerma
Religions Muslim 85%, Traditional beliefs 14%, other 1%
Ethnic mix Hausa 54%, Djerma and Songhai 21%, Fulani 10%, Tuareg 9%, other 6%
Government Multiparty republic
Currency CFA franc = 100 centimes
Literacy rate 15.9%
Calorie consumption 2,089 kilocalories

Niger 75 F4 river W Africa
Nigeria 75 F4 Country W Africa

Nigeria 75

Official name Federal Republic of Nigeria
Formation 1960
Capital Abuja
Population 116.9 million / 328 people per sq mile (127 people per sq km)
Total area 356,667 sq miles (923,768 sq km)
Languages English, Hausa, Yoruba, Ibo
Religions Muslim 50%, Christian 40%, Traditional beliefs 10%
Ethnic mix Hausa 21%, Yoruba 21%, Ibo 18%, Fulani 11%, other 29%
Government Multiparty republic
Currency Naira = 100 kobo

Nigeria (continued)

Literacy rate 63.9%
Calorie consumption 2,850
kilocalories

Niger, Mouths of the 75 F5 *delta*
S Nigeria
Nihon *see* Japan
Niigata 131 D5 Niigata, Honshū,
C Japan
Niihama 131 B7 Ehime, Shikoku,
SW Japan
Niihau 47 A7 *island* Hawaii, USA,
C Pacific Ocean
Nii-jima 131 D6 *island* E Japan
Nijkerk 86 D3 Gelderland,
C Netherlands
Nijlen 87 C5 Antwerpen,
N Belgium
Nijmegen 86 D4 *Ger.* Nimwegen;
anc. Noviomagus. Gelderland,
SE Netherlands
Nikaria *see* Ikaría
Nikel' 110 C2 Murmanskaya
Oblast', NW Russian Federation
Nikiniki 139 E5 Timor,
S Indonesia
Nikopol' 109 F3 Pleven, N Bulgaria
Nikšić 101 C5 Montenegro,
SW Serbia and Montenegro
(Yugo.)
Nikumaroro 145 E3 *prev.* Gardner
Island, Kemins Island. *Atoll*
Phoenix Islands, C Kiribati
Nikunau 145 E3 *var.* Nukunau; *prev.*
Byron Island. *Atoll* Tungaru,
W Kiribati
Nile 68 D3 *Ar.* Nahr an Nīl. *River*
N Africa
Nile 72 B2 *former province*
NW Uganda
Nile Delta 72 B1 *delta* N Egypt
Nîmes 91 C6 *anc.* Nemausus,
Nismes. Gard, S France
Nine Degree Channel 132 B3
channel India/Maldives
Ninetyeast Ridge 141 D5 *undersea
feature* E Indian Ocean
Ninety Mile Beach 150 C1 *beach*
North Island, NZ
Ningbo 128 D4 *var.* Ning-po, Yin-
hsien; *prev.* Ninghsien. Zhejiang,
SE China
Ninghsien *see* Ningbo
Ning-po *see* Ningbo
Ningxia 128 B4 *off.* Ningxia Huizu
Zizhiqu, *var.* Ning-hsia, Ningsia,
Eng. Ningsia Hui, Ningsia Hui
Autonomous Region. Admin.
region *autonomous region* N China
Ningxia Huizu Zizhiqu *see*
Ningxia
Nio *see* Íos
Niobrara River 45 E3 *river*
Nebraska/Wyoming, C USA
Nioro 74 D3 *var.* Nioro du Sahel.
Kayes, W Mali
Nioro du Sahel *see* Nioro
Niort 90 B4 Deux-Sèvres,
W France
Nipigon 38 B4 Ontario,
S Canada
Nipigon, Lake 38 B3 *lake* Ontario,
S Canada
Nippon *see* Japan
Niš 101 E5 *Eng.* Nish, *Ger.* Nisch;
anc. Naissus. Serbia, SE Serbia
and Montenegro (Yugo.)
Nişab 120 B4 Al Ḥudūd ash
Shamālīyah, N Saudi Arabia
Nisibin *see* Nusaybin
Nísiros *see* Nísyros
Nisko 98 F4 Podkarpackie,
SE Poland
Nísyros 105 E7 *var.* Nisiros. *Island*
Dodekánisos, Greece, Aegean Sea
Nitra 99 C6 *Ger.* Neutra, *Hung.*
Nyitra. *River* W Slovakia
Nitra 99 C6 *Ger.* Neutra, *Hung.*
Nyitra. Nitriansky Kraj,
SW Slovakia
Niuatoputapu *see* Niuatoputapu
Niuatoputapu 145 E4 *var.*
Niuatobutabu; *prev.* Keppel
Island. *Island* N Tonga

Niue 145 F4 *self-governing territory
in free association with NZ* S Pacific
Ocean
Niulakita 145 E3 *var.* Nurakita.
Atoll S Tuvalu
Niutao 145 E3 *atoll* NW Tuvalu
Nivernais 90 C4 *cultural region*
C France
Nizāmābād 134 D5 Andhra
Pradesh, C India
Nizhnekamsk 111 C5 Respublika
Tatarstan, W Russian Federation
Nizhnevartovsk 114 D3 Khanty-
Mansiyskiy Avtonomnyy Okrug,
C Russian Federation
Nizhniy Novgorod 111 C5 *prev.*
Gor'kiy. Nizhegorodskaya
Oblast', W Russian Federation
Nizhniy Odes 110 D4 Respublika
Komi, NW Russian Federation
Nizhnyaya Tunguska 115 E3 *Eng.*
Lower Tunguska. *River* N Russian
Federation
Nizhyn 109 E1 *Rus.* Nezhin.
Chernihivs'ka Oblast',
NE Ukraine
Njazidja *see* Grande Comore
Njombe 73 C8 Iringa, S Tanzania
Nkayi 77 B6 *prev.* Jacob. La
Bouenza, S Congo
Nkongsamba 76 A4 *var.*
N'Kongsamba. Littoral,
W Cameroon
Nmai Hka 136 B2 *var.* Me Hka.
River N Myanmar
Nobeoka 131 B7 Miyazaki, Kyūshū,
SW Japan
Noboribetsu 130 D3 *var.*
Noboribetu. Hokkaidō,
NE Japan
Noboribetu *see* Noboribetsu
Nogales 48 B3 Arizona, SW USA
Nogales 50 B1 Sonora, NW Mexico
Nogal Valley *see* Dooxo Nugaaleed
Nokia 85 D5 Länsi-Suomi,
W Finland
Nokou 76 B3 Kanem, W Chad
Nola 77 B5 Sangha-Mbaéré,
SW Central African Republic
Nolinsk 111 C5 Kirovskaya Oblast',
NW Russian Federation
Nongkaya *see* Nong Khai
Nong Khai 136 C4 *var.* Mi Chai,
Nongkaya. Nong Khai,
E Thailand
Nonouti 144 D2 *prev.* Sydenham
Island. *Atoll* Tungaru, W Kiribati
Noord-Beveland 86 B4 *var.* North
Beveland. *Island*
SW Netherlands
Noordwijk aan Zee 86 C3 Zuid-
Holland, W Netherlands
Nora 85 C6 Örebro, C Sweden
Norak 123 E3 *Rus.* Nurek.
W Tajikistan
Nord 83 F1 N Greenland
Nordaustlandet 83 G1 *island*
NE Svalbard
Norden 94 A3 Niedersachsen,
NW Germany
Norderstedt 94 B3 Schleswig-
Holstein, N Germany
Nordfriesische Inseln *see* North
Frisian Islands
Nordhausen 94 C4 Thüringen,
C Germany
Nordhorn 94 A3 Niedersachsen,
NW Germany
Nordkapp 84 D1 *Eng.* North Cape.
Headland N Norway
Norfolk 45 E3 Nebraska, C USA
Norfolk 41 F5 Virginia, NE USA
Norfolk Island 142 D4 *Australian
external territory* SW Pacific Ocean
Norfolk Ridge 142 D4 *undersea
feature* W Pacific Ocean
Norias 49 G5 Texas, SW USA
Noril'sk 114 D3 Taymyrskiy
(Dolgano-Nenetskiy)
Avtonomnyy Okrug, N Russian
Federation
Norman 49 G1 Oklahoma, USA
Normandie 90 B3 *Eng.* Normandy.
Cultural region N France
Normandy *see* Normandie
Normanton 148 D2 Queensland,
NE Australia

Norrköping 85 C6 Östergötland,
S Sweden
Norrtälje 85 C6 Stockholm,
C Sweden
Norseman 147 B6 Western Australia
North Albanian Alps 101 C5 *Alb.*
Bjeshkët e Namuna, *SCr.*
Prokletije. *Mountain range*
Albania/Serbia and Montenegro
(Yugo.)
Northallerton 89 D5 N England,
UK
Northam 147 A6 Western Australia
North America 34 *continent*
Northampton 89 D6 C England, UK
North Andaman 133 F2 *island*
Andaman Islands, India,
NE Indian Ocean
North Australian Basin 141 E5 *Fr.*
Bassin Nord de l' Australie.
Undersea feature E Indian Ocean
North Bay 38 D4 Ontario, S Canada
North Beveland *see* Noord-
Beveland
North Cape 66 D1 *headland* New
Ireland, NE PNG
North Cape 150 C1 *headland* North
Island, NZ
North Cape *see* Nordkapp
North Carolina 43 E1 *off.* State of
North Carolina; also known as
Old North State, Tar Heel State,
Turpentine State. *State* SE USA
North Channel 40 D2 *lake channel*
Canada/USA
North Charleston 43 F2 South
Carolina, SE USA
North Dakota 44 D2 *off.* State of
North Dakota; also known as
Flickertail State, Peace Garden
State, Sioux State. *State* N USA
Northeast Providence Channel 54
C1 *channel* N Bahamas
Northeim 94 B4 Niedersachsen,
C Germany
Northern Cook Islands 145 F4
island group N Cook Islands
Northern Cyprus, Turkish
Republic of 102 D5 *disputed region*
N Cyprus
Northern Dvina *see* Severnaya
Dvina
Northern Ireland 88 B4 *var.* The Six
Counties. *Political division* UK
Northern Mariana Islands 142 B1
US commonwealth territory
W Pacific Ocean
Northern Sporades *see* Vóreioi
Sporádes
Northern Territory 144 A5 *territory*
N Australia
North European Plain 81 E3 *plain*
N Europe
Northfield 45 F2 Minnesota,N USA
North Fiji Basin 142 D3 *undersea
feature* N Coral Sea
North Frisian Islands 94 B2 *var.*
Nordfriesische Inseln. *Island group*
N Germany
North Huvadhu Atoll 132 B5 *var.*
Gaafu Alifu Atoll. *Atoll*
S Maldives
North Island 150 B2 *island* N NZ
North Korea 129 E3 *Kor.* Chosŏn-
minjujuŭi-inmin-kanghwaguk.
Country E Asia

North Korea 129

Official name Democratic People's
Republic of Korea
Formation 1948
Capital Pyongyang
Population 22.4 million /481 people
per sq mile (186 people per sq km)
Total area 46,540 sq miles
(120,540 sq km)
Languages Korean, Chinese
Religions Atheist 100%
Ethnic mix Korean 100%
Government One-party republic
Currency N Korean won
= 100 chon
Literacy rate 95%
Calorie consumption 2,185
kilocalories

North Little Rock 42 B1 Arkansas,
C USA
North Minch *see* Minch, The
North Mole 93 G4 *harbour wall*
NW Gibraltar
North Platte 45 E4 Nebraska, C USA
North Platte River 44 D4 *river*
C USA
North Pole 155 B3 *pole* Arctic Ocean
North Saskatchewan 37 F5 *river*
Alberta/Saskatchewan, S Canada
North Sea *C3 Dan.* Nordsøen, *Dut.*
Noordzee, *Fr.* Mer du Nord, *Ger.*
Nordsee, *Nor.* Nordsjøen; *prev.*
German Ocean, *Lat.* Mare
Germanicum. *Sea* NW Europe
North Siberian Lowland *see*
Severo-Sibirskaya Nizmennosť
North Siberian Plain *see* Severo-
Sibirskaya Nizmennosť
North Taranaki Bight 150 C3 *gulf*
North Island, NZ
North Uist 88 B3 *island*
NW Scotland, UK
Northwest Atlantic Mid-Ocean
Canyon 34 E4 *undersea feature*
N Atlantic Ocean
North West Highlands 88 C3
mountain range N Scotland, UK
Northwest Pacific Basin 113 G4
undersea feature NW Pacific Ocean
Northwest Providence Channel 54
C1 *channel* N Bahamas
Northwest Territories 37 E3 *Fr.*
Territoires du Nord-Ouest.
Territory NW Canada (the eastern
part is now the territory of
Nunavut)
Northwind Plain 155 B2 *undersea
feature* Arctic Ocean
Norton Sound 36 C2 *inlet* Alaska,
USA
Norway 85 A5 *Nor.* Norge. *Country*
N Europe

Norway 85

Official name Kingdom of Norway
Formation 1905
Capital Oslo
Population 4.5 million /36 people
per sq mile (14 people per sq km)
Total area 125,181 sq miles
(324,220 sq km)
Languages Norwegian, Sami
Religions Evangelical Lutheran
89%, Roman Catholic 1%, other and
non-religious 10%
Ethnic mix Norwegian 93%, Sami
1%, other 6%
Government Parliamentary
democracy
Currency Norwegian krone = 100
ore
Literacy rate 99%
Calorie consumption 3,414
kilocalories

Norwegian Basin 83 F4 *undersea
feature* NW Norwegian Sea
Norwegian Sea 83 F4 *Nor.* Norske
Havet. *Sea* NE Atlantic Ocean
Norwich 89 E6 E England, UK
Noshiro 130 D4 *var.* Nosiro; *prev.*
Noshirominato. Akita, Honshū,
C Japan
Noshirominato *see* Noshiro
Nosiro *see* Noshiro
Nosivka 109 E1 *Rus.* Nosovka.
Chernihivs'ka Oblast', NE Ukraine
Noşratābād 120 E3 Sīstān va
Balūchestān, E Iran
Nossob 72 C4 *river* E Namibia
Notéč 98 C3 *Ger.* Netze. *River*
NW Poland
Nóties Sporádes *see* Dodekánisos
Nottingham 89 D6 C England, UK
Nouâdhibou 74 B2 *prev.* Port-
Étienne. Dakhlet Nouâdhibou,
W Mauritania
Nouakchott 74 B2 *country capital*
(Mauritania) Nouakchott District,
SW Mauritania
Nouméa 144 C5 *dependent territory
capital* (New Caledonia) Province
Sud, S New Caledonia

Nouvelle-Calédonie *see* New Caledonia
Nova Gorica 95 D8 W Slovenia
Nova Gradiška 100 C3 *Ger.* Neugradisk, *Hung.* Újgradiska. Brod-Posavina, NE Croatia
Nova Iguaçu 63 F4 Rio de Janeiro, SE Brazil
Novara 96 B2 *anc.* Novaria. Piemonte, NW Italy
Nova Scotia 39 F4 *Fr.* Nouvelle Écosse. *Province* SE Canada
Nova Scotia 35 E5 *physical region* SE Canada
Novaya Sibir', Ostrov 115 F1 *island* Novosibirskiye Ostrova, NE Russian Federation
Novaya Zemlya 110 D1 *island group* N Russian Federation
Novaya Zemlya Trench *see* East Novaya Zemlya Trench
Novgorod 110 B4 Novgorodskaya Oblast', W Russian Federation
Novi Grad *see* Bosanski Novi
Novi Iskŭr 104 C2 Sofiya-Grad, W Bulgaria
Novi Pazar 101 D5 *Turk.* Yenipazar. Shumen, NE Bulgaria
Novi Sad 100 D3 *Ger.* Neusatz, *Hung.* Újvidék. Serbia, N Serbia and Montenegro (Yugo.)
Novoazovs'k 109 G4 *Rus.* Novoazovsk. Donets'ka Oblast', E Ukraine
Novocheboksarsk 111 C5 Chuvashskaya Respublika, W Russian Federation
Novocherkassk 111 B7 Rostovskaya Oblast', SW Russian Federation
Novodvinsk 110 C3 Arkhangel'skaya Oblast', NW Russian Federation
Novohrad-Volyns'kyy 108 D2 *Rus.* Novograd-Volynskiy. Zhytomyrs'ka Oblast', N Ukraine
Novokazalinsk *see* Ayteke Bi
Novokuznetsk 114 D4 *prev.* Stalinsk. Kemerovskaya Oblast', S Russian Federation
Novolazarevskaya 154 C2 Russian *research station* Antarctica
Novo Mesto 95 E8 *Ger.* Rudolfswert; *prev. Ger.* Neustadtl. SE Slovenia
Novomoskovs'k 109 F3 *Rus.* Novomoskovsk. Dnipropetrovs'ka Oblast', E Ukraine
Novomoskovsk 111 B5 Tul'skaya Oblast', W Russian Federation
Novorossiysk 111 A7 Krasnodarskiy Kray, SW Russian Federation
Novoshakhtinsk 111 B6 Rostovskaya Oblast', SW Russian Federation
Novosibirsk 114 D4 Novosibirskaya Oblast', C Russian Federation
Novosibirskiye Ostrova 115 F1 *Eng.* New Siberian Islands. *Island group* N Russian Federation
Novotroitsk 111 D6 Orenburgskaya Oblast', W Russian Federation
Novotroyits'ke 109 F4 *Rus.* Novotroitskoye. Khersons'ka Oblast', S Ukraine
Novovolyns'k 108 C1 *Rus.* Novovolynsk. Volyns'ka Oblast', NW Ukraine
Novy Dvor 107 B6 *Rus.* Novyy Dvor. Hrodzyenskaya Voblasts', W Belarus
Novyy Buh 109 E3 *Rus.* Novyy Bug. Mykolayivs'ka Oblast', S Ukraine
Novyy Uzen' *see* Zhanaözen
Nowa Sól 98 B4 *var.* Nowasól, *Ger.* Neusalz an der Oder. Lubuskie, W Poland
Nowogard 98 B2 *var.* Nowógard, *Ger.* Naugard. Zachodniopomorskie, NW Poland
Nowógard *see* Nowogard
Nowo-Minsk *see* Miusk Mazowiecki
Nowy Dwór Mazowiecki 98 D3 Mazowieckie, C Poland

Nowy Sącz 99 D5 *Ger.* Neu Sandec. Małopolskie, S Poland
Nowy Tomyśl 98 B3 *var.* Nowy Tomysl. Wielkopolskie, C Poland
Noyon 90 C3 Oise, N France
Nsanje 79 E3 Southern, S Malawi
Nsawam 75 E5 SE Ghana
Ntomba, Lac 77 C6 *var.* Lac Tumba. *Lake* NW Dem. Rep. Congo
Nubian Desert 72 B3 *desert* NE Sudan
Nu'eima 119 E7 E West Bank
Nueva Gerona 54 B2 Isla de la Juventud, S Cuba
Nueva Rosita 50 D2 Coahuila de Zaragoza, NE Mexico
Nuevitas 54 C2 Camagüey, E Cuba
Nuevo, Bajo 53 G1 *island* NW Colombia
Nuevo Casas Grandes 50 C1 Chihuahua, N Mexico
Nuevo, Golfo 65 C6 *gulf* S Argentina
Nuevo Laredo 51 E2 Tamaulipas, NE Mexico
Nui Atoll 145 E3 *atoll* W Tuvalu
Nûk *see* Nuuk
Nuku'alofa 145 E5 *country capital* (Tonga) Tongatapu, S Tonga
Nukufetau Atoll 145 E3 *atoll* C Tuvalu
Nukulaelae Atoll 145 E3 *var.* Nukulailai. *Atoll* E Tuvalu
Nukulailai *see* Nukulaelae Atoll
Nukunau *see* Nikunau
Nukunonu Atoll 145 E3 *island* C Tokelau
Nukus 122 C2 Qoraqalpoghiston Respublikasi, W Uzbekistan
Nullarbor Plain 147 C6 *plateau* South Australia/Western Australia
Nunap Isua 98 B5 *var.* Uummannarsuaq, *Dan.* Kap Farvel, *Eng.* Cape Farewell. *Headland* S Greenland
Nunavut 37 F3 *territory* N Canada
Nuneaton 89 D6 C England, UK
Nunivak Island 36 B2 *island* Alaska, USA
Nunspeet 86 D3 Gelderland, E Netherlands
Nuoro 97 A5 Sardegna, Italy, C Mediterranean Sea
Nuquí 58 A3 Chocó, W Colombia
Nurakita *see* Niulakita
Nuremberg *see* Nürnberg
Nurmes 84 E4 Itä-Suomi, E Finland
Nürnberg 95 C5 *Eng.* Nuremberg. Bayern, S Germany
Nurota 123 E2 *Rus.* Nurata. Nawoiy Wiloyati, C Uzbekistan
Nusa Tenggara 139 E5 *Eng.* Lesser Sunda Islands. East Timor / C Indonesia
Nusaybin 117 F4 *var.* Nisibin. Manisa, SE Turkey
Nuuk 82 C4 *var.* Nûk, *Dan.* Godthaab, Godthåb. *Dependent territory capital* (Greenland) SW Greenland
Nyagan' 114 C3 Khanty-Mansiyskiy Avtonomnyy Okrug, N Russian Federation
Nyaingêntanglha Shan 126 C5 *mountain range* W China
Nyala 72 A4 Southern Darfur, W Sudan
Nyamapanda 78 D3 Mashonaland East, NE Zimbabwe
Nyamtumbo 73 C8 Ruvuma, S Tanzania
Nyandoma 110 C4 Arkhangel'skaya Oblast', NW Russian Federation
Nyantakara 73 B7 Kagera, NW Tanzania
Nyasa, Lake 79 E2 *var.* Lake Malawi; *prev.* Lago Nyassa. *Lake* E Africa
Nyasvizh 107 C6 *Pol.* Nieświez, *Rus.* Nesvizh. Minskaya Voblasts', C Belarus
Nyaunglebin 136 B4 Pegu, SW Myanmar
Nyeri 73 C6 Central, C Kenya
Nyima 126 C5 Xizang Zizhiqu, W China

Nyíregyháza 99 D6 Szabolcs-Szatmár-Bereg, NE Hungary
Nykøbing 85 B8 Storstrøm, SE Denmark
Nyköping 85 C6 Södermanland, S Sweden
Nylstroom *see* Modimolle
Nyngan 149 D6 New South Wales, SE Australia
Nyurba 115 F3 Respublika Sakha (Yakutiya), NE Russian Federation
Nyzhn'ohirs'kyy 109 F4 *Rus.* Nizhnegorskiy. Respublika Krym, S Ukraine
Nzega 73 C7 Tabora, C Tanzania
Nzérékoré 74 D4 Guinée-Forestière, SE Guinea
Nzwani *see* Anjouan

O

Oahu 47 A7 *Haw.* O'ahu. *Island* Hawaii, USA, C Pacific Ocean
Oak Harbor 46 B1 Washington, NW USA
Oakland 47 B6 California, W USA
Oamaru 151 B7 Otago, South Island, NZ
Oaxaca 51 F5 *var.* Oaxaca de Juárez; *prev.* Antequera. Oaxaca, SE Mexico
Oaxaca de Juárez *see* Oaxaca
Ob' 112 C2 *river* C Russian Federation
Obal' 107 D5 *Rus.* Obol'. Vitsyebskaya Voblasts', N Belarus
Oban *see* Halfmoon Bay
Oban 88 C4 W Scotland, UK
Obando *see* Puerto Inírida
Obeliai 106 C4 Rokiškis, NE Lithuania
Oberhollabrunn *see* Tulln
Ob, Gulf of *see* Obskaya Guba
Obihiro 130 D2 Hokkaidō, NE Japan
Obo 76 D4 Haut-Mbomou, E Central African Republic
Obock 72 D4 E Djibouti
Oborniki 98 C3 Wielkopolskie, C Poland
Obskaya Guba 114 D3 *Eng.* Gulf of Ob'. *Gulf* N Russian Federation
Ob' Tablemount 141 B7 *undersea feature* S Indian Ocean
Ocala 43 E4 Florida, SE USA
Ocaña 59 D2 Castilla-La Mancha, C Spain
Ocaña 58 B2 Norte de Santander, N Colombia
O Carballiño 108 C1 *var.* Carballiño. Gallicia, NW Spain
Occidental, Cordillera 61 E4 *mountain range* W South America
Occidental, Cordillera 58 B2 *mountain range* W Colombia
Occidental, Cordillera 60 D4 *mountain range* W Peru
Ocean Falls 36 D5 British Columbia, SW Canada
Ocean Island *see* Banaba
Oceanside 47 C8 California, W USA
Ochakiv 109 E4 *Rus.* Ochakov. Mykolayivs'ka Oblast', S Ukraine
Och'amch'ire 117 E2 *Rus.* Ochamchira. W Georgia
Ocho Rios 54 B4 C Jamaica
Ochrida, Lake *see* Ohrid, Lake
Ocotal 52 D3 Nueva Segovia, NW Nicaragua
Ocozocuautla 51 G5 Chiapas, SE Mexico
Ocú 53 F5 Herrera, S Panama
Ōdate 130 D3 Akita, Honshū, C Japan
Oddur *see* Xuddur
Ödemiş 116 A4 Izmir, SW Turkey
Odense 85 B7 Fyn, C Denmark
Oder 98 B3 *Cz./Pol.* Odra. *River* C Europe
Oderhaff *see* Szczeciński, Zalew
Odesa 109 E4 *Rus.* Odessa. Odes'ka Oblast', SW Ukraine
Odessa 49 E3 Texas, SW USA
Odienné 74 D4 NW Côte d'Ivoire
Ôdôngk 137 D6 Kâmpóng Spoe, S Cambodia

Odoorn 86 E2 Drenthe, NE Netherlands
Of 117 E2 Trabzon, NE Turkey
Ofanto 97 D5 *river* S Italy
Offenbach 95 B5 *var.* Offenbach am Main. Hessen, W Germany
Offenbach am Main *see* Offenbach
Offenburg 95 B6 Baden-Württemberg, SW Germany
Ogaden 73 D5 *Som.* Ogaadeen. *Plateau* Ethiopia/Somalia
Ōgaki 131 C6 Gifu, Honshū, SW Japan
Ogallala 44 D4 Nebraska, C USA
Ogbomosho 75 F4 Oyo, W Nigeria
Ogden 44 B4 Utah, W USA
Ogdensburg 41 F2 New York, NE USA
Ogulin 100 A3 Karlovac, NW Croatia
Ohio 40 C4 *off.* State of Ohio; also known as The Buckeye State. *State* N USA
Ohio River 40 C4 *river* N USA
Ohrid 101 D6 *Turk.* Ochrida, Ohri. SW FYR Macedonia
Ohrid, Lake 101 D6 *var.* Lake Ochrida, *Alb.* Liqeni i Ohrit, *Mac.* Ohridsko Ezero. *Lake* Albania/FYR Macedonia
Ohridsko Ezero *see* Ohrid, Lake
Ohura 150 D3 Manawatu-Wanganui, North Island, NZ
Oirschot 87 C5 Noord-Brabant, S Netherlands
Oise 90 C3 *river* N France
Oistins 55 G2 S Barbados
Ōita 131 B7 Ōita, Kyūshū, SW Japan
Ojinaga 50 D2 Chihuahua, N Mexico
Ojos del Salado, Cerro 64 B3 *mountain* W Argentina
Okaihau 150 C2 Northland, North Island, NZ
Okāra 134 C2 Punjab, E Pakistan
Okavanggo *see* Cubango
Okavango *see* Cubango
Okavango 78 C3 *district* NW Namibia
Okavango Delta 78 C3 *wetland* N Botswana
Okayama 131 B6 Okayama, Honshū, SW Japan
Okazaki 131 C6 Aichi, Honshū, C Japan
Okeechobee, Lake 43 E4 *lake* Florida, SE USA
Okefenokee Swamp 43 E3 *wetland* Georgia, SE USA
Okhotsk 115 G3 Khabarovskiy Kray, E Russian Federation
Okhotskoye More 115 G3 *sea* NW Pacific Ocean
Okhotsk, Sea of 113 F3 *sea* NW Pacific Ocean
Okhtyrka 109 F2 *Rus.* Akhtyrka. Sums'ka Oblast', NE Ukraine
Oki-guntō *see* Oki-shotō
Okinawa 130 A3 *island* SW Japan
Okinawa-shotō 130 A3 *island group* SW Japan
Oki-shotō 131 B6 *var.* Oki-guntō. *Island group* SW Japan
Oklahoma 49 F2 *off.* State of Oklahoma; also known as The Sooner State. *State* C USA
Oklahoma City 49 G1 *state capital* Oklahoma, C USA
Okmulgee 49 G1 Oklahoma, C USA
Oko, Wadi 72 C3 *river* NE Sudan
Oktyabr'skiy 111 D6 Volgogradskaya Oblast', SW Russian Federation
Oktyabr'skoy Revolyutsii, Ostrov 115 E2 *Eng.* October Revolution Island. *Island* Severnaya Zemlya, N Russian Federation
Okulovka *see* Uglovka
Okushiri-tō 130 C3 *var.* Okusiri Tô. *Island* NE Japan
Okusiri Tô *see* Okushiri-tō
Öland 85 C7 *island* S Sweden
Olavarría 65 D5 Buenos Aires, E Argentina
Oława 98 C4 *Ger.* Ohlau. Dolnośląskie, SW Poland

Ibia 97 *A5 prev.* Terranova Pausania. Sardegna, Italy, C Mediterranean Sea
Idebroek 86 *D3* Gelderland, E Netherlands
Idenburg 94 *B3* Niedersachsen, NW Germany
Idenburg 94 *C2* Schleswig-Holstein, N Germany
Idenzaal 86 *E3* Overijssel, E Netherlands
Id Harbour 54 *B5* C Jamaica
Iékma 115 *F4 river* C Russian Federation
Iékminsk 115 *F3* Respublika Sakha (Yakutiya), NE Russian Federation
Ieksandrivka 109 *E3 Rus.* Aleksandrovka. Kirovohrads'ka Oblast', C Ukraine
Ieksandriya 109 *F3 Rus.* Aleksandriya. Kirovohrads'ka Oblast', C Ukraine
Ienegorsk 110 *C2* Murmanskaya Oblast', NW Russian Federation
Ienёk 115 *E3* Respublika Sakha (Yakutiya), NE Russian Federation
Ienёk 115 *E3 river* NE Russian Federation
Iéron, Île d' 91 *A5 island* W France
Ievs'k 108 *D1 Rus.* Olevsk. Zhytomyrs'ka Oblast', N Ukraine
Igiy 126 *C2* Bayan-Ölgiy, W Mongolia
Ihão 92 *B5* Faro, S Portugal
Ilifa 78 *B3* Kunene, NW Namibia
Iimbos *see* Ólympos
Iimpo *see* Fuerte Olimpo
Iiva 93 *F4* País Valenciano, E Spain
Iivet 90 *C4* Loiret, C France
Imaliq 123 *E2 Rus.* Almalyk. Toshkent Wiloyati, E Uzbekistan
Iomouc 99 *C5 Ger.* Olmütz, *Pol.* Ołomuniec. Olomoucký Kraj, E Czech Republic
Ionets 110 *B3* Respublika Kareliya, NW Russian Federation
Iovyannaya 115 *F4* Chitinskaya Oblast', S Russian Federation
Ilpe 94 *B4* Nordrhein-Westfalen, W Germany
Isztyn 98 *D2 Ger.* Allenstein. Warmińsko-Mazurskie, NE Poland
Ilt 108 *B5 var.* Oltul, *Ger.* Alt. *River* S Romania
Iteniţa 108 *C5 prev. Eng.* Oltenitsa, *anc.* Constantiola. Călăraşi, SE Romania
Iltul *see* Olt
Ilvera 92 *D5* Andalucía, S Spain
Ilympia 46 *B2 state capital* Washington, NW USA
Ilympic Mountains 46 *A2 mountain range* Washington, NW USA
Ilympos 104 *B4 var.* Ólimbos, *Eng.* Mount Olympus. *Mountain* N Greece
Ilympus, Mount *see* Ólympos
Imagh 89 *B5 Ir.* An Ómaigh. W Northern Ireland, UK
Imaha 45 *F4* Nebraska, C USA
Iman 120 *D6 Ar.* Salţanat 'Umān; *prev.* Muscat and Oman. *Country* SW Asia

---

Iman 121

Ifficial name Sultanate of Oman
Iormation 1951
Capital Muscat
Population 2.6 million / 32 people per sq mile (12 people per sq km)
Total area 82,031 sq miles (212,460 sq km)
Languages Arabic, Baluchi
Religions Ibadi Muslim 75%, other Muslim and Hindu 25%
Ethnic mix Arab 88%, Baluch 4%, Persian 3%, Indian and Pakistani 4%, African 2%
Government Monarchy
Currency Omani rial = 1,000 baizas
Literacy rate 71.8%
Calorie consumption not available

Oman, Gulf of 120 *E4 Ar.* Khalīj 'Umān. *Gulf* N Arabian Sea
Omboué 77 *A6* Ogooué-Maritime, W Gabon
Omdurman 72 *B4 var.* Umm Durmān. Khartoum, C Sudan
Ometepe, Isla de 52 *D4 island* S Nicaragua
Ommen 86 *E3* Overijssel, E Netherlands
Omsk 114 *C4* Omskaya Oblast', C Russian Federation
Ōmuta 131 *A7* Fukuoka, Kyūshū, SW Japan
Onda 93 *F3* País Valenciano, E Spain
Ondjiva *see* N'Giva
Öndörhaan 127 *E2* Hentiy, E Mongolia
Onega 110 *B4 river* NW Russian Federation
Onega 110 *C3* Arkhangel'skaya Oblast', NW Russian Federation
Onega, Lake *see* Onezhskoye Ozero
Onex 95 *A7* Genève, SW Switzerland
Onezhskoye Ozero 110 *B4 Eng.* Lake Onega. *Lake* NW Russian Federation
Ongole 132 *D1* Andhra Pradesh, E India
Onitsha 75 *G5* Anambra, S Nigeria
Onon Gol 127 *E2 river* N Mongolia
Ononte *see* Orantes
Onslow 146 *A4* Western Australia
Onslow Bay 43 *F1 bay* North Carolina, E USA
Ontario 38 *B3 province* S Canada
Ontario, Lake 41 *E3 lake* Canada/USA
Onteniente *see* Ontinyent
Ontinyent 93 *F4 var.* Onteniente. País Valenciano, E Spain
Ontong Java Rise 125 *H4 undersea feature* W Pacific Ocean
Oostakker 87 *B5* Oost-Vlaanderen, NW Belgium
Oostburg 87 *B5* Zeeland, SW Netherlands
Oostende 87 *A5 Eng.* Ostend, *Fr.* Ostende. West-Vlaanderen, NW Belgium
Oosterbeek 86 *D4* Gelderland, SE Netherlands
Oosterhout 86 *C4* Noord-Brabant, S Netherlands
Opatija 100 *A2 It.* Abbazia. Primorsko-Gorski Kotar, NW Croatia
Opava 99 *C5 Ger.* Troppau. Ostravský Kraj, E Czech Republic
Opelika 42 *D2* Alabama, S USA
Opelousas 42 *B3* Louisiana, S USA
Opmeer 86 *C2* Noord-Holland, NW Netherlands
Opochka 110 *A4* Pskovskaya Oblast', W Russian Federation
Opole 98 *C4 Ger.* Oppeln. Opolskie, S Poland
Opotiki 150 *E3* Bay of Plenty, North Island, NZ
Oppidum Ubiorum *see* Köln
Oqtosh 123 *E2 Rus.* Aktash. Samarqand Wiloyati, C Uzbekistan
Oradea 108 *B3 prev.* Oradea Mare, *Ger.* Grosswardein, *Hung.* Nagyvárad. Bihor, NW Romania
Orahovac 101 *D5 Alb.* Rahovec. Serbia, S Serbia and Montenegro (Yugo.)
Oran 70 *D2 var.* Ouahran, Wahran. NW Algeria
Orange 91 *D6 anc.* Arausio. Vaucluse, SE France
Orange 149 *D6* New South Wales, SE Australia
Orangeburg 43 *E2* South Carolina, SE USA
Orange Cone *see* Orange Fan
Orange Fan 69 *C7 var.* Orange Cone. *Undersea feature* SW Indian Ocean
Orange Mouth *see* Oranjemund
Orangemund *see* Oranjemund
Orange River 78 *B4 Afr.* Oranjerivier. *River* S Africa
Orange Walk 52 *C1* Orange Walk, N Belize

Oranienburg 94 *D3* Brandenburg, NE Germany
Oranjemund 78 *B4 var.* Orangemund; *prev.* Orange Mouth. Karas, SW Namibia
Oranjestad 55 *E5 dependent territory capital* (Aruba) W Aruba
Orantes 118 *B3 var.* Ononte, *Ar.* Nahr el Aassi, Nahr al 'Aşī. *River* SW Asia
Oraviţa 108 *A4 Ger.* Orawitza, *Hung.* Oravicabánya. Caraş-Severin, SW Romania
Orbetello 96 *B4* Toscana, C Italy
Orcadas 154 *A1 Argentinian research station* South Orkney Islands, Antarctica
Orchard Homes 44 *B1* Montana, NW USA
Ordino 91 *A8* NW Andorra
Ordos Desert *see* Mu Us Shamo
Ordu 116 *D2 anc.* Cotyora. Ordu, N Turkey
Ordzhonikidze 109 *F3* Dnipropetrovs'ka Oblast', E Ukraine
Orealla 59 *G3* E Guyana
Örebro 85 *C6* Örebro, C Sweden
Oregon 46 *B3 off.* State of Oregon; also known as Beaver State, Sunset State, Valentine State, Webfoot State. *State* NW USA
Oregon City 46 *B3* Oregon, NW USA
Orël 111 *B5* Orlovskaya Oblast', W Russian Federation
Orem 44 *B4* Utah, W USA
Orenburg 111 *D6 prev.* Chkalov. Orenburgskaya Oblast', W Russian Federation
Orense *see* Ourense
Oreor 144 *A2 var.* Koror. *Country capital* (Palau) Oreor, N Palau
Orestiáda 104 *D3 prev.* Orestiás. Anatolikí Makedonía kai Thráki, NE Greece
Organ Peak 48 *D3 mountain* New Mexico, SW USA
Orgeyev *see* Orhei
Orhei 108 *D3 var.* Orheiu, *Rus.* Orgeyev. N Moldova
Orheiu *see* Orhei
Oriental, Cordillera 60 *D3 mountain range* Bolivia/Peru
Oriental, Cordillera 61 *F4 mountain range* C Bolivia
Oriental, Cordillera 58 *B3 mountain range* C Colombia
Orihuela 93 *F4* País Valenciano, E Spain
Orikhiv 109 *G3 Rus.* Orekhov. Zaporiz'ka Oblast', SE Ukraine
Orinoco, Río 59 *E2 river* Colombia/Venezuela
Orissa 135 *F4 state* NE India
Orissaare 106 *C2 var.* Orissaar. Saaremaa, W Estonia
Oristano 97 *A5* Sardegna, Italy, C Mediterranean Sea
Orito 58 *A4* Putumayo, SW Colombia
Orizaba, Volcán Pico de 35 *C7 var.* Citlaltépetl. *Mountain* S Mexico
Orkney *see* Orkney Islands
Orkney Islands 88 *C2 var.* Orkney, Orkneys. *Island group* N Scotland, UK
Orkneys *see* Orkney Islands
Orlando 43 *E4* Florida, SE USA
Orléanais 90 *C4 cultural region* C France
Orléans 90 *C4 anc.* Aurelianum. Loiret, C France
Orléansville *see* Chlef
Orly 90 *E2 international airport* (Paris) Essonne, N France
Orlya 107 *B6 Rus.* Orlya. Hrodzyenskaya Voblasts', W Belarus
Ormuz, Strait of *see* Hormuz, Strait of
Örnsköldsvik 85 *C5* Västernorrland, C Sweden
Oromocto 39 *F4* New Brunswick, SE Canada
Orona 145 *F3 prev.* Hull Island. *Atoll* Phoenix Islands, C Kiribati

---

Orosirá Rodhópis *see* Rhodope Mountains
Orpington 89 *B8* SE England, UK
Orsha 107 *E6 Rus.* Orsha. Vitsyebskaya Voblasts', NE Belarus
Orsk 114 *B4* Orenburgskaya Oblast', W Russian Federation
Orşova 108 *A4 Ger.* Orschowa, *Hung.* Orsova. Mehedinţi, SW Romania
Orthez 91 *B6* Pyrénées-Atlantiques, SW France
Ortona 96 *D4* Abruzzo, C Italy
Oruba *see* Aruba
Oruro 61 *F4* Oruro, W Bolivia
Ōsaka 131 *C6 hist.* Naniwa. Ōsaka, Honshū, SW Japan
Osa, Península de 53 *E5 peninsula* S Costa Rica
Osborn Plateau 141 *D5 undersea feature* E Indian Ocean
Osh 123 *F2* Oshskaya Oblast', SW Kyrgyzstan
Oshawa 38 *D5* Ontario, SE Canada
Oshikango 78 *B3* Ohangwena, N Namibia
Ō-shima 131 *D6 island* S Japan
Oshkosh 40 *B2* Wisconsin, N USA
Osijek 100 *C3 prev.* Osiek, Osjek, *Ger.* Esseg, *Hung.* Eszék. Osijek-Baranja, E Croatia
Oskaloosa 45 *G4* Iowa, C USA
Oskarshamn 85 *C7* Kalmar, S Sweden
Oskil 109 *G2 Rus.* Oskol. *River* Russian Federation/Ukraine
Oslo 85 *B6 prev.* Christiania, Kristiania. *Country capital* (Norway) Oslo, S Norway
Osmaniye 116 *D4* Osmaniye, admin. region *province* S Turkey
Osnabrück 94 *A3* Niedersachsen, NW Germany
Osogovo Mountains 120 *B3 var.* Osogovske Planine, Osogovski Planina, *Mac.* Osogovski Planini. *mountain range* Bulgaria/FYR, Macedonia
Osogovske Planine/Osogovski Planina/Osogovski Planini *see* Osogov Mountains
Osorno 65 *B5* Los Lagos, C Chile
Oss 86 *D4* Noord-Brabant, S Netherlands
Ossa, Serra d' 92 *C4 mountain range* SE Portugal
Ossora 115 *H2* Koryakskiy Avtonomnyy Okrug, E Russian Federation
Ostend *see* Oostende
Ostende *see* Oostende
Oster 109 *E1* Chernihiv's'ka Oblast', N Ukraine
Östersund 85 *C5* Jämtland, C Sweden
Ostfriesische Inseln 94 *A3 Eng.* East Frisian Islands. *Island group* NW Germany
Ostiglia 96 *C2* Lombardia, N Italy
Ostrava 99 *C5* Ostravský Kraj, E Czech Republic
Ostróda 98 *D3 Ger.* Osterode. Osterode in Ostpreussen. Warmińsko-Mazurskie, NE Poland
Ostrołęka 98 *D3 Ger.* Wiesenhof, *Rus.* Ostrolenka. Mazowieckie, C Poland
Ostrov 110 *A4 Latv.* Austrava. Karlovarský Kraj, W Czech Republic
Ostrovets *see* Ostrowiec Świętokrzyski
Ostrów *see* Ostrów Wielkopolski
Ostrowiec *see* Ostrowiec Świętokrzyski
Ostrowiec Świętokrzyski 98 *D4 var.* Ostrowiec, *Rus.* Ostrovets. Świętokrzyskie, C Poland
Ostrów Mazowiecka 98 *D3 var.* Ostrów Mazowiecki. Mazowieckie, C Poland
Ostrów Mazowiecki *see* Ostrów Mazowiecka
Ostrowo *see* Ostrów Wielkopolski
Ostrów Wielkopolski 98 *C4 var.* Ostrów, *Ger.* Ostrowo. Wielkopolskie, C Poland

Osum *see* Osumit, Lumi i
Ōsumi-shotō 131 *A8 island group*
SW Japan
Osumit, Lumi i 101 *D7 var.* Osum.
River SE Albania
Osuna 92 *D4* Andalucía, S Spain
Oswego 41 *F2* New York, NE USA
Otago Peninsula 151 *B7 peninsula*
South Island, NZ
Otaki 150 *D4* Wellington, North
Island, NZ
Otaru 130 *C2* Hokkaidō, NE Japan
Otavalo 60 *B1* Imbabura,
N Ecuador
Otavi 78 *B3* Otjozondjupa,
N Namibia
Oţelu Roşu 108 *B4 Ger.*
Ferdinandsberg, *Hung.*
Nándorhgy. Caras-Severin,
SW Romania
Otepää 106 *D3 Ger.* Odenpäh.
Valgamaa, SE Estonia
Oti 75 *E4 river* W Africa
Otira 151 *C6* West Coast, South
Island, NZ
Otjiwarongo 78 *B3* Otjozondjupa,
N Namibia
Otorohanga 150 *D3* Waikato, North
Island, NZ
Otranto, Strait of 101 *C6 It.* Canale
d'Otranto. *Strait* Albania/Italy
Otrokovice 99 *C5 Ger.* Otrokowitz.
Zlínský Kraj, E Czech Republic
Ōtsu 131 *C6 var.* Ōtu. Shiga,
Honshū, SW Japan
Ottawa 41 *E2 Fr.* Outaouais. Admin.
region *river* Ontario/Quebec,
SE Canada
Ottawa 38 *D5 country capital*
(Canada) Ontario, SE Canada
Ottawa 40 *B3* Illinois, N USA
Ottawa 45 *F5* Kansas, C USA
Ottawa Islands 38 *C1 island group*
Northwest Territories, C Canada
Ottignies 87 *C6* Wallon Brabant,
C Belgium
Ottumwa 45 *G4* Iowa, C USA
Ōtu *see* Ōtsu
Ouachita Mountains 42 *A1*
mountain range
Arkansas/Oklahoma, C USA
Ouachita River 42 *B2 river*
Arkansas/Louisiana, C USA
Ouadi Howa *see* Howar, Wādi
Ouagadougou 75 *E4 var.*
Wagadugu. *Country capital*
(Burkina Faso) C Burkina Faso
Ouahigouya 75 *E3* NW Burkina
faso
Ouahran *see* Oran
Oualata *see* Oualâta
Oualâta 74 *D3 var.* Oualata. Hodh
ech Chargui, SE Mauritania
Ouanary 59 *H3* E French Guiana
Ouanda Djallé 76 *D4* Vakaga,
NE Central African Republic
Ouarâne 74 *D2 desert* C Mauritania
Ouargla 71 *E2 var.* Wargla.
NE Algeria
Ouarzazate 70 *C3* S Morocco
Oubangui *see* Ubangi
Oubangui-Chari *see* Central
African Republic
Ouessant, Île d' 90 *A3 Eng.* Ushant.
Island NW France
Ouésso 77 *B5* La Sangha,
NW Congo
Oujda 70 *D2 Ar.* Oudjda, Ujda.
NE Morocco
Oujeft 74 *C2* Adrar, C Mauritania
Oulu 84 *D4 Swe.* Uleåborg. Oulu,
C Finland
Oulujärvi 84 *D4 Swe.* Uleträsk. *Lake*
C Finland
Oulujoki 84 *D4 Swe.* Uleälv. *River*
C Finland
Ounasjoki 84 *D3 river* N Finland
Ounianga Kébir 76 *C2* Borkou-
Ennedi-Tibesti, N Chad
Oup *see* Auob
Oupeye 87 *D6* Liège, E Belgium
Our 87 *D5 river* NW Europe
Ourense 92 *C1 var. Cast.* Orense;
Lat. Aurium. Galicia, NW Spain
Ourique 92 *B4* Beja, S Portugal
Ourthe 87 *D7 river* E Belgium
Ouse 89 *D5 river* N England, UK

Outer Hebrides 88 *B3 var.* Western
Isles. *Island group* NW Scotland,
UK
Outer Islands 79 *G1 island group*
SW Seychelles
Outes 92 *B1* Galicia, NW Spain
Ouvéa 144 *D5 island* Îles Loyauté,
NE New Caledonia
Ouyen 149 *C6* Victoria, SE Australia
Ovalle 64 *B3* Coquimbo, N Chile
Ovar 92 *B2* Aveiro, N Portugal
Overflakkee 86 *B4 island*
SW Netherlands
Overijse 87 *C6* Vlaams Brabant,
C Belgium
Oviedo 92 *C1 anc.* Asturias.
Asturias, NW Spain
Ovruch 108 *D1* Zhytomyrs'ka
Oblast', N Ukraine
Owando 77 *B5 prev.* Fort-Rousset.
Cuvette, C Congo
Owase 131 *C6* Mie, Honshū,
SW Japan
Owatonna 45 *F3* Minnesota, N USA
Owen Fracture Zone 140 *B4 tectonic*
feature W Arabian Sea
Owen, Mount 151 *C5 mountain*
South Island, NZ
Owensboro 40 *B5* Kentucky, S USA
Owen Stanley Range 144 *B3*
mountain range S PNG
Owerri 75 *F5* Imo, S Nigeria
Owo 75 *F5* Ondo, SW Nigeria
Owyhee River 46 *C4 river*
Idaho/Oregon, NW USA
Oxford 89 *D6 Lat.* Oxonia.
S England, UK
Oxford 151 *C6* Canterbury, South
Island, NZ
Oxkutzcab 51 *H4* Yucatán,
SE Mexico
Oxnard 47 *B7* California, W USA
Oyama 131 *D5* Tochigi, Honshū,
S Japan
Oyem 77 *B5* Woleu-Ntem, N Gabon
Oyo 77 *B6* Cuvette, C Congo
Oyo 75 *F4* Oyo, W Nigeria
Ozark 42 *D3* Alabama, S USA
Ozark Plateau 45 *G5 plain*
Arkansas/Missouri, C USA
Ozarks, Lake of the 45 *F5 reservoir*
Missouri, C USA
Ozbourn Seamount 152 *D4*
undersea feature W Pacific Ocean
Ózd 99 *D6* Borsod-Abaúj-Zemplén,
NE Hungary
Ozero Khanka *see* Khanka, Lake
Ozero Ubsu-Nur *see* Uvs Nuur
Ozieri 97 *A5* Sardegna, Italy,
C Mediterranean Sea

P

Paamiut 82 *B4 var.* Pâmiut, *Dan.*
Frederikshåb. S Greenland
Pa-an 136 *B4* Karen State, S Myanmar
Pabianice 98 *C4* Łódz, C Poland
Pabna 135 *G4* Rajshahi,
W Bangladesh
Pachuca 51 *E4 var.* Pachuca de Soto.
Hidalgo, C Mexico
Pachuca de Soto *see* Pachuca
Pacific-Antarctic Ridge 152 *B5*
undersea feature S Pacific Ocean
Pacific Ocean 152 *D3 ocean*
Padalung *see* Phatthalung
Padang 138 *B4* Sumatera,
W Indonesia
Paderborn 94 *B4* Nordrhein-
Westfalen, NW Germany
Padma *see* Brahmaputra
Padova 96 *C2 Eng.* Padua; *anc.*
Patavium. Veneto, NE Italy
Padre Island 49 *G5 island* Texas,
SW USA
Padua *see* Padova
Paducah 40 *B5* Kentucky, S USA
Paeroa 150 *D3* Waikato, North
Island, NZ
Páfos 102 *C5 var.* Paphos.
W Cyprus
Pag 100 *A3 It.* Pago. *Island* Zadar
SW Croatia
Page 48 *B1* Arizona, SW USA
Pago Pago 145 *F4 dependent territory*
capital (American Samoa) Tutuila,
W American Samoa

Pahiatua 150 *D4* Manawatu-
Wanganui, North Island, NZ
Pahsien *see* Chongqing
Paide 106 *D2 Ger.* Weissenstein.
Järvamaa, N Estonia
Paihia 150 *D2* Northland, North
Island, NZ
Päijänne 85 *D3 lake* S Finland
Paine, Cerro 65 *A7 mountain* S Chile
Painted Desert 48 *B1 desert*
Arizona, SW USA
Paisley 88 *C4* W Scotland, UK
País Valenciano 93 *F3 cultural region*
NE Spain
País Vasco 93 *E1 cultural region*
N Spain
Paita 60 *B3* Piura, NW Peru
Pakanbaru *see* Pekanbaru
Pakaraima Mountains 59 *E3 var.*
Serra Pacaraim, Sierra Pacaraima.
Mountain range N South America
Pakistan 134 *A2 var.* Islami
Jamhuriya e Pakistan. *Country* S Asia

Pakistan 134

Official name Islamic Republic of
Pakistan
Formation 1947
Capital Islamabad
Population 145 million / 467 people
per sq mile (180 people per sq km)
Total area 310,401 sq miles
(803,940 sq km)
Languages Urdu, Punjabi, Sindhi
Religions Sunni Muslim 77%, Shi'a
Muslim 20%, Hindu 2%,
Christian 1%
Ethnic mix Punjabi 50%, Sindhi
15%, Pashto 15%, Mohajir 8%,
other 12%
Government Military-based regime
Currency Pakistani rupee = 100
paisa
Literacy rate 46.1%
Calorie consumption 2,452
kilocalories

Paknam *see* Samut Prakan
Pakokku 136 *A3* Magwe,
C Myanmar
Pak Phanang 137 *C7 var.* Ban Pak
Phanang. Nakhon Si Thammarat,
SW Thailand
Pakruojis 106 *C4* Pakruojis,
N Lithuania
Paks 99 *C7* Tolna, S Hungary
Paksé *see* Pakxé
Pakxé 137 *D5 var.* Paksé.
Champasak, S Laos
Palafrugell 93 *G2* Cataluña, NE Spain
Palagruža 101 *B5 It.* Pelagosa. *Island*
SW Croatia
Palaiá Epídavros 105 *C6*
Pelopónnisos, S Greece
Palaiseau 90 *D2* Essonne, N France
Palamós 93 *G2* Cataluña, NE Spain
Palamuse 106 *E2 Ger.* Sankt-
Bartholomäi. Jõgevamaa,
E Estonia
Pālanpur 134 *C4* Gujarāt, W India
Palapye 78 *D3* Central,
SE Botswana
Palau 144 *A2 var.* Belau. *Country*
W Pacific Ocean

Palau 144

Official name Republic of Palau
Formation 1994
Capital Koror
Population 19,100 / 108 people per
sq mile (42 people per sq km)
Total area 177 sq miles (458 sq km)
Languages Palauan, English,
Japanese, Angaur, Tobi,
Sonsorolese
Religions Christian 66%,
Modekngei 34%
Ethnic mix Micronesian 87%,
Filipino 8%, Chinese 5%
Government Non-party democracy
Currency US dollar = 100 cents
Literacy rate 92%
Calorie consumption not available

Palawan 139 *E2 island*
W Philippines
Palawan Passage 138 *D2 passage*
W Philippines
Paldiski 106 *D2 prev.* Baltiski, *Eng.*
Baltic Port, *Ger.* Baltischport.
Harjumaa, NW Estonia
Palembang 138 *B4* Sumatera,
W Indonesia
Palencia 92 *D2 anc.* Palantia,
Pallantia. Castilla-León,
NW Spain
Palermo 97 *C7 Fr.* Palerme; *anc.*
Panhormus, Panormus. Sicilia,
Italy, C Mediterranean Sea
Pāli 134 *C3* Rājasthān, N India
Palikir 144 *C2 country capital*
(Micronesia) Pohnpei,
E Micronesia
Palimé *see* Kpalimé
Palioúri, Akrotírio 104 *C4 var.* Akra
Kanestron. *Headland* N Greece
Palk Strait 132 *C3 strait* India/Sri
Lanka
Palliser, Cape 151 *D5 headland*
North Island, NZ
Palma 93 *G3 var.* Palma de
Mallorca. Mallorca, Spain,
W Mediterranean Sea
Palma del Río 92 *D4* Andalucía,
S Spain
Palma de Mallorca *see* Palma
Palmar Sur 53 *E5* Puntarenas,
SE Costa Rica
Palma Soriano 54 *C3* Santiago de
Cuba, E Cuba
Palm Beach 148 *E1* New South
Wales, SE Australia
Palmer 154 *A2* US research station
Antarctica
Palmer Land 154 *A3 physical region*
Antarctica
Palmerston 145 *F4 island* S Cook
Islands
Palmerston North 150 *D4*
Manawatu-Wanganui, North
Island, NZ
Palmi 97 *D7* Calabria, SW Italy
Palmira 58 *B3* Valle del Cauca,
W Colombia
Palm Springs 47 *D7* California,
W USA
Palmyra *see* Tudmur
Palmyra Atoll 145 *G2* US privately
owned unincorporated territory
C Pacific Ocean
Palo Alto 47 *B6* California, W USA
Palu 139 *E4 prev.* Paloe. Sulawesi,
C Indonesia
Pamiers 91 *B6* Ariège, S France
Pamir *var.* Daryâ-ye Pāmīr, *Taj.*
Dar''yoi Pomir. *River*
Afghanistan/Tajikistan *see also*
Pāmīr, Daryâ-ye
Pamirs 123 *F3 Pash.* Daryâ-ye
Pāmīr, *Rus.* Pamir. *Mountain range*
C Asia
Pâmiut *see* Paamiut
Pamlico Sound 43 *G1 sound* North
Carolina, SE USA
Pampa 49 *E1* Texas, SW USA
Pampas 64 *C4 plain* C Argentina
Pamplona 93 *E1 Basq.* Iruña; *prev.*
Pampeluna, *anc.* Pompaelo.
Navarra, N Spain
Pamplona 58 *C2* Norte de
Santander, N Colombia
Panaji *see* Pānji
Panamá 53 *G5 Country* Central
America

Panama 53

Official name Republic of Panama
Formation 1903
Capital Panama City
Population 2.9 million / 96 people
per sq mile (37 people per sq km)
Total area 30,193 sq miles
(78,200 sq km)
Languages Spanish, English Creole
Amerindian languages, Chibchan
Religions Roman Catholic 86%,
Protestant 6%, other 8%
Ethnic mix Mestizo 60%, White
14%, Black 12%, Amerindian 8%,
Asian 4%, other 2%

Panama (continued)

Government Presidential democracy
Currency Balboa = 100 centesimos
Literacy rate 91.9%
Calorie consumption 2,488 kilocalories

Panamá 53 G4 *var.* Ciudad de Panamá, *Eng.* Panama City. *Country capital* (Panama) Panamá, C Panama
Panama Basin 35 C8 *undersea feature* E Pacific Ocean
Panama Canal 53 F4 *canal* E Panama
Panama City *see* Panamá
Panama City 42 D3 Florida, SE USA
Panamá, Golfo de 53 G5 *var.* Gulf of Panama. *Gulf* S Panama
Panama, Gulf of *see* Panamá, Golfo de
Panamá, Isthmus of *see* Panamá, Istmo de
Panamá, Istmo de 53 G4 *Eng.* Isthmus of Panama; *prev.* Isthmus of Darien. *Isthmus* E Panama
Panay Island 139 E2 *island* C Philippines
Pančevo 100 D3 *Ger.* Pantschowa, *Hung.* Pancsova. Serbia, N Serbia and Montenegro (Yugo.)
Paneas *see* Bāniyās
Panevėžys 106 C4 Panevėžys, C Lithuania
Pangim *see* Panji
Pangkalpinang 138 C4 Pulau Bangka, W Indonesia
Pang-Nga *see* Phang-Nga
Panjim *see* Panji
Panji 132 B1 *var.* Pangim, Panaji, Panjim, New Goa. Goa, W India
Pánormos 105 C7 Kriti, Greece, E Mediterranean Sea
Pantanal 63 E3 *var.* Pantanalmato-Grossense. *Swamp* SW Brazil
Pantanalmato-Grossense *see* Pantanal
Pantelleria, Isola di 97 B7 *island* SW Italy
Pánuco 51 E3 Veracruz-Llave, E Mexico
Pao-chi *see* Baoji
Paoki *see* Baoji
Paola 102 B5 E Malta
Pao-shan *see* Baoshan
Pao-t'ou *see* Baotou
Paotow *see* Baotou
Papagayo, Golfo de 52 C4 *gulf* NW Costa Rica
Papakura 150 D3 Auckland, North Island, NZ
Papantla 51 F4 *var.* Papantla de Olarte. Veracruz-Llave, E Mexico
Papantla de Olarte *see* Papantla
Papeete 145 F4 *dependent territory capital* (French Polynesia) Tahiti, W French Polynesia
Paphos *see* Páfos
Papile 106 B3 Akmenė, NW Lithuania
Papillion 45 F4 Nebraska, C USA
Papua 139 H4 *var.* Irian Barat, Irian Jaya, West Irian, West New Guinea, West Papua; *prev.* Dutch New Guinea, Netherlands New Guinea. Admin. region *province* E Indonesia
Papua, Gulf of 144 B3 *gulf* S PNG
Papua New Guinea 144 B3 *prev.* Territory of Papua and New Guinea, *abbrev.* PNG. *Country* NW Melanesia

Papua New Guinea 144

Official name Independent State of Papua New Guinea
Formation 1975
Capital Port Moresby
Population 5.2 million / 29 people per sq mile (11 people per sq km)
Total area 178,703 sq miles (462,840 sq km)

Papua New Guinea (continued)

Languages English, Pidgin English, Papuan, Motu, c.750 native languages
Religions Protestant 60%, Roman Catholic 37%, other 3%
Ethnic mix Melanesian and mixed 100%
Government Multiparty republic
Currency Kina = 100 toea
Literacy rate 63.9%
Calorie consumption 2,175 kilocalories

Papuk 100 C3 *mountain range* NE Croatia
Pará 63 E2 *off.* Estado do Pará. *State* N Brazil
Pará *see* Belém
Paracel Islands 125 E3 *disputed territory* SE Asia
Paraćin 100 D4 Serbia, C Serbia and Montenegro (Yugo.)
Paragua 59 E3 *river* SE Venezuela
Paraguay *see* Paraguay, Río
Paraguay, Río 64 C2 *var.* Río Paraguay. *River* C South America
Paraguay 64 C2 *country* C South America

Paraguay 64

Official name Republic of Paraguay
Formation 1811
Capital Asunción
Population 5.6 million / 36 people per sq mile (14 people per sq km)
Total area 157,046 sq miles (406,750 sq km)
Languages Spanish, Guaraní
Religions Roman Catholic 96%, Protestant (including Mennonite) 4%
Ethnic mix Mestizo 90%, Amerindian 2%, other 8%
Government Presidential democracy
Currency Guaraní = 100 centimos
Literacy rate 93.3%
Calorie consumption 2,533 kilocalories

Paraguay, Río *see* Paraguay
Paraíba 63 G2 *off.* Estado da Paraíba; *prev.* Parahiba, Parahyba. *State* E Brazil
Parakou 75 F4 C Benin
Paramaribo 59 G3 *country capital* (Suriname) Paramaribo, N Suriname
Paramushir, Ostrov 115 H3 *island* SE Russian Federation
Paraná 63 E4 *off.* Estado do Paraná. *State* S Brazil
Paraná 64 C5 *var.* Alto Paraná. *River* C South America
Paraná 64 E4 Entre Ríos, E Argentina
Paranéstio 104 C3 Anatolikí Makedonía kai Thráki, NE Greece
Paraparaumu 151 D5 Wellington, North Island, NZ
Parchim 94 C3 Mecklenburg-Vorpommern, N Germany
Parczew 98 E4 Lubelskie, E Poland
Pardubice 99 B5 *Ger.* Pardubitz. Pardubický Kraj, C Czech Republic
Parechcha 107 B5 *Rus.* Porech'ye. Hrodzyenskaya Voblasts', NE Belarus
Parecis, Chapada dos 62 D3 *var.* Serra dos Parecis. *Mountain range* W Brazil
Parepare 139 E4 Sulawesi, C Indonesia
Párga 105 A5 Ípeiros, W Greece
Paria, Golfo de *see* Paria, Gulf of
Paria, Gulf of 59 E1 *var.* Golfo de Paria. *Gulf* Trinidad and Tobago/Venezuela
Parika 59 F2 NE Guyana

Paris 90 D1 *anc.* Lutetia, Lutetia Parisiorum, Parisii. *Country capital* (France) Paris, N France
Paris 49 G2 Texas, SW USA
Parkersburg 40 D4 West Virginia, NE USA
Parkes 149 D6 New South Wales, SE Australia
Parma 96 B2 Emilia-Romagna, N Italy
Parnaíba *see* Parnaíba
Parnaíba 63 F2 *var.* Parnahyba. Piauí, E Brazil
Pärnu 106 D2 *Ger.* Pernau, *Latv.* Pērnava; *prev.* Rus. Pernov. Pärnumaa, SW Estonia
Pärnu 106 D2 *var.* Pärnu Jõgi, *Ger.* Pernau. *River* SW Estonia
Pärnu-Jaaguppi 106 D2 *Ger.* Sankt-Jakobi. Pärnumaa, SW Estonia
Pärnu Jõgi *see* Pärnu
Pärnu Laht 106 D2 *Ger.* Pernauer Bucht. *Bay* SW Estonia
Páros 105 C6 *island* Kykládes, Greece, Aegean Sea
Páros 105 D6 Páros, Kykládes, Greece, Aegean Sea
Parral *see* Hidalgo del Parral
Parral 64 B4 Maule, C Chile
Parramatta 148 D1 New South Wales, SE Australia
Parras 50 D3 *var.* Parras de la Fuente. Coahuila de Zaragoza, NE Mexico
Parras de la Fuente *see* Parras
Parsons 45 F5 Kansas, C USA
Pasadena 47 C7 California, W USA
Pasadena 49 H4 Texas, SW USA
Paşcani 108 C3 *Hung.* Páskán. Iaşi, NE Romania
Pasco 46 C2 Washington, NW USA
Pas de Calais *see* Dover, Strait of
Pasewalk 94 D3 Mecklenburg-Vorpommern, NE Germany
Pasinler 117 F3 Erzurum, NE Turkey
Pasłęk 98 D2 *Ger.* Preußisch Holland. Warmińsko-Mazurskie, NE Poland
Pasni 134 A3 Baluchistān, SW Pakistan
Paso de Indios 65 B6 Chubut, S Argentina
Passau 95 D6 Bayern, SE Germany
Passo del Brennero *see* Brenner Pass
Passo Fundo 63 E5 Rio Grande do Sul, S Brazil
Pastavy 107 C5 *Pol.* Postawy, *Rus.* Postavy. Vitsyebskaya Voblasts', NW Belarus
Pastaza, Río 60 B2 *river* Ecuador/Peru
Pasto 58 A4 Nariño, SW Colombia
Pasvalys 106 C4 Pasvalys, N Lithuania
Patagonia 57 B7 *physical region* Argentina/Chile
Patalung *see* Phatthalung
Patani *see* Pattani
Patavium *see* Padova
Patea 150 D4 Taranaki, North Island, NZ
Paterson 41 F3 New Jersey, NE USA
Pathein *see* Bassein
Pátmos 105 D6 *island* Dodekánisos, Greece, Aegean Sea
Patna 135 F3 *var.* Azimabad. Bihār, N India
Patnos 117 F3 Ağrı, E Turkey
Patos, Lagoa dos 63 E5 *lagoon* S Brazil
Pátra 105 B5 *Eng.* Patras; *prev.* Pátrai. Dytikí Ellás, S Greece
Pattani 137 C7 *var.* Patani. Pattani, SW Thailand
Pattaya 137 C5 Chon Buri, S Thailand
Patuca, Río 52 D2 *river* E Honduras
Pau 91 B6 Pyrénées-Atlantiques, SW France
Paulatuk 37 E3 Northwest Territories, NW Canada
Paungde 136 B4 Pegu, C Myanmar
Pavia 96 B2 *anc.* Ticinum. Lombardia, N Italy
Pāvilosta 106 B3 Liepāja, W Latvia

Pavlikeni 104 D2 Veliko Tŭrnovo, N Bulgaria
Pavlodar 114 C4 Pavlodar, NE Kazakhstan
Pavlohrad 109 G3 *Rus.* Pavlograd. Dnipropetrovs'ka Oblast', E Ukraine
Pawn 136 B3 *river* C Myanmar
Paxoí 105 A5 *island* Iónioi Nísoi, Greece, C Mediterranean Sea
Payo Obispo *see* Chetumal
Paysandú 64 D4 Paysandú, W Uruguay
Pazar 117 E2 Rize, NE Turkey
Pazardzhik 104 C3 *prev.* Tatar Pazardzhik. Pazardzhik, C Bulgaria
Pearl River 42 B3 *river* Louisiana/Mississippi, S USA
Pearsall 49 F4 Texas, SW USA
Peć 101 D5 *Alb.* Pejë, *Turk.* Ipek. Serbia, S Serbia and Montenegro (Yugo.)
Pechora 110 D3 *river* NW Russian Federation
Pechora 110 D3 Respublika Komi, NW Russian Federation
Pechorskoye More 110 D2 *Eng.* Pechora Sea. *Sea* NW Russian Federation
Pecos 49 E3 Texas, SW USA
Pecos River 49 E3 *river* New Mexico/Texas, SW USA
Pécs 99 C7 *Ger.* Fünfkirchen; *Lat.* Sopianae. Baranya, SW Hungary
Pedra Lume 74 A3 Sal, NE Cape Verde
Pedro Cays 54 C3 *island group* S Jamaica
Pedro Juan Caballero 64 D2 Amambay, E Paraguay
Peer 87 D5 Limburg, NE Belgium
Pegasus Bay 151 C6 *bay* South Island, NZ
Pegu 136 B4 *var.* Bago. Pegu, SW Myanmar
Pehuajó 64 C4 Buenos Aires, E Argentina
Pei-ching *see* Beijing
Peine 94 B3 Niedersachsen, C Germany
Pei-p'ing *see* Beijing
Peipus, Lake *E3 Est.* Peipsi Järv, *Ger.* Peipus-See, *Rus.* Chudskoye Ozero. *Lake* Estonia/Russian Federation
Peiraías 105 C6 *prev.* Piraiévs, *Eng.* Piraeus. Attikí, C Greece
Pèk 136 D4 *var.* Xieng Khouang; *prev.* Xiangkhoang. Xiangkhoang, N Laos
Pekalongan 138 C4 Jawa, C Indonesia
Pekanbaru 138 B3 *var.* Pakanbaru. Sumatera, W Indonesia
Pekin 40 B4 Illinois, N USA
Peking *see* Beijing
Pelagie, Isole 97 B8 *island group* SW Italy
Pelly Bay 37 G3 Nunavut, N Canada
Peloponnese *see* Pelopónnisos
Peloponnesus *see* Pelopónnisos
Pelopónnisos 105 B6 *var.* Morea, *Eng.* Peloponnese; *anc.* Peloponnesus. *Peninsula* S Greece
Pematangsiantar 138 B3 Sumatera, W Indonesia
Pemba 79 F2 *prev.* Port Amelia, Porto Amélia. Cabo Delgado, NE Mozambique
Pemba 73 D7 *island* E Tanzania
Pembroke 38 D4 Ontario, SE Canada
Penang *see* George Town
Penang *see* Pinang, Pulau
Penas, Golfo de 65 A7 *gulf* S Chile
Penderma *see* Bandırma
Pendleton 46 C3 Oregon, NW USA
Pend Oreille, Lake 46 D2 *lake* Idaho, NW USA
Peneius *see* Pineiós
Peng-pu *see* Bengbu
Peniche 92 B3 Leiria, W Portugal
Péninsule de la Gaspésie *see* Gaspé, Péninsule de

Pennine Alps 95 A8 Fr. Alpes
Pennines, It. Alpi Pennine; Lat.
Alpes Penninae. Mountain range
Italy/Switzerland
Pennine Chain see Pennines
Pennines 89 D5 var. Pennine Chain.
Mountain range N England, UK
Pennsylvania 40 D3 off.
Commonwealth of Pennsylvania;
also known as The Keystone
State. State NE USA
Penobscot River 41 G2 river Maine,
NE USA
Penong 149 A6 South Australia
Penonomé 53 F5 Coclé, C Panama
Penrhyn 145 G3 atoll N Cook
Islands
Penrhyn Basin 143 F3 undersea
feature C Pacific Ocean
Penrith 148 D1 New South Wales,
SE Australia
Penrith 89 D5 NW England, UK
Pensacola 42 C3 Florida, SE USA
Pentecost 144 D4 Fr. Pentecôte.
Island C Vanuatu
Penza 111 C6 Penzenskaya Oblast',
W Russian Federation
Penzance 89 C7 SW England, UK
Peoria 40 B4 Illinois, N USA
Perchtoldsdorf 95 E6
Niederösterreich, NE Austria
Percival Lakes 146 C4 lakes Western
Australia
Perdido, Monte 93 F1 mountain
NE Spain
Perece Vela Basin see West
Mariana Basin
Pereira 58 B3 Risaralda, W Colombia
Pergamino 64 C4 Buenos Aires,
E Argentina
Périgueux 91 C5 anc. Vesuna.
Dordogne, SW France
Perito Moreno 65 B6 Santa Cruz,
S Argentina
Perlas, Archipiélago de las 53 G5
Eng. Pearl Islands. Island group
SE Panama
Perlas, Laguna de 53 E3 Eng. Pearl
Lagoon. Lagoon E Nicaragua
Perleberg 94 C3 Brandenburg,
N Germany
Perm' 114 C3 prev. Molotov.
Permskaya Oblast', NW Russian
Federation
Pernambuco 63 G2 off. Estado de
Pernambuco. State E Brazil
Pernambuco Abyssal Plain see
Pernambuco Plain
Pernambuco Plain 67 C5 var.
Pernambuco Abyssal Plain.
Undersea feature E Atlantic Ocean
Pernau see Pärnu
Pernik 104 B2 prev. Dimitrovo.
Pernik, W Bulgaria
Perote 51 F4 Veracruz-Llave,
E Mexico
Perovsk see Kyzylorda
Perpignan 91 C6 Pyrénées-
Orientales, S France
Perryton 49 F1 Texas, SW USA
Perryville 45 H5 Missouri, C USA
Persian Gulf see Gulf, The
Perth 147 A6 state capital Western
Australia
Perth 88 C4 C Scotland, UK
Perth Basin 141 E6 undersea feature
SE Indian Ocean
Peru 60 C2 Country W South America

Peru 60

Official name Republic of Peru
Formation 1824
Capital Lima
Population 26.1 million / 53 people
per sq mile (20 people per sq km)
Total area 496,223 sq miles
(1,285,220 sq km)
Languages Spanish, Quechua,
Aymará
Religions Roman Catholic 95%,
other 5%
Ethnic mix Amerindian 54%,
Mestizo 32%, White 12%, other 2%
Government Presidential
democracy

Peru (continued)

Currency New sol = 100 centimos
Literacy rate 89.9%
Calorie consumption 2,624
kilocalories

Peru see Beru
Peru Basin 67 A5 undersea feature
E Pacific Ocean
Peru-Chile Trench 56 A4 undersea
feature E Pacific Ocean
Perugia 96 C4 Fr. Pérouse; anc.
Perusia. Umbria, C Italy
Péruwelz 87 B6 Hainaut,
SW Belgium
Pervomays'k 109 E3 prev.
Ol'viopol'. Mykolayivs'ka Oblast',
S Ukraine
Pervyy Kuril'skiy Proliv 115 H3
strait E Russian Federation
Pesaro 96 C3 anc. Pisaurum.
Marche, C Italy
Pescara 96 D4 anc. Aternum, Ostia
Aterni. Abruzzo, C Italy
Peshāwar 134 C1 North-West
Frontier Province, N Pakistan
Peshkopi 101 C4 var. Peshkopia,
Peshkopija. Dibër, NE Albania
Peshkopia see Peshkopi
Peshkopija see Peshkopi
Peski Karakumy see Garagumy
Pessac 91 B5 Gironde,
SW France
Petach-Tikva see Petah Tiqwa
Petah Tiqva see Petah Tiqwa
Petah Tiqwa 119 A6 var. Petach-
Tikva, Petah Tiqva, Petakh Tikva.
Tel Aviv, C Israel
Petakh Tikva see Petah Tiqwa
Pétange 87 D8 Luxembourg,
SW Luxembourg
Petchaburi see Phetchaburi
Peterborough 89 E6 prev.
Medeshamstede. E England, UK
Peterborough 38 D5 Ontario,
SE Canada
Peterborough 149 B6 South
Australia
Peterhead 88 D3 NE Scotland, UK
Peter I Island 154 A3 Norwegian
dependency Antarctica
Petermann Bjerg 83 E3 mountain
C Greenland
Petersburg 41 E5 Virginia,
NE USA
Peters Mine 59 F3 var. Peter's Mine.
N Guyana
Peto 51 H4 Yucatán, SE Mexico
Petoskey 40 C2 Michigan, N USA
Petra see Wādī Mūsā
Petrich 104 C3 Blagoevgrad,
SW Bulgaria
Petrinja 100 B3 Sisak-Moslavina,
C Croatia
Petrodvorets 110 A4 Fin. Pietarhovi.
Leningradskaya Oblast',
NW Russian Federation
Petrograd see Sankt-Peterburg
Petropavl see Petropavlovsk
Petropavlovsk 114 C4 Kaz.
Petropavl. Severnyy Kazakhstan,
N Kazakhstan
Petropavlovsk-Kamchatskiy 115
H3 Kamchatskaya Oblast',
E Russian Federation
Petroşani 108 B4 var. Petroşeni, Ger.
Petroschen, Hung. Petrozsény.
Hunedoara, W Romania
Petroschen see Petroşani
Petroşeni see Petroşani
Petrozavodsk 114 B2 Fin. Petroskoi.
Respublika Kareliya, NW Russian
Federation
Petrozsény see Petroşani
Pevek 115 G1 Chukotskiy
Avtonomnyy Okrug, NE Russian
Federation
Pezinok 99 C6 Ger. Bösing, Hung.
Bazin. Bratislavský Kraj,
W Slovakia
Pforzheim 95 B6 Baden-
Württemberg, SW Germany
Pfungstadt 95 B5 Hessen,
W Germany
Phangan, Ko 137 C6 island
SW Thailand

Phang-Nga 137 B7 var. Pang-Nga,
Phangnga. Phangnga,
SW Thailand
Phangnga see Phang-Nga
Phanom Dang Raek see Dângrêk,
Chuŏr Phnum
Phanom Dong Rak see Dângrêk,
Chuŏr Phnum
Phan Rang see Phan Rang-Thap
Cham
Phan Rang-Thap Cham 137 E6 var.
Phanrang, Phan Rang, Phan Rang
Thap Cham. Ninh Thuân,
S Vietnam
Phan Thiêt 137 E6 Binh Thuân,
S Vietnam
Pharnacia see Giresun
Phatthalung 137 C7 var. Padalung,
Patalung. Phatthalung,
SW Thailand
Phayao 136 C4 var. Muang Phayao.
Phayao, NW Thailand
Phenix City 42 D2 Alabama, S USA
Phet Buri see Phetchaburi
Phetchaburi 137 C5 var. Bejraburi,
Petchaburi, Phet Buri.
Phetchaburi, SW Thailand
Philadelphia see Amman
Philadelphia 41 F4 Pennsylvania,
NE USA
Philippine Basin 125 F3 undersea
feature W Pacific Ocean
Philippines 139 E1 Country SE Asia

Philippines 139

Official name Republic of the
Philippines
Formation 1946
Capital Manila
Population 77.1 million / 666
people per sq mile (257 people
per sq km)
Total area 115,830 sq miles
(300,000 sq km)
Languages Filipino, English,
Cebuano
Religions Roman Catholic 83%,
Protestant 9%, Muslim 5%, other 3%
Ethnic mix Filipino 50%,
Indonesian and Polynesian 30%,
other 20%
Government Presidential
democracy
Currency Peso = 100 centavos
Literacy rate 95.3%
Calorie consumption 2,379
kilocalories

Philippines 139 E1 island group
W Pacific Ocean
Philippine Sea 125 F3 sea W Pacific
Ocean
Philippine Trench 141 A1 undersea
feature W Philippine Sea
Phitsanulok 136 C4 var. Bisnulok,
Muang Phitsanulok, Pitsanulok.
Phitsanulok, C Thailand
Phlórina see Flórina
Phnom Penh see Phnum Pénh
Phnum Pénh 137 D6 var. Phnom
Penh. Country capital (Cambodia)
Phnum Penh, S Cambodia
Phoenix 48 B2 state capital Arizona,
SW USA
Phoenix Islands 145 E3 island group
C Kiribati
Phôngsali 136 C3 var. Phong Saly.
Phôngsali, N Laos
Phong Saly see Phôngsali
Phrae 136 C4 var. Muang Phrae,
Prae. Phrae, NW Thailand
Phra Nakhon Si Ayutthaya see
Ayutthaya
Phra Thong, Ko 137 B6 island
SW Thailand
Phuket 137 B7 var. Bhuket, Puket,
Mal. Ujung Salang; prev.
Junkseylon, Salang. Phuket,
SW Thailand
Phuket, Ko 137 B7 island
SW Thailand
Phumĭ Kâmpóng Trâbêk 137 D5
Kâmpóng Chhnăng, C Cambodia
Phumĭ Sâmraông 137 D5 Poŭthĭsăt,
NW Cambodia

Phu Vinh see Tra Vinh
Piacenza 96 B2 Fr. Paisance; anc.
Placentia. Emilia-Romagna,
N Italy
Piatra-Neamţ 108 C4 Hung.
Karácsonkő. Neamţ, NE Romania
Piauí 63 F2 off. Estado do Piauí;
prev. Piauhy. State E Brazil
Picardie 90 C3 Eng. Picardy.
Cultural region N France
Pichilemu 64 B4 Libertador, C Chile
Pico 92 A5 var. Ilha do Pico. Island
Azores, Portugal, NE Atlantic
Ocean
Picos 63 F2 Piauí, E Brazil
Picton 151 C5 Marlborough, South
Island, NZ
Piedras Negras 51 E2 var. Ciudad
Porfirio Díaz. Coahuila de
Zaragoza, NE Mexico
Pielinen 84 E4 var. Pielisjärvi. Lake
E Finland
Pielisjärvi see Pielinen
Piemonte 96 A2 Eng. Piedmont.
Cultural region NW Italy
Pierre 45 E3 state capital South
Dakota, N USA
Piešt'any 99 C6 Ger. Pistyan, Hung.
Pöstyén. Trnavský Kraj,
W Slovakia
Pietermaritzburg 78 C5 var.
Maritzburg. KwaZulu/Natal,
E South Africa
Pietersburg see Polokwane
Pigs, Bay of see Cochinos, Bahía de
Pijijiapán 51 G5 Chiapas,
SE Mexico
Pikes Peak 44 C5 mountain
Colorado, C USA
Pikeville 40 D5 Kentucky, S USA
Pikinni see Bikini Atoll
Piła 98 B3 Ger. Schneidemühl.
Wielkopolskie, C Poland
Pilar 64 D3 var. Villa del Pilar.
Ñeembucú, S Paraguay
Pilcomayo 57 C5 river C South
America
Pilos see Pýlos
Pinang see George Town
Pinang, Pulau 138 B3 var. Penang,
Pinang; prev. Prince of Wales
Island. Island Peninsular Malaysia
Pinar del Río 54 A2 Pinar del Río,
W Cuba
Píndhos see Píndos
Píndhos Óros see Píndos
Píndos 104 A4 var. Píndhos Óros,
Eng. Pindus Mountains; prev.
Píndhos. Mountain range C Greece
Pindus Mountains see Píndos
Pine Bluff 42 B2 Arkansas, C USA
Pine Creek 146 D2 Northern
Territory, N Australia
Pinega 110 C3 river NW Russian
Federation
Pineiós 104 B4 var. Piniós; anc.
Peneius. River C Greece
Pineland 49 H3 Texas, SW USA
Pines, The Isle of the see Juventud,
Isla de la
Pingdingshan 128 C4 Henan,
C China
Pingkiang see Harbin
Ping, Mae Nam 136 B4 river
W Thailand
Piniós see Pineiós
Pinkiang see Harbin
Pínnes, Akrotírio 104 C4 headland
N Greece
Pinos, Isla de see Juventud, Isla de
la
Pinotepa Nacional 51 F5 var.
Santiago Pinotepa Nacional.
Oaxaca, SE Mexico
Pinsk 107 B7 Pol. Pińsk. SW Belarus
Pinta, Isla 60 A5 var. Abingdon.
Island Galapagos Islands,
Ecuador, E Pacific Ocean
Piombino 96 B3 Toscana, C Italy
Pioneer Mountains 46 D3 mountain
range Montana, NW USA
Pionerskiy 106 A4 Ger. Neukuhren.
Kaliningradskaya Oblast',
W Russian Federation
Piotrków Trybunalski 98 D4 Ger.
Petrikau, Rus. Petrokov. Łódzkie,
C Poland

Piraeus see Peiraiás
Pírgos see Pýrgos
Piripiri 63 F2 Piauí, E Brazil
Pirna 94 D4 Sachsen, E Germany
Pirot 101 E5 Serbia, SE Serbia and Montenegro (Yugo.)
Pisa 96 B3 var. Pisae. Toscana, C Italy
Pisae see Pisa
Pisco 60 D4 Ica, SW Peru
Písek 99 A5 Budějovicky Kraj, S Czech Republic
Pishan 126 A3 var. Guma. Xinjiang Uygur Zizhiqu, NW China
Pishpek see Bishkek
Pistoia 96 B3 anc. Pistoria, Pistoriæ. Toscana, C Italy
Pisz 98 D3 Ger. Johannisburg. Warminsko-Mazurskie, NE Poland
Pita 74 C4 Moyenne-Guinée, NW Guinea
Pitalito 58 B4 Huila, S Colombia
Pitcairn Island 143 G4 island S Pitcairn Islands
Pitcairn Islands 143 G4 UK dependent territory C Pacific Ocean
Piteå 84 D4 Norrbotten, N Sweden
Pitești 108 B3 Argeş, S Romania
Pitsanulok see Phitsanulok
Pittsburg 45 F5 Kansas, C USA
Pittsburgh 41 E4 Pennsylvania, NE USA
Pittsfield 41 F3 Massachusetts, NE USA
Piura 60 B2 Piura, NW Peru
Pivdennyy Buh 109 E3 Rus. Yuzhnyy Bug. River S Ukraine
Placetas 54 B2 Villa Clara, C Cuba
Plainview 49 E2 Texas, SW USA
Planeta Rica 58 B2 Córdoba, NW Colombia
Planken 94 E1 C Liechtenstein
Plano 49 G2 Texas, SW USA
Plasencia 92 C3 Extremadura, W Spain
Plata, Río de la 64 D4 var. River Plate. Estuary Argentina/Uruguay
Plateau du Bemaraha see Bemaraha
Platinum 36 C3 Alaska, USA
Plattensee see Balaton
Platte River 45 E4 river Nebraska, C USA
Plattsburgh 41 F2 New York, NE USA
Plauen 95 C5 var. Plauen im Vogtland. Sachsen, E Germany
Plauen im Vogtland see Plauen
Plavinas 106 D4 Ger. Stockmannshof. Aizkraukle, S Latvia
Plây Cu 137 E5 var. Pleiku. Gia Lai, C Vietnam
Pleiku see Plây Cu
Plenty, Bay of 150 E3 bay North Island, NZ
Plérin 90 A3 Côtes d'Armor, NW France
Plesetsk 110 C3 Arkhangel'skaya Oblast', NW Russian Federation
Pleszew 98 C4 Wielkopolskie, C Poland
Pleven 100 C2 prev. Plevna. Pleven, N Bulgaria
Plevlja see Pljevlja
Pljevlja 100 C4 prev. Plevlja, Plevlje. Montenegro, N Serbia and Montenegro (Yugo.)
Ploče 100 B4 It. Plocce; prev. Kardeljevo. Dubrovnik-Neretva, SE Croatia
Płock 98 D3 Ger. Plozk. Mazowieckie, C Poland
Plöcken Pass 95 C7 Ger. Plöckenpass, It. Passo di Monte Croce Carnico. Pass SW Austria
Ploiești 108 C5 prev. Ploești. Prahova, SE Romania
Plomári 105 D5 prev. Plomárion. Lésvos, E Greece
Płońsk 98 D3 Mazowieckie, C Poland
Plovdiv 104 C3 prev. Eumolpias, anc. Evmolpia, Philippopolis, Lat. Trimontium. Plovdiv, C Bulgaria
Plunge 106 B3 Plungė, W Lithuania

Plyeshchanitsy 107 D5 Rus. Pleshchenitsy. Minskaya Voblasts', N Belarus
Plymouth 55 G3 dependent territory capital (Montserrat) SW Montserrat
Plymouth 89 C7 SW England, UK
Plzeň 99 A5 Ger. Pilsen, Pol. Pilzno. Plzeňský Kraj, W Czech Republic
Po 80 D4 river N Italy
Pobeda Peak see Pobedy, Pik
Pobedy, Pik 126 B3 var. Pobeda Peak, Chin. Tomur Feng. Mountain China/Kyrgyzstan see also Tomur Feng
Pocahontas 42 B1 Arkansas, C USA
Pocatello 46 E4 Idaho, NW USA
Pochinok 111 A5 Smolenskaya Oblast', W Russian Federation
Pocking 95 D6 Bayern, SE Germany
Poděbrady 99 B5 Ger. Podiebrad. Středočeský Kraj, C Czech Republic
Podgorica 101 C5 prev. Titograd. Montenegro, SW Serbia and Montenegro (Yugo.)
Podil's'ka Vysochina 108 D3 Rus. Podol'skaya Vozvyshennost'. Mountain range SW Ukraine
Podkarpackie admin. region province SE Poland
Podol'sk 111 B5 Moskovskaya Oblast', W Russian Federation
Podravska Slatina see Slatina
Podujevo 101 D5 Serbia, S Serbia and Montenegro (Yugo.)
Po, Foci del 96 C2 var. Bocche del Po. River NE Italy
Pogradec 101 D6 var. Pogradeci. Korçë, SE Albania
Pogradeci see Pogradec
Pohnpei 144 C2 prev. Ponape Ascension Island. Island E Micronesia
Poinsett, Cape 154 D4 headland Antarctica
Pointe-à-Pitre 55 G3 Grande Terre, C Guadeloupe
Pointe-Noire 77 B6 Le Kouilou, S Congo
Point Lay 36 C2 Alaska, USA
Poitiers 90 B4 prev. Poictiers, anc. Limonum. Vienne, W France
Poitou 90 B4 cultural region W France
Pokhara 135 E3 Western, C Nepal
Pokrovs'ke 109 G3 Rus. Pokrovskoye. Dnipropetrovs'ka Oblast', E Ukraine
Pola de Lena 92 D1 Asturias, N Spain
Poland 98 B4 var. Polish Republic, Pol. Polska, Rzeczpospolita Polska; prev. Pol. Polska Rzeczpospolita Ludowa, Polish People's Republic. Country C Europe

---

Poland 98

Official name Republic of Poland
Formation 1918
Capital Warsaw
Population 38.6 million / 320 people per sq mile (123 peopleper sq km)
Total area 120,728 sq miles (312,685 sq km)
Languages Polish
Religions Roman Catholic 93%, Eastern Orthodox 2%, other and non-religious 5%
Ethnic mix Polish 98%, German 1%, other 1%
Government Parliamentary democracy
Currency Zloty = 100 groszy
Literacy rate 99%
Calorie consumption 3,376 kilocalories

Poland 81 E3 Kiritimati, E Kiribati
Polatli 116 C3 Ankara, C Turkey
Polatsk 107 D5 Rus. Polotsk. Vitsyebskaya Voblasts', N Belarus
Pol-e Khomrí 123 E4 var. Pul-i-Khumri. Baghlān, NE Afghanistan

Poli see Pólis
Polikastro see Polýkastro
Políkastron see Polýkastro
Polikrayshte 104 D2 Veliko Tŭrnovo, N Bulgaria
Pólis 102 C5 var. Poli. W Cyprus
Polkowice 98 B4 Ger. Heerwegen. Dolnośląskie, SW Poland
Pollença 93 G3 var. Pollensa. Mallorca, Spain, W Mediterranean Sea
Pollensa see Pollença
Polohy 109 G3 Rus. Pologi. Zaporiz'ka Oblast', SE Ukraine
Polokwane 56 D4 Var. Pietersburg, NE South Africa
Polonne 108 D2 Rus. Polonnoye. Khmel'nyts'ka Oblast', NW Ukraine
Polska Kosovo 104 D2 Ruse, N Bulgaria
Poltava 109 F2 Poltavs'ka Oblast', NE Ukraine
Pōlva 104 E3 Ger. Pōlwe. Pōlvamaa, SE Estonia
Polyarnyy 110 C2 Murmanskaya Oblast', NW Russian Federation
Polýkastro 104 B3 var. Polikastro; prev. Políkastron. Kentrikí Makedonía, N Greece
Polynesia 143 F4 island group C Pacific Ocean
Pomeranian Bay 94 D2 Ger. Pommersche Bucht, Pol. Zatoka Pomorska. Bay Germany/Poland
Pomorskiy Proliv 110 D2 strait NW Russian Federation
Pompano Beach 43 F5 Florida, SE USA
Ponca City 49 G1 Oklahoma, C USA
Ponce 55 F3 C Puerto Rico
Pondicherry 132 C2 var. Puduchcheri, Fr. Pondichéry. Pondicherry, SE India
Pondichéry see Pondicherry
Ponferrada 92 C1 Castilla-León, NW Spain
Poniatowa 98 E4 Lublin, E Poland
Pons Aelii see Newcastle upon Tyne
Ponta Delgada 92 B5 São Miguel, Azores, Portugal, NE Atlantic Ocean
Ponta Grossa 63 E4 Paraná, S Brazil
Pontarlier 90 D4 Doubs, E France
Ponteareas 92 B2 Galicia, NW Spain
Ponte da Barca 92 B2 Viana do Castelo, N Portugal
Pontevedra 92 B1 anc. Pons Vetus. Galicia, NW Spain
Pontiac 40 D3 Michigan, N USA
Pontianak 138 C4 Borneo, C Indonesia
Pontivy 90 A3 Morbihan, NW France
Pontoise 90 C5 anc. Briva Isarae, Cergy-Pontoise, Pontisarae. Val-d'Oise, N France
Ponziane, Isole 97 C5 island C Italy
Poole 89 D7 S England, UK
Poopó, Lago 61 F4 var. Lago Pampa Aullagas. Lake W Bolivia
Popayán 58 B4 Cauca, SW Colombia
Poperinge 87 A6 West-Vlaanderen, W Belgium
Poplar Bluff 45 G5 Missouri, C USA
Popocatépetl 51 E4 volcano S Mexico
Poprad 99 D5 Ger. Deutschendorf, Hung. Poprád. Prešovský Kraj, E Slovakia
Poprad 99 D5 Ger. Popper, Hung. Poprád. River Poland/Slovakia
Porbandar 134 B4 Gujarāt, W India
Porcupine Plain 80 B3 undersea feature E Atlantic Ocean
Pordenone 96 C2 anc. Portenau. Friuli-Venezia Giulia, NE Italy
Poreč 96 A2 It. Parenzo. Istra, NW Croatia
Pori 85 D5 Swe. Björneborg. Länsi-Suomi, W Finland
Porirua 151 D5 Wellington, North Island, NZ

Porkhov 110 A4 Pskovskaya Oblast', W Russian Federation
Porlamar 59 E1 Nueva Esparta, NE Venezuela
Póros 105 A5 Kefallinía, Iónioi Nísoi, Greece, C Mediterranean Sea
Póros 105 C6 Póros, S Greece
Porsangen 84 D2 fjord N Norway
Porsgrunn 85 B6 Telemark, S Norway
Portachuelo 61 G4 Santa Cruz, C Bolivia
Portadown 89 B5 Ir. Port An Dúnáin. S Northern Ireland, UK
Portalegre 92 C3 anc. Ammaia, Amoea. Portalegre, E Portugal
Port Alexander 36 D4 Baranof Island, Alaska, USA
Port Alfred 78 D5 Eastern Cape, S South Africa
Port An Dúnáin see Portadown
Port Angeles 46 B1 Washington, NW USA
Port Antonio 54 B5 NE Jamaica
Port Arthur 49 H4 Texas, SW USA
Port Augusta 149 B6 South Australia
Port-au-Prince 54 D3 country capital (Haiti) C Haiti
Port-au-Prince 55 D7 international airport E Haiti
Port Blair 133 F2 Andaman and Nicobar Islands, SE India
Port Charlotte 43 E4 Florida, SE USA
Port d'Envalira 91 B8 E Andorra
Port Douglas 148 D3 Queensland, NE Australia
Port Elizabeth 78 C5 Eastern Cape, S South Africa
Porterville 47 C7 California, W USA
Port-Gentil 77 A6 Ogooué-Maritime, W Gabon
Port Harcourt 75 G5 Rivers, S Nigeria
Port Hardy 36 D5 Vancouver Island, British Columbia, SW Canada
Port Harrison see Inukjuak
Port Hedland 146 B4 Western Australia
Port Huron 40 D3 Michigan, N USA
Portimão 92 B4 var. Vila Nova de Portimão. Faro, S Portugal
Port Jackson 148 E1 harbour New South Wales, SE Australia
Port Láirge see Waterford
Portland 41 G2 Maine, NE USA
Portland 46 B3 Oregon, NW USA
Portland 49 G4 Texas, SW USA
Portland 149 B7 Victoria, SE Australia
Portland Bight 54 B5 bay S Jamaica
Portlaoighise see Portlaoise
Portlaoise 89 B6 Ir. Portlaoighise; prev. Maryborough. C Ireland
Port Lavaca 49 G4 Texas, SW USA
Port Lincoln 149 A6 South Australia
Port Louis 79 H3 country capital (Mauritius) NW Mauritius
Port Macquarie 149 E6 New South Wales, SE Australia
Portmore 54 B5 C Jamaica
Port Moresby 144 B3 country capital (PNG) Central/National Capital District, SW PNG
Port Musgrave 149 B9 bay Queensland, N Australia
Porto 92 B2 Eng. Oporto; anc. Portus Cale. Porto, NW Portugal
Porto Alegre 63 F5 State capital Rio Grande do Sul, S Brazil
Porto Alegre 76 E2 São Tomé, S Sao Tome and Principe
Porto Bello see Portobelo
Portobelo 53 G4 var. Porto Bello, Puerto Bello. Colón, N Panama
Port O'Connor 49 G4 Texas, SW USA
Porto Edda see Sarandë
Portoferraio 96 B4 Toscana, C Italy
Port-of-Spain 55 H5 country capital (Trinidad and Tobago) Trinidad, Trinidad and Tobago

Porto Grande see Mindelo
Portogruaro 96 C2 Veneto, NE Italy
Porto-Novo 75 F5 country capital
  (Benin) S Benin
Porto Santo 70 A2 var. Ilha do Porto
  Santo. Island Madeira, Portugal,
  NE Atlantic Ocean
Porto Torres 97 A5 Sardegna, Italy,
  C Mediterranean Sea
Porto Velho 62 D2 var. Velho. State
  capital Rondônia, W Brazil
Portoviejo 60 A2 var. Puertoviejo.
  Manabí, W Ecuador
Port Pirie 149 B6 South Australia
Port Said 72 B1 Ar. Bûr Sa'îd.
  N Egypt
Portsmouth 41 G3 New Hampshire,
  NE USA
Portsmouth 40 D4 Ohio, N USA
Portsmouth 89 D7 S England, UK
Portsmouth 41 F5 Virginia, NE USA
Port Stanley see Stanley
Port Sudan 72 C3 Red Sea,
  NE Sudan
Port Swettenham see Klang
Port Talbot 89 C7 S Wales, UK
Portugal 92 B3 Country SW Europe

Portugal 92

Official name Republic of Portugal
Formation 1139
Capital Lisbon
Population 10 million / 280 people
  per sq mile (108 people per sq km)
Total area 35,672 sq miles
  (92,391 sq km)
Languages Portuguese
Religions Roman Catholic 97%,
  Protestant 1%, other 2%
Ethnic mix Portuguese 98%,
  African and other 2%
Government Parliamentary
  democracy
Currency Euro (Portuguese escudo
  until 2002)
Literacy rate 92.3%
Calorie consumption 3,716
  kilocalories

Portuguese Timor see East Timor
Port-Vila 144 D4 var. Vila. Country
  capital (Vanuatu) Éfaté, C Vanuatu
Porvenir 65 B8 Magallanes, S Chile
Porvenir 61 E3 Pando, NW Bolivia
Porvoo 85 E6 Swe. Borgå. Etelä-
  Suomi, S Finland
Posadas 64 D3 Misiones,
  NE Argentina
Poschega see Požega
Posterholt 87 D5 Limburg,
  SE Netherlands
Postojna 95 D8 Ger. Adelsberg, It.
  Postumia. SW Slovenia
Potamós 105 C7 Antikýthira,
  S Greece
Potenza 97 D5 anc. Potentia.
  Basilicata, S Italy
P'ot'i 117 F2 W Georgia
Potiskum 75 G4 Yobe, NE Nigeria
Potomac River 41 E5 river
  NE USA
Potosí 61 F4 Potosí, S Bolivia
Potsdam 94 D3 Brandenburg,
  NE Germany
Potwar Plateau 134 C2 plateau
  NE Pakistan
Poûthisăt 137 D6 prev. Pursat.
  Poûthisăt, W Cambodia
Po Valley 96 C2 It. Valle del Po.
  Valley N Italy
Považská Bystrica 99 C5 Ger.
  Waagbistritz, Hung. Vágbeszterce.
  Trenčiansky Kraj, W Slovakia
Poverty Bay 150 E4 inlet North
  Island, NZ
Póvoa de Varzim 92 B2 Porto,
  NW Portugal
Powder River 44 D2 river
  Montana/Wyoming, NW USA
Powell 44 C2 Wyoming, C USA
Powell, Lake 44 B5 lake Utah,
  W USA
Požarevac 100 D4 Ger. Passarowitz.
  Serbia, NE Serbia and
  Montenegro (Yugo.)

Poza Rica 51 F4 var. Poza Rica de
  Hidalgo. Veracruz-Llave,
  E Mexico
Poza Rica de Hidalgo see Poza Rica
Požega 100 D4 prev. Slavonska
  Požega. Ger. Poschega, Hung.
  Pozsega. Požega-Slavonija, NE
  Croatia
Pozsega see Požega
Poznań 98 C3 Ger. Posen, Posnania.
  Wielkopolskie, C Poland
Pozoblanco 92 D4 Andalucía,
  S Spain
Pozzallo 97 C8 Sicilia, Italy,
  C Mediterranean Sea
Prachatice 99 A5 Ger. Prachatitz.
  Budějovický Kraj, S Czech
  Republic
Prado del Ganso see Goose Green
Prae see Phrae
Prague 80 D3 Oklahoma, C USA
Praha 99 A5 Eng. Prague, Ger. Prag,
  Pol. Praga. Country capital (Czech
  Republic) Středočesky Kraj,
  NW Czech Republic
Praia 74 A3 country capital (Cape
  Verde) Santiago, S Cape Verde
Prato 96 B3 Toscana, C Italy
Pratt 45 E5 Kansas, C USA
Prattville 42 D2 Alabama, S USA
Pravda 104 D1 prev. Dogrular.
  Silistra, NE Bulgaria
Pravia 92 C1 Asturias, N Spain
Prenzlau 94 D3 Brandenburg,
  NE Germany
Přerov 99 C5 Ger. Prerau.
  Olomoucký Kraj, E Czech
  Republic
Presa de la Amistad see Amistad
  Reservoir
Preschau see Prešov
Prescott 48 B2 Arizona, SW USA
Prešovo 101 D5 Serbia, SE Serbia
  and Montenegro (Yugo.)
Presidente Epitácio 63 E4 São
  Paulo, S Brazil
Prešov 99 D5 var. Preschau, Ger.
  Eperies, Hung. Eperjes. Prešouský
  Kraj, E Slovakia
Prespa, Lake 101 D6 Alb. Liqen i
  Prespës, Gk. Límni Megáli Préspa,
  Límni Prespa, Mac. Prespansko
  Ezero, Serb. Prespansko Jezero.
  Lake SE Europe
Presque Isle 41 H1 Maine, NE USA
Preston 89 D5 NW England, UK
Prestwick 88 C4 W Scotland, UK
Pretoria 78 D4 var. Epitoli, Tshwane.
  Country capital(South Africa-
  administrative capital) Gauteng,
  NE South Africa
Préveza 105 A5 Ípeiros, W Greece
Pribilof Islands 36 A3 island group
  Alaska, USA
Priboj 100 C4 Serbia, W Serbia and
  Montenegro (Yugo.)
Price 44 B4 Utah, W USA
Prichard 42 C3 Alabama, S USA
Priekulė 106 B3 Ger. Prökuls.
  Gargždai, W Lithuania
Prienai 107 B5 Pol. Preny. Prienai,
  S Lithuania
Prieska 78 C4 Northern Cape,
  C South Africa
Prijedor 100 B3 Republika
  Srpska, NW Bosnia and
  Herzegovina
Prijepolje 100 D4 Serbia, W Serbia
  and Montenegro (Yugo.)
Prilep 101 D6 Turk. Perlepe. S FYR
  Macedonia
Primorsk 106 A4 Ger. Fischhausen.
  Kaliningradskaya Oblast',
  W Russian Federation
Primorsko 104 E2 prev. Keupriya.
  Burgas, E Bulgaria
Prince Albert 37 F5 Saskatchewan,
  S Canada
Prince Edward Island 39 F4 Fr. Île-
  du Prince-Édouard. Province
  SE Canada
Prince Edward Islands 69 E8 island
  group S South Africa
Prince George 37 E5 British
  Columbia, SW Canada
Prince of Wales Island 37 F2 island
  Queen Elizabeth Islands,
  Nunavut, NW Canada

Prince of Wales Island 148 B1 island
  Queensland, E Australia
Prince Patrick Island 37 E2 island
  Parry Islands, Northwest
  Territories, NW Canada
Prince Rupert 36 D4 British
  Columbia, SW Canada
Prince's Island see Príncipe
Princess Charlotte Bay 148 C2 bay
  Queensland, NE Australia
Princess Elizabeth Land 154 C3
  physical region Antarctica
Príncipe 77 A5 var. Príncipe Island,
  Eng. Prince's Island. Island N Sao
  Tome and Principe
Príncipe Island see Príncipe
Prinzapolka 53 E3 Región
  Autónoma Atlántico Norte,
  NE Nicaragua
Pripet 107 C7 Bel. Prypyats', Ukr.
  Pryp″yat'. River Belarus/Ukraine
Pripet Marshes 107 B7 wetland
  Belarus/Ukraine
Priština 101 D5 Alb. Prishtinë.
  Serbia, S Serbia and Montenegro
  (Yugo.)
Privas 91 D5 Ardèche, E France
Prizren 101 D5 Alb. Prizreni. Serbia,
  S Serbia and Montenegro (Yugo.)
Probolinggo 138 D5 Jawa,
  C Indonesia
Progreso 51 H3 Yucatán, SE Mexico
Prokhladnyy 111 B8 Kabardino-
  Balkarskaya Respublika,
  SW Russian Federation
Prokuplje 101 D5 Serbia, SE Serbia
  and Montenegro (Yugo.)
Prome 136 B4 var. Pyè. Pegu,
  C Myanmar
Promyshlennyy 110 E3 Respublika
  Komi, NW Russian Federation
Prostějov 99 C5 Ger. Prossnitz, Pol.
  Prościejów. Olomoucký Kraj,
  E Czech Republic
Provence 91 D6 cultural region
  SE France
Providence see Fort Providence
Providence 41 G3 state capital
  Rhode Island, NE USA
Providencia, Isla de 53 F3 island
  NW Colombia
Provideniya 172 B1 Chukotskiy
  Avtonomnyy Okrug, NE Russian
  Federation
Provo 44 B4 Utah, W USA
Prudhoe Bay 36 D2 Alaska, USA
Prusa see Bursa
Pruszków 98 D3 Ger. Kaltdorf.
  Mazowieckie, C Poland
Prut 108 D4 Ger. Pruth. River
  E Europe
Pruzhany 107 B6 Pol. Prużana.
  Brestskaya Voblasts', SW Belarus
Prydz Bay 154 D3 bay Antarctica
Pryluky 109 E2 Rus. Priluki.
  Cherníhivs'ka Oblast',
  NE Ukraine
Prymors'k 109 G4 Rus. Primorsk;
  prev. Primorskoye. Zaporiz'ka
  Oblast', SE Ukraine
Przemyśl 99 E5 Rus. Peremyshl.
  Podkarpackie, SE Poland
Psará 105 D5 island E Greece
Psël 109 F2 river Russian
  Federation/Ukraine
Pskov 114 B2 Ger. Pleskau, Latv.
  Pleskava. Pskovskaya Oblast',
  W Russian Federation
Pskov, Lake E3 Est. Pihkva Järv,
  Ger. Pleskauer See, Rus.
  Pskovskoye Ozero. Lake
  Estonia/Russian Federation
Ptich 107 C7 Rus. Ptich'. River
  SE Belarus
Ptich 107 C7 Rus. Ptich'.
  Homyel'skaya Voblasts',
  SE Belarus
Ptuj 95 E7 Ger. Pettau; anc.
  Poetovio. NE Slovenia
Pucallpa 60 C3 Ucayali, C Peru
Puck 98 C2 Pomorskie, N Poland
Pudasjärvi 84 D4 Oulu, C Finland
Puducherri see Pondicherry
Puebla 51 F4 var. Puebla de
  Zaragoza. Puebla, S Mexico
Puebla de Zaragoza see Puebla
Pueblo 44 D5 Colorado, C USA

Puerto Acosta 61 E4 La Paz,
  W Bolivia
Puerto Aisén 65 B6 Aisén, S Chile
Puerto Ángel 51 F5 Oaxaca,
  SE Mexico
Puerto Argentino see Stanley
Puerto Ayacucho 58 D3 Amazonas,
  SW Venezuela
Puerto Baquerizo Moreno 60 B5
  var. Baquerizo Moreno. Galapagos
  Islands, Ecuador, E Pacific Ocean
Puerto Barrios 52 C2 Izabal,
  E Guatemala
Puerto Bello see Portobelo
Puerto Berrío 58 B2 Antioquia,
  C Colombia
Puerto Cabello 58 D1 Carabobo,
  N Venezuela
Puerto Cabezas 53 E2 var. Bilwi.
  Región Autónoma Atlántico
  Norte, NE Nicaragua
Puerto Carreño 58 D3 Vichada,
  E Colombia
Puerto Cortés 52 C2 Cortés,
  NW Honduras
Puerto Cumarebo 58 C1 Falcón,
  N Venezuela
Puerto Deseado 65 C7 Santa Cruz,
  SE Argentina
Puerto Escondido 51 F5 Oaxaca,
  SE Mexico
Puerto Francisco de Orellana 60 B1
  var. Coca. Napo, N Ecuador
Puerto Gallegos see Río Gallegos
Puerto Inírida 58 D3 var. Obando.
  Guainía, E Colombia
Puerto La Cruz 59 E1 Anzoátegui,
  NE Venezuela
Puerto Lempira 53 E2 Gracias a
  Dios, E Honduras
Puerto Limón see Limón
Puertollano 92 D4 Castilla-La
  Mancha, C Spain
Puerto López 58 C1 La Guajira,
  N Colombia
Puerto Maldonado 61 E3 Madre de
  Dios, E Peru
Puerto México see Coatzacoalcos
Puerto Montt 65 B5 Los Lagos,
  C Chile
Puerto Natales 65 B7 Magallanes,
  S Chile
Puerto Obaldía 53 H5 San Blas,
  NE Panama
Puerto Plata 55 E3 var. San Felipe
  de Puerto Plata. N Dominican
  Republic
Puerto Princesa 139 E2 off. Puerto
  Princesa City. Palawan,
  W Philippines
Puerto Rico 55 F3 off.
  Commonwealth of Puerto Rico;
  prev. Porto Rico. US
  commonwealth territory C West
  Indies
Puerto Rico 56 B1 island C West
  Indies
Puerto Rico Trench 56 B1 undersea
  feature NE Caribbean Sea
Puerto San José see San José
Puerto San Julián 65 B7 var. San
  Julián. Santa Cruz, SE Argentina
Puerto Suárez 61 H4 Santa Cruz,
  E Bolivia
Puerto Vallarta 50 D4 Jalisco,
  SW Mexico
Puerto Varas 65 B5 Los Lagos,
  C Chile
Puerto Viejo 53 E4 Heredia,
  NE Costa Rica
Puertoviejo see Portoviejo
Puget Sound 46 B1 sound
  Washington, NW USA
Puglia 97 E5 Eng. Apulia. Cultural
  region SE Italy
Pukaki, Lake 151 B6 lake South
  Island, NZ
Pukekohe 150 D3 Auckland, North
  Island, NZ
Puket see Phuket
Pukhovichy 107 C6 Rus.
  Pukhovichi. Minskaya Voblasts',
  C Belarus
Pula 100 A3 It. Pola; prev. Pulj. Istra,
  NW Croatia
Pulaski 40 D5 Virginia, NE USA
Pulau Butung see Buton, Pulau

Puławy 98 D4 Ger. Neu Amerika. Lublin, E Poland
Pul-i-Khumri see Pol-e Khomrī
Pullman 46 C2 Washington, NW USA
Pułtusk 98 D3 Mazowieckie, C Poland
Puná, Isla 60 A2 island SW Ecuador
Pune 134 C5 prev. Poona. Mahārāshtra, W India
Punjab 134 C2 prev. West Punjab, Western Punjab. Province E Pakistan
Puno 61 E4 Puno, SE Peru
Punta Alta 65 C5 Buenos Aires, E Argentina
Punta Arenas 65 B8 prev. Magallanes. Magallanes, S Chile
Punta Gorda 53 E4 Región Autónoma Atlántico Sur, SE Nicaragua
Punta Gorda 52 C2 Toledo, SE Belize
Puntarenas 52 D4 Puntarenas, W Costa Rica
Punto Fijo 58 C1 Falcón, N Venezuela
Pupuya, Nevado 61 E4 mountain W Bolivia
Puri 135 F5 var. Jagannath. Orissa, E India
Puriramya see Buriram
Purmerend 86 C3 Noord-Holland, C Netherlands
Purus, Rio 62 C2 Sp. Río Purús. River Brazil/Peru
Pusan 129 E4 off. Pusan-gwangyōksi, var. Busan, Jap. Fusan. SE South Korea
Püspökladány 99 D6 Hajdú-Bihar, E Hungary
Putorana Mountains 114 D3 var. Gory Putorana, Eng. Putorana Mountains. Mountain range N Russian Federation
Puttalam 132 C3 North Western Province, W Sri Lanka
Puttgarden 94 C2 Schleswig-Holstein, N Germany
Putumayo, Río 58 B5 var. Rio Içá. River NW South America see also Içá, Rio
Putumayo, Río see Içá, Rio
Puurmani 106 D2 Ger. Talkhof. Jōgevamaa, E Estonia
Pyatigorsk 111 B7 Stavropol'skiy Kray, SW Russian Federation
P"yatykhatky 109 F3 Rus. Pyatikhatki. Dnipropetrovs'ka Oblast', E Ukraine
Pyè see Prome
Pyetrykaw 107 C7 Rus. Petrikov. Homyel'skaya Voblasts', SE Belarus
Pyinmana 136 B4 Mandalay, C Myanmar
Pýlos 105 B6 var. Pilos. Pelopónnisos, S Greece
P'yōngyang 129 E4 var. P'yōngyang-si, Eng. Pyongyang. Country capital (North Korea) SW North Korea
P'yōngyang-si see P'yōngyang
Pyramid Lake 47 C5 lake Nevada, W USA
Pyrenees 102 B2 Fr. Pyrénées, Sp. Pirineos; anc. Pyrenaei Montes. Mountain range SW Europe
Pýrgos 105 B6 var. Pírgos. Dytikí Ellás, S Greece
Pyryatyn 109 E2 Rus. Piryatin. Poltava'ka Oblast', NE Ukraine
Pyrzyce 98 B3 Ger. Pyritz. Zachodniopomorskie, NW Poland
Pyu 136 B4 Pegu, C Myanmar
Pyuntaza 136 B4 Pegu, SW Myanmar

Q

Qā' al Jafr 119 C7 lake S Jordan
Qaanaaq 82 C4 var. Qânâq, Dan. Thule. N Greenland
Qabātiya 119 E6 N West Bank
Qābis see Gabès
Qafşah see Gafsa
Qagan Us see Dulan
Qahremānshahr see Bākhtarān
Qaidam Pendi 126 C4 basin C China
Qal'aikhum 123 F3 Rus. Kalaikhum. S Tajikistan
Qal'at Bīshah 121 B5 'Asīr, SW Saudi Arabia
Qalqīlya 119 D6 N West Bank
Qamdo 126 D5 Xizang Zizhiqu, W China
Qamishly see Al Qāmishlī
Qânâq see Qaanaaq
Qaqortoq 82 C4 Dan. Julianehåb. S Greenland
Qara Qum see Garagumy
Qarkilik see Ruoqiang
Qarokül 123 F3 Rus. Karakul'. E Tajikistan
Qars see Kars
Qarshi 123 E3 Rus. Karshi; prev. Bek-Budi. Qashqadaryo Wiloyati, S Uzbekistan
Qasigianguit see Qasigiannguit
Qasigiannguit 82 C3 var. Qasigianguit, Dan. Christianshåb. C Greenland
Qasr Farâfra 72 B2 W Egypt
Qaṭanā 119 B5 var. Katana. Dimashq, S Syria
Qatar 120 C4 Ar. Dawlat Qaṭar. Country SW Asia

Qatar 120

Official name State of Qatar
Formation 1971
Capital Doha
Population 575,000 / 130 people per sq mile (50 people per sq km)
Total area 4,416 sq miles (11,437 sq km)
Languages Arabic
Religions Muslim (mainly Sunni) 95%, other 5%
Ethnic mix Arab 40%, Pakistani 18%, Indian 18%, Iranian 10%, other 14%
Government Monarchy
Currency Qatar riyal = 100 dirhams
Literacy rate 81.2%
Calorie consumption not available

Qattara Depression see Qaṭṭâra, Monkhafad el
Qattâra, Monkhafad el 88 A1 var. Munkhafaḍ al Qaṭṭārah, Eng. Qattara Depression. Desert NW Egypt
Qazimämmäd 117 H3 Rus. Kazi Magomed. SE Azerbaijan
Qazvīn 120 C2 var. Kazvin. Qazvin, N Iran
Qena 72 B2 var. Qinā; anc. Caene, Caenepolis. E Egypt
Qeqertarssuaq see Qeqertarsuaq
Qeqertarsuaq 82 C3 var. Qeqertarssuaq, Dan. Godhavn. S Greenland
Qeqertarsuaq 82 C3 island W Greenland
Qeqertarsuup Tunua 82 C3 Dan. Disko Bugt. Inlet W Greenland
Qerveh see Qorveh
Qeshm 120 D4 var. Jazīreh-ye Qeshm, Qeshm Island. Island S Iran
Qeshm Island see Qeshm
Qian see Guizhou
Qilian Shan 126 D3 var. Kilien Mountains. Mountain range N China
Qimusseriarsuaq 82 C2 Dan. Melville Bugt, Eng. Melville Bay. Bay NW Greenland
Qinā see Qena
Qing see Qinghai
Qingdao 128 D4 var. Ching-Tao, Ch'ing-tao, Tsingtao, Tsintao, Ger. Tsingtau. Shandong, E China
Qinghai 126 C4 var. Chinghai, Koko Nor, Qing, Qinghai Sheng, Tsinghai. Admin. region province C China
Qinghai Hu 126 D4 var. Ch'ing Hai, Tsing Hai, Mong. Koko Nor. lake C China

Qinghai Sheng see Qinghai
Qingzang Gaoyuan 126 B4 var. Xizang Gaoyuan, Eng. Plateau of Tibet. Plateau W China
Qinhuangdao 128 D3 Hebei, E China
Qinzhou 128 B6 Guangxi Zhuangzu Zizhiqu, S China
Qiong see Hainan
Qiqihar 128 D2 var. Ch'i-ch'i-ha-erh, Tsitsihar; prev. Lungkiang. Heilongjiang, NE China
Qira 126 B4 Xinjiang Uygur Zizhiqu, NW China
Qitai 126 C3 Xinjiang Uygur Zizhiqu, NW China
Qīzān see Jīzān
Qizil Orda see Kyzylorda
Qizil Qum see Kyzyl Kum
Qizilrabot 123 G3 Rus. Kyzylrabot. SE Tajikistan
Qom 120 C3 var. Kum, Qum. Qom, N Iran
Qomul see Hami
Qondūz see Kunduz
Qorveh 120 C3 var. Qerveh, Qurveh. Kordestān, W Iran
Qostanay see Kostanay
Qoubaïyât 118 B4 var. Al Qubayyāt. N Lebanon
Qoussantina see Constantine
Quang Ngai 137 E5 var. Quangngai, Quang Nghia. Quang Ngai, C Vietnam
Quangngai see Quang Ngai
Quang Nghia see Quang Ngai
Quanzhou 128 D6 var. Ch'uan-chou, Tsinkiang; prev. Chin-chiang. Fujian, SE China
Quanzhou 128 C6 Guangxi Zhuangzu Zizhiqu, S China
Qu'Appelle 37 F5 river Saskatchewan, S Canada
Quarles, Pegunungan 139 E4 mountain range Sulawesi, C Indonesia
Quarnero see Kvarner
Quartu Sant' Elena 97 A6 Sardegna, Italy, C Mediterranean Sea
Quba 117 H2 Rus. Kuba. N Azerbaijan
Qubba see Ba'qūbah
Québec 39 E4 var. Quebec. Quebec, SE Canada
Quebec 38 D3 var. Quebec. Admin. region province SE Canada
Queen Charlotte Islands 36 C5 Fr. Îles de la Reine-Charlotte. Island group British Columbia, SW Canada
Queen Charlotte Sound 36 C5 sea area British Columbia, W Canada
Queen Elizabeth Islands 37 F2 Fr. Îles de la Reine-Élisabeth. Island group Northwest Territories/Nunavut, N Canada
Queensland 148 B4 state N Australia
Queenstown 78 D5 Eastern Cape, S South Africa
Queenstown 151 B7 Otago, South Island, NZ
Quelimane 79 E3 var. Kilimane, Kilmain, Quilimane. Zambézia, NE Mozambique
Quepos 53 E4 Puntarenas, S Costa Rica
Querétaro 51 E4 Querétaro de Arteaga, C Mexico
Quesada 53 E4 var. Ciudad Quesada, San Carlos. Alajuela, N Costa Rica
Quetta 134 B2 Baluchistān, SW Pakistan
Quetzalcoalco see Coatzacoalcos
Quetzaltenango see Quezaltenango
Quezaltenango 52 A2 var. Quetzaltenango. Quezaltenango, W Guatemala
Quibdó 58 A3 Chocó, W Colombia
Quilimane see Quelimane
Quillabamba 60 D3 Cusco, C Peru
Quilon 132 C6 var. Kolam, Kollam. Kerala, SW India
Quimper 90 A3 anc. Quimper Corentin. Finistère, NW France
Quimperlé 90 A3 Finistère, NW France

Quincy 40 A4 Illinois, N USA
Qui Nhon see Quy Nhon
Quissico 79 E4 Inhambane, S Mozambique
Quito 60 B1 country capital (Ecuador) Pichincha, N Ecuador
Qullai Garmo see Kommunizm, Qullai
Qum see Qom
Qunaytra see Al Qunayṭirah
Qŭqon 123 F2 var. Khokand, Rus. Kokand. Farghona Wiloyati, E Uzbekistan
Qurein see Al Kuwayt
Qŭrghonteppa 123 E3 Rus. Kurgan-Tyube. SW Tajikistan
Qurlurtuuq see Kugluktuk
Qurveh see Qorveh
Quşayr see Al Quşayr
Quy Nhon 137 E5 var. Quinhon, Qui Nhon. Binh Ðinh, C Vietnam
Qyteti Stalin see Kuçovë
Qyzylorda see Kyzylorda

R

Raab 100 B1 Hung. Rába. River Austria/Hungary see also Rába
Raahe 84 D4 Swe. Brahestad. Oulu, W Finland
Raalte 86 D3 Overijssel, E Netherlands
Raamsdonksveer 86 C4 Noord-Brabant, S Netherlands
Raasiku 106 D2 Ger. Rasik. Harjumaa, NW Estonia
Rába 99 B7 Ger. Raab. River Austria/Hungary see also Raab
Rabat 70 C2 var. al Dar al Baida. Country capital (Morocco) NW Morocco
Rabat see Victoria
Rabat 102 B3 W Malta
Rabbah Ammon see 'Ammān
Rabbath Ammon see 'Ammān
Rabinal 52 B2 Baja Verapaz, C Guatemala
Rabka 99 D5 Małopolskie, S Poland
Râbniţa see Ribniţa
Rabyanāh, Ramlat 71 G4 var. Rebiana Sand Sea, ṣaḥrā' Rabyanāh. Desert SE Libya
Race, Cape 39 H3 headland Newfoundland, Newfoundland and Labrador, E Canada
Rach Gia 137 D6 Kiên Giang, S Vietnam
Rach Gia, Vinh 137 D6 bay S Vietnam
Racine 40 B3 Wisconsin, N USA
Rădăuţi 108 C3 Ger. Radautz, Hung. Rádóc. Suceava, N Romania
Radom 98 D4 Mazowieckie, C Poland
Radomsko 98 D4 Rus. Novorodomsk. Łódzkie, C Poland
Radomyshl' 108 D2 Zhytomyrs'ka Oblast', N Ukraine
Radoviš 101 E6 prev. Radovište. E FYR Macedonia
Radviliškis 106 B4 Radviliškis, N Lithuania
Radzyń Podlaski 98 E4 Lubelskie, E Poland
Rae-Edzo see Edzo
Raetihi 150 D4 Manawatu-Wanganui, North Island, NZ
Rafa see Rafah
Rafaela 64 C3 Santa Fe, E Argentina
Rafah 119 A7 var. Rafa, Rafaḥ, Heb. Rafiaḥ, Raphiah. SW Gaza Strip
Rafaḥ see Rafah
Rafḥah 120 B4 Al Ḥudūd ash Shamālīyah, N Saudi Arabia
Rafiaḥ see Rafah
Raga 73 A5 Western Bahr el Ghazal, SW Sudan
Ragged Island Range 54 C2 island group S Bahamas
Ragusa 97 C7 Sicilia, Italy, C Mediterranean Sea
Rahachow 107 D7 Rus. Rogachëv. Homyel'skaya Voblasts', SE Belarus
Rahaeng see Tak

231

Rahaṭ, Ḥarrat 121 B5 *lavaflow* W Saudi Arabia
Rahīmyār Khān 134 C3 Punjab, SE Pakistan
Raiatea 145 G4 *island* Îles Sous le Vent, W French Polynesia
Rāichūr 132 C1 Karnātaka, C India
Rainier, Mount 34 A4 *volcano* Washington, NW USA
Rainy Lake 38 A4 *lake* Canada/USA
Raipur 135 E4 Madhya Pradesh, C India
Rājahmundry 135 E5 Andhra Pradesh, E India
Rajang *see* Rajang, Batang
Rajang, Batang 138 D3 *var.* Rajang. *River* East Malaysia
Rājapālaiyam 132 C3 Tamil Nādu, SE India
Rājasthān 134 C3 *state* NW India
Rājkot 134 C4 Gujarāt, W India
Rāj Nāndgaon 135 E4 Madhya Pradesh, C India
Rajshahi 135 G3 *prev.* Rampur Boalia. Rajshahi, W Bangladesh
Rakahanga 145 F3 *atoll* N Cook Islands
Rakaia 151 B6 *river* South Island, NZ
Rakka *see* Ar Raqqah
Rakke 106 E2 Lääne-Virumaa, NE Estonia
Rakvere 106 E2 Ger. Wesenberg. Lääne-Virumaa, N Estonia
Ralik Chain 144 D1 *island group* Ralik Chain, W Marshall Islands
Ramadi *see* Ar Ramādī
Ramlat Ahl Wahībah *see* Wahībah, Ramlat Āl
Ramlat Al Wahaybah *see* Wahībah, Ramlat Āl
Râmnicu Sărat 108 C4 *prev.* Râmnicul-Sărat, Rîmnicu-Sărat. Buzău, E Romania
Râmnicu Vâlcea 108 B4 *prev.* Rîmnicu Vîlcea. Vâlcea, C Romania
Ramree Island 136 A4 *island* W Myanmar
Ramtha *see* Ar Ramthā
Rancagua 64 B4 Libertador, C Chile
Rānchi 135 F4 Bihār, N India
Randers 85 B7 Århus, C Denmark
Rangiora 151 C6 Canterbury, South Island, NZ
Rangitikei 150 D4 *river* North Island, NZ
Rangoon *see* Yangon
Rangpur 135 G3 Rajshahi, N Bangladesh
Rankin Inlet 37 G3 Nunavut, C Canada
Ranong 137 B6 Ranong, SW Thailand
Rapa Nui *see* Easter Island
Raphiah *see* Rafah
Rapid City 44 D3 South Dakota, N USA
Räpina 106 E3 Ger. Rappin. Põlvamaa, SE Estonia
Rapla 106 D2 Ger. Rappel. Raplamaa, NW Estonia
Rarotonga 145 G5 *island* S Cook Islands, C Pacific Ocean
Ras al 'Ain *see* Ra's al 'Ayn
Ra's al 'Ayn 118 D1 *var.* Ras al 'Ain. Al Ḥasakah, N Syria
Ra's an Naqb 119 B7 Ma'ān, S Jordan
Raseiniai 106 B4 Raseiniai, C Lithuania
Ras Hafun *see* Xaafuun, Raas
Rasht 120 C2 *var.* Resht. Gīlān, NW Iran
Râşnov 108 C4 *prev.* Rîşno, Rozsnyó, *Hung.* Barcarozsnyó. Braşov, C Romania
Ratak Chain 144 D1 *island group* Ratak Chain, E Marshall Islands
Ratan 85 C5 Jämtland, C Sweden
Rat Buri *see* Ratchaburi
Ratchaburi 137 C5 *var.* Rat Buri. Ratchaburi, W Thailand
Rastenburg *see* Kętrzyn
Rat Islands 36 A2 *island group* Aleutian Islands, Alaska, USA

Ratlām 134 D4 *prev.* Rutlam. Madhya Pradesh, C India
Ratnapura 132 D4 Sabaragamuwa Province, S Sri Lanka
Raton 48 D1 New Mexico, SW USA
Rättvik 85 C5 Kopparberg, C Sweden
Raudhatain *see* Ar Rawḍatayn
Raufarhöfn 83 E4 Nordhurland Eystra, NE Iceland
Raukawa *see* Cook Strait
Raukumara Range 150 E3 *mountain range* North Island, NZ
Rāulakela 151 F4 *var.* Rāurkela, *prev.* Rourkela. Orissa, E India
Rauma 85 D5 *Swe.* Raumo. Länsi-Suomi, W Finland
Raurkela *see* Raulakela
Ravenna 96 C3 Emilia-Romagna, N Italy
Rāvi 134 C2 *river* India/Pakistan
Rāwalpindi 134 C1 Punjab, NE Pakistan
Rawa Mazowiecka 98 D4 Łódzkie, C Poland
Rawicz 98 C4 Ger. Rawitsch. Wielkopolskie, C Poland
Rawlins 44 C3 Wyoming, C USA
Rawson 65 C6 Chubut, SE Argentina
Rayak 118 B4 *var.* Rayaq, Riyāq. E Lebanon
Rayaq *see* Rayak
Rayleigh 43 F1 *state capital* North Carolina, SE USA
Rayong 137 C5 Rayong, S Thailand
Razāzah, Buhayrat ar 120 B3 *var.* Bahr al Milh. *Lake* C Iraq
Razgrad 104 D2 Razgrad, N Bulgaria
Razim, Lacul 108 D5 *prev.* Lacul Razelm. *Lagoon* NW Black Sea
Reading 89 D7 S England, UK
Reading 41 F4 Pennsylvania, NE USA
Realicó 64 C4 La Pampa, C Argentina
Reàng Kesei 137 D5 Bătdâmbâng, W Cambodia
Rebecca, Lake 147 C6 *lake* Western Australia
Rebiana Sand Sea *see* Rabyānah, Ramlat
Rebun-tō 130 C2 *island* NE Japan
Rechytsa 107 D7 *Rus.* Rechitsa. Brestskaya Voblasts', SW Belarus
Recife 63 H2 *prev.* Pernambuco. *State capital* Pernambuco, E Brazil
Recklinghausen 94 A4 Nordrhein-Westfalen, W Germany
Recogne 87 C7 Luxembourg, SE Belgium
Reconquista 64 D3 Santa Fe, C Argentina
Red Deer 37 E5 Alberta, SW Canada
Redding 47 B5 California, W USA
Redon 90 B4 Ille-et-Vilaine, NW France
Red River 136 C2 *var.* Yuan, *Chin.* Yuan Jiang, *Vtn.* Sông Hông Hà. *River* China/Vietnam
Red River 45 E1 *river* Canada/USA
Red River 42 B3 *river* Louisiana, S USA
Red River 35 C6 *river* S USA
Red Sea 72 C3 *anc.* Sinus Arabicus. *Sea* Africa/Asia
Red Wing 45 G2 Minnesota, N USA
Reefton 151 C5 West Coast, South Island, NZ
Reese River 47 C5 *river* Nevada, W USA
Refahiye 117 E3 Erzincan, C Turkey
Regensburg 95 C6 *Eng.* Ratisbon, *Fr.* Ratisbonne; *hist.* Ratisbona, *anc.* Castra Regina, Reginum. Bayern, SE Germany
Regenstauf 95 C6 Bayern, SE Germany
Reggane 70 D3 C Algeria
Reggio *see* Reggio nell' Emilia
Reggio Calabria *see* Reggio di Calabria
Reggio di Calabria 97 D7 *var.* Reggio Calabria, *Gk.* Rhegion; *anc.* Regium, Rhegium. Calabria, SW Italy

Reggio Emilia *see* Reggio nell' Emilia
Reggio nell' Emilia 96 B2 *var.* Reggio Emilia, *abbrev.* Reggio; *anc.* Regium Lepidum. Emilia-Romagna, N Italy
Reghin 108 C4 *Ger.* Sächsisch-Reen, *Hung.* Szászrégen; *prev.* Reghinul Săsesc, *Ger.* Sächsisch-Regen. Mureş, C Romania
Regina 37 F5 Saskatchewan, S Canada
Registan *see* Rīgestān
Regium *see* Reggio di Calabria
Regium Lepidum *see* Reggio nell' Emilia
Rehoboth *see* Reḥovot
Rehoboth 78 B3 Hardap, C Namibia
Reḥovot 119 A6 *var.* Rehoboth, Rehovoth, Rekhovot. Central, C Israel
Rehovoth *see* Reḥovot
Reid 147 D6 Western Australia
Reikjavik *see* Reykjavík
Ré, Île de 90 A4 *island* W France
Reims 90 D3 *Eng.* Rheims; *anc.* Durocortorum, Remi. Marne, N France
Reindeer Lake 37 F4 *lake* Manitoba/Saskatchewan, C Canada
Reinga, Cape 150 C1 *headland* North Island, NZ
Reinosa 92 D1 Cantabria, N Spain
Rekhovot *see* Reḥovot
Reliance 37 F4 Northwest Territories, C Canada
Rendina *see* Rentína
Rendsburg 94 B2 Schleswig-Holstein, N Germany
Rengat 138 B4 Sumatera, W Indonesia
Reni 108 D4 Odes'ka Oblast', SW Ukraine
Rennell 144 C3 *var.* Mu Nggava. *Island* S Solomon Islands
Rennes 90 B3 Bret. Roazon; *anc.* Condate. Ille-et-Vilaine, NW France
Reno 47 C5 Nevada, W USA
Renqiu 128 C2 Hebei, E China
Rentína 105 B5 *var.* Rendina. Thessalía, C Greece
Republika Srpska Admin. region *republic* Bosnia and Herzegovina
République Centrafricaine *see* Central African Republic
Repulse Bay 37 G3 Nunavut, N Canada
Resht *see* Rasht
Resistencia 64 D3 Chaco, NE Argentina
Reşiţa 108 A4 *Ger.* Reschitza, *Hung.* Resicabánya. Caraş-Severin, W Romania
Resolute 37 F2 Cornwallis Island, Nunavut, N Canada
Resolution Island 39 E1 *island* Northwest Territories, NE Canada
Resolution Island 151 A7 *island* SW NZ
Réunion 79 H4 *off.* La Réunion. *French overseas department* W Indian Ocean
Réunion 141 B5 *island* W Indian Ocean
Reus 93 F2 Cataluña, E Spain
Reutlingen 95 B6 Baden-Württemberg, S Germany
Reuver 87 D5 Limburg, SE Netherlands
Revillagigedo Islands *see* Revillagigedo, Islas
Revillagigedo, Islas 50 B5 *Eng.* Revillagigedo Islands. *Island group* W Mexico
Rexburg 46 E3 Idaho, NW USA
Reyes 61 F3 Beni, NW Bolivia
Rey, Isla del 53 G5 *island* Archipiélago de las Perlas, SE Panama
Reykjanes Basin 82 C5 *var.* Irminger Basin. *Undersea feature* N Atlantic Ocean
Reykjanes Ridge 80 A1 *undersea feature* N Atlantic Ocean

Reykjavík 83 E5 *var.* Reikjavik. *Country capital* (Iceland) Höfudhborgarsvaedhi, W Iceland
Reynosa 51 E2 Tamaulipas, C Mexico
Rezé 90 A4 Loire-Atlantique, NW France
Rēzekne 106 D4 *Ger.* Rositten; *prev.* Rus. Rezhitsa. Rēzekne, SE Latvia
Rezovo 104 E3 *Turk.* Rezve. Burgas, E Bulgaria
Rhegion *see* Reggio di Calabria
Rhegium *see* Reggio di Calabria
Rhein *see* Rhine
Rheine 94 A3 *var.* Rheine in Westfalen. Nordrhein-Westfalen, NW Germany
Rheine in Westfalen *see* Rheine
Rheinisches Schiefergebirge 95 A5 *var.* Rhine State Uplands, *Eng.* Rhenish Slate Mountains. *Mountain range* W Germany
Rhenish Slate Mountains *see* Rheinisches Schiefergebirge
Rhine 80 D4 *Dut.* Rijn, *Fr.* Rhin, *Ger.* Rhein. *River* W Europe
Rhinelander 40 B2 Wisconsin, N USA
Rhine State Uplands *see* Rheinisches Schiefergebirge
Rho 96 B2 Lombardia, N Italy
Rhode Island 41 G3 *off.* State of Rhode Island and Providence Plantations; *also known as* Little Rhody, Ocean State. *State* NE USA
Rhodes *see* Ródos
Rhodope Mountains 104 C3 *var.* Rodhópi, *Bul.* Rhodope Planina, Rodopi, *Gk.* Orosirá Rodhópis, *Turk.* Dospad Dagh. *Mountain range* Bulgaria/Greece
Rhodope Planina *see* Rhodope Mountains
Rhodos *see* Ródos
Rhône 80 D4 *river* France/Switzerland
Rhône 91 D6 *department* E France
Rhum 88 B3 *var.* Rum. *Island* W Scotland, UK
Ribble 89 D5 *river* NW England, UK
Ribeira 92 B1 Galicia, NW Spain
Ribeirão Preto 63 F4 São Paulo, S Brazil
Riberalta 61 F2 Beni, N Bolivia
Ribnița 108 D3 *var.* Râbnița, *Rus.* Rybnitsa. NE Moldova
Rice Lake 40 A2 Wisconsin, N USA
Richard Toll 74 B3 N Senegal
Richfield 44 B4 Utah, W USA
Richland 46 C2 Washington, NW USA
Richmond 41 E5 *state capital* Virginia, NE USA
Richmond 40 C5 Kentucky, S USA
Richmond 151 C5 Tasman, South Island, NZ
Richmond Range 151 C5 *mountain range* South Island, NZ
Ricobayo, Embalse de 92 C2 *reservoir* NW Spain
Ridgecrest 47 C7 California, W USA
Ried *see* Ried im Innkreis
Ried im Innkreis 95 D6 *var.* Ried. Oberösterreich, NW Austria
Riemst 87 D6 Limburg, NE Belgium
Riesa 94 D4 Sachsen, E Germany
Rift Valley *see* Great Rift Valley
Rīga 106 C3 *Eng.* Riga. *Country capital* (Latvia) Rīga, C Latvia
Riga, Gulf of 106 C3 *Est.* Liivi Laht, *Ger.* Rigaer Bucht, *Latv.* Rīgas Jūras Līcis, *Rus.* Rizhskiy Zaliv; *prev. Est.* Riia Laht. *Gulf* Estonia/Latvia
Rīgān 120 E4 Kermān, SE Iran
Rīgestān 122 D4 *var.* Registan. *Desert region* S Afghanistan
Riihimäki 85 D5 Etelä-Suomi, S Finland
Rijeka 100 A2 *Ger.* Sankt Veit am Flaum, *It.* Fiume, *Slvn.* Reka; *anc.* Tarsatica. Primorje-Gorski Kotar, NW Croatia
Rijssel *see* Lille
Rijssen 86 E3 Overijssel, E Netherlands

Rimah, Wādī ar 120 B4 var. Wādī ar
Rummah. Dry watercourse C Saudi
Arabia
Rimini 96 C3 anc. Ariminum.
Emilia-Romagna, N Italy
Rimouski 39 E4 Quebec,
SE Canada
Ringebu 85 B5 Oppland, S Norway
Ringkøbing Fjord 85 A7 fjord
W Denmark
Ringvassøya 84 C2 island N Norway
Rio see Rio de Janeiro
Riobamba 60 B1 Chimborazo,
C Ecuador
Rio Branco 56 B3 state capital Acre,
W Brazil
Río Bravo 51 E2 Tamaulipas,
C Mexico
Río Cuarto 64 C4 Córdoba,
C Argentina
Rio de Janeiro 63 F4 var. Rio. State
capital Rio de Janeiro, SE Brazil
Río Gallegos 65 B7 var. Gallegos,
Puerto Gallegos. Santa Cruz,
S Argentina
Rio Grande 63 E5 var. São Pedro do
Rio Grande do Sul. Rio Grande do
Sul, S Brazil
Río Grande 50 D3 Zacatecas,
C Mexico
Rio Grande do Norte 63 G2 off.
Estado do Rio Grande do Norte.
State E Brazil
Rio Grande do Sul 63 E5 off. Estado
do Rio Grande do Sul. State
S Brazil
Rio Grande Plateau see Rio Grande
Rise
Rio Grande Rise 57 E6 var. Rio
Grande Plateau. Undersea feature
SW Atlantic Ocean
Ríohacha 58 B1 La Guajira,
N Colombia
Río Lagartos 51 H3 Yucatán,
SE Mexico
Riom 91 C5 anc. Ricomagus. Puy-
de-Dôme, C France
Río San Juan 53 E4 department
S Nicaragua
Rioverde see Río Verde
Río Verde 51 F4 var. Rioverde. San
Luis Potosí, C Mexico
Ripoll 93 G2 Cataluña, NE Spain
Rishiri-tō 130 C2 var. Risiri Tô.
Island NE Japan
Risiri Tô see Rishiri-tō
Risti 106 D2 Ger. Kreuz. Läänemaa,
W Estonia
Rivas 52 D4 Rivas, SW Nicaragua
Rivera 64 D3 Rivera, NE
Uruguay
River Falls 40 A2 Wisconsin,
N USA
River Plate see Plata, Río de la
Riverside 47 C7 California, W USA
Riverton 151 A7 Southland, South
Island, NZ
Riverton 44 C3 Wyoming, C USA
Rivière-du-Loup 39 E4 Quebec,
SE Canada
Rivne 108 C2 Pol. Równe, Rus.
Rovno. Rivnens'ka Oblast',
NW Ukraine
Rivoli 96 A2 Piemonte, NW Italy
Riyadh see Ar Riyāḍ
Riyāq see Rayak
Rize 117 E2 Rize, NE Turkey
Rizhao 128 D4 Shandong, E China
Rkîz 74 C3 Trarza, W Mauritania
Road Town 55 F3 dependent territory
capital (British Virgin Islands)
Tortola, C British Virgin Islands
Roanne 91 C5 anc. Rodunma. Loire,
E France
Roanoke 41 E5 Virginia, NE USA
Roanoke River 43 F1 river North
Carolina/Virginia, SE USA
Roatán 52 C2 var. Coxen Hole,
Coxin Hole. Islas de la Bahía,
N Honduras
Robbie Ridge 143 E3 undersea
feature W Pacific Ocean
Robert Williams see Caála
Robinson Range 147 B5 mountain
range Western Australia
Robson, Mount 37 E5 mountain
British Columbia, SW Canada

Robstown 49 G4 Texas, SW USA
Roca Partida, Isla 50 B5 island
W Mexico
Rocas, Atol das 63 G2 island
E Brazil
Rochefort 90 B4 var. Rochefort sur
Mer. Charente-Maritime, W France
Rochefort 87 C7 Namur, SE Belgium
Rochefort sur Mer see Rochefort
Rochester 45 G3 Minnesota, N USA
Rochester 41 G2 New Hampshire,
NE USA
Rochester 41 E3 New York, NE USA
Rockall Bank 80 B2 undersea feature
N Atlantic Ocean
Rockall Trough 80 B2 undersea
feature N Atlantic Ocean
Rockdale 148 E2 New South Wales,
SE Australia
Rockford 40 B3 Illinois, N USA
Rockhampton 148 D4 Queensland,
E Australia
Rock Hill 43 E1 South Carolina,
SE USA
Rockies see Rocky Mountains
Rockingham 147 A6 Western
Australia
Rock Island 40 B3 Illinois, N USA
Rock Sound 54 C1 Eleuthera Island,
C Bahamas
Rock Springs 44 C3 Wyoming,
C USA
Rockstone 59 F3 C Guyana
Rocky Mount 43 F1 North Carolina,
SE USA
Rocky Mountains 34 B4 var.
Rockies, Fr. Montagnes
Rocheuses. Mountain range
Canada/USA
Roden 86 E2 Drenthe,
NE Netherlands
Rodez 91 C5 anc. Segodunum.
Aveyron, S France
Rodhópi Óri see Rhodope
Mountains
Ródhos see Ródos
Rodi see Ródos
Rodopi see Rhodope Mountains
Ródos 105 E7 var. Ródhos, Eng.
Rhodes, It. Rodi; anc. Rhodos.
Island Dodekánisos, Greece,
Aegean Sea
Roermond 87 D5 Limburg,
SE Netherlands
Roeselare 87 A6 Fr. Roulers; prev.
Rousselaere. West-Vlaanderen,
W Belgium
Rogatica 100 C4 Republika Srpska,
SE Bosnia and Herzegovina
Rogers 42 A1 Arkansas, C USA
Roger Simpson Island see
Abemama
Roi Et see Roi Et
Roi Et 137 D5 var. Muang Roi Et,
Roi Et. Roi Et, E Thailand
Roja 106 C2 Talsi, NW Latvia
Rokiškis 106 C4 Rokiškis,
NE Lithuania
Rokycany 99 A5 Ger. Rokytzan.
Plzeňský Kraj, W Czech Republic
Rokytzan see Rokycany
Rôlas, Ilha das 76 E2 island S Sao
Tome and Principe
Rolla 45 G5 Missouri, C USA
Roma 96 C4 Eng. Rome. Country
capital (Italy) Lazio, C Italy
Roma 149 D5 Queensland,
E Australia
Roman 108 C4 Hung. Románvásár.
Neamț, NE Romania
Roman 104 C2 Vratsa, NW Bulgaria
Romania 88 B4 Bul. Rumŭniya,
Ger. Rumänien, Hung. Románia,
Rom. România, SCr. Rumunija,
Ukr. Rumuniya; prev. Republica
Socialistă România, Roumania,
Rumania, Socialist Republic of
Romania, Rom. Romînia. Country
SE Europe

Romania 108

Official name Romania
Formation 1878
Capital Bucharest
Population 21.7 million / 237

Romania (continued)

Population 21.7 million / 237
people per sq mile (91 people
per sq km)
Total area 91,699 sq miles
(237,500 sq km)
Languages Romanian, Hungarian,
German, Romany
Religions Romanian Orthodox 87%,
Roman Catholic 5%, other 8%
Ethnic mix Romanian 89%, Magyar
9%, Romany 1%, other 1%
Government Multiparty republic
Currency Romanian Leu = 100 bani
Literacy rate 98.1%
Calorie consumption 3,274
kilocalories

Rome see Roma
Rome 42 D2 Georgia, SE USA
Romny 109 F2 Sums'ka Oblast',
NE Ukraine
Rømø 85 A7 Ger. Röm. Island
SW Denmark
Roncador, Serra do 56 D4 mountain
range C Brazil
Ronda 92 D5 Andalucía, S Spain
Rondônia 62 D3 off. Estado de
Rondônia; prev. Território de
Rondônia. State W Brazil
Rondonópolis 63 E3 Mato Grosso,
W Brazil
Rongelap Atoll 144 D1 var. Rönļap.
Atoll Ralik Chain, NW Marshall
Islands
Rõngu 106 D3 Ger. Ringen.
Tartumaa, SE Estonia
Rönļap see Rongelap Atoll
Rønne 85 B8 Bornholm,
E Denmark
Ronne Ice Shelf 154 A3 ice shelf
Antarctica
Roosendaal 87 C5 Noord-Brabant,
S Netherlands
Roosevelt Island 154 B4 island
Antarctica
Roraima 62 D1 off. Estado de
Roraima; prev. Território do Rio
Branco, Território de Roraima.
State N Brazil
Roraima, Mount 59 E3 mountain
N South America
Røros 85 B5 Sør-Trøndelag,
S Norway
Rosa, Lake 54 D2 lake Great Inagua,
S Bahamas
Rosario 64 D2 San Pedro,
C Paraguay
Rosario 64 D4 Santa Fe,
C Argentina
Rosarito 50 A1 Baja California,
NW Mexico
Roscommon 40 C2 Michigan,
N USA
Roseau 55 G4 prev. Charlotte Town.
Country capital (Dominica)
SW Dominica
Roseburg 46 B4 Oregon, NW USA
Rosenberg 49 G4 Texas, SW USA
Rosengarten 94 B3 Niedersachsen,
N Germany
Rosenheim 95 C6 Bayern,
S Germany
Rosia 93 H5 W Gibraltar
Rosia Bay 93 H5 bay SW Gibraltar
Roșiori de Vede 108 B5 Teleorman,
S Romania
Roslavl' 111 A5 Smolenskaya
Oblast', W Russian Federation
Rosmalen 86 C4 Noord-Brabant,
S Netherlands
Ross 151 B6 West Coast, South
Island, NZ
Rossano 97 E6 anc. Roscianum.
Calabria, SW Italy
Ross Ice Shelf 154 B4 ice shelf
Antarctica
Rosso 74 B3 Trarza, SW Mauritania
Rossosh' 111 B6 Voronezhskaya
Oblast', W Russian Federation
Ross Sea 154 B4 sea Antarctica
Rostak see Ar Rustāq
Rostock 94 C2 Mecklenburg-
Vorpommern, NE Germany
Rostov see Rostov-na-Donu

Rostov-na-Donu 111 B7 var. Rostov,
Eng. Rostov-on-Don. Rostovskaya
Oblast', SW Russian Federation
Rostov-on-Don see Rostov-na-
Donu
Roswell 48 D2 New Mexico,
SW USA
Rota 144 B1 island S Northern
Mariana Islands
Rothera 154 A2 UK research station
Antarctica
Rotorua 150 D3 Bay of Plenty,
North Island, NZ
Rotorua, Lake 150 D3 lake North
Island, NZ
Rotterdam 86 C4 Zuid-Holland,
SW Netherlands
Rottweil 95 B6 Baden-
Württemberg, S Germany
Rotuma 145 E4 island NW Fiji
Roubaix 90 C2 Nord, N France
Rouen 90 C3 anc. Rotomagus.
Seine-Maritime, N France
Round Rock 49 G3 Texas, SW USA
Rourkela see Râulakela
Roussillon 91 C6 cultural region
S France
Rouyn-Noranda 38 D4 Quebec,
SE Canada
Rovaniemi 84 D3 Lappi,
N Finland
Rovigo 96 C2 Veneto, NE Italy
Rovinj 100 A3 It. Rovigno. Istra,
NW Croatia
Rovuma, Rio 79 F2 var. Ruvuma.
River Mozambique/Tanzania see
also Ruvuma
Rovuma, Rio see Ruvuma
Roxas City 139 E2 Panay Island,
C Philippines
Royale, Isle 40 B1 island Michigan,
N USA
Royan 91 B5 Charente-Maritime,
W France
Rozdol'ne 109 F4 Rus. Razdolnoye.
Respublika Krym, S Ukraine
Rožňava 99 D6 Ger. Rosenau,
Hung. Rozsnyó. Košický Kraj,
E Slovakia
Ruapehu, Mount 150 D4 mountain
North Island, NZ
Ruapuke Island 151 B8 island
SW NZ
Ruatoria 150 E3 Gisborne, North
Island, NZ
Ruawai 150 D2 Northland, North
Island, NZ
Rubizhne 109 H3 Rus. Rubezhnoye.
Luhans'ka Oblast', E Ukraine
Ruby Mountains 47 D5 mountain
range Nevada, W USA
Rucava 106 B3 Liepāja, SW Latvia
Rūd-e Hīrmand see Helmand,
Daryā-ye
Rūdiškės 107 B5 Trakai,
S Lithuania
Rudnik 104 E2 Varna, E Bulgaria
Rudny see Rudnyy
Rudnyy 114 C4 var. Rudny.
Kostanay, N Kazakhstan
Rudolf, Lake see Turkana, Lake
Rudolfswert see Novo Mesto
Rudzyensk 107 C6 Rus. Rudensk.
Minskaya Voblasts', C Belarus
Rufiji 73 C7 river E Tanzania
Rufino 64 C4 Santa Fe, C Argentina
Rugāji 106 D4 Balvi, E Latvia
Rügen 94 D2 headland
NE Germany
Ruggell 94 E1 N Liechtenstein
Ruhnu 106 C2 var. Ruhnu Saar, Swe.
Runö. Island SW Estonia
Ruhnu Saar see Ruhnu
Rüjiena 106 D3 Est. Ruhja, Ger.
Rujen. Valmiera, N Latvia
Rukwa, Lake 73 B7 lake
SE Tanzania
Rum see Rhum
Ruma 100 D3 Serbia, N Serbia and
Montenegro (Yugo.)
Rumadiya see Ar Ramādī
Rumbek 73 B5 El Buhayrat,
S Sudan
Rum Cay 54 D2 island C Bahamas
Rumia 98 C2 Pomorskie, N Poland
Rummah, Wādī ar see Rimah,
Wādī ar

Runanga 151 B5 West Coast, South Island, NZ
Runaway Bay 54 B4 C Jamaica
Rundu 78 C3 var. Runtu. Okavango, NE Namibia
Runö see Ruhnu
Runtu see Rundu
Ruoqiang 126 C3 var. Jo-ch'iang, Uigh. Charkhlik, Charkhliq, Qarklilik. Xinjiang Uygur Zizhiqu, NW China
Rupea 108 C4 Ger. Reps, Hung. Kőhalom; prev. Cohalm. Braşov, C Romania
Rupel 87 B5 river N Belgium
Rupert, Rivière de 38 D3 river Quebec, C Canada
Ruschuk see Ruse
Rusçuk see Ruse
Ruse 104 D1 var. Ruschuk, Rustchuk, Turk. Rusçuk. Ruse, N Bulgaria
Rus Krymskaya ASSR see Crimea
Russellville 42 A1 Arkansas, C USA

Russian Federation 112

Official name Russian Federation
Formation 1991
Capital Moscow
Population 144.7 million / 22 people per sq mile (8 people per sq km)
Total area 6,592,735 sq miles (17,075,200 sq km)
Languages Russian
Religions Russian Orthodox 75%, other 25%
Ethnic mix Russian 82%, Tatar 4%, Ukranian 3%, Chavash 1%, other 10%
Government Presidential democracy
Currency Rouble = 100 kopeks
Literacy rate 99%
Calorie consumption 2,917 kilocalories

Rustaq see Ar Rustāq
Rust'avi 117 G2 SE Georgia
Rustchuk see Ruse
Ruston 42 B2 Louisiana, S USA
Rutanzige I M, Lake see Edward, Lake
Rutba see Ar Ruţbah
Rutland 41 F2 Vermont, NE USA
Rutog 126 A4 var. Rutok. Xizang Zizhiqu, W China
Rutok see Rutog
Ruvuma 69 E5 var. Rio Rovuma. River Mozambique/Tanzania see also Rovuma, Rio
Ruvuma see Rovuma, Rio
Ruwenzori 77 E5 mountain range Uganda/Dem. Rep. Congo
Ruzhany 107 B6 Rus. Ruzhany. Brestskaya Voblasts', SW Belarus
Ružomberok 99 C5 Ger. Rosenberg, Hung. Rózsahegy. Žilinsky Kraj, N Slovakia
Rwanda 73 B6 prev. Ruanda. Country C Africa

Rwanda 73

Official name Republic of Rwanda
Formation 1962
Capital Kigali
Population 7.9 million / 777 people per sq mile (300 people per sq km)
Total area 10,169 sq miles (26,338 sq km)
Languages French, Kinyarwanda, Kiswahili, English
Religions Roman Catholic 65%, Traditional beliefs 25%, Protestant 9%, Muslim 1%
Ethnic mix Hutu 90%, Tutsi 9%, other (including Twa) 1%

Rwanda (continued)

Government Transitional regime
Currency Rwanda franc = 100 centimes
Literacy rate 66.8%
Calorie consumption 2,077 kilocalories

Ryazan' 111 B5 Ryazanskaya Oblast', W Russian Federation
Rybinsk 110 B4 prev. Andropov. Yaroslavskaya Oblast', W Russian Federation
Rybnik 99 C5 Śląskie, S Poland
Rybnitsa see Rîbniţa
Ryde 104 E1 New South Wales, SE Australia
Ryki 98 D4 Lublin, E Poland
Rypin 98 C3 Kujawsko-pomorskie, C Poland
Ryssel see Lille
Rysy 99 C5 mountain S Poland
Ryukyu Islands 125 E3 island group SW Japan
Ryukyu Trench 125 F3 var. Nansei Syotō Trench. Undersea feature S East China Sea
Rzeszów 99 E5 Podkarpackie, SE Poland
Rzhev 110 B4 Tverskaya Oblast', W Russian Federation

S

Saale 94 C4 river C Germany
Saalfeld 95 C5 var. Saalfeld an der Saale. Thüringen, C Germany
Saalfeld an der Saale see Saalfeld
Saarbrücken 95 A6 Fr. Sarrebruck. Saarland, SW Germany
Säare 106 C2 var. Sjar. Saaremaa, W Estonia
Saaremaa 106 C2 Ger. Oesel, Ösel; prev. Saare. Island W Estonia
Saariselkä 84 D2 Lapp. Suoločielgi. Lappi, N Finland
Sab' Abar 118 C4 var. Sab'a Biyar, Sa'b Bi'ār. Ḩimş, C Syria
Sab'a Biyar see Sab' Ābār
Šabac 100 D3 Serbia, W Serbia and Montenegro (Yugo.)
Sabadell 93 G2 Cataluña, E Spain
Sabah 138 D3 cultural region Borneo, SE Asia
Sabanalarga 58 B1 Atlántico, N Colombia
Sabaneta 58 C1 Falcón, N Venezuela
Sab'atayn, Ramlat as 121 C6 desert C Yemen
Sabaya 61 F4 Oruro, S Bolivia
Sa'b Bi'ār see Sab' Ābār
Şāberī, Hāmūn-e var. Daryācheh-ye Hāmūn, Daryācheh-ye Sīstān. Lake Afghanistan/Iran see also Sīstān, Daryācheh-ye
Sabhā 71 F3 C Libya
Sabi, Rio see Save, Rio
Sabinas 51 E2 Coahuila de Zaragoza, NE Mexico
Sabinas Hidalgo 51 E2 Nuevo León, NE Mexico
Sabine River 49 H3 river Louisiana/Texas, SW USA
Sabkha see As Sabkhah
Sable, Cape 43 E5 headland Florida, SE USA
Sable Island 39 G4 island Nova Scotia, SE Canada
Şabyā 121 B6 Jīzān, SW Saudi Arabia
Sabzawar see Sabzevār
Sabzevār 120 D2 var. Sabzawar. Khorāsān, NE Iran
Sachsen 94 D4 Eng. Saxony, Fr. Saxe. State E Germany
Sachs Harbour 37 E2 Banks Island, Northwest Territories, N Canada
Sacramento 47 B5 state capital California, W USA
Sacramento Mountains 48 D2 mountain range New Mexico, SW USA
Sacramento River 47 B5 river California, W USA

Sacramento Valley 47 B5 valley California, W USA
Şa'dah 121 B6 NW Yemen
Sado 131 C5 var. Sadoga-shima. Island C Japan
Sadoga-shima see Sado
Safad see Zefat
Safed see Zefat
Säffle 85 B6 Värmland, C Sweden
Safford 48 C3 Arizona, SW USA
Safi 70 B2 W Morocco
Safid Kūh, Selseleh-ye 122 D4 Eng. Paropamisus Range. Mountain range W Afghanistan
Sagaing 136 B3 Sagaing, C Myanmar
Sagami-nada 131 D6 inlet SW Japan
Sagan see Żagań
Sāgar 134 D4 prev. Saugor. Madhya Pradesh, C India
Saghez see Saqqez
Saginaw 40 C3 Michigan, N USA
Saginaw Bay 40 D2 lake bay Michigan, N USA
Sagua la Grande 54 B2 Villa Clara, C Cuba
Sagunt see Sagunto
Sagunto 93 F3 var. Sagunt, Ar. Murviedro; anc. Saguntum. País Valenciano, E Spain
Saguntum see Sagunto
Sahara 68 B3 desert Libya/Algeria
Sahara el Gharbîya 72 B2 var. Aş Şaḩrā' al Gharbīyah, Eng. Western Desert. Desert C Egypt
Saharan Atlas see Atlas Saharien
Sahel 74 D3 physical region C Africa
Sāḩiliyah, Jibāl as 118 B3 mountain range NW Syria
Sāhīwāl 134 C2 prev. Montgomery. Punjab, E Pakistan
şahrā' Rabyanāh see Rabyanāh, Ramlat
Saïda 119 A5 var. Şaydā, Sayida; anc. Sidon. W Lebanon
Saidpur 135 G3 var. Syedpur. Rajshahi, NW Bangladesh
Saigon see Hồ Chi Minh
Sai Hun see Syr Darya
Saimaa 85 E5 lake SE Finland
St Albans 89 E6 anc. Verulamium. E England, UK
Saint Albans 40 D5 West Virginia, NE USA
St Andrews 88 C4 E Scotland, UK
Saint Anna Trough see Svyataya Anna Trough
St.Ann's Bay 54 B4 C Jamaica
St.Anthony 39 G3 Newfoundland, Newfoundland and Labrador, SE Canada
Saint Augustine 43 E3 Florida, SE USA
St Austell 89 C7 SW England, UK
St-Brieuc 90 A3 Côtes d'Armor, NW France
St. Catharines 38 D5 Ontario, S Canada
St-Chamond 91 D5 Loire, E France
St.Clair, Lake 40 D3 Fr. Lac à L'Eau Claire. Lake Canada/USA
St-Claude 91 D5 anc. Condate. Jura, E France
Saint Cloud 45 F2 Minnesota, N USA
St Croix 55 F3 island S Virgin Islands (US)
Saint Croix River 40 A2 river Minnesota/Wisconsin, N USA
St David's Island 42 B5 island E Bermuda
St-Denis 79 G4 dependent territory capital (Réunion) NW Réunion
St-Dié 90 E4 Vosges, NE France
St-Egrève 91 D5 Isère, E France
Saintes 91 B5 anc. Mediolanum. Charente-Maritime, W France
St-Étienne 91 D5 Loire, E France
St-Flour 91 C5 Cantal, C France
Saint Gall see Sankt Gallen
St-Gaudens 91 B6 Haute-Garonne, S France
St George 42 B4 N Bermuda
Saint George 109 D5 Queensland, E Australia
Saint George 44 A5 Utah, W USA
St.George's 55 G5 country capital (Grenada) SW Grenada

St-Georges 59 H3 E French Guiana
St-Georges 39 E4 Quebec, SE Canada
St George's Channel 89 B6 channel Ireland/Wales, UK
St George's Island 42 B4 island E Bermuda
Saint Helena 69 B6 UK dependent territory C Atlantic Ocean
St.Helena Bay 78 B5 bay SW South Africa
St Helier 89 D8 dependent territory capital (Jersey) S Jersey, Channel Islands
Saint Ignace 40 C2 Michigan, N USA
St-Jean, Lac 39 E4 lake Quebec, SE Canada
Saint Joe River 46 D2 river Idaho, NW USA
Saint John 41 H1 river Canada/USA
Saint John 39 F4 New Brunswick, SE Canada
St John's 55 G3 country capital (Antigua and Barbuda) Antigua, Antigua and Barbuda
St.John's 39 H3 Newfoundland, Newfoundland and Labrador, E Canada
Saint Joseph 45 F4 Missouri, C USA
St Julian's 102 B5 N Malta
St Kilda 88 A3 island NW Scotland, UK
Saint Kitts and Nevis 55 F3 var. Saint Christopher-Nevis. Country E West Indies

Saint Kitts & Nevis 55

Official name Federation of Saint Christopher and Nevis
Formation 1983
Capital Basseterre
Population 41,000 / 407 people per sq mile (157 people per sq km)
Languages English, English Creole
Religions Anglican 33%, Methodist 29%, Moravian 9%, Roman Catholic 7%, other 22%
Ethnic mix Black 94%, Mixed 3%, Other and Amerindian 2%, other 1%
Government Parliamentary democracy
Currency Eastern Caribbean dollar = 100 cents
Literacy rate 90%
Calorie consumption 2,685 kilocalories

St-Laurent-du-Maroni 59 H3 var. St-Laurent. NW French Guiana
St.Lawrence 39 E4 Fr. Fleuve St-Laurent. River Canada/USA
St.Lawrence, Gulf of 39 F3 gulf NW Atlantic Ocean
Saint Lawrence Island 36 B2 island Alaska, USA
St-Lô 90 B3 anc. Briovera, Laudus. Manche, N France
St-Louis 90 E4 Haut-Rhin, NE France
Saint Louis 45 G4 Missouri, C USA
Saint Louis 74 B3 NW Senegal
Saint Lucia 55 E1 country SE West Indies

Saint Lucia 55

Official name Saint Lucia
Formation 1979
Capital Castries
Population 156,300 / 653 people per sq mile (252 people per sq km)
Total area 239 sq miles (620 sq km)
Languages English, French Creole
Religions Roman Catholic 90%, other 10%
Ethnic mix Black 90%, Mulatto 6%, Asian 3%, White 1%
Government Parliamentary democracy
Currency Eastern Caribbean dollar = 100 cents

Saint Lucia (continued)

Literacy rate 82%
Calorie consumption 2,838
kilocalories

Saint Lucia Channel 55 H4 channel
Martinique/Saint Lucia
St-Malo 90 B3 Ille-et-Vilaine,
NW France
St-Malo, Golfe de 90 A3 gulf
NW France
St Matthew's Island see Zadetkyi
Kyun
St.Matthias Group 144 B3 island
group NE PNG
St-Maur-des-Fossés 90 E2 Val-de-
Marne, N France
St.Moritz 95 B7 Ger. Sankt Moritz,
Rmsch. San Murezzan.
Graubünden, SE Switzerland
St-Nazaire 90 A4 Loire-Atlantique,
NW France
St-Omer 90 C2 Pas-de-Calais,
N France
Saint Paul 45 F2 state capital
Minnesota, N USA
St-Paul, Île 141 C6 var. St.Paul
Island. Island NE French Southern
and Antarctic Territories
St Peter Port 89 D8 dependent
territory capital (Guernsey)
C Guernsey, Channel Islands
Saint Petersburg see Sankt-
Peterburg
Saint Petersburg 43 E4 Florida,
SE USA
St-Pierre and Miquelon 35 E5 Fr.
Îles St-Pierre et Miquelon. French
territorial collectivity NE North
America
St-Quentin 90 C3 Aisne,
N France
Saint Vincent 55 G4 island
N Saint Vincent and the
Grenadines
Saint Vincent and the Grenadines
55 H4 country SE West Indies

Saint Vincent & The
Grenadines 55

Official name Saint Vincent and the
Grenadines
Formation 1979
Capital Kingston
Population 115,500 / 769 people
per sq mile (297 people per sq km)
Total area 150 sq miles (389 sq km)
Languages English, English Creole
Religions Anglican 42%,
Methodist 20%, Roman Catholic
19%, other 19%
Ethnic mix Black 66%, Mulatto 19%,
Asian 6%, White 4%, other 5%
Government Parliamentary
democracy
Currency Eastern Caribbean dollar
= 100 cents
Literacy rate 82%
Calorie consumption 2,579
kilocalories

Saint Vincent Passage 55 H4
passage Saint Lucia/Saint Vincent
and the Grenadines
Saipan 142 B1 island country capital
(Northern Mariana Islands)
S Northern Mariana Islands
Sajama, Nevado 61 F4 mountain
W Bolivia
Sajószentpéter 99 D6 Borsod-
Abaúj-Zemplén, NE Hungary
Sakākah 120 B4 Al Jawf, NW Saudi
Arabia
Sakakawea, Lake 44 D1 reservoir
North Dakota, N USA
Sakata 130 D4 Yamagata, Honshū,
C Japan
Sakhalin see Sakhalin, Ostrov
Sakhalin, Ostrov 115 G4 var.
Sakhalin. Island SE Russian
Federation
Sakhon Nakhon see Sakon Nakhon
Şäki 117 G2 Rus. Sheki; prev.
Nukha. NW Azerbaijan

Sakishima-shotō 130 A3 var.
Sakisima Syotô. Island group
SW Japan
Sakisima Syotô see Sakishima-shotō
Sakiz see Saqqez
Sakiz-Adasi see Chíos
Sakon Nakhon 136 D4 var. Muang
Sakon Nakhon, Sakhon Nakhon.
Sakon Nakhon, E Thailand
Saky 109 F5 Rus. Saki. Respublika
Krym, S Ukraine
Sal 74 A3 island Ilhas de Barlavento,
NE Cape Verde
Sala 85 C6 Västmanland, C Sweden
Salacgrīva 106 C3 Est. Salatsi.
Limbaži, N Latvia
Sala Consilina 97 D5 Campania,
S Italy
Salado, Río 63 C7 river C Argentina
Salado, Río 62 D5 river E Argentina
Şalālah 121 D6 SW Oman
Salamá 52 B2 Baja Verapaz,
C Guatemala
Salamanca 92 D2 anc. Helmantica,
Salmantica. Castilla-León,
NW Spain
Salamanca 64 B4 Coquimbo, C Chile
Salamīyah 118 B3 var. As
Salamīyah. Ḥamāh, W Syria
Salang see Phuket
Salantai 106 B3 Kretinga,
NW Lithuania
Salavan 137 D5 var. Saravan,
Saravane. Salavan, S Laos
Salavat 111 D6 Respublika
Bashkortostan, W Russian
Federation
Sala y Gomez 153 F4 island Chile,
E Pacific Ocean
Sala y Gomez Fracture Zone see
Sala y Gomez Ridge
Sala y Gomez Ridge 153 G4 var.
Sala y Gomez Fracture Zone.
Tectonic feature SE Pacific Ocean
Šalčininkai 107 C5 Šalčininkai,
SE Lithuania
Saldus 106 B3 Ger. Frauenburg.
Saldus, W Latvia
Sale 149 C7 Victoria, SE Australia
Salé 70 C2 NW Morocco
Salekhard 114 D3 prev. Obdorsk.
Yamalo-Nenetskiy Avtonomnyy
Okrug, N Russian Federation
Salem 46 B3 state capital Oregon,
NW USA
Salem 132 C2 Tamil Nādu, SE India
Salerno 97 D5 anc. Salernum.
Campania, S Italy
Salerno, Golfo di 97 C5 Eng. Gulf
of Salerno. Gulf S Italy
Salihorsk 107 C7 Rus. Soligorsk.
Minskaya Voblasts', S Belarus
Salima 79 E2 Central, C Malawi
Salina 45 E5 Kansas, C USA
Salina Cruz 51 F5 Oaxaca,
SE Mexico
Salinas 47 B6 California, W USA
Salinas 60 A2 Guayas, W Ecuador
Salisbury 89 D7 var. New Sarum.
S England, UK
Sallyana see Salyan
Salmon River 46 D3 river Idaho,
NW USA
Salmon River Mountains 46 D3
mountain range Idaho, NW USA
Salo 85 D6 Länsi-Suomi, W
Finland
Salon-de-Provence 91 D6 Bouches-
du-Rhône, SE France
Salonta 108 A3 Hung.
Nagyszalonta. Bihor, W Romania
Sal'sk 111 B7 Rostovskaya Oblast',
SW Russian Federation
Salt see As Salt
Salta 64 C2 Salta, NW Argentina
Saltash 89 C7 SW England, UK
Saltillo 51 E3 Coahuila de
Zaragoza, NE Mexico
Salt Lake City 44 B4 state capital
Utah, W USA
Salto 64 D3 Salto, N Uruguay
Salton Sea 47 D8 lake California,
W USA
Salvador 63 G3 prev. São Salvador.
Bahia, E Brazil
Salween 124 C2 Bur. Thanlwin,
Chin. Nu Chiang, Nu Jiang. River
SE Asia

Salyan 135 E3 var. Sallyana. Mid
Western, W Nepal
Salzburg 95 D6 anc. Juvavum.
Salzburg, N Austria
Salzgitter 94 C4 prev. Watenstedt-
Salzgitter. Niedersachsen,
C Germany
Salzwedel 94 C3 Sachsen-Anhalt,
N Germany
Šamac see Bosanski Šamac
Samakhixai 137 E5 var. Attapu,
Attopeu. Attapu, S Laos
Samalayuca 50 C1 Chihuahua,
N Mexico
Samar 139 F2 island C Philippines
Samara 111 C6 prev. Kuybyshev.
Samarskaya Oblast', W Russian
Federation
Samarang see Semarang
Samarinda 138 D4 Borneo,
C Indonesia
Samarqand 123 E2 Rus. Samarkand.
Samarqand Wiloyati,
C Uzbekistan
Samawa see As Samāwah
Sambalpur 135 F4 Orissa, E India
Sambava 79 G2 Antsirañana,
NE Madagascar
Sambir 108 B2 Rus. Sambor.
L'vivs'ka Oblast', NW Ukraine
Sambre 90 D2 river Belgium/France
Samfya 78 D2 Luapula, N Zambia
Saminatal 94 E2 valley
Austria/Liechtenstein
Samnān see Semnān
Sam Neua see Xam Nua
Samoa 145 E4 var. Sāmoa; prev.
Western Samoa. Country
W Polynesia

Samoa 145

Official name Independent State of
Samoa
Formation 1962
Capital Apia
Population 159,000 / 144 people per
sq mile (56 people per sq km)
Total area 1,104 sq miles
(2,860 sq km)
Languages Samoan, English
Religions Christian 99%, other 1%
Ethnic mix Polynesian 90%,
Euronesian 9%, other 1%
Government Parliamentary
democracy
Currency Tala = 100 sene
Literacy rate 80.2%
Calorie consumption not available

Samoa Basin 143 E3 undersea feature
W Pacific Ocean
Samobor 100 A2 Zagreb, N Croatia
Sámos 105 E6 prev. Limín Vathéos.
Sámos, Dodekánisos, Greece,
Aegean Sea
Sámos 105 D6 island Dodekánisos,
Greece, Aegean Sea
Samosch see Someş
Samothráki 104 C4 anc.
Samothrace. Island NE Greece
Samothráki 104 D4 Samothráki,
NE Greece
Sampit 138 C4 Borneo, C Indonesia
Samsun 116 D2 anc. Amisus.
Samsun, N Turkey
Samtredia 117 F2 W Georgia
Samui, Ko 137 C6 island
SW Thailand
Samut Prakan 137 C5 var. Muang
Samut Prakan, Paknam. Samut
Prakan, C Thailand
San 59 E5 river SE Poland
San 74 D3 Ségou, C Mali
Şan'ā' 121 B6 Eng. Sana. Country
capital (Yemen) W Yemen
Sana 100 B3 river NW Bosnia and
Herzegovina
Sanae see Şan'ā'
Sanae 154 B2 South African research
station Antarctica
Sanaga 77 B5 river C Cameroon
San Ambrosio Island. Island W Chile
San Ambrosio, Isla 57 A5 Eng. San
Ambrosio Island. Island W Chile
Sanandaj 120 C3 prev. Sinneh.
Kordestān, W Iran

San Andrés, Isla de 53 F3 island
NW Colombia
San Andrés Tuxtla 51 F4 var. Tuxtla.
Veracruz-Llave, E Mexico
San Angelo 49 F3 Texas, SW USA
San Antonio 49 F4 Texas, SW USA
San Antonio 52 B2 Toledo, S Belize
San Antonio 64 B4 Valparaíso,
C Chile
San Antonio Oeste 65 C5 Río
Negro, E Argentina
San Antonio River 49 G4 river
Texas, SW USA
Sanāw 121 C6 var. Sanaw.
NE Yemen
San Benedicto, Isla 50 B4 island
W Mexico
San Benito 52 B1 Petén,
N Guatemala
San Benito 49 G5 Texas, SW USA
San Bernardino 47 C7 California,
W USA
San Blas 50 C3 Sinaloa, C Mexico
San Blas, Cape 42 D3 headland
Florida, SE USA
San Blas, Cordillera de 53 G4
mountain range NE Panama
San Carlos see Quesada
San Carlos 48 B2 Arizona, SW USA
San Carlos 52 D4 Río San Juan,
S Nicaragua
San Carlos de Bariloche 65 B5 Río
Negro, SW Argentina
San Carlos del Zulia 58 C2 Zulia,
W Venezuela
San Clemente Island 47 B8 island
Channel Islands, California,
W USA
San Cristobal 144 C4 var. Makira.
Island SE Solomon Islands
San Cristóbal see San Cristóbal de
Las Casas
San Cristóbal 58 C2 Táchira,
W Venezuela
San Cristóbal de Las Casas 51 G5
var. San Cristóbal. Chiapas,
SE Mexico
San Cristóbal, Isla 60 B5 var.
Chatham Island. Island Galapagos
Islands, Ecuador, E Pacific Ocean
Sancti Spíritus 54 B2 Sancti
Spíritus, C Cuba
Sandakan 138 D3 Sabah, East
Malaysia
Sandanski 104 C3 prev. Sveti Vrach.
Blagoevgrad, SW Bulgaria
Sanday 88 D2 island NE Scotland,
UK
Sanders 48 C2 Arizona, SW USA
Sand Hills 44 D3 mountain range
Nebraska, C USA
San Diego 47 C8 California, W USA
Sandnes 85 A6 Rogaland,
S Norway
Sandomierz 98 D4 Rus. Sandomir.
Świętokrzyskie, C Poland
Sandoway 136 A4 Arakan State,
W Myanmar
Sandpoint 46 C1 Idaho, NW USA
Sand Springs 49 G1 Oklahoma,
C USA
Sandusky 40 D3 Ohio, N USA
Sandvika 85 A6 Akershus,
S Norway
Sandviken 85 C6 Gävleborg,
C Sweden
Sandy Bay 93 H7 bay E Gibraltar
Sandy City 44 B4 Utah, W USA
Sandy Lake 38 B3 lake Ontario,
C Canada
San Esteban 52 D2 Olancho,
C Honduras
San Felipe 58 D1 Yaracuy,
NW Venezuela
San Felipe de Puerto Plata see
Puerto Plata
San Félix, Isla 57 A5 Eng. San Felix
Island. Island W Chile
San Fernando 92 C5 prev. Isla de
León. Andalucía, S Spain
San Fernando 58 D2 var. San
Fernando de Apure. Apure,
C Venezuela
San Fernando 46 D1 California,
W USA
San Fernando 55 H5 Trinidad,
Trinidad and Tobago

San Fernando de Apure *see* San Fernando
San Fernando del Valle de Catamarca 64 C3 *var.* Catamarca. Catamarca, NW Argentina
San Fernando de Monte Cristi *see* Monte Cristi
San Francisco 47 B6 California, W USA
San Francisco del Oro 50 C2 Chihuahua, N Mexico
San Francisco de Macorís 55 E3 C Dominican Republic
San Gabriel 60 B1 Carchi, N Ecuador
San Gabriel Mountains 46 E1 *mountain range* California, W USA
Sangir, Kepulauan 139 F3 *var.* Kepulauan Sangihe. *Island group* N Indonesia
Sāngli 132 B1 Mahārāshtra, W India
Sangmélima 77 B5 Sud, S Cameroon
Sangre de Cristo Mountains 48 D1 *mountain range* Colorado/New Mexico, C USA
San Ignacio 52 B1 *prev.* Cayo, El Cayo. Cayo, W Belize
San Ignacio 50 B2 Baja California Sur, W Mexico
San Ignacio 61 F3 Beni, N Bolivia
San Joaquin Valley 47 B7 *valley* California, W USA
San Jorge, Golfo 65 C6 *var.* Gulf of San Jorge. *Gulf* S Argentina
San Jorge, Gulf of *see* San Jorge, Golfo
San José *see* San José del Guaviare
San José 47 B6 California, W USA
San José 52 B3 *var.* Puerto San José. Escuintla, S Guatemala
San José 61 G3 *var.* San José de Chiquitos. Santa Cruz, E Bolivia
San José 53 E4 *country capital* (Costa Rica) San José, C Costa Rica
San José de Chiquitos *see* San José
San José de Cúcuta *see* Cúcuta
San José del Guaviare 58 C4 *var.* San José. Guaviare, S Colombia
San Juan 55 F3 *dependent territory capital* (Puerto Rico) NE Puerto Rico
San Juan *see* San Juan de los Morros
San Juan 64 B4 San Juan, W Argentina
San Juan Bautista 64 D3 Misiones, S Paraguay
San Juan Bautista Tuxtepec *see* Tuxtepec
San Juan de Alicante 93 F4 País Valenciano, E Spain
San Juan del Norte 53 E4 *var.* Greytown. Río San Juan, SE Nicaragua
San Juan de los Morros 58 D2 *var.* San Juan. Guárico, N Venezuela
San Juanito, Isla 50 C4 *island* C Mexico
San Juan Mountains 48 D1 *mountain range* Colorado, C USA
San Juan River 48 C1 *river* Colorado/Utah, W USA
San Julián *see* Puerto San Julián
Sankt Gallen 95 B7 *var.* St.Gallen, *Eng.* Saint Gall, *Fr.* St-Gall. Sankt Gallen, NE Switzerland
Sankt-Peterburg 110 B4 *prev.* Leningrad, Petrograd, *Eng.* Saint Petersburg, *Fin.* Pietari. Leningradskaya Oblast', NW Russian Federation
Sankt Pölten 95 E6 Niederösterreich, N Austria
Sankuru 77 D6 *river* C Dem. Rep. Congo
Şanlıurfa 117 E4 *prev.* Sanli Urfa, Urfa, *anc.* Edessa. Şanlıurfa, S Turkey
San Lorenzo 60 A1 Esmeraldas, N Ecuador
San Lorenzo 61 G5 Tarija, S Bolivia
San Lorenzo, Isla 60 C4 *island* W Peru
Sanlúcar de Barrameda 92 C5 Andalucía, S Spain

San Luis 50 A1 *var.* San Luis Río Colorado. Sonora, NW Mexico
San Luis 52 B2 Petén, NE Guatemala
San Luis 64 C4 San Luis, C Argentina
San Luis Obispo 47 B7 California, W USA
San Luis Potosí 51 E3 San Luis Potosí, C Mexico
San Luis Río Colorado *see* San Luis
San Marcos 52 A2 San Marcos, W Guatemala
San Marcos 49 G4 Texas, SW USA
San Marino 96 D1 *Country* S Europe

San Marino 96

Official name Republic of San Marino
Formation 1631
Capital San Marino
Population 26,900 / 1,138 people per sq mile (440 people per sq km)
Total area 24 sq miles (61 sq km)
Languages Italian
Religions Roman Catholic 93%, other and non-religious 7%
Ethnic mix Sammarinese 80%, Italian 19%, other 1%
Government Parliamentary democracy
Currency Euro (Lira until 2002)
Literacy rate 99%
Calorie consumption not available

San Marino 96 E1 *country capital* (San Marino) C San Marino
San Martín 154 A2 *Argentinian research station* Antarctica
San Mateo 59 E2 Anzoátegui, NE Venezuela
San Matías 61 H3 Santa Cruz, E Bolivia
San Matías, Golfo 65 C5 *var.* Gulf of San Matías. *Gulf* E Argentina
San Matías, Gulf of *see* San Matías, Golfo
Sanmenxia 128 C4 *var.* Shan Xian. Henan, C China
San Miguel 50 D2 Coahuila de Zaragoza, N Mexico
San Miguel 52 C3 San Miguel, SE El Salvador
San Miguel de Ibarra *see* Ibarra
San Miguel de Tucumán 64 C3 *var.* Tucumán. Tucumán, N Argentina
San Miguelito 53 G4 Panamá, C Panama
San Miguel, Río 61 G3 *river* E Bolivia
Sannär *see* Sennar
Sānnicolaul-Mare *see* Sânnicolau Mare
Sânnicolau Mare 108 A4 *var.* Sânnicolaul-Mare, *Hung.* Nagyszentmiklós; *prev.* Sânmiclăuş Mare, Sînnicolau Mare. Timiş, W Romania
Sanok 99 E5 Podkarpackie, SE Poland
San Pablo 61 F5 Potosí, S Bolivia
San Pedro 50 D3 *var.* San Pedro de las Colonias. Coahuila de Zaragoza, NE Mexico
San Pedro 52 C1 Corozal, NE Belize
San-Pédro 74 D5 S Côte d'Ivoire
San Pedro de la Cueva 50 C2 Sonora, NW Mexico
San Pedro de las Colonias *see* San Pedro
San Pedro de Lloc 60 B3 La Libertad, NW Peru
San Pedro Mártir, Sierra 50 A1 *mountain range* NW Mexico
San Pedro Sula 52 C2 Cortés, NW Honduras
San Rafael 64 B4 Mendoza, W Argentina
San Rafael Mountains 47 C7 *mountain range* California, W USA
San Ramón de la Nueva Orán 64 C2 Salta, N Argentina

San Remo 96 A3 Liguria, NW Italy
San Salvador 52 B3 *country capital* (El Salvador) San Salvador, SW El Salvador
San Salvador de Jujuy 64 C2 *var.* Jujuy. Jujuy, N Argentina
San Salvador, Isla 60 A4 *prev.* Watlings Island. *Island* E Bahamas
Sansanné-Mango 75 E4 *var.* Mango. N Togo
Sansepolcro 96 C3 Toscana, C Italy
San Severo 97 D5 Puglia, SE Italy
Santa Ana 61 F3 Beni, N Bolivia
Santa Ana 46 D2 California, W USA
Santa Ana 52 B3 Santa Ana, NW El Salvador
Santa Ana Mountains 46 E2 *mountain range* California, W USA
Santa Barbara 47 C7 California, W USA
Santa Barbara 50 C2 Chihuahua, N Mexico
Santa Catalina Island 47 B8 *island* Channel Islands, California, W USA
Santa Catarina 63 E5 *off.* Estado de Santa Catarina. *State* S Brazil
Santa Clara 54 B2 Villa Clara, C Cuba
Santa Clarita 46 D1 California, W USA
Santa Comba 92 B1 Galicia, NW Spain
Santa Cruz 61 G4 *var.* Santa Cruz de la Sierra. Santa Cruz, C Bolivia
Santa Cruz 47 B6 California, W USA
Santa Cruz 76 F2 São Tomé, E Sao Tome and Principe
Santa Cruz Barillas *see* Barillas
Santa Cruz de la Sierra *see* Santa Cruz
Santa Cruz del Quiché 52 B2 Quiché, W Guatemala
Santa Cruz de Tenerife 70 A3 Tenerife, Islas Canarias, Spain, NE Atlantic Ocean
Santa Cruz, Isla 60 B5 *var.* Indefatigable Island, Isla Chávez. *Island* Galapagos Islands, Ecuador, E Pacific Ocean
Santa Cruz Islands 144 D3 *island group* E Solomon Islands
Santa Cruz, Río 65 B7 *river* S Argentina
Santa Elena 52 B1 Cayo, W Belize
Santa Fe 48 D1 *state capital* New Mexico, SW USA
Santa Fe 64 C4 Santa Fe, C Argentina
Santa Genoveva 50 B3 *mountain* W Mexico
Santa Isabel 144 C3 *var.* Bughotu. *Island* N Solomon Islands
Santa Lucia Range 47 B7 *mountain range* California, W USA
Santa Margarita, Isla 50 B3 *island* W Mexico
Santa Maria 92 A5 *island* Azores, Portugal, NE Atlantic Ocean
Santa Maria 47 B7 California, W USA
Santa Maria 63 E5 Rio Grande do Sul, S Brazil
Santa María, Isla 60 A5 *var.* Isla Floreana, Charles Island. *Island* Galapagos Islands, Ecuador, E Pacific Ocean
Santa Marta 58 B1 Magdalena, N Colombia
Santa Monica 46 D1 California, W USA
Santana 76 E2 São Tomé, S Sao Tome and Principe
Santander 92 D1 Cantabria, N Spain
Santanilla, Islas 53 E1 *Eng.* Swan Islands. *Island* NE Honduras
Santarém 92 B3 *anc.* Scalabis. Santarém, W Portugal
Santarém 63 E2 Pará, N Brazil
Santa Rosa *see* Santa Rosa de Copán
Santa Rosa 47 B6 California, W USA
Santa Rosa 64 C4 La Pampa, C Argentina
Santa Rosa de Copán 52 C2 *var.* Santa Rosa. Copán, W Honduras

Santa Rosa Island 47 B8 *island* California, W USA
Sant Carles de la Ràpida *see* Sant Carles de la Ràpita
Sant Carles de la Ràpita 93 F3 *var.* Sant Carles de la Ràpida. Cataluña, NE Spain
Santiago 64 B4 *var.* Gran Santiago. *Country capital* (Chile) Santiago, C Chile
Santiago 92 B1 *var.* Santiago de Compostela, *Eng.* Compostella; *anc.* Campus Stellae. Galicia, NW Spain
Santiago 55 E3 *var.* Santiago de los Caballeros. N Dominican Republic
Santiago 74 A3 *var.* São Tiago. *Island* Ilhas de Sotavento, S Cape Verde
Santiago *see* Santiago de Cuba
Santiago 53 F5 Veraguas, S Panama
Santiago de Compostela *see* Santiago
Santiago de Cuba 54 C3 *var.* Santiago. Santiago de Cuba, E Cuba
Santiago de Guayaquil *see* Guayaquil
Santiago del Estero 64 C3 Santiago del Estero, C Argentina
Santiago de los Caballeros *see* Santiago
Santiago Pinotepa Nacional *see* Pinotepa Nacional
Santiago, Río 60 B2 *river* N Peru
Santi Quaranta *see* Sarandë
Santissima Trinidad *see* Chilung
Sant Julià de Lòria 91 A8 SW Andorra
Santo *see* Espiritu Santo
Santo Antão 74 A2 *island* Ilhas de Barlavento, N Cape Verde
Santo António 76 E1 Príncipe, N Sao Tome and Principe
Santo Domingo 54 D3 *prev.* Ciudad Trujillo. *Country capital* (Dominican Republic) SE Dominican Republic
Santo Domingo de los Colorados 60 B1 Pichincha, NW Ecuador
Santo Domingo Tehuantepec *see* Tehuantepec
Santos 63 F4 São Paulo, S Brazil
Santos Plateau 57 D5 *undersea feature* SW Atlantic Ocean
Santo Tomé 64 D3 Corrientes, NE Argentina
San Valentín, Cerro 65 A6 *mountain* S Chile
San Vicente 52 C3 San Vicente, C El Salvador
São Francisco, Rio 63 F3 *river* E Brazil
Sao Hill 73 C7 Iringa, S Tanzania
São João da Madeira 92 B2 Aveiro, N Portugal
São Jorge 92 A5 *island* Azores, Portugal, NE Atlantic Ocean
São Luís 63 F2 *state capital* Maranhão, NE Brazil
São Mandol *see* São Manuel, Rio
São Manuel, Rio 63 E3 *var.* São Mandol, Teles Pires. *River* C Brazil
São Marcos, Baía de 63 F1 *bay* N Brazil
São Miguel 92 A5 *island* Azores, Portugal, NE Atlantic Ocean
Saona, Isla 55 E3 *island* SE Dominican Republic
Saône 91 D5 *river* E France
São Nicolau 74 A3 *Eng.* Saint Nicholas. *Island* Ilhas de Barlavento, N Cape Verde
São Paulo 63 E4 *off.* Estado de São Paulo. *State* S Brazil
São Paulo 63 E4 *state capital* São Paulo, S Brazil
São Pedro do Rio Grande do Sul *see* Rio Grande
São Roque, Cabo de 63 G2 *headland* E Brazil
São Salvador *see* M'Banza Congo
São Salvador do Congo *see* M'Banza Congo
São Tiago *see* Santiago

São Tomé *76 E2 Eng.* Saint Thomas.
Island S Sao Tome and Principe
São Tomé *77 A5 country capital* (Sao Tome and Principe) São Tomé,
S Sao Tome and Principe
Sao Tome and Principe *76 D1 Country* E Atlantic Ocean

Sao Tome & Príncipe 76

Official name Democratic Republic of São Tomé and Príncipe
Formation 1975
Capital São Tomé
Population 159,900 / 414 people per sq mile (160 people per sq km)
Total area 386 sq miles (1,001 sq km)
Languages Portuguese, Portuguese Creole
Religions Roman Catholic 84%, other Christian 16%
Ethnic mix Black 90%, Portuguese and Creole 10%
Government Multiparty republic
Currency Dobra = 100 centimos
Literacy rate 75%
Calorie consumption 2,390 kilocalories

São Tomé, Pico de *76 D2 mountain* São Tomé, S Sao Tome and Principe
São Vicente, Cabo de *92 B5 Eng.* Cape Saint Vincent, *Port.* Cabo de São Vicente. *Headland* S Portugal
São Vincente *74 A3 Eng.* Saint Vincent. *Island* Ilhas de Barlavento, N Cape Verde
Sápai *see* Sápes
Sapele *75 F5* Delta, S Nigeria
Sápes *104 D3 var.* Sápai. Anatolikí Makedonía kai Thráki, NE Greece
Sapir *see* Sappir
Sa Pobla *93 G3 var.* La Puebla. Mallorca, Spain, W Mediterranean Sea
Sappir *119 B7 var.* Sapir. Southern, S Israel
Sapporo *130 D2* Hokkaidō, NE Japan
Sapri *97 D6* Campania, S Italy
Sapulpa *49 G1* Oklahoma, C USA
Saqqez *120 C2 var.* Saghez, Sakiz, Saqqiz. Kordestān, NW Iran
Saqqiz *see* Saqqez
Sara Buri *137 C5 var.* Saraburi. Saraburi, C Thailand
Saragt *see* Serakhs
Saraguro *60 B2* Loja, S Ecuador
Sarajevo *100 C4 country capital* (Bosnia and Herzegovina). Federacija Bosna I Hercegovina, SE Bosnia and Herzegovina
Sarakhs *120 E2* Khorāsān, NE Iran
Saraktash *111 D6* Orenburgskaya Oblast', W Russian Federation
Saran' *114 C4 Kaz.* Saran. Karaganda, C Kazakhstan
Saranda *see* Sarandë
Sarandë *101 C7 var.* Saranda, *It.* Porto Edda; *prev.* Santi Quaranta. Vlorë, S Albania
Saransk *111 C5* Respublika Mordoviya, W Russian Federation
Sarasota *43 E4* Florida, SE USA
Saratov *114 B3* Saratovskaya Oblast', W Russian Federation
Saravan *see* Salavan
Saravane *see* Salavan
Sarawak *138 D3 cultural region* Borneo, SE Asia
Sarawak and Sabah (North Borneo) and Singapore *see* Malaysia
Sarcelles *90 D1* Val-d'Oise, N France
Sardegna *97 A5 Eng.* Sardinia. *Island* Italy, C Mediterranean Sea
Sardinia *see* Sardegna
Sarera, Teluk *see* Cenderawasih, Teluk

Sarh *76 C4 prev.* Fort-Archambault. Moyen-Chari, S Chad
Sārī *120 D2 var.* Sari, Sári. Māzandarān, N Iran
Saría *105 E7 island* SE Greece
Sarıkamış *117 F3* Kars, NE Turkey
Sarikol Range *123 G3 Rus.* Sarykol'skiy Khrebet. *Mountain range* China/Tajikistan
Sark *89 D8 Fr.* Sercq. *Island* Channel Islands
Şarkışla *116 D3* Sivas, C Turkey
Sarmiento *65 B6* Chubut, S Argentina
Sarnia *38 C5* Ontario, S Canada
Sarny *108 C1* Rivnens'ka Oblast', NW Ukraine
Sarochina *107 D5 Rus.* Sorochino. Vitsyebskaya Voblasts', N Belarus
Sarpsborg *85 B6* Østfold, S Norway
Sartène *91 E7* Corse, France, C Mediterranean Sea
Sarthe *90 B4 cultural region* N France
Sárti *104 C4* Kentrikí Makedonía, N Greece
Saruhan *see* Manisa
Saryesik-Atyrau, Peski *123 G1 desert* E Kazakhstan
Sary-Tash *123 F2* Oshskaya Oblast', SW Kyrgyzstan
Sasebo *131 A7* Nagasaki, Kyūshū, SW Japan
Saskatchewan *37 F5 river* Manitoba/Saskatchewan, C Canada
Saskatchewan *37 F5 province* SW Canada
Saskatoon *37 F5* Saskatchewan, S Canada
Sasovo *111 B5* Ryazanskaya Oblast', W Russian Federation
Sassandra *74 D5* S Côte d'Ivoire
Sassandra Fleuve *see* Sassandra
Sassandra *74 D5 S* Côte d'Ivoire, C Mediterranean Sea
Sassari *97 A5* Sardegna, Italy, C Mediterranean Sea
Sassenheim *86 C3* Zuid-Holland, W Netherlands
Sassnitz *94 D2* Mecklenburg-Vorpommern, NE Germany
Sátoraljaújhely *99 D6* Borsod-Abaúj-Zemplén, NE Hungary
Sātpura Range *134 D4 mountain range* C India
Satsuna-shotō *130 A3 var.* Satunan Syotô. *Island group* SW Japan
Sattanen *84 D3* Lappi, NE Finland
Satu Mare *108 B3 Ger.* Sathmar, *Hung.* Szatmárrnémeti. Satu Mare, NW Romania
Satunan Syotô *see* Satsunan-shotō
Saudi Arabia *121 B5 Ar.* Al 'Arabīyah as Su'ūdīyah, Al Mamlakah al 'Arabīyah as Su'ūdīyah. *Country* SW Asia

Saudi Arabia 121

Official name Kingdom of Saudi Arabia
Formation 1932
Capital Riyadh
Population 21 million / 28 people per sq mile (11 people per sq km)
Total area 756,981 sq miles (1,960,582 sq km)
Languages Arabic
Religions Sunni Muslim 85%, Shi'a Muslim 15%
Ethnic mix Arab 90%, Afro-Asian 10%
Government Monarchy
Currency Saudi riyal = 100 malalah
Literacy rate 77%
Calorie consumption 2,875 kilocalories

Sauer *see* Sûre
Saulkrasti *106 C3* Rīga, C Latvia
Sault Sainte Marie *40 C1* Michigan, N USA

Sault Ste.Marie *38 C4* Ontario, S Canada
Saumur *90 B4* Maine-et-Loire, NW France
Saurimo *78 C1 Port.* Henrique de Carvalho, Vila Henrique de Carvalho. Lunda Sul, NE Angola
Sava *100 B3 Eng.* Save, *Ger.* Sau, *Hung.* Száva. *River* SE Europe
Sava *107 E4 Rus.* Sava. Mahilyowskaya Voblasts', E Belarus
Savá *52 D2* Colón, N Honduras
Savai'i *145 E4 island* NW Samoa
Savannah *43 E2* Georgia, SE USA
Savannah River *43 E2 river* Georgia/South Carolina, SE USA
Savanna-La-Mar *54 A5 W* Jamaica
Save, Rio *79 E3 var.* Rio Sabi. *River* Mozambique/Zimbabwe
Saverne *90 E3 var.* Zabern; *anc.* Tres Tabernae. Bas-Rhin, NE France
Savigliano *96 A2* Piemonte, NW Italy
Savigsivik *see* Savissivik
Savinski *see* Savinskiy
Savinskiy *110 C4 var.* Savinski. Arkhangel'skaya Oblast', NW Russian Federation
Savissivik *82 D1 var.* Savigsivik. N Greenland
Savoie *91 D5 cultural region* E France
Savona *96 A2* Liguria, NW Italy
Savu Sea *139 E5 Ind.* Laut Sawu, *Sea* S Indonesia
Sawakin *see* Suakin
Sawdirī *see* Sodiri
Sawhāj *see* Sohâg
Şawqirah *121 D6 var.* Suqrah. S Oman
Sayanskiy Khrebet *112 D3 mountain range* S Russian Federation
Sayat *122 D3* Lebapskiy Velayat, É Turkmenistan
Sayaxché *52 B2* Petén, N Guatemala
Şaydā *see* Saïda
Sayhūt *121 D6* E Yemen
Sayida *see* Saïda
Saynshand *127 E2* Dornogovĭ, SE Mongolia
Sayre *41 E3* Pennsylvania, NE USA
Say'ūn *121 C6 var.* Saywūn. C Yemen
Saywūn *see* Say'ūn
Scandinavia *66 D2 geophysical region* NW Europe
Scarborough *89 D5* N England, UK
Schaan *94 E1* W Liechtenstein
Schaerbeek *87 C6* Brussels, C Belgium
Schaffhausen *95 B7 Fr.* Schaffhouse. Schaffhausen, N Switzerland
Schagen *86 C2* Noord-Holland, NW Netherlands
Schebschi Mountains *see* Shebshi Mountains
Scheessel *94 B3* Niedersachsen, NW Germany
Schefferville *39 E2* Quebec, E Canada
Scheldt *87 B5 Dut.* Schelde, *Fr.* Escaut. *River* W Europe
Schell Creek Range *47 D5 mountain range* Nevada, W USA
Schenectady *41 F3* New York, NE USA
Schertz *49 G4* Texas, SW USA
Schiermonnikoog *86 D1 Fris.* Skiermûntseach. *Island* Skiermûntseach, N Netherlands
Schijndel *86 D4* Noord-Brabant, S Netherlands
Schiltigheim *90 E3* Bas-Rhin, NE France
Schleswig *94 B2* Schleswig-Holstein, N Germany
Schleswig-Holstein *94 B2 cultural region* N Germany
Schönebeck *94 C4* Sachsen-Anhalt, C Germany
Schooten *see* Schoten
Schoten *87 C5 var.* Schooten. Antwerpen, N Belgium

Schouwen *86 B4 island* SW Netherlands
Schwabenalb *see* Schwäbische Alb
Schwäbische Alb *95 B6 var.* Schwabenalb, *Eng.* Swabian Jura. *Mountain range* S Germany
Schwandorf *95 C5* Bayern, SE Germany
Schwarzwald *95 B6 Eng.* Black Forest. *Mountain range* SW Germany
Schwaz *95 C7* Tirol, W Austria
Schweinfurt *95 B5* Bayern, SE Germany
Schwerin *94 C3* Mecklenburg-Vorpommern, N Germany
Schwiz *see* Schwyz
Schwyz *95 C7 var.* Schwiz. Schwyz, C Switzerland
Scilly, Isles of *89 B8 island group* SW England, UK
Scio *see* Chíos
Scoresby Sound *see* Ittoqqortoormiit
Scoresbysund *see* Ittoqqortoormiit
Scotia Sea *57 C8 sea* SW Atlantic Ocean
Scotland *88 C3 national region* UK
Scott Base *154 B4 NZ research station* Antarctica
Scott Island *154 B5 island* Antarctica
Scottsbluff *44 D3* Nebraska, C USA
Scottsboro *42 D1* Alabama, S USA
Scottsdale *48 B2* Arizona, SW USA
Scranton *41 F3* Pennsylvania, NE USA
Scupi *see* Skopje
Scutari *see* Shkodër
Scutari, Lake *101 C5 Alb.* Liqeni i Shkodrës, *SCr.* Skadarsko Jezero. *Lake* Albania/Serbia and Montenegro (Yugo.)
Scyros *see* Skýros
Searcy *42 B1* Arkansas, C USA
Seattle *46 B2* Washington, NW USA
Sébaco *52 D3* Matagalpa, W Nicaragua
Sebastián Vizcaíno, Bahía *50 A2 bay* NW Mexico
Sechura, Bahía de *60 A3 bay* NW Peru
Secunderābād *134 D5 var.* Sikandarabad. Andhra Pradesh, C India
Sedan *90 D3* Ardennes, N France
Seddon *151 D5* Marlborough, South Island, NZ
Seddonville *151 C5* West Coast, South Island, NZ
Sédhiou *74 B3* SW Senegal
Sedona *48 B2* Arizona, SW USA
Seesen *94 B4* Niedersachsen, C Germany
Segestica *see* Sisak
Segezha *110 B3* Respublika Kareliya, NW Russian Federation
Ségou *74 D3 var.* Segu. Ségou, C Mali
Segovia *92 D2* Castilla-León, C Spain
Segoviao Wangkí *see* Coco, Río
Segu *see* Ségou
Séguédine *75 H2* Agadez, NE Niger
Seguin *49 G4* Texas, SW USA
Segura *93 E4 river* S Spain
Seinäjoki *85 D5 Swe.* Östermyra. Länsi-Suomi, W Finland
Seine *90 D1 river* N France
Seine, Baie de la *90 B3 bay* N France
Sekondi *see* Sekondi-Takoradi
Sekondi-Takoradi *75 E5 var.* Sekondi. S Ghana
Selat Balabac *see* Balabac Strait
Selenga *127 E1 Mong.* Selenge Mörön. *River* Mongolia/Russian Federation
Sélestat *90 E3* Bas-Rhin, NE France
Selfoss *83 E5* Sudhurland, SW Iceland
Sélibabi *74 C3 var.* Sélibaby. Guidimaka, S Mauritania
Sélibaby *see* Sélibabi
Selma *47 C6* California, W USA
Selway River *46 D2 river* Idaho, NW USA

Selwyn Range 148 B3 mountain range Queensland, C Australia
Selzaete see Zelzate
Semarang 138 C5 var. Samarang. Jawa, C Indonesia
Sembé 77 B5 La Sangha, NW Congo
Semey see Semipalatinsk
Seminole 49 E3 Texas, SW USA
Seminole, Lake 42 D3 reservoir Florida/Georgia, SE USA
Semipalatinsk 114 D4 Kaz. Semey. Vostochnyy kazakhstan, E Kazakhstan
Semnān 120 D3 var. Samnān.
Semnān, N Iran
Semois 87 C8 river SE Belgium
Sendai 131 A8 Kagoshima, Kyūshū, SW Japan
Sendai 130 D4 Miyagi, Honshū, C Japan
Sendai-wan 130 D4 bay E Japan
Senec 99 C6 Ger. Wartberg, Hung. Szenc; prev. Szempcz. Bratislavský Kraj, W Slovakia
Senegal 74 C3 Fr. Sénégal. River W Africa
Senegal 74 B3 Fr. Sénégal. Country W Africa

Senegal 74

Official name Republic of Senegal
Formation 1960
Capital Dakar
Population 9.7 million / 128 people per sq mile (49 people per sq km)
Total area 75,749 sq miles (196,190 sq km)
Languages French, Wolof, Fulani, Serer, Diola, Malinke, Soninke, Arabic
Religions Sunni Muslim 90%, Christian (mainly Roman Catholic) 5%, Traditional beliefs 5%
Ethnic mix Wolof 44%, Serer 15%, Fula 12%, Diola 5%, Malinke 4%, other 20%
Government Presidential democracy
Currency CFA franc = 100 centimes
Literacy rate 37.4%
Calorie consumption 2,257 kilocalories

Senftenberg 94 D4 Brandenburg, E Germany
Senica 99 C6 Ger. Senitz, Hung. Szenice. Trnavský Kraj, W Slovakia
Senj 100 A3 Ger. Zengg, It. Segna; anc. Senia. Lika-Senj, NW Croatia
Senja 84 C2 prev. Senjen. Island N Norway
Senkaku-shotō 130 A3 island group SW Japan
Senlis 90 C3 Oise, N France
Sennar 72 C4 var. Sannār. Sinnar, C Sudan
Sens 90 C3 anc. Agendicum, Senones. Yonne, C France
Sên, Stœng 137 D5 river C Cambodia
Senta 100 D3 Hung. Zenta. Serbia, N Serbia and Montenegro (Yugo.)
Seo de Urgel see La See d'Urgel
Seoul see Sŏul
Sept-Îles 39 E3 Quebec, SE Canada
Seraing 87 D6 Liège, E Belgium
Serakhs 122 D3 var. Saragt. Akhalskiy Velayat, S Turkmenistan
Seram, Pulau 139 F4 var. Serang, Eng. Ceram. Island Maluku, E Indonesia
Serang see Seram, Pulau
Serang 138 C5 Jawa, C Indonesia
Serasan, Selat 138 C3 strait Indonesia/Malaysia
Serbia 100 D4 Ger. Serbien, Serb. Srbija. Admin. region republic Serbia and Montenegro (Yugo.)
Serbia and Montenegro (Yugo.) 100 D4 SCr. Jugoslavija, Savezna Republika Jugoslavija. Country SE Europe

Serbia and Montenegro (Yugo.) 100

Official name Serbia and Montenegro
Formation 1992
Capital Belgrade
Population 10.5 million / 266 people per sq mile (103 people per sq km)
Total area 39,449 sq miles (102,173 sq km)
Languages Serbo-Croat, Albanian, Hungarian
Religions Eastern Orthodox 65, Muslim 19%, Roman Catholic 4%, other 12%
Ethnic mix Serb 62%, Albanian 17%, Montenegrin 5%, other 16%
Government Multiparty republic
Currency Dinar (Euro widely used in Montenegro)
Literacy rate 93.3%
Calorie consumption 2,570 kilocalories

Serdica see Sofiya
Seremban 138 B3 Negeri Sembilan, Peninsular Malaysia
Serenje 78 D2 Central, E Zambia
Seres see Sérres
Seret see Siret
Sereth see Siret
Sérifos 105 C6 anc. Seriphos. Island Kykládes, Greece, Aegean Sea
Serov 114 C3 Sverdlovskaya Oblast', C Russian Federation
Serowe 78 D3 Central, SE Botswana
Serpa Pinto see Menongue
Serpent's Mouth, The 59 F2 Sp. Boca de la Serpiente. Strait Trinidad and Tobago/Venezuela
Serpukhov 111 B5 Moskovskaya Oblast', W Russian Federation
Serra dos Parecis see Parecis, Chapada dos
Sérrai see Sérres
Serrana, Cayo de 53 F2 island group NW Colombia
Serranilla, Cayo de 53 F2 island group NW Colombia
Serra Pacaraim see Pakaraima Mountains
Serra Tumucumaque see Tumuc Humac Mountains
Serravalle 96 E1 N San Marino
Sérres 104 C3 var. Seres; prev. Sérrai. Kentriki Makedonía, NE Greece
Sert see Siirt
Sesto San Giovanni 96 B2 Lombardia, N Italy
Sesvete 100 B2 Zagreb, N Croatia
Setabis see Xàtiva
Sète 91 C6 prev. Cette. Hérault, S France
Setesdal 85 A6 valley S Norway
Sétif 71 E2 var. Stif. N Algeria
Setté Cama 77 A6 Ogooué-Maritime, SW Gabon
Setúbal 92 B4 Eng. Saint Ubes, Saint Yves. Setúbal, W Portugal
Setúbal, Baía de 92 B4 bay W Portugal
Seul, Lac 38 B3 lake Ontario, S Canada
Sevan 117 G2 C Armenia
Sevana Lich 117 G2 Lake Sevan, Rus. Ozero Sevan. Lake E Armenia
Sevastopol' 109 F5 Eng. Sebastopol. Respublika Krym, S Ukraine
Severn 89 D6 Wel. Hafren. River England/Wales, UK
Severn 38 B2 river Ontario, S Canada
Severnaya Dvina 110 C4 var. Northern Dvina. River NW Russian Federation
Severnaya Zemlya 115 E2 var. Nicholas II Land. Island group N Russian Federation
Severnyy 110 E3 Respublika Komi, NW Russian Federation
Severodvinsk 110 C3 prev. Molotov, Sudostroy. Arkhangel'skaya Oblast', NW Russian Federation

Severomorsk 110 C2 Murmanskaya Oblast', NW Russian Federation
Severo-Sibirskaya Nizmennost' 115 E2 var. North Siberian Plain, Eng. North Siberian Lowland. Lowlands N Russian Federation
Severskiy Donets see Donets
Sevier Lake 44 A4 lake Utah, W USA
Sevilla 92 C4 Eng. Seville; anc. Hispalis. Andalucía, SW Spain
Seville see Sevilla
Sevlievo 104 D2 Gabrovo, N Bulgaria
Seychelles 79 G1 Country W Indian Ocean

Seychelles 79

Official name Republic of the Seychelles
Formation 1976
Capital Victoria
Population 79,300/ 451 people per sq mile (174 people per sq km)
Total area 176 sq miles (455 sq km)
Languages French Creole (Seselwa), English, French
Religions Roman Catholic 90%, Anglican 8%, other 2%
Ethnic mix Creole 89%, Indian 5%, Chinese 2%, other 4%
Government Multiparty republic
Currency Seychelles rupee = 100 cents
Literacy rate 84%
Calorie consumption 2,432 kilocalories

Seydhisfjördhur 83 E5 Austurland, É Iceland
Seydi 122 D2 prev. Neftezavodsk. Lebapskiy Velayat, E Turkmenistan
Seyhan see Adana
Sfákia 105 C8 Kríti, Greece, E Mediterranean Sea
Sfântu Gheorghe 108 C4 Ger. Sankt-Georgen, Hung. Sepsiszentgyörgy; prev. Sepsi-Sângeorz, Sfîntu Gheorghe. Covasna, C Romania
Sfax 71 F2 Ar. Şafāqis. E Tunisia
's-Gravenhage 86 B4 var. Den Haag, Eng. The Hague, Fr. La Haye. Country capital (Netherlands-seat of government) Zuid-Holland, W Netherlands
's-Gravenzande 86 B4 Zuid-Holland, W Netherlands
Shaan see Shaanxi
Shaanxi 128 B5 var. Shaan, Shaanxi Sheng, Shan-hsi, Shenshi, Shensi. Admin. region province C China
Shaanxi Sheng see Shaanxi
Shache 126 A3 var. Yarkant. Xinjiang Uygur Zizhiqu, NW China
Shackleton Ice Shelf 154 D3 ice shelf Antarctica
Shaddādī see Ash Shadādāh
Shāhābād see Eslāmābād
Shahjanabad see Delhi
Shahr-e Kord 120 C3 var. Shahr Kord. Chahār Maḩall va Bakhtīārī, C Iran
Shahr Kord see Shahr-e Kord
Shāhrūd 120 D2 prev. Emāmrūd, Emāmshahr. Semnān, N Iran
Shandī see Shendi
Shandong 128 D4 var. Lu, Shandong Sheng, Shantung. Admin. region province C China
Shandong Sheng see Shandong
Shanghai 128 D5 var. Shang-hai. Shanghai Shi, E China
Shang-hai see Shanghai
Shangrao 128 D5 Jiangxi, S China
Shan-hsi see Shaanxi
Shan-hsi see Shanxi
Shannon 89 A6 Ir. An tSionainn. River W Ireland
Shan Plateau 136 B3 plateau E Myanmar
Shansi see Shanxi
Shantarskiye Ostrova 115 G3 Eng. Shantar Islands. Island group E Russian Federation

Shantou 128 D6 var. Shan-t'ou, Swatow. Guangdong, S China
Shantung see Shandong
Shanxi 128 C4 var. Jin, Shan-hsi, Shansi, Shanxi Sheng. Admin. region province C China
Shan Xian see Sanmenxia
Shanxi Sheng see Shanxi
Shaoguan 128 C6 var. Shao-kuan, Cant. Kukong; prev. Ch'u-chiang. Guangdong, S China
Shao-kuan see Shaoguan
Shaqrā' see Shuqrah
Shaqrā' 120 B4 Ar Riyāḑ, C Saudi Arabia
Shar 130 D5 var. Charsk. Vostochnyy Kazakhstan, E Kazakhstan
Shari see Chari
Shari 130 D2 Hokkaidō, NE Japan
Shark Bay 147 A5 bay Western Australia
Shashe 78 D3 var. Shashi. River Botswana/Zimbabwe
Shashi see Shashe
Shatskiy Rise 125 G1 undersea feature N Pacific Ocean
Shatt al-Hodna see Hodna, Chott El
Shatt al Jarīd see Jerid, Chott el
Shawnee 49 G1 Oklahoma, C USA
Shchadryn 107 D7 Rus. Shchedrin. Homyel'skaya Voblasts', SE Belarus
Shchëkino 111 B5 Tul'skaya Oblast', W Russian Federation
Shchors 109 E1 Chernihivs'ka Oblast', N Ukraine
Shchuchinsk 114 C4 prev. Shchuchye. Severnyy kazakhstan, N Kazakhstan
Shchychyn 107 B5 Pol. Szczuczyn Nowogródzki, Rus. Shchuchin. Hrodzyenskaya Voblasts', W Belarus
Shebekino 111 A6 Belgorodskaya Oblast', W Russian Federation
Shebeli 73 D5 Amh. Wabē Shebelē Wenz, It. Scebeli, Som. Webi Shabeelle. River Ethiopia/Somalia
Sheberghān 123 E3 var. Shibarghān, Shiberghan, Shiberghān. Jowzjān, N Afghanistan
Sheboygan 40 B2 Wisconsin, N USA
Shebshi Mountains 76 A4 var. Schebschi Mountains. Mountain range E Nigeria
Shechem see Nablus
Shedadi see Ash Shadādāh
Sheffield 89 D5 N England, UK
Shekhem see Nablus
Shelby 44 B1 Montana, NW USA
Sheldon 45 F3 Iowa, C USA
Shelekhov Gulf see Shelikhova, Zaliv
Shelikhova, Zaliv 115 G2 Eng. Shelekhov Gulf. Gulf E Russian Federation
Shendi 72 C4 var. Shandī. River Nile, NE Sudan
Shengking see Liaoning
Shenking see Liaoning
Shenshi see Shaanxi
Shensi see Shaanxi
Shenyang 128 D3 Chin. Shen-yang, Eng. Moukden, Mukden; prev. Fengtien. Liaoning, NE China
Shepetivka 108 D2 Rus. Shepetovka. Khmel'nyts'ka Oblast', NW Ukraine
Shepparton 149 C7 Victoria, SE Australia
Sherbrooke 39 E4 Quebec, SE Canada
Shereik 72 C3 River Nile, N Sudan
Sheridan 44 C2 Wyoming, C USA
Sherman 49 G2 Texas, SW USA
's-Hertogenbosch 86 C4 Fr. Bois-le-Duc, Ger. Herzogenbusch. Noord-Brabant, S Netherlands
Shetland Islands 88 D1 island group NE Scotland, UK
Shibarghān see Sheberghān
Shiberghan see Sheberghān
Shibetsu 130 D2 var. Sibetu. Hokkaidō, NE Japan

Shibh Jazīrat Sīnā' *see* Sinai
Shibushi-wan 131 B8 *bay* SW Japan
Shigatse *see* Xigazê
Shih-chia-chuang *see* Shijiazhuang
Shihezi 126 C2 Xinjiang Uygur
  Zizhiqu, NW China
Shihmen *see* Shijiazhuang
Shijiazhuang 128 C4 *var.* Shih-chia-
  chuang; *prev.* Shihmen. Hebei,
  E China
Shikārpur 134 B3 Sind, S Pakistan
Shikoku 131 C7 *var.* Sikoku. *Island*
  SW Japan
Shikoku Basin 125 F2 *var.* Sikoku
  Basin. *Undersea feature*
  N Philippine Sea
Shikotan, Ostrov 130 E2 *Jap.*
  Shikotan-tō. *Island* NE Russian
  Federation
Shilabo 73 D5 E Ethiopia
Shiliguri 135 F3 *prev.* Siliguri. West
  Bengal, NE India
Shilka 115 F4 *river* S Russian
  Federation
Shilong 113 G3 E India
Shimbir Berris *see* Shimbiris
Shimbiris 72 E4 *var.* Shimbir Berris.
  Mountain N Somalia
Shimoga 132 C2 Karnātaka, W India
Shimonoseki 131 A7 *var.*
  Simonoseki; *hist.* Akamagaseki,
  Bakan. Yamaguchi, Honshū,
  SW Japan
Shinano-gawa 131 C5 *var.* Sinano
  Gawa. *River* Honshū, C Japan
Shīndand 122 D4 Farāh,
  W Afghanistan
Shingū 131 C6 *var.* Singū.
  Wakayama, Honshū, SW Japan
Shinjō 130 D4 *var.* Sinzyô.
  Yamagata, Honshū, C Japan
Shinyanga 73 C7 Shinyanga,
  NW Tanzania
Shiprock 48 C1 New Mexico,
  SW USA
Shīrāz 120 D4 *var.* Shīrāz. Fārs,
  S Iran
Shivpuri 134 D3 Madhya Pradesh,
  C India
Shizugawa 130 D4 Miyagi, Honshū,
  NE Japan
Shizuoka 131 D6 *var.* Sizuoka.
  Shizuoka, Honshū, S Japan
Shklow 107 D6 *Rus.* Shklov.
  Mahilyowskaya Voblasts',
  E Belarus
Shkodër 101 C5 *var.* Shkodra, *It.*
  Scutari, *SCr.* Skadar. Shkodër,
  NW Albania
Shkodra *see* Shkodër
Shkubinit, Lumi i 101 C6 *var.*
  Shkumbî, Shkumbin. *River*
  C Albania
Shkumbî *see* Shkubinit, Lumi i
Shkumbin *see* Shkubinit, Lumi i
Sholāpur *see* Solāpur
Shostka 109 F1 Sums'ka Oblast',
  NE Ukraine
Show Low 48 B2 Arizona, SW USA
Shpola 109 E3 Cherkas'ka Oblast',
  N Ukraine
Shreveport 42 A2 Louisiana, S USA
Shrewsbury 89 D6 *hist.*
  Scrobesbyrig'. W England, UK
Shu 114 C5 *Kaz.* Shū. Zhambyl,
  SE Kazakhstan
Shuang-liao *see* Liaoyuan
Shumagin Islands 36 B3 *island
  group* Alaska, USA
Shumen 104 D2 Shumen,
  NE Bulgaria
Shumilina 107 E5 *Rus.* Shumilino.
  Vitsyebskaya Voblasts', NE Belarus
Shuqrah 121 B7 *var.* Shaqrā.
  SW Yemen
Shwebo 136 B3 Sagaing, C Myanmar
Shyichy 107 C7 *Rus.* Shiichi.
  Homyel'skaya Voblasts',
  SE Belarus
Shymkent 114 B5 *prev.* Chimkent.
  Yuzhnyy Kazakhstan,
  S Kazakhstan
Shyshchytsy 107 C6 *Rus.*
  Shishchitsy. Minskaya Voblasts',
  C Belarus
Si *see* Syr Darya
Siam, Gulf of *see* Thailand, Gulf of

Sian *see* Xi'an
Siang *see* Brahmaputra
Siangtan *see* Xiangtan
Šiauliai 106 B4 *Ger.* Schaulen.
  Šiauliai, N Lithuania
Sibay 111 D6 Respublika
  Bashkortostan, W Russian
  Federation
Šibenik 116 B4 *It.* Sebenico.
  Šibenik-Knin, S Croatia
Siberia *see* Sibir'
Siberut, Pulau 138 A4 *prev.*
  Siberoet. *Island* Kepulauan
  Mentawai, W Indonesia
Sibetu *see* Shibetsu
Sibi 134 B2 Baluchistān,
  SW Pakistan
Sibir' 115 E3 *var.* Siberia. *Physical
  region* NE Russian Federation
Sibiti 77 B6 La Lékoumou, S Congo
Sibiu 108 B4 *Ger.* Hermannstadt,
  Hung. Nagyszeben. Sibiu,
  C Romania
Sibolga 138 B3 Sumatera,
  W Indonesia
Sibu 138 D3 Sarawak, East
  Malaysia
Sibut 76 C4 *prev.* Fort-Sibut. Kémo,
  S Central African Republic
Sibuyan Sea 139 E2 *sea* C Philippines
Sichon 137 C6 *var.* Ban Sichon, Si
  Chon. Nakhon Si Thammarat,
  SW Thailand
Sichuan 128 B5 *var.* Chuan, Sichuan
  Sheng, Ssu-ch'uan, Szechuan,
  Szechwan. Admin. region *province*
  C China
Sichuan Pendi 128 B5 *depression*
  C China
Sichuan Sheng *see* Sichuan
Sicilia 97 C7 *Eng.* Sicily; *anc.*
  Trinacria. *Island* Italy,
  C Mediterranean Sea
Sicilian Channel *see* Sicily, Strait of
Sicily *see* Sicilia
Sicily, Strait of 97 B7 *var.* Sicilian
  Channel. *Strait* C Mediterranean
  Sea
Sicuani 61 E4 Cusco, S Peru
Sidári 104 A4 Kérkyra, Iónioi Nísoi,
  Greece, C Mediterranean Sea
Sidas 138 C4 Borneo, C Indonesia
Siderno 97 D7 Calabria, SW Italy
Sîdi Barrâni 72 A1 NW Egypt
Sidi Bel Abbès 70 D2 *var.* Sidi bel
  Abbès, Sidi-Bel-Abbès.
  NW Algeria
Sidirókastro 104 C3 *prev.*
  Sidhirókastron. Kentrikí
  Makedonía, NE Greece
Sidley, Mount 154 B4 *mountain*
  Antarctica
Sidney 44 D1 Montana, NW USA
Sidney 44 D3 Nebraska, C USA
Sidney 40 C4 Ohio, N USA
Sidon *see* Saïda
Sidra *see* Surt
Siedlce 98 E3 *Ger.* Sedlez, *Rus.*
  Sesdlets. Mazowieckie, C Poland
Siegen 94 B4 Nordrhein-Westfalen,
  W Germany
Siemiatycze 98 E3 Podlaskie,
  NE Poland
Siena 96 B3 *Fr.* Sienne; *anc.* Saena
  Julia. Toscana, C Italy
Sieradz 98 C4 Łódzkie, C Poland
Sierpc 98 D3 Mazowieckie,
  C Poland
Sierra de Soconusco *see* Sierra
  Madre
Sierra Leone 74 C4 *Country*
  W Africa

Sierra Leone 74

Official name Republic of Sierra
  Leone
Formation 1961
Capital Freetown
Population 4.6 million / 166 people
  per sq mile (64 people per sq km)
Total area 27,699 sq miles
  (71,740 sq km)
Languages English, Mende, Temne,
  Krio
Religions Traditional beliefs 30%,
  Muslim 30%, Christian 10%,
  other 30%

Sierra Leone (continued)

Ethnic mix Mende 35%, Temne
  32%, Limba 8%, Kuranko 4%, other
  21%
Government Multiparty republic
Currency Leone = 100 cents
Literacy rate 36.3%
Calorie consumption 1,863
  kilocalories

Sierra Leone Basin 66 C4 *undersea
  feature* E Atlantic Ocean
Sierra Leone Ridge *see* Sierra
  Leone Rise
Sierra Leone Rise 66 C4 *var.* Sierra
  Leone Ridge, Sierra Leone
  Schwelle. *Undersea feature*
  E Atlantic Ocean
Sierra Leone Schwelle *see* Sierra
  Leone Rise
Sierra Madre 52 B2 *var.* Sierra de
  Soconusco. *Mountain range*
  Guatemala/Mexico
Sierra Madre *see* Madre
  Occidental, Sierra
Sierra Nevada 47 C6 *mountain range*
  W USA
Sierra Pacaraima *see* Pakaraima
  Mountains
Sierra Vieja 48 D3 *mountain range*
  Texas, SW USA
Sierra Vista 48 B3 Arizona,
  SW USA
Sífnos 105 C6 *anc.* Siphnos. *Island*
  Kykládes, Greece, Aegean Sea
Sigli 138 A3 Sumatera, W Indonesia
Siglufjördhur 83 E4 Nordhurland
  Vestra, N Iceland
Signal Peak 48 A2 *mountain*
  Arizona, SW USA
Signan *see* Xi'an
Signy 152 A2 *UK research station*
  South Orkney Islands, Antarctica
Siguatepeque 52 C2 Comayagua,
  W Honduras
Siguiri 74 D4 Haute-Guinée,
  NE Guinea
Siilinjärvi 84 E4 Itä-Suomi,
  C Finland
Siirt 117 F4 *var.* Sert; *anc.*
  Tigranocerta. Siirt, SE Turkey
Sikandarabad *see* Secunderābād
Sikasso 74 D4 Sikasso, S Mali
Sikeston 45 H5 Missouri, C USA
Sikhote-Alin', Khrebet 115 G4
  mountain range SE Russian
  Federation
Siking *see* Xi'an
Siklós 99 C7 Baranya, SW Hungary
Sikoku *see* Shikoku
Sikoku Basin *see* Shikoku Basin
Šilalė 106 B4 Šilalė, W Lithuania
Silchar 135 G3 Assam, NE India
Silesia 98 B4 *physical region* SW
  Poland
Silifke 116 C4 *anc.* Seleucia. İçel,
  S Turkey
Siling Co 126 C5 *lake* W China
Silinhot *see* Xilinhot
Silistra 104 E1 *var.* Silistria; *anc.*
  Durostorum. Silistra, NE Bulgaria
Silistria *see* Silistra
Sillamäe 106 E2 *Ger.* Sillamäggi.
  Ida-Virumaa, NE Estonia
Šilutė 106 B4 *Ger.* Heydekrug.
  Šilutė, W Lithuania
Silvan 117 F4 Diyarbakır, SE Turkey
Silverek 117 F4 Şanlıurfa,
  SE Turkey
Simanggang *see* Sri Aman
Simanichy 107 C7 *Rus.* Simonichi.
  Homyel'skaya Voblasts',
  SE Belarus
Simav 116 B3 Kütahya, W Turkey
Simav Çayı 116 A3 *river*
  NW Turkey
Simeto 97 C7 *river* Sicilia, Italy,
  C Mediterranean Sea
Simeulue, Pulau 138 A3 *island*
  NW Indonesia
Simferopol' 109 F5 Respublika
  Krym, S Ukraine
Simitli 104 C3 Blagoevgrad,
  SW Bulgaria

Šimleu Silvaniei 108 B3 *Hung.*
  Szilágysomlyó; *prev.* Şimlăul
  Silvaniei, Şimleul Silvaniei. Sălaj,
  NW Romania
Simonoseki *see* Shimonoseki
Simpelveld 87 D6 Limburg,
  SE Netherlands
Simplon Pass 95 B8 *pass*
  S Switzerland
Simpson *see* Fort Simpson
Simpson Desert 148 B4 *desert*
  Northern Territory/South
  Australia
Sinā' *see* Sinai
Sinai 72 C2 *var.* Sinai Peninsula, *Ar.*
  Shibh Jazīrat Sīnā', Sīnā'. *Physical
  region* NE Egypt
Sinaia 108 C4 Prahova, SE Romania
Sinai Peninsula *see* Sinai
Sinano Gawa *see* Shinano-gawa
Sincelejo 58 B2 Sucre,
  NW Colombia
Sind 134 B3 *var.* Sindh. Admin.
  region *province* SE Pakistan
Sindelfingen 95 B6 Baden-
  Württemberg, SW Germany
Sindh *see* Sind
Sindi 106 D2 *Ger.* Zintenhof.
  Pärnumaa, SW Estonia
Sines 92 B4 Setúbal, S Portugal
Singan *see* Xi'an
Singapore 138 A1 *Country* SE Asia

Singapore 138

Official name Republic of
  Singapore
Formation 1965
Capital Singapore
Population 4.1 million /
  16,400 people per sq mile (6,332
  people per sq km)
Total area 250 sq miles (648 sq km)
Languages Malay, English,
  Mandarin, Tamil
Religions Buddhist 55%,
  Taoism 22%, Muslim 16%, Hindu,
  Christian, Sikh 7%
Ethnic mix Chinese 77%, Malay
  14%, Indian 8%, other 1%
Government Parliamentary
  democracy
Currency Singapore dollar = 100
  cents
Literacy rate 92.4%
Calorie consumption not available

Singapore 138 B3 *country capital*
  (Singapore) S Singapore
Singen 95 B6 Baden-Württemberg,
  S Germany
Singida 73 C7 Singida,
  C Tanzania
Singkang 139 E4 Sulawesi,
  C Indonesia
Singkawang 138 C3 Borneo,
  C Indonesia
Singora *see* Songkhla
Singū *see* Shingū
Sining *see* Xining
Siniscola 97 A5 Sardegna, Italy,
  C Mediterranean Sea
Sinj 100 B4 Split-Dalmacija,
  SE Croatia
Sinkiang *see* Xinjiang Uygur
  Zizhiqu
**Sinkiang Uighur Autonomous
  Region** *see* Xinjiang Uygur
  Zizhiqu
Sinnamarie *see* Sinnamary
Sinnamary 59 H3 *var.* Sinnamarie.
  N French Guiana
Sînnicolau Mare *see* Sânnicolau
  Mare
Sinoie, Lacul 108 D5 *prev.* Lacul
  Sinoe. *Lagoon* SE Romania
Sinop 116 D2 *anc.* Sinope. Sinop,
  N Turkey
Sinsheim 95 B6 Baden-
  Württemberg,
  SW Germany
Sint Maarten 55 G3 *Eng.* Saint
  Martin. *Island* N Netherlands
  Antilles
Sint-Michielsgestel 86 C4 Noord-
  Brabant, S Netherlands

239

Sint-Niklaas 87 B5 Fr. Saint-Nicolas. Oost-Vlaanderen, N Belgium
Sint-Pieters-Leeuw 87 B6 Vlaams Brabant, C Belgium
Sintra 92 B3 prev. Cintra. Lisboa, W Portugal
Sinujiif 73 E5 Nugaal, NE Somalia
Sinus Aelaniticus see Aqaba, Gulf of
Sinyang see Xinyang
Sinzyô see Shinjō
Sion 95 A7 Ger. Sitten; anc. Sedunum. Valais, SW Switzerland
Sioux City 45 F3 Iowa, C USA
Sioux Falls 45 F3 South Dakota, N USA
Siping 128 D3 var. Ssu-p'ing, Szeping; prev. Ssu-p'ing-chieh. Jilin, NE China
Siple, Mount 154 A4 mountain Siple Island, Antarctica
Siquirres 53 E4 Limón, E Costa Rica
Siracusa 97 D7 Eng. Syracuse. Sicilia, Italy, C Mediterranean Sea
Sir Darya see Syr Darya
Sir Edward Pellew Group 148 B2 island group Northern Territory, NE Australia
Siret 108 C3 var. Siretul, Ger. Sereth, Rus. Seret, Ukr. Siret. River Romania/Ukraine
Siret see Siret
Siretul see Siret
Sirikit Reservoir 136 C4 lake N Thailand
Sirjān 120 D4 prev. Sa'īdābād. Kermān, S Iran
Sirna see Sýrna
Şırnak 117 F4 Şırnak, SE Turkey
Síros see Sýros
Sirte see Surt
Sirte, Gulf of see Surt, Khalīj
Sisak 100 B3 var. Siscia, Ger. Sissek, Hung. Sziszek; anc. Segestica. Sisak-Moslavina, C Croatia
Siscia see Sisak
Sisimiut 82 C3 var. Holsteinborg, Holsteinsborg, Holstenborg, Holstensborg. S Greenland
Sissek see Sisak
Sistema Penibético see Béticos, Sistemas
Siteía 105 D8 var. Sitía. Kríti, Greece, E Mediterranean Sea
Sitges 93 G2 Cataluña, NE Spain
Sitía see Siteía
Sittang 136 B4 var. Sittoung. River S Myanmar
Sittard 87 D5 Limburg, SE Netherlands
Sittoung see Sittang
Sittwe 136 A3 var. Akyab. Arakan State, W Myanmar
Siuna 52 D3 Región Autónoma Atlántico Norte, NE Nicaragua
Siut see Asyūt
Sivas 116 D3 anc. Sebastia, Sebaste. Sivas, C Turkey
Sivers'kyy Donets' see Donets
Siwa 72 A2 var. Siwah. NW Egypt
Siwah see Siwa
Six-Fours-les-Plages 91 D6 Var, SE France
Siyäzän 117 H2 Rus. Siazan'. NE Azerbaijan
Sizuoka see Shizuoka
Sjar see Sääre
Sjælland 88 Eng. Zealand, Ger. Seeland. Island E Denmark
Sjenica 101 D5 Turk. Seniça. Serbia, SW Serbia and Montenegro (Yugo.)
Skadar see Shkodër
Skagerak see Skagerrak
Skagerrak 85 A6 var. Skagerak. Channel N Europe
Skagit River 46 B1 river Washington, NW USA
Skalka 84 D1 lake N Sweden
Skarżysko-Kamienna 98 D4 Świętokrzyskie, C Poland
Skaudvilė 106 B4 Tauragė, SW Lithuania
Skegness 89 E6 E England, UK
Skellefteå 84 D4 Västerbotten, N Sweden

Skellefteälven 84 C4 river N Sweden
Ski 85 B6 Akershus, S Norway
Skíathos 105 C5 Skíathos, Vóreioi Sporádes, Greece, Aegean Sea
Skidal' 107 B5 Rus. Skidel'. Hrodzyenskaya Voblasts', W Belarus
Skierniewice 98 D3 Lodzkie, C Poland
Skiftet 106 C1 Fin. Kihti. Strait Gulf of Bothnia/Gulf of Finland
Skíros see Skýros
Skópelos 105 C5 Skópelos, Vóreioi Sporádes, Greece, Aegean Sea
Skopje 101 D6 var. Üsküb, Turk. Üsküp; prev. Skoplje, anc. Scupi. Country capital (FYR Macedonia) N FYR Macedonia
Skoplje see Skopje
Skovorodino 115 F4 Amurskaya Oblast', SE Russian Federation
Skuodas 106 B3 Ger. Schoden, Pol. Szkudy. Skuodas, NW Lithuania
Skye, Isle of 88 B3 island NW Scotland, UK
Skýros 105 C5 var. Skíros. Skýros, Vóreioi Sporádes, Greece, Aegean Sea
Skýros 105 C5 var. Skíros; anc. Scyros. Island Vóreioi Sporádes, Greece, Aegean Sea
Slagelse 85 B7 Vestsjælland, E Denmark
Slatina 108 B5 Olt, S Romania
Slatina 100 C3 Hung. Szlatina, prev. Podravska Slatina. Virovitica-Podravina, NE Croatia
Slavonska Požega see Požega
Slavonski Brod 100 C3 Ger. Brod, Hung. Bród; prev. Brod, Brod na Savi. Brod-Posavina, NE Croatia
Slavuta 108 C2 Khmel'nyts'ka Oblast', W Ukraine
Slawharad 107 E7 Rus. Slavgorod. Mahilyowskaya Voblasts', E Belarus
Stawno 98 C2 Zachodniopomorskie, NW Poland
Sléibhte Chill Mhantáin see Wicklow Mountains
Slēmānī see As Sulaymānīyah
Sliema 102 B5 N Malta
Sligeach see Sligo
Sligo 89 A5 Ir. Sligeach. NW Ireland
Sliven 104 D2 var. Slivno. Sliven, C Bulgaria
Slivnitsa 104 B2 Sofiya, W Bulgaria
Slivno see Sliven
Slobozia 108 C5 Ialomiţa, SE Romania
Slonim 107 B6 Pol. Słonim, Rus. Slonim. Hrodzyenskaya Voblasts', W Belarus
Slovakia 99 C6 Ger. Slowakei, Hung. Szlovákia, Slvk. Slovensko. Country C Europe

Slovakia 99

Official name Slovak Republic
Formation 1993
Capital Bratislava
Population 5.4 million / 286 people per sq mile (111 people per sq km)
Total area 18,859 sq miles (48,845 sq km)
Languages Slovak, Hungarian, Czech
Religions Roman Catholic 60%, Atheist 10%, Protestant 8%, Orthodox 4%, other 18%
Ethnic mix Slovak 85%, Magyar 11%, Romany 1%, Czech 1%, other 2%
Government Parliamentary democracy
Currency Koruna = 100 halierov
Literacy rate 99%
Calorie consumption 3,133 kilocalories

Slovak Ore Mountains see Slovenské rudohorie

Slovenia 95 D8 Ger. Slowenien, Slvn. Slovenija. Country SE Europe

Slovenia 95

Official name Republic of Slovenia
Formation 1991
Capital Ljubljana
Population 2 million /256 people per sq mile (99 people per sq km)
Total area 7820 sq miles (20,253 sq km)
Languages Slovene, Serbo-Croat
Religions Roman Catholic 96%, Muslim 1%, other 3%
Ethnic mix Slovene 88%, Croat 3%, Serb 2%, Muslim 1%, other 6%
Government Parliamentary democracy
Currency Tolar = 100 stotins
Literacy rate 99%
Calorie consumption 3,168 kilocalories

Slovenské rudohorie 99 D6 Eng. Slovak Ore Mountains, Ger. Slowakisches Erzgebirge, Ungarisches Erzgebirge. Mountain range C Slovakia
Slov''yans'k 109 G3 Rus. Slavyansk. Donets'ka Oblast', E Ukraine
Slowakisches Erzgebirge see Slovenské rudohorie
Stubice 98 B3 Ger. Frankfurt. Lubuskie, W Poland
Sluch 108 D1 river NW Ukraine
Słupsk 98 C2 Ger. Stolp. Pomorskie, N Poland
Slutsk 107 C6 Rus. Slutsk. Minskaya Voblasts', S Belarus
Smallwood Reservoir 39 F2 lake Newfoundland and Labrador, S Canada
Smara 70 B3 var. Es Semara. N Western Sahara
Smarhon' 107 C5 Pol. Smorgonie, Rus. Smorgon'. Hrodzyenskaya Voblasts', W Belarus
Smederevo 100 D4 Ger. Semendria. Serbia, N Serbia and Montenegro (Yugo.)
Smederevska Palanka 100 D4 Serbia, C Serbia and Montenegro (Yugo.)
Smila 109 E2 Rus. Smela. Cherkas'ka Oblast', C Ukraine
Smiltene 106 D3 Ger. Smilten. Valka, N Latvia
Smola 84 A4 island W Norway
Smolensk 111 A5 Smolenskaya Oblast', W Russian Federation
Snake 34 B4 river Yukon Territory, NW Canada
Snake River 46 C3 river NW USA
Snake River Plain 46 D4 plain Idaho, NW USA
Sneek 86 D2 Friesland, N Netherlands
Snězka 98 B4 Ger. Schneekoppe. Mountain N Czech Republic
Śniardwy, Jezioro 114 D2 Ger. Spirdingsee. Lake NE Poland
Snina 99 E5 Hung. Szinna. Prešovský Kraj, E Slovakia
Snowdonia 89 C6 mountain range NW Wales, UK
Snyder 49 F3 Texas, SW USA
Sobradinho, Represa de 63 F2 var. Barragem de Sobradinho. Reservoir E Brazil
Sochi 111 A7 Krasnodarskiy Kray, SW Russian Federation
Société, Archipel de la 145 G4 var. Archipel de Tahiti, Îles de la Société, Eng. Society Islands. Island group W French Polynesia
Society Islands see Société, Archipel de la
Socorro 48 D2 New Mexico, SW USA
Socorro, Isla 50 B5 island W Mexico
Socotra see Suquţrā
Soc Trăng 137 D6 var. Khanh. Soc Trăng, S Vietnam
Socuéllamos 93 E3 Castilla-La Mancha, C Spain

Sodankylä 84 D3 Lappi, N Finland
Sodari see Sodiri
Söderhamn 85 C5 Gävleborg, C Sweden
Södertälje 85 C6 Stockholm, C Sweden
Sodiri 72 B4 var. Sawdirī, Sodari. Northern Kordofan, C Sudan
Sofia see Sofiya
Sofiya 104 C2 var. Sophia, Eng. Sofia; Lat. Serdica. Country capital (Bulgaria) Sofiya-Grad, W Bulgaria
Sogamoso 58 B3 Boyacá, C Colombia
Sognefjorden 85 A5 fjord NE North Sea
Sohâg 72 B2 var. Sawhāj, Suliag. C Egypt
Sohar see Şuhār
Sohm Plain 66 B3 undersea feature NW Atlantic Ocean
Sohrau see Żory
Sokal' 108 C2 Rus. Sokal. L'vivs'ka Oblast', NW Ukraine
Söke 116 A4 Aydın, SW Turkey
Sokhumi 117 E1 Rus. Sukhumi. NW Georgia
Sokodé 75 F4 C Togo
Sokol 110 C4 Vologodskaya Oblast', NW Russian Federation
Sokółka 98 E3 Białystok, NE Poland
Sokolov 99 A5 Ger. Falkenau an der Eger; prev. Falknov nad Ohří. Karlovarský Kraj, W Czech Republic
Sokone 74 B3 W Senegal
Sokoto 75 F4 river NW Nigeria
Sokoto 75 F3 Sokoto, NW Nigeria
Sokotra see Suquţrā
Solāpur 124 B3 var. Sholápur. Mahārāshtra, W India
Solca 108 C3 Ger. Solka. Suceava, N Romania
Sol, Costa del 92 D5 coastal region S Spain
Soldeu 91 B7 NE Andorra
Solec Kujawski 98 C3 Kujawski-pomorskie, C Poland
Soledad, Isla see East Falkland
Soledad 58 B1 Anzoátegui, NE Venezuela
Solikamsk 114 C3 Permskaya Oblast', NW Russian Federation
Sol'-Iletsk 111 D6 Orenburgskaya Oblast', W Russian Federation
Solingen 94 A4 Nordrhein-Westfalen, W Germany
Sollentuna 85 C6 Stockholm, C Sweden
Solok 138 B4 Sumatera, W Indonesia
Solomon Islands 144 C3 prev. British Solomon Islands Protectorate. Country W Pacific Ocean

Solomon Islands 144

Official name Solomon Islands
Formation 1978
Capital Honiara
Population 463,000 / 42 people per sq mile (16 people per sq km)
Total area 10,985 sq miles (28,450 sq km)
Languages English, Pidgin English, Melanesian Pidgin
Religions Anglican 34%, Roman Catholic 19%, South Seas Evangelical Church 17%, Methodist 11%, other 19%
Ethnic mix Melanesian 94%, other 6%
Government Parliamentary democracy
Currency Solomon Islands dollar = 100 cents
Literacy rate 62%
Calorie consumption 2,277 kilocalories

Solomon Islands 144 C3 island group PNG/Solomon Islands

Solomon Sea *144 B3 sea* W Pacific Ocean
Soltau *94 B3* Niedersachsen, NW Germany
Sol'tsy *110 A4* Novgorodskaya Oblast', W Russian Federation
Solwezi *78 D2* North Western, NW Zambia
Sōma *130 D4* Fukushima, Honshū, C Japan
Somalia *73 D5 Som.* Jamuuriyada Demuqraadiga Soomaaliyeed, Soomaaliya; *prev.* Italian Somaliland, Somaliland Protectorate. *Country* E Africa

Somalia 73

Official name Somali
Formation 1960
Capital Mogadishu
Population 9.2 million / 37 people per sq mile (14 people per sq km)
Total area 246,199 sq miles (637,657 sq km)
Languages Arabic, Somali, English, Italian
Religions Sunni Muslim 98%, other 2%
Ethnic mix Somali 85%, other 15%
Government Transitional regime
Currency Somali shilling = 100 cents
Literacy rate 24.1%
Calorie consumption 1,628 kilocalorie

Somali Basin *69 E5 undersea feature* W Indian Sea
Sombor *100 C3 Hung.* Zombor. Serbia, NW Serbia and Montenegro (Yugo.)
Someren *87 D5* Noord-Brabant, SE Netherlands
Somerset *42 A5 var.* Somerset Village. W Bermuda
Somerset *40 C5* Kentucky, S USA
Somerset Island *37 F2 island* Queen Elizabeth Islands, Nunavut, NW Canada
Somerset Island *42 A5 island* W Bermuda
Somerset Village *see* Somerset
Somers Islands *see* Bermuda
Somerton *48 A2* Arizona, SW USA
Someș *108 B3 var.* Somesch, Someșul, Szamos, *Ger.* Samosch. *River* Hungary/Romania
Somesch *see* Someș
Someșul *see* Someș
Somme *90 C2 river* N France
Somotillo *52 C3* Chinandega, NW Nicaragua
Somoto *52 D3* Madriz, NW Nicaragua
Songea *73 C8* Ruvuma, S Tanzania
Sông Hồng Hà *see* Red River
Songkhla *137 C7 var.* Songkla, *Mal.* Singora. Songkhla, SW Thailand
Songkla *see* Songkhla
Sông Srepok *see* Srêpôk, Tônle
Sông Tiên Giang *see* Mekong
Sonoran Desert *48 A3 var.* Desierto de Altar. *Desert* Mexico/USA *see also* Altar, Desierto de
Sonsonate *52 B3* Sonsonate, W El Salvador
Soochow *see* Suzhou
Sop Hao *136 D3* Houaphan, N Laos
Sophia *see* Sofiya
Sopot *98 C2 Ger.* Zoppot. Plovdiv, C Bulgaria
Sopron *99 B6 Ger.* Ödenburg. Győr-Moson-Sopron, NW Hungary
Sorgues *91 D6* Vaucluse, SE France
Sorgun *116 D3* Yozgat, C Turkey
Soria *93 E2* Castilla-León, N Spain
Soroca *108 D3 Rus.* Soroki. N Moldova
Sorong *139 F4* Papua, E Indonesia
Sørøy *see* Sørøya
Sørøya *84 C2 var.* Sørøy. *Island* N Norway
Sortavala *110 B3* Respublika Kareliya, NW Russian Federation

Sotavento, Ilhas de *74 A3 var.* Leeward Islands. *Island group* S Cape Verde
Sotkamo *84 E4* Oulu, C Finland
Souanké *77 B5* La Sangha, NW Congo
Soueida *see* As Suwaydā'
Soufli *104 D3 prev.* Souflíon. Anatolikí Makedonía kai Thráki, NE Greece
Soufrière *55 F2 volcano* S Dominica
Soukhné *see* As Sukhnah
Sŏul *129 E4 off.* Sŏul-t'ŭkpyŏlsi, *Eng.* Seoul, *Jap.* Keijō; *prev.* Kyŏngsŏng. *Country capital* (South Korea) NW South Korea
Soûr *119 A5 var.* Şūr; *anc.* Tyre. SW Lebanon
Souris River *45 E1 var.* Mouse River. *River* Canada/USA
Sourpi *105 B5* Thessalía, C Greece
Sousse *71 F2 var.* Sūsah. NE Tunisia
South Africa *78 C4 Afr.* Suid-Afrika. *Country* S Africa

South Africa 78

Official name Republic of South Africa
Formation 1934
Capital Pretoria (administrative)
Population 43.8 million / 93 people per sq mile (36 people per sq km)
Languages Afrikaans, English, 9 other African languages
Religions Black Independent 17%, Dutch reformed 11%, Roman Catholic 8%, Methodist 6%, other 58%
Ethnic mix Zulu 23%, other Black 38%, White 16%, Mixed 10%, other 13%
Government Parliamentary democracy
Currency Rand = 100 cents
Literacy rate 85.3%
Calorie consumption 2,886 kilocalorie

South America *56 continent*
Southampton *89 D7 hist.* Hamwih, *Lat.* Clausentum. S England, UK
Southampton Island *37 G3 island* Nunavut, NE Canada
South Andaman *133 F2 island* Andaman Islands, India, NE Indian Ocean
South Australia *149 A5 state* S Australia
South Australian Basin *142 B5 undersea feature* SW Indian Ocean
South Bend *40 C3* Indiana, N USA
South Beveland *see* Zuid-Beveland
South Bruny Island *149 C8 island* Tasmania, SE Australia
South Carolina *43 E2 off.* State of South Carolina; *also known as* The Palmetto State. *State* SE USA
South Carpathians *see* Carpații Meridionali
South China Basin *125 E4 undersea feature* SE South China Sea
South China Sea *124 D4 Chin.* Nan Hai, *Ind.* Laut Cina Selatan, *Vtn.* Biển Đông. *Sea* SE Asia
South Dakota *44 D2 off.* State of South Dakota; *also known as* The Coyote State, Sunshine State. *State* N USA
Southeast Indian Ridge *141 D7 undersea feature* Indian Ocean/Pacific Ocean
Southeast Pacific Basin *153 E5 var.* Belling Hausen Mulde. *Undersea feature* SE Pacific Ocean
South East Point *149 C7 headland* Victoria, S Australia
Southend-on-Sea *89 E6* E England, UK
Southern Alps *151 B6 mountain range* South Island, NZ
Southern Cook Islands *145 F4 island group* S Cook Islands

Southern Cross *147 B6* Western Australia
Southern Indian Lake *37 F4 lake* Manitoba, C Canada
Southern Ocean *67 B7 ocean*
Southern Uplands *88 C4 mountain range* S Scotland, UK
South Fiji Basin *142 D4 undersea feature* S Pacific Ocean
South Geomagnetic Pole *154 B3 pole* Antarctica
South Georgia *57 D8 island* South Georgia and the South Sandwich Islands, SW Atlantic Ocean
South Goulburn Island *146 E2 island* Northern Territory, N Australia
South Huvadhu Atoll *132 A5 var.* Gaafu Dhaalu Atoll. *Atoll* S Maldives
South Indian Basin *141 D7 undersea feature* Indian Ocean/Pacific Ocean
South Island *151 C6 island* S NZ
South Korea *129 E4 Kor.* Taehan Min'guk. *Country* E Asia

South Korea 129

Official name Republic of Korea
Formation 1948
Capital Seoul
Population 47.1 million / 1,239 people per sq mile (478 people per sq km)
Total area 38,023 sq miles (98,480 sq km)
Languages Korean, Chinese
Religions Mahayana Buddhist 47%, Protestant 38%, Roman Catholic 11%, Confucian 3%, other 1%
Ethnic mix Korean 100%
Government Presidential democracy
Currency Korean won = 100 chon
Literacy rate 97.8%
Calorie consumption 3,093 kilocalories

South Lake Tahoe *47 C5* California, W USA
South Orkney Islands *154 A2 island group* Antarctica
South Ossetia *117 F2 former autonomous region* SW Georgia
South Pacific Basin *see* Southwest Pacific Basin
South Platte River *44 D4 river* Colorado/Nebraska, C USA
South Pole *154 B3 pole* Antarctica
South Sandwich Islands *57 D8 island group* SE South Georgia and South Sandwich Islands
South Sandwich Trench *57 E8 undersea feature* SW Atlantic Ocean
South Shetland Islands *154 A2 island group* Antarctica
South Shields *88 D4* NE England, UK
South Sioux City *45 F3* Nebraska, C USA
South Taranaki Bight *150 C4 bight* SE Tasman Sea
South Tasmania Plateau *see* Tasman Plateau
South Uist *88 B3 island* NW Scotland, UK
South West Cape *151 A8 headland* Stewart Island, NZ
Southwest Indian Ocean Ridge *see* Southwest Indian Ridge
Southwest Indian Ridge *141 B6 var.* Southwest Indian Ocean Ridge. *Undersea feature* SW Indian Ocean
Southwest Pacific Basin *143 E4 var.* South Pacific Basin. *Undersea feature* SE Pacific Ocean
Sovereign Base Area *102 C5 UK military installation* E Cyprus
Sovereign Base Area *102 C5 UK military installation* S Cyprus
Soweto *78 D4* Gauteng, NE South Africa
Spain *92 D3 Sp.* España; *anc.* Hispania, Iberia, *Lat.* Hispana. *Country* SW Europe

Spain 92

Official name Kingdom of Spain
Formation 1492
Capital Madrid
Population 39.9 million / 205 people per sq mile (79 people per sq km)
Total area 194,896 sq miles (504,782 sq km)
Languages Spanish, Catalan, Galician, Basque
Religions Roman Catholic 96%, other 4%
Ethnic mix Castilian Spanish 72%, Catalan 17%, Galician 6%, other 5%
Government Parliamentary democracy
Currency Euro (peseta until 2002)
Literacy rate 97.7%
Calorie consumption 3,352 kilocalories

Spanish Town *54 B5 hist.* St.Iago de la Vega. C Jamaica
Sparks *47 C5* Nevada, W USA
Spartanburg *43 E1* South Carolina, SE USA
Spárti *105 B6 Eng.* Sparta. Pelopónnisos, S Greece
Spearfish *44 D2* South Dakota, N USA
Speightstown *55 G1* NW Barbados
Spencer *45 F3* Iowa, C USA
Spencer Gulf *149 B6 gulf* South Australia
Spey *88 C3 river* NE Scotland, UK
Spiess Seamount *67 C7 undersea feature* S Atlantic Ocean
Spijkenisse *86 B4* Zuid-Holland, SW Netherlands
Spili *105 C8* Kriti, Greece, E Mediterranean Sea
Spin Būldak *123 E5* Kandahār, S Afghanistan
Spirdingsee *see* Śniardwg, Jezioro
Spitsbergen *83 F2 island* NW Svalbard
Split *100 B4 It.* Spalato. Split-Dalmacija, S Croatia
Špogi *106 D4* Daugvapils, SE Latvia
Spokane *46 C2* Washington, NW USA
Spratly Islands *138 B2 Chin.* Nansha Qundao. *Disputed territory* SE Asia
Spree *94 D4 river* E Germany
Springfield *40 B4 state capital* Illinois, N USA
Springfield *41 G3* Massachusetts, NE USA
Springfield *45 G5* Missouri, C USA
Springfield *40 C4* Ohio, N USA
Springfield *46 B3* Oregon, NW USA
Spring Garden *59 F2* NE Guyana
Spring Hill *43 E4* Florida, SE USA
Springs Junction *151 C5* West Coast, South Island, NZ
Springsure *148 D4* Queensland, E Australia
Spruce Knob *41 E4 mountain* West Virginia, NE USA
Srbinje *see* Foča
Srbobran *100 C4* Republika Srpska, E Bosnia and Herzegovina
Sredets *104 E2 prev.* Grudovo. Burgas, E Bulgaria
Sredets *104 E2 prev.* Syulemeshlii. Stara Zagora, C Bulgaria
Srednerusskaya Vozvyshennost' *109 G1 Eng.* Central Russian Upland. *Mountain range* W Russian Federation
Srednesibirskoye Ploskogor'ye *114 D3 var.* Central Siberian Uplands, *Eng.* Central Siberian Plateau. *Mountain range* N Russian Federation
Sremska Mitrovica *100 C3 prev.* Mitrovica, *Ger.* Mitrowitz. Serbia, NW Serbia and Montenegro(Yugo.)

Srêpôk, Tônle *137 E5 var.*
Sông Srepok. *River*
Cambodia/Vietnam
Sri Aman *138 C3 var.* Bandar Sri
Aman, Simanggang. Borneo, East
Malaysia
Sri Jayawardanapura *132 D3 var.*
Sri Jayawardenepura; *prev.*
Kotte. Western Province, W Sri
Lanka
Sri Jayawardenepura *see* Sri
Jayawardanapura
Srīkākulam *135 F5* Andhra
Pradesh, E India
Sri Lanka *132 D3 prev.* Ceylon.
Country S Asia

Sri Lanka 132

Official name Democratic Socialist
Republic of Sri Lanka
Formation 1948
Capital Colombo
Population 19.1 million / 754
people per sq mile (291 people per
sq km)
Total area 25,332 sq miles
(65,610 sq km)
Languages Sinhalese, Tamil,
English
Religions Buddhist 69%, Hindu
15%, Christian 8%, Muslim 8%
Ethnic mix Sinhalese 74%, Tamil
18%, Moor 7%, other 1%
Government Presidential
democracy
Currency Sri Lanka rupee = 100
cents
Literacy rate 91.7%
Calorie consumption 2,405
kilocalories

Srpska, Republika *100 B3* Admin.
region *variant* NE Bosnia and
Herzegovina
Srinagarind Reservoir *137 C5 lake*
W Thailand
Ssu-ch'uan *see* Sichuan
Ssu-p'ing *see* Siping
Ssu-p'ing-chieh *see* Siping
Stabroek *87 B5* Antwerpen,
N Belgium
Stade *94 B3* Niedersachsen,
NW Germany
Stadskanaal *86 E2* Groningen,
NE Netherlands
Stafford *89 D6* C England, UK
Staicele *106 D3* Limbaži, N Latvia
Stakhanov *109 H3* Luhans'ka
Oblast', E Ukraine
Stalinabad *see* Dushanbe
Stalingrad *see* Volgograd
Stalinobod *see* Dushanbe
Stalin Peak *see* Kommunizm,
Qullai
Stalowa Wola *98 E4* Podkarpackie,
SE Poland
Stamford *41 F3* Connecticut, NE USA
Stampalia *see* Astypálaia
Stanley *65 D7 var.* Port Stanley,
Puerto Argentino. *Dependent
territory capital* (Falkland Islands)
East Falkland, Falkland Islands
Stanovoy Khrebet *113 E3 mountain
range* SE Russian Federation
Stanthorpe *149 D5* Queensland,
E Australia
Staphorst *86 D2* Overijssel,
E Netherlands
Starachowice *98 D4*
Świętokrzyskie, C Poland
Stara Pazova *100 D3 Ger.* Altpasua,
Hung. Ópazova. Serbia, N Serbia
and Montenegro (Yugo.)
Stara Zagora *104 D2 Lat.* Augusta
Trajana. Stara Zagora, C Bulgaria
Starbuck Island *145 G3 prev.*
Volunteer Island. *Island* E Kiribati
Stargard Szczeciński *98 B3 Ger.*
Stargard in Pommern.
Zachodniopomorskie, NW Poland
Starobíl's'k *109 H2 Rus.* Starobel'sk.
Luhans'ka Oblast',
E Ukraine
Starobyn *107 C7 Rus.* Starobin.
Minskaya Voblasts', S Belarus

Starogard Pomorskiei *98 C2 Ger.*
Preussisch-Stargard. Pomorskie,
N Poland
Starokostyantyniv *108 D2 Rus.*
Starokonstantinov. Khmel'nyts'ka
Oblast', NW Ukraine
Starominskaya *111 A7*
Krasnodarskiy Kray, SW Russian
Federation
Staryya Darohi *107 C6 Rus.* Staryye
Dorogi. Minskaya Voblasts',
S Belarus
Staryy Oskol *111 B6* Belgorodskaya
Oblast', W Russian Federation
State College *41 E4* Pennsylvania,
NE USA
Statesboro *43 E2* Georgia, SE USA
Staunton *41 E5* Virginia, NE USA
Stavanger *85 A6* Rogaland,
S Norway
Stavers Island *see* Vostok Island
Stavropol' *111 B7 prev.*
Voroshilovsk. Stavropol'skiy Kray,
SW Russian Federation
Steamboat Springs *44 C4* Colorado,
C USA
Steenwijk *86 D2* Overijssel,
N Netherlands
Steier *see* Steyr
Steinkjer *84 B4* Nord-Trøndelag,
C Norway
Stendal *94 C3* Sachsen-Anhalt,
C Germany
Stephenville *49 F3* Texas, SW USA
Sterling *44 D4* Colorado, C USA
Sterling *40 B3* Illinois, N USA
Sterlitamak *114 B3* Respublika
Bashkortostan, W Russian
Federation
Stettiner Haff *see* Szczeciński,
Zalew
Stevenage *89 E6* E England, UK
Stevens Point *40 B2* Wisconsin,
N USA
Stewart Island *151 A8 island* S NZ
Steyr *95 D6 var.* Steier.
Oberösterreich, N Austria
St-Gall *see* Sankt Gallen
StGallen *see* Sankt Gallen
Stif *see* Sétif
Stillwater *49 G1* Oklahoma, C USA
Stirling *88 C4* C Scotland, UK
Stjørdal *84 B4* Nord-Trøndelag,
C Norway
St-Laurent *see* St-Laurent-du-
Maroni
Stockach *95 B6* Baden-
Württemberg, S Germany
Stockholm *85 C6 country capital*
(Sweden) Stockholm, C Sweden
Stockton *47 B6* California, W USA
Stockton Plateau *49 E4 plain* Texas,
SW USA
Stœng Trêng *137 D5 prev.* Stung
Treng. Stœng Trêng,
NE Cambodia
Stoke *see* Stoke-on-Trent
Stoke-on-Trent *89 D6 var.* Stoke.
C England, UK
Stómio *104 B4* Thessalía, C Greece
Stony Tunguska *112 D2 river*
C Russian Federation
Store Bælt *see* Storebælt
Storebælt *85 B8 var.* Store Bælt, *Eng.*
Great Belt, Storebelt. *Channel*
Baltic Sea/Kattegat
Storebelt *see* Storebælt
Støren *85 B5* Sør-Trøndelag,
S Norway
Storfjorden *83 G2 fjord* S Norway
Stornoway *88 B2* NW Scotland,
UK
Storsjön *85 B5 lake* C Sweden
Storuman *84 C4 lake* N Sweden
Storuman *84 C4* Västerbotten,
N Sweden
Stowbtsy *107 C6 Pol.* Stołbce, *Rus.*
Stolbtsy. Minskaya Voblasts',
C Belarus
St.Paul Island *see* St-Paul, Île
St-Pierre and Miquelon *39 G4 Fr.*
Îles St-Pierre et Miquelon. *French
territorial collectivity* NE North
America

Strabane *89 B5 Ir.* An Srath Bán.
W Northern Ireland, UK
Strakonice *99 A5 Ger.* Strakonitz.
Budějovický Kraj, S Czech
Republic
Stralsund *94 D2* Mecklenburg-
Vorpommern, NE Germany
Stranraer *89 C5* S Scotland,
UK
Strasbourg *90 E3 Ger.* Strassburg;
anc. Argentoratum. Bas-Rhin,
NE France
Strǎșeni *108 D3 var.* Strasheny.
C Moldova
Strasheny *see* Strǎșeni
Stratford *150 D4* Taranaki, North
Island, NZ
Strathfield *148 E2* New South
Wales, SE Australia
Straubing *95 C6* Bayern,
SE Germany
Strehaia *108 B5* Mehedinți,
SW Romania
Strelka *114 D4* Krasnoyarskiy Kray,
C Russian Federation
Strofiliá *see* Strofyliá
Strofyliá *105 C5 var.* Strofilia.
Évvoia, C Greece
Stromboli, Isola *97 D6 island* Isole
Eolie, S Italy
Stromeferry *88 C3* N Scotland, UK
Strömstad *85 B6* Västra Götaland,
S Sweden
Strömsund *84 C4* Jämtland,
C Sweden
Struga *101 D6* SW FYR Macedonia
Strumica *101 E6* E FYR Macedonia
Strumyani *104 C3* Blagoevgrad,
SW Bulgaria
Strymónas *104 C3 Bul.* Struma.
River Bulgaria/Greece *see also*
Struma
Stryy *108 B2* L'vivs'ka Oblast',
NW Ukraine
Studholme *151 B6* Canterbury,
South Island, NZ
Sturgis *44 D3* South Dakota, N USA
Stuttgart *95 B6* Baden-
Württemberg, SW Germany
Stykkishólmur *83 E4* Vesturland,
W Iceland
Styr *108 C1 Rus.* Styr'. *River*
Belarus/Ukraine
Su *see* Jiangsu
Suakin *72 C3 var.* Sawakin. Red Sea,
NE Sudan
Subačius *106 C4* Kupiškis,
NE Lithuania
Subaykhān *118 E3* Dayr az Zawr,
E Syria
Subotica *100 D2 Ger.* Maria-
Theresiopel, *Hung.* Szabadka.
Serbia, N Serbia and Montenegro
(Yugo.)
Suceava *108 C3 Ger.* Suczawa,
Hung. Szucsava. Suceava,
NE Romania
Su-chou *see* Suzhou
Suchow *see* Xuzhou
Sucre *61 F4 hist.* Chuquisaca, La
Plata. *Country capital* (Bolivia-legal
capital) Chuquisaca, S Bolivia
Sudan *72 A4 Ar.* Jumhuriyat as-
Sudan; *prev.* Anglo-Egyptian
Sudan. *country* N Africa

Sudan 72

Official name Republic of the
Sudan
Formation 1956
Capital Khartoum
Population 31.8 million / 33 people
per sq mile (13 people per sq km)
Total area 967,493 sq miles
(2,505,810 sq km)
Languages Arabic, Dinka, Nuer,
Zande, Nubian, Beja, Bari, Fur,
Shilluk, Lotuko
Religions Muslim (mainly Sunni)
70%, Traditional beliefs 20%,
other 10%
Ethnic mix Arab 40%, Tribal 30%,
Dinka and Beja 7%, other 23%

Sudan (continued)

Government Presidential regime
Currency Sudanese pound or dinar
= 100 piastres
Literacy rate 58%
Calorie consumption 2,348
kilocalories

Sudbury *38 C4* Ontario, S Canada
Sudd *73 B5 swamp region*
S Sudan
Sudeten *98 B4 var.* Sudetes, Sudetic
Mountains, Cz./Pol. Sudety.
Mountain range Czech
Republic/Poland
Sudetes *see* Sudeten
Sudetic Mountains *see* Sudeten
Sudety *see* Sudeten
Südkarpaten *see* Carpații
Meridionali
Sue *73 B5 river* S Sudan
Sueca *93 F3* País Valenciano,
E Spain
Sue Wood Bay *42 B5 bay*
W Bermuda
Suez *72 B1 Ar.* As Suways,
El Suweis. NE Egypt
Suez Canal *72 B1 Ar.* Qanāt as
Suways. *Canal* NE Egypt
Suez, Gulf of *72 B2 Ar.* Khalīj as
Suways. *Gulf* NE Egypt
Suğla Gölü *116 C4 lake* SW Turkey
Şuḩār *121 D5 var.* Sohar.
N Oman
Sühbaatar *127 E1* Selenge,
N Mongolia
Suhl *95 C5* Thüringen, C Germany
Suixi *128 C6* Guangdong,
S China
Sujāwal *134 B3* Sind, SE Pakistan
Sukabumi *138 C5 prev.* Soekaboemi.
Jawa, C Indonesia
Sukagawa *131 D5* Fukushima,
Honshū, C Japan
Sukarnapura *see* Jayapura
Sukhne *see* As Sukhnah
Sukhona *110 C4 var.* Tot'ma. *River*
NW Russian Federation
Sukkertoppen *see* Maniitsoq
Sukkur *134 B3* Sind, SE Pakistan
Sukumo *131 B7* Kōchi, Shikoku,
SW Japan
Sulaimaniya *see* As Sulaymānīyah
Sulaimān Range *134 C2 mountain
range* C Pakistan
Sula, Kepulauan *139 E4 island
group* C Indonesia
Sulawesi *139 E4 Eng.* Celebes.
Island C Indonesia
Sulechów *98 B3 Ger.* Züllichau.
Lubuskie, W Poland
Suliag *see* Sohâg
Sullana *60 B2* Piura, NW Peru
Sulphur Springs *49 G2* Texas,
SW USA
Sulu Archipelago *139 E3 island
group* SW Philippines
Sulu Sea *139 E2 Ind.* Laut Sulu. *Sea*
SW Philippines
Sulyukta *123 E2 Kir.* Sülüktü.
Oshskaya Oblast', SW
Kyrgyzstan
Sumatera *137 B8 Eng.* Sumatra.
Island W Indonesia
Sumatra *see* Sumatera
Sumba, Pulau *139 E5 Eng.*
Sandalwood Island; *prev.* Soemba.
Island Nusa Tenggara,
C Indonesia
Sumba, Selat *139 E5 strait* Nusa
Tenggara, S Indonesia
Sumbawanga *73 B7* Rukwa,
W Tanzania
Sumbe *78 B2 prev.* N'Gunza, *Port.*
Novo Redondo. Cuanza Sul,
W Angola
Sumeih *73 B5* Southern Darfur,
S Sudan
Summer Lake *46 B4 lake* Oregon,
NW USA
Summit *93 H5 mountain*
C Gibraltar

Sumqayıt 117 H2 Rus. Sumgait.
E Azerbaijan
Sumy 109 F2 Sums'ka Oblast',
NE Ukraine
Sunbury 149 C7 Victoria,
SE Australia
Sunda Islands see Greater Sunda
Islands
Sunda, Selat 138 B5 strait
Jawa/Sumatera, SW Indonesia
Sunda Trench see Java Trench
Sunderland 88 D4 var. Wearmouth.
NE England, UK
Sundsvall 85 C5 Västernorrland,
C Sweden
Sungaipenuh 138 B4 prev.
Soengaipenoeh. Sumatera,
W Indonesia
Sunnyvale 47 A6 California,
W USA
Suntar 115 F3 Respublika Sakha
(Yakutiya), NE Russian
Federation
Sunyani 75 E5 W Ghana
Suomussalmi 84 E4 Oulu,
E Finland
Suŏng 137 D6 Kâmpóng Cham,
C Cambodia
Suoyarvi 110 B3 Respublika
Kareliya, NW Russian Federation
Supe 60 C3 Lima, W Peru
Superior 40 A1 Wisconsin, N USA
Superior, Lake 40 B1 Fr. Lac
Supérieur. Lake Canada/USA
Suqrah see Şawqirah
Suquţrā 121 C7 var. Sokotra, Eng.
Socotra. Island SE Yemen
Şūr see Soûr
Şūr 121 E5 NE Oman
Surabaya 138 D5 prev. Soerabaja,
Surabaja. Jawa, C Indonesia
Surakarta 138 C5 Eng. Solo; prev.
Soerakarta. Jawa, S Indonesia
Šurany 99 C6 Hung. Nagysurány.
Nitriansky Kraj, SW Slovakia
Sūrat 134 C4 Gujarāt, W India
Suratdhani see Surat Thani
Surat Thani 137 C6 var. Suratdhani.
Surat Thani, SW Thailand
Surazh 107 E5 Rus. Surazh.
Vitsyebskaya Voblasts',
NE Belarus
Surdulica 101 E5 Serbia, SE Serbia
and Montenegro (Yugo.)
Sûre 87 D7 var. Sauer. River
W Europe see also Sauer
Surendranagar 134 C4 Gujarāt,
W India
Surfers Paradise 149 E5
Queensland, E Australia
Surgut 114 D3 Khanty-Mansiyskiy
Avtonomnyy Okrug, C Russian
Federation
Surin 137 D5 Surin, E Thailand
Surinam see Suriname
Suriname 59 G3 var. Surinam; prev.
Dutch Guiana, Netherlands
Guiana. Country N S America

Suriname 59

Official name Republic of Suriname
Formation 1975
Capital Paramaribo
Population 419,000 / 7 people
per sq mile (3 people per sq km)
Total area 63,039 sq miles
(163,270 sq km)
Languages Dutch, Sranan,
Saramaccan, Javanese, Sarnami
Hindi, Chinese
Religions Christian 48%, Hindu
27%, Muslim 20%, other 5%
Ethnic mix Indo South Asian 34%, Creole
34%, Javanese 18%, Black 9%,
other 5%
Government Parliamentary
democracy
Currency Suriname guilder = 100
cents
Literacy rate 94.2%
Calorie consumption 2,652
kilocalories

Surkhob 123 F3 river
C Tajikistan
Surt 71 G2 var. Sidra, Sirte.
N Libya
Surt, Khalīj 71 F2 Eng. Gulf of
Sidra, Gulf of Sirti, Sidra. Gulf
N Libya
Surtsey 83 E5 island S Iceland
Suruga-wan 131 D6 bay
SE Japan
Susa 96 A2 Piemonte, NE Italy
Süsah see Sousse
Susanville 47 B5 California,
W USA
Susitna 36 C3 Alaska, USA
Susteren 87 D5 Limburg,
SE Netherlands
Susuman 115 G3 Magadanskaya
Oblast', E Russian Federation
Sutherland 148 E2 New South
Wales, SE Australia
Sutlej 134 C2 river India/Pakistan
Suur Munamägi 106 D3 var.
Munamägi, Ger. Eier-Berg.
Mountain SE Estonia
Suur Väin 106 C2 Ger. Grosser
Sund. Strait W Estonia
Suva 145 E4 country capital (Fiji) Viti
Levu, W Fiji
Suwałki 98 E2 Lith. Suvalkai, Rus.
Suvalki. Podlaskie, NE Poland
Şuwār see Aş Şuwār
Suweida see As Suwaydā'
Suzhou 128 D5 var. Soochow, Su-
chou, Suchow; prev. Wuhsien.
Jiangsu, E China
Svalbard 83 E1 Norwegian
dependency Arctic Ocean
Svartisen 84 C3 glacier
C Norway
Svay Riêng 137 D6 Svay Riêng,
S Cambodia
Sveg 85 B5 Jämtland,
C Sweden
Svenstavik 85 C5 Jämtland,
C Sweden
Svetlograd 111 B7 Stavropol'skiy
Kray, SW Russian Federation
Svilengrad 104 D3 prev. Mustafa-
Pasha. Khaskovo, S Bulgaria
Svitlovods'k 109 F3 Rus.
Svetlovodsk. Kirovohrads'ka
Oblast', C Ukraine
Svobodnyy 115 G4 Amurskaya
Oblast', SE Russian
Federation
Svyataya Anna Trough 172 C4 var.
Saint Anna Trough. Undersea
feature N Kara Sea
Svyetlahorsk 107 D7 Rus.
Svetlogorsk. Homyel'skaya
Voblasts', SE Belarus
Swabian Jura see Schwäbische Alb
Swakopmund 78 B3 Erongo,
W Namibia
Swansea 89 C7 Wel. Abertawe.
S Wales, UK
Swarzędz 98 C3 Wielkopolskie,
C Poland
Swatow see Shantou
Swaziland 78 D4 Country S Africa

Swaziland 78

Official name Kingdom of
Swaziland
Formation 1968
Capital Mbabane
Population 938,000 / 140 people
per sq mile (54 people per sq km)
Total area 6,704 sq miles
(17,363 sq km)
Languages Siswati, English, Zulu,
Tsonga
Religions Christian 60%,
Traditional beliefs 40%
Ethnic mix Swazi 97%, other 3%
Government Constitutional
monarchy
Currency Lilangeni = 100 cents
Literacy rate 79.6%
Calorie consumption 2,620
kilocalories

Sweden 84 B4 Swe. Sverige. Country
N Europe

Sweden 84

Official name Kingdom of Sweden
Formation 1523
Capital Stockholm
Population 8.8 million /
51 people per sq mile (20 people
per sq km)
Total area 173,731 sq miles
(449,964 sq km)
Languages Swedish, Finnish,
Sami
Religions Evangelical Lutheran
89%, Roman Catholic 2%, other 9%
Ethnic mix Swedish 91%, Finnish
and Sami 3%, other European 6%
Government Parliamentary
democracy
Currency Swedish krona = 100 ore
Literacy rate 99%
Calorie consumption 3,109
kilocalories

Swed Ormsö see Vormsi
Sweetwater 49 F3 Texas,
SW USA
Świdnica 98 B4 Ger. Schweidnitz.
Wałbrzych, SW Poland
Świdwin 98 B2 Ger. Schivelbein.
Zachodniopomorskie, NW Poland
Świebodzice 98 B4 Ger. Freiburg in
Schlesien, Swiebodzice.
Wałbrzych, SW Poland
Świebodzin 98 B3 Ger. Schwiebus.
Lubuskie, W Poland
Świecie 98 C3 Ger. Schwertberg.
Kujawsko-pomorskie, C Poland
Swindon 89 D7 S England, UK
Świnoujście 98 B2 Ger.
Swinemünde.
Zachodniopomorskie, NW Poland
Switzerland 95 A7 Fr. La Suisse,
Ger. Schweiz, It. Svizzera; anc.
Helvetia. Country C Europe

Switzerland 95

Official name Swiss Confederation
Formation 1291
Capital Bern
Population 7.2 million / 469 people
per sq mile (174 people per sq km)
Total area 15,942 sq miles
(41,290 sq km)
Languages German, French, Italian,
Swiss German, Romansch
Religions Roman Catholic 46%,
Protestant 40%, other 14%
Ethnic mix German 65%, French
18%, Italian 10%, Romansh 1%,
other 6%
Government Parliamentary
democracy
Currency Swiss franc = 100
centimes
Literacy rate 99%
Calorie consumption 3,293
kilocalories

Sycaminum see Hefa
Sydney 148 D1 state capital New
South Wales, SE Australia
Sydney 39 G4 Cape Breton Island,
Nova Scotia, SE Canada
Syedpur see Saidpur
Syemyezhava 107 C6 Rus.
Semezhevo. Minskaya Voblasts',
C Belarus
Syene see Aswān
Syeverodonets'k 109 H3 Rus.
Severodonetsk. Luhans'ka
Oblast', E Ukraine
Syktyvkar 110 D4 prev. Ust'-
Sysol'sk. Respublika Komi,
NW Russian Federation
Sylhet 135 G3 Chittagong,
NE Bangladesh
Synel'nykove 109 G3
Dnipropetrovs'ka Oblast',
E Ukraine

Syowa 154 C2 Japanese research
station Antarctica
Syracuse 41 F3 New York, NE USA
Syrdariya see Syr Darya
Syr Darya 114 B4 var. Sai Hun, Sir
Darya, Syrdariya, Kaz. Syrdariya,
Rus. Syrdar'ya, Uzb. Sirdaryo; anc.
Jaxartes. River C Asia
Syria 118 B3 var. Siria, Syrie, Ar. Al-
Jumhūrīyah al-'Arabīyah as-
Sūrīyah, Sūrīya. Country SW Asia

Syria 118

Official name Syrian Arab Republic
Formation 1941
Capital Damascus
Population 16.6 million / 232
people per sq mile (90 people
per sq km)
Total area 71,498 sq miles
(185,180 sq km)
Languages Arabic, French, Kurdish
Religions Sunni Muslim 74%, other
Muslim 16%, Christian 10%
Ethnic mix Arab 89%, Kurdish 6%,
Armenian, Turkmen, Circassian 2%,
other 3%
Government One-party republic
Currency Syrian pound = 100
piastres
Literacy rate 74.5%
Calorie consumption 3,038
kilocalories

Syrian Desert 119 D5 Ar.
Al Hamad, Bādiyat ash Shām.
Desert SW Asia
Sýrna 105 E7 var. Sirna. Island
Kykládes, Greece, Aegean Sea
Sýros 105 C6 var. Síros. Island
Kykládes, Greece, Aegean Sea
Syvash, Zatoka 109 F4 Rus. Zaliv
Syvash. Inlet S Ukraine
Syzran' 111 C6 Samarskaya Oblast',
W Russian Federation
Szamos see Someş
Szamotuły 98 B3 Wielkopolskie,
C Poland
Szczecin 98 B3 Eng./Ger. Stettin.
Zachodniopomorskie, NW Poland
Szczecinek 98 B2 Ger. Neustettin.
Zachodniopomorskie, NW Poland
Szczeciński, Zalew 98 A2 var.
Stettiner Haff, Ger. Oderhaff. Bay
Germany/Poland
Szczytno 98 D3 Ger. Ortelsburg.
Olsztyn, NE Poland
Szechuan see Sichuan
Szechwan see Sichuan
Szeged 99 D7 Ger. Szegedin, Rom.
Seghedin. Csongrád, SE Hungary
Székesfehérvár 99 C6 Ger.
Stuhlweissenberg; anc. Alba
Regia. Fejér, W Hungary
Szekszárd 99 C7 Tolna, S Hungary
Szenttamás see Srbobran
Szeping see Siping
Sziszek see Sisak
Szlatina see Slatina
Szolnok 99 D6 Jász-Nagykun-
Szolnok, C Hungary
Szombathely 99 B6 Ger.
Steinamanger; anc. Sabaria,
Savaria. Vas, W Hungary
Szprotawa 98 B4 Ger. Sprottau.
Lubuskie, W Poland

T

Table Rock Lake 49 G1 reservoir
Arkansas/Missouri, C USA
Tábor 99 B5 Budějovický Kraj,
S Czech Republic
Tabora 73 B7 Tabora, W Tanzania
Tabrīz 120 C2 var. Tebriz; anc.
Tauris. Āzarbāyjān-e Khāvarī,
NW Iran
Tabuaeran 145 G2 prev. Fanning
Island. Atoll Line Islands,
E Kiribati
Tabūk 120 A4 Tabūk, NW Saudi
Arabia

Täby *85 C6* Stockholm, C Sweden
Tachov *99 A5 Ger.* Tachau. Plzeňský Kraj, W Czech Republic
Tacloban *139 F2 off.* Tacloban City. Leyte, C Philippines
Tacna *61 E4* Tacna, SE Peru
Tacoma *46 B2* Washington, NW USA
Tacuarembó *64 D4 prev.* San Fructuoso. Tacuarembó, C Uruguay
Tademaït, Plateau du *70 D3 plateau* C Algeria
Tadmor *see* Tudmur
Tadmur *see* Tudmur
Tādpatri *132 C2* Andhra Pradesh, E India
Taegu *129 E4 off.* Taegugwangyŏksi, *var.* Daegu, *Jap.* Taikyū. SE South Korea
Taejŏn *129 E4 off.* Taejŏngwangyŏksi, *Jap.* Taiden. C South Korea
Tafassâsset, Ténéré du *75 G2 desert* N Niger
Tafila *see* Aṭ Ṭafilah
Taganrog *111 A7* Rostovskaya Oblast', SW Russian Federation
Taganrog, Gulf of *109 G4 Rus.* Taganrogskiy Zaliv, *Ukr.* Tahanroz'ka Zatoka. *Gulf* Russian Federation/Ukraine
Taguatinga *63 F3* Tocantins, C Brazil
Tagus *92 C3 Port.* Rio Tejo, *Sp.* Río Tajo. *River* Portugal/Spain
Tagus Plain *80 A4 undersea feature* E Atlantic Ocean
Tahat *71 E4 mountain* SE Algeria
Tahiti *145 H4 island* Îles du Vent, W French Polynesia
Tahlequah *49 G1* Oklahoma, C USA
Tahoe, Lake *47 B5 lake* California/Nevada, W USA
Tahoua *75 F3* Tahoua, W Niger
T'aichung *128 D6 Jap.* Taichū; *prev.* Taiwan. C Taiwan
Taieri *151 B7 river* South Island, NZ
Taihape *150 D4* Manawatu-Wanganui, North Island, NZ
Tailem Bend *149 B7* South Australia
T'ainan *128 D6 Jap.* Tainan; *prev.* Dainan. S Taiwan
T'aipei *128 D6 Jap.* Taihoku; *prev.* Daihoku. *Country capital* (Taiwan) N Taiwan
Taiping *138 B3* Perak, Peninsular Malaysia
Taiwan *128 D6 var.* Formosa, Formo'sa. *Country* E Asia

Taiwan 128

Official name Republic of China (Taiwan)
Formation 1949
Capital Taipei
Population 22.2 million / 1,598 people per sq mile (617 people per sq km)
Total area 13,892 sq miles (35,980 sq km)
Languages Mandarin Chinese, Amoy Chinese, Hakka Chinese
Religions Buddhist, Confucian, Taoist 93%, Christian 5%, other 2%
Ethnic mix Indigenous Chinese 84%, Mainland Chinese 14%, Aborigine 2%
Government Multiparty republic
Currency Taiwan dollar = 100 cents
Literacy rate 94%
Calorie consumption not available

T'aiwan Haihsia *see* Taiwan Strait
Taiwan Haixia *see* Taiwan Strait
Taiwan Strait *128 D6 var.* Formosa Strait, *Chin.* T'aiwan Haihsia, Taiwan Haixia. *Strait* China/Taiwan
Taiyuan *128 C4 prev.* T'ai-yuan, T'ai-yüan, Yangku. Shanxi, C China

Ta'izz *121 B7* SW Yemen
Tajikistan *123 E3 Rus.* Tadzhikistan, *Taj.* Jumhurii Tojikiston; *prev.* Tajik S.S.R. *Country* C Asia

Tajikistan 123

Official name Republic of Tajikistan
Formation 1991
Capital Dushanbe
Population 6.1 million / 110 people per sq mile (43 people per sq km)
Total area 55,251 sq miles (143,100 sq km)
Languages Tajik, Russian
Religions Sunni Muslim 80%, Shi'a Muslim 5%, other 15%
Ethnic mix Tajik 62%, Uzbek 24%, Russian 8%, Tatar 1%, Kyrgyz 1%, other 4%
Government Multiparty republic
Currency Somoni
Literacy rate 99%
Calorie consumption 1720 kilocalories

Tak *136 C4 var.* Rahaeng. Tak, W Thailand
Takao *see* Kaohsiung
Takaoka *131 C5* Toyama, Honshū, SW Japan
Takapuna *150 D2* Auckland, North Island, NZ
Takhiatosh *122 C2 Rus.* Takhiatash. Qoraqalpoghiston Respublikasi, W Uzbekistan
Takhtakŭpir *122 D1 Rus.* Takhtakupyr. Qoraqalpoghiston Respublikasi, NW Uzbekistan
Takikawa *130 D2* Hokkaidō, NE Japan
Takla Makan Desert *see* Taklimakan Shamo
Taklimakan Shamo *126 B3 Eng.* Takla Makan Desert. *Desert* NW China
Takow *see* Kaohsiung
Takutea *145 G4 island* S Cook Islands
Talachyn *107 D6 Rus.* Tolochin. Vitsyebskaya Voblasts', NE Belarus
Talamanca, Cordillera de *53 E5 mountain range* S Costa Rica
Talara *60 B2* Piura, NW Peru
Talas *123 F2* Talasskaya Oblast', NW Kyrgyzstan
Talaud, Kepulauan *139 F3 island group* E Indonesia
Talavera de la Reina *92 D3 anc.* Caesarobriga, Talabriga. Castilla-La Mancha, C Spain
Talca *64 B4* Maule, C Chile
Talcahuano *65 B5* Bío Bío, C Chile
Taldykorgan *114 C5 Kaz.* Taldyqorghan; *prev.* Taldy-Kurgan. Almaty, SE Kazakhstan
Taldy-Kurgan/Taldyqorghan *see* Taldykorgan
Ta-lien *see* Dalian
Taliq-an *see* Tāloqān
Tal'ka *107 C6 Rus.* Tal'ka. Minskaya Voblasts', C Belarus
Tallahassee *42 D3 prev.* Muskogean. *State capital* Florida, SE USA
Tall al Abyaḍ *see* At Tall al Abyaḍ
Tallinn *106 D2 Ger.* Reval, *Rus.* Tallin; *prev.* Revel. *Country capital* (Estonia) Harjumaa, NW Estonia
Tall Kalakh *118 B4 var.* Tell Kalakh. Ḥimṣ, C Syria
Tallulah *42 B2* Louisiana, S USA
Talnakh *114 D3* Taymyrskiy (Dolgano-Nenetskiy) Avtonomnyy Okrug, N Russian Federation
Tal'ne *109 E3 Rus.* Tal'noye. Cherkas'ka Oblast', C Ukraine
Taloga *49 F1* Oklahoma, C USA
Tāloqān *123 E3 var.* Taliq-an. Takhār, NE Afghanistan

Talsi *106 C3 Ger.* Talsen. Talsi, NW Latvia
Taltal *64 B2* Antofagasta, N Chile
Talvik *84 D2* Finnmark, N Norway
Tamabo, Banjaran *138 D3 mountain range* East Malaysia
Tamale *75 E4* C Ghana
Tamana *145 E3 prev.* Rotcher Island. *Atoll* Tungaru, W Kiribati
Tamanrasset *71 E4 var.* Tamenghest. S Algeria
Tamar *89 C7 river* SW England, UK
Tamar *see* Tudmur
Tamatave *see* Toamasina
Tamazunchale *51 E4* San Luis Potosí, C Mexico
Tambacounda *74 C3* SE Senegal
Tambov *111 B6* Tambovskaya Oblast', W Russian Federation
Tambura *73 B5* Western Equatoria, SW Sudan
Tamchaket *see* Tâmchekkeṭ
Tâmchekkeṭ *74 C3 var.* Tamchaket. Hodh el Gharbi, S Mauritania
Tamenghest *see* Tamanrasset
Tamiahua, Laguna de *51 F4 lagoon* E Mexico
Tamil Nādu *132 C3 prev.* Madras. *State* SE India
Tam Ky *137 E5* Quang Nam-Da Nâng, C Vietnam
Tampa *43 E4* Florida, SE USA
Tampa Bay *43 E4 bay* Florida, SE USA
Tampere *85 D5 Swe.* Tammerfors. Länsi-Suomi, W Finland
Tampico *51 E3* Tamaulipas, C Mexico
Tamworth *149 D6* New South Wales, SE Australia
Tana *84 D2 var.* Tenojoki, *Fin.* Teno, *Lapp.* Dealnu. *River* Finland/Norway *see also* Teno
Tana *84 D2* Finnmark, N Norway
Tanabe *131 C7* Wakayama, Honshū, SW Japan
T'ana Hāyk' *72 C4 Eng.* Lake Tana. *Lake* NW Ethiopia
Tanais *see* Don
Tanami Desert *146 D3 desert* Northern Territory, N Australia
Tandil *65 D5* Buenos Aires, E Argentina
Tanega-shima *131 B8 island* Nansei-shotō, SW Japan
Tane Range *136 B4 Bur.* Tanen Taunggyi. *Mountain range* W Thailand
Tanezrouft *70 D4 desert* Algeria/Mali
Ṭanf, Jabal aṭ *118 D4 mountain* SE Syria
Tanga *73 C7* Tanga, E Tanzania
Tanga *73 C7 region* E Tanzania
Tanganyika, Lake *73 B7 lake* E Africa
Tangeh-ye Hormoz *see* Hormuz, Strait of
Tanger *70 C2 var.* Tangiers, Tangier, *Fr./Ger.* Tangerk, *Sp.* Tánger; *anc.* Tingis. NW Morocco
Tangier *see* Tanger
Tangiers *see* Tanger
Tangla Range *see* Tanggula Shan
Tangra Yumco *126 B5 var.* Tangro Tso. *Lake* W China
Tangro Tso *see* Tangra Yumco
Tangshan *128 D3 var.* T'ang-shan. Hebei, E China
T'ang-shan *see* Tangshan
Tanimbar, Kepulauan *139 F5 island group* Maluku, E Indonesia
Tanna *144 D4 island* S Vanuatu
Tannenhof *see* Krynica
Tan-Tan *70 B3* SW Morocco
Tan-tung *see* Dandong

Talsi *106 C3 Ger.* Talsen. Talsi, NW Latvia

Tanzania *73 C7 Swa.* Jamhuri ya Muungano wa Tanzania; *prev.* German East Africa, Tanganyika and Zanzibar. *Country* E Africa

Tanzania 73

Official name United Republic of Tanzania
Formation 1961
Capital Dodoma
Population 36 million / 99 people per sq mile (38 people per sq km)
Total area 364,898 sq miles (945,087 sq km)
Languages English, Kiswahili, Sukuma
Religions Muslim 33%, Christian 33%, Traditional beliefs 30%, other 4%
Ethnic mix Native African (over 120 tribes) 99%, European and Asian 1%
Government Presidential democracy
Currency Tanzanian shilling = 100 cents
Literacy rate 75.8%
Calorie consumption 1,906 kilocalories

Taoudenit *see* Taoudenni
Taoudenni *75 E2 var.* Taoudenit. Tombouctou, N Mali
Tapa *106 E2 Ger.* Taps. Lääne-Virumaa, NE Estonia
Tapachula *51 G5* Chiapas, SE Mexico
Tapajós, Rio *63 E2 var.* Tapajóz. *River* NW Brazil
Tapajóz *see* Tapajós, Rio
Ṭarābulus *71 F2 var.* Ṭarābulus al Gharb, *Eng.* Tripoli.*Country capital* (Libya) NW Libya
Ṭarābulus *see* Tripoli
Ṭarābulus al Gharb *see* Ṭarābulus
Ṭarābulus ash Shām *see* Tripoli
Taraclia *108 D4 Rus.* Tarakilya. S Moldova
Taranaki, Mount *150 C4 var.* Egmont, Mount. *Mountain* North Island, NZ
Tarancón *93 E3* Castilla-La Mancha, C Spain
Taranto *97 E5 var.* Tarentum. Puglia, SE Italy
Taranto, Golfo di *97 E6 Eng.* Gulf of Taranto. *Gulf* S Italy
Tarapoto *60 C2* San Martín, N Peru
Tarare *91 D5* Rhône, E France
Tarascon *91 D6* Bouches-du-Rhône, SE France
Tarawa *144 D2 atoll* Tungaru, W Kiribati
Taraz *114 C5 prev.* Aulie Ata, Auliye-Ata, Dzhambul, Zhambyl. Zhambyl, S Kazakhstan
Tarazona *93 E2* Aragón, NE Spain
Tarbes *91 B6 anc.* Bigorra. Hautes-Pyrénées, S France
Tarcoola *149 A6* South Australia
Taree *149 D6* New South Wales, SE Australia
Tarentum *see* Taranto
Târgoviște *108 C3 var.* Tîrgoviște. Dâmbovița, S Romania
Târgu Jiu *108 B4 prev.* Tîrgu Jiu. Gorj, W Romania
Târgu-Neamț *see* Târgu-Neamț
Târgu Mures *108 B4 prev.* Oșorhei, Tîrgu Mures, *Ger.* Neumarkt, *Hung.* Marosvásárhely. Mureș, C Romania
Târgu-Neamț *108 C3 var.* Târgu-Neamț; *prev.* Tîrgu-Neamț. Neamț, NE Romania
Târgu Ocna *108 C4 Hung.* Aknavásár; *prev.* Tîrgu Ocna. Bacău, E Romania
Târgu Secuiesc *108 C4 Ger.* Neumarkt, Szekler Neumarkt, *Hung.* Kezdivásárhely; *prev.* Chezdi-Oșorheiu, Târgul-Săcuiesc, Tîrgu Secuiesc. Covasna, E Romania

Tarija *61 G5* Tarija, S Bolivia
Tarīm *121 C6* C Yemen
Tarim Basin *124 C2 basin* NW China
Tarim He *126 B3 river* NW China
Tarma *60 C3* Junín, C Peru
Tarn *91 C6 cultural region* S France
Tarn *91 C6 river* S France
Tarnobrzeg *98 D4* Podkarpackie, SE Poland
Tarnów *99 D5* Małopolskie, S Poland
Tarragona *93 G2 anc.* Tarraco. Cataluña, E Spain
Tàrrega *93 F2 var.* Tarrega. Cataluña, NE Spain
Tarsus *116 C4* İçel, S Turkey
Tartu *106 D3 Ger.* Dorpat; *prev.* Rus. Yurev, Yur'yev. Tartumaa, SE Estonia
Ţarţūs *118 A3 Fr.* Tartouss; *anc.* Tortosa. Tarţūs, W Syria
Ta Ru Tao, Ko *137 B7 island* S Thailand
Tarvisio *96 D2* Friuli-Venezia Giulia, NE Italy
Tashi Chho Dzong *see* Thimphu
Tashkent *see* Toshkent
Tash-Kumyr *123 F2 Kir.* Tash-Kömür. Dzhalal-Abadskaya Oblast', W Kyrgyzstan
Tashqurghan *see* Kholm
Tasikmalaya *138 C5 prev.* Tasikmalaja. Jawa, C Indonesia
Tasman Basin *142 C5 var.* East Australian Basin. *Undersea feature* S Tasman Sea
Tasman Bay *151 C5 inlet* South Island, NZ
Tasmania *149 B8 prev.* Van Diemen's Land. *State* SE Australia
Tasmania *152 B4 island* SE Australia
Tasman Plateau *142 C5 var.* South Tasmania Plateau. *Undersea feature* SW Tasman Sea
Tasman Sea *142 C5 sea* SW Pacific Ocean
Tassili-n-Ajjer *71 E4 plateau* E Algeria
Tatabánya *99 C6* Komárom-Esztergom, NW Hungary
Tathlīth *121 B5 'Asīr,* S Saudi Arabia
Tatra Mountains *99 D5 Ger.* Tatra, *Hung.* Tátra, *Pol./Slvk.* Tatry. *Mountain range* Poland/Slovakia
Ta-t'ung *see* Datong
Tatvan *117 F3* Bitlis, SE Turkey
Ta'ū *145 F4 var.* Tau. *Island* Manua Islands, E American Samoa
Tau *see* Ta'ū
Taukum, Peski *123 G1 desert* SE Kazakhstan
Taumarunui *150 D4* Manawatu-Wanganui, North Island, NZ
Taungdwingyi *136 B3* Magwe, C Myanmar
Taunggyi *136 B3* Shan State, C Myanmar
Taunton *89 C7* SW England, UK
Taupo *150 D3* Waikato, North Island, NZ
Taupo, Lake *150 D3 lake* North Island, NZ
Tauragė *106 B4 Ger.* Tauroggen. Tauragė, SW Lithuania
Tauranga *150 D3* Bay of Plenty, North Island, NZ
Tauris *see* Tabrīz
Tavas *116 B4* Denizli, SW Turkey
Tavira *92 C5* Faro, S Portugal
Tavoy *137 B5 var.* Dawei. Tenasserim, S Myanmar
Tavoy Island *see* Mali Kyun
Tawakoni, Lake *49 G2 reservoir* Texas, SW USA
Tawau *138 D3* Sabah, East Malaysia
Ţawkar *see* Tokar
Tawzar *see* Tozeur
Taxco *51 E4 var.* Taxco de Alarcón. Guerrero, S Mexico
Taxco de Alarcón *see* Taxco
Tay *88 C3 river* C Scotland, UK

Taylor *49 G3* Texas, SW USA
Taymā' *120 A4* Tabūk, NW Saudi Arabia
Taymyr, Ozero *115 E2 lake* N Russian Federation
Taymyr, Poluostrov *115 E2 peninsula* N Russian Federation
Taz *114 D3 river* N Russian Federation
T'bilisi *117 G2 Eng.* Tiflis. *Country capital* (Georgia) SE Georgia
T'bilisi *112 B4 international airport* S Georgia
Tchien *see* Zwedru
Tchongking *see* Chongqing
Tczew *98 C2 Ger.* Dirschau. Pomorskie, N Poland
Te Anau *151 A7* Southland, South Island, NZ
Te Anau, Lake *151 A7 lake* South Island, NZ
Teapa *51 G4* Tabasco, SE Mexico
Teate *see* Chieti
Tebingtinggi *138 B3* Sumatera, N Indonesia
Tebriz *see* Tabrīz
Techirghiol *108 D5* Constanţa, SE Romania
Tecomán *50 D4* Colima, SW Mexico
Tecpan *51 E4 var.* Tecpan de Galeana. Guerrero, S Mexico
Tecpan de Galeana *see* Tecpan
Tecuci *108 C4* Galaţi, E Romania
Tedzhen *122 C3 Turkm.* Tejen. Akhalskiy Velayat, S Turkmenistan
Tedzhen *see* Harīrūd
Tees *89 D5 river* N England, UK
Tefé *62 D2* Amazonas, N Brazil
Tegal *138 C4* Jawa, C Indonesia
Tegelen *87 D5* Limburg, SE Netherlands
Tegucigalpa *52 C3 country capital* (Honduras) Francisco Morazán, SW Honduras
Teheran *see* Tehrān
Tehrān *120 C3 var.* Teheran. *Country capital* (Iran) Tehrān, N Iran
Tehuacán *51 F4* Puebla, S Mexico
Tehuantepec *51 F5 var.* Santo Domingo Tehuantepec. Oaxaca, SE Mexico
Tehuantepec, Golfo de *51 F5 var.* Gulf of Tehuantepec. *Gulf* S Mexico
Tehuantepec, Gulf of *see* Tehuantepec, Golfo de
Tehuantepec, Isthmus of *see* Tehuantepec, Istmo de
Tehuantepec, Istmo de *51 F5 var.* Isthmus of Tehuantepec. *Isthmus* SE Mexico
Tejen *see* Harīrūd
Te Kao *150 C1* Northland, North Island, NZ
Tekax *51 H4 var.* Tekax de Álvaro Obregón. Yucatán, SE Mexico
Tekax de Álvaro Obregón *see* Tekax
Tekeli *114 C5* Almaty, SE Kazakhstan
Tekirdağ *116 A2 It.* Rodosto; *anc.* Bisanthe, Raidestos, Rhaedestus. Tekirdağ, NW Turkey
Te Kuiti *150 D3* Waikato, North Island, NZ
Tela *52 C2* Atlántida, NW Honduras
Telanaipura *see* Jambi
Tel Aviv-Jaffa *see* Tel Aviv-Yafo
Tel Aviv-Yafo *119 A6 var.* Tel Aviv-Jaffa. Tel Aviv, C Israel
Teles Pirés *see* São Manuel, Rio
Telish *104 C2 prev.* Azizie. Pleven, NW Bulgaria
Tell Abiad *see* At Tall al Abyaḍ
Tell Abyad *see* At Tall al Abyaḍ
Tell Kalakh *see* Tall Kalakh
Tell Shedadi *see* Ash Shaddādah
Telšiai *106 B3 Ger.* Telschen. Telšiai, NW Lithuania
Teluk Irian *see* Cenderawasih, Teluk

Teluk Serera *see* Cenderawasih, Teluk
Temerin *100 D3* Serbia, N Serbia and Montenegro (Yugo.)
Temirtau *114 C4 prev.* Samarkandski, Samarkandskoye. Karaganda, C Kazakhstan
Tempio Pausania *97 A5* Sardegna, Italy, C Mediterranean Sea
Temple *49 G3* Texas, SW USA
Temuco *65 B5* Araucanía, C Chile
Temuka *151 B6* Canterbury, South Island, NZ
Tenasserim *137 B6* Tenasserim, S Myanmar
Ténenkou *74 D3* Mopti, C Mali
Ténéré *75 G3 physical region* C Niger
Tenerife *70 A3 island* Islas Canarias, Spain, NE Atlantic Ocean
Tengger Shamo *127 E3 desert* N China
Tengréla *74 D4 var.* Tingréla. N Côte d'Ivoire
Tenkodogo *75 E4* S Burkina faso
Tennant Creek *148 A3* Northern Territory, C Australia
Tennessee *42 C1 off.* State of Tennessee; *also known as* The Volunteer State. *State* SE USA
Tennessee River *42 C1 river* S USA
Teno *see* Tana
Tenojoki *see* Tana
Tepelena *see* Tepelenë
Tepelenë *101 C7 var.* Tepelena, *It.* Tepeleni. Gjirokastër, S Albania
Tepeleni *see* Tepelenë
Tepic *50 D4* Nayarit, C Mexico
Teplice *98 A4 Ger.* Teplitz; *prev.* Teplice-Šanov, Teplitz-Schönau. Ústecký Kraj, NW Czech Republic
Tequila *50 D4* Jalisco, SW Mexico
Teraina *145 G2 prev.* Washington Island. *Atoll* Line Islands, E Kiribati
Teramo *96 C4 anc.* Interamna. Abruzzo, C Italy
Tercan *117 E3* Erzincan, NE Turkey
Terceira *92 A5 var.* Ilha Terceira. *Island* Azores, Portugal, NE Atlantic Ocean
Teresina *63 F2 var.* Therezina. *State capital* Piauí, NE Brazil
Termia *see* Kýthnos
Términos, Laguna de *51 G4 lagoon* SE Mexico
Termiz *123 E3 Rus.* Termez. Surkhondaryo Wiloyati, S Uzbekistan
Termoli *96 D4* Molise, C Italy
Terneuzen *87 B5 var.* Neuzen. Zeeland, SW Netherlands
Terni *96 C4 anc.* Interamna Nahars. Umbria, C Italy
Ternopil' *108 C2 Pol.* Tarnopol, *Rus.* Ternopol'. Ternopil's'ka Oblast', W Ukraine
Terracina *97 C5* Lazio, C Italy
Terrassa *93 G2 Cast.* Tarrasa. Cataluña, E Spain
Terre Adélie *154 C3 disputed region* SE Antarctica
Terre Haute *40 B4* Indiana, N USA
Territoire du Yukon *see* Yukon Territory
Terschelling *86 C1 Fris.* Skylge. *Island* Waddeneilanden, N Netherlands
Teruel *93 F3 anc.* Turba. Aragón, E Spain
Tervel *104 E1 prev.* Kurtbunar, *Rom.* Curtbunar. Dobrich, NE Bulgaria
Tervueren *see* Tervuren
Tervuren *87 C6 var.* Tervueren. Vlaams Brabant, C Belgium
Teseney *72 C4 var.* Tesseney. W Eritrea
Tessalit *75 E2* Kidal, NE Mali
Tessaoua *75 G3* Maradi, S Niger
Tessenderlo *87 C5* Limburg, NE Belgium
Tesseney *see* Teseney
Testigos, Islas los *59 E1 island group* N Venezuela

Tete *79 E2* Tete, NW Mozambique
Teterow *94 C3* Mecklenburg-Vorpommern, NE Germany
Tétouan *70 C2 var.* Tetouan, Tetuán. N Morocco
Tetovo *101 D5 Alb.* Tetova, Tetovë, *Turk.* Kalkandelen. Razgrad, N Bulgaria
Tetuán *see* Tétouan
Tevere *96 C4 Eng.* Tiber. *River* C Italy
Teverya *119 B5 var.* Tiberias, Tverya. Northern, N Israel
Te Waewae Bay *151 A7 bay* South Island, NZ
Texarkana *42 A2* Arkansas, C USA
Texarkana *49 H2* Texas, SW USA
Texas *49 F3 off.* State of Texas; *also known as* The Lone Star State. *State* S USA
Texas City *49 H4* Texas, SW USA
Texel *86 C2 island* Waddeneilanden, NW Netherlands
Texoma, Lake *49 G2 reservoir* Oklahoma/Texas, C USA
Teziutlán *51 F4* Puebla, S Mexico
Thaa Atoll *see* Kolhumadulu Atoll
Thai Binh *136 D3* Thai Binh, N Vietnam
Thailand *137 C5 Th.* Prathet Thai; *prev.* Siam. *Country* SE Asia

Thailand 137

Official name Kingdom of Thailand
Formation 1238
Capital Bangkok
Population 63.6 million /
322 people per sq mile (124 people per sq km)
Total area 197,254 sq miles (510,890 sq km)
Languages Thai, Chinese, Malay, Khmer, Mon, Karen, Miao
Religions Buddhist 90%, Muslim 3%, Christian 1%, other 1%
Ethnic mix Thai 83%, Chinese 12%, Malay 3%, Khmer and other 2%
Government Parliamentary democracy
Currency Baht = 100 stangs
Literacy rate 95.5%
Calorie consumption 2,506 kilocalories

Thailand, Gulf of *137 C6 var.* Gulf of Siam, *Th.* Ao Thai, *Vtn.* Vinh Thai Lan. *Gulf* SE Asia
Thai Nguyên *136 D3* Bắc Thai, N Vietnam
Thakhèk *136 D4 prev.* Muang Khammouan. Khammouan, C Laos
Thamarīd *see* Thamarīt
Thamarīt *121 D6 var.* Thamarīd, Thumrayt. SW Oman
Thames *89 B8 river* S England, UK
Thames *150 D3* Waikato, North Island, NZ
Thanh Hoa *136 D3* Vinh Phu, N Vietnam
Thanintari Taungdan *see* Bilauktaung Range
Thar Desert *134 C3 var.* Great Indian Desert, Indian Desert. *Desert* India/Pakistan
Tharthār, Buḩayrat ath *120 B3 lake* C Iraq
Thásos *104 C4 island* E Greece
Thásos *104 C4* Thásos, E Greece
Thaton *136 B4* Mon State, S Myanmar
Thayetmyo *136 A4* Magwe, C Myanmar
The Crane *55 H2 var.* Crane. S Barbados
The Dalles *46 B3* Oregon, NW USA
The Flatts Village *see* Flatts Village
The Hague *see* 's-Gravenhage
The Pas *37 F5* Manitoba, C Canada
Theodosia *see* Feodosiya
Therezina *see* Teresina

Thérma 105 D6 Ikaría,
Dodekánisos, Greece, Aegean Sea
Thermaïkós Kólpos 104 B4 Eng.
Thermaic Gulf; anc. Thermaicus
Sinus. Gulf N Greece
Thermiá see Kýthnos
Thérmo 105 B5 Dytikí Ellás,
C Greece
The Rock 93 H4 E Gibraltar
The Six Counties see Northern
Ireland
Thessaloníki 104 C3 Eng. Salonica,
Salonika, SCr. Solun, Turk.
Selânik. Kentrikí Makedonía,
N Greece
The Valley 55 G3 dependent territory
capital (Anguilla) E Anguilla
The Village 49 G1 Oklahoma,
C USA
Thiamis see Thýamis
Thibet see Xizang Zizhiqu
Thief River Falls 45 F1 Minnesota,
N USA
Thienen see Tienen
Thiers 91 C5 Puy-de-Dôme,
C France
Thiès 74 B3 W Senegal
Thimbu see Thimphu
Thimphu 135 G3 var. Thimbu; prev.
Tashi Chho Dzong. Country capital
(Bhutan) W Bhutan
Thionville 90 D3 Ger. Diedenhofen.
Moselle, NE France
Thíra 105 D7 prev. Santorin,
Santoríni, anc. Thera. Island
Kykládes, Greece, Aegean Sea
Thíra 105 D7 Thíra, Kykládes,
Greece, Aegean Sea
Thiruvananthapuram see
Trivandrum
Thitu Island 128 C8 island
NW Spratly Islands
Tholen 86 B4 island
SW Netherlands
Thomasville 42 D3 Georgia,
SE USA
Thompson 37 F4 Manitoba,
C Canada
Thonon-les-Bains 91 D5 Haute-
Savoie, E France
Thorlákshöfn 83 E5 Sudhurland,
SW Iceland
Thornton Island see Millennium
Island
Thouars 90 B4 Deux-Sèvres,
W France
Thracian Sea 104 D4 Gk. Thrakikó
Pélagos; anc. Thracium Mare. Sea
Greece/Turkey
Three Kings Islands 150 C1 island
group N NZ
Thrissur see Trichūr
Thuin 87 B7 Hainaut, S Belgium
Thule see Qaanaaq
Thumrayt see Thamarīt
Thun 95 A7 Fr. Thoune. Bern,
W Switzerland
Thunder Bay 38 B4 Ontario,
S Canada
Thuner See 95 A7 lake
C Switzerland
Thung Song 137 C7 var. Cha Mai.
Nakhon Si Thammarat,
SW Thailand
Thurso 88 C2 N Scotland, UK
Thýamis 104 A4 var. Thiamis. River
W Greece
Tianjin 128 D4 var. Tientsin. Tianjin
Shi, E China
Tianjin see Tianjin Shi
Tianjin Shi 128 D4 var. Jin, Tianjin,
T'ien-ching, Tientsin. Admin.
region municipality E China
Tianshui 128 B4 Gansu, C China
Tiba see Chiba
Tiberias see Teverya
Tiberias, Lake 119 B5 var.
Chinnereth, Sea of Bahr Tabariya,
Sea of Galilee, Ar. Bahrat
Tabariya, Heb. Yam Kinneret. Lake
N Israel
Tibesti 76 C2 var. Tibesti Massif, Ar.
Tībistī. Mountain range N Africa

Tibesti Massif see Tibesti
Tibet see Xizang Zizhiqu
Tibetan Autonomous Region see
Xizang Zizhiqu
Tibet, Plateau of see Qingzang
Gaoyuan
Tibistī see Tibesti
Tibnī see At Tibnī
Tiburón, Isla 50 B2 var. Isla del
Tiburón. Island NW Mexico
Tiburón, Isla del see Tiburón, Isla
Tichît 74 D2 var. Tichitt. Tagant,
C Mauritania
Tichitt see Tichît
Ticul 51 H3 Yucatán, SE Mexico
Tidjikdja see Tidjikdja
Tidjikdja 74 C2 var. Tidjikdja; prev.
Fort-Cappolani. Tagant,
C Mauritania
T'ien-ching see Tianjin Shi
Tienen 87 C6 var. Thienen, Fr.
Tirlemont. Vlaams Brabant,
C Belgium
Tien Shan 126 B3 Chin. Thian Shan,
Tian Shan, T'ien Shan, Rus. Tyan'-
Shan'. Mountain range C Asia
Tientsin see Tianjin Shi
Tierp 85 C6 Uppsala, C Sweden
Tierra del Fuego 65 B8 off. Provincia
de la Tierra del Fuego. Admin.
region province S Argentina
Tierra del Fuego 57 B8 island
Argentina/Chile
Tifton 42 D3 Georgia, SE USA
Tifu 139 F4 Pulau Buru,
E Indonesia
Tighina 108 D4 Rus. Bendery; prev.
Bender. E Moldova
Tigranocerta see Siirt
Tigris 120 B2 Ar. Dijlah, Turk. Dicle.
River Iraq/Turkey
Tiguentourine 71 E3 E Algeria
Ti-hua see Ürümqi
Tihwa see Ürümqi
Tijuana 50 A1 Baja California,
NW Mexico
Tikhoretsk 111 A7 Krasnodarskiy
Kray, SW Russian Federation
Tikhvin 110 B4 Leningradskaya
Oblast', NW Russian Federation
Tiki Basin 143 G3 undersea feature
S Pacific Ocean
Tiksi 115 F2 Respublika Sakha
(Yakutiya), NE Russian
Federation
Tilburg 86 C4 Noord-Brabant,
S Netherlands
Tilimsen see Tlemcen
Tillabéri 75 F3 var. Tillabéry.
Tillabéri, W Niger
Tillabéry see Tillabéri
Tílos 105 E7 island Dodekánisos,
Greece, Aegean Sea
Timanskiy Kryazh 110 D3 Eng.
Timan Ridge. Ridge NW Russian
Federation
Timaru 151 B6 Canterbury, South
Island, NZ
Timbaki see Tympáki
Timbákion see Tympáki
Timbedgha 74 D3 var. Timbédra.
Hodh ech Chargui, SE Mauritania
Timbédra see Timbedgha
Timbuktu see Tombouctou
Timiş 108 A4 river W Romania
Timişoara 108 A4 Ger. Temeschwar,
Temeswar, Hung. Temesvár; prev.
Temeschburg. Timiş, W Romania
Timmins 38 C4 Ontario, S Canada
Timor 125 F5 island Nusa Tenggara,
East Timor/Indonesia
Timor Timur see East Timor
Timor Sea 125 F5 sea E Indian
Ocean
Timor Trench see Timor Trough
Timor Trough 125 F5 var. Timor
Trench. Undersea feature NE Timor
Sea
Timrå 85 C5 Västernorrland,
C Sweden
Tindouf 70 C3 W Algeria
Tineo 92 C1 Asturias, N Spain
Tingis I MM see Tanger

Tingo María 60 C3 Huánuco,
C Peru
Tingréla see Tengréla
Tinhosa Grande 76 E2 island N Sao
Tome and Principe
Tinhosa Pequena 76 E1 island
N Sao Tome and Principe
Tinian 144 B1 island S Northern
Mariana Islands
Tínos 105 D6 anc. Tenos. Island
Kykládes, Greece, Aegean Sea
Tínos 105 D6 Tínos, Kykládes,
Greece, Aegean Sea
Tip 101 E6 Papua, E Indonesia
Tipitapa 52 D3 Managua,
W Nicaragua
Tip Top Mountain 38 C4 mountain
Ontario, S Canada
Tirana see Tiranë
Tiranë 101 C6 var. Tirana. Country
capital (Albania) Tiranë, C Albania
Tiraspol 108 D4 Rus. Tiraspol'.
E Moldova
Tiree 88 B3 island W Scotland, UK
Tîrgu-Neamţ see Târgu-Neamţ
Tirlemont see Tienen
Tírnavos see Týrnavos
Tirol 95 C7 cultural region
Austria/Italy
Tiruchchirāppalli 132 C3 prev.
Trichinopoly. Tamil Nādu,
SE India
Tiruppattūr 132 C2 Tamil Nādu,
SE India
Tisa 103 F1 Ger. Theiss,
Rom./Slvn./SCr. Tisa, Rus. Tissa,
Ukr. Tysa. River SE Europe see also
Tisza
Tiszakécske 99 D7 Bács-Kiskun,
C Hungary
Titano, Monte 96 E1 mountain
C San Marino
Titicaca, Lake 61 E4 lake
Bolivia/Peru
Titose see Chitose
Titu 108 C5 Dâmboviţa,
S Romania
Titule 77 D5 Orientale, N Dem.
Rep. Congo
Tiverton 89 C7 SW England, UK
Tivoli 96 C4 anc. Tiber. Lazio,
C Italy
Tizimín 51 H3 Yucatán,
SE Mexico
Tizi Ouzou 71 E1 var. Tizi-Ouzou.
N Algeria
Tiznit 70 B3 SW Morocco
Tlaquepaque 50 D4 Jalisco,
C Mexico
Tlascala see Tlaxcala
Tlaxcala 51 F4 var. Tlascala,
Tlaxcala de Xicohténcatl. Tlaxcala,
C Mexico
Tlaxcala de Xicohténcatl see
Tlaxcala
Tlemcen 70 D2 var. Tilimsen,
Tlemsen. NW Algeria
Tlemsen see Tlemcen
Toamasina 79 G3 var. Tamatave.
Toamasina, E Madagascar
Toba, Danau 138 B3 lake Sumatera,
W Indonesia
Tobago 55 H5 island NE Trinidad
and Tobago
Tobol 114 C4 Kaz. Tobyl. River
Kazakhstan/Russian Federation
Tobol'sk 114 C3 Tyumenskaya
Oblast', C Russian Federation
Tocantins 63 E3 off. Estado do
Tocantins. State C Brazil
Tocantins, Rio 63 F2 river N Brazil
Tocoa 52 D2 Colón, N Honduras
Tocopilla 64 B2 Antofagasta,
N Chile
Todi 96 C4 Umbria, C Italy
Todos os Santos, Baía de 63 G3 bay
E Brazil
Toetoes Bay 151 B8 bay South
Island, NZ
Tofua 145 E4 island Ha'apai Group,
C Tonga
Togo 75 E4 French Togoland.
Country W Africa

Togo 75

Official name Republic of Togo
Formation 1960
Capital Lomé
Population 4.7 million / 214 people
per sq mile (83 people per sq km)
Total area 21,925 sq miles
(56,785 sq km) **Languages** French,
Ewe, Kabye, Gurma
Religions Traditional beliefs 50%,
Christian 35%, Muslim 15%
Ethnic mix Ewe 46%, other African
53%, European 1%
Government Presidential regime
Currency CFA franc = 100 centimes
Literacy rate 57.3%
Calorie consumption 2,329
kilocalories

Tokanui 151 B7 Southland, South
Island, NZ
Tokar 72 C3 var. Ṭawkar. Red Sea,
NE Sudan
Tokat 116 D3 Tokat, N Turkey
Tokelau 145 E3 NZ overseas territory
W Polynesia
Tokio see Tōkyō
Tokmak 123 G2 Kir. Tokmok.
Chuyskaya Oblast',
N Kyrgyzstan
Tokmak 109 G4 var. Velykyy
Tokmak. Zaporiz'ka Oblast',
SE Ukraine
Tokoroa 150 D3 Waikato, North
Island, NZ
Tokounou 74 C4 Haute-Guinée,
C Guinea
Tokushima 131 C6 var. Tokusima.
Tokushima, Shikoku, SW Japan
Tokusima see Tokushima
Tōkyō 130 A1 var. Tokio. Country
capital (Japan) Tōkyō, Honshū,
S Japan
Tōkyō Bay 130 A2 bay SW Japan
Toledo 92 D3 anc. Toletum. Castilla-
La Mancha, C Spain
Toledo 40 D3 Ohio, N USA
Toledo Bend Reservoir 49 G3
reservoir Louisiana/Texas,
SW USA
Toliara 79 F4 var. Toliary; prev.
Tuléar. Toliara, SW Madagascar
Toliary see Toliara
Tolmin 95 D7 Ger. Tolmein, It.
Tolmino. W Slovenia
Tolna 99 C7 Ger. Tolnau. Tolna,
S Hungary
Tolosa 93 E1 País Vasco, N Spain
Toluca 51 E4 var. Toluca de Lerdo.
México, S Mexico
Toluca de Lerdo see Toluca
Tol'yatti 111 C6 prev. Stavropol'.
Samarskaya Oblast', W Russian
Federation
Tomah 40 B2 Wisconsin, N USA
Tomakomai 130 D2 Hokkaidō,
NE Japan
Tomar 92 B3 Santarém, W Portugal
Tomaschow see Tomaszów
Mazowiecki
Tomaschow see Tomaszów
Mazowiecki
Tomaszów Lubelski 98 E4 Ger.
Tomaschow. Lubelskie,
E Poland
Tomaszów Mazowiecka see
Tomaszów Mazowiecki
Tomaszów Mazowiecki 98 D4 var.
Tomaszów Mazowiecka; prev.
Tomaszów, Ger. Tomaschow.
Łódzkie, C Poland
Tombigbee River 42 C3 river
Alabama/Mississippi, S USA
Tombouctou 75 E3 Eng. Timbuktu.
Tombouctou, N Mali
Tombua 78 A2 Port. Porto
Alexandre. Namibe, SW Angola
Tomelloso 93 E3 Castilla-La
Mancha, C Spain
Tomini, Gulf of 139 E4 var. Teluk
Tomini; prev. Teluk Gorontalo. Bay
Sulawesi, C Indonesia

Tomini, Teluk see Tomini, Gulf of
Tomsk 114 D4 Tomskaya Oblast', C Russian Federation
Tomur Feng see Pobedy, Pik
Tonga 145 E4 var. Friendly Islands. Country SW Pacific Ocean

Tonga 145

Official name Kingdom of Tonga
Formation 1970
Capital Nuku'alofa
Population 102,200 / 354 people per sq mile (137 people per sq km)
Total area 289 sq miles (748 sq km)
Languages Tongan, English
Religions Free Wesleyan 64%, Roman Catholic 15%, Other 21%
Ethnic mix Polynesian 99%, other Pacific groups and European 1%
Government Monarchy
Currency Pa'anga (Tongan dollar) = 100 seniti
Literacy rate 98.5%
Calorie consumption not available

Tongatapu 145 E5 island Tongatapu Group, S Tonga
Tonga Trench 143 E3 undersea feature S Pacific Ocean
Tongchuan 128 C4 Shaanxi, C China
Tongeren 87 D6 Fr. Tongres. Limburg, NE Belgium
Tongking, Gulf of 128 B7 Chin. Beibu Wan, Vtn. Vinh Bắc Bộ. Gulf China/Vietnam
Tongliao 127 G2 Nei Mongol Zizhiqu, N China
Tongshan see Xuzhou
Tongtian He 126 C4 river C China
Tonj 73 B5 Warab, SW Sudan
Tônlé Sap 137 D5 Eng. Great Lake. Lake W Cambodia
Tonopah 47 C6 Nevada, W USA
Tonyezh 107 C7 Rus. Tonezh. Homyel'skaya Voblasts', SE Belarus
Tooele 44 B4 Utah, W USA
Toowoomba 149 E5 Queensland, E Australia
Topeka 45 F4 state capital Kansas, C USA
Toplița 108 C3 Ger. Töplitz, Hung. Maroshévíz; prev. Toplița Română, Hung. Oláh-Toplicza, Toplicza. Harghita, C Romania
Topol'čany 99 C6 Hung. Nagytapolcsány. Nitriansky Kraj, SW Slovakia
Topolovgrad 104 D3 prev. Kavakli. Khaskovo, S Bulgaria
Top Springs Roadhouse 146 D3 Northern Territory, N Australia
Torez 109 H3 Donets'ka Oblast', SE Ukraine
Torgau 94 D4 Sachsen, E Germany
Torhout 87 A5 West-Vlaanderen, W Belgium
Torino 96 A2 Eng. Turin. Piemonte, NW Italy
Tornacum see Tournai
Torneälven see Tornionjoki
Torneträsk 84 C3 lake N Sweden
Tornio 84 D4 Swe. Torneå. Lappi, NW Finland
Torniojoki see Tornionjoki
Tornionjoki 84 D3 var. Torniojoki, Swe. Torneälven. River Finland/Sweden
Toro 92 D2 Castilla-León, N Spain
Toronto 38 D5 Ontario, S Canada
Toros Dağları 116 C4 Eng. Taurus Mountains. Mountain range S Turkey
Torquay 89 C7 SW England, UK
Torrance 46 D2 California, W USA
Torre, Alto da 92 B3 mountain C Portugal
Torre del Greco 97 D5 Campania, S Italy
Torrejón de Ardoz 93 E3 Madrid, C Spain

Torrelavega 92 D1 Cantabria, N Spain
Torrens, Lake 149 A6 salt lake South Australia
Torrent see Torrente
Torrent de l'Horta see Torrente
Torrente 93 F3 var. Torrent, Torrent de l'Horta. País Valenciano, E Spain
Torreón 50 D3 Coahuila de Zaragoza, NE Mexico
Torres Strait 148 C1 strait Australia/PNG
Torres Vedras 92 B3 Lisboa, C Portugal
Torrington 44 D3 Wyoming, C USA
Tórshavn 83 F5 Dan. Thorshavn. Dependent territory capital (Faeroe Islands) N Faeroe Islands
Tortoise Islands see Galapagos Islands
Tortosa 93 F2 anc. Dertosa. Cataluña, E Spain
Tortue, Montagne 59 H3 mountain range C French Guiana
Tortuga, Isla see La Tortuga, Isla
Toruń 98 C3 Ger. Thorn. Kujawskie-pomorskie, C Poland
Tôrva 106 D3 Ger. Törwa. Valgamaa, S Estonia
Torzhok 110 B4 Tverskaya Oblast', W Russian Federation
Tosa-wan 131 B7 bay SW Japan
Toscana 96 B3 Eng. Tuscany. Cultural region C Italy
Toscano, Archipelago 96 B4 Eng. Tuscan Archipelago. Island group C Italy
Toshkent 123 E2 Eng./Rus. Tashkent. Country capital (Uzbekistan) Toshkent Wiloyati, E Uzbekistan
Totana 93 E4 Murcia, SE Spain
Tot'ma see Sukhona
Totness 59 G3 Coronie, N Suriname
Tottori 131 B6 Tottori, Honshū, SW Japan
Touâjîl 74 C2 Tiris Zemmour, N Mauritania
Touggourt 71 E2 NE Algeria
Toukoto 74 C3 Kayes, W Mali
Toul 90 D3 Meurthe-et-Moselle, NE France
Toulon 91 D6 anc. Telo Martius, Tilio Martius. Var, SE France
Toulouse 91 B6 anc. Tolosa. Haute-Garonne, S France
Toungoo 136 B4 Pegu, C Myanmar
Touraine 90 B4 cultural region C France
Tourcoing 90 C2 Nord, N France
Tournai 87 A6 var. Tournay, Dut. Doornik; anc. Tornacum. Hainaut, SW Belgium
Tournay see Tournai
Tours 90 B4 anc. Caesarodunum, Turoni. Indre-et-Loire, C France
Tovarkovskiy 111 B5 Tul'skaya Oblast', W Russian Federation
Tower Island see Genovesa, Isla
Townsville 148 D3 Queensland, NE Australia
Towraghoudī 122 D4 Herāt, NW Afghanistan
Towson 41 F4 Maryland, NE USA
Towuti, Danau 139 E4 Dut. Towoeti Meer. Lake Sulawesi, C Indonesia
Toyama 131 C5 Toyama, Honshū, SW Japan
Toyama-wan 131 B5 bay W Japan
Toyota 131 C6 Aichi, Honshū, SW Japan
Tozeur 71 E2 var. Tawzar. W Tunisia
Trâblous see Tripoli
Trabzon 117 E2 Eng. Trebizond; anc. Trapezus. Trabzon, NE Turkey
Traiectum Tungrorum see Maastricht
Traietum ad Mosam see Maastricht
Traiskirchen 95 E6 Niederösterreich, NE Austria
Trakai 107 C5 Ger. Traken, Pol. Troki. Trakai, SE Lithuania

Tralee 89 A6 Ir. Trá Lí. SW Ireland
Trá Lí see Tralee
Tralles see Aydın
Trang 137 C7 Trang, S Thailand
Transantarctic Mountains 154 B3 mountain range Antarctica
Transsylvanische Alpen see Carpații Meridionali
Transylvania 108 B4 Eng. Ardeal, Transilvania, Ger. Siebenbürgen, Hung. Erdély. Cultural region NW Romania
Transylvanian Alps see Carpații Meridionali
Trapani 97 B7 anc. Drepanum. Sicilia, Italy, C Mediterranean Sea
Trâpeăng Vêng 137 D5 Kâmpóng Thum, C Cambodia
Traralgon 149 C7 Victoria, SE Australia
Trasimeno, Lago C4 Eng. Lake of Perugia, Italy. Trasimenischersee. Lake C Italy
Traverse City 40 C2 Michigan, N USA
Tra Vinh 137 D6 var. Phu Vinh. Tra Vinh, S Vietnam
Travis, Lake 49 F3 reservoir Texas, SW USA
Travnik 100 C4 Federacija Bosna I Hercegovina, C Bosnia and Herzegovina
Trbovlje 95 E7 Ger. Trifail. C Slovenia
Třebíč 99 B5 Ger. Trebitsch. Jihlavský Kraj, C Czech Republic
Trebinje 101 C5 Republika Srpska, S Bosnia and Herzegovina
Trebišov 99 D6 Hung. Tőketerebes. Košický Kraj, E Slovakia
Trélazé 90 B4 Maine-et-Loire, NW France
Trelew 65 C6 Chubut, SE Argentina
Tremelo 87 C5 Vlaams Brabant, C Belgium
Trenčín 99 C5 Ger. Trentschin, Hung. Trencsén. Trenčiansky Kraj, W Slovakia
Trenque Lauquen 64 C4 Buenos Aires, E Argentina
Trento 96 C2 Eng. Trent, Ger. Trient; anc.Tridentum. Trentino-Alto Adige, N Italy
Trenton 41 F4 state capital New Jersey, NE USA
Tres Arroyos 65 D5 Buenos Aires, E Argentina
Treskavica 100 C4 mountain range SE Bosnia and Herzegovina
Tres Tabernae see Saverne
Treviso 96 C2 anc. Tarvisium. Veneto, NE Italy
Trichūr 132 C3 var. Thrissur. Kerala, SW India
Trier 95 A5 Eng. Treves, Fr. Trèves; anc. Augusta Treverorum. Rheinland-Pfalz, SW Germany
Triesen 94 E2 SW Liechtenstein
Triesenberg 94 E2 SW Liechtenstein
Trieste 96 D2 Slvn. Trst. Friuli-Venezia Giulia, NE Italy
Tríkala 104 B4 prev. Trikkala. Thessalía, C Greece
Trincomalee 132 D3 var. Trinkomali. Eastern Province, NE Sri Lanka
Trindade, Ilha da 67 C5 island Brazil, W Atlantic Ocean
Trinidad 55 H5 island C Trinidad and Tobago
Trinidad 61 F3 Beni, N Bolivia
Trinidad 44 D5 Colorado, C USA
Trinidad 64 D4 Flores, S Uruguay
Trinidad and Tobago 55 H5 Country SE West Indies

Trinidad & Tobago 55

Official name Republic of Trinidad and Tobago
Formation 1962
Capital Port-of-Spain
Population 1.3 million / 657 people per sq mile (254 people per sq km)

Trinidad & Tobago (continued)

Total area 1980 sq miles (5,128 sq km)
Languages English, English Creole, Hindi. French, Spanish
Religions Christian 61%, Hindu 24%, other and non-religious 15%
Ethnic mix Asian 40%, Black 40%, Mixed 19%, White and Chinese 1%
Government Parliamentary democracy
Currency Trinidad and Tobago dollar = 100 cents
Literacy rate 93.8%
Calorie consumption 2,777 kilocalories

Trinité, Montagnes de la 59 H3 mountain range C French Guiana
Trinity River 49 G3 river Texas, SW USA
Trinkomali see Trincomalee
Tripoli 118 B4 var. Tarābulus, Țarābulus ash Shām, Trâblous; anc. Tripolis. N Lebanon
Tripoli see Țarābulus
Tripoli 105 B6 prev. Trípolis. Pelopónnisos, S Greece
Tripolis see Tripoli
Tristan da Cunha 69 B7 dependency of Saint Helena SE Atlantic Ocean
Triton Island 128 B7 island S Paracel Islands
Trivandrum 132 C3 var. Thiruvananthapuram. Kerala, SW India
Trnava 99 C6 Ger. Tyrnau, Hung. Nagyszombat. Trnavský Kraj, W Slovakia
Trogir 100 B4 It. Traù. Split-Dalmacija, S Croatia
Troglav 100 B4 mountain Bosnia and Herzegovina/Croatia
Trois-Rivières 39 E4 Quebec, SE Canada
Trollhättan 85 B6 Västra Götaland, S Sweden
Tromsø 84 C2 Fin. Tromssa. Troms, N Norway
Trondheim 84 B4 Ger. Drontheim; prev. Nidaros, Trondhjem. Sør-Trøndelag, S Norway
Trondheimsfjorden 84 B4 fjord S Norway
Troódos 102 C5 var. Troodos Mountains. Mountain range C Cyprus
Troodos Mountains see Troódos
Troy 42 D3 Alabama, S USA
Troy 41 F3 New York, NE USA
Troyan 104 C2 Lovech, N Bulgaria
Troyes 90 D3 anc. Augustobona Tricassium. Aube, N France
Trstenik 100 E4 Serbia, C Serbia and Montenegro (Yugo.)
Trujillo 52 D2 Colón, NE Honduras
Trujillo 92 C3 Extremadura, W Spain
Trujillo 60 B3 La Libertad, NW Peru
Truk Islands see Chuuk Islands
Trŭn 104 B2 Pernik, W Bulgaria
Truro 39 F4 Nova Scotia, SE Canada
Truro 89 C7 SW England, UK
Trzcianka 98 B3 Ger. Schönlanke. Wielkopolskie, C Poland
Trzebnica 98 C4 Ger. Trebnitz. Dolnośląskie, SW Poland
Tsalka 117 F2 S Georgia
Tsamkong see Zhanjiang
Tsangpo see Brahmaputra
Tsarevo 104 E2 prev. Michurin. Burgas, E Bulgaria
Tsaritsyn see Volgograd
Tsefat see Zefat
Tsetserleg 126 D2 Arhangay, C Mongolia
Tsevat see Zefat
Tshela 77 B6 Bas-Zaïre, W Dem. Rep. Congo
Tshikapa 77 C7 Kasai Occidental, SW Dem. Rep. Congo

Tshuapa 77 D6 river C Dem. Rep.
Congo

Tshwane see Pretoria

Tsinan see Jinan

Tsing Hai see Qinghai Hu

Tsingtao see Qingdao

Tsingtau see Qingdao

Tsinkiang see Quanzhou

Tsintao see Qingdao

Tsitsihar see Qiqihar

Tsu 131 C6 var. Tu. Mie, Honshū,
SW Japan

Tsugaru-kaikyō 130 C3 strait
N Japan

Tsumeb 78 B3 Otjikoto, N Namibia

Tsuruga 131 C6 var. Turuga. Fukui,
Honshū, SW Japan

Tsuruoka 130 D4 var. Turuoka.
Yamagata, Honshū, C Japan

Tsushima 131 A7 var. Tsushima-tō,
Tusima. Island group SW Japan

Tsushima-tō see Tsushima

Tsyerakhowka 107 D8 Rus.
Terekhovka. Homyel'skaya
Voblasts', SE Belarus

Tsyurupyns'k 109 E4 Rus.
Tsyurupinsk. Khersons'ka Oblast',
S Ukraine

Tu see Tsu

Tuamotu Fracture Zone 143 H3
tectonic feature E Pacific Ocean

Tuamotu, Îles 145 H4 var. Archipel
des Tuamotu, Dangerous
Archipelago, Tuamotu Islands.
Island group N French Polynesia

Tuamotu Islands see Tuamotu, Îles

Tuapi 53 E2 Región Autónoma
Atlántico Norte, NE Nicaragua

Tuapse 111 A7 Krasnodarskiy Kray,
SW Russian Federation

Tuba City 48 B1 Arizona, SW USA

Tubbergen 86 E3 Overijssel,
E Netherlands

Tubize 87 B6 Dut. Tubeke. Wallon
Brabant, C Belgium

Tubmanburg 74 C5 NW Liberia

Ţubruq 71 H2 Eng. Tobruk, It.
Tobruch. NE Libya

Tubuai Islands see Australes,
Îles

Tucker's Town 42 B5 E Bermuda

Tucson 48 B3 Arizona, SW USA

Tucumán see San Miguel de
Tucumán

Tucumcari 49 E2 New Mexico,
SW USA

Tucupita 59 E2 Delta Amacuro,
NE Venezuela

Tucuruí, Represa de 63 F2 reservoir
NE Brazil

Tudela 93 E2 Basq. Tutera; anc.
Tutela. Navarra, N Spain

Tudmur 118 C3 var. Tadmur, Tamar,
Gk. Palmyra; Bibl. Tadmor. Ḩimş,
C Syria

Tuguegarao 139 E1 Luzon,
N Philippines

Tuktoyaktuk 37 E3 Northwest
Territories, NW Canada

Tukums 106 C3 Ger. Tuckum.
Tukums, W Latvia

Tula 111 B5 Tul'skaya Oblast',
W Russian Federation

Tulancingo 51 E4 Hidalgo,
C Mexico

Tulare Lake Bed 47 C7 salt flat
California, W USA

Tulcán 60 B1 Carchi, N Ecuador

Tulcea 108 D5 Tulcea, E Romania

Tul'chyn 108 D3 Rus. Tul'chin.
Vinnyts'ka Oblast', C Ukraine

Tuléar see Toliara

Tulia 49 E2 Texas, SW USA

Tulle 91 C5 anc. Tutela. Corrèze,
C France

Tulln 95 E6 var. Oberhollabrunn.
Niederösterreich,
NE Austria

Tully 148 D3 Queensland,
NE Australia

Tulsa 49 G1 Oklahoma, C USA

Tuluá 58 B3 Valle del Cauca,
W Colombia

Tulun 115 E4 Irkutskaya Oblast',
S Russian Federation

Tumaco 58 A4 Nariño,
SW Colombia

Tumba, Lac see Ntomba, Lac

Tumbes 60 A2 Tumbes, NW Peru

Tumkür 132 C2 Karnātaka,
W India

Tumuc Humac Mountains 63 E1
var. Serra Tumucumaque.
Mountain range N South America

Tunduru 73 C8 Ruvuma, S Tanzania

Tundzha 104 D3 Turk. Tunca Nehri.
River Bulgaria/Turkey see also
Tunca Nehri

Tungabhadra Reservoir 132 C2 lake
S India

Tungaru 145 E2 prev. Gilbert
Islands. Island group W Kiribati

T'ung-shan see Xuzhou

Tungsten 36 D4 Northwest
Territories, W Canada

Tung-t'ing Hu see Dongting Hu

Tunis 71 E1 var. Tūnis. Country
capital (Tunisia) NE Tunisia

Tūnis see Tunis

Tunis, Golfe de 102 D3 Ar. Khalīj
Tūnis. Gulf NE Tunisia

Tunisia 71 F2 Ar. Al Jumhūrīyah at
Tūnisīyah, Fr. République
Tunisienne. Country N Africa

Tunisia 71

Official name Republic of Tunisia
Formation 1956
Capital Tunis
Population 9.6 million / 152 people
per sq mile (59 people per sq km)
Total area 63,170 sq miles
(163,610 sq km)
Languages Arabic, French
Religions Muslim (mainly Sunni)
98%, Christian 1%, Jewish 1%
Ethnic mix Arab and Berber 98%,
European 1%, other 1%
Government Presidential
democracy
Currency Tunisian dinar =
1,000 millimes
Literacy rate 71%
Calorie consumption 3,299
kilocalories

Tunja 58 B3 Boyacá, C Colombia

Tuong Buong see T,ong Ð,ong

Tupelo 42 C2 Mississippi, S USA

Tupiza 61 G5 Potosí, S Bolivia

Turabah 121 B5 Makkah, W Saudi
Arabia

Turangi 150 D4 Waikato, North
Island, NZ

Turan Lowland 122 C2 var. Turan
Plain, Kaz. Turan Oypaty, Rus.
Turanskaya Nizmennost', Turk.
Turan Pesligi, Uzb. Turon
Pasttekisligi. Plain C Asia

Turan Oypaty see Turan
Lowland

Turan Pesligi see Turan Lowland

Turan Plain see Turan Lowland

Turanskaya Nizmennost' see Turan
Lowland

Ţurayf 120 A3 Al Ḩudūd ash
Shamālīyah, NW Saudi Arabia

Turbat 134 A3 Baluchistān,
SW Pakistan

Turda 108 B4 Ger. Thorenburg,
Hung. Torda. Cluj, NW
Romania

Turek 98 C3 Wielkopolskie, C
Poland

Turfan see Turpan

Turin see Torino

Turkana, Lake 89 C6 var. Lake
Rudolph. Lake N Kenya

**Turkish Republic of Northern
Cyprus** 102 D5 Dependent
territory, disputed territory.
Cyprus

Turkestan 114 B5 Kaz. Türkistan.
Yuzhnyy Kazakhstan,
S Kazakhstan

Turkey 116 B3 Turk. Türkiye
Cumhuriyeti. Country SW Asia

Turkey 116

Official name Republic of Turkey
Formation 1923
Capital Ankara
Population 67.6 million / 224
people per sq mile (87 people
per sq km)
Total area 301,382 sq miles
(780,580 sq km)
Languages Turkish, Kurdish,
Arabic, Circassian, Armenian, Greek,
Georgian
Religions Muslim (mainly Sunni)
99%, other 1%
Ethnic mix Turkish 70%, Kurdish
20%, Arab 2%, other 8%
Government Parliamentary
democracy
Currency Turkish lira = 100 krural
Literacy rate 85.1%
Calorie consumption 3,416
kilocalories

Turkmenbashi 122 B2 prev.
Krasnovodsk. Balkanskiy Velayat,
W Turkmenistan

Turkmenistan 122 B2 prev.
Turkmenskaya Soviet Socialist
Republic. Country C Asia

Turkmenistan 122

Official name Turkmenistan
Formation 1991
Capital Ashgabat
Population 4.8 million /
25 people per sq mile (10 people
per sq km)
Total area 188,455 sq miles
(488,100 sq km)
Languages Turkmen, Uzbek,
Russian
Religions Sunni Muslim 87%,
Eastern Orthodox 11%, other 2%
Ethnic mix Turkmen 73%, Russian
10%, Uzbek 9%, Kazakh 2%, Tatar
1%, other 5%
Government One-party state
Currency Manat = 100 tenge
Literacy rate 98%
Calorie consumption 2,675
kilocalories

Turkmenskiy Zaliv 122 B2 Turkm.
Türkmen Aylagy. Lake gulf
W Turkmenistan

Turks and Caicos Islands 55 E2 UK
dependent territory N West Indies

Turlock 47 B6 California, W USA

Turnagain, Cape 150 D4 headland
North Island, NZ

Turnhout 87 C5 Antwerpen,
N Belgium

Turnov 98 B4 Ger. Turnau.
Liberecký Kraj, N Czech Republic

Turnu Măgurele 108 B5 var. Turnu-
Măgurele. Teleorman, S Romania

Turon Pasttekisligi see Turan
Lowland

Turpan 126 C3 var. Turfan. Xinjiang
Uygur Zizhiqu, NW China

Turpan Pendi 126 C3 Eng. Turpan
Depression. Depression NW China

Türtkül 122 D2 Rus. Turtkul'; prev.
Petroaleksandrovsk.
Qoraqalpoghiston Respublikasi,
W Uzbekistan

Turuga see Tsuruga

Turuoka see Tsuruoka

Tuscaloosa 42 C2 Alabama, S USA

Tusima see Tsushima

Tuticorin 132 C3 Tamil Nādu,
SE India

Tutrakan 104 D1 Silistra,
NE Bulgaria

Tutuila 145 F4 island W American
Samoa

Tuvalu 145 E3 prev. Ellice Islands.
Country SW Pacific Ocean

Tuvalu 145

Official name Tuvalu
Formation 1978
Capital Fongafale, on Funafuti Atoll
Population 10,800 / 1,076 people
per sq mile (415 people per sq km)
Total area 10 sq miles (26 sq km)
Languages English, Tuvaluan,
Kiribati
Religions Church of Tuvalu 97%,
Seventh-day Adventist 1%, Baha'i
1%, other 1%
Ethnic mix Polynesian 96%,
other 4%
Government Non-party democracy
Currency Australian dollar and
Tuvaluan dollar = 100 cents
Literacy rate 95%
Calorie consumption not available

Ţuwayq, Jabal 121 C5 mountain
range C Saudi Arabia

Tuxpán 51 F4 var. Tuxpán de
Rodríguez Cano. Veracruz-Llave,
E Mexico

Tuxpan 50 D4 Jalisco, C Mexico

Tuxpan 50 D4 Nayarit, C Mexico

Tuxpán de Rodríguez Cano see
Tuxpán

Tuxtepec 51 F4 var. San Juan Bautista
Tuxtepec. Oaxaca, S Mexico

Tuxtla see San Andrés Tuxtla

Tuxtla Gutiérrez see Tuxtla

Tuy Hoa 137 E5 Phu Yên, S Vietnam

Tuz Gölü 116 C3 lake C Turkey

Tuzla 100 C3 Federacija Bosna I
Hercegovina, NE Bosnia and
Herzegovina

Tver' 110 B4 prev. Kalinin. Tverskaya
Oblast', W Russian Federation

Tverya see Teverya

Twin Falls 46 D4 Idaho, NW USA

Tychy 99 D5 Ger. Tichau. Śląskie,
S Poland

Tyler 49 G3 Texas, SW USA

Týmpáki 105 C8 var. Timbaki; prev.
Timbákion. Kríti, Greece,
E Mediterranean Sea

Tynda 115 F4 Amurskaya Oblast',
SE Russian Federation

Tyne 88 D4 river N England, UK

Tyósi see Chōshi

Tyre see Soûr

Týrnavos 104 B4 var. Tírnavos.
Thessalía, C Greece

Tyrrhenian Sea 97 B6 It. Mare
Tirreno. Sea N Mediterranean Sea

Tyumen' 114 C3 Tyumenskaya
Oblast', C Russian Federation

Tyup 123 G2 Kir. Tüp. Issyk-
Kul'skaya Oblast', NE Kyrgyzstan

Tywyn 89 C6 W Wales, UK

Tzekung see Zigong

T,ong Ð,ong 136 D4 var. Tuong
Buong. Nghê An, N Vietnam

U

Uanle Uen see Wanlaweyn

Uaupés, Rio see Vaupés, Río

Ubangi 77 C5 Fr. Oubangui. River
C Africa

Ubangi-Shari see Central African
Republic

Ube 131 B7 Yamaguchi, Honshū,
SW Japan

Ubeda 93 E4 Andalucía, S Spain

Uberaba 63 F4 Minas Gerais,
SE Brazil

Uberlândia 63 F4 Minas Gerais,
SE Brazil

Ubol Rajadhani see Ubon
Ratchathani

Ubol Ratchathani see Ubon
Ratchathani

Ubon Ratchathani 137 D5 var.
Muang Ubon, Ubol Rajadhani,
Ubol Ratchathani, Udon
Ratchathani. Ubon Ratchathani,
E Thailand

Ubrique 92 D5 Andalucía, S Spain
Ucayali, Río 60 D3 river C Peru
Uchiura-wan 130 D3 bay
NW Pacific Ocean
Uchqudug 122 D2 Rus. Uchkuduk.
Nawoiy Wiloyati, N Uzbekistan
Uchtagan, Peski 122 C2 Turkm.
Uchtagan Gumy. Desert
NW Turkmenistan
Udaipur 134 C3 prev. Oodeypore.
Rājasthān, N India
Uddevalla 85 B6 Västra Götaland,
S Sweden
Udine 96 D2 anc. Utina. Friuli-
Venezia Giulia, NE Italy
Udintsev Fracture Zone 154 A5
tectonic feature S Pacific Ocean
Udipi see Udupi
Udon Ratchathani see Ubon
Ratchathani
Udon Thani 136 C4 var. Ban Mak
Khaeng, Udorndhani. Udon
Thani, N Thailand
Udorndhani see Udon Thani
Udupi 132 B2 var. Udipi. Karnātaka,
SW India
Uele 77 D5 var. Welle. River
NE Dem. Rep. Congo
Uelzen 94 C3 Niedersachsen,
N Germany
Ufa 111 D6 Respublika
Bashkortostan, W Russian
Federation
Ugāle 106 C2 Ventspils, NW Latvia
Uganda 73 B6 Country E Africa

Uganda 73

Official name Republic of Uganda
Formation 1962
Capital Kampala
Population 24 million / 263 people
per sq mile (102 people per sq km)
Total area 91,135 sq miles
(236,040 sq km)
Languages English, Nkole, Luganda
Religions Roman Catholic 38%,
Protestant 33%, Traditional beliefs
13%, Muslim (mainly Sunni) 5%,
other 11%
Ethnic mix Bantu Tribes 50%,
other 50%
Government Non-party democracy
Currency New Uganda shilling =
100 cents
Literacy rate 67.1%
Calorie consumption 2,359
kilocalories

Uglovka 110 B4 var. Okulovka.
Novgorodskaya Oblast',
W Russian Federation
Uhuru Peak see Kilimanjaro
Uíge 78 B1 Port. Carmona, Vila
Marechal Carmona. Uíge,
NW Angola
Uinta Mountains 44 B4 mountain
range Utah, W USA
Uitenhage 78 C5 Eastern Cape,
S South Africa
Uithoorn 86 C3 Noord-Holland,
C Netherlands
Ujelang Atoll 144 C1 var. Wujlān.
Atoll Ralik Chain, W Marshall
Islands
Ujungpandang 139 E4 var.
Macassar, Makassar; prev.
Makasar. Sulawesi, C Indonesia
Ujung Salang see Phuket
Ukhta 114 C3 Respublika Komi,
NW Russian Federation
Ukiah 47 B5 California, W USA
Ukmergė see Lithuania
Ukmergė 106 C4 Pol. Wiłkomierz.
Ukmergė, C Lithuania
Ukraine 108 C2 Ukr. Ukrayina; prev.
Ukrainian Soviet Socialist
Republic, Ukrainskaya S.S.R.
Country SE Europe

Ukraine 108

Official name Ukraine
Formation 1991

Ukraine (continued)

Official name Ukraine
Formation 1991
Capital Kiev
Population 48.4 million / 208
people per sq mile (80 people
per sq km)
Total area 223,089 sq miles
(603,700 sq km)
Languages Ukrainian, Russian,
Tartar
Religions Christian (mainly
Ukrainian Orthodox) 95%, Jewish
1%, other 4%
Ethnic mix Ukrainian 73%, Russian
22%, Jewish 1%, other 4%
Government Presidential
democracy
Currency Hryvnia = 100 kopiykas
Literacy rate 99%
Calorie consumption 2,871
kilocalories

Ulaanbaatar 127 E2 Eng. Ulan
Bator. Country capital (Mongolia)
Töv, C Mongolia
Ulaangom 126 C2 Uvs,
NW Mongolia
Ulan Bator see Ulaanbaatar
Ulanhad see Chifeng
Ulan-Ude 115 E4 prev.
Verkhneudinsk. Respublika
Buryatiya, S Russian Federation
Ulft 86 E4 Gelderland, E Netherlands
Ullapool 88 C3 N Scotland, UK
Ulm 95 B6 Baden-Württemberg,
S Germany
Ulsan 129 E4 Jap. Urusan. SE South
Korea
Ulster 89 B5 cultural region N Ireland
Ulungur Hu 126 B2 lake NW China
Uluru 147 D5 var. Ayers Rock. Rocky
outcrop Northern Territory,
C Australia
Ulyanivka 109 E3 Rus. Ul'yanovka.
Kirovohrads'ka Oblast',
C Ukraine
Ul'yanovsk 111 C5 prev. Simbirsk.
Ul'yanovskaya Oblast',
W Russian Federation
Uman' 109 E3 Rus. Uman.
Cherkas'ka Oblast', C Ukraine
Umán 51 H3 Yucatán, SE Mexico
Umanak see Uummannaq
Umanaq see Uummannaq
Umbro-Marchigiano, Appennino
96 C3 Eng. Umbrian-Machigian
Mountains. Mountain range C Italy
Umeå 84 C4 Västerbotten,
N Sweden
Umeälven 84 C4 river N Sweden
Umiat 36 D2 Alaska, USA
Umm Buru 72 A4 Western Darfur,
W Sudan
Umm Durmān see Omdurman
Umm Ruwaba 72 C4 var. Umm
Ruwābah, Um Ruwāba. Northern
Kordofan, C Sudan
Umm Ruwābah see Umm Ruwaba
Umnak Island 36 A3 island
Aleutian Islands, Alaska, USA
Um Ruwāba see Umm Ruwaba
Umtali see Mutare
Umtata 78 D5 Eastern Cape,
SE South Africa
Una 100 B3 river Bosnia and
Herzegovina/Croatia
Unac 100 B3 river W Bosnia and
Herzegovina
Unalaska Island 36 A3 island
Aleutian Islands, Alaska, USA
'Unayzah 120 B4 var. Anaiza.
Al Qaşīm, C Saudi Arabia
Uncía 61 F4 Potosí, C Bolivia
Uncompahgre Peak 44 B5 mountain
Colorado, C USA
Ungarisches Erzgebirge see
Slovenské rudohorie
Ungava Bay 39 E1 bay Quebec,
E Canada
Ungava, Péninsule d' 38 D1
peninsula Quebec, SE Canada

Ungheni 108 D3 Rus. Ungeny.
W Moldova
Unimak Island 36 B3 island
Aleutian Islands, Alaska, USA
Union 43 E1 South Carolina, SE USA
Union City Tennessee, S USA
United Arab Emirates 121 C5 Ar.
Al Imārāt al 'Arabīyah
al Muttaḥidah, abbrev. UAE; prev.
Trucial States. Country SW Asia

United Arab Emirates 121

Official name United Arab
Emirates
Formation 1971
Capital Abu Dhabi
Population 2.7 million /
84 people per sq mile (33 people
per sq km)
Total area 32,000 sq miles
(82,880 sq km)
Languages Arabic, Farsi, English,
Indian and Pakistani languages
Religions Muslim (mainly Sunni)
96%, Christian, Hindu and other 4%
Ethnic mix Asian 60%, Emirian
25%, other Arab 12%, European 3%
Government Monarchy
Currency UAE dirham = 100 fils
Literacy rate 75.6%
Calorie consumption 3,192
kilocalories

United Kingdom 89 B5 abbrev. UK.
Country NW Europe

United Kingdom 89

Official name United Kingdom of
Great Britain and Northern Ireland
Formation 1707
Capital London
Population 59.5 million / 629
people per sq mile (243 people per
sq km)
Total area 94,525 sq miles
(244,820 sq km)
Languages English, Welsh, Scottish
Religions Anglican 47%,
Presbyterian 4%, Roman Catholic
9% , other 40%
Ethnic mix English 80%, Scottish
9%, Northern Irish 3%, Welsh 3%,
other 5%
Government Parliamentary
democracy
Currency Pound sterling = 100
pence
Literacy rate 99%
Calorie consumption 3,334
kilocalories

United States of America 35 B5 var.
America, The States, abbrev. U.S.,
USA. Country

United States of America 35

Official name United States of
America
Formation 1776
Capital Washington DC
Population 281.4 million /76 people
per sq mile (29 people per sq km)
Total area 3,717,792 sq miles
(9,629,091 sq km)
Languages English, Spanish, Italian,
German, French, Polish, Chinese,
Greek
Religions Protestant 61%, Roman
Catholic 25%, Jewish 2%,
other 12%
Ethnic mix White (including
Hispanic) 81%, Native American 2%,
Asia 4%, Black American
African 13%
Government Presidential
democracy
Currency US dollar = 100 cents
Literacy rate 99%
Calorie consumption 3,772
kilocalories

Unst 88 D1 island NE Scotland, UK
Ünye 116 D2 Ordu, W Turkey
Upala 52 D4 Alajuela, NW Costa
Rica
Upata 59 E2 Bolívar, E Venezuela
Upemba, Lac 77 D7 lake SE Dem.
Rep. Congo
Upernavik 82 C2 var. Upernivik.
C Greenland
Upernivik see Upernavik
Upington 78 C4 Northern Cape,
W South Africa
Upolu 145 F4 island SE Samoa
Upper Klamath Lake 46 A4 lake
Oregon, NW USA
Upper Lough Erne 89 A5 lake
SW Northern Ireland, UK
Upper Red Lake 45 F1 lake
Minnesota, N USA
Uppsala 85 C6 Uppsala, C
Sweden
Ural 112 B3 Kaz. Zayyq. River
Kazakhstan/Russian Federation
Ural Mountains see Ural'skiye
Gory
Ural'sk 114 B3 Kaz. Oral. Zapadnyy
Kazakhstan, NW Kazakhstan
Ural'skiye Gory 114 C3 var.
Ural'skiy Khrebet, Eng. Ural
Mountains. Mountain range
Kazakhstan/Russian Federation
Ural'skiy Khrebet see Ural'skiye
Gory
Uraricoera 62 D1 Roraima,
N Brazil
Urbandale 45 F3 Iowa, C USA
Uren' 111 C5 Nizhegorodskaya
Oblast', W Russian Federation
Urganch 122 D2 Rus. Urgench; prev.
Novo-Urgench. Khorazm
Wiloyati, W Uzbekistan
Urgut 123 E3 Samarqand Wiloyati,
C Uzbekistan
Uroševac 101 D5 Alb. Ferizaj.
Serbia, S Serbia and Montenegro
(Yugo.)
Úroteppa 123 E2 Rus. Ura-Tyube.
NW Tajikistan
Uruapan 51 E4 var. Uruapan del
Progreso. Michoacán de Ocampo,
SW Mexico
Uruapan del Progreso see Uruapan
Uruguai, Rio see Uruguay
Uruguay 64 D4 prev. La Banda
Oriental. Country E South
America

Uruguay 64

Official name Eastern Republic of
Uruguay
Formation 1828
Capital Montevideo
Population 3.4 million /50 people
per sq mile (19 people per sq km)
Total area 68,039 sq miles
(176,220 sqkm)
Languages Spanish
Religions Roman Catholic 66%,
non-religious 30%, Jewish 2%,
Protestant 2%
Ethnic mix White 90%, other 10%
Government Presidential
democracy
Currency Uruguayan peso =
100 centimes
Literacy rate 97.8%
Calorie consumption 2,879
kilocalories

Uruguay 64 D3 var. Rio Uruguai,
Río Uruguay. River E South
America
Uruguay, Río see Uruguay
Urumchi see Ürümqi
Urumqi see Ürümqi
Ürümqi 126 C3 var. Tihwa,
Urumchi, Urumqi, Urumtsi,
Wu-lu-k'o-mu-shi, Wu-lu-mu-ch'i;
prev. Ti-hua. Autonomous region
capital Xinjiang Uygur Zizhiqu,
NW China
Urumtsi see Ürümqi

Urup, Ostrov 115 H4 *island*
Kuril'skiye Ostrova, SE Russian
Federation
Urziceni 108 C5 Ialomiţa,
SE Romania
Usa 110 E3 *river* NW Russian
Federation
Uşak 116 B3 *prev.* Ushak. Uşak,
W Turkey
Ushuaia 65 B8 Tierra del Fuego,
S Argentina
Usinsk 110 E3 Respublika Komi,
NW Russian Federation
Üsküb *see* Skopje
Üsküp *see* Skopje
Usmas Ezers 106 B3 *lake* NW Latvia
Usol'ye-Sibirskoye 115 E4
Irkutskaya Oblast', C Russian
Federation
Ussel 91 C5 Corrèze, C France
Ussuriysk 115 G5 *prev.* Nikol'sk,
Nikol'sk-Ussuriyskiy, Voroshilov.
Primorskiy Kray, SE
Ustica, Isola d' 97 B6 *island* S Italy
Ust'-Ilimsk 115 E4 Irkutskaya
Oblast', C Russian Federation
Ústí nad Labem 98 A4 *Ger.* Aussig.
Ústecký Kraj, NW Czech Republic
Ustka 98 C2 *Ger.* Stolpmünde.
Pomorskie, N Poland
Ust'-Kamchatsk 115 H2
Kamchatskaya Oblast', E Russian
Federation
Ust'-Kamenogorsk 114 D5 *Kaz.*
Öskemen. Vostochnyy
Kazakhstan, E Kazakhstan
Ust'-Kut 115 E4 Irkutskaya Oblast',
C Russian Federation
Ust'-Olenëk 115 E3 Respublika
Sakha (Yakutiya), NE Russian
Federation
Ustrzyki Dolne 99 E5
Podkarpackie, SE Poland
Ust Urt *see* Ustyurt Plateau
Ustyurt Plateau 122 B1 *var.* Ust Urt,
Uzb. Ustyurt Platosi. *Plateau*
Kazakhstan/Uzbekistan
Ustyurt Platosi *see* Ustyurt Plateau
Usulután 52 C3 Usulután,
SE El Salvador
Usumacinta, Río 52 B1 *river*
Guatemala/Mexico
Utah 48 A1 *off.* State of Utah; also
known as Beehive State, Mormon
State. *State* W USA
Utah Lake 44 B4 *lake* Utah, W USA
Utena 106 C4 Utena, E Lithuania
Utica 41 F3 New York, NE USA
Utrecht 86 C4 *Lat.* Trajectum ad
Rhenum. Utrecht, C Netherlands
Utsunomiya 131 D5 *var.*
Utunomiya. Tochigi, Honshū,
S Japan
Uttar Pradesh 135 E3 *prev.* United
Provinces, United Provinces of
Agra and Oudh. *State* N India
Utunomiya *see* Utsunomiya
Uulu 106 D2 Pärnumaa,
SW Estonia
Uummannaq 82 C3 *var.* Umanak,
Umanaq. C Greenland
Uummannarsuaq *see* Nunap Isua
Uvalde 49 F4 Texas, SW USA
Uvaravichy 107 D7 *Rus.* Uvarovichi.
Homyel'skaya Voblasts',
SE Belarus
Uvea, Île 145 E4 *island* N Wallis and
Futuna
Uvs Nuur 126 C1 *var.* Ozero Ubsu-
Nur. *Lake* Mongolia/Russian
Federation
'Uwaynāt, Jabal al 88 A3 *var.* Jebel
Uweinat. *Mountain* Libya/Sudan
Uyo 75 G5 Akwa Ibom, S Nigeria
Uyuni 61 F5 Potosí, W Bolivia
Uzbekistan 122 D2 *Country* C Asia

Uzbekistan 122

Official name Republic of
Uzbekistan
Formation 1991
Capital Tashkent

Uzbekistan (continued)

Population 25.3 million / 146
people per sq mile (57 people
per sq km)
Total area 172,741 sq miles
(447,400 sq km)
Languages Uzbek, Russian
Religions Sunni Muslim 88%,
Eastern Orthodox 9%, other 3%
Ethnic mix Uzbek 71%, Russian 8%,
Tajik 5%, Kazakh 4%, other 12%
Government Presidential
democracy
Currency Som = 100 teen
Literacy rate 88.9%
Calorie consumption 2,317
kilocalories

Uzhhorod 108 B2 *Rus.* Uzhgorod;
prev. Ungvár. Zakarpats'ka
Oblast', W Ukraine
Užice 100 D4 *prev.* Titovo Užice.
Serbia, W Serbia and Montenegro
(Yugo.)

V

Vaal 78 D4 *river* C South Africa
Vaals 87 D6 Limburg,
SE Netherlands
Vaasa 85 D5 *Swe.* Vasa; *prev.*
Nikolainkaupunki. Länsi-Suomi,
W Finland
Vaassen 86 D3 Gelderland,
E Netherlands
Vác 99 C6 *Ger.* Waitzen. Pest,
N Hungary
Vadodara 134 C4 *prev.* Baroda.
Gujarāt, W India
Vaduz 94 E2 *country capital*
(Liechtenstein) W Liechtenstein
Váh 99 C5 *Ger.* Waag, *Hung.* Vág.
River W Slovakia
Väinameri 106 C2 *prev.* Muhu Väin,
Ger. Moon-Sund. *Sea* E Baltic Sea
Valachia *see* Wallachia
Valday 110 B4 Novgorodskaya
Oblast', W Russian Federation
Valdecañas, Embalse de 92 D3
reservoir W Spain
Valdepeñas 93 E4 Castilla-La
Mancha, C Spain
Valdés, Península 65 C6 *peninsula*
SE Argentina
Valdez 36 C3 Alaska, USA
Valdia *see* Weldiya
Valdivia 65 B5 Los Lagos, C Chile
Val-d'Or 38 D4 Quebec, SE Canada
Valdosta 43 E3 Georgia, SE USA
Valence 91 D5 *anc.* Valentia, Valentia
Julia, Ventia. Drôme, E France
Valencia 46 D1 California, W USA
Valencia 58 D1 Carabobo,
N Venezuela
Valencia 93 F3 País Valenciano,
E Spain
Valencia, Golfo de 93 F3 *var.* Gulf
of Valencia. *Gulf* E Spain
Valencia, Gulf of *see* Valencia,
Golfo de
Valenciennes 90 D2 Nord,
N France
Valera 58 C2 Trujillo,
NW Venezuela
Valga 106 D3 *Ger.* Walk, *Latv.* Valka.
Valgamaa, S Estonia
Valira 91 A8 *river* Andorra/Spain
Valjevo 100 C4 Serbia, W Serbia
and Montenegro (Yugo.)
Valjok *see* Válljohka
Valka 106 D3 *Ger.* Walk. Valka,
N Latvia
Valkenswaard 87 D5 Noord-
Brabant, S Netherlands
Valladolid 92 D2 Castilla-León,
NW Spain
Valladolid 51 H3 Yucatán,
SE Mexico
Vall d'Uxó 93 F3 País Valenciano,
E Spain
Valle de La Pascua 58 D2 Guárico,
N Venezuela

Valledupar 58 B1 Cesar,
N Colombia
Vallejo 47 B6 California, W USA
Vallenar 64 B3 Atacama, N Chile
Valletta 97 C8 *prev.* Valetta. *Country
capital* (Malta) E Malta
Valley City 45 E2 North Dakota,
N USA
Válljohka 84 D2 *var.* Valjok.
Finnmark, N Norway
Valls 93 G2 Cataluña, NE Spain
Valmiera 106 D3 *Est.* Volmari, *Ger.*
Wolmar. Valmiera, N Latvia
Valozhyn 107 C5 *Pol.* Wołożyn, *Rus.*
Volozhin. Minskaya Voblasts',
C Belarus
Valparaíso 40 C3 Indiana, N USA
Valparaíso 64 B4 Valparaíso,
C Chile
Valverde del Camino 92 C4
Andalucía, S Spain
Van 117 F3 Van, E Turkey
Vanadzor 117 F2 *prev.* Kirovakan.
N Armenia
Vancouver 36 D5 British Columbia,
SW Canada
Vancouver 46 B3 Washington,
NW USA
Vancouver Island 36 D5 *island*
British Columbia, SW Canada
Van Diemen Gulf 146 D2 *gulf*
Northern Territory, N Australia
Vänern 85 B6 *Eng.* Lake Vaner; *prev.*
Lake Vener. *Lake* S Sweden
Vangaindrano 79 G4 Fianarantsoa,
SE Madagascar
Van Gölü 117 F3 *Eng.* Lake Van;
anc. Thospitis. *Salt lake* E Turkey
Van Horn 48 D3 Texas, SW USA
Van, Lake *see* Van Gölü
Vannes 90 A3 *anc.* Dariorigum.
Morbihan, NW France
Vantaa 85 D6 *Swe.* Vanda. Etelä-
Suomi, S Finland
Vanua Levu 145 E4 *island* N Fiji
Vanuatu 144 C4 *prev.* New
Hebrides. *Country* SW Pacific
Ocean

Vanuatu 144

Official name Republic of Vanuatu
Formation 1980
Capital Port Vila
Population 200,000 / 42 people per
sq mile (16 people per sq km)
Total area 4,710 sq miles
(12,200 sq km)
Languages Bislama, English, French
Religions Presbyterian 37%,
Anglican 15%, Roman Catholic 15%,
Indigenous beliefs 8%, Seventh-day
Adventist 6%, other 19%
Ethnic mix Melanesian 94%,
Polynesian 3%, other 3%
Government Parliamentary
democracy
Currency Vatu = 100 centimes
Literacy rate 64%
Calorie consumption 2,587
kilocalories

Van Wert 40 C4 Ohio, N USA
Varakļāni 106 D4 Madona,
C Latvia
Vārānasi 135 E3 *prev.* Banaras,
Benares, *hist.* Kasi. Uttar Pradesh,
N India
Varangerfjorden 84 E2 *fjord*
N Norway
Varangerhalvøya 84 D2 *peninsula*
N Norway
Varannó *see* Vranov nad Topl'ou
Varaždin 100 B2 *Ger.* Warasdin,
Hung. Varasd. Varaždin,
N Croatia
Varberg 85 B7 Halland, S Sweden
Vardar 101 E6 *Gk.* Axiós. *River* FYR
Macedonia/Greece *see also* Axiós
Varde 85 A7 Ribe, W Denmark
Varéna 107 B5 *Pol.* Orany. Varéna,
S Lithuania
Varese 96 B2 Lombardia, N Italy

Vârful Moldoveanu 108 B4 *var.*
Moldoveanul; *prev.* Vîrful
Moldoveanu. *Mountain*
C Romania
Varkaus 85 E5 Itä-Suomi,
C Finland
Varna 104 E2 *prev.* Stalin, *anc.*
Odessus. Varna, E Bulgaria
Varnenski Zaliv 104 E2 *prev.*
Stalinski Zaliv. Bay E Bulgaria
Vasiliki 105 A5 Lefkáda, Iónioi
Nísoi, Greece, C Mediterranean
Sea
Vasilishki 107 B5 *Pol.* Wasiliszki,
Rus. Vasilishki. Hrodzyenskaya
Voblasts', W Belarus
Vaslui 108 D4 Vaslui, C Romania
Västerås 85 C6 Västmanland,
C Sweden
Vasyl'kiv 109 E2 *Rus.* Vasil'kov.
Kyyivs'ka Oblast', N Ukraine
Vaté *see* Efate
Vatican City 97 A7 *Country*
S Europe

Vatican City 97

Official name State of the
Vatican City
Formation 1929
Capital Vatican City
Population 524 / 3,082 people per
sq mile (1,191 people per sq km)
Total area 0.17 sq miles (0.44 sq km)
Languages Italian, Latin
Religions Roman Catholic 100%
Ethnic mix The current pope is
Polish, ending nearly 500 years of
Italian popes. Cardinals are from
many nationalities, but Italians form
the largest group. Most of the
resident lay persons are Italian.
Government Papal state
Currency Euro (Lira until 2002)
Literacy rate 99%
Calorie consumption not available

Vatnajökull 83 E5 *glacier* SE Iceland
Vättern 85 B6 *Eng.* Lake Vetter; *prev.*
Lake Vetter. *Lake* S Sweden
Vaughn 48 D2 New Mexico,
SW USA
Vaupés, Río 58 C4 *var.* Rio Uaupés.
River Brazil/Colombia *see also*
Uaupés, Rio
Vava'u Group 145 E4 *island group*
N Tonga
Vavuniya 132 D3 Northern
Province, N Sri Lanka
Vawkavysk 107 B6 *Pol.*
Wołkowysk, *Rus.* Volkovysk.
Hrodzyenskaya Voblasts',
W Belarus
Växjö 85 C7 *var.* Vexiö. Kronoberg,
S Sweden
Vaygach, Ostrov 110 E2 *island*
NW Russian Federation
Veendam 86 E2 Groningen,
NE Netherlands
Veenendaal 86 D4 Utrecht,
C Netherlands
Vega 84 B4 *island* C Norway
Veisiejai 107 B5 Lazdijai,
S Lithuania
Vejer de la Frontera 92 C5
Andalucía, S Spain
Veldhoven 87 D5 Noord-Brabant,
S Netherlands
Velebit 100 A3 *mountain range*
C Croatia
Velenje 95 E7 *Ger.* Wöllan.
N Slovenia
Veles 101 E6 *Turk.* Köprülü. C FYR
Macedonia
Velho *see* Porto Velho
Velika Morava 100 D4 *var.* Glavn'a
Morava, Morava, *Ger.* Grosse
Morava. *River* C Serbia and
Montenegro (Yugo.)
Velikaya 113 G2 *river* NE Russian
Federation
Velikiye Luki 110 A4 Pskovskaya
Oblast', W Russian Federation

Veliko Tŭrnovo *104 D2 prev.*
Trnovo, Trnovo, Tŭrnovo. Veliko
Tŭrnovo, N Bulgaria
Velingrad *104 C3* Pazardzhik,
C Bulgaria
Vel´ký Krtíš *99 D6* Banskobystrický
Kraj, C Slovakia
Vellore *132 C2* Tamil Nādu,
SE India
Velobriga *see* Viana do Castelo
Velsen *see* Velsen-Noord
Velsen-Noord *86 C3 var.* Velsen.
Noord-Holland, W Netherlands
Vel´sk *110 C4 var.* Velsk.
Arkhangel´skaya Oblast´,
NW Russian Federation
Velsk *see* Vel´sk
Velvendós *see* Velvendós
Velvendós *104 B4 var.* Velvendos.
Dytikí Makedonía, N Greece
Velykyy Tokmak *see* Tokmak
Vendôme *90 C4* Loir-et-Cher,
C France
Venezia *96 C2 Eng.* Venice, *Fr.*
Venise, *Ger.* Venedig; *anc.*Venetia.
Veneto, NE Italy
Venezuela *58 D2 prev.* Estados
Unidos de Venezuela, United
States of Venezuela. *Country*
N South America

Venezuela 58

Official name Bolivarian Republic
of Venezuela
Formation 1830
Capital Caracas
Population 24.6 million /70 people
per sq mile (27 people per sq km)
Total area 352,143 sq miles
(912,050 sq km)
Languages Spanish, Amerindian
languages
Religions Roman Catholic 89%,
Protestant and other 11%
Ethnic mix Mestizo 69%, White
20%, Black 9%, Amerindian 2%
Government Presidential
democracy
Currency Bolívar = 100 centimos
Literacy rate 92.6%
Calorie consumption 2,256
kilocalories

Venezuela, Golfo de *58 C1 Eng.*
Gulf of Maracaibo, Gulf of
Venezuela. *Gulf* NW Venezuela
Venezuelan Basin *56 B1 undersea
feature* E Caribbean Sea
Venice *see* Venezia
Venice *42 C4* Louisiana, S USA
Venice, Gulf of *96 C2 It.* Golfo di
Venezia, *Slvn.* Beneški Zaliv. *Gulf*
N Adriatic Sea
Venlo *87 D5 prev.* Venloo. Limburg,
SE Netherlands
Venta *106 B3 Ger.* Windau. *River*
Latvia/Lithuania
Ventimiglia *96 A3* Liguria,
NW Italy
Ventspils *106 B2 Ger.* Windau.
Ventspils, NW Latvia
Vera *64 D3* Santa Fe, C Argentina
Veracruz *51 F4 var.* Veracruz Llave.
Veracruz-Llave, E Mexico
Veracruz Llave *see* Veracruz
Vercelli *96 A2 anc.* Vercellae.
Piemonte, NW Italy
Verdalsøra *84 B4* Nord-Trøndelag,
C Norway
Verde, Costa *92 D1 coastal region*
N Spain
Verden *94 B3* Niedersachsen,
NW Germany
Veria *see* Véroia
Verkhoyanskiy Khrebet *115 F3
mountain range* NE Russian
Federation
Vermillion *45 F3* South Dakota,
N USA
Vermont *41 F2 off.* State of Vermont;
also known as The Green
Mountain State. *State* NE USA

Vernal *44 B4* Utah, W USA
Vernon *49 F2* Texas, SW USA
Véroia *104 B4 var.* Veria, Vérroia,
Turk. Karaferiye. Kentrikí
Makedonía, N Greece
Verona *96 C2* Veneto, NE Italy
Vérroia *see* Véroia
Versailles *90 D1* Yvelines,
N France
Verviers *87 D6* Liège, E Belgium
Vesdre *87 D6 river* E Belgium
Veselinovo *104 D2* Shumen,
NE Bulgaria
Vesoul *90 D4 anc.* Vesulium,
Vesulum. Haute-Saône, E France
Vesterålen *84 B2 island group*
N Norway
Vestfjorden *84 C3 fjord* C Norway
Vestmannaeyjar *83 E5* Sudhurland,
S Iceland
Vesuvio *97 D5 Eng.* Vesuvius.
Volcano S Italy
Veszprém *99 C7 Ger.* Veszprim.
Veszprém, W Hungary
Vetrino *104 E2* Varna, E Bulgaria
Veurne *87 A5 var.* Furnes. West-
Vlaanderen, W Belgium
Vexiö *see* Växjö
Viacha *61 F4* La Paz, W Bolivia
Viana do Castelo *see* Viana do
Castelo
Viana do Castelo *92 B2 var.* Viana
de Castelo; *anc.* Velobriga. Viana
do Castelo, NW Portugal
Vianen *86 C4* Zuid-Holland,
C Netherlands
Viangchan *136 C4 Eng./Fr.*
Vientiane. *Country capital* (Laos)
C Laos
Viangphoukha *136 C3 var.* Vieng
Pou Kha. Louang Namtha,
N Laos
Viareggio *96 B3* Toscana, C Italy
Viborg *85 A7* Viborg,
NW Denmark
Vic *93 G2 var.* Vich; *anc.* Ausa, Vicus
Ausonensis. Cataluña, NE Spain
Vicenza *96 C2 anc.* Vicentia. Veneto,
NE Italy
Vich *see* Vic
Vichy *90 C5* Allier, C France
Vicksburg *42 B2* Mississippi, S USA
Victoria *102 A5 var.* Rabat. Gozo,
NW Malta
Victoria *79 H1 country capital*
(Seychelles) Mahé, SW Seychelles
Victoria *49 G4* Texas, SW USA
Victoria *36 D5* Vancouver Island,
British Columbia, SW Canada
Victoria *149 C7 state* SE Australia
Victoria Bank *see* Vitória
Seamount
Victoria de Durango *see* Durango
Victoria de las Tunas *see* Las Tunas
Victoria Falls *78 C2 waterfall*
Zambia/Zimbabwe
Victoria Falls *78 C3* Matabeleland
North, W Zimbabwe
Victoria Island *37 F3 island*
Northwest Territories/Nunavut,
NW Canada
Victoria, Lake *73 B6 var.* Victoria
Nyanza. *Lake* E Africa
Victoria Land *154 C4 physical region*
Antarctica
Victoria Nyanza *see* Victoria, Lake
Victoria River *146 D3 river*
Northern Territory, N Australia
Victorville *47 C7* California, W
USA
Vicus Ausonensis *see* Vic
Vidalia *43 E2* Georgia, SE USA
Vidin *104 B1 anc.* Bononia. Vidin,
NW Bulgaria
Vidzy *107 C5 Rus.* Vidzy.
Vitsyebskaya Voblasts´,
NW Belarus
Viedma *65 C5* Río Negro,
E Argentina
Vieng Pou Kha *see* Viangphoukha
Vienna *see* Wien
Vienne *91 D5 anc.* Vienna. Isère,
E France

Vienne *90 B4 river* W France
Vientiane *see* Viangchan
Vierzon *90 C4* Cher, C France
Viesīte *106 C4 Ger.* Eckengraf.
Jēkabpils, S Latvia
Vietnam *136 D4 Vtn.* Công Hoa Xa
Hôi Chu Nghia Viêt Nam.
Country SE Asia

Vietnam 136

Official name Socialist Republic
of Vietnam
Formation 1976
Capital Hanoi
Population 79.2 million / 622
people per sq mile (240 people per
sq km)
Total area 127,243 sq miles
(329,560 sq km)
Languages Vietnamese, Chinese,
Thai, Khmer, Muong, Nung, Miao,
Yao
Religions Buddhist 55%, Christian
7%, other and non-religious 38%
Ethnic mix Vietnamese 88%,
Chinese 4%, Thai 2%, other 6%
Government One-party republic
Currency Dông = 10 hao = 100 xu
Literacy rate 93.4%
Calorie consumption 2,583
kilocalories

Vietri *see* Viêt Tri
Viêt Tri *136 D3 var.* Vietri. Vinh
Phu, N Vietnam
Vieux Fort *55 F2* S Saint Lucia
Vigo *92 B2* Galicia, NW Spain
Vijayawāda *132 D1 prev.* Bezwada.
Andhra Pradesh, SE India
Vijosa *see* Vjosës, Lumi i
Vijosë *see* Vjosës, Lumi i
Vila *see* Port-Vila
Vila Artur de Paiva *see* Cubango
Vila da Ponte *see* Cubango
Vila de Mocímboa da Praia *see*
Mocímboa da Praia
Vila do Conde *92 B2* Porto,
NW Portugal
Vila do Zumbo *78 D2 prev.* Vila do
Zumbu, Zumbo. Tete,
NW Mozambique
Vilafranca del Penedés *93 G2 var.*
Villafranca del Panadés. Cataluña,
NE Spain
Vila General Machado *see*
Camacupa
Viļaka *106 D4 Ger.* Marienhausen.
Balvi, NE Latvia
Vilalba *92 C1* Galicia, NW Spain
Vila Nova de Gaia *92 B2* Porto,
NW Portugal
Vila Nova de Portimão *see*
Portimão
Vila Pereira de Eça *see* N'Giva
Vila Real *92 C2 var.* Vila Rial. Vila
Real, N Portugal
Vila Rial *see* Vila Real
Vila Robert Williams *see* Caála
Vila Serpa Pinto *see* Menongue
Vilhelmina *84 C4* Västerbotten,
N Sweden
Vilhena *62 D3* Rondônia, W Brazil
Vília *105 C5* Attikí, C Greece
Viliya *107 C5 Lith.* Neris, *Rus.*
Viliya. *River* W Belarus
Viljandi *106 D2* Ger. Fellin.
Viljandimaa, S Estonia
Vilkaviškis *106 B4 Pol.*
Wyłkowyszki. Vilkaviškis,
SW Lithuania
Villa Acuña *50 D2 var.* Ciudad
Acuña. Coahuila de Zaragoza, NE
Mexico
Villa Bella *61 F2* Beni, N Bolivia
Villacarrillo *93 E4* Andalucía,
S Spain
Villa Cecilia *see* Ciudad Madero
Villach *95 D7 Slvn.* Beljak. Kärnten,
S Austria
Villacidro *97 A5* Sardegna, Italy,
C Mediterranean Sea
Villa Concepción *see* Concepción

Villa del Pilar *see* Pilar
Villafranca de los Barros *92 C4*
Extremadura, W Spain
Villafranca del Panadés *see*
Vilafranca del Penedès
Villahermosa *51 G4 prev.* San Juan
Bautista. Tabasco, SE Mexico
Villajoyosa *93 F4 var.* La Vila Jojosa.
País Valenciano, E Spain
Villa María *64 C4* Córdoba,
C Argentina
Villa Martín *61 F5* Potosí,
SW Bolivia
Villa Mercedes *64 C4 prev.*
Mercedes. San Luis,
C Argentina
Villanueva *50 D3* Zacatecas,
C Mexico
Villanueva de la Serena *92 C3*
Extremadura, W Spain
Villanueva de los Infantes *93 E4*
Castilla-La Mancha, C Spain
Villarrica *64 D2* Guairá,
SE Paraguay
Villavicencio *58 B3* Meta,
C Colombia
Villaviciosa *92 D1* Asturias,
N Spain
Villazón *61 G5* Potosí, S Bolivia
Villena *93 F4* País Valenciano,
E Spain
Villeurbanne *91 D5* Rhône,
E France
Villingen-Schwenningen *95 B6*
Baden-Württemberg, S Germany
Vilnius *107 C5 Pol.* Wilno, *Ger.*
Wilna; *prev. Rus.* Vilna. *Country
capital* (Lithuania) Vilnius,
SE Lithuania
Vil'shanka *109 E3 Rus.* Olshanka.
Kirovohrads'ka Oblast',
C Ukraine
Vilvoorde *87 C6 Fr.* Vilvorde.
Vlaams Brabant, C Belgium
Vilyeyka *107 C5 Pol.* Wilejka, *Rus.*
Vileyka. Minskaya Voblasts',
NW Belarus
Vilyuy *115 F3 river* NE Russian
Federation
Viña del Mar *64 B4* Valparaíso,
C Chile
Vinaròs *93 F3* País Valenciano,
E Spain
Vincennes *40 B4* Indiana, N USA
Vindhya Mountains *see* Vindhya
Range
Vindhya Range *134 D4 var.*
Vindhya Mountains. *Mountain
range* N India
Vineland *41 F4* New Jersey,
NE USA
Vinh *136 D4* Nghê An, N Vietnam
Vinh Loi *see* Bac Liêu
Vinh Thai Lan *see* Thailand,
Gulf of
Vinishte *104 C2* Montana,
NW Bulgaria
Vinita *49 G1* Oklahoma, C USA
Vinkovci *100 C3 Ger.* Winkowitz,
Hung. Vinkovcze. Vukovar-Srijem,
E Croatia
Vinnytsya *108 D2 Rus.* Vinnitsa.
Vinnyts'ka Oblast', C Ukraine
Vinson Massif *154 A3 mountain*
Antarctica
Viranşehir *117 E4* Şanlıurfa,
SE Turkey
Vîrful Moldoveanu *see* Vârful
Moldoveanu
Virginia *41 E5 off.* Commonwealth
of Virginia; also known as Mother
of Presidents, Mother of States,
Old Dominion. *State* NE USA
Virginia *45 G1* Minnesota, N USA
Virginia Beach *41 F5* Virginia,
NE USA
Virgin Islands *see* British Virgin
Islands
Virgin Islands (US) *55 F3 var.*
Virgin Islands of the United
States; *prev.* Danish West Indies.
US unincorporated territory E West
Indies

Virgin Islands of the United States
see Virgin Islands (US)
Virôchey 137 E5 Rôtânôkiri,
NE Cambodia
Virovitica 100 C2 Ger. Virovititz,
Hung. Verôcze; *prev. Ger.*
Werowitz. Virovitica-Podravina,
NE Croatia
Virton 87 D8 Luxembourg,
SE Belgium
Virtsu 106 D2 Ger. Werder.
Läänemaa, W Estonia
Vis 100 B4 *It.* Lissa; *anc. Issa. Island*
S Croatia
Vis see Fish
Visaginas 106 C4 *prev.* Sniečkus.
Ignalina, E Lithuania
Visākhapatnam 135 E5 Andhra
Pradesh, SE India
Visalia 47 C6 California, W USA
Visby 85 C7 Ger. Wisby. Gotland,
SE Sweden
Viscount Melville Sound 37 F2
prev. Melville Sound. *Sound*
Northwest Territories/Nunavut,
N Canada
Visé 87 D6 Liège, E Belgium
Viseu 92 C2 *prev.* Vizeu. Viseu,
N Portugal
Visoko 100 C4 Federacija Bosna I
Hercegovina, C Bosnia and
Herzegovina
Vistula see Wisła
Vistula Lagoon 98 C2 Ger. Frisches
Haff, *Pol.* Zalew Wiślany, *Rus.*
Vislinskiy Zaliv. *Lagoon*
Poland/Russian Federation
Viterbo 96 C4 *anc.* Vicus Elbii.
Lazio, C Italy
Viti Levu 145 E4 *island* W Fiji
Vitim 115 F4 *river* C Russian
Federation
Vitoria see Vitoria-Gasteiz
Vitória 63 F4 Espírito Santo,
SE Brazil
Vitória Bank see Vitória Seamount
Vitória da Conquista 63 F3 Bahia,
E Brazil
Vitoria-Gasteiz 93 E1 *var.* Vitoria,
Eng. Vittoria. País Vasco, N Spain
Vitória Seamount 67 B5 *var.*
Victoria Bank, Vitoria Bank.
Undersea feature C Atlantic Ocean
Vitré 90 B3 Ille-et-Vilaine,
NW France
Vitsyebsk 107 E5 *Rus.* Vitebsk.
Vitsyebskaya Voblasts',
NE Belarus
Vittoria see Vitoria-Gasteiz
Vittoria 97 C7 Sicilia, Italy,
C Mediterranean Sea
Vizianagaram 135 E5 *var.*
Vizianagram. Andhra Pradesh,
E India
Vizianagram see Vizianagaram
Vjosës, Lumi i 101 C7 *var.* Vijosa,
Vijosë, *Gk.* Aóos. *River*
Albania/Greece *see also* Aóos
Vlaardingen 86 B4 Zuid-Holland,
SW Netherlands
Vladikavkaz 111 B8 *prev.*
Dzaudzhikau, Ordzhonikidze.
Severnaya Osetiya-Alaniya,
SW Russian Federation
Vladimir 111 B5 Vladimirskaya
Oblast', W Russian Federation
Vladivostok 115 G5 Primorskiy
Kray, SE Russian Federation
Vlagtwedde 86 E2 Groningen,
NE Netherlands
Vlasotince 101 E5 Serbia, SE Serbia
and Montenegro (Yugo.)
Vlieland 86 C1 Fris. Flylân. *Island*
Waddeninseln, N Netherlands
Vlijmen 86 C4 Noord-Brabant,
S Netherlands
Vlissingen 87 B5 Eng. Flushing, *Fr.*
Flessingue. Zeeland,
SW Netherlands
Vlorë 101 C7 *prev.* Vlonë, *It.* Valona,
Vlora. Vlorë, SW Albania
Vöcklabruck 95 D6 Oberösterreich,
NW Austria

Vohimena, Tanjona 79 F4 Fr. Cap
Sainte Marie. *Headland*
S Madagascar
Voiron 91 D5 Isère, E France
Vojvodina 100 D3 Ger. Wojwodina.
Region N Serbia and Montenegro
(Yugo.)
Volcán de Chiriquí see Barú,
Volcán
Volga 111 B7 *river* NW Russian
Federation
Volga Uplands 81 G3 *Russ.*
Privolzhskaya Vozvyshennost'
mountain range W Russian
Federation
Volgodonsk 111 B7 Rostovskaya
Oblast', SW Russian Federation
Volgograd 111 B7 *prev.* Stalingrad,
Tsaritsyn. Volgogradskaya
Oblast', SW Russian Federation
Volkhov 110 B4 Leningradskaya
Oblast', NW Russian Federation
Volnovakha 109 G3 Donets'ka
Oblast', SE Ukraine
Volodymyr-Volyns'kyy 108 C1 Pol.
Włodzimierz, *Rus.* Vladimir-
Volynskiy. Volyns'ka Oblast',
NW Ukraine
Vologda 110 B4 Vologodskaya
Oblast', W Russian Federation
Vólos 105 B5 Thessalía, C Greece
Vol'sk 111 C6 Saratovskaya Oblast',
W Russian Federation
Volta 75 E5 *river* SE Ghana
Volta Blanche see White Volta
Volta, Lake 75 E5 *reservoir*
SE Ghana
Volta Noire see Black Volta
Volturno 97 D5 *river* S Italy
Volzhskiy 111 B6 Volgogradskaya
Oblast', SW Russian Federation
Võnnu 106 E3 Ger. Wendau.
Tartumaa, SE Estonia
Voorst 86 D3 Gelderland,
E Netherlands
Voranava 107 C5 Pol. Werenów, *Rus.*
Voronovo. Hrodzyenskaya
Voblasts', W Belarus
Vorderrhein 95 B7 *river*
SE Switzerland
Vóreioi Sporádes 105 C5 *var.* Vórioi
Sporádhes, *Eng.* Northern
Sporades. *Island group* E Greece
Vórioi Sporádhes see Vóreioi
Sporádes
Vorkuta 114 C2 Respublika Komi,
NW Russian Federation
Vormsi 106 C2 *var.* Vormsi Saar, *Ger.*
Worms, Swed. Ormsö. *Island*
W Estonia
Vormsi Saar see Vormsi
Voronezh 111 B6 Voronezhskaya
Oblast', W Russian Federation
Võru 106 D3 Ger. Werro. Võrumaa,
SE Estonia
Vosges 90 E4 *mountain range*
NE France
Vostochno-Sibirskoye More 115 F1
Eng. East Siberian Sea. *Sea* Arctic
Ocean
Vostock Island see Vostok Island
Vostok 154 C3 *Russian research*
station Antarctica
Vostok Island 145 G3 *var.* Vostock
Island; *prev.* Stavers Island. *Island*
Line Islands, SE Kiribati
Voznesens'k 109 E3 *Rus.*
Voznesensk. Mykolayivs'ka
Oblast', S Ukraine
Vrangelya, Ostrov 115 F1 *Eng.*
Wrangel Island. *Island* NE Russian
Federation
Vranje 101 E5 Serbia, SE Serbia and
Montenegro (Yugo.)
Vranov see Vranov nad Topl'ou
Vranov nad Topl'ou 99 D5 *var.*
Vranov, *Hung.* Varannó.
Prešovský Kraj, E Slovakia
Vratsa 104 C2 Vratsa, NW Bulgaria
Vrbas 100 C3 *river* N Bosnia and
Herzegovina
Vrbas 100 C3 Serbia, NW Serbia
and Montenegro (Yugo.)

Vsetín 99 C5 Ger. Wsetin. Zlínský
Kraj, E Czech Republic
Vučitrn 101 D5 Serbia, S Serbia and
Montenegro (Yugo.)
Vukovar 100 C3 Hung. Vukovár.
Vukovar-Srijem, E Croatia
Vulcano, Isola 97 C7 *island* Isole
Eolie, S Italy
Vung Tau 137 E6 *prev.* Fr. Cape
Saint Jacques, Cap Saint-Jacques.
Ba Ria-Vung Tau, S Vietnam
Vyatka 111 C5 *river* NW Russian
Federation
Vyborg 110 B3 Fin. Viipuri.
Leningradskaya Oblast',
NW Russian Federation
Vyerkhnyadzvinsk 107 D5 *Rus.*
Verkhnedvinsk. Vitsyebskaya
Voblasts', N Belarus
Vyetryna 107 D5 *Rus.* Vetrino.
Vitsyebskaya Voblasts', N Belarus
Vynohradiv 108 B3 Cz. Sevluš,
Hung. Nagyszöllôs, *Rus.*
Vinogradov; *prev.* Sevlyush.
Zakarpats'ka Oblast', W Ukraine

W

Wa 75 E4 NW Ghana
Waal 86 C4 *river* S Netherlands
Wabash 40 C4 Indiana, N USA
Wabash River 40 B5 *river* N USA
Waco 49 G3 Texas, SW USA
Waddān 71 F3 NW Libya
Waddeneilanden 86 C1 *Eng.* West
Frisian Islands. *Island group*
N Netherlands
Waddenzee 86 C1 *var.* Wadden Zee.
Sea SE North Sea
Waddington, Mount 36 D5
mountain British Columbia,
SW Canada
Wādī as Sīr 119 B6 *var.* Wadi es Sir.
'Ammān, NW Jordan
Wadi es Sir see Wādī as Sīr
Wadi Halfa 72 B3 *var.* Wādī Ḥalfā'.
Northern, N Sudan
Wādī Mūsā 119 B7 *var.* Petra.
Ma'ān, S Jordan
Wad Madanī see Wad Medani
Wad Medani 72 C4 *var.* Wad
Madanī. Gezira, C Sudan
Waflia 139 F4 Pulau Buru,
E Indonesia
Wagadugu see Ouagadougou
Wagga Wagga 149 C7 New South
Wales, SE Australia
Wagin 147 B7 Western Australia
Wāh 134 C1 Punjab, NE Pakistan
Wahai 139 F4 Pulau Seram,
E Indonesia
Wahiawa 47 A8 *Haw.* Wahiawā.
Oahu, Hawaii, USA, C Pacific
Ocean
Wahībah, Ramlat Āl 121 E5 *var.*
Ramlat Ahl Wahībah, Ramlat
Al Wahaybah, *Eng.* Wahibah
Sands. *Desert* N Oman
Wahibah Sands see Wahībah,
Ramlat Āl
Wahpeton 45 F2 North Dakota,
N USA
Wahran see Oran
Waiau 151 A7 *river* South Island,
NZ
Waigeo, Pulau 139 G4 *island*
Maluku, E Indonesia
Waikaremoana, Lake 150 E4 *lake*
North Island, NZ
Wailuku 47 B8 Maui, Hawaii, USA,
C Pacific Ocean
Waimate 151 B6 Canterbury, South
Island, NZ
Waiouru 150 D4 Manawatu-
Wanganui, North Island, NZ
Waipara 151 C6 Canterbury, South
Island, NZ
Waipawa 150 E4 Hawke's Bay,
North Island, NZ
Waipukurau 150 D4 Hawke's Bay,
North Island, NZ
Wairau 151 C5 *river*
South Island, NZ

Wairoa 150 D2 *river* North Island,
NZ
Wairoa 150 E4 Hawke's Bay, North
Island, NZ
Waitaki 151 B6 *river* South Island,
NZ
Waitara 150 D4 Taranaki, North
Island, NZ
Waiuku 150 D3 Auckland, North
Island, NZ
Wakasa-wan 131 C6 *bay* C Japan
Wakatipu, Lake 151 A7 *lake* South
Island, NZ
Wakayama 131 C6 Wakayama,
Honshū, SW Japan
Wake Island 142 D1 *atoll*
NW Pacific Ocean
Wake Island 152 C2 US
unincorporated territory NW Pacific
Ocean
Wakkanai 130 C1 Hokkaidō,
NE Japan
Walachei see Wallachia
Walachia see Wallachia
Wałbrzych 98 B4 Ger. Waldenburg,
Waldenburg in Schlesien.
Dolnośląskie, SW Poland
Walcourt 87 C7 Namur, S Belgium
Wałcz 98 B3 Ger. Deutsch Krone.
Zachodniopomorskie, NW Poland
Waldia see Weldiya
Wales 89 C6 Wel. Cymru. *National*
region UK
Wales 36 C2 Alaska, USA
Wales Island, Prince of see Pinang,
Pulau
Walgett 149 D5 New South Wales,
SE Australia
Walker Lake 47 C5 *lake* Nevada,
W USA
Wallachia 108 B5 *var.* Walachia, Ger.
Walachei, *Rom.* Valachia. *Cultural*
region S Romania
Walla Walla 46 C2 Washington,
NW USA
Wallis and Futuna 145 E4 Fr.
Territoire de Wallis et Futuna.
French overseas territory C Pacific
Ocean
Walnut Ridge 42 B1 Arkansas,
C USA
Walthamstow 89 B7 SE England,
UK
Walvis Bay 78 A4 Afr. Walvisbaai.
Erongo, NW Namibia
Walvish Ridge see Walvis Ridge
Walvis Ridge 69 B7 *var.* Walvish
Ridge. *Undersea feature* E Atlantic
Ocean
Wan see Anhui
Wanaka 151 B6 Otago, South
Island, NZ
Wanaka, Lake 151 A6 *lake* South
Island, NZ
Wanchuan see Zhangjiakou
Wandel Sea 83 E1 *sea* Arctic Ocean
Wandsworth 89 A8 SE England,
UK
Wanganui 150 D4 Manawatu-
Wanganui, North Island, NZ
Wangaratta 149 C7 Victoria,
SE Australia
Wanki, Río see Coco, Río
Wanlaweyn 73 D6 *var.* Wanle Weyn,
It. Uanle Uen. Shabeellaha Hoose,
SW Somalia
Wanle Weyn see Wanlaweyn
Wanxian 128 B5 Chongqing,
C China
Warangal 135 E5 Andhra Pradesh,
C India
Warburg 94 B4 Nordrhein-
Westfalen, W Germany
Ware 37 E4 British Columbia,
W Canada
Waremme 87 C6 Liège, E Belgium
Waren 94 C3 Mecklenburg-
Vorpommern, NE Germany
Wargla see Ouargla
Warkworth 150 D2 Auckland,
North Island, NZ
Warnemünde 94 C2 Mecklenburg-
Vorpommern, NE Germany

Warner 49 G1 Oklahoma, C USA
Warnes 61 G4 Santa Cruz, C Bolivia
Warrego River 149 C5 *seasonal river*
New South Wales/Queensland,
E Australia
Warren 40 D3 Michigan, N USA
Warren 40 D3 Ohio, N USA
Warren 41 E3 Pennsylvania,
NE USA
Warri 75 F5 Delta, S Nigeria
Warrnambool 149 B7 Victoria,
SE Australia
Warsaw *see* Mazowieckie
Warszawa 98 D3 *Eng.* Warsaw, *Ger.*
Warschau, *Rus.* Varshava. *Country
capital* (Poland) Mazowieckie,
C Poland
Warta 98 B3 *Ger.* Warthe. *River*
W Poland
Warwick 149 E5 Queensland,
E Australia
Washington 44 A2 *off.* State of
Washington; also known as
Chinook State, Evergreen State.
State NW USA
Washington DC 41 E4 *country
capital* (USA) District of
Columbia, NE USA
Washington, Mount 41 G2 *mountain*
New Hampshire, NE USA
Wash, The 89 E6 *inlet* E England,
UK
Waspam 53 E2 *var.* Waspán. Región
Autónoma Atlántico Norte,
NE Nicaragua
Waspán *see* Waspam
Watampone 139 E4 *var.* Bone.
Sulawesi, C Indonesia
Waterbury 41 F3 Connecticut,
NE USA
Waterford 89 B6 *Ir.* Port Láirge.
S Ireland
Waterloo 45 G3 Iowa, C USA
Watertown 41 F2 New York,
NE USA
Watertown 45 F2 South Dakota,
N USA
Waterville 41 G2 Maine, NE USA
Watford 89 E7 SE England, UK
Watsa 77 E5 Orientale, NE Dem.
Rep. Congo
Watts Bar Lake *reservoir* Tennessee,
S USA
Wau 73 B5 *var.* Wāw. Western Bahr
el Ghazal, S Sudan
Waukegan 40 B3 Illinois, N USA
Waukesha 40 B3 Wisconsin, N USA
Wausau 40 B2 Wisconsin, N USA
Waverly 45 G3 Iowa, C USA
Wavre 87 C6 Wallon Brabant,
C Belgium
Wāw *see* Wau
Wawa 38 C4 Ontario, S Canada
Waycross 43 E3 Georgia, SE USA
Wearmouth *see* Sunderland
Webster City 45 F3 Iowa, C USA
Weddell Plain 154 A2 *undersea
feature* SW Atlantic Ocean
Weddell Sea 154 A2 *sea* SW Atlantic
Ocean
Weener 94 A3 Niedersachsen,
NW Germany
Weert 87 D5 Limburg,
SE Netherlands
Weesp 86 C3 Noord-Holland,
C Netherlands
Węgorzewo 98 D2 *Ger.* Angerburg.
Warmińsko-Mazurskie,
NE Poland
Weimar 94 C4 Thüringen,
C Germany
Weissenburg 95 C6 Bayern,
SE Germany
Weiswampach 87 D7 Diekirch,
N Luxembourg
Wejherowo 98 C2 Pomorskie,
NW Poland
Welchman Hall 55 G1 C Barbados
Weldiya 72 C4 *var.* Waldia, *It.*
Valdia. N Ethiopia
Welkom 78 D4 Free State, C South
Africa
Welle *see* Uele

Wellesley Islands 148 B2 *island
group* Queensland, N Australia
Wellington 151 D5 *country capital*
(NZ) Wellington, North
Island, NZ
Wellington *see* Wellington, Isla
Wellington 45 F5 Kansas, C USA
Wellington, Isla 65 A7 *var.*
Wellington. *Island* S Chile
Wells 46 D4 Nevada, W USA
Wellsford 150 D2 Auckland, North
Island, NZ
Wells, Lake 147 C5 *lake* Western
Australia
Wels 95 *D6 anc.* Ovilava.
Oberösterreich, N Austria
Wembley 89 A8 SE England, UK
Wemmel 87 B6 Vlaams Brabant,
C Belgium
Wenatchee 46 B2 Washington,
NW USA
Wenchi 75 E4 W Ghana
Wen-chou *see* Wenzhou
Wenchow *see* Wenzhou
Wenmen Island *see* Wolf, Isla
Wenzhou 128 D5 *var.* Wen-chou,
Wenchow. Zhejiang, SE China
Werda 78 C4 Kgalagadi, S Botswana
Werkendam 86 C4 Noord-Brabant,
S Netherlands
Weser 94 B3 *river* NW Germany
Wessel Islands 148 B1 *island group*
Northern Territory, N Australia
West Antarctica *see* Lesser
Antarctica
West Bank 119 A6 *disputed region*
SW Asia
West Bend 40 B3 Wisconsin, N USA
West Bengal 135 F4 *state* NE India
West Cape 151 A7 *headland* South
Island, NZ
West Des Moines 45 F3 Iowa,
C USA
Westerland 94 B2 Schleswig-
Holstein, N Germany
Western Australia 146 B4 *state*
W Australia
Western Desert *see* Sahara
Western Dvina 85 E7 *Bel.* Dzvina,
Ger. Düna, *Latv.* Daugava, *Rus.*
Zapadnaya Dvina. *River*
W Europe
Western Ghats 134 C5 *mountain
range* SW India
Western Isles *see* Outer
Hebrides
Western Sahara 70 B3 *UK disputed
territory* N Africa
Western Samoa *see* Samoa
Westerschelde 87 B5 *Eng.* Western
Scheldt; *prev.* Honte. *Inlet* S North
Sea
West Falkland 65 C7 *var.* Isla Gran
Malvina. *Island* W Falkland
Islands
West Fargo 45 F2 North Dakota,
N USA
West Irian *see* Papua
West Mariana Basin 142 B1 *var.*
Perece Vela Basin. *Undersea feature*
W Pacific Ocean
West Memphis 42 B1 Arkansas,
C USA
West New Guinea *see* Papua
West Papua *see* Papua
Weston-super-Mare 89 D7
SW England, UK
West Palm Beach 43 F4 Florida,
SE USA
Westport 151 C5 West Coast, South
Island, NZ
West River *see* Xi Jiang
West Siberian Plain *see* Zapadno-
Sibirskaya Ravnina
West Virginia 40 D4 *off.* State of
West Virginia; also known as The
Mountain State. *State* NE USA
Wetar, Pulau 139 F5 *island*
Kepulauan Damar, E Indonesia
Wetzlar 95 B5 Hessen, W Germany
Wevok 36 C2 *var.* Wewuk. Alaska,
USA

Wewuk *see* Wevok
Wexford 89 B6 *Ir.* Loch Garman.
SE Ireland
Weyburn 37 F5 Saskatchewan,
S Canada
Weymouth 89 D7 S England, UK
Wezep 86 D3 Gelderland,
E Netherlands
Whakatane 150 E3 Bay of Plenty,
North Island, NZ
Whale Cove 37 G3 Nunavut,
C Canada
Whangarei 150 D2 Northland,
North Island, NZ
Wharton Basin 141 D5 *var.* West
Australian Basin. *Undersea feature*
E Indian Ocean
Whataroa 151 B6 West Coast, South
Island, NZ
Wheatland 44 D3 Wyoming, C USA
Wheeler Peak 48 D1 *mountain* New
Mexico, SW USA
Wheeling 40 D4 West Virginia,
NE USA
Whitby 89 D5 N England, UK
Whitefish 44 B1 Montana,
NW USA
Whitehaven 89 C5 NW England,
UK
Whitehorse 36 D4 *territory capital*
Yukon Territory, W Canada
White Nile 72 B4 *Ar.* Al Baḥr
al Abyaḍ, An Nīl al Abyaḍ, Bahr
el Jebel. *River* SE Sudan
White Nile 72 B4 *var.* Bahr el Jebel.
River S Sudan
White River 44 D3 *river* South
Dakota, N USA
White Sea *see* Beloye More
White Volta 75 E4 *var.* Nakambé, *Fr.*
Volta Blanche. *River* Burkina
faso/Ghana
Whitianga 150 D2 Waikato, North
Island, NZ
Whitney, Mount 47 C6 *mountain*
California, W USA
Whitsunday Group 148 D3 *island
group* Queensland, E Australia
Whyalla 149 B6 South Australia
Wichita 45 F5 Kansas, C USA
Wichita Falls 49 F2 Texas, SW
USA
Wichita River 49 F2 *river* Texas,
SW USA
Wickenburg 48 B2 Arizona,
SW USA
Wicklow 89 B6 *Ir.* Cill Mhantáin.
Cultural region E Ireland
Wicklow Mountains 89 B6 *Ir.*
Sléibhte Chill Mhantáin. *Mountain
range* E Ireland
Wieliczka 99 D5 Małopolskie,
S Poland
Wieluń 98 C4 Łódzkie, C Poland
Wien 95 E6 *Eng.* Vienna, *Hung.*
Bécs, *Slvk.* Vídeň, *Slvn.* Dunaj; *anc.*
Vindobona. *Country capital*
(Austria) Wien, NE Austria
Wiener Neustadt 95 E6
Niederösterreich, E Austria
Wierden 86 E3 Overijssel,
E Netherlands
Wiesbaden 95 B5 Hessen,
W Germany
Wight, Isle of 89 D7 *island*
S England, UK
Wijchen 86 D4 Gelderland,
SE Netherlands
Wijk bij Duurstede 86 D4 Utrecht,
C Netherlands
Wilcannia 149 C6 New South
Wales, SE Australia
Wilhelm, Mount 144 B3 *mountain*
C PNG
Wilhelm-Pieck-Stadt *see* Guben
Wilhelmshaven 94 B3
Niedersachsen, NW Germany
Wilkes Barre 41 F3 Pennsylvania,
NE USA
Wilkes Land 154 C4 *physical region*
Antarctica
Willard 48 D2 New Mexico,
SW USA

Willcox 48 C3 Arizona, SW USA
Willebroek 87 B5 Antwerpen,
C Belgium
Willemstad 55 E5 *dependent territory
capital* (Netherlands Antilles)
Curaçao, Netherlands Antilles
Williston 44 D1 North Dakota,
N USA
Wilmington 41 F4 Delaware,
NE USA
Wilmington 43 F2 North Carolina,
SE USA
Wilmington 40 C4 Ohio, N USA
Wilrijk 87 C5 Antwerpen,
N Belgium
Winchester 89 D7 *hist.*
Wintanceaster, *Lat.* Venta
Belgarum. S England, UK
Winchester 41 E4 Virginia, NE USA
Windhoek 78 B3 *Ger.* Windhuk.
Country capital (Namibia)
Khomas, C Namibia
Windorah 148 C4 Queensland,
C Australia
Windsor 41 G3 Connecticut,
NE USA
Windsor 148 D1 New South Wales,
SE Australia
Windsor 38 C5 Ontario, S Canada
Windsor 89 D7 S England, UK
Windward Islands 55 H4 *island
group* E West Indies
Windward Islands *see* Barlavento,
Ilhas de
Windward Passage 54 D3 *Sp.* Paso
de los Vientos. *Channel*
Cuba/Haiti
Winisk 38 C2 *river* Ontario,
S Canada
Winisk 38 C2 Ontario, C Canada
Winnebago, Lake 40 B2 *lake*
Wisconsin, N USA
Winnemucca 47 C5 Nevada,
W USA
Winnipeg 37 G5 Manitoba,
S Canada
Winnipeg, Lake 37 G5 *lake*
Manitoba, C Canada
Winnipegosis, Lake 38 A3 *lake*
Manitoba, C Canada
Winona 45 G3 Minnesota, N USA
Winschoten 86 E2 Groningen,
NE Netherlands
Winsen 94 B3 Niedersachsen,
N Germany
Winston Salem 43 E1 North
Carolina, SE USA
Winsum 86 D1 Groningen,
NE Netherlands
Winterswijk 86 E4 Gelderland,
E Netherlands
Winterthur 95 B7 Zürich,
NE Switzerland
Winton 148 C4 Queensland,
E Australia
Winton 151 A7 Southland, South
Island, NZ
Wisconsin 40 A2 *off.* State of
Wisconsin; also known as The
Badger State. *State* N USA
Wisconsin Rapids 40 B2 Wisconsin,
N USA
Wisconsin River 40 B3 *river*
Wisconsin, N USA
Wisła 98 C2 *Eng.* Vistula, *Ger.*
Weichsel. *River* Śląskie, S Poland
Wismar 94 C2 Mecklenburg-
Vorpommern, N Germany
Wittenberge 94 C3 Brandenburg,
N Germany
Wittlich 95 A5 Rheinland-Pfalz,
SW Germany
Wittstock 94 C3 Brandenburg,
NE Germany
W.J. van Blommesteinmeer 59 G3
reservoir E Suriname
Władysławowo 98 C2 Pomorskie,
N Poland
Włocławek 98 C3 *Ger./Rus.*
Vlotslavsk. Kujawsko-pomorskie,
C Poland
Włodawa 98 E4 *Rus.* Vlodava.
Lubelskie, E Poland

Wlotzkasbaken 78 B3 Erongo, W Namibia
Wodonga 149 C7 Victoria, SE Australia
Wodzisław Śląski 99 C5 Ger. Loslau. Śląskie, S Poland
Wōjjā see Wotje Atoll
Woking 89 D7 SE England, UK
Wolf, Isla 60 A4 var. Wenmen Island. Island W Ecuador
Wolfsberg 95 D7 Kärnten, SE Austria
Wolfsburg 94 C3 Niedersachsen, N Germany
Wolgast 94 D2 Mecklenburg-Vorpommern, NE Germany
Wollaston Lake 37 F4 Saskatchewan, C Canada
Wollongong 149 D6 New South Wales, SE Australia
Wolvega 86 D2 Fris. Wolvegea. Friesland, N Netherlands
Wolverhampton 89 D6 C England, UK
Wŏnsan 129 E3 SE North Korea
Woodburn 46 B3 Oregon, NW USA
Woodland 47 B5 California, W USA
Woodruff 40 B2 Wisconsin, N USA
Woods, Lake of the 38 A3 Fr. Lac des Bois. Lake Canada/USA
Woodville 150 D4 Manawatu-Wanganui, North Island, NZ
Woodward 49 F1 Oklahoma, C USA
Worcester 89 D6 hist. Wigorna Ceaster. W England, UK
Worcester 41 G3 Massachusetts, NE USA
Worcester 78 C5 Western Cape, SW South Africa
Workington 89 C5 NW England, UK
Worland 44 C3 Wyoming, C USA
Worms 95 B5 anc. Augusta Vangionum, Borbetomagus, Wormatia. Rheinland-Pfalz, SW Germany
Worms see Vormsi
Worthington 45 F3 Minnesota, N USA
Wotje Atoll 144 D1 var. Wōjjā. Atoll Ratak Chain, E Marshall Islands
Woudrichem 86 C4 Noord-Brabant, S Netherlands
Wrangel Island see Vrangelya, Ostrov
Wrangel Plain 155 B2 undersea feature Arctic Ocean
Wrocław 98 C4 Eng./Ger. Breslau. Dolnośląskie, SW Poland
Września 98 C3 Wielkopolskie, C Poland
Wuchang see Wuhan
Wuday 'ah 121 C6 Najrān, S Saudi Arabia
Wuhai 127 E3 Nei Mongol Zizhiqu, N China
Wuhan 128 C5 var. Han-kou, Han-k'ou, Hanyang, Wuchang, Wu-han; prev. Hankow. Hubei, C China
Wuhsi see Wuxi
Wuhsien see Suzhou
Wuhu 128 D5 var. Wu-na-mu. Anhui, E China
Wujlān see Ujelang Atoll
Wukari 75 G4 Taraba, E Nigeria
Wuliang Shan 128 A6 mountain range SW China
Wu-lu-k'o-mu-shi see Ürümqi
Wu-lu-mu-ch'i see Ürümqi
Wu-na-mu see Wuhu
Wuppertal 94 A4 prev. Barmen-Elberfeld. Nordrhein-Westfalen, W Germany
Würzburg 95 B5 Bayern, SW Germany
Wusih see Wuxi
Wuxi 128 D5 var. Wuhsi, Wu-hsi, Wusih. Jiangsu, E China
Wuyi Shan 125 E3 mountain range SE China

Wye 89 C6 Wel. Gwy. River England/Wales, UK
Wyndham 146 D3 Western Australia
Wyoming 44 B3 off. State of Wyoming; also known as The Equality State. State C USA
Wyoming 40 C3 Michigan, N USA
Wyszków 98 D3 Ger. Probstberg. Mazowieckie, C Poland

X

Xaafuun, Raas 72 E4 var. Ras Hafun. Headland NE Somalia
Xaçmaz 117 H2 Rus. Khachmas. N Azerbaijan
Xaignabouli 136 C4 prev. Muang Xaignabouri, Fr. Sayaboury. Xaignabouli, N Laos
Xai-Xai 79 E4 prev. João Belo, Vila de João Bel. Gaza, S Mozambique
Xalapa 51 F4 var. Jalapa, Jalapa Enríquez. Veracruz-Llave, SE Mexico
Xam Nua 136 D3 var. Sam Neua. Houaphan, N Laos
Xankändi 117 G3 Rus. Khankendi; prev. Stepanakert. SW Azerbaijan
Xánthi 104 C3 Anatolikí Makedonía kai Thráki, NE Greece
Xátiva 93 F3 var. Jativa;anc. Setabis. País Valenciano, E Spain
Xauen see Chefchaouen
Xeres see Jeréz de la Frontera
Xiaguan see Dali
Xiamen 128 D6 var. Hsia-men; prev. Amoy. Fujian, SE China
Xi'an 128 C4 var. Changan, Sian, Signan, Siking, Singan, Xian. Shaanxi, C China
Xian see Xi'an
Xiangkhoang see Pèk
Xiangtan 128 C5 var. Hsiang-t'an, Siangtan. Hunan, S China
Xiao Hinggan Ling 128 D2 Eng. Lesser Khingan Range. Mountain range NE China
Xichang 128 B5 Sichuan, C China
Xieng Khouang see Pèk
Xieng Ngeun see Muong Xiang Ngeun
Xigazê see Xigazê
Xigazê 126 C5 var. Jih-k'a-tse, Shigatse, Xigaze. Xizang Zizhiqu, W China
Xi Jiang 124 D3 var. Hsi Chiang, Eng. West River. River S China
Xilinhot 127 F2 var. Silinhot. Nei Mongol Zizhiqu, N China
Xilokastro see Xylókastro
Xin see Xinjiang Uygur Zizhiqu
Xingkai Hu see Khanka, Lake
Xingu, Rio 63 E2 river C Brazil
Xingxingxia 126 D3 Xinjiang Uygur Zizhiqu, NW China
Xining 127 E4 var. Hsining, Hsi-ning, Sining. Province capital Qinghai, C China
Xinjiang see Xinjiang Uygur Zizhiqu
Xinjiang Uygur Zizhiqu 126 B3 var. Sinkiang, Sinkiang Uighur Autonomous Region, Xin, Xinjiang. Admin. region autonomous region NW China
Xinpu see Lianyungang
Xinxiang 128 C4 Henan, C China
Xinyang 128 C5 var. Hsin-yang, Sinyang. Henan, C China
Xinzo de Limia 92 C2 Galicia, NW Spain
Xiqing Shan 124 D2 mountain range C China
Xixón see Gijón
Xizang see Xizang Zizhiqu
Xizang Gaoyuan see Qingzang Gaoyuan
Xizang Zizhiqu 126 B4 var. Thibet, Tibetan Autonomous Region of Xizang, Eng. Tibet. Admin. region autonomous region W China

Xolotlán see Managua, Lago de
Xuddur 73 D5 var. Hudur, It. Oddur. Bakool, SW Somalia
Xuwen 128 C7 Guangdong, S China
Xuzhou 128 D4 var. Hsu-chou, Suchow, Tongshan; prev. T'ung-shan. Jiangsu, E China
Xylókastro 105 B5 var. Xilokastro. Pelopónnisos, S Greece

Y

Ya'an 128 B5 var. Yaan. Sichuan, C China
Yabēlo 73 C5 C Ethiopia
Yablis 53 E2 Región Autónoma Atlántico Norte, NE Nicaragua
Yablonovyy Khrebet 115 F4 mountain range S Russian Federation
Yabrai Shan 127 E3 mountain range NE China
Yafran 71 F2 NW Libya
Yaghan Basin 67 B7 undersea feature SE Pacific Ocean
Yahotyn 109 E2 Rus. Yagotin. Kyyivs'ka Oblast', N Ukraine
Yahualica 50 D4 Jalisco, SW Mexico
Yakima 46 B2 Washington, NW USA
Yakima River 46 B2 river Washington, NW USA
Yakoruda 104 C3 Blagoevgrad, SW Bulgaria
Yaku-shima 131 B8 island Nansei-shotō, SW Japan
Yakutat 36 D4 Alaska, USA
Yakutsk 115 F3 Respublika Sakha (Yakutiya), NE Russian Federation
Yala 137 C7 Yala, SW Thailand
Yalizava 107 D6 Rus. Yelizovo. Mahilyowskaya Voblasts', E Belarus
Yalong Jiang 128 A5 river C China
Yalova 116 B3 Yalova, NW Turkey
Yalpuh, Ozero 108 D4 Rus. Ozero Yalpug. Lake SW Ukraine
Yalta 109 F5 Respublika Krym, S Ukraine
Yalu 125 E2 Chin. Yalu Jiang, Jap. Oryokko, Kor. Amnok-kang. River China/North Korea
Yamaguchi 131 B7 var. Yamaguti. Yamaguchi, Honshū, SW Japan
Yamaguti see Yamaguchi
Yamal, Poluostrov 114 D2 peninsula N Russian Federation
Yambio 73 B5 var. Yambiyo. Western Equatoria, S Sudan
Yambiyo see Yambio
Yambol 104 D2 Turk. Yanboli. Yambol, E Bulgaria
Yamdena, Pulau 139 G5 prev. Jamdena. Island Kepulauan Tanimbar, E Indonesia
Yam HaMelah see Dead Sea
Yam Kinneret see Tiberias, Lake
Yamoussoukro 74 D5 country capital (Côte d'Ivoire) C Côte d'Ivoire
Yamuna 134 D3 prev. Jumna. River N India
Yana 115 F2 river NE Russian Federation
Yanbu 'al Baḥr 121 A5 Al Madīnah, W Saudi Arabia
Yangambi 77 D5 Orientale, N Dem. Rep. Congo
Yangchow see Yangzhou
Yangiyŭl 123 E2 Rus. Yangiyul'. Toshkent Wiloyati, E Uzbekistan
Yangon 136 B4 Eng. Rangoon. Country capital (Myanmar) Yangon, S Myanmar
Yangtze see Chang Jiang
Yangtze Kiang see Chang Jiang
Yangzhou 128 D5 var. Yangchow. Jiangsu, E China
Yankton 45 E3 South Dakota, N USA
Yannina see Ioánnina
Yanskiy Zaliv 113 F2 bay N Russian Federation

Yantai 128 D4 var. Yan-t'ai; prev. Chefoo, Chih-fu. Shandong, E China
Yan-t'ai see Yantai
Yaoundé 77 B5 var. Yaunde. Country capital (Cameroon) Centre, S Cameroon
Yap 144 A1 island Caroline Islands, W Micronesia
Yapanskoye More see Japan, Sea of
Yapen, Pulau 139 G4 prev. Japen. Island E Indonesia
Yap Trench 142 B2 var. Yap Trough. Undersea feature SE Philippine Sea
Yap Trough see Yap Trench
Yapurá see Caquetá, Río
Yapurá see Japurá, Rio
Yaqui, Río 50 C2 river NW Mexico
Yaransk 111 C5 Kirovskaya Oblast', NW Russian Federation
Yarega 110 D4 Respublika Komi, NW Russian Federation
Yarkant see Shache
Yarlung Zangbo Jiang see Brahmaputra
Yarmouth see Great Yarmouth
Yarmouth 39 F5 Nova Scotia, SE Canada
Yaroslavl' 110 B4 Yaroslavskaya Oblast', W Russian Federation
Yarumal 58 B2 Antioquia, NW Colombia
Yasyel'da 107 B7 river SW Belarus
Yatsushiro 131 A7 var. Yatusiro. Kumamoto, Kyūshū, SW Japan
Yatusiro see Yatsushiro
Yaunde see Yaoundé
Yavarí see Javari, Rio
Yaviza 53 H5 Darién, SE Panama
Yavoriv 108 B2 Pol. Jaworów, Rus. Yavorov. L'vivs'ka Oblast', NW Ukraine
Yazd 120 D3 var. Yezd. Yazd, C Iran
Yazoo City 42 B2 Mississippi, S USA
Yding Skovhøj 85 A7 hill C Denmark
Ýdra 105 C6 var. Ídhra. Island S Greece
Ye 137 B5 Mon State, S Myanmar
Yecheng 126 A3 var. Kargilik. Xinjiang Uygur Zizhiqu, NW China
Yefremov 111 B5 Tul'skaya Oblast', W Russian Federation
Yekaterinburg 114 C3 prev. Sverdlovsk. Sverdlovskaya Oblast', C Russian Federation
Yelets 111 B5 Lipetskaya Oblast', W Russian Federation
Yell 88 D1 island NE Scotland, UK
Yellowknife 37 E4 territory capital Northwest Territories, W Canada
Yellow River see Huang He
Yellow Sea 128 D4 Chin. Huang Hai, Kor. Hwang-Hae. Sea E Asia
Yellowstone River 44 C2 river Montana/Wyoming, NW USA
Yel'sk 107 C7 Rus. Yel'sk. Homyel'skaya Voblasts', SE Belarus
Yelwa 75 F4 Kebbi, W Nigeria
Yemen 121 C7 Ar. Al Jumhūrīyah al Yamanīyah, Al Yaman. Country SW Asia

---

Yemen 121

Official name Republic of Yemen
Formation 1990
Capital Sana
Population 19.1 million / 94 people per sq mile (36 people per sq km)
Total area 203,849 sq miles (527,970 sq km)
Languages Arabic
Religions Shi'a Muslim 42%, Sunni Muslim 55%, Christian, Hindu and Jewish 3%
Ethnic mix Arab 95%, Afro-Arab 3%, Indian, Somali and European 2%

Yemen (continued)

Government Multiparty republic
Currency Yemeni Rial
Literacy rate 46.3%
Calorie consumption 2,038 kilocalories

Yemva 110 D4 *prev.*
Zheleznodorozhnyy. Respublika Komi, NW Russian Federation
Yenakiyeve 109 G3 *Rus.*
Yenakiyevo; *prev.* Ordzhonikidze, Rykovo. Donets'ka Oblast', E Ukraine
Yenangyaung 136 A3 Magwe, W Myanmar
Yendi 75 E4 NE Ghana
Yengisar 126 A3 Xinjiang Uygur Zizhiqu, NW China
Yenierenköy *see* Agialoúsa
Yenisey 114 D3 *river* Mongolia/Russian Federation
Yenping *see* Nanping
Yeovil 89 D7 SW England, UK
Yeppoon 148 D4 Queensland, E Australia
Yerevan 117 F3 *var.* Erevan, *Eng.* Erivan. *Country capital* (Armenia) C Armenia
Yeriho *see* Jericho
Yerushalayim *see* Jerusalem
Yeu, Île d' 90 A4 *island* NW France C Azerbaijan
Yevlax 117 G2 *Rus.* Yevlakh. C Azerbaijan
Yevpatoriya 109 F5 Respublika Krym, S Ukraine
Yeya 109 H4 *river* SW Russian Federation
Yezd *see* Yazd
Yezyaryshcha 107 E5 *Rus.* Yezerishche. Vitsyebskaya Voblasts', NE Belarus
Yiannitsá *see* Giannitsá
Yichang 128 C5 Hubei, C China
Yıldızeli 116 D3 Sivas, N Turkey
Yinchuan 128 B4 *var.* Yinch'uan, Yin-ch'uan, Yinchwan. Ningxia, N China
Yinchwan *see* Yinchuan
Yin-hsien *see* Ningbo
Yining 126 B2 *var.* I-ning, *Uigh.* Gulja, Kuldja. Xinjiang Uygur Zizhiqu, NW China
Yíthion *see* Gýtheio
Yogyakarta 138 C5 *prev.* Djokjakarta, Jogjakarta, Jokyakarta. Jawa, C Indonesia
Yokohama 131 D5 Aomori, Honshū, C Japan
Yokohama 130 A2 Kanagawa, Honshū, S Japan
Yokote 130 D4 Akita, Honshū, C Japan
Yola 75 H4 Adamawa, E Nigeria
Yonago 131 B6 Tottori, Honshū, SW Japan
Yong'an 128 D6 *var.* Yongan. Fujian, SE China
Yonkers 41 F3 New York, NE USA
Yonne 90 C4 *river* C France
Yopal 58 C3 *var.* El Yopal. Casanare, C Colombia
York 89 D5 *anc.* Eboracum, Eburacum. N England, UK
York 45 E4 Nebraska, C USA
York, Cape 148 C1 *headland* Queensland, NE Australia
Yorkton 37 F5 Saskatchewan, S Canada
Yoro 52 C2 Yoro, C Honduras
Yoshkar-Ola 111 C5 Respublika Mariy El, W Russian Federation
Youngstown 40 D4 Ohio, N USA
Youth, Isle of *see* Juventud, Isla de la
Yreka 46 B4 California, W USA
Yssel *see* IJssel
Ysyk-Köl *see* Issyk-Kul', Ozero
Yu *see* Henan
Yuan *see* Red River
Yuan Jiang *see* Red River
Yuba City 47 B5 California, W USA

Yucatan Channel 51 H3 *Sp.* Canal de Yucatán. *Channel* Cuba/Mexico
Yucatan Peninsula 35 C7 *peninsula* Guatemala/Mexico
Yuci 128 C4 Shanxi, C China
Yue *see* Guangdong
Yueyang 128 C5 Hunan, S China
Yukhavichy 107 D5 *Rus.* Yukhovichi. Vitsyebskaya Voblasts', N Belarus
Yukon 36 C2 *river* Canada/USA
Yukon *see* Yukon Territory
Yukon Territory 36 D3 *var.* Yukon, *Fr.* Territoire du Yukon. Admin. *region territory* NW Canada
Yulin 128 C6 Guangxi Zhuangzu Zizhiqu, S China
Yuma 48 A2 Arizona, SW USA
Yumen 128 A3 *var.* Laojunmiao, Yümen. Gansu, N China
Yun *see* Yunnan
Yungki *see* Jilin
Yung-ning *see* Nanning
Yunjinghong *see* Jinghong
Yunki *see* Jilin
Yunnan 128 A6 *var.* Yun, Yunnan Sheng, Yun-nan, Yun-nan. Admin. *region province* SW China
Yunnan *see* Kunming
Yunnan Sheng *see* Yunnan
Yuruá, Río *see* Juruá, Rio
Yushu 126 D4 Qinghai, C China
Yuty 64 D3 Caazapá, S Paraguay
Yuzhno-Sakhalinsk 115 H4 *Jap.* Toyohara; *prev.* Vladimirovka. Ostrov Sakhalin, Sakhalinskaya Oblast', SE Russian Federation
Yuzhou *see* Chongqing
Yylanly *see* Il'yaly

Z

Zaanstad 86 C3 *prev.* Zaandam. Noord-Holland, C Netherlands
Zabaykal'sk 115 F5 Chitinskaya Oblast', S Russian Federation
Zabern *see* Saverne
Zabīd 121 B7 W Yemen
Ząbkowice *see* Ząbkowice Śląskie
Ząbkowice Śląskie 98 B4 *var.* Ząbkowice, *Ger.* Frankenstein, Frankenstein in Schlesien. Wałbrzych, SW Poland
Zábřeh 99 C5 *Ger.* Hohenstadt. Olomoucký Kraj, E Czech Republic
Zacapa 52 B2 Zacapa, E Guatemala
Zacatecas 50 D3 Zacatecas, C Mexico
Zacatepec 51 E4 Morelos, S Mexico
Zacháro 50 B6 *var.* Zaharo, Zakháro. Dytikí Ellás, S Greece
Zadar 100 A3 *It.* Zara; *anc.* Iader. Zadar, SW Croatia
Zadetkyi Kyun 137 B6 *var.* St. Matthew's Island. *Island* Mergui Archipelago, S Myanmar
Zafra 92 C4 Extremadura, W Spain
Żagań 98 B4 *var.* Zagań, Żegań; *Ger.* Sagan. Lubuskie, W Poland
Zagazig 72 B1 *var.* Az Zaqāzīq. N Egypt
Zágráb *see* Zagreb
Zagreb 100 B2 *Ger.* Agram, *Hung.* Zágráb. *Country capital* (Croatia) Zagreb, N Croatia
Zagros, Kūhhā-ye 120 C3 *Eng.* Zagros Mountains. *Mountain range* W Iran
Zāgros Mountains *see* Zagros, Kūhhā-ye
Zaharo *see* Zacháro
Zāhedān 120 E4 *var.* Zahidan; *prev.* Duzdab. Sīstān va Balūchestān, SE Iran
Zahidan *see* Zāhedān
Zaḥlah *see* Zahlé
Zahlé 118 B4 *var.* Zaḥlah. C Lebanon
Záhony 99 E6 Szabolcs-Szatmár-Bereg, NE Hungary
Zaire *see* Congo
Zaječar 100 E4 Serbia, E Serbia and Montenegro (Yugo.)
Zakháro *see* Zacháro

Zākhō 120 B2 *var.* Zākhū. N Iraq
Zākhū *see* Zākhō
Zákinthos *see* Zákynthos
Zakopane 99 D5 Małopolskie, S Poland
Zakota Pomorskiea *see* Danzig, Gulf of
Zákynthos 105 A6 *var.* Zákinthos, *It.* Zante. *Island* Iónioi Nísoi, Greece, C Mediterranean Sea
Zalaegerszeg 99 B7 Zala, W Hungary
Zalău 108 B3 *Ger.* Waltenberg, *Hung.* Zilah; *prev.* Ger. Zillenmarkt. Sălaj, NW Romania
Zalim 121 B5 Makkah, W Saudi Arabia
Zambesi *see* Zambezi
Zambeze *see* Zambezi
Zambezi 78 D2 *var.* Zambesi, *Port.* Zambeze. *River* S Africa
Zambezi 78 C2 North Western, W Zambia
Zambia 78 C2 *off.* Republic of Zambia; *prev.* Northern Rhodesia. *Country* S Africa

Zambia 78

Official name Republic of Zambia
Formation 1964
Capital Lusaka
Population 10.6 million / 36 people per sq mile (14 people per sq km)
Total area 290,584 sq miles (752,612 sq km)
Languages English, Bemba, Nyanja, Tonga, Kaonde, Lunda, Luvale, Lozi
Religions Christian 63%, Indigenous beliefs 36%, other 1%
Ethnic mix Bemba 34%, European 1%, other African 65%
Government Presidential democracy
Currency Zambian kwacha = 100 ngwee
Literacy rate 78.1%
Calorie consumption 1,912 kilocalories

Zamboanga 139 E3 *off.* Zamboanga City. Mindanao, S Philippines
Zambrów 98 E3 Podlaskie, E Poland
Zamora 92 D2 Castilla-León, NW Spain
Zamora de Hidalgo 50 D4 Michoacán de Ocampo, SW Mexico
Zamość 98 E4 Rus. Zamoste. Lubelskie, E Poland
Zancle *see* Messina
Zanda 126 A4 Xizang Zizhiqu, W China
Zanesville 40 D4 Ohio, N USA
Zanjān 120 C2 *var.* Zenjan, Zinjan. Zanjān, NW Iran
Zante *see* Zákynthos
Zanthus 147 C6 Western Australia
Zanzibar 73 C7 *Swa.* Unguja. *Island* E Tanzania
Zanzibar 73 D7 Zanzibar, E Tanzania
Zaozhuang 128 D4 Shandong, E China
Zapadna Morava 100 D4 *Ger.* Westliche Morava. *River* C Serbia and Montenegro (Yugo.)
Zapadnaya Dvina 110 A4 Tverskaya Oblast', W Russian Federation
Zapadno-Sibirskaya Ravnina 114 C3 *Eng.* West Siberian Plain. *Plain* C Russian Federation
Zapadnyy Sayan 114 D4 *Eng.* Western Sayans. *Mountain range* S Russian Federation
Zapala 65 B5 Neuquén, W Argentina
Zapiola Ridge 67 B6 *undersea feature* SW Atlantic Ocean

Zapolyarnyy 110 C2 Murmanskaya Oblast', NW Russian Federation
Zaporizhzhya 109 F3 *Rus.* Zaporozh'ye; *prev.* Aleksandrovsk. Zaporiz'ka Oblast', SE Ukraine
Zapotiltic 50 D4 Jalisco, SW Mexico
Zaqatala 117 G2 *Rus.* Zakataly. NW Azerbaijan
Zara 116 D3 Sivas, C Turkey
Zarafshon 122 D2 *Rus.* Zarafshan. Nawoiy Wiloyati, N Uzbekistan
Zaragoza 93 F2 *Eng.* Saragossa; *anc.* Caesaraugusta, Salduba. Aragón, NE Spain
Zarand 120 D3 Kermān, C Iran
Zaranj 122 D5 Nīmrūz, SW Afghanistan
Zarasai 106 C4 Zarasai, E Lithuania
Zárate 64 D4 *prev.* General José F.Uriburu. Buenos Aires, E Argentina
Zarautz 93 E1 *var.* Zarauz. País Vasco, N Spain
Zarauz *see* Zarautz
Zaraza 59 E2 Guárico, N Venezuela
Zarghūn Shahr 123 E4 *var.* Katawaz. Paktīkā, SE Afghanistan
Zaria 75 G4 Kaduna, C Nigeria
Zarós 105 D8 Kriti, Greece, E Mediterranean Sea
Zarqa *see* Az Zarqā'
Żary 98 B4 *Ger.* Sorau, Sorau in der Niederlausitz. Lubuskie, W Poland
Zaunguzskiye Garagumy 122 C2 *Turkm.* Üngüz Angyrsyndaky Garagum. *Desert* N Turkmenistan
Zavet 104 D1 Razgrad, N Bulgaria
Zavidovići 100 C3 Federacija Bosna I Hercegovina, N Bosnia and Herzegovina
Zawia *see* Az Zāwiyah
Zawiercie 98 D4 *Rus.* Zavertse. Śląskie, S Poland
Zawīlah 71 F3 *var.* Zuwaylah, *It.* Zueila. C Libya
Zaysan, Ozero 114 D5 *Kaz.* Zaysan Köl. *Lake* E Kazakhstan
Zbarazh 108 C2 Ternopil's'ka Oblast', W Ukraine
Zduńska Wola 98 C4 Łódzkie, C Poland
Zeebrugge 87 A5 West-Vlaanderen, NW Belgium
Zeewolde 86 D3 Flevoland, C Netherlands
Żegań *see* Żagań
Zefat 119 B5 *var.* Safed, Tsefat, *Ar.* Safad. Northern, N Israel
Zeist 86 C4 Utrecht, C Netherlands
Zele 87 B5 Oost-Vlaanderen, NW Belgium
Zelenoborskiy 110 B2 Murmanskaya Oblast', NW Russian Federation
Zelenograd 111 B5 Moskovskaya Oblast', W Russian Federation
Zelenogradsk 106 A4 *Ger.* Cranz, Kranz. Kaliningradskaya Oblast', W Russian Federation
Zelle *see* Celle
Zel'va 107 B6 *Pol.* Zelwa. Hrodzyenskaya Voblasts', W Belarus
Zelzate 87 B5 *var.* Selzaete. Oost-Vlaanderen, NW Belgium
Žemaičiu Aukštumas 106 B4 *physical region* W Lithuania
Zemst 87 C5 Vlaams Brabant, C Belgium
Zemun 100 D3 Serbia, N Serbia and Montenegro (Yugo.)
Zenica 100 C4 Federacija Bosna I Hercegovina, C Bosnia and Herzegovina
Zenjan *see* Zanjān
Zeravshan 123 E3 *Taj./Uzb.* Zarafshon. *River* Tajikistan/Uzbekistan
Zevenaar 86 D4 Gelderland, SE Netherlands

Zevenbergen *86 C4* Noord-Brabant,
S Netherlands
Zeya *113 E3 river* SE Russian
Federation
Zgierz *98 C4 Ger.* Neuhof, *Rus.*
Zgerzh. Łódź, C Poland
Zgorzelec *98 B4 Ger.* Görlitz.
Dolnośląskie, SW Poland
Zhabinka *107 A6 Pol.* Żabinka, *Rus.*
Zhabinka. Brestskaya Voblasts',
SW Belarus
Zhambyl *see* Taraz
Zhanaozen *114 A4 Kaz.*
Zhangaözen, *prev.* Novyy Uzen'.
Mangistau, W Kazakhstan
Zhangaözen *see* Zhanaozen
Zhangaqazaly *see* Ayteke Bi
Zhang-chia-k'ou *see* Zhangjiakou
Zhangdian *see* Zibo
Zhangjiakou *128 C3 var.*
Changkiakow, Zhang-chia-k'ou,
Eng. Kalgan; *prev.* Wanchuan.
Hebei, E China
Zhangzhou *128 D6* Fujian,
SE China
Zhanjiang *128 C7 var.* Chanchiang,
Chan-chiang, *Cant.* Tsamkong, *Fr.*
Fort-Bayard. Guangdong, S China
Zhaoqing *128 C6* Guangdong,
S China
Zhe *see* Zhejiang
Zhejiang *128 D5 var.* Che-chiang,
Chekiang, Zhe, Zhejiang Sheng.
Admin. region *province* SE China
Zhejiang Sheng *see* Zhejiang
Zhelezndoroznyy *106 A4 Ger.*
Gerdauen. Kaliningradskaya
Oblast', W Russian Federation
Zheleznogorsk *111 A5* Kurskaya
Oblast', W Russian Federation
Zhengzhou *128 C4 var.* Ch'eng-
chou, Chengchow; *prev.*
Chenghsien. Henan, C China
Zhezkazgan *114 C4 Kaz.*
Zhezqazghan; *prev.* Dkaraganda.
Karaganda, C Kazakhstan
Zhlobin *107 D7* Homyel'skaya
Voblasts', SE Belarus
Zhmerynka *108 D2 Rus.*
Zhmerinka. Vinnyts'ka Oblast',
C Ukraine
Zhodzina *107 D6 Rus.* Zhodino.
Minskaya Voblasts', C Belarus
Zhovkva *108 B2 Pol.* Żółkiew, *Rus.*
Zholkev, Zholkva; *prev.* Nesterov.
L'vivs'ka Oblast', NW Ukraine
Zhovti Vody *109 F3 Rus.* Zhëltyye
Vody. Dnipropetrovs'ka Oblast',
E Ukraine
Zhovtneve *109 E4 Rus.*
Zhovtnevoye. Mykolayivs'ka
Oblast', S Ukraine
Zhydachiv *108 B2 Pol.* Żydaczów,
Rus. Zhidachov. L'vivs'ka Oblast',
NW Ukraine
Zhytkavichy *107 C7 Rus.*
Zhitkovichi. Homyel'skaya
Voblasts', SE Belarus
Zhytomyr *108 D2 Rus.* Zhitomir.
Zhytomyrs'ka Oblast',
NW Ukraine
Zibo *128 D4 var.* Zhangdian.
Shandong, E China
Zielona Góra *98 B4 Ger.* Grünberg,
Grünberg in Schlesien,
Grüneberg. Lubuskie,
W Poland
Zierikzee *86 B4* Zeeland,
SW Netherlands
Zigong *128 B5 var.* Tzekung.
Sichuan, C China
Ziguinchor *74 B3* SW Senegal
Žilina *99 C5 Ger.* Sillein, *Hung.*
Zsolna. Žilinský Kraj, N Slovakia
Zimbabwe *78 D3 prev.* Rhodesia.
Country S Africa

Zimbabwe 78

Official name Republic of
Zimbabwe
Formation 1980
Capital Harare

Zimbabwe (continued)

Population 12.9 million / 86 people
per sq mile (33 people per sq km)
Total area 150,803 sq miles
(390,580 sq km)
Languages English, Shona, Ndebele
Religions Syncretic (Christian and
traditional beliefs) 50%,
Christian 25%, Traditional beliefs
24%, other 1%
Ethnic mix Shona 71%, Ndebele
16%, other African 11%, Asian 1%,
White 1%
Government Presidential regime
Currency Zimbabwe dollar = 100
cents
Literacy rate 88.7%
Calorie consumption 2,117
kilocalories

Zimnicea *108 C5* Teleorman,
S Romania
Zimovniki *111 B7* Rostovskaya
Oblast', SW Russian Federation
Zinder *75 G3* Zinder, S Niger
Zinjan *see* Zanjān
Zipaquirá *58 B3* Cundinamarca,
C Colombia
Zittau *94 D4* Sachsen, E
Germany
Zlatni Pyasŭtsi *104 E2* Dobrich,
NE Bulgaria
Zlín *99 C5 prev.* Gottwaldov.
Zlínský Kraj, E Czech Republic
Złotów *98 C3* Wielkopolskie,
C Poland
Znam"yanka *109 F3 Rus.*
Znamenka. Kirovohrads'ka
Oblast', C Ukraine
Żnin *98 C3* Kujawski-pomorskie,
C Poland
Znojmo *99 B5 Ger.* Znaim.
Brněnský Kraj, SE Czech Republic
Zoetermeer *86 C4* Zuid-Holland,
W Netherlands
Zolochiv *108 C2 Pol.* Złoczów, *Rus.*
Zolochev. L'vivs'ka Oblast',
W Ukraine
Zolochiv *109 G2 Rus.* Zolochev.
Kharkivs'ka Oblast', E Ukraine
Zolote *109 H3 Rus.* Zolotoye.
Luhans'ka Oblast', E Ukraine
Zolotonosha *109 E2* Cherkas'ka
Oblast', C Ukraine
Zomba *79 E2* Southern, S Malawi
Zongo *77 C5* Equateur, N Dem.
Rep. Congo
Zonguldak *116 C2* Zonguldak,
NW Turkey
Zonhoven *87 D6* Limburg,
NE Belgium
Żory *99 C5 var.* Zory, *Ger.* Sohrau.
Śląskie, S Poland
Zouar *76 C2* Borkou-Ennedi-Tibesti,
N Chad
Zouérat *74 C2 var.* Zouérate,
Zouîrât. Tiris Zemmour,
N Mauritania
Zouérate *see* Zouérat
Zouîrât *see* Zouérat
Zrenjanin *100 D3 prev.* Petrovgrad,
Veliki Bečkerek, *Ger.*
Grossbetschkerek, *Hung.*
Nagybecskerek. Serbia, N Serbia
and Montenegro (Yugo.)
Zubov Seamount *67 D5 undersea
feature* E Atlantic Ocean
Zueila *see* Zawīlah
Zug *95 B7 Fr.* Zoug. Zug,
C Switzerland
Zugspitze *95 C7 mountain*
S Germany
Zuid-Beveland *87 B5 var.* South
Beveland. *Island* SW Netherlands
Zuidhorn *86 E1* Groningen,
NE Netherlands
Zuidlaren *86 E2* Drenthe,
NE Netherlands
Zula *72 C4* E Eritrea
Züllichau *see* Sulechów
Zundert *87 C5* Noord-Brabant,
S Netherlands

Zunyi *128 B5* Guizhou, S China
Županja *100 C3 Hung.* Zsupanya.
Vukovar-Srijem, E Croatia
Zürich *95 B7 Eng./Fr.* Zurich, *It.*
Zurigo. Zürich, N Switzerland
Zürichsee *95 B7 Eng.* Lake Zurich.
Lake NE Switzerland
Zutphen *86 D3* Gelderland,
E Netherlands
Zuwārah *71 F2* NW Libya
Zuwaylah *see* Zawīlah
Zuyevka *111 D5* Kirovskaya
Oblast', NW Russian Federation
Zvenyhorodka *109 E2 Rus.*
Zvenigorodka. Cherkas'ka
Oblast', C Ukraine
Zvishavane *78 D3 prev.* Shabani.
Matabeleland South, S Zimbabwe
Zvolen *99 C6 Ger.* Altsohl, *Hung.*
Zólyom. Banskobystricky Kraj,
C Slovakia
Zvornik *100 C4* E Bosnia and
Herzegovina
Zwedru *74 D5 var.* Tchien. E Liberia
Zwettl *95 E6* Wien, NE Austria
Zwevegem *87 A6* West-Vlaanderen,
W Belgium
Zwickau *95 C5* Sachsen, E Germany
Zwolle *86 D3* Overijssel,
E Netherlan
Zyōetu *see* Jōetsu
Żyardów *98 D3* Mazowieckie, C
Poland
Zyryanovsk *114 D5* Vostochnyy
Kazakhstan, E Kazakhstan

KEY TO MAP PAGES

NORTH & WEST ASIA 112-113

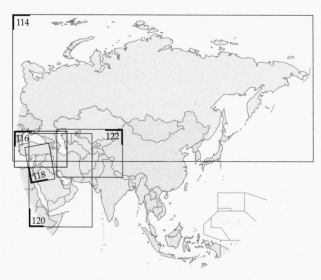

SOUTH & EAST ASIA 124-125

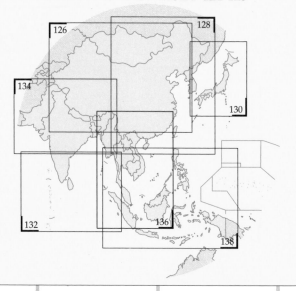